Trust and Connection in Digital Spaces:

From Homes to Classrooms

Ruqia Safdar Bajwa
Bahauddin Zakariya University, Pakistan

Sarwat Sultan
https://orcid.org/0000-0001-7439-1559
Bahauddin Zakariya University, Pakistan

Asma Yunus
University of Sargodha, Pakistan

IGI Global
Scientific Publishing
Publishing Tomorrow's Research Today

Vice President of Editorial — Melissa Wagner
Director of Acquisitions — Mikaela Felty
Director of Book Development — Jocelynn Hessler
Production Manager — Mike Brehm
Cover Design — Jose Rosado

Published in the United States of America by
IGI Global Scientific Publishing
701 East Chocolate Avenue
Hershey, PA, 17033, USA
Tel: 717-533-8845 | Fax: 717-533-7115
Website: https://www.igi-global.com E-mail: cust@igi-global.com

Library of Congress Cataloging-in-Publication Data

(CIP Data Pending)
ISBN13: 979-8-2600-0934-5
Isbn13Softcover: 979-8-2600-0935-2
EISBN13: 979-8-2600-0936-9
British Cataloguing in Publication Data
A Cataloguing in Publication record for this book is available from the British Library.

Table of Contents

Detailed Table of Contents

The proliferation of digital technologies has reshaped family interaction, creating a dual potential for "virtual closeness" and "digital distance." This chapter analyzes how technology mediates family life, fostering connection yet risking emotional withdrawal. Guided by Attachment and Social Presence Theories, it examines tools like video calls, messaging apps, co-parenting platforms, and monitoring software. These can sustain bonds across distances but also introduce challenges like "technoference," parental "phubbing," and uneven closeness. The analysis reveals that outcomes hinge not on the technology itself, but on its application. Positive results are tied to authoritative parenting and open communication. Negative consequences, such as child anxiety, attachment insecurity, and conflict, are linked to parental distraction and intrusive monitoring. It concludes with a conceptual model illustrating how digital tools and attachment behaviors interact to affect family satisfaction, offering practical recommendations and future research directions for nurturing strong family bonds.

This chapter introduces "digital kinship," arguing that technology actively transforms family bonds, rather than just facilitating communication. It posits that digital tools are a primary arena where the familial self is constructed. By integrating Symbolic Interactionism (for identity work) and Family Systems Theory (for emotional dynamics), the analysis examines sites like social media feeds and group chats. It reveals how platform features shape family processes, using emojis for identity, creating digital hearths for support, and navigating digital fog. The proposed model frames digital kinship as an ongoing achievement, offering insights for theory and practical application in therapy and education.

This chapter examines the evolving dynamics of psychological safety in virtual and hybrid work environments. As digital interaction replaces physical co-presence, psychological safety becomes a critical yet complex goal, requiring intentional leadership and thoughtful design. We explore how remote settings can foster inclusivity, autonomy, and flexibility, while also posing risks of isolation, miscommunication, and surveillance. The role of leadership, technology, and team rituals in shaping safe virtual spaces is emphasized, along with future considerations involving AI-mediated collaboration. Ultimately, psychological safety is positioned as a strategic necessity for performance, innovation, and resilience in distributed teams.

This chapter advances a programmatic blueprint that treats psychological safety as an engineered control parameter in hybrid classrooms, integrating social identity, self-categorization, Community of Inquiry, Self Determination, Control Value, cognitive load, procedural justice, value sensitive design, cybernetics, and adoption science. We specify a defense in depth architecture across interaction, facilitation, moderation, and institutional strata, with bounded roles for human and artificial cofacilitators constrained by provenance, refusal rules, and least privilege access. The framework codifies patterns such as anonymous first submissions with named replies, paced queues, progressive disclosure, week zero norm co-authoring, tiered moderation with evidentiary logging, and WCAG aligned accessibility. A compact measurement suite couples psychometrics to behavioral telemetry including parity indices, turn entropy, responsiveness, and repair depth, enabling quasi experimental inference and weekly decision routines. Procurement and data governance render pedagogy auditable.

The shift to online learning has transformed traditional classroom dynamics, placing emphasis on student engagement and collaborative learning in virtual spaces. Engagement, either cognitive, emotional, and behavioral, is essential for meaningful learning experiences, yet fostering it online presents unique challenges. Similarly, effective group collaboration in digital environments requires instructional design to build social presence, trust, and equitable participation. This chapter explores the interplay of these factors to offer evidence-based strategies for enhancing engagement and collaboration in virtual classrooms. This chapter also presents directions for future research.

Within the context of online classrooms, this chapter investigates the effect that virtual group dynamics have on student engagement. It focuses on the ways in which collaborative interactions within digital learning environments affect involvement, motivation, and the overall learning experience. Peer-to-peer contact, small group discussions, and participatory activities with the purpose of fostering a sense of community and reducing feelings of isolation that are widespread in online education are all examples of virtual group dynamics. By fostering active learning and social presence, effective management of these dynamics via techniques such as rotating breakout groups, informal peer exchanges, and real-time chat functionalities, in addition to other methods, increases engagement. The research provides a synthesis of studies on the ways in which dynamic virtual group interactions lead to deeper reflection, enhanced comfort in participation, and higher academic achievements.

The digital transformation of education has redefined the way learners engage with content, instructors, and peers in virtual classrooms. Engagement and collaboration are pivotal in ensuring knowledge retention, learner satisfaction, and academic achievement in online learning environments. This chapter explores the dimensions of online engagement behavioral, cognitive, and emotional and examines the role of group collaboration in fostering active participation, critical thinking, and social interaction. It highlights the pedagogical models, technological tools, and instructional strategies that enhance collaborative learning while addressing the challenges of virtual teamwork. Practical insights and case studies illustrate best practices for promoting inclusivity, motivation, and equal participation. The chapter concludes by discussing future directions in online engagement, including the integration of artificial intelligence, learning analytics, and immersive technologies, to create more personalized and interactive digital classrooms.

The rapid digitalization of higher education, accelerated by COVID-19, has reshaped teaching practices and faculty identity. This study examines how Indian faculty construct identity in avatar-based classrooms, drawing on impression management and social cognition frameworks. Interviews with 25 teachers reveal heightened emotional labor and "digitally mediated burnout," driven by reduced social cues, performance pressures, and institutional demands. The study proposes a model

Preface

INTRODUCTION

As editors of *Trust and Connection in Digital Spaces: From Homes to Classrooms*, we are pleased to present a volume that responds to one of the most significant transformations of our time: the rapid and pervasive integration of digital technologies into the fabric of everyday social life. Human interaction is no longer confined to physical settings; instead, it unfolds across complex, mediated environments that reshape how individuals construct identity, form relationships, express emotions, and exert social influence.

This collection, *Examining Social Psychology in Virtual Environments*, brings together diverse scholarly perspectives to explore the evolving nature of social behaviour in digitally mediated contexts. From social media platforms and online gaming communities to virtual classrooms, metaverses, and AI-integrated communication systems, the chapters in this volume reflect the breadth and depth of contemporary digital experience. As editors, we have sought to curate contributions that not only document these changes but also critically engage with their psychological implications.

A central aim of this book is to integrate foundational theories of social psychology with emerging empirical research from immersive and algorithmically driven environments. The contributors draw upon established frameworks while extending them to account for new modes of interaction shaped by anonymity, persistence, scalability, and automation. In doing so, the volume offers fresh insights into core processes such as identity formation, social cognition, group dynamics, emotional expression, and behavioural influence in digital contexts.

Importantly, this work also bridges theoretical and applied domains. The chapters collectively address pressing issues including digital well-being, online activism, learning and engagement in virtual classrooms, and the ethical dimensions of technologically mediated interaction. By synthesising interdisciplinary perspectives, the volume highlights both the opportunities and challenges inherent in digital spaces, emphasising the role of trust and connection as foundational elements of meaningful human experience.

We envision this book as a valuable resource for academics, researchers, and postgraduate students across social psychology, digital media, education, sociology, and behavioural science. At the same time, it is intended to inform practitioners: educators, instructional designers, mental health professionals, and technology developers, who are navigating and shaping the psychological landscapes of virtual environments.

As digital technologies continue to evolve, so too must our understanding of their impact on human thought and behaviour. It is our hope that this volume will not only contribute to scholarly discourse but also inspire ongoing inquiry into how trust, connection, and social meaning are constructed and sustained in an increasingly digital world.

ORGANIZATION OF THE BOOK

As editors, we open this volume by foregrounding the intimate and often underexamined terrain of family life in digital contexts. In Chapter 1, the contributors develop a nuanced framework for understanding how technology-mediated communication reshapes parent–child relationships, revealing a delicate balance between "virtual closeness" and "digital distance." Drawing on attachment and social presence perspectives, the chapter demonstrates that digital tools, from messaging platforms to monitoring applications, are not inherently beneficial or harmful; rather, their impact depends on patterns of use embedded within parenting styles and communication practices. By mapping the interplay between technoference, emotional availability, and relational outcomes, the authors offer both a conceptual model and practical guidance for fostering trust, intimacy, and stability in increasingly mediated family environments.

Extending this focus on the family, Chapter 2 reconceptualizes the home as a digitally constructed social space through the lens of "digital kinship." Here, the authors compellingly argue that technologies do more than facilitate interaction, they actively constitute the arena in which familial identities are negotiated and performed. Integrating symbolic interactionism with family systems theory, the chapter explores how everyday digital practices, from emoji use to shared online spaces, shape emotional bonds and collective meaning-making. The notion of the "digital hearth" captures how families cultivate connection amid the ambiguities of what the authors term “digital fog,” ultimately framing kinship as an ongoing, co-constructed achievement in technologically saturated lives.

Shifting from homes to workplaces, Chapter 3 addresses the critical construct of psychological safety within virtual and hybrid teams. The author highlights how the absence of physical co-presence transforms both the opportunities and vulnerabilities of collaboration, requiring leaders to intentionally cultivate trust, inclusivity, and open communication. While digital environments can empower autonomy and broaden participation, they also introduce risks of isolation, misinterpretation, and perceived surveillance. This chapter positions psychological safety not merely as an interpersonal ideal but as a strategic imperative, essential for sustaining innovation, resilience, and collective performance in distributed organizational contexts.

Chapter 4 advances the discussion into the domain of hybrid learning environments, offering a sophisticated and forward-looking framework for engineering psychological safety through sociotechnical design. The contributor conceptualizes trust not as an emergent byproduct but as a system-level parameter that can be intentionally structured across layers of interaction, facilitation, and governance. By integrating multiple theoretical traditions with design principles and measurable indicators, the chapter outlines actionable architectures for human–AI co-facilitation in networked classrooms. In doing so, it challenges educators and institutions to reconceptualize pedagogy as an auditable, data-informed system in which equity, participation, and safety are systematically cultivated.

In Chapter 5, attention turns to the foundational elements of student engagement and collaboration in online classrooms. The authors synthesize research on cognitive, emotional, and behavioral engagement, emphasizing the central role of social presence and instructional design in shaping meaningful learning experiences. They demonstrate that effective collaboration in virtual environments depends not only on technological affordances but also on intentional pedagogical strategies that promote trust, inclusivity, and active participation. The chapter provides evidence-based recommendations that speak directly to educators navigating the complexities of digital instruction.

Complementing this perspective, Chapter 6 delves deeper into the role of virtual group dynamics in shaping student engagement. The contributors highlight how structured peer interaction, through small group work, discussion forums, and informal exchanges, can mitigate isolation and foster a sense of community in online learning environments. By synthesizing empirical findings, the chapter illustrates how well-managed group dynamics enhance motivation, participation comfort, and academic outcomes. It reinforces the idea that connection and collaboration are not incidental but must be deliberately designed into virtual learning experiences.

Chapter 7 further builds on these themes by offering a comprehensive exploration of teaching strategies that promote active engagement and collaboration in online courses. The authors examine pedagogical models, digital tools, and instructional practices that support behavioral, cognitive, and emotional engagement, while also addressing the challenges of virtual teamwork. Through practical insights and illustrative case studies, the chapter highlights best practices for fostering inclusivity, motivation, and equitable participation. It also looks ahead to emerging innovations, including artificial intelligence and immersive technologies, positioning them as key drivers of more personalized and interactive digital learning environments.

Finally, Chapter 8 turns to the experiences of educators themselves, examining faculty identity in avatar-mediated classrooms. Drawing on impression management and social cognition frameworks, the authors reveal how digital teaching environments reshape professional self-presentation and emotional labor. The findings point to the intensification of performance pressures and the emergence of "digitally mediated burnout," underscoring the psychological costs of reduced social cues and heightened institutional expectations. By proposing an integrative model of identity, cognition, and well-being, the chapter calls for systemic interventions—including training, infrastructure, and ethical design—to support educators navigating the complexities of the avatar age.

Finally, Chapter 9 highlights important factors that may contribute to the disengaged social behaviors of Gen-Z students in virtual classrooms. Educators are struggling to hold the attention of Gen-Z students as they compete with the notifications, bells, and vibrations of smart phones. Grounded in social learning theory and social comparison theory, the authors synthesize and connect research findings that explain how this generation developed during a unique sociocultural period that likely influenced their online social behavior.

Taken together, these chapters illuminate the multifaceted nature of trust and connection across digital spaces, from the intimacy of the home to the structured environments of classrooms and organizations. As editors, we see these contributions as collectively advancing a critical understanding of how social psychological processes are not only transformed but also reconstituted in virtual contexts.

CONCLUSION

As editors, we close this volume with a recognition that digital environments are no longer peripheral to human interaction, they are central to how relationships are formed, sustained, and understood across the lifespan. The chapters in this collection collectively demonstrate that trust and connection, long studied within traditional social contexts, must now be reconsidered within technologically mediated spaces that are dynamic, layered, and often opaque. From family relationships and identity construction to classroom engagement and organizational collaboration, the contributions in this volume underscore that social psychological processes are not diminished in digital environments, they are reconfigured in profound and consequential ways.

A unifying insight across the chapters is that technology itself is neither inherently connective nor isolating. Rather, its impact depends on the social practices, institutional structures, and design choices that shape its use. Whether in the context of parent–child intimacy, virtual teamwork, or online learning, trust emerges as both a fragile and essential condition—one that must be intentionally cultivated through communication, transparency, inclusivity, and ethical design. Similarly, connection is shown to be an active, ongoing achievement, requiring thoughtful engagement from individuals, educators, leaders, and system designers alike.

The volume also highlights the increasing convergence of human and technological agency. As artificial intelligence, immersive platforms, and data-driven systems become more deeply embedded in everyday interactions, the boundaries between social and technical systems continue to blur. This shift calls for interdisciplinary approaches that integrate psychological theory with insights from education, design, and computational sciences. It also demands new frameworks for accountability, ensuring that digital environments support well-being, equity, and meaningful participation.

Importantly, the chapters do not merely diagnose challenges; they offer pathways forward. Through conceptual models, empirical findings, and practical strategies, the contributors provide tools for fostering psychologically safe, engaging, and inclusive digital spaces. These insights are particularly vital for those designing and facilitating environments where trust and connection are foundational; homes, classrooms, and collaborative workplaces.

As we look ahead, we see this volume as part of an ongoing conversation rather than a final statement. The rapid evolution of digital technologies ensures that the questions raised here will continue to develop in new and unexpected ways. We hope that this collection not only advances scholarly understanding but also inspires further inquiry, innovation, and critical reflection.

Ultimately, to understand social life in the twenty-first century is to understand it as inherently intertwined with digital mediation. It is our hope that this volume equips readers to engage with this reality thoughtfully and responsibly, contributing to the creation of digital spaces that genuinely support human connection, trust, and flourishing.

Chapter 1

A Framework for Analyzing the Impact of Technology-Mediated Communication on Parent-Child Intimacy and Conflict

Zeinab Zaremohzzabiehh
http://orcid.org/0009-0005-1282-989X
University of Religions and Denominations, Iran

Hamed Mohammadi
University of Religions and Denominations, Iran

Mansoureh Zarean
http://orcid.org/0000-0003-0824-9305
Alzahra University, Iran

ABSTRACT

The proliferation of digital technologies has reshaped family interaction, creating a dual potential for "virtual closeness" and "digital distance." This chapter analyzes how technology mediates family life, fostering connection yet risking emotional withdrawal. Guided by Attachment and Social Presence Theories, it examines tools like video calls, messaging apps, co-parenting platforms, and monitoring software. These can sustain bonds across distances but also introduce challenges like "technoference," parental "phubbing," and uneven closeness. The analysis reveals that

DOI: 10.4018/979-8-2600-0934-5.ch001

outcomes hinge not on the technology itself, but on its application. Positive results are tied to authoritative parenting and open communication. Negative consequences, such as child anxiety, attachment insecurity, and conflict, are linked to parental distraction and intrusive monitoring. It concludes with a conceptual model illustrating how digital tools and attachment behaviors interact to affect family satisfaction, offering practical recommendations and future research directions for nurturing strong family bonds.

INTRODUCTION

Social connection is a cornerstone of human well-being, yet rapid technological change has profoundly transformed how families sustain emotional closeness and navigate physical separation. Decades of research have consistently shown that social isolation is linked to adverse health outcomes, including poor physical health (Shankar et al., 2017), increased mortality (Holt-Lunstad et al., 2015), diminished well-being (Golden et al., 2009), and heightened loneliness (Burholt et al., 2017). Loneliness itself has been associated with mortality (Holwerda et al., 2014), cognitive decline and dementia (Holwerda et al., 2014), and reduced functional capacity (Shankar et al., 2017). Early sociological studies suggested that structural transformations in family life and increasing population mobility heightened risks of isolation, particularly among older adults (Hareven, 2018). The World Health Organization (2015) has also emphasized that global trends such as declining fertility rates, shrinking family sizes, and transnational migration are likely to exacerbate social isolation worldwide.

Within this context, technology-mediated communication has emerged as both a solution and a source of tension. On one hand, digital tools from video calls to instant messaging are celebrated for bridging geographical distances and preserving kinship ties (Burholt et al., 2020). Indeed, the technological revolution has been described as "the death of distance" (Cairncross, 2002) and "the end of geography" (Couclelis, 1996). On the other hand, some evidence suggests that technology may inadvertently displace face-to-face interaction, weaken social networks, and intensify isolation (Kraut et al., 1998). This divide between utopian promises of connection and dystopian fears of disconnection remains unresolved, particularly within the intimate sphere of family life. Few studies have systematically explored how digital communication affects families' everyday emotional experiences, attachment patterns, and sense of presence.

Social relations are commonly evaluated through the quantity and quality of meaningful social contacts or network size, with low levels indicating social isolation (Lubben, 2017). For geographically dispersed families, sustaining in-person interaction requires significant emotional, financial, and temporal investment. Consequently, many families increasingly rely on digital communication to maintain relationships. Research depicts a complex landscape of virtual family connections (Wilding, 2006). While digital media platforms such as Facebook and WhatsApp can strengthen emotional bonds across distances, these connections are unevenly shaped by inequalities of access, age, gender, and class (Cabalquinto, 2021). Such disparities produce what Cabalquinto (2018) described as "asymmetrical mobile intimacy," a condition where some family members feel more connected, while others experience surveillance, exclusion, or emotional detachment. Thus, the promise of digital intimacy is both real and ambivalent, reflecting an ongoing tension between connection and control, accessibility and fatigue.

Against this backdrop, this chapter examines how digital technologies reshape family intimacy, simultaneously fostering connection and generating new forms of emotional distance. It draws on two foundational theoretical frameworks: Attachment Theory (Bowlby, 1982) and Social Presence Theory (Short et al., 1976). Together, these perspectives illuminate how emotional bonds are formed, maintained, or strained when relationships are mediated by screens, apps, and artificial intelligence. Furthermore, the chapter considers emerging parasocial and AI-mediated forms of intimacy that challenge traditional understandings of family connection. Increasingly, children and adolescents develop one-sided emotional attachments to influencers, streamers, and even AI companions such as chatbots or virtual assistants. While these interactions may offer comfort or fill emotional gaps, they also risk distorting expectations of authentic intimacy. The chapter therefore asks whether these connections compensate for absent familial care or, conversely, reinforce emotional detachment by substituting artificial empathy for genuine relational engagement. Through an integrated application of Attachment Theory and Social Presence Theory, this chapter proposes a conceptual model explaining how digital tools can both support and strain family relationships. In doing so, it contributes to contemporary debates in family studies, psychology, and media research about what intimacy means in a hyper-connected yet emotionally fragmented world.

Mediated Family Communication

Extensive research has explored how transnational families use technology to maintain emotional bonds and a shared sense of identity (Abel et al., 2021; Baldassar, 2016; Madianou & Miller, 2013). Yet, digital mediation has become just as common among families who live together (Räisä, 2022; Stæhr & Nørreby, 2021). Understanding this phenomenon requires looking beyond the distinction between speaking and writing to focus on the affordances of digital tools themselves. It is now routine for family members to send WhatsApp voice notes from separate rooms or post in a family group chat while sitting together on the sofa. This blending of physical co-presence and digital interaction redefines what everyday family communication looks like.

Choosing a specific digital platform or communication mode is a meaningful act, closely tied to language practices, identity, and emotional expression. Studies on multilingual families show that digital tools play a vital role in maintaining heritage languages and facilitating informal learning. For instance, children often create different WhatsApp groups with relatives to practice distinct heritage languages and cultural identities, turning these chats into informal classrooms for writing in languages not taught at school (Palviainen & Kędra, 2020). The choice of language for emotional expression is also deliberate. A study of Chinese and Polish transnational families in the United Kingdom found that heritage languages were preferred over English for sending affectionate messages on WhatsApp and WeChat (Curdt-Christiansen & Iwaniec, 2023). This finding suggests that digital spaces are essential for reinforcing family language policies and nurturing both linguistic and emotional bonds.

The unique features, or affordances, of communication modes such as text, voice, and video strongly shape these interactions. The choice among them depends on factors like personal comfort, language ability, and cultural norms. Research with Senegalese families in Norway illustrates this complexity: while one family member might send voice messages blending Joola, Wolof, and French, another might find such messages "embarrassing" and prefer replying with written French texts (Gonçalves & Lexander, 2023). For that person, texting provided the time to think, translate, and express themselves more confidently showing how families adapt media choices to fit diverse linguistic competencies and comfort levels.

Video calls are especially significant in fostering emotional closeness and supporting language development among geographically separated families. Video communication offers rich multimodal cues (visual and auditory) that simulate face-to-face interaction and help maintain relationships. For example, Arabic-speaking families in the United Kingdom used Skype to expose children to different dialects and forms of Arabic (Said, 2021). Similarly, a Russian-speaking mother in Finland maintained daily Viber video calls with grandparents in Russia to keep Russian an active part of family life (Palviainen, 2020). These interactions are more than functional—they are emotional rituals that preserve cultural continuity and the feeling of "being together" across borders.

Despite its advantages, the digital mediation of family life also brings challenges and inequalities. Seamless communication can be disrupted by technical limitations, especially for families using languages with non-Latin scripts like Arabic, Thai, or Vietnamese. When digital platforms lack full language support, families may be forced to choose between texting, which can limit literacy development in the heritage language or using only voice and video calls. These constraints can lead to what Cabalquinto (2018) terms "asymmetrical mobile intimacy," where technologies meant to connect instead create feelings of exclusion, surveillance, or emotional detachment.

In conclusion, mediated family communication represents a complex ecosystem where technology, language, and emotion are deeply intertwined. Digital tools provide unparalleled opportunities to sustain intimacy and reinforce cultural identity, especially within multilingual and geographically dispersed families. Yet the quality of these connections depends on individual choices, linguistic ability, and platform design. As families continue to navigate this evolving landscape, they redefine what kinship and emotional presence mean in a hyper-connected world, turning a simple voice note, video call, or bilingual text into a powerful expression of love, identity, and belonging.

Virtual Intimacies and Family Bond

Digital technologies have profoundly reshaped family life, creating an environment where emotional connection must be deliberately cultivated alongside everyday coordination. This balance is particularly crucial in post-divorce or dual-household families, where digital tools are essential for sustaining functional co-parenting relationships. Research with divorced parents shows that asynchronous communication tools such as texting or shared calendars enable coordination while preserving healthy boundaries. For example, a text about a schedule change or health update can replace potentially contentious face-to-face discussions (Palviainen, 2020).

However, the effectiveness of these tools largely depends on the quality of the parents' pre-existing relationship. Cooperative co-parents often find that technology enhances communication and reduces conflict, while parents with adversarial relationships may use the same tools to limit information sharing or control interactions (Ganong et al., 2012).

Specialized co-parenting applications such as *OurFamilyWizard* (Figure 1) illustrate this dual nature. These platforms provide shared calendars, expense tracking, and secure messaging designed for separated families. For cooperative parents, such features streamline logistics and reduce misunderstandings. Yet, in high-conflict situations, the same tools, particularly those with permanent, court-admissible message logs can transform everyday exchanges into formal, legalistic communications. This can escalate tension and create what researchers describe as a "cold" operational environment, where technology reinforces emotional detachment rather than cooperation (Hodgkinson & Healey, 2014).

Figure 1. OurFamilyWizard app

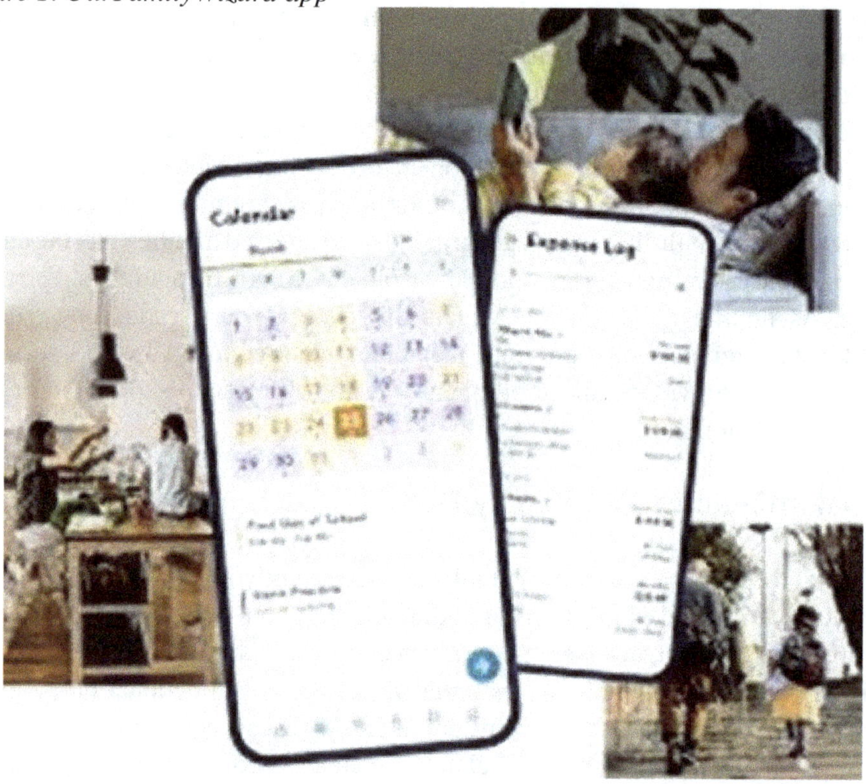

Beyond co-parenting, digital technologies have redefined how parents monitor their children's safety and daily activities. Tools such as GPS tracking, device monitoring, and regular digital check-ins are now common (Lim, 2019). Research suggests that positive digital communication between parents and adolescents strengthens offline relationships (Jensen et al., 2021). However, these practices also raise concerns: 76% of children report feeling that parental monitoring apps are invasive and represent a breach of trust (Ghosh et al., 2018). When monitoring crosses into surveillance, it can damage parent–child trust and emotional security.

The key difference between constructive monitoring and harmful surveillance lies in communication style and parenting approach. Effective digital monitoring reflects the principles of authoritative parenting—balancing appropriate oversight with respect for adolescent autonomy (Jonas et al., 2023). For instance, a location check framed as "Hope you arrived safely at the library!" conveys care, while "Where are you?" suggests control. The former strengthens emotional bonds; the latter risks eroding trust.

This distinction underscores the vital interplay between emotional warmth and instrumental communication in digital family interactions. These two forms of communication are not contradictory but mutually reinforcing. Practical support often carries emotional significance when delivered with warmth and engagement (Morelli et al., 2015; Semmer et al., 2008). A simple message such as "I transferred your lunch money—hope you have a great day!" seamlessly blends instrumental and emotional connection, fostering a sense of care and closeness.

Ultimately, the influence of digital technology on children's well-being depends more on parental behavior than on the technology itself. Studies indicate that a parent's preoccupation with their own device predicts a child's attachment insecurity more strongly than the child's own screen time (Linder et al., 2021). Moreover, some forms of digital communication, particularly between mothers and daughters are linked with increased depressive symptoms (He et al., 2024). The relationship between technology use and well-being often follows a U-shaped curve, where both minimal and excessive use correlate with poorer outcomes, while moderate, intentional engagement tends to be most beneficial (Dienlin & Johannes, 2020).

In sum, evidence consistently highlights that in the digital age, the quality of emotional communication matters far more than the quantity of technological monitoring. Effective digital parenting requires modeling healthy engagement, maintaining emotional presence, and ensuring that digital tools enhance rather than replace genuine human connection.

Digital Distance and Family Bond

The pervasive integration of digital technology into everyday family life has created a paradoxical situation: the very tools designed to enhance connection can also produce emotional distance between parents and children, thereby altering family dynamics and developmental outcomes. This sense of digital distance emerges via several mechanisms, chief among them parental emotional withdrawal—behaviours that significantly disrupt children's socio-emotional development. For example, Gallegos et al. (2017) found that father–infant emotional withdrawal at eight months postpartum was negatively associated with toddlers' emotion regulation, whereas mother–infant withdrawal did not show a comparable effect. The implications are that paternal emotional disengagement may carry unique risks in early childhood.

The consequences of parental emotional unavailability extend throughout childhood. Interparental withdrawal negatively affects children's adjustment in multiple domains, and paternal emotional withdrawal frequently precedes maternal rejecting parenting practices, which in turn predict children's internalising behaviours (Sturge-Apple et al., 2006). Children with socially withdrawn temperaments appear especially vulnerable to parental disengagement, suggesting that individual differences moderate the impact of emotional withdrawal (Zarra-Nezhad et al., 2014).

In contemporary families, emotional withdrawal often takes the form of "technoference"—the frequent everyday interruptions of parent–child interaction by digital devices. McDaniel and Radesky (2018) describe how parental technology use and child withdrawal behaviours can become mutually reinforcing, escalating over time. Even toddlers show physiological stress responses such as vagal withdrawal when parents are distracted by devices (Porter et al., 2024). Similarly, adolescents report that perceived parental device distraction reduces their sense of companionship and raises parent–child conflict (Meeus et al., 2021). Research also links parental technoference to increased adolescent anxiety and depression, highlighting how device-induced interference may reshape the emotional climate of the family.

A particular manifestation of technoference is "phubbing" — prioritizing smartphone interactions over in-person communication. Experimental studies show that phubbing reduces perceived communication quality and lowers relationship satisfaction (Chotpitayasunondh & Douglas, 2018). The concept of digital akrasia—the inability to resist digital engagement despite awareness of its social inappropriateness—helps to explain the ubiquity of phubbing (Aagaard, 2019). Research links frequent phubbing to higher levels of Internet addiction and lower self-control, raising concerns about broader implications such as increased social isolation (Brkljačić et al., 2018). Because most studies are cross-sectional, there remains a pressing need for longitudinal and experimental work to clarify causal chains.

These issues have substantial global relevance, especially in settings such as China, where Internet penetration surpasses 78%. Parental phubbing defined as phone use in the presence of children without meaningful engagement has been shown to significantly increase preschoolers' behavioural problems during a critical developmental period. Such behaviours are associated with both internalising outcomes (e.g., anxiety, depression) and externalising outcomes (e.g., aggression), and are linked with reduced autonomy, increased risk of depressive symptoms, and technological dependency (Glickman et al., 2021). Given that parents of preschool children show high rates of device-related interference understanding these mechanisms is now a vital research priority.

According to the displacement hypothesis, parents who are absorbed in mobile devices shift their attention away from children, which may lead to less responsive, more punitive parenting (Valkenburg & Peter, 2007). Empirical work shows that excessive device use undermines parent–child interaction quality through delayed responsiveness, lower emotional engagement, and harsher discipline (Lemish et al., 2020). Over time, this pattern cultivates a sense of emotional neglect and rejection in children, eroding attachment security and increasing rejection sensitivity (Pietromonaco & Powers, 2015). Consistent with Parental Acceptance–Rejection Theory (PART), device-focused inattention may function as a subtle form of parental rejection, with strong associations between technology-induced neglect and children's perceptions of exclusion (Rohner & Lansford, 2017). Children's perceptions often diverge from parental self-reports of device use, with children reporting higher levels of parental device use, a gap that undermines relational trust (Hiniker et al., 2017).

Cultural factors introduce additional complexity. In many Asian societies, higher levels of authoritarian parenting are observed compared with Western contexts (Wilcox, 1998). In China, parental phubbing correlates with authoritarian parenting styles, which have negative implications for preschoolers' executive functioning when parental overcontrol and monitoring replace emotional responsiveness (Fay-Stammbach et al., 2014). Parental attempts to capture children's attention from devices often trigger stricter control, reinforcing cycles of detachment and frustration.

Repeated incidents of phubbing also threaten core emotional bonds in the family. Children often interpret repeated device-based neglect as rejection, which undermines attachment security and leads to maladaptive coping behaviours (Wolfers et al., 2020). Because young children often cannot articulate disappointment verbally, they may respond with attention-seeking behaviours like tantrums or crying. Meanwhile many mothers use devices to manage childcare stress or personal time (Oduor et al., 2016). Tragically, children may internalise these patterns and replicate similar behaviours, contributing to insecure attachment in their own future relationships (Smetana, 2017). According to Attachment Theory (Ainsworth et al., 2015), such patterns of detachment undermine the "secure base" essential for healthy psychological development, and parent–child conflict remains a key risk factor for emotional and behavioural problems.

Parenting roles themselves have been transformed in the digital era. Parents now manage dual roles—providing access to technology and establishing boundaries—yet often face a "generational reversal" in digital expertise, wherein children become the "home gurus" of technology (Livingstone, 2007; Mitchell et al., 2005). Research indicates that fewer than two-thirds of parents consistently engage in meaningful discussions about online experiences with their children, even though such dialogues reduce internet-related risks and promote healthier usage patterns (Fleming et al., 2006; Lee & Chae, 2007; Young, 2008).

Family functioning and marital conflict further complicate this digital landscape. Bowen's family systems theory (Bowen, 1966) emphasizes that emotional conflict between family members affects the entire family system. In this context, adolescents living in conflict-ridden households show higher vulnerability to Internet addiction, and low family cohesion both predicts and results from problematic digital use (De Leo & Wulfert, 2013; Lin & Tsai, 2002).

In sum, the dynamic interplay between digital distance and family bonds underscores the urgent need for emotionally present, technologically mindful parenting that prioritises connection over connectivity. While cultural and contextual variations exist, the quality of parent–child relationships remains the primary determinant of healthy development in this increasingly hyperconnected yet emotionally fragmented age. This is especially relevant in cultural contexts such as China, where the *Family Education Promotion Law* emphasises parents' moral and behavioural guidance. As research continues to evolve, the central challenge for families is to integrate technology thoughtfully while preserving the essential human connections that underpin psychological well-being across generations.

Attachment Theory and Family Bonds in the Digital Age

Attachment Theory, first developed by John Bowlby (1969/1982), posits that early emotional bonds between children and caregivers form the foundation for psychological security and social functioning throughout life. Bowlby identified four core dimensions of attachment: proximity maintenance, safe haven, secure base, and separation distress. These interrelated functions collectively promote a child's sense of safety, emotional regulation, and capacity for exploration (see Figure 1). When caregivers are responsive and emotionally available, children internalize a "secure base" from which to engage with the world and a "safe haven" to return to when distressed (Waters et al., 1991). Over time, these interactions give rise to internal working models, or mental representations of self and others, that guide future relational expectations and behaviors (Mikulincer & Shaver, 2020).

Building on these foundational ideas, empirical research consistently demonstrates that attachment patterns influence a wide range of family dynamics, including conflict resolution, emotional expression, and perceived cohesiveness (Sanyal et al., 2015; Sutton et al., 2019). Securely attached individuals typically exhibit emotional openness and adaptive communication patterns. In contrast, insecure attachment styles such as preoccupied, dismissing, and fearful (Vieira et al., 2012) are often linked to relational avoidance, anxiety, and inconsistent caregiving. These relational scripts tend to persist into adulthood, shaping how parents interact with their children, partners, and extended family members across the lifespan.

As society enters the digital age, the nature of attachment-related interactions has been profoundly transformed. Digital technologies now play a central role in how attachment needs are expressed, negotiated, and managed. Mobile phones, messaging apps, and social media platforms mediate proximity, reassurance, and emotional expression within families. On one hand, these technologies create new opportunities for emotional closeness by enabling continuous connection and immediate access to loved ones. On the other hand, they may foster dependence on technology, constant monitoring, or emotional disengagement. Thus, technology functions as both a bridge and a barrier in modern attachment dynamics.

Emerging research underscores how individual attachment orientations shape digital behaviors. For instance, attachment anxiety predicts more frequent digital checking, reassurance seeking, and electronic monitoring (Konok et al., 2016). For anxiously attached individuals, the smartphone may function as a compensatory attachment object, offering an illusion of closeness during physical separation. Conversely, avoidantly attached individuals often prefer asynchronous communication, such as text or email, which allows for greater emotional distance and control (Morey et al., 2013). In this sense, digital media can simultaneously amplify preexisting attachment insecurities while serving as a coping mechanism for emotional regulation.

Beyond individual tendencies, specific digital behaviors further illustrate how technology disrupts or distorts attachment processes. A particularly salient phenomenon is phubbing, the act of ignoring family members to engage with one's phone. Experimental evidence shows that phubbing undermines relationship satisfaction and perceived communication quality (Chotpitayasunondh & Douglas, 2018). Among couples, frequent phubbing predicts lower relational fulfillment and heightened feelings of exclusion (David & Roberts, 2017). Moreover, attachment style moderates these effects, as insecurely attached individuals are both more likely to engage in phubbing and to feel distressed when it occurs (Shams et al., 2019). Collectively, these findings suggest that digital technologies not only mediate attachment but also reshape its behavioral manifestations, influencing emotional availability and perceived intimacy within family life.

At the same time, for many contemporary families, particularly those separated by geography, digital communication has become essential for maintaining attachment bonds. For migrant or transnational parents, video calls, messaging apps, and shared digital spaces facilitate proximity maintenance and emotional reassurance (Wilding et al., 2006). Yet, these same technologies can produce what Cabalquinto et al. (2018) describe as asymmetrical mobile intimacy, in which emotional closeness is unevenly distributed: some family members feel deeply connected, while others experience surveillance, obligation, or detachment. These disparities often mirror broader inequalities in access, digital literacy, and communicative competence. Consequently, digital intimacy emerges as an ambivalent phenomenon—it sustains emotional connection while simultaneously fragmenting the felt sense of togetherness.

Ultimately, applying Attachment Theory to the digital age illuminates how technology mediates humanity's enduring need for closeness, security, and belonging. Digital communication reshapes the core dimensions of attachment, transforming proximity into constant connectivity, the secure base into digital reassurance, and separation distress into notification anxiety. Understanding these shifts is essential for reimagining emotional availability, caregiving, and family bonding in an increasingly connected world.

Figure 2. The digital-age adaptation of Bowlby's attachment framework

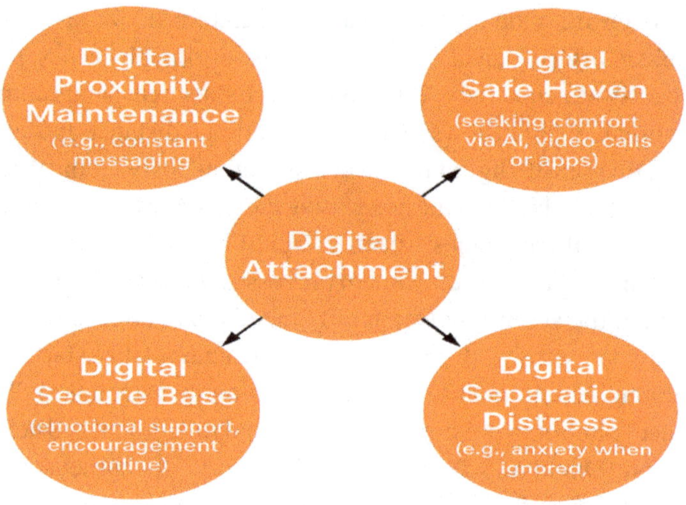

Figure 2 illustrates how core attachment mechanisms—proximity maintenance, secure base, safe haven, and separation distress—are reinterpreted through technology-mediated communication. Digital platforms provide new ways to sustain emotional bonds but also introduce novel vulnerabilities such as surveillance, dependency, and emotional fatigue.

Social Presence Theory and Perceived Closeness

Social Presence Theory offers a foundational lens for understanding how technology-mediated environments shape the perception of relational closeness and emotional connection. The concept of *social presence* refers to the degree to which individuals perceive others as being psychologically and socially "present" during communication. According to Short et al.(1976), different communication media vary in their ability to convey such presence due to differences in the richness of cues they transmit such as facial expressions, gestures, gaze, posture, or vocal tone. Media that enable more nonverbal and paralinguistic cues, such as face-to-face interactions, telephone calls, or video conferencing, provide higher social presence than leaner media such as emails or text messages. Consequently, higher-presence media are often more effective in relational communication, facilitating intimacy, trust, and empathy among family members. In contrast, leaner media are better suited for task-oriented exchanges that rely less on emotional nuance.

Social Presence Theory assumes that the perceived outcome of an interaction largely depends on the medium's capacity to support the desired level of social and emotional communication. In other words, when communication involves personal, relational, or affective content, richer and more synchronous media tend to foster greater satisfaction and closeness. Early studies (Short et al., 1976; Daft & Lengel, 1983) argued that face-to-face communication given its rich repertoire of social cues remains the most effective form for maintaining relationships, while text-based media such as emails, which filter out visual and vocal information, constrain the expression of emotion and empathy. This idea was echoed by "Cues-Filtered-Out" theories (Markus, 1987), which posited that the absence of nonverbal cues in computer-mediated communication (CMC) limits the efficacy of emotional expression and interpersonal understanding. These perspectives characterized early CMC as cold, impersonal, and inferior to face-to-face communication for relational bonding.

However, subsequent theoretical developments challenged these assumptions. Walther's (1992) Social Information Processing (SIP) Theory argued that users adapt to cue-lean environments over time, developing creative strategies to convey emotion and intimacy through textual and temporal features, such as emojis, punctuation, message timing, or linguistic style. Walther suggested that relationships in CMC may develop more slowly but can ultimately reach the same level of relational depth as those formed face-to-face. Later theories, such as Media Richness Theory (Daft & Lengel, 1983) and the Hyperpersonal Model (Walther, 1996), further expanded understanding of how individuals use available technological affordances such as modality, interactivity, and synchronicity to maintain emotional connection and manage impressions in mediated contexts. These developments demonstrated that social presence is not a fixed property of a medium, but rather an *emergent phenomenon* shaped by users' motivations, adaptivity, and communication behaviors.

In the digital age, social presence extends beyond interpersonal communication to include mediated interactions with technology itself. The work of Fogg (2002) highlights the persuasive and affective capacities of digital platforms, where interface design, interactivity, and navigability can amplify the user's sense of social and emotional engagement. In family communication, this translates into the experience of *mediated co-presence* the feeling of "being together apart." For example, shared photos, video calls, and voice messages allow family members to remain emotionally connected across distance, fostering a sense of immediacy and intimacy even without physical proximity. Al-Ghaith (2015) and Anderson (2009) emphasized that immediacy, the perception of rapid and responsive communication—and intimacy, the willingness to disclose and share personal experiences—are two central components of social presence. When these qualities are present, family members perceive greater emotional satisfaction and relational warmth. Conversely, delays in response or lack of affective cues can evoke feelings of neglect or misunderstanding.

Empirical research supports the strong relationship between perceived social presence and emotional outcomes. Richardson et al. (2003) found that higher levels of social presence in online environments correlate with increased satisfaction, trust, and perceived relational quality. Similarly, Rourke (1999) argued that social presence is not merely a technical feature of communication media but a psychological and affective construct that sustains community and belonging. In family contexts, this means that technologies high in social presence such as video calls or synchronous voice communication facilitate emotional regulation, empathy, and the maintenance of familial bonds. However, media low in social presence, such as text-based messaging, may increase ambiguity, reduce emotional expressiveness, and heighten the risk of misinterpretation. For instance, a brief text or delayed reply may be perceived as emotional withdrawal or disinterest, leading to misunderstandings that can erode relational harmony.

The degree of social presence also varies across media forms. Srivastava and Chandra (2018) found that text-based chat produces lower levels of perceived presence compared to audio and video communication, which convey richer cues of tone and facial expression. However, other studies, such as Rickard et al. (2012), noted that text can sometimes elicit greater cognitive involvement and reflective engagement, suggesting that social presence is multidimensional and context-dependent. Interestingly, Connell et al. (2001) found that telephone communication often provides an "optimum blend of richness and presence," allowing emotional expression through vocal tone while maintaining psychological comfort. Similarly, Lee et al. (2003) demonstrated that even subtle voice characteristics such as tone congruent with personality can significantly enhance perceived social presence. Together, these findings suggest that perceived closeness and satisfaction in digital family communication depend not only on technological affordances but also on users' interpretive processes and relational expectations.

Within families, social presence functions as both a *bridge* and a *boundary*. It can bridge emotional distance by enabling ongoing connection through digital proximity—messaging, calls, and social media updates that sustain everyday awareness and affection. Yet, it can also create new forms of misunderstanding, particularly when emotional nuance is lost in translation through mediated cues. For instance, asynchronous communication may fail to convey immediacy, leading to emotional ambiguity or feelings of exclusion. This tension highlights that mediated presence does not replace physical co-presence but redefines it, allowing families to negotiate closeness through hybrid forms of connection where love, intimacy, and misunderstanding coexist in the same digital space. Ultimately, the theory underscores that perceived presence is not only about being "connected" but about being *emotionally available*, and this distinction determines whether digital family interactions foster warmth and satisfaction or distance and confusion.

Figure 3. Dimensions of social presence theory in technology-mediated familial communication

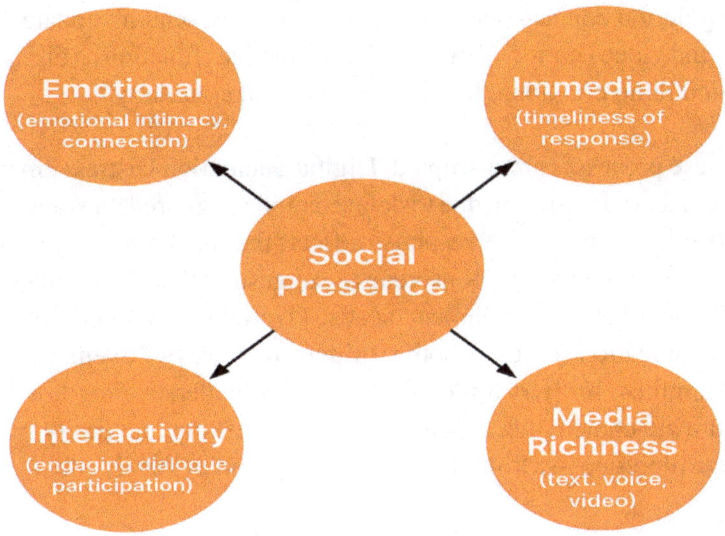

Adapted from Al-Ghaith (2015); Short et al. (1976)

Figure 3 presents a conceptual framework outlining the core components of *digital attachment dynamics* within technology-mediated family relationships. Drawing upon Attachment Theory (Bowlby, 1969/1982), the model illustrates how individuals—particularly children and adolescents—form and maintain emotional bonds through digital communication tools such as messaging apps, video calls, and social media platforms. At the center of the model is Digital Attachment, representing the overarching emotional connection sustained through technological mediation. This construct is supported by three interrelated components: Digital Safe Haven, Digital Secure Base, and Digital Proximity Maintenance.

1. Digital Safe Haven refers to the use of technology for emotional comfort and reassurance during moments of distress. Examples include seeking support through video calls with family members, chatting with a parent via messaging apps, or interacting with AI-driven companions for emotional soothing. This digital comfort-seeking behavior mirrors the traditional attachment function of turning to caregivers for safety and security.

2. Digital Secure Base captures how technology enables individuals to explore their environments confidently while maintaining access to emotional support. Through constant connectivity, family members can provide encouragement and guidance, reinforcing feelings of stability and belonging even when physically apart.
3. Digital Proximity Maintenance involves efforts to sustain closeness through ongoing digital contact—such as frequent texting, sending updates, or sharing photos and videos on social media. These practices function as digital strategies for maintaining emotional bonds and relational continuity.

When these processes are disrupted, Digital Separation Distress emerges, manifesting as anxiety or frustration due to delayed replies, ignored messages, or reduced online presence. This emotional response reflects the attachment system's activation in the absence of perceived responsiveness, suggesting that digital interactions can both fulfill and frustrate attachment needs. Overall, the model emphasizes that digital communication serves as both a bridge and a barrier to emotional intimacy in modern families. It offers a theoretical lens for understanding how technology reshapes core attachment mechanisms—comfort-seeking, proximity maintenance, and secure exploration—within the digital ecosystem of family life.

CONCEPTUAL MODEL AND THEORETICAL PROPOSITIONS

The proposed conceptual model integrates Attachment Theory (1982) and Social Presence Theory (Short et al., 1976) to explain how digital communication technologies influence emotional closeness and satisfaction within family relationships. As illustrated in Figure 3, the model conceptualizes digital attachment behaviors including proximity maintenance, separation distress, and secure base functions as primary predictors of emotional outcomes, while social presence variables (i.e., immediacy, media richness, and perceived presence) serve as mediators and moderators in these relationships.

Attachment Theory posits that human beings seek proximity and emotional security through close relationships. In the digital age, these attachment functions are increasingly enacted through technology, which provides a channel for maintaining emotional connection despite physical separation. The model identifies three key dimensions of digital attachment: *digital proximity maintenance*, or the tendency to remain in frequent digital contact (e.g., constant messaging or video calls) to preserve emotional reassurance; *digital separation distress*, referring to the anxiety or insecurity experienced when messages go unanswered or online presence cues are absent; and *digital secure base*, which reflects the perception that family members are emotionally supportive and available through digital means, such as offering comfort or encouragement online. In technology-mediated family life, individuals who maintain digital proximity and perceive a secure base experience emotional safety, whereas inconsistent or delayed communication may heighten distress and undermine attachment satisfaction. Accordingly, the following propositions are offered:

Proposition 1: Digital proximity maintenance is positively associated with emotional closeness and satisfaction in family relationships.
Proposition 2: Digital separation distress is negatively associated with emotional closeness and satisfaction.
Proposition 3: Perceived digital secure base is positively associated with emotional well-being and relational harmony.

While Attachment Theory explains *why* individuals seek connection, Social Presence Theory explains *how* the sense of connectedness is psychologically and communicatively achieved in mediated environments. Social Presence Theory suggests that individuals' experience of "being with" another person through digital interaction depends on two affordances: *media richness* and *immediacy*, both of which influence the perceived quality of interaction. *Media richness* refers to the capacity of a medium such as text, voice, or video to convey social and emotional cues. Richer media, such as video calls, allow for nonverbal and affective expression, enhancing interpersonal understanding. *Immediacy* reflects the timeliness, responsiveness, and warmth of communication how quickly and attentively family members respond to one another. These affordances shape *perceived presence*, defined as the subjective feeling that one's family member is emotionally and psychologically "there" despite physical distance. When media richness and immediacy are high, perceived presence increases, strengthening emotional bonds and reducing separation anxiety. Conversely, low immediacy or limited media richness can evoke frustration, miscommunication, or emotional detachment. From these assumptions, the following propositions emerge:

Proposition 4: Higher media richness in digital communication enhances perceived presence among family members.
Proposition 5: Greater immediacy in online exchanges increases perceived presence and feelings of connectedness.
Proposition 6: Perceived presence mediates the relationship between digital affordances (media richness, immediacy) and emotional outcomes.

Integrating the two frameworks suggests that social presence variables explain *how and when* digital attachment behaviors lead to positive or negative emotional outcomes. Perceived presence functions as a mediating bridge between digital attachment and emotional satisfaction: rich and immediate media amplify psychological closeness, fulfilling attachment needs for safety, reassurance, and connectedness. However, when immediacy is low or communication lacks expressiveness, attachment functions may be disrupted, resulting in separation distress or emotional fatigue. Thus, technology operates both as a *mediator* facilitating emotional exchange and as a *moderator*, influencing the intensity of attachment outcomes depending on its affordances. Accordingly:

> **Proposition 7:** Perceived presence mediates the relationship between digital attachment dimensions (proximity maintenance, separation distress, and secure base) and emotional outcomes.
>
> **Proposition 8:** The effects of digital attachment dimensions on emotional outcomes are moderated by media richness and immediacy; higher levels of these affordances strengthen the positive impact of attachment behaviors.

Emotional outcomes represent the relational consequences of digitally mediated attachment. Positive outcomes, such as intimacy, trust, and satisfaction, arise when communication is rich, responsive, and emotionally expressive. In contrast, negative outcomes including anxiety, jealousy, or emotional exhaustion emerge when communication lacks immediacy or consistency. Overall, this model demonstrates that digital intimacy depends not merely on connectivity but on the quality of mediated presence and the extent to which technology supports attachment needs. It highlights the dynamic interplay between psychological processes and technological affordances in shaping emotional well-being and family cohesion in the digital era.

Figure 4. A conceptual model of tech-mediated family intimacy integrating Attachment Theory and Social Presence Theory

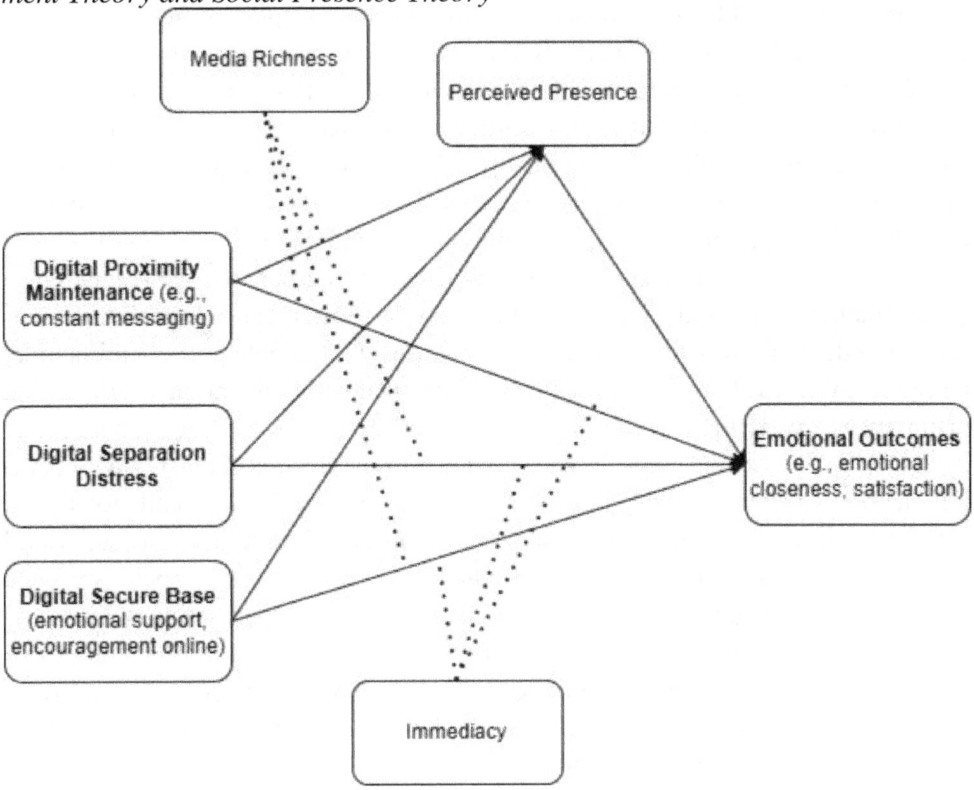

INTERVENTIONS AND RECOMMENDATIONS

To navigate the complex terrain of digital family life, evidence-based interventions must address both technological habits and emotional competencies. First, families should establish "technology-free zones" and designated times that prioritize uninterrupted interaction, particularly during meals, bedtime routines, and special family occasions. These practices help mitigate the effects of technoference and phubbing by creating protected spaces for attachment-building interactions. Research suggests that structured digital boundaries, when collaboratively developed and consistently maintained, can significantly reduce parent-child conflict while increasing perceived emotional availability. Furthermore, families should engage in regular "digital literacy" conversations that go beyond safety concerns to address the emotional impact of different communication mediums. For instance, parents and children can discuss how a hastily sent text might convey unintended emotional tones, or how video calls, while rich in social cues, might sometimes feel intrusive. Educational institutions and healthcare providers can support these efforts through workshops that teach "emotionally intelligent digital communication"—skills that help family members choose appropriate mediums for different emotional needs, recognize the limitations of digital cues, and develop strategies for repairing misunderstandings that inevitably occur in mediated communication. These interventions acknowledge that digital tools are permanent fixtures in family life; thus, the goal is not elimination but mindful integration that preserves emotional connection.

For families navigating specific challenges such as co-parenting arrangements or geographical separation, tailored technological solutions can help maintain emotional bonds while respecting healthy boundaries. Co-parenting applications like OurFamilyWizard should be implemented with clear communication protocols that distinguish between instrumental coordination and emotional exchanges, potentially designating specific platforms for each type of communication. Transnational families can benefit from creating "digital rituals" such as weekly video calls for shared activities, virtual storytimes for grandparents and grandchildren, or private social media groups for sharing everyday moments. These rituals leverage social presence theory by maximizing media richness and immediacy to sustain emotional connection across distances. However, it's crucial to recognize and address "asymmetrical mobile intimacy" by ensuring all family members have equal access, digital literacy, and comfort with chosen platforms. For families with young children, parents should practice "engaged mediation" during digital interactions—verbally narrating their actions when they must use devices in their children's presence and explaining why certain digital boundaries exist. These practices transform potential sources of conflict into opportunities for teaching digital citizenship and emotional awareness.

At a broader societal level, policymakers and technology developers share responsibility for fostering digital environments that support rather than undermine family intimacy. This requires moving beyond individual behavior change to address structural factors that contribute to digital distance. Technology companies should design products with "family-friendly" defaults that encourage mindful usage, such as features that highlight screen time patterns or suggest breaks during prolonged use. Educational systems should integrate digital wellness into standard curricula, teaching children and parents alike to critically evaluate how technology affects their relationships and emotional well-being. Workplace policies must recognize the impact of "digital leash" expectations on family life, establishing norms that respect non-work hours and discourage constant connectivity. Additionally, public health campaigns should raise awareness about the developmental consequences of parental phubbing, particularly during early childhood, and promote the concept of "emotional availability" as a crucial component of digital citizenship. By addressing these issues at multiple levels (individual, familial, and societal), we can cultivate a digital ecosystem that truly serves human connection, ensuring that technological advancement enhances rather than diminishes the emotional bonds that form the foundation of family life and human well-being.

FUTURE RESEARCH DIRECTIONS

The investigation of technology-mediated family relationships, while growing rapidly, reveals several critical avenues for future scholarly inquiry. First, there is a pressing need for longitudinal studies that track how digital communication patterns evolve across the family life cycle and how these patterns influence long-term attachment security and relational satisfaction. Most current research provides snapshot views of family digital practices, yet the psychological impact of sustained technoference or digitally-mediated attachment may accumulate or transform over years and developmental stages. Future research should examine how early experiences with parental phubbing affect children's relational templates in adolescence and adulthood, and whether certain family communication practices can buffer these effects. Furthermore, as new technologies continually emerge, research must investigate how increasingly immersive platforms such as virtual reality family gatherings or AI-facilitated communication reshape the experience of presence and emotional intimacy. These studies should particularly focus on vulnerable populations, including transnational families, single-parent households, and families experiencing socioeconomic disadvantage, who may experience both the benefits and drawbacks of digital communication with particular intensity. The cultural dimensions of digital family intimacy also demand greater attention, as current research remains predominantly Western-focused, while family communication norms, attachment styles, and technology adoption patterns vary significantly across cultural contexts.

A second crucial direction involves developing more sophisticated methodological approaches to capture the complex, multi-layered nature of digital family communication. Most existing studies rely on self-report measures, which are subject to social desirability biases and may not accurately reflect actual digital behaviors. Future research should incorporate objective data tracking alongside qualitative methods to create richer understandings of how technology is interwoven into daily family interactions. Ecological momentary assessment could provide real-time insights into how specific digital communications affect mood and relational connectedness throughout the day. Additionally, dyadic and family-level analyses are needed to move beyond individual experiences and examine how technology shapes and is shaped by family system dynamics. Neurophysiological methods could illuminate the biological correlates of digital connection and disconnection, building on existing research showing that parental phone use triggers physiological stress responses in children. As family communication becomes increasingly mediated through multiple simultaneous channels, research must also develop frameworks for understanding "multi-channel intimacy"—how families navigate different platforms for different relational purposes and how this segmentation affects overall family functioning.

Finally, future research should focus on developing and testing evidence-based interventions that help families harness technology for connection while minimizing its disruptive potential. This includes designing and evaluating "digital mindfulness" programs tailored to different family structures and cultural contexts, creating tools that help families establish healthy digital boundaries, and developing clinical approaches for addressing technology-related family conflict. Research is particularly needed on how to adapt existing family therapies to address digital intrusion as a presenting problem, especially for families where technology has become a focal point for conflict or emotional disengagement. Additionally, as artificial intelligence becomes increasingly integrated into family life, research must investigate the ethical and psychological implications of children forming attachment-like bonds with AI entities, and how these relationships affect human family dynamics. By pursuing these research directions with methodological rigor and theoretical sophistication, scholars can provide the insights needed to help families navigate an increasingly digital world while preserving the human connections that remain fundamental to psychological well-being across the lifespan.

CONCLUSION

The chapter through the landscape of technology-mediated family life reveals a complex and often contradictory reality: digital tools simultaneously bridge and create distance, fostering virtual intimacies while risking emotional disconnection. This chapter has demonstrated that the fundamental question is not whether technology is good or bad for family bonds, but *how* it is integrated into the delicate fabric of family relationships. The evidence consistently shows that the quality of connection depends less on the technology itself and more on the human communication and emotional intentionality that surrounds it. Digital tools can streamline co-parenting logistics, sustain heritage languages across continents, and provide a digital safe haven for adolescents, yet these same platforms can become conduits for conflict, instruments of surveillance, and sources of profound emotional neglect when used as substitutes for genuine engagement.

The integration of Attachment Theory and Social Presence Theory provides a powerful lens for understanding these dynamics. It illuminates how our innate need for a secure base and safe haven is now negotiated through screens and notifications, and how the perceived closeness in these interactions is shaped by the richness and immediacy of the digital medium. The conceptual model presented offers a pathway for future research to systematically investigate how digital attachment behaviors (proximity maintenance, separation distress, and the secure base function) interact with technological affordances to produce either relational satisfaction or dysfunction. This theoretical synthesis moves the discourse beyond simplistic screen-time metrics toward a more nuanced understanding of how technology mediates our most fundamental human need for connection.

Ultimately, the challenge for contemporary families is not to resist technological change, but to master the art of digital mindfulness to consciously shape their digital ecosystems in ways that protect and nurture human connection. This requires establishing boundaries that safeguard quality time, developing literacy in the emotional nuances of different communication platforms, and, most importantly, ensuring that technology serves as a tool to enhance rather than replace the irreplaceable elements of human interaction: shared presence, emotional attachments, and the secure, loving bonds that form the foundation of family life across the lifespan. The future of family intimacy in the digital age will be determined by our collective ability to harness the connective potential of our tools while fiercely protecting the human spaces where true relationship resides.

REFERENCES

Aagaard, J. (2019). Multitasking as distraction: A conceptual analysis of media multitasking research. *Theory & Psychology*, *29*(1), 87–99. DOI: 10.1177/0959354318815766

Abel, S., Machin, T., & Brownlow, C. (2021). Social media, rituals, and long-distance family relationship maintenance: A mixed-methods systematic review. *New Media & Society*, *23*(3), 632–654. DOI: 10.1177/1461444820958717

Ainsworth, M. D. S., Blehar, M. C., Waters, E., & Wall, S. N. (2015). *Patterns of attachment: A psychological study of the strange situation*. Psychology press. DOI: 10.4324/9780203758045

Al-Ghaith, W. (2015). Understanding social network usage: Impact of co-presence, intimacy, and immediacy. *International Journal of Advanced Computer Science and Applications*, *6*(8), 99–111. DOI: 10.14569/IJACSA.2015.060813

Anderson, T. L. (2009). Online instructor immediacy and instructor-student relationships in Second Life. *Higher Education in Virtual Worlds: Teaching and Learning in Second Life*, *1*, 101–114.

Baldassar, L. (2016). De-demonizing distance in mobile family lives: Co-presence, care circulation and polymedia as vibrant matter. *Global Networks*, *16*(2), 145–163. DOI: 10.1111/glob.12109

Bowlby, J. (1982). Attachment and loss: Retrospect and prospect. *The American Journal of Orthopsychiatry*, *52*(4), 664–678. DOI: 10.1111/j.1939-0025.1982.tb01456.x PMID: 7148988

Brkljačić, T., Šakić, V., & Kaliterna-Lipovčan, L. J. (2018). Phubbing among Croatian students. *Protection and Promotion of the Well-Being of Children, Youth, and Families: Selected Proceedings of the 1st International Scientific Conference of the Department of Psychology at the Catholic University of Croatia*, 109–126.

Burholt, V., Windle, G., Gott, M., & Morgan, D. J. (2020). Technology-mediated communication in familial relationships: Moderated-mediation models of isolation and loneliness. *The Gerontologist*, *60*(7), 1202–1212. DOI: 10.1093/geront/gnaa040 PMID: 32369112

Burholt, V., Windle, G., Morgan, D. J., & Team, C. W. (2017). A social model of loneliness: The roles of disability, social resources, and cognitive impairment. *The Gerontologist*, *57*(6), 1020–1030. DOI: 10.1093/geront/gnw125 PMID: 27831482

Cabalquinto, E. C. (2018). Home on the move: Negotiating differential domesticity in family life at a distance. *Media Culture & Society*, *40*(6), 795–816. DOI: 10.1177/0163443717737611

Cabalquinto, E. C. B. (2021). Telecocooning in the age of (im) mobility. *Communication, Culture & Critique*, *14*(2), 351–355. DOI: 10.1093/ccc/tcab024

Cairncross, F. (2002). The death of distance. *RSA Journal*, *149*(5502), 40–42.

Chotpitayasunondh, V., & Douglas, K. M. (2018). Measuring phone snubbing behavior: Development and validation of the Generic Scale of Phubbing (GSP) and the Generic Scale of Being Phubbed (GSBP). *Computers in Human Behavior*, *88*, 5–17. DOI: 10.1016/j.chb.2018.06.020

Connell, D., & Goldberg, J. P.David Connell, Jeanne P. Goldberg. (2001). An Intervention to Increase Fruit and Vegetable Consumption Using Audio Communications: In-Store Public Service Announcements and AudioTapes. *Journal of Health Communication*, *6*(1), 31–43. DOI: 10.1080/10810730150501396 PMID: 11317422

Couclelis, H. (1996). The Death of Distance. *Environment and Planning. B, Planning & Design*, *23*(4), 387–389. DOI: 10.1068/b230387

Curdt-Christiansen, X. L., & Iwaniec, J. (2023). ' , I miss you ': Emotional multilingual practices in transnational families. *The International Journal of Bilingualism*, *27*(2), 159–180. DOI: 10.1177/13670069221125342

Daft, R. L., & Lengel, R. H. (1983). Information richness. A new approach to managerial behavior and organization design. *Research in Organizational Behavior*, *6*, 191–233.

David, M. E., & Roberts, J. A. (2017). Phubbed and Alone: Phone Snubbing, Social Exclusion, and Attachment to Social Media. *Journal of the Association for Consumer Research*, *2*(2), 155–163. DOI: 10.1086/690940

De Leo, J. A., & Wulfert, E. (2013). Problematic Internet use and other risky behaviors in college students: An application of problem-behavior theory. *Psychology of Addictive Behaviors*, *27*(1), 133–141. DOI: 10.1037/a0030823 PMID: 23276311

Dienlin, T., & Johannes, N. (2020). The impact of digital technology use on adolescent well-being. *Dialogues in Clinical Neuroscience*, *22*(2), 135–142. DOI: 10.31887/DCNS.2020.22.2/tdienlin PMID: 32699513

Fay-Stammbach, T., Hawes, D. J., & Meredith, P. (2014). Parenting influences on executive function in early childhood: A review. *Child Development Perspectives*, *8*(4), 258–264. DOI: 10.1111/cdep.12095

Fleming, L. E., Broad, K., Clement, A., Dewailly, E., Elmir, S., Knap, A., Pomponi, S. A., Smith, S., Solo Gabriele, H., & Walsh, P. (2006). Oceans and human health: Emerging public health risks in the marine environment. *Marine Pollution Bulletin, 53*(10-12), 545–560. DOI: 10.1016/j.marpolbul.2006.08.012 PMID: 16996542

Fogg, B. J. (2002). Persuasive technology: Using computers to change what we think and do. *Ubiquity, 2002*(December), 2. DOI: 10.1145/764008.763957

Gallegos, M. I., Murphy, S. E., Benner, A. D., Jacobvitz, D. B., & Hazen, N. L. (2017). Marital, parental, and whole-family predictors of toddlers' emotion regulation: The role of parental emotional withdrawal. *Journal of Family Psychology, 31*(3), 294–303. DOI: 10.1037/fam0000245 PMID: 27617477

Ganong, L. H., Coleman, M., Feistman, R., Jamison, T., & Stafford Markham, M. (2012). Communication technology and postdivorce coparenting. *Family Relations, 61*(3), 397–409. DOI: 10.1111/j.1741-3729.2012.00706.x

Ghosh, A. K., Badillo-Urquiola, K., Guha, S., LaViola, J. J.Jr, & Wisniewski, P. J. (2018). Safety vs. surveillance: What children have to say about mobile apps for parental control. *Proceedings of the 2018 CHI Conference on Human Factors in Computing Systems*, 1–14. DOI: 10.1145/3173574.3173698

Glickman, E. A., Choi, K. W., Lussier, A. A., Smith, B. J., & Dunn, E. C. (2021). Childhood emotional neglect and adolescent depression: Assessing the protective role of peer social support in a longitudinal birth cohort. *Frontiers in Psychiatry, 12*, 681176. DOI: 10.3389/fpsyt.2021.681176 PMID: 34434126

Golden, J., Conroy, R. M., Bruce, I., Denihan, A., Greene, E., Kirby, M., & Lawlor, B. A. (2009). Loneliness, social support networks, mood and wellbeing in community-dwelling elderly. *International Journal of Geriatric Psychiatry, 24*(7), 694–700. DOI: 10.1002/gps.2181 PMID: 19274642

Gonçalves, K., & Lexander, K. V. (2023). Permanent or temporary homes?: Investigating the discourses of lifestyle migration, lifestyle mobilities and multilingualism within a Norwegian context. *AILA Review, 36*(2), 299–320. DOI: 10.1075/aila.00057.gon

Hareven, T. K. (2018). *Families, history and social change: Life course and cross-cultural perspectives*. Routledge. DOI: 10.4324/9780429500572

He, R., Suitor, J. J., & Gilligan, M. (2024). Digital Contact as Strain or Support: How Does Type of Contact Shape the Association Between Mother–Child Interactions and Adult Children's Depressive Symptoms in Later-Life Families? *The Gerontologist, 64*(12), 1–11. DOI: 10.1093/geront/gnae158 PMID: 39487712

Hiniker, A., Lee, B., Sobel, K., & Choe, E. K. (2017). Plan & play: supporting intentional media use in early childhood. In *Proceedings of the 2017 conference on interaction design and children* (pp. 85-95). DOI: 10.1145/3078072.3079752

Hodgkinson, G. P., & Healey, M. P. (2014). Coming in from the cold: The psychological foundations of radical innovation revisited. *Industrial Marketing Management, 43*(8), 1306–1313. DOI: 10.1016/j.indmarman.2014.08.012

Holt-Lunstad, J., Smith, T. B., Baker, M., Harris, T., & Stephenson, D. (2015). Loneliness and Social Isolation as Risk Factors for Mortality: A Meta-Analytic Review. *Perspectives on Psychological Science, 10*(2), 227–237. DOI: 10.1177/1745691614568352 PMID: 25910392

Holwerda, T. J., Deeg, D. J., Beekman, A. T., Van Tilburg, T. G., Stek, M. L., Jonker, C., & Schoevers, R. A. (2014). Feelings of loneliness, but not social isolation, predict dementia onset: Results from the Amsterdam Study of the Elderly (AMS). *Journal of Neurology, Neurosurgery, and Psychiatry, 85*(2), 135–142. DOI: 10.1136/jnnp-2012-302755 PMID: 23232034

Jensen, M., George, M. J., Russell, M. A., Lippold, M. A., & Odgers, C. L. (2021). Does Adolescent Digital Technology Use Detract from the Parent–Adolescent Relationship? *Journal of Research on Adolescence, 31*(2), 469–481. DOI: 10.1111/jora.12618 PMID: 33829598

Jonas, R. M., Hanrahan, B. V., Sloan, C. J., & Fosco, G. M. (2023). Supporting from the Background: How a Mobile Application for Parent Skills Development Encourages Authoritative Parenting. *Computer Supported Cooperative Work and Social Computing*, 105–111. DOI: 10.1145/3584931.3606969

Konok, V., Gigler, D., Bereczky, B. M., & Miklósi, Á. (2016). Humans' attachment to their mobile phones and its relationship with interpersonal attachment style. *Computers in Human Behavior, 61*, 537–547. DOI: 10.1016/j.chb.2016.03.062

Kraut, R., Patterson, M., Lundmark, V., Kiesler, S., Mukophadhyay, T., & Scherlis, W. (1998). Internet paradox: A social technology that reduces social involvement and psychological well-being? *The American Psychologist, 53*(9), 1017–1031. DOI: 10.1037/0003-066X.53.9.1017 PMID: 9841579

Lee, S. J., & Chae, Y. G. (2007). Children's Internet use in a family context: Influence on family relationships and parental mediation. *Cyberpsychology & Behavior, 10*(5), 640–644. DOI: 10.1089/cpb.2007.9975 PMID: 17927531

Lemish, D., Elias, N., & Floegel, D. (2020). "Look at me!" Parental use of mobile phones at the playground. *Mobile Media & Communication*, *8*(2), 170–187. DOI: 10.1177/2050157919846916

Lim, S. S. (2019). *Transcendent parenting: Raising children in the digital age*. Oxford University Press.

Lin, S. S., & Tsai, C. C. (2002). Sensation seeking and internet dependence of Taiwanese high school adolescents. *Computers in Human Behavior*, *18*(4), 411–426. DOI: 10.1016/S0747-5632(01)00056-5

Linder, L. K., McDaniel, B. T., Stockdale, L., & Coyne, S. M. (2021). The impact of parent and child media use on early parent–infant attachment. *Infancy*, *26*(4), 551–569. DOI: 10.1111/infa.12400 PMID: 33773012

Lubben, J. (2017). Addressing social isolation as a potent killer! *The Public Policy and Aging Report*, *27*(4), 136–138. DOI: 10.1093/ppar/prx026

Madianou, M., & Miller, D. (2013). *Migration and new media: Transnational families and polymedia*. Routledge. DOI: 10.4324/9780203154236

Markus, M. L. (1987). Toward a "critical mass" theory of interactive media: Universal access, interdependence and diffusion. *Communication Research*, *14*(5), 491–511. DOI: 10.1177/009365087014005003

McDaniel, B. T., & Radesky, J. S. (2018). Technoference: Parent Distraction With Technology and Associations With Child Behavior Problems. *Child Development*, *89*(1), 100–109. DOI: 10.1111/cdev.12822 PMID: 28493400

Meeus, A., Coenen, L., Eggermont, S., & Beullens, K. (2021). Family technoference: Exploring parent mobile device distraction from children's perspectives. *Mobile Media & Communication*, *9*(3), 584–604. DOI: 10.1177/2050157921991602

Mikulincer, M., & Shaver, R., P. (. (2020). Enhancing the "broaden and build" cycle of attachment security in adulthood: From the laboratory to relational contexts and societal systems. *International Journal of Environmental Research and Public Health*, *17*(6), 2054. DOI: 10.3390/ijerph17062054 PMID: 32244872

Mitchell, J. P., Macrae, C. N., & Banaji, M. R. (2005). Forming impressions of people versus inanimate objects: Social-cognitive processing in the medial prefrontal cortex. *NeuroImage*, *26*(1), 251–257. DOI: 10.1016/j.neuroimage.2005.01.031 PMID: 15862225

Morelli, S. A., Lee, I. A., Arnn, M. E., & Zaki, J. (2015). Emotional and instrumental support provision interact to predict well-being. *Emotion (Washington, D.C.)*, *15*(4), 484–493. DOI: 10.1037/emo0000084 PMID: 26098734

Morey, J. N., Gentzler, A. L., Creasy, B., Oberhauser, A. M., & Westerman, D. (2013). Young adults' use of communication technology within their romantic relationships and associations with attachment style. *Computers in Human Behavior*, *29*(4), 1771–1778. DOI: 10.1016/j.chb.2013.02.019

Oduor, E., Neustaedter, C., Odom, W., Tang, A., Moallem, N., Tory, M., & Irani, P. (2016). The frustrations and benefits of mobile device usage in the home when co-present with family members. In *Proceedings of the 2016 ACM conference on designing interactive systems* (pp. 1315-1327). DOI: 10.1145/2901790.2901809

Palviainen, Å. (2020). Video calls as a nexus of practice in multilingual translocal families. *Zeitschrift Für Interkulturellen Fremdsprachenunterricht*, *25*(1), 85–108.

Palviainen, Å., & Kędra, J. (2020). What's in the family app? *Journal of Multilingual Theories and Practices*, *1*(1), 89–111. DOI: 10.1558/jmtp.15363

Pietromonaco, P. R., & Powers, S. I. (2015). Attachment and health-related physiological stress processes. *Current Opinion in Psychology*, *1*, 34–39. DOI: 10.1016/j.copsyc.2014.12.001 PMID: 25729755

Porter, C. L., Coyne, S. M., Chojnacki, N. A., McDaniel, B. T., Reschke, P. J., & Stockdale, L. A. (2024). Toddlers' physiological response to parent's mobile device distraction and technoference. *Developmental Psychobiology*, *66*(2), e22460. DOI: 10.1002/dev.22460

Räisä, T. (2022). Family relations: Emotional overload. In *Mediatisation of emotional life* (pp. 151–167). Routledge. DOI: 10.4324/9781003254287-13

Richardson, D. C., Spivey, M. J., Barsalou, L. W., & McRae, K. (2003). Spatial representations activated during real-time comprehension of verbs. *Cognitive Science*, *27*(5), 767–780.

Rickard, N. S., Bambrick, C. J., & Gill, A. (2012). Absence of widespread psychosocial and cognitive effects of school-based music instruction in 10–13-year-old students. *International Journal of Music Education*, *30*(1), 57–78. DOI: 10.1177/0255761411431399

Rohner, R. P., & Lansford, J. E. (2017). Deep structure of the human affectional system: Introduction to interpersonal acceptance–rejection theory. *Journal of Family Theory & Review*, *9*(4), 426–440. DOI: 10.1111/jftr.12219

Rourke, L. (1999). Assessing social presence in asynchronous text-based computer conferencing. *Journal of Distance Education*.

Said, F. F. (2021). 'Ba-SKY-a P with her each day at dinner': Technology as supporter in the learning and management of home languages. *Journal of Multilingual and Multicultural Development, 42*(8), 747–762. DOI: 10.1080/01434632.2021.1924755

Sanyal, D., Grassitelli, L., Langer, N., & Bestenlehner, J. M. (2015). Massive main-sequence stars evolving at the Eddington limit. *Astronomy & Astrophysics, 580*, A20. DOI: 10.1051/0004-6361/201525945

Semmer, N. K., Elfering, A., Jacobshagen, N., Perrot, T., Beehr, T. A., & Boos, N. (2008). The emotional meaning of instrumental social support. *International Journal of Stress Management, 15*(3), 235–251. DOI: 10.1037/1072-5245.15.3.235

Shams, M., Iftikhar, U., & Raja, A. A. (2019). Impact of attachment styles on relationship satisfaction: Mediating role of phubbing behavior. *IBT Journal of Business Studies (JBS), 1*(1).

Shankar, A., McMunn, A., Demakakos, P., Hamer, M., & Steptoe, A. (2017). Social isolation and loneliness: Prospective associations with functional status in older adults. *Health Psychology, 36*(2), 179–187. DOI: 10.1037/hea0000437 PMID: 27786518

Short, J., Williams, E., & Christie, B. (1976). *The social psychology of telecommunications*. Wiley. https://cir.nii.ac.jp/crid/1130282268777950720

Smetana, J. G. (2017). Current research on parenting styles, dimensions, and beliefs. *Current Opinion in Psychology, 15*, 19–25. DOI: 10.1016/j.copsyc.2017.02.012 PMID: 28813261

Srivastava, S. C., & Chandra, S. (2018). Social presence in virtual world collaboration. *Management Information Systems Quarterly, 42*(3), 779–A16. DOI: 10.25300/MISQ/2018/11914

Stæhr, A. C., & Nørreby, T. R. (2021). The metapragmatics of mode choice. *Pragmatics and Society, 12*(5), 756–781. DOI: 10.1075/ps.20050.can

Sturge-Apple, M. L., Davies, P. T., & Cummings, E. M. (2006). Impact of Hostility and Withdrawal in Interparental Conflict on Parental Emotional Unavailability and Children's Adjustment Difficulties. *Child Development, 77*(6), 1623–1641. DOI: 10.1111/j.1467-8624.2006.00963.x PMID: 17107450

Sutton, A., Clowes, M., Preston, L., & Booth, A. (2019). Meeting the review family: Exploring review types and associated information retrieval requirements. *Health Information and Libraries Journal, 36*(3), 202–222. DOI: 10.1111/hir.12276 PMID: 31541534

Valkenburg, P. M., & Peter, J. (2007). Online communication and adolescent well-being: Testing the stimulation versus the displacement hypothesis. *Journal of Computer-Mediated Communication, 12*(4), 1169–1182. DOI: 10.1111/j.1083-6101.2007.00368.x

Vieira, A. D. P., De Passillé, A. M., & Weary, D. M. (2012). Effects of the early social environment on behavioral responses of dairy calves to novel events. *Journal of Dairy Science, 95*(9), 5149–5155. DOI: 10.3168/jds.2011-5073 PMID: 22916920

Walther, J. B. (1996). Computer-mediated communication: Impersonal, interpersonal, and hyperpersonal interaction. *Communication Research, 23*(1), 3–43. DOI: 10.1177/009365096023001001

Waters, C. L., Menk, F. W., & Fraser, B. J. (1991). The resonance structure of low latitude Pc3 geomagnetic pulsations. *Geophysical Research Letters, 18*(12), 2293–2296. DOI: 10.1029/91GL02550

Wilcox, D. C. (1998). *Turbulence modeling for CFD* (Vol. 2, pp. 103-217). La Canada, CA: DCW industries.

Wilding, R. (2006). 'Virtual' intimacies? Families communicating across transnational contexts. *Global Networks, 6*(2), 125–142. DOI: 10.1111/j.1471-0374.2006.00137.x

Wolfers, L. N., Kitzmann, S., Sauer, S., & Sommer, N. (2020). Phone use while parenting: An observational study to assess the association of maternal sensitivity and smartphone use in a playground setting. *Computers in Human Behavior, 102*, 31–38. DOI: 10.1016/j.chb.2019.08.013

Zarra-Nezhad, M., Kiuru, N., Aunola, K., Zarra-Nezhad, M., Ahonen, T., Poikkeus, A., Lerkkanen, M., & Nurmi, J. (2014). Social withdrawal in children moderates the association between parenting styles and the children's own socioemotional development. *Journal of Child Psychology and Psychiatry, and Allied Disciplines, 55*(11), 1260–1269. DOI: 10.1111/jcpp.12251 PMID: 24827990

Chapter 2
The Digital Hearth and the Curated Self in Modern Family Life

Seyedali Ahrari
http://orcid.org/0009-0009-8947-6147
Umiversity of Religions and Denominations, Iran

Ali Farsimadan
University of Religions and Denominations, Iran

ABSTRACT

This chapter introduces "digital kinship," arguing that technology actively transforms family bonds, rather than just facilitating communication. It posits that digital tools are a primary arena where the familial self is constructed. By integrating Symbolic Interactionism (for identity work) and Family Systems Theory (for emotional dynamics), the analysis examines sites like social media feeds and group chats. It reveals how platform features shape family processes, using emojis for identity, creating digital hearths for support, and navigating digital fog. The proposed model frames digital kinship as an ongoing achievement, offering insights for theory and practical application in therapy and education.

1. INTRODUCTION

Kinship is also a sociocultural construction, one that creates a network of social and biological relationships between individuals. Through kinship systems, humans create meaning by interpreting social and biological relationships (McKinlay, 2023). The contemporary family is increasingly a digitally-mediated institution (Nichols

DOI: 10.4018/979-8-2600-0934-5.ch002

& Selim, 2022). The rapid proliferation of communication platforms has fundamentally altered the fabric of kinship. No longer confined to shared physical spaces or synchronous time, family life now unfolds across a hybrid sphere, intertwining the material and the digital (Qian & Hu, 2024). This digital layer is not merely a supplementary channel for logistics and updates; it has become a primary site for the ongoing, dynamic processes of being and doing family (Rondi et al., 2024). It is within this context that the concepts of identity construction and emotional regulation, long central to understanding family systems, demand re-examination.

Existing scholarship has effectively mapped the terrain of computer-mediated communication (CMC) within families, establishing that digital tools are crucial for maintaining relational ties across geographical distance (Baruah, 2025). Research has documented the use of these technologies for instrumental support, the exchange of social capital, and the performance of family rituals online. Simultaneously, a rich body of work in psychology and sociology has detailed how identity is formed and negotiated within the family unit, and how individuals develop strategies to manage their emotions in response to familial interactions (Abel et al., 2021). However, these two streams of inquiry have largely run in parallel. The specific, intricate ways in which digital platforms are harnessed not just for communication, but as active arenas for the construction of a familial self and the regulation of complex emotions, remains underexplored.

This gap in the literature forms the central problem for this study. While we know that families communicate online, we lack a deep, qualitative understanding of how the architectural affordances and constraints of digital platforms, such as asynchronicity, editability, persistence, and public/private audience management, shape core psychosocial processes (Xu, 2024). For instance, how does the ability to edit a message in a family group chat before sending it facilitate a new form of emotional regulation? In what ways do curate family posts on Instagram or Facebook contribute to an individual's identity narrative, both within the family and to the outside world? The current research landscape often treats the digital as a neutral conduit, failing to interrogate it as a transformative medium that actively co-constitutes kinship practices (Cruz, 2025).

Therefore, this study seeks to bridge this gap by investigating the phenomenon of digital kinship (DK), the experience and practice of family relationships as mediated and constituted through digital technologies. The primary research questions guiding this inquiry are:

1. How do individuals utilize digital communication platforms to construct, perform, and negotiate their identities within the family context?

2. What strategies of emotional regulation do individuals employ in online family interactions, and how are these strategies influenced by the specific features of digital media?

By addressing these questions, this study aims to contribute a nuanced theoretical framework that integrates media studies with family sociology and psychology. It positions digital platforms not as passive tools, but as agentic forces in the ongoing drama of family life, where the self is made and remade, and emotions are meticulously managed. Through an exploration of DK, this research will illuminate the profound and subtle ways in which our most intimate relationships are being reshaped in the digital age.

Historically, digital technology was often framed within family studies as an external force, a potential disruptor that existed on the periphery of "real" kinship (Abel, 2021). Early research focused on concerns about time displacement, where screen time was seen as competing with face-to-face interaction, and the internet was characterized as a separate "cyberspace" one could log into and, crucially, log out of (Waterworth, 2025). This perspective positioned the digital as a distinct and often intrusive realm, threatening the sanctity of the home as a purely physical and unmediated environment. The family, in this view, was a bounded entity that needed to manage its relationship with technology, defending its organic core against digital encroachment.

This framing, however, has been rendered obsolete by the pervasive normalization of connected media. The contemporary family is now a digitally saturated unit, where technology is not a separate sphere but an embedded, ubiquitous, and essential infrastructure of daily life (Willett & Wheeler, 2021). Smartphones are constant companions, social media (SM) groups serve as the continuous "heartbeat" of the household, cloud albums are the default family photo album, and smart speakers manage domestic schedules (Rogers-Whitehead, 2025). Digital tools have moved from the periphery to the very center of familial practice, becoming the primary medium for coordinating logistics, sharing milestones, performing care, and navigating conflicts. This shift demands a fundamental reconceptualization: the digital is no longer a layer on top of family life; it is a constitutive element of it, fundamentally reshaping the how, when, and where of kinship itself.

The integration of digital media into the family sphere is not merely a change in communication tools, but a fundamental transformation of kinship itself (Kang, 2012). Core experiences of relatedness are being reshaped through technological affordances. For instance, the creation of persistent, semi-public family groups on platforms generates a new kind of "always-on" kinship, where the family unit exists as a continuous, accessible background presence regardless of physical location. This transforms rituals; a daily check-in evolves from a phone call into a cascading thread of emoji reactions, photos of meals, and voice notes, creating a distributed and asynchronous form of co-presence. Similarly, the use of shared cloud albums for storing family photos redefines collective memory. Curating these albums becomes a collaborative project of identity formation, where what is saved, tagged, and commented on actively constructs the family's official narrative, making kinship a consciously authored and archived project in ways that traditional photo albums never allowed.

This digitally-mediated environment also profoundly alters the processes of identity construction and emotional regulation (Carter & Asencio, 2019). The self that one presents to the family is no longer forged solely in spontaneous, face-to-face interactions but is increasingly curated and edited (Pauwels, 2008). The asynchronous and editable nature of text-based communication, for example, provides a "buffer" that allows individuals to carefully craft messages, rehearse emotional disclosures, or strategically delay responses to manage familial expectations and tensions. This affords new forms of control over self-presentation, enabling individuals to manage impressions and regulate emotional output with a precision unavailable in the fluid, high-stakes context of the family dinner table. Conversely, the constant connectivity can also amplify emotional labor, creating new anxieties around availability and the performance of familial closeness. Thus, the digital sphere becomes a crucial psychological workspace where the familial self is continuously assembled, performed, and emotionally managed, blurring the lines between the organic and the curated, the felt and the performed.

2. THEORETICAL FOUNDATIONS: A DUAL LENS FOR DIGITAL KINSHIP

To adequately analyze the complexities of DK, this study adopts an integrated theoretical framework, merging the sociological insights of Symbolic Interactionism (SI) with the media-centric approach of Affordance Theory (AT). SI, with its premise that the self is constructed through social interaction and the interpretation of symbols, provides a vital lens for understanding identity construction within the family (Stryker, 1959). It posits that individuals derive their sense of self from the reflected appraisals of significant others; a process traditionally located in physical co-presence. In the context of this research, it raises a crucial question: how is this "looking-glass self" reconfigured when the "mirror" is a digital platform, and the "symbols" of interaction include curated images, edited texts, and reaction emojis? This perspective allows us to view online family spaces not as mere channels of information, but as dynamic arenas where meanings are negotiated, roles are performed, and the familial self is continuously made and remade through digital dialogue.

However, to understand how these interactions are shaped, we must examine the medium itself. This is where AT becomes essential. Rather than treating technology as a neutral pipe, this lens focuses on the specific action possibilities that digital platforms invite, constrain, and shape. Key affordances such as persistence (the lasting nature of messages and photos), editability (the ability to craft and revise a message before sending), asynchronicity (communication outside of real-time), and audience management (controlling who sees what) fundamentally alter the conditions for social interaction (de Carvalho, 2022). When applied to the family context, these affordances directly influence the processes of identity and emotion. For instance, editability and asynchronicity afford new strategies for emotional regulation, allowing a family member to pause, reflect, and carefully formulate a response to a provocative message. By applying this dual lens, this study argues that identity and emotion in the digital family cannot be understood by social theory alone; they must be seen as the product of a continuous interplay between interpersonal meaning-making and the specific architectural logic of the digital platforms that mediate it.

2.1. Symbolic Interactionism: Meaning-Making and the Performed Self

SI, rooted in the work of Mead (1913) and Blumer (1986), provides a foundational lens for understanding how the self is socially constructed through ongoing interpretation and interaction. Its core tenets posit that human action is based on the meanings that individuals assign to things; these meanings arise from social interaction with others; and these meanings are handled and modified through an interpretive process. This process is facilitated by language and symbols, which allow for complex thought and self-reflection. Central to the theory is the concept of the "self" as not an innate entity, but a dynamic product that emerges as individuals see themselves from the perspective of others; a process Cooley termed the "looking-glass self."(Zhao, 2015) Through this continuous loop of interpretation and adjustment, individuals learn and perform their social roles.

Applying this framework to the digitally saturated family reveals how identity performance is both amplified and altered in online contexts (Qian & Hu, 2024). The family group chat, a shared SM post, or a curated photo album becomes a primary stage for this symbolic work. In these spaces, identity is performed and negotiated through a new lexicon of digital symbols: a carefully selected emoji can convey affection or sarcasm, a strategically shared article can position oneself as the informed child, and a curated post about a family event creates an official narrative for both internal and external audiences. The "self" that emerges is shaped by the anticipated interpretations of family members—the "significant others" whose digital reactions (likes, comments, heart reactions) serve as immediate, tangible reflections (Gore, 2018). Thus, the digital family sphere is not a passive channel but a vibrant, symbolic ecosystem where kinship roles and individual identities are continuously authored, contested, and reaffirmed through everyday digital interactions.

2.2. Family Systems Theory: The Digital Family as an Emotional Unit

Family Systems Theory (FST) posits that the family is a complex, interconnected emotional unit whose members cannot be understood in isolation (Berry, 2020). Its core tenets include interconnectedness, where a change in one member's functioning predictably impacts all others; homeostasis, referring to the family's innate tendency to maintain its stability and resist change through unwritten rules and patterns; and the mechanisms that sustain this balance, namely feedback loops and the management of boundaries between the family and the outside world. Within this framework, communication is the central nervous system of the family—the primary process through which feedback is exchanged, rules are enforced, and the emotional climate is regulated to preserve the system's equilibrium.

Applying this systemic lens to the digital realm, we see that online communication platforms have become a critical infrastructure for these very processes. The SM groups act as a powerful, persistent feedback loop. A delayed reply to a group message can trigger corrective responses from multiple members, enforcing a rule about expected responsiveness. The "seen" receipt or a lack of "likes" on a post provides immediate, non-verbal feedback that regulates behavior and emotional expression to maintain homeostasis. Furthermore, digital tools actively reshape family boundaries; a private SM group can strengthen internal boundaries by creating an exclusive space for family matters, while a public post about a family achievement manages the boundary between the family and the wider community (Sharaievska & Stodolska, 2015). In this way, digital communication is not merely a tool for conversation but a fundamental mechanism for the emotional regulation and systemic maintenance of the modern family unit.

2.3. The Affordances of Connection: How Platform Architectures Shape Interaction

To move beyond a technologically deterministic or neutral view, this analysis is guided by the concept of affordances—the perceived and actual properties of a technology that determine how it might be used to facilitate action (De Boer, 2023). The architectural logic of digital platforms is not a passive backdrop but an active participant in shaping familial interaction (Barns, 2019). This section delineates four key affordances central to the construction of DK: persistence, editability, asynchronicity, and audience management. These features fundamentally reconfigure the conditions under which identity construction and emotional regulation occur, transforming the temporal, stylistic, and contextual rules of family communication. Understanding these affordances is a prerequisite for analyzing how the "digital self" is built and how the "family system" is maintained online.

Persistence creates a durable, searchable digital family archive, where shared photos and message histories become a permanent, often idealized, record of collective memory (Woodham et al., 2017). Editability provides a crucial buffer for emotional regulation, allowing individuals to craft, revise, and perfect messages before sending, thus introducing a calculated element into traditionally spontaneous familial exchanges. Asynchronicity liberates communication from real-time conversation, fostering a rhythm of perpetual, yet fragmented, connection that can sustain bonds across time zones but also generates anxiety through delayed responses. Finally, audience management forces families to constantly navigate collapsed contexts, where a single post must simultaneously address diverse audiences (immediate family, extended kin, friends), complicating the performance of a coherent familial identity. Together, these affordances constitute the very architecture within which the drama of digital family life unfolds.

2.4. Synthesizing the Framework: Identity, Emotion, and System

The true analytical power for understanding DK emerges from the synergy between Symbolic Interactionism (SI) and Family Systems Theory (FST). While SI provides a micro-level lens focused on the individual's performance and interpretation of symbols, FST offers a macro-level view of the family as an interdependent emotional circuit. Synthesized, these theories reveal a dynamic feedback loop: the continuous, individual identity work described by SI constitutes the very data and energy that flows through the family system described by FST. Each curated post, carefully worded message, or strategic use of an emoji is not merely a personal act of self-presentation; it is a communicative input into the family system that carries emotional weight, reinforces or challenges relational rules, and contributes to the collective homeostasis.

This integrated framework posits that the "digital self" is never constructed in a vacuum. The individual, through the SI process of taking the role of the "generalized family other," anticipates the systemic consequences of their digital performances. They regulate their emotional expression and curate their identity based on an internalized map of the family's emotional landscape—knowing that a certain post might trigger a parent's worry or that a specific meme will solidify a bond with a sibling. Conversely, the FST is maintained and transformed by the aggregate of these digital performances. A conflict erupting in a group chat is both a series of individual symbolic acts and a systemic event that tests boundaries and requires recalibration (Shumate & Fulk, 2004). Thus, the digital realm becomes the primary site where the individual and the system mutually constitute one another, where the performed self is both a product and a producer of the family's emotional world.

3. THE ARCHITECTURE OF DIGITAL KINSHIP: KEY FOCUS AREAS

Building upon the synthesized framework of SI and FST, this study investigates the concrete architectures where DK is built and lived. It moves from theoretical abstraction to empirical focus by examining three key platforms that constitute the primary habitats for online family life. These are not neutral channels but distinct environments with their own affordances, norms, and communicative pressures. By analyzing these specific domains, we can dissect how the general processes of identity construction and emotional regulation are concretely enacted and shaped by the digital spaces families inhabit.

This chapter concentrates on three pivotal areas: first, the persistent, multi-generational family group chat, which serves as the central nervous system for daily coordination, emotional support, and conflict, characterized by its immediacy and collapsed contexts. Second, the curated space of SM feeds, where family narratives are crafted for a blended audience of kin and non-kin, focusing on the performance of familial identity and the management of the family's public image. Finally, the shared digital archives, which function as the family's collective memory bank, where the past is actively constructed, preserved, and commemorated. By examining interactions across these three distinct yet often overlapping architectural layers, this study aims to provide a comprehensive map of the ecosystem in which the modern family is forged.

3.1. The Family Group Chat: The Central Nervous System

Within the hybrid family ecosystem, the persistent, multi-participant group chat—hosted on platforms like WhatsApp, Facebook Messenger, or iMessage—functions as the central nervous system of DK (Mone et al., 2024). It is the primary, always-on channel for the daily flow of information, emotion, and coordination that constitutes modern family life. This digital space collapses the distance between household members and dispersed relatives, creating a continuous, low-fidelity form of co-presence where logistics about dinner, photos from a vacation, heartfelt support during a crisis, and humorous memes all intermingle in a single, flowing stream (Watson et al., 2021). Unlike the curated performances of SM feeds, the group chat is often characterized by a sense of raw, informal immediacy, making it a rich site for observing the largely unvarnished, real-time interplay of identity construction and emotional regulation within the familial collective.

The architecture of the group chat directly shapes these core processes. The affordances of asynchronicity and persistence allow conversations to unfold over hours or days, creating a shared, searchable transcript of family life that serves as both a practical log and an emotional record. However, this very structure also generates unique pressures. The expectation of perpetual availability can lead to tensions when responses are delayed, and the read receipts function transforms simple notifications into loaded signifiers of attention and care, requiring constant micro-management of one's digital presence. Within this space, family roles are incessantly performed and affirmed—the organizer, the jester, the nurturer—and the emotional labor of maintaining the family's bond is made visible through the daily work of checking in, coordinating plans, and offering digital comfort, solidifying the group chat as the operational heart of the digital family.

The most immediate function of the family group chat is logistical, serving as the digital command center for the practical management of domestic life. It replaces the physical family bulletin board and shouted reminders, streamlining the coordination of schedules, grocery lists, pick-up times, and household chores into a single, persistent, and accessible thread. This constant, low-level stream of logistical updates—"Running 10 mins late," "Can someone grab milk?", "What's the plan for dinner?"—does more than just organize; it creates a rhythmic, ambient awareness of other members' activities and whereabouts. This steady pulse of mundane communication forms the functional "heartbeat" of the home, generating a foundational sense of shared life and mutual involvement even when family members are physically apart. This logistical layer is the essential, often invisible, infrastructure upon which the more complex emotional aspects of DK are built.

Beyond mere efficiency, this continuous logistical flow serves a crucial psychosocial purpose, acting as a primary mechanism for emotional regulation through the reinforcement of stability and care. The predictable rhythm of check-ins and updates provides a sense of order and reliability, mitigating the anxiety of dislocation and reinforcing the family system's homeostasis. In this way, the coordination of daily life becomes a continuous, low-stakes performance of familial roles and responsibilities. Each logistical message is a subtle reaffirmation of membership and mutual dependence, weaving a durable fabric of DK through the seemingly ordinary threads of shared domestic life.

While the family group chat fosters connection, its persistent and semi-public nature within the family unit also makes it a potent arena for conflict. The very affordances that enable closeness—asynchronicity, persistence, and the lack of non-verbal cues—can amplify disagreements. A hastily typed comment, stripped of tone, can fester in the "digital fog," its meaning warped by the anxieties of other members. Unlike a fleeting verbal spat, a conflict in the group chat is archived, creating a permanent, searchable record of the dispute that can be revisited and re-interpreted, often intensifying the original hurt. This forces a new form of emotional regulation, where members must navigate the dual challenge of managing their immediate feelings while also contending with the long-term, visible residue of their digital interactions.

The family system's innate drive for homeostasis is thus tested and must adapt within this persistent space. The group chat becomes a visible feedback loop where the system works to recalibrate after a disruption. This can manifest in several ways: a flurry of appeasing emojis or changing the subject to diffuse tension; members privately "side-texting" to manage the conflict outside the main channel; or the enforcement of new, tacit rules, such as a moratorium on certain topics. The audience management affordance collapses, meaning a conflict with one member is often witnessed by all, turning a dyadic disagreement into a systemic event that requires collective emotional management. The group chat, therefore, does not eliminate conflict but transposes it into a new key, making the family's struggle to maintain equilibrium a visible, archived, and continuously negotiated process.

3.2. Curated Selves: Self-Presentation and Role-Taking in Online Family Spaces

Online family spaces function as dynamic stages for the conscious curation of identity, where individuals engage in sophisticated impression management and role performance. The family unit, once a backdrop for more private self-exploration, is now a primary audience for a deliberate digital self. Members strategically enact familiar familial roles—such as the "dutiful daughter" who shares photos of a visit home, the "proud parent" chronicling a child's milestones, or the "supportive sibling" leaving public, affectionate comments. This performance is not merely an individual pursuit but a relational process that actively constructs and reinforces the family's collective narrative. Through these curated acts, individuals do not just present themselves to their family; they negotiate and solidify their place within the family structure, engaging in a continuous process of what you term "identity construction" within the sphere of " DK."

This identity work is inherently collaborative and often involves a delicate negotiation of visibility. The decision to post, tag, or join a group chat is never neutral;

it is a act of social inclusion or exclusion that carries emotional weight. A tagged photo can serve as a public affirmation of belonging, while an untagged post might signal a desire to partition an identity. To illustrate this, consider analyzing a family's interactions on a Facebook birthday post. The celebrant's initial post is a curated self-image, receiving reinforcements of love and social validation from relatives. Simultaneously, an Instagram "graduation dump" becomes a site of collective pride, where the family's shared identity is performatively bolstered through congratulatory comments and shares. These micro-interactions are the bedrock of online family life, where emotional regulation is practiced through the careful management of a shared digital front, balancing individual self-presentation with the expectations and bonds of the familial collective.

3.3. The Symbolic Toolkit: Emojis, Filters, and the Construction of Relational Identity

In the absence of the non-verbal cues that anchor face-to-face interaction—tone of voice, facial expressions, and physical touch—family members co-opt a shared symbolic toolkit to navigate the ambiguities of digital communication. Emojis, GIFs, photo filters, and even punctuation become crucial prosthetic devices for conveying emotional subtext. A simple "okay" can be transformed by its symbolic framing: "okay." reads as resigned or annoyed, "okay!" as enthusiastic, and "okay emoji" as genuine assent (Zhou, 2022). This digital paraprosody allows individuals to perform the emotional labor necessary to maintain familial bonds, ensuring that affection, sarcasm, or concern is not lost in translation. The toolkit, therefore, is not merely decorative; it is a functional necessity for the emotional regulation required to sustain connection across digital mediums.

The use of these symbols extends beyond clarifying tone to actively constructing a shared relational identity (Li et al., 2023). A family photo uniformly edited with a warm, nostalgic filter does more than enhance aesthetics; it publicly projects an image of harmony, unity, and shared warmth—a curated ideal of the family unit. Similarly, the strategic deployment of a "emoji" or a family-specific inside joke via GIF in a group chat reinforces a unique, collective sense of humor and belonging. These small, daily acts of symbolic communication constitute a process of mutual identity formation. Through this collaborative semiotics, families develop their own distinctive dialect, building what can be understood as a DK that is both performed and solidified through a shared lexicon of care, humor, and connection.

3.4. Navigating the Digital Fog: Boundaries, Misunderstandings, and Emotional Fallout

The very tools that facilitate DK also create a pervasive "digital fog"—a layer of ambiguity inherent in text-based and asynchronous communication where non-verbal cues are absent (Patel, 2024). This fog routinely obscures intent and amplifies emotional risk. A hastily typed message, stripped of affectionate tone, can be misread as coldness; a delayed reply can spiral into anxiety over withheld affection or simmering conflict; and the ominous "read receipt" can transform a simple notification into a source of intense scrutiny and hurt. These are not minor glitches but central stressors in online family life, demanding constant emotional regulation as members attempt to interpret often-ambiguous signals. The family chat, intended as a space for connection, can thus become a minefield of potential misunderstandings, where the identity construction of one member—for instance, as "available" or "responsive"—is constantly being assessed and reassessed by others through an imperfect and often unforgiving digital lens.

In response to this emotional fallout, families can actively adapt, developing a unique set of norms and digital boundaries to manage relational strain. This adaptive process is a practical manifestation of emotional regulation at the group level. Families collectively institute new rules: muting overwhelming group chats to preserve sanity, creating private SM "vaults" or "finstas" to carve out spaces free from familial surveillance, or establishing tacit agreements to avoid contentious topics in digital forums. These are not acts of disconnection but rather sophisticated strategies for sustaining connection by mitigating its digital-era hazards. By negotiating these boundaries, families engage in a continuous redefinition of their DK, determining which parts of their collective life and individual identities can thrive online and which must be reserved for the more nuanced realm of offline interaction.

3.5. The Digital Hearth: Emotional Labor and Support Roles

Beyond the stages for curated selves and the minefields of misunderstanding, online platforms function as a modern "digital hearth"—a central, warm space where the crucial work of familial care, coordination, and emotional support is conducted. This digital hearth is maintained through a constant stream of what is fundamentally emotional labor: the daily "good morning" text that signals presence, the group chat meticulously organized to coordinate care for an aging parent, or the voice note filled with laughter that offers comfort across miles (Wang & Haapio-Kirk, 2021). These micro-interactions, whether a carefully chosen meme that perfectly captures a shared feeling or the scheduling of a video call to celebrate a small achievement, are the rituals that sustain DK. They transform utilitarian platforms into intimate spaces where identity construction is reinforced through affirmation and where belonging is actively practiced and felt, providing a stable anchor in the fluidity of online and offline life.

However, the responsibility for tending this digital hearth is rarely distributed equally, and its upkeep often falls along predictable gendered and generational lines. The role of "family communicator"—the person who remembers birthdays, facilitates planning, mediates tensions, and provides consistent emotional support—disproportionately falls on women, mirroring the traditional distribution of emotional labor in offline domestic spheres. Simultaneously, a generational divide emerges, where younger, often more digitally native members may be tasked with providing technical support or managing shared digital assets like family photos in the cloud, while older generations might specialize in different forms of outreach, such as lengthy phone calls or emails. This intersectional analysis reveals that DK is not just a product of connection but also of often-invisible work, and that the emotional regulation required to maintain family bonds online is a form of labor that reflects and can even exacerbate existing social hierarchies within the family structure.

4. TOWARD A CONCEPTUAL MODEL OF DIGITAL KINSHIP

The preceding analysis demonstrates that online family life is not a mere digital replica of offline interaction but a distinct relational domain governed by its own unique dynamics. To fully capture this phenomenon, we must move beyond isolated observations and consolidate them into a cohesive theoretical framework. This chapter proposes a conceptual model of DK, defined as the technologically-mediated, actively constructed network of familial bonds that is continuously negotiated through practices of identity performance and emotional regulation. This model posits that kinship in the digital age is not a given state but an ongoing achievement, built and sustained through the conscious efforts detailed in this chapter: the curation of selves, the use of a symbolic toolkit, the navigation of digital ambiguity, and the unequal distribution of emotional labor. The model thus integrates the core processes of identity construction and emotional regulation as the twin pillars upon which modern familial connection is built and maintained.

The utility of this model lies in its ability to frame the complexities and contradictions of online family life not as paradoxes, but as interconnected elements of a single system. It illustrates how the same platform that fosters connection through a "digital hearth" can also be a source of tension in the "digital fog," and how the tools that enable "curated selves" also necessitate a "symbolic toolkit" for emotional nuance. By mapping these interactions, the model provides a lens through which to analyze the evolving family. It encourages future research to investigate how different family structures enact DK, how these processes impact individual well-being, and how the model might adapt to emerging technologies. Ultimately, conceptualizing DK in this way allows us to better understand the profound, multifaceted, and deeply human effort to cultivate belonging in a connected world.

4.1. Core Tenets of the Digital Kinship Model

The Digital Kinship Model (DKM) is built upon three foundational principles that reframe our understanding of family connection in the digital age. First, it posits that kinship is an ongoing achievement, not a static biological or legal fact. In the pre-digital era, family bonds were largely sustained through routine, co-located rituals and shared physical space. The digital era, however, demands that kinship be actively and continuously performed through deliberate communicative labour (Cordova, 2024). A family group chat does not constitute kinship simply by existing; it becomes a site of kinship only through the daily, often mundane, acts of sharing photos, coordinating schedules, offering support, and exchanging humorous memes (Bakuri & Amoabeng, 2023). This relentless, collaborative effort—this achievement—is what sustains the feeling of "family" across dispersed networks, transforming the digital channel from a mere tool into a vital lifeline of relational maintenance.

Second, the model elucidates the symbiotic interplay of identity construction and emotional regulation. Online family spaces become crucial arenas where individuals, particularly adolescents and young adults, negotiate their personal identities in relation to the family unit (Hällgren & Björk, 2023). A teenager may curate a specific self by selectively sharing academic successes on a platform, knowing their extended family is watching, while simultaneously seeking emotional validation for more vulnerable struggles within the private confines of a SM family group (Weinstein & James, 2022). This curation is a dual-purpose process: it shapes how one is perceived by the kin network (identity construction) while also managing the emotional responses of family members and regulating one's own affective state (emotional regulation). This interplay highlights that what is shared, how it is shared, and, just as importantly, what is withheld are all strategic choices in the performance of DK. Finally, and crucially, the model recognizes the platform as an active agent in these dynamics. Digital platforms are not neutral conduits; their architectures and affordances directly shape family interactions. The persistent, searchable nature of a Facebook timeline archives family history, influencing how the past is remembered (Cannelli, 2024). The ephemerality of Snapchat stories creates a context for more casual, in-the-moment sharing, lowering the stakes of communication. Algorithms that prioritize certain types of content can dictate which family member's posts are most seen, subtly influencing family hierarchies and attention. By granting platforms this agentic role, the model acknowledges that the very texture of modern kinship is co-constructed with the digital environments families inhabit.

4.2. Reconfiguring, Not Replacing: The Hybrid Family Ecosystem

Online platforms have become a new social territory where the timeless functions of the family—nurturance, support, conflict, and identity formation—are transposed and transformed (Erstad et al., 2024). The impulse to perform familial roles, manage emotional exchanges, and maintain connection is ancient; however, the digital stage upon which these dramas now unfold is fundamentally new. This is not a story of displacement but of integration, where the "digital hearth" exists alongside the physical dinner table, and the curated self-online informs the offline sense of identity. The very concept of kinship is thus stretched and adapted, becoming a continuous negotiation between physical presence and digital co-presence, between the spontaneity of the home and the performativity of the platform.

This hybrid ecosystem is characterized by its own distinct rhythms, tools, and challenges, which collectively redefine the experience of family life. The rhythm of interaction is now punctuated by the ping of a notification and the anxiety of the "read receipt," creating an expectation of perpetual availability that conflicts with the boundaries necessary for individual well-being. The tools for connection—from emojis that compensate for a lack of tone to group chats that coordinate care—have become as central to relational maintenance as a hug or a phone call. Yet, these same tools introduce novel challenges, such as the "digital fog" of ambiguity and the heightened potential for misinterpretation. Ultimately, the modern family exists in a state of fluid movement across this hybrid ecosystem, where the work of identity construction and emotional regulation is no longer confined to a physical place but is a continuous, multi-platform effort to sustain DK across time, space, and the interface of a screen.

5. THEORETICAL AND PRACTICAL IMPLICATIONS

5.1 Theoretical Contribution

The conceptual model of DK advanced in this chapter makes a significant theoretical contribution by integrating SI with FST, creating a robust lens for understanding contemporary family life. While SI provides the tools to analyze the micro-level "curated selves" and "symbolic toolkit" families use online, FST illuminates the macro-level relational patterns, boundaries, and emotional processes that these interactions sustain or disrupt. This integrated framework allows researchers to see that a seemingly individual act, like choosing a filter for a family photo, is simultaneously an act of personal identity construction and a communication that regulates the emotional climate of the entire family system. By bridging the individual-focused tradition of media studies with the relational focus of family studies, this model offers a more holistic and dynamic understanding of how families co-construct their reality and navigate intimacy in a digitally saturated world.

This SI/FST synthesis moves the field beyond simplistic debates about whether technology connects or isolates, reframing it instead as a new and complex environment for relational dynamics. It provides a structured way to analyze how the "digital hearth" and the "digital fog" are two sides of the same coin—both emerging from the same processes of symbolic communication and emotional feedback loops within the family unit. This theoretical model invites future research to investigate, for example, how different family structures (e.g., single-parent, multi-generational, transnational) develop distinct DK patterns, or how the model holds when applied to emerging technologies like virtual reality. It establishes a foundation for studying the family not as a static entity buffeted by technological change, but as an adaptive, meaning-making system that is actively, if not always consciously, designing its own digital future.

5.2 Practical Implications

The findings of this analysis offer crucial practical utility for professionals supporting family well-being. For family therapists, the model of DK provides a new diagnostic lens and a vocabulary to help families articulate conflicts that often feel vague and intangible. A therapist can now frame a teenage client's frustration over a parent's "overposting" not as a mere preference, but as a breach in the collectively negotiated identity construction and a failure of attuned emotional regulation. By mapping a family's "digital ecosystem"—including their group chat norms, SM boundaries, and use of symbolic tools—therapists can help clients identify specific friction points and co-create healthier digital communication contracts, moving from reactive conflict to proactive management of their online interactions.

Beyond the therapy room, these insights are vital for educators and individuals seeking to navigate digital family life more mindfully. Educational programs on digital literacy can be expanded to include modules on "digital emotional literacy," teaching adolescents and parents alike how to interpret tone in text, the relational weight of tagging, and the importance of establishing mutual expectations around availability. For the individual, understanding that online family spaces are sites of active identity construction and emotional labor can foster a more conscious and intentional approach. Recognizing the gendered distribution of digital kin-work can prompt a more equitable sharing of this labor, and appreciating the ambiguity of the "digital fog" can cultivate greater empathy and the habit of seeking clarification. Ultimately, this knowledge empowers families to move from being passive consumers of technology to becoming architects of their own DK, using digital tools to enrich, rather than erode, their foundational bonds.

6. LIMITATIONS AND FUTURE RESEARCH DIRECTIONS

While this chapter has proposed an integrated model for understanding DK, it is crucial to acknowledge its primary limitation: as a conceptual analysis, it establishes a framework requiring robust empirical validation. The arguments presented here are derived from synthesizing existing literature and theorizing the interaction between identity construction and emotional regulation. The next critical step is to test these propositions through qualitative and quantitative research to determine how these processes manifest across diverse family contexts. Do the dynamics of the "curated self" and the "digital hearth" hold true in families experiencing economic precarity, or those separated by migration? Without such empirical grounding, the model remains a heuristic tool, albeit a powerful one, whose precise applicability and boundaries are yet to be fully determined.

This conceptual starting point, however, opens several fertile avenues for future research. First, studies could conduct platform-specific ethnographies, comparing how the affordances of WhatsApp, TikTok, or private gaming servers shape the expression of DK differently. Second, longitudinal research is vital to understand the long-term effects of these digital practices. How does growing up in a family with pervasive "connected presence" influence an individual's core identity and capacity for emotional regulation in adulthood? Finally, cross-cultural comparative studies are essential to de-center potentially Western perspectives. Investigating how collectivist versus individualist societies, or cultures with different communication norms, negotiate DK would reveal the extent to which these dynamics are universal or culturally specific, significantly enriching our understanding of the global digital family.

7. CONCLUSION

In conclusion, this chapter has argued that the contemporary family is a hybrid entity, whose very fabric is woven from both physical and digital threads. Through the integrated lens of SI and FST, we have reframed DK not as a diminished form of connection, but as an active, ongoing project where identity construction and emotional regulation are continuously negotiated. The analysis has illuminated the central paradoxes of this new reality: digital platforms serve simultaneously as a stage for curated selves and a symbolic toolkit, a source of digital fog and a comforting hearth, a site of both intensified emotional labor and profound support. The proposed conceptual model of DK provides a vital framework for navigating this complexity, underscoring that family bonds are no longer simply given, but are dynamically made and remade through our digital interactions. As technology continues to evolve, this model offers a foundational understanding for grasping the profound, and deeply human, endeavor of building belonging in an increasingly connected world.

REFERENCES

Abel, S. (2021). *Making time online: Exploring social media as a tool for family connection* [PhD Thesis]. University of Southern Queensland.

Abel, S., Machin, T., & Brownlow, C. (2021). Social media, rituals, and long-distance family relationship maintenance: A mixed-methods systematic review. *New Media & Society*, *23*(3), 632–654. DOI: 10.1177/1461444820958717

Bakuri, A. Z., & Amoabeng, D. (2023). Doing kin work among Ghanaians home and abroad: A paradigm shift to ICT. *Family Relations*, *72*(2), 585–600. DOI: 10.1111/fare.12838

Barns, S. (2019). Negotiating the platform pivot: From participatory digital ecosystems to infrastructures of everyday life. *Geography Compass*, *13*(9), e12464. DOI: 10.1111/gec3.12464

Baruah, A. (2025). The Impact of Computer-Mediated Communication on Relationships and Social Interactions. *International Journal of Human-Computer Interaction*, *41*(18), 11245–11251. DOI: 10.1080/10447318.2024.2442755

Berry, N. (2020). *Students as Thinking Systems: A Phenomenological Inquiry on Learning Natural Family Systems Theory* [PhD Thesis]. Barry University.

Blumer, H. (1986). *Symbolic interactionism: Perspective and method.* University of California Press. https://books.google.com/books?hl=en&lr=&id=HVuognZFofoC&oi=fnd&pg=PA1&dq=Blumer&ots=4pUcHawP6u&sig=ZZhAdigNsE6x96qiPNYD5S24Eqo

Cannelli, B. (2024). *Archiving Social Media: A Comparative Study of the Practices, Obstacles, and Opportunities Related to the Development of Social Media Archives* [PhD Thesis]. School of Advanced Study.

Carter, M. J., & Asencio, E. K. (2019). Identity Processes in Face-to-Face and Digitally Mediated Environments. *Sociological Perspectives*, *62*(2), 220–239. DOI: 10.1177/0731121418786247

Cordova, J. C. (2024). *Creating a Digital House of Knowledge: Ensuring the Continuation and Integrity of Indigenous Knowledge Transfers in the Digital Era* [Master's Thesis]. University of Alaska Fairbanks.

Cruz, F. (2025). *Digital specters of colony: Securitization, Moros, and the age of social media* [PhD Thesis]. University of Antwerp.

De Boer, B. (2023). Explaining multistability: Postphenomenology and affordances of technologies. *AI & Society, 38*(6), 2267–2277. DOI: 10.1007/s00146-021-01272-3

de Carvalho, E. M. (2022). Social affordance. In *Encyclopedia of animal cognition and behavior* (pp. 6497–6500). Springer. DOI: 10.1007/978-3-319-55065-7_1870

Erstad, O., Hegna, K., Livingstone, S., Negru-Subtirica, O., & Stoilova, M. (2024). How digital technologies become embedded in family life across generations: Scoping the agenda for researching 'platformised relationality.'. *Families, Relationships and Societies, 13*(2), 164–180. DOI: 10.1332/20467435Y2024D000000023

Gore, M. C. (2018). *The digital self: A qualitative approach to studying female college students' use of social-networking platforms* [PhD Thesis]. Eastern Michigan University.

Hällgren, C., & Björk, Å. (2023). Young people's identities in digital worlds. *The International Journal of Information and Learning Technology, 40*(1), 49–61. DOI: 10.1108/IJILT-06-2022-0135

Kang, T. (2012). Gendered media, changing intimacy: Internet-mediated transnational communication in the family sphere. *Media Culture & Society, 34*(2), 146–161. DOI: 10.1177/0163443711430755

Li, J., Adnan, H. M., & Gong, J. (2023). Exploring Cultural Meaning Construction in Social Media: An Analysis of Liziqi's YouTube Channel. *Journal of Intercultural Communication, 23*(4), 1–12. DOI: 10.36923/jicc.v23i4.237

McKinlay, S. N. (2023). Kinship and Family. In *Teaching Cultural Anthropology for 21st Century Learners*. Viva.

Mead, G. H. (1913). The social self. *The Journal of Philosophy, Psychology, and Scientific Methods, 10*(14), 374–380. DOI: 10.2307/2012910

Mone, F., Visan, M., & Simionescu, M. (2024). Multi-participant Decision-making Based on Digital Platforms: A Case Study for the Romanian Academy. *Science and Technology, 27*(1), 94–105.

Nichols, S., & Selim, N. (2022). Digitally mediated parenting: A review of the literature. *Societies (Basel, Switzerland), 12*(2), 60. DOI: 10.3390/soc12020060

Patel, S. (2024). Digital Kinship: The Future Calling. *Anthropology & Aging, 45*(2), 75–81. DOI: 10.5195/aa.2024.550

Pauwels, L. (2008). A private visual practice going public? Social functions and sociological research opportunities of Web-based family photography. *Visual Studies, 23*(1), 34–49. DOI: 10.1080/14725860801908528

Qian, Y., & Hu, Y. (2024). The digitalization of family life: A multilevel conceptual framework. *Journal of Marriage and Family, 86*(5), 1160–1183. DOI: 10.1111/jomf.12983

Rogers-Whitehead, C. (2025). *Technology for Littles: Helping Young Children Navigate the Internet Responsibly*. Rowman & Littlefield.

Rondi, E., Magrelli, V., Debellis, F., & De Massis, A. (2024). The evolution of craft work in the strategic development of a family enterprise. *Strategic Entrepreneurship Journal, 18*(4), 811–840. DOI: 10.1002/sej.1503

Sharaievska, I., & Stodolska, M. (2015). Redefining Boundaries in Families through Social Networking Leisure. *Leisure Sciences, 37*(5), 431–446. DOI: 10.1080/01490400.2015.1021882

Shumate, M., & Fulk, J. (2004). Boundaries and Role Conflict When Work and Family are Colocated: A Communication Network and Symbolic Interaction Approach. *Human Relations, 57*(1), 55–74. DOI: 10.1177/0018726704042714

Stryker, S. (1959). Symbolic interaction as an approach to family research. *Marriage and Family Living, 21*(2), 111–119. DOI: 10.2307/348099

Wang, X., & Haapio-Kirk, L. (2021). Emotion work via digital visual communication: A comparative study between China and Japan. *Global Media and China, 6*(3), 325–344. DOI: 10.1177/20594364211008044

Waterworth, J. A. (2025). Disembodied Social Interaction. In J. A. Waterworth, *The Displaced Self* (pp. 15–34). Springer Nature Switzerland. DOI: 10.1007/978-3-031-99832-4_2

Watson, A., Lupton, D., & Michael, M. (2021). The COVID digital home assemblage: Transforming the home into a work space during the crisis. *Convergence (London), 27*(5), 1207–1221. DOI: 10.1177/13548565211030848

Weinstein, E., & James, C. (2022). *Behind their screens: What teens are facing (and adults are missing)*. MIT press. DOI: 10.7551/mitpress/14088.001.0001

Willett, R., & Wheeler, N. (2021). Maintaining family stability in the age of digital technologies: An analysis of d/Discourse informing domestic screen media practices in three US families. *Children & Society, 35*(5), 722–735. DOI: 10.1111/chso.12443

Woodham, A., King, L., Gloyn, L., Crewe, V., & Blair, F. (2017). We Are What We Keep: The "Family Archive", Identity and Public/Private Heritage. *Heritage & Society, 10*(3), 203–220. DOI: 10.1080/2159032X.2018.1554405

Xu, Y. (2024). *Negotiating "privacy" in the digital age: A study on the new live/work home* [PhD Thesis]. University of Nottingham.

Zhao, S. (2015). Reconceptualizing the Self Phenomenon: Toward an Emic Conception of the Self. *Symbolic Interaction*, *38*(2), 235–260. DOI: 10.1002/symb.151

Zhou, Z. (2022). *VibEmoji: Exploring User-authoring Multi-modal Emoticons in Social Communication* [PhD Thesis]. University of Waterloo.

Chapter 3

Psychological Safety in Virtual Teams: Opportunities and Challenges

Munir Ahmad
http://orcid.org/0000-0003-4836-6151
Survey of Pakistan, Pakistan

ABSTRACT

This chapter examines the evolving dynamics of psychological safety in virtual and hybrid work environments. As digital interaction replaces physical co-presence, psychological safety becomes a critical yet complex goal, requiring intentional leadership and thoughtful design. We explore how remote settings can foster inclusivity, autonomy, and flexibility, while also posing risks of isolation, miscommunication, and surveillance. The role of leadership, technology, and team rituals in shaping safe virtual spaces is emphasized, along with future considerations involving AI-mediated collaboration. Ultimately, psychological safety is positioned as a strategic necessity for performance, innovation, and resilience in distributed teams.

INTRODUCTION

Psychological safety is the shared belief that the team is safe to take interpersonal risks, in the sense that members are not afraid to speak up without fear of being embarrassed, retaliated, or marginalized (A. Edmondson, 1999). It was initially conceived by Edmondson, who has, throughout this concept, become relevant in learning, engagement, creativity, and performance in teams (Frazier et al., 2017).

DOI: 10.4018/979-8-2600-0934-5.ch003

Members of such psychologically safe environments (including psychologically safe teams) are open to asking questions, sharing ideas, accepting errors, and challenging assumptions that exist, which are important aspects of creating innovation and navigating resilience.

With the trend of organizations shifting to virtual and hybrid work paradigms, the interaction within the team has altered dramatically. Remote collaboration tools, such as Zoom, Slack, Teams, etc., have empowered international connectivity and helped create new complications within the need to maintaining trust, connection, and mutual understanding (Ford et al., 2017; Morrison-Smith & Ruiz, 2020). The absence of physical closeness and informality has resulted in difficulty in establishing and maintaining the psychological prerequisites promoting transparent communication and exposure.

Learning how to create and manage psychological safety in the digital world is becoming more pressing than ever. In virtual settings, even minor cases of miscommunication have a high potential of escalating, silence may be mistaken as an expression of disapproval, and a sense of isolation may undermine the strength of the team. The lack of psychological safety subjects the virtual teams to the risk of being transactional, disengaged, and unwilling to innovate, which can eventually influence organizational performance and its well-being.

This chapter addresses the ambivalence of psychological safety in virtual teams: the potential of the distributed work to increase team inclusiveness and flexibility, and those forces that reduce psychological team cohesiveness when the usual face-to-face communication is lacking. It also describes feasible strategies that leaders and organizations can adopt to create and maintain psychological safety in virtual conditions. With this design, the chapter presents actionable information and a moderate picture of the changes in the needs of remote work.

OPPORTUNITIES TO ENHANCE PSYCHOLOGICAL SAFETY

Although a significant amount of the narrative currently hovering around virtual work centers on the constraints of that world, the virtual collaborating environments also present unique and, under certain circumstances, even enhanced opportunities to foster psychological safety-even in a mode not inferior to traditional face-to-face applications. When well crafted, virtual teams can amplify voices that have traditionally gone unheard, allow diverse participation, allow individuals to work at their own cadence, and accommodate each person in terms of communication style. These factors may form powerful psychological enablers to further openness, belonging, and innovation in remote and hybrid teams.

Psychological Safety & Asynchronous Communication

The face-to-face meetings tend to support the implicit authority. Equal participation may be discouraged through dominant personalities and seniority, or by social rules of operation that do not allow equal participation, especially by junior, quiet, or culturally reserved members of the team. By contrast, however, even though virtual spaces at the surface tend to be an utter nightmare when it comes to democratization and inclusivity of engagement, they present a distinct opportunity to address those issues head-on when approached deliberately (Edmondson & Lei, 2014). Technology-enhanced learning features, such as chat options, anonymous polls, emoticons, digital hand-raising, and whiteboard-sharing, can enable each person to make their input at a degree of comfort and frequency. The asynchronous nature of communication allows time to reflect and widen discussion--e.g., conversation that occurs through Slack, Microsoft Teams, Miro, etc., relieves the intense feeling of thinking and responding immediately.

As an example, a worldwide marketing department at a multinational technological company found that in live video conference calls, junior staff members would stay quiet and would not offer raw ideas as they worried about possible judgment or language insecurity. To solve this, the team implemented asynchronous idea boards and pre-meeting Slack threads that the members were able to post in beforehand. In a short time frame, the number of individuals joining the program grew, especially among younger workers and people who were not native speakers of English. Such modifications were not only able to increase psychological safety but also bring a considerable jump in the diversity of creativity and originality of brainstorming results. Well-orchestrated virtual teamwork can even the playing field, allowing the hearing of those who otherwise might not be heard. Bringing down real-time social pressure and multiple input mechanisms to virtual teams, one can realize a much wider range of ideas and may create a culture that welcomes everyone to talk out.

Flexibility and Autonomy in Remote Work

Among the most popular affordances of remote work is flexibility, which is directly related to the psychological safety of the latter. Working in virtual places provides human beings with more independence in terms of time, physical environment, and work pace. Such self-direction creates feelings of trust, dignity, and self-efficacy, upon which the building of environments where individuals psychologically feel safe to express issues, reveal faults, or be involved in interpersonal risks is based (Gajendran & Harrison, 2007). By having employees who are not under the strict time allocation, extra meetings, or micromanaging in real-time, among other factors, it becomes more likely that employees can feel professional judgment is valued.

This not only performs against stress levels and mental pressure but also builds a mutual responsibility and emotional genuineness culture.

Psychological safety and this connection to autonomy have been evidenced in remote-first companies like Buffer and Doist. These organizations prioritize goal-oriented management, non-concentrated work processes, as opposed to continuous monitoring. Consequently, team members experience greater feelings of being willing to be honest in opinions, produce incomplete ideas, and seek guidance, all activities which are essential to perpetual learning and innovation. It is important to note that such environments prove that flexibility is not the cause of worse performance, but it increases psychological well-being and fosters more trust among group members (Knight & Haslam, 2010).

Global & Asynchronous Collaboration

Virtual teams can allow an organization to have access to a wide and international talent pool that promotes diversity in thought and experience. Yet, at the same time, the same characteristics of these teams, which render them dynamic, namely, geographical dispersion and cultural difference, bring in obstacles synchronicity of communication. Differences in time zones, language barriers, and incongruent communication expectations may become an obstacle to real-time communication and undermine team unity unless handled properly (Hinds & Bailey, 2003).

When done intentionally, asynchronous collaboration can make a potent equalizer on virtual terrain. It takes away the burden and feeling that one should be accessible all the time, takes away the mental stress as well as gives the individuals the time and mind space to process information and formulate answers, and gives meaningful input. This is especially beneficial to neurodiverse team members or colleagues who have to manage caregiving obligations or those employees who have to communicate in their second language, as these groups might find themselves strained or ostracized by the traditional, synchronous communication environments. The tools that facilitate asynchronous work processes include platforms like Loom, Notion, and Google Docs. Rather than being about speed and verbal control, asynchronous systems provide an incentive to provide clarity, purposefulness, and thoughtful input, which are psychological safety catalysts.

One of the most prominent examples of such practice is GitLab, a completely technological company operating in more than 60 different countries. GitLab is an asynchronous communication tool according to default settings and focuses more on documentation rather than meetings. The model fits diverse communication preferences and time differences; it also supports transparency or a sharing culture. The employees say they feel morally strong and psychologically secure with the knowledge that they have the same chance to express their views without being limited by geography, time, or style of communicating. Asynchronous collaboration creates the grounds in which psychological safety is formed through the change in focus from immediacy to intentionality, in which people are listened to, their respect, and their ability to contribute on their time are present. Table 1 provides a snapshot of GitLab's asynchronous-first model, showcasing specific practices and how they contribute to psychological safety in a globally distributed workforce.

Table 1. GitLab's asynchronous communication practices supporting psychological safety

Practice	Tool/Approach	Contribution to Psychological Safety
Default to asynchronous communication	GitLab Handbook, Notion	Removes pressure to respond immediately; allows for thoughtful input
Extensive documentation culture	Internal Wiki, Git Repos	Builds shared understanding; reduces ambiguity and reliance on memory
Recorded updates & video messages	Loom	Supports accessibility across time zones; aids clarity through visuals
Open feedback loops and version control	GitLab Issues, Merge Requests	Encourages transparent collaboration and iterative improvement
"Write it down" culture	Google Docs, Markdown	Empowers quieter voices; democratizes contribution

Virtual Psychological Safety

The examples of establishing psychological safety are the well-planned behavior in online worlds described by a few organizations are presented below and summarized in Table 2.

- In Trello (since acquired by Atlassian), a no-blame postmortem process was pioneered in which the Trello asynchronous boards are used where teams share their stories of project failures and successes openly, without persecuting individuals, but rather focusing on systems (Atlassian, 2025). This developed a culture in which team members were not feared to indicate errors and learn based on them.
- In Automattic (maker of WordPress), they have internal blogging and asynchronous feedback loops where every employee can comment on important decisions without action being real-time based (Luis, 2020). This makes all employees feel that they are represented regardless of their remote time zones and locations.

- IDEO is among the companies that welcomed the use of digital collaboration tools to execute virtual design sprints during the pandemic. They found out that even the silent members of the team were more engaged through digital whiteboards and asynchronous prototyping tools, and contributed to better teamwork and results.

Table 2. Case studies of virtual psychological safety practices

Organization	Practice	Tool(s)/Method	Psychological Safety Outcome
Trello (Atlassian)	"No Blame" Postmortems	Asynchronous Trello Boards	Encouraged learning from failure without fear of blame
Automattic	Asynchronous Feedback for Decision-Making	Internal Blogs, Async Comment Threads	Equalized participation across global team members
IDEO	Inclusive Virtual Design Sprints	Digital Whiteboards (e.g., Miro), Async Tools	Amplified voices of quieter participants, leading to better outcomes

Table 3 summarizes the key virtual work features that, when intentionally designed, can serve as enablers of psychological safety.

Table 3. Enablers of psychological safety in virtual teams

Opportunity Area	Key Enabler	How It Enhances Psychological Safety
Inclusivity & Participation	Text/chat tools, anonymous input, async collaboration platforms	Reduces fear of judgment; gives everyone a voice
Flexibility & Autonomy	Remote scheduling, self-paced work, autonomy in task execution	Builds trust; allows authentic expression without constant supervision
Diverse Communication Styles	Support for written, visual, and asynchronous inputs	Accommodates neurodiverse and multilingual team members
Global Collaboration	Teams spanning multiple regions and time zones	Encourages diverse perspectives and flattens hierarchies
Tool-Enabled Safety	Collaborative whiteboards, reaction emojis, and psychological safety check-ins	Allows expression of ideas/emotions in low-risk ways
Intentional Culture Design	Inclusive rituals, safe feedback loops, and open leadership communication	Normalizes mistake-sharing and feedback; fosters belonging

KEY CHALLENGES TO PSYCHOLOGICAL SAFETY IN VIRTUAL TEAMS

Besides having its benefits, remote and hybrid workplaces pose a unique group of challenges that risk psychological safety. As opposed to physical environments where informal leadership and dynamic interactions may lead to building trust, the digital landscapes need a close intention to provide team members with the feeling of safety, being heard, and appreciated. Without such initiatives, there is an increase in misunderstanding and a decrease in engagement and psychological insecurity of the team, which harms its performance and well-being.

Loss of Nonverbal Communication and Its Effect on Trust and Empathy

Nonverbal communication forms the background of how human beings have developed trust, empathy, and mutual understanding in dealings amongst people and includes facial expressions, eye contact, tone of voice, gestures, as well as posture. During in-person interaction, these signals act as feedback tools in real-time that aid the process of controlling conversation dynamics, indicating paying attention, and emotional validation (Hess, 2023). Nevertheless, the subtle but important signals are reduced or lacking altogether in virtual environments, mostly in text-only or audio-only virtual environments, which may have drastic implications on team dynamics.

Considering an example, in a remote meeting, when video cameras are disabled, a colleague who proposes a new idea does not have visual confirmation of acceptance, no nodding, smiling, or tilting toward the person. When such a situation arises, the absence of some form of visible support may cause a vacuum whereby one starts to query the relevance of their input or even its comprehension. Such uncertainty has the potential to undermine confidence and limit future engagement. A mere nonverbal expression, such as the words, would denote an implication of mildness with a clear implication of hostility, whereas in nature it is not so. A study conducted by Kruger et al., (2005) Revealed that the use of emails and other text-driven communications channels commonly creates a sense of overconfidence about the clarity of tone and intent, which has proven to be a major cause of misunderstanding and inability to connect emotionally.

This lack of proportion is also a detriment to the visual and emotional display and understanding of empathy, especially in emotionally tense or high-stakes encounters. Leaders, who would otherwise pay a kind gesture, e.g., a nod of the head or speak in a soft tone, now have to speak only, which may sound empty or dishonest. Under such circumstances, it is more difficult to develop psychological safety, which can be defined as a belief that a person can speak up, ask questions, or expose their susceptibility without fear of humiliation and retaliation (A. Edmondson, 1999). This leads to the creation of a culture of risk-averse communication where the team members do not express their opinions, especially when they are neither confirming nor agreeing to an inference or an emotion.

To remedy the above effects, organizations and leaders should be more conscious of how they utilize digital communication channels. Some of the methods to restore this warmth and clarity are the encouragement of video engagements (when possible), inclusion of expressive characteristics, including emojis or GIFs, and a change in communication conventions that articulate intention, such as the use of clarifying tone, e.g., "Excited about this! ". Applications such as the reaction icons in Zoom, live emoji responses in MS Teams, and asynchronous video messages (such as Loom) partly replace real-time nonverbal expression to help deal with the empathy gap in remote teams.

Nonetheless, as useful as the technology is, it can never compete with the full depth of face-to-face indicators. It is even more important that there should be organized rules about feedback, recognition, and emotional check-ins in remote and hybrid teams. In an example, one can ease nonverbal affirmation by checking in on feelings at the beginning of a meeting ("On a scale of 1-5, how are you feeling regarding energy today?") or reinstating reflection listening skills ("What I am hearing is...") to restore interpersonal trust. The negation of nonverbal communication can be countered, yet it needs a purposeful design, a cultural consideration, and sensitivity in leadership to make digital cooperation human-friendly.

Digital Fatigue, Disengagement, and Perceived Surveillance

Within virtual workspaces, there has been an unintentional byproduct of digital fatigue, or more directly, Zoom fatigue, due to the heightened usage of digital communication tools like Zoom, Microsoft Teams, and Slack. This can be defined as the mental and emotional fatigue as a result of the tedious virtual interactions. As opposed to face-to-face meetings, the situation with video conferencing is that it requires a constant alertness to various screens, faces, and nonverbal communication messages, which are often distorted or delayed. Researchers have indicated that it has the potential to saturate the brain in processing social and visual information, leading to an earlier depletion of brainpower (Bailenson, 2021). The obligatory urge to keep eye contact, control the facial expressions, and keep track of his/her representation presents another system of stress where certain team members become involved or simply turn into a state of passive involvement.

In that hyperconnected condition, people can start emotionally or even intellectually pulling out of the meetings, not out of disinterest but due to exhaustion of the information bandwidth. As the participatory turn is performative, the genuine dialogue and psychological security are under duress. Individuals can nod in agreement and still disengage, be reluctant to state an outrageous suggestion, or feel intimidated to make important things clearer because they do not want to disrupt the meeting.

To add to this problem, there is also the increased adoption of digital surveillance and monitoring as a pretense of managing productivity. With the help of such applications as Time Doctor, Hubstaff, or Teramind, an employer can monitor keystrokes being used, what is shown on a screen, and even the webcam video feed. Though it is positive to hold people accountable in distant environments, these technologies can more likely demonstrate contradictory appreciative results on psychology. Organizational behavior research emphasizes the decreased trust, autonomy, and intrinsic motivation as a result of perceived surveillance, staples of psychological safety (Jeske & Santuzzi, 2015). Once team members believe they are being observed and judged versus nurtured at the interpersonal level, they develop a dark cloud over interpersonal risk taking (admitting a mistake, seeking assistance, and offering constructive dissent). This can create a culture of compliance as opposed to creativity, collaboration, or continuous learning. Surveillance has also resulted in underground forms of resistance or detachment in other scenarios, and this has seen employees seek alternative ways around the system or just give the least possible, thus making it a culture of mistrust and micromanaging. As an example, an employee working at home and knowing that he is network-monitored will not want to switch tabs during a meeting, even when he has to take notes or refer to the relevant document, lest he appear inattentive. Such hypervigilance will, over a period of time, result in job dissatisfaction and burnout. To the extent that leaders use such tools without offsetting them with trusting behaviors, the innovation and openness that are desirable are hampered by the actions of the leaders themselves.

In order to reduce these risks, deliberate design of work norms and tech policies is essential. Instead of imposing intrusive monitoring, organizations ought to focus on output, not input, individual agency, rather than authority, and psychological safety, instead of performative productivity. Considering break time in between the gatherings, promoting camera-optional ideology, and building trust by maintaining transparency in communication are some of the techniques that can potentially maintain engagement and safeguard well-being in virtual teams.

Misinterpretations, Delays, and Asynchronous Silos

Communication in virtual teams is mostly unfamiliar with the immediacy and contextual richness of face-to-face. Communication, via emails, Slack messages, or project management comments, is asynchronous, always leaving a temporal and emotional distance. Often, when sending out a message, team members cannot tell the recipient about the state of his or her cognitive load, emotional state, and availability. For example, the unresponsiveness, brought on by time zone or work overload, upon receipt of a message, can be interpreted differently as a lack of engagement or inclusion, in cases when that is not the intention (Byron, 2008).

All these misunderstandings can add up over time and can silently destroy trust. There is no follow-up or real-time clarification in place; thus, all persons are left to make assumptions, and these assumptions may breed resentment, confusion, or isolation. Also, in the case of asynchronous remote work, there may be what can be termed as communication silos where smaller groups or individuals become so inward-facing in work and with communications. These silos obstruct cross-functional interaction, diminish the rate at which spontaneous feedback is provided, and de-power the collective psychological cohesion in the team (Olson & Olson, 2009).

Such a virtual drift may be disastrous, especially among mixed groups, wherein differences in culture or even language already bring into the fray. Misunderstandings could not be solved without the formal means of checking the comprehension or consistency, which could be further enhanced with the progression of time, leading to breakdowns in communication. Such incidents may be explained and resolved almost instantaneously in a high-trust organization, whereas in a low-trust, low-security one, such incidents tend to simmer. The objective relies on continuous and receptive communication, which synchronous platforms can pursue without an explicit and succinct design, but asynchronous platforms challenge (Nguyen, 2021).

To suitably address them, overlapping communication strategies should be applied in organizations like regular check-ins, team-wide digital norms, and shared protocols to respond to messages (i.e., acknowledging receipt where the detailed reply cannot follow immediately). The negative effect of asynchronous miscommunication can also be mitigated by encouraging what some call interpretive generosity positivism in a context of ambiguity.

Cultural and Time-Zone Differences Complicating Shared Understanding

Virtual teams have one of their distinctive features or even paradoxes: they are global. Geographic dispersion adds a degree of cognitive diversity and a diversified skill set or abundance of cultural points of view, but can complicate the psychology of working in groups. There are very different cultural conventions related to communication styles, such as directness and assertiveness are interpreted as clarity and confidence in one society but as obnoxious or rude in another. High-context cultures (e.g. Japan, India) stress the use of subtle clues and implicit knowledge, but low-context (e.g. Germany, the U.S.) cultures are more likely to like unambiguous, explicit communications. In case team members are not aware of such differences, the subsequent improper actions or misconceptions may take place, which can often be traced to a matter of blame on personal defects and not cultural differences (Eckhardt, 2002; Sabella & Hall, 1978).

These cultural differences may weaken psychological safety in insidious and far-reaching terms. As an example, a team member of a culture that is collectivist in nature may not speak up or openly disagree with ideas in a team dominated by individualistic standards. When they do not speak, and people misunderstand them as not having ambitions or interest, this may influence their inclusion and credibility. In contrast, the rest of the cultural backgrounds tend to be more vocal and can control conversations, which can be unintended but in effect lead to silencing others.

These problems are worsened by the fact that real-time interaction is not easy due to the differences in time zones. It is not always easy to organize meetings that fit the agendas of all the participants, many of whom are working on different continents, and thus, there is one group of participants who remain constantly disadvantaged. In the same vein, providing rituals during inopportune times to the members of the team may convey implicit messages of preferred attendance and contributions. By progressive asymmetry, this could in the long-term result in lesser participation, marginalization, and/or withdrawal.

Moreover, asynchronous teamwork, although it is an attractive option, inhibits the random moments of direct human-to-human connection, be it a less straightforward check-in or a discussion during a break in the hallway, which would otherwise occur without prior coordination and always build connections and understanding. Lack of these micro interactions raises obstruction to empathy and relational trust, which are the compulsory components of psychological safety.

These cultural and temporal gaps need strategic leadership and design to fill the gap. Organizations should ensure cultural intelligence (CQ) is fostered among the teams by being curious, open, and humble in dealing with intercultural interactions. Equity in time zones must also become part of scheduling policies, and it should be achieved by rotating meeting times or making use of asynchronous video tools to offer a wider range of access. Communication norms and expectations can be codified in team charters so that all members have a common protocol that can minimize the ambiguity in interpretation. They can only do so using deliberate strategies that would enable teams to change their global diversity into a psychological asset. Table 4 provides a comparison of psychological safety threats in physical vs virtual teams.

Table 4. Comparison of threats to psychological safety in physical vs. virtual teams

Challenge Area	Physical Teams	Virtual Teams
Nonverbal Communication	Reliant on facial expressions, body language, and tone	Largely absent or distorted; video fatigue discourages use
Participation Dynamics	Dominated by extroverts or senior voices in person	Often silenced by tech barriers or uneven access
Feedback and Empathy	Informal feedback is possible in hallway chats or post-meeting talks	Feedback is delayed or misinterpreted in asynchronous platforms
Surveillance and Monitoring	Rare or visible (e.g., supervisor watching work)	Invisible but intrusive (e.g., tracking software)
Fatigue and Engagement	Occasional fatigue from meetings; physical breaks are possible	High digital fatigue, screen burnout, and lack of boundaries
Communication Clarity	Tone and context are often clearer; instant clarification is possible	Prone to misinterpretation; message lag causes confusion
Cultural Awareness	Easier to observe and adapt to others' styles in person	Harder to detect subtle cultural cues online
Time Zone Coordination	Less relevant in co-located teams	Major barrier to real-time interaction and shared rhythm
Team Bonding and Trust Building	Spontaneous social interactions help build trust	Requires intentional effort; often overlooked in virtual settings

Consequences of Poor Psychological Safety in Virtual Teams

In virtual teams, psychological safety is missing, which may cause cascading failures by destroying trust, performance, and increasing attrition. Although virtual collaboration is flexible and scalable, it is less tangible and it could hide the early inferences of disengagement or distraught, and thus its effects are sneakier.

For example, the product development team in a software company is going global, remotely. The leadership also assumed that the existing norms could be easily adapted to virtual environments and did not provide new feedback mechanisms and informal areas of open communication. Junior members of the team, afraid to break a taboo, did not even want to discuss dubious design assumptions in the open Slack threads-relying on avoidance and fearing public condemnation, reprimand, or reprisal in their careers. Their unsaid fears finally found their way into the critical faults of the product, which found its way to the customer without any curb. The repercussion was loss of contracts, relationships with clients, and a blame orientation, further reinforcing the culture of silence based on fear throughout the team.

In another example, a digital marketing agency used real-time performance monitoring software that helped to monitor the remote workflow during the COVID-19 pandemic. The change was meant to enhance accountability, but it did the opposite. As far as its impact was concerned, this change had taken the form of an indicator of a lack of trust. The employees claimed to be micromanaged, spied on, and detached from leaders. There was no cushion to absorb this change of rapport since offices lacked the casual interpersonal interactions in life. Scores in engagement diminished with time, and teambuilding meetings became less active, and the motivated employees started leaving for other companies that promote individuality and psychological comfort. Even when it spent money on the latest digital equipment, the agency lost much of its morale and productivity, which showed that technology is not able to replace the culture of safety and respect.

BUILDING AND SUSTAINING PSYCHOLOGICAL SAFETY IN DISTRIBUTED TEAMS

Building and sustaining psychological safety in distributed teams does not happen by accident or automatically, but requires purposeful leadership and team design and selective use of technology. Whereas in co-located teams, informal cues and closeness can easily breed trust, virtual teams need structure, clarity, and empathy to offset the deficiency that the distance creates. Organizations and leaders who make a priority of psychological safety in the culture of their digital workplace can achieve a more resilient, creative, and inclusive team.

Leadership is an overemphasized feature of promoting psychological safety in a virtual and a hybrid team environment. Distributed teams only have the most deliberate leadership actions to foster trust, open communication, or work as a team when they have no informal hall meetings, shared lunches, and the face-to-face emotional feedback that is a symbol of co-located teams. The leadership in such situations should not be confined to the classic responsibilities of a manager but must be aimed at creating an environment of interpersonal risk-taking where the members of the team freely speak up when they see problems, offer suggestions, and make mistakes without fear of punishment.

Modeling vulnerability is considered to be one of the best leadership strategies. This is because when leaders accept their inefficiency, request assistance, or request open feedback through virtual meetings, they demonstrate that mistakes are expected and learning should be valued over extremes. To illustrate, when a team leader says at the start of a remote stand-up meeting, I got our timeline wrong last week, and I think you were very patient, they accept accountability and make transparency easy to do. Other individuals can also be open since this is the way things are done. As the studies by Edmondson, (1999) Psychological safety demonstrates a high relationship with team learning and performance, and the leaders are at the center of the process when setting this norm.

The other behavior that is essential is the non-punitive reaction to disagreement with views or opinions, or questions. Leaders should be particularly sensitive to welcoming dissent in a virtual environment where it is very easy to misunderstand the intent of the other party due to communication being based on text. In a related example, when a remote worker takes an opposing view in a Slack conversation or dares an uncomfortable question in a Zoom call, what the leader says can either break down communication or reinforce the free flow of information. When a leader responds to a comment made by another member, saying, that's a great way of looking at it, I hadn't thought of it in this fashion, he or she is showing recognition that cognitive diversity exists. Stimulating a culture in which disagreement serves as a way to create a safer, healthier culture.

Communication practices also need to be inclusive. This might make quiet voices or introverts and persons with marginalized backgrounds to speak up even more difficult in a distributed team. Successful virtual leaders encourage people to participate by asking questions like round-robin sharing, anonymous polls, or directing questions by saying, "Sarah, we have not heard your thoughts yet- how do you see this? With such behaviors, every member of the team has a chance to contribute, no matter where they are, what time zone they belong to, or their personality.

It may be even more vital in the virtual world where nonverbal communication is weakened or absent, and active listening and empathy are highly valuable. Leaders are required to consciously recognize the emotions and contributions of team members. As an example, a reply that may help contain emotion and affirm psychological safety can include, "That would be frustrating, so thanks for raising it," or "You have been quiet lately, so how are you doing?"

Intentional Design of Digital Rituals and Norms

Psychological safety in the environment of a distributed team does not always occur naturally; it should be purposefully developed in well-built and all-inclusive digital rituals and norms. Such team rituals act as social scaffolding, in that they assist in substituting the informal interactions and emotional aspects that abound in co-located settings. Designed intentionally, digital rituals create mutual understanding, predictability, and the feeling of emotions, which are essential to the psychological safety prerequisites (A. Edmondson, 1999).

An effective variant is the emotional check-in at the beginning of the meeting, and it assists in bringing the emotional statuses of team members to light and makes empathy ready. Occasions to open up can be low-stakes, such as prompts like: What is one word you would use to describe how you are coming today? What is something distracting you right now? According to studies conducted by the NeuroLeadership Institute, those rituals stimulate the social reward center of the brain and make the participants feel trust and end up less threatened (Rock, 2008). Such rituals are also repeated often in meetings conducted by teams at GitLab and Buffer, and at other fully remote companies, as a means of bridging the connection across time zones.

The other best practice is that of rotating roles in participation in various meetings, which is a democratic manner of participation and sends a strong message that everyone holds leadership and a voice. Having the different members of a team facilitating meetings in rotation helps demote hierarchy as well as increases participation of the people who would otherwise be sidelined. It also aids in fighting the so-called halo effect, where more vocal team members accidentally take the center stage of psychological safety in virtual groups. Peer shout-outs, virtual kudos boards, asynchronous praise walls (e.g., in channels of Slack or on Miro boards), all invigorate a culture of recognition and belonging. Appreciation in the digital environment is out in the open and long-lasting, thus enabling the establishment of an atmosphere in which team members feel appreciated even beyond the touchpoints in synchronous learning.

Are also equally important rituals of reflection, like the retrospectives done at the end of a project that adhere to a no-blame philosophy. Applying such frameworks as Start-Stop-Continue or What went well, what did not, and what can we learn allows open feedback without the fear of being judged. Such tools as Confluence, Trello, or FunRetro can assist in such a process in both asynchronous and hybrid environments. To take one example, instead of allowing their engineering teams to take a relatively calm and centered approach to failure, Atlassian encourages its engineers to explicitly process failure during these rituals, which serve as a formalized means of reminding everyone that psychological safety is a good thing.

Digital ritual design is also associated with cultural sensitivity. In transnational work groups, it is crucially important to acknowledge that certain cultures might esteem the hierarchy more or be more silent in the manifestation of conflict. The approach in including individuals who might not feel free to participate in live discussions could use anonymous feedback tools, chat-based feedback before a discussion, or simple written language of meeting summaries.

Technology's Role in Supporting Transparency and Voice

Technology plays a more crucial role in virtual teams than in traditional ones: technology is not merely the tool that facilitates the process of working in a team, but it is the tool that allows experiencing organizational culture. Each tool chosen and each feature enabled can have the effect of affecting psychological safety, either by allowing voices to be heard and visibility, or by alienating members and creating fear. Therefore, one of the guiding principles in the technology adoption by distributed teams should be psychological usability, i.e., how much tools create a sense of trust, inclusion, and agency.

Among the most important roles of technology, one can note the role of increasing transparency. Much of the contextual and other project-related information is discussed in informal hallway conversations or spontaneous interactions in co-located teams. Virtual teams use such knowledge-management tools as Notion, Confluence, or Google Docs as a central storage of what has been decided, when, by whom, and why. Such transparent documentation eliminates doubt and limits the sense of isolation, especially of teammates who are newer or in remote areas and may not be a part of every discussion. Transparency also assists in accountability without being threatening since it is known and seen what is expected of one.

No less significant is the fact that any team member can feel safe, inspired, and ready to explore personality in detail and use the words in a preferred language without fear of the reaction of others due to the level on the organizational ladder. Anonymous input, such as with the use of a tool like Slido, Mentimeter, or Google Forms in a virtual meeting, can be used to bring difficult subjects or opposing views out into the open without putting a person at interpersonal risk. A study by Edmondson, (1999) Points out that in high psychological safety teams, there is an increased likelihood of team members reporting errors and providing ideas, which can become a critical milestone in bridging teams that are still in an early phase of developing this trust by using an anonymous tool.

Also, with the elimination of physical signals, technology-based emotionally expressive features promote the humanization of digital communication. Other add-ons (the emoji reaction, mood check-ins, or applications such as Range and Donut) can imbue otherwise impersonal communications with affective context. Although their features have sometimes been denounced as trivial, they serve, at least, to support feelings, promote empathy, and offer support by means of a lightweight yet strong gesture. An example of this is the feelings of approval by sending a thumbs up or heart on a colleague's message, or a brief mood survey could be done with a green/yellow/red thumbs up to who might need some added support that day.

An additional factor is the adoption of asynchronous tools, i.e., Slack threads, Microsoft Teams channels, or internal forums where people can be thoughtful and unhurried. Not every member of the team feels at ease talking during real-time video conference calls, particularly during inter-zonal calls or when they are in a second-language situation. The asynchronous spaces provide psychological safety in that people are able to process, reflect, and respond at their own pace, thereby evening the communicative playing field.

Meanwhile, it is necessary to note that technological advances have another side, making psychological safety vulnerable. Over-surveillance, such as tracking the screen, monitoring keystrokes, or making webcams compulsory, can be interpreted as an indicator of distrust and lead to anxiety and inhibition of natural behaviour. Trivedi & Patel, (2021) Reported that employee surveillance had gone up during the pandemic, though a large number of employees said that they had lost morale and developed a sense of violation as a result. These invasive technologies may lead to an atmosphere of fear as opposed to transparency, especially when done without consent or a strategic aim.

Key Methods and Models

Bringing psychological safety to virtual teams can never be dealt with by mere goodwill, but by strategic approaches that are based upon tried frameworks. A number of theoretical frameworks, together with diagnostic instruments, can inform leaders on how to design psychologically safe environments, particularly within the distributed working environment context. These models can easily be converted to the virtual environment and provide practical research findings that can optimize trust, openness, and connection among team members.

Amy Edmondson's Model of Psychological Safety

According to seminal works by Amy Edmondson, psychological safety is defined as a belief expressed in terms that the team is safe to take interpersonal risks (A. Edmondson, 1999). This theory explains three important behaviours that can create such an environment: leader inclusiveness, constructive responses to failure, and encouragement of voice. This model is specifically effective within the virtual environment when incorporated into digital workflows.

As a notable example, evidence of inclusive leadership within distributed teams can be given through frequent open forums wherein members of the team are encouraged to express queries or present ideas without any form of criticism. Leaders need to move on effectively when failures happen, e.g., due to the failure to meet a deadline or due to a misconceived project launch, by engaging in open discussions of the lessons learned instead of allocating blame. This creates a connotation of learning and not fear. Moreover, the encouragement of voice is one of the dimensions that can be implemented into the interaction of virtual teams through asynchronous channels, asking introverted or distant team members to provide their say via dedicated Slack threads or Google Forms.

SCARF Model (David Rock)

The SCARF model, as proposed by David Rock, is a neuroscience-grounded model of explaining what makes human beings tick as far as social interactions are concerned. It also establishes five domains that affect psychological safety by either triggering a reward or a threat system in the brain: status, certainty, autonomy, relatedness, and fairness (Rock, 2008). Virtual teams can reflectively address each of these domains.

- Appreciate input in visible, fair manners. For example, virtual shout-outs at team gatherings or leaderboards of accomplishments nominated by peers might assist in keeping the status quo.
- Be clear on expectations, goals, and deadlines with team members by constructive planning in applications such as Trello or Asana. The ambiguity can be minimized by regularly updated dashboards or project briefs.
- Provide freedom within work hours and how to go about tasks, and believe in the employee to take care of his/her time-essential in cross-time zone set-ups.
- Establish a bonding mechanism using digital watercooler conversations, group storytelling, or cross-functional interactions.
- Promote the distribution of the information and resources fairly and oversee decision-making with transparency.

Through the incorporation of the SCARF model in virtual leadership training, organizations can have an opportunity to mitigate social threats proactively and improve a psychologically safe culture.

Team Psychological Safety Scales

We need to measure to proceed. Questionnaires like the 7-item Team Psychological Safety Scale created by Edmondson provide quantitative ways of measuring the psychological climate of teams. Such items as "When you commit an error in this team, it does not count against you" or "You can afford to risk this team" can serve as pieces that elucidate the subtexts that might not be visible in virtual environments (A. Edmondson, 1999). Such surveys are able to be done quarterly and then reviewed by the HR or team leads to determine trends or red flags. To illustrate, a precipitous decline in scores on questions touching on risk-taking could be an indication of a culture dominated by fear following some failure involving the management, or a change in the management team. It is based on such insights that leaders can take specific action by revisiting team norms or introducing open Q and sessions to restore lost trust. Also, it is always possible to combine a psychological safety scale with a sentiment analysis tool or anonymous pulse surveys (e.g., Officevibe, Culture Amp) to have a more comprehensive picture of team health over platforms and time zones. Table 5 summarizes actionable strategies and tools that support psychological safety in distributed teams across leadership, cultural, and technological dimensions.

Table 5. Key strategies for psychological safety in distributed teams

Category	Strategy / Tool	How It Supports Psychological Safety
Leadership Behaviors	Model vulnerability (admit mistakes, ask for feedback)	Normalizes openness and reduces fear of negative judgment
	Inclusive facilitation (invite diverse input)	Ensures all voices are heard, including quieter or remote members
	Emotional check-ins & empathetic listening	Builds trust and demonstrates care
	Non-punitive response to dissent or error	Encourages risk-taking and idea sharing
Digital Rituals	Start-of-meeting emotional check-ins	Creates space for vulnerability and mutual understanding
	Rotating facilitation roles	Distributes power and increases team ownership
	Virtual kudos boards, feedback walls	Reinforces appreciation and recognition in remote environments
	Retrospectives & post-mortems with a "no-blame" culture	Enables open discussion of mistakes and continuous learning
Technology Tools	Asynchronous input tools (e.g., Google Forms, Slido)	Enables participation from hesitant or time-shifted members
	Collaboration platforms (e.g., Notion, Confluence)	Promotes transparency and access to shared knowledge
	Reaction buttons, emojis, check-in apps (e.g., Range)	Enhances emotional signaling and human connection
	Avoidance of surveillance software	Maintains trust and autonomy in virtual work
Frameworks & Diagnostics	Edmondson's Team Psychological Safety Model	Guides leader behavior and team norms to foster safety
	SCARF Model (Status, Certainty, Autonomy, Relatedness, Fairness)	Identifies social threat/reward factors in team dynamics
	Team Psychological Safety Survey Tools	Diagnoses safety levels and monitors cultural health

CONCLUSION

The move to a virtual and hybrid work model has changed the way teams can meet and work together, and build trust. In these pages, we have discussed the pluralism of psychological safety in the distributed environments- both the opportunities it delivers and the problems that one can experience in replacing physical co-presence in digital interaction.

The first lesson is that psychological safety does not just happen in virtual teams; rather, it has to be purposefully designed, fostered, and guided. A virtual environment can make the process of communication more inclusive, accommodate various communication styles and preferences of different team members, and grant them freedom and independence in a new working environment. Nonetheless, the digital medium brings the hazards of loneliness, misunderstanding, and distrust, particularly the nonverbal signals can be lost, and individual control is put in danger because of monitoring gadgets. The important role that leaders have in the development and maintenance of psychological safety is best observed. Their actions, including being vulnerable, valuing different opinions, and establishing inclusive practices, can fundamentally affect the perception of the participants in terms of safety to make their voice heard, to take a chance, and to offer their whole selves. Coupled with this, technological decisions and team rituals should be used to strengthen openness, transparency, and the fair voice of the team- and not just productivity.

Going forward, it is likely that new developments such as AI-facilitated collaboration and emotion-sensitive systems can raise novel challenges regarding what role digital means can play in advancing and/or compromising psychological safety. Like, AI assistants who summarize meetings or express team sentiment could be helpful--but are also ethically questionable in terms of spying and independence. Such changes require interdisciplinary research, which would allow uniting the knowledge of organizational psychology, human-computer interaction, and data ethics research. Psychological safety is still a key to good teamwork, whether in-person or online. With the way organizations are reinventing workspaces, this chapter reminds its readers, in the form of leadership, human resource managers, platform designers, and other researchers, about the issue of psychological safety that should not be a side issue, but a strategic need. Safety design is performance, inclusion, and long-term resilience design.

REFERENCES

Atlassian. (2025). *How to run a blameless postmortem*. https://www.atlassian.com/incident-management/postmortem/blameless

Bailenson, J. N. (2021). Nonverbal Overload: A Theoretical Argument for the Causes of Zoom Fatigue. *Technology, Mind, and Behavior*, *2*(1), 1–6. Advance online publication. DOI: 10.1037/tmb0000030

Byron, K. (2008). Carrying too heavy a load? The communication and miscommunication of emotion by email. *Academy of Management Review*, *33*(2), 309–327. Advance online publication. DOI: 10.5465/amr.2008.31193163

Eckhardt, G. (2002). Culture's Consequences: Comparing Values, Behaviors, Institutions and Organisations Across Nations. In *Australian Journal of Management* (Vol. 27, Issue 1). DOI: 10.1177/031289620202700105

Edmondson, A. (1999). Psychological safety and learning behavior in work teams. *Administrative Science Quarterly*, *44*(2), 350–383. Advance online publication. DOI: 10.2307/2666999

Edmondson, A. C., & Lei, Z. (2014). Psychological Safety: The History, Renaissance, and Future of an Interpersonal Construct. In *Annual Review of Organizational Psychology and Organizational Behavior* (Vol. 1). DOI: 10.1146/annurev-orgpsych-031413-091305

Ford, R. C., Piccolo, R. F., & Ford, L. R. (2017). Strategies for building effective virtual teams: Trust is key. *Business Horizons*, *60*(1), 25–34. Advance online publication. DOI: 10.1016/j.bushor.2016.08.009

Frazier, M. L., Fainshmidt, S., Klinger, R. L., Pezeshkan, A., & Vracheva, V. (2017). Psychological Safety: A Meta-Analytic Review and Extension. *Personnel Psychology*, *70*(1), 113–165. Advance online publication. DOI: 10.1111/peps.12183

Gajendran, R. S., & Harrison, D. A. (2007). The Good, the Bad, and the Unknown About Telecommuting: Meta-Analysis of Psychological Mediators and Individual Consequences. *The Journal of Applied Psychology*, *92*(6), 1524–1541. Advance online publication. DOI: 10.1037/0021-9010.92.6.1524 PMID: 18020794

Hess, U. (2023). Nonverbal communication. In *Encyclopedia of Mental Health, Third Edition: Volume 1-3* (Vol. 2). DOI: 10.1016/B978-0-323-91497-0.00133-8

Hinds, P. J., & Bailey, D. E. (2003). Out of Sight, Out of Sync: Understanding Conflict in Distributed Teams. *Organization Science*, *14*(6), 615–632. Advance online publication. DOI: 10.1287/orsc.14.6.615.24872

Jeske, D., & Santuzzi, A. M. (2015). Monitoring what and how: Psychological implications of electronic performance monitoring. *New Technology, Work and Employment*, *30*(1), 62–78. Advance online publication. DOI: 10.1111/ntwe.12039

Knight, C., & Haslam, S. A. (2010). Your place or mine? organizational identification and comfort as mediators of relationships between the managerial control of workspace and employees' satisfaction and well-being. *British Journal of Management*, *21*(3), 717–735. Advance online publication. DOI: 10.1111/j.1467-8551.2009.00683.x

Kruger, J., Epley, N., Parker, J., & Ng, Z. W. (2005). Egocentrism over E-mail: Can we communicate as well as we think? *Journal of Personality and Social Psychology*, *89*(6), 925–936. Advance online publication. DOI: 10.1037/0022-3514.89.6.925 PMID: 16393025

Luis, M. (2020). *Case Study: Meet Automattic, a Remote Worker Success Story | DistantJob - Remote Recruitment Agency*. https://distantjob.com/blog/2017-02-09-case-study-meet-automattic-a-remote-worker-success-story/

Morrison-Smith, S., & Ruiz, J. (2020). Challenges and barriers in virtual teams: A literature review. *SN Applied Sciences*, *2*(6), 1096. Advance online publication. DOI: 10.1007/s42452-020-2801-5

Nguyen, N. (2021). The Fearless Organization: Creating Psychological Safety in the Workplace for Learning, Innovation, and Growth. In *Learning Organization* (Vol. 28, Issue 3). DOI: 10.1108/TLO-04-2021-266

Olson, G. M., & Olson, J. S. (2009). Human –Computer Interaction Distance Matters. *International Journal of Human Computer Interaction, 0024*(July 2014).

Rock, D. (2008). SCARF: A brain-based model for collaborating with and influencing others. *NeuroLeadership Journal, 1*(1).

Sabella, E. Z., & Hall, E. T. (1978). Beyond Culture. *Contemporary Sociology*, *7*(4), 503. Advance online publication. DOI: 10.2307/2064404

Trivedi, S., & Patel, N. (2021). Virtual Employee Monitoring: A Review on Tools, Opportunities, Challenges, and Decision Factors. *Empirical Quests for Management Essences, 1*(1).

Chapter 4
Human-AI Cofacilitation, Psychological Safety, and the Engineering of Trust in Networked Learning:
Sociotechnical Architectures in Hybrid Classrooms

Ashraf Alam
http://orcid.org/0000-0001-6178-1187
Alliance University, Bengaluru, India

ABSTRACT

This chapter advances a programmatic blueprint that treats psychological safety as an engineered control parameter in hybrid classrooms, integrating social identity, self-categorization, Community of Inquiry, Self Determination, Control Value, cognitive load, procedural justice, value sensitive design, cybernetics, and adoption science. We specify a defense in depth architecture across interaction, facilitation, moderation, and institutional strata, with bounded roles for human and artificial cofacilitators constrained by provenance, refusal rules, and least privilege access. The framework codifies patterns such as anonymous first submissions with named replies, paced queues, progressive disclosure, week zero norm co-authoring, tiered moderation with evidentiary logging, and WCAG aligned accessibility. A compact measurement suite couples psychometrics to behavioral telemetry including parity indices, turn entropy, responsiveness, and repair depth, enabling quasi experimental inference and weekly decision routines. Procurement and data governance render pedagogy auditable.

DOI: 10.4018/979-8-2600-0934-5.ch004

1. INTRODUCTION

1.1 Epistemic Prolegomenon to Sociotechnical Safety Engineering in Hybrid Pedagogy

Psychological safety functions as a tunable systems parameter rather than a soft attribute, governing utterance likelihood, error disclosure latency, and consolidation fidelity of newly acquired schemas (Dutton, 2025; West & Mudaliar, 2025). Edmondson's multicite field investigations in 1999 demonstrated that a shared belief in interpersonal risk tolerance predicts learning behavior and performance in complex work systems, a finding that transfers to instructional ecologies when instantiated through explicit roles, interface affordances, and auditable protocols stabilized by feedback control. The pandemic shock in early 2020 displaced more than 1.6 billion learners across over 190 jurisdictions into mediated settings, revealing structural bottlenecks that persist. By 2023 the International Telecommunication Union estimated internet use near 67 percent, approximately 5.4 billion people, with pronounced urban rural and regional disparities that compress feasible design space. The GSMA in the same period described a usage gap near 38 percent among populations already under mobile broadband coverage, implicating affordability and skills rather than infrastructure alone. These figures define a pragmatic feasibility envelope for any safety by design program (Wu, 2025; Firth & Preston, 2025). The chapter therefore posits a programmatic agenda that engineers safety as an institutional capability, not a classroom anecdote, and situates the argument within audit friendly instrumentation, repeatable facilitation routines, and governance that preserves dignity while enabling cumulative improvement in participation bandwidth and knowledge resilience.

1.2 Human Machine Cofacilitation and the Multi-Theoretic Drivetrain for Architectural Translation

Artificial intelligence now saturates hybrid learning and requires calibrated task partitioning, bounded autonomy, provenance signaling, and human adjudication (Ionescu et al., 2021; Bardin & Ferrari, 2022). Guidance from the Department for Education in England in 2023 framed generative tools as assistive when professional judgment remains decisive, while sector surveys in 2024 and 2025 reported student adoption above ninety percent with limited formal training that necessitates refusal rules, transparency notes, and recovery drills. UNESCO's global guidance in 2023 emphasized human centered policy and educator capacity with provenance cues embedded in workflow. The analytical drivetrain integrates social identity and self-categorization theories to explain status linked speaking asymmetries, the SIDE model to specify conformity under constrained identifiability, the Community of Inquiry to align social, cognitive, and teaching presence with transactional distance, Self Determination Theory to couple autonomy support with persistence, Control Value Theory to forecast achievement emotions from appraisals, cognitive load research to bound extraneous demands, and organizational justice to sustain legitimacy through procedural, informational, and interactional fairness (Harris et al., 2025; Chatzithanos et al., 2021). These lenses translate into interface defaults that invite participation without exposure, workflow constraints that minimize anchoring and dominance spirals, and measurement targets that capture parity, entropy, and responsiveness with sufficient reliability for weekly decision making in heterogeneous cohorts (Ji et al., 2024; Le & Ta, 2024).

1.3 Defence in Depth Architecture With Measurement for Decision and Governance for Durability

The chapter specifies four interlocking strata that generate redundancy against local failures. The interaction stratum governs identity presentation, two stage responses, paced queues, progressive disclosure for sensitive topics, and quiet help channels that reduce stigma while preserving knowledge diffusion (Safron & Sheikhbahaee, 2023; Nöth, 2021). The facilitation stratum conducts week zero norm co-authoring, rotating roles such as inclusion sentinel and scribe, scripted repair dialogues, and a predictable cadence that interleaves micro lectures, structured dialogue, and off-screen consolidation (Parker et al., 2025; West & Mudaliar, 2025). The moderation stratum operationalizes severity tiers, evidentiary logging, timelines, restorative options when safe, and privacy preserving redaction that together sustain legitimacy (Mizraji, 2024; Azarian, 2022). The institutional stratum aligns codes of conduct, accessibility conformance consistent with WCAG 2.2, data minimization and retention consistent with GDPR principles, procurement due diligence, and auditability across accreditation cycles. Measurement operates as communal feedback rather than surveillance through compact psychometrics for safety, belonging, justice, inclusivity, fatigue, and collaboration, married to behavioral indicators including participation parity, turn entropy, responsiveness, escalation latency, and repair depth (Araneda, 2022; Jeon, 2022). Credible inference in live courses uses difference in differences, matched sections, generalized linear mixed models, stepped wedge and interrupted time series with multiverse sensitivity. Implementation is lifecycle orchestration that includes low resource pathways such as SMS decision trees, phone based IVR, and community radio. A forward research program targets dose response, durability across cohorts, transfer to offline teamwork, and distributional effects of artificial cofacilitation with preregistration, privacy preserving experimentation, and dashboards that bind evidence to action.

2. CONCEPTUAL FOUNDATIONS WITH A SYNTHETIC LENS FOR DESIGN

Psychological safety functions as a controllable group climate that modulates speaking probability, error disclosure latency, and schema consolidation fidelity in hybrid classrooms. The construct becomes an explicit parameter when educators render safety visible, rehearsed, and measurable through repair scripts, rubric aligned examples, curiosity-oriented response stems, quiet think time, paced queues, and private help conduits that later diffuse anonymized learning to the cohort (Osejo-Bucheli, 2024; Osejo-Bucheli, 2024). Social identity theory and self-categorization theory explain status linked asymmetries in airtime and help seeking, while stereotype threat clarifies performance suppression under identity risk. The SIDE model predicts conformity when identifiability is constrained and cues are sparse, and expectancy violation logic anticipates sanction under large audiences. Interface choreography therefore staggers visibility using anonymous first moves with named follow ups, progressive disclosure for sensitive prompts, cooldown intervals, and small room rehearsal that preserves exploratory cognition without reputational hazard (Zukowski, 2023; Michels, 2025). Justice theory adds the legitimacy substrate through procedural, interactional, and informational fairness, and epistemic justice highlights testimonial and hermeneutical deficits that silence particular speakers. Operational translation follows with published response timelines, redacted evidence logs, bounded appeals, and restorative options when safe, all written in plain language. These convergent lenses yield a compact grammar of interaction that elevates participation parity, reduces dominance spirals, accelerates error correction, and normalizes repair as routine pedagogical work.

Table 1. Theory-to-design map for safety by design in hybrid learning

Construct (Scope)	Mechanism-of-Action (Causal Microfoundations)	Design Operationalization (Hybrid/Online)	KPIs & Failure Modes (Quantifiable Readouts; Anti-Patterns)
Psychological Safety as Control Parameter	Attenuates evaluation apprehension; elevates error-disclosure rate and corrective-feedback throughput; shifts system from defensive routines to double-loop learning.	Publish repair protocols; rubric-linked examples; mandated curiosity stems; quiet think-time; paced queues; privacy-preserving help routes; short transparency notes post-incident.	Safety pulse $\geq 4/5$; time-to-first-reply $< 24h$; zero-reply $< 10\%$; parity Gini ≤ 0.20; failures: performative consensus, anonymity misuse, slow closure inducing learned silence.
Identity, Self-Categorization, Stereotype Threat	Social categorization drives norm-congruent speech; identity threat suppresses risk-taking; status cues skew airtime and help-seeking.	Identity-safety cues in prompts/examples; cross-status dialogue with equalized airtime; role rotation (inclusion sentinel, scribe, norms steward); co-authored Week-0 norms.	Airtime share within $\pm10\%$ of enrollment per subgroup; help-seeking parity; confidence $\Delta \geq 0.3$ SD; failures: token roles, example bias, norm drift under time pressure.
Visibility, Conformity, Audience Effects	Constrained identifiability heightens conformity to salient norms; cue scarcity and large audiences amplify sanction risk; persistent transcripts raise perceived cost of novice error.	Anonymous-first then named-reply; progressive disclosure on sensitive topics; small-room rehearsal; cooldown timers; time-boxed queues with exit without penalty.	Turn-entropy ≥ 0.70; $\geq 60\%$ two-stage use on high-risk prompts; moderation latency $<12h$; failures: pile-ons, anchor bias, queue gaming, incivility under blanket anonymity.

continued on following page

Table 1. Continued

Construct (Scope)	Mechanism-of-Action (Causal Microfoundations)	Design Operationalization (Hybrid/Online)	KPIs & Failure Modes (Quantifiable Readouts; Anti-Patterns)
Presence, Engagement, Knowledge Building	Triadic presence synergy; dialogue–structure co-tuning reduces transactional distance; interactive moves catalyze idea improvement cycles.	6–8 min micro-lectures + ICAP-grade prompts; explicit KB moves; reflective consolidation; paced, timely teacher presence without saturation.	≥50% interactive moves; ≥1 idea-improvement cycle per analytic thread; fewer unclosed threads; failures: teacher over-presence, passive content dumps, stalled revisions.
Motivation, Appraisal, Flow	Autonomy–competence–relatedness drive persistence; emotions follow control×value appraisals; challenge–skill equilibrium sustains deep work.	Choice of modality/ pacing; annotated examples and transparent criteria; task chunking with recoverable steps; buffered high-stakes windows; ritualized relatedness.	SDT index ≥4/5; on-time submissions ≥90% without grade inflation; stable stress markers; failures: over-constraint, opaque grading, deadline clustering.
Cognition, Load, Distributed Activity	WM capacity constraints demand extraneous-load minimization; cognition externalized across artifacts, peers, conventions; representations scaffold schema growth.	Reduce tool-switching; single-window prompts for complex reasoning; captions/transcripts; shared boards; structured note templates/checklists; quiet pre-speech think time.	Navigation hops ≤2; extraneous-load <3/5; artifact reuse rising across modules; failures: parallel-chat overload, fragmented UI, missing captions, absent memory scaffolds.

continued on following page

Table 1. Continued

Construct (Scope)	Mechanism-of-Action (Causal Microfoundations)	Design Operationalization (Hybrid/Online)	KPIs & Failure Modes (Quantifiable Readouts; Anti-Patterns)
Procedural/Interactional/Informational Justice; Epistemic Justice	Legitimacy via consistency, respectful treatment, sufficiency of reasons; counters testimonial and hermeneutical injustice that suppress credibility and voice.	Publish triage tiers and SLAs; minimal-exposure evidence logs; plain-language rationales; bounded appeals; credibility repair; diversified examples and validated non-dominant registers.	Justice score ≥4/5; appeal turnaround ≤7d; relapse <10% at 30d; failures: opaque sanctions, uneven enforcement, testimonial discounting, reason-giving deficits.
Affordances, Value-Sensitive Design, Choice Architecture	Perceived action possibilities steer behavior; stakeholder values encoded as requirements; defaults frame trajectories; dark patterns erode trust and safety.	Privacy-by-default; friction for risky public tagging; provenance labels on summaries; rapid quiet-help affordances; explicit dark-pattern bans; accessibility as default.	Informed-consent public-share ≥95%; provenance exposure 100%; zero dark-pattern audit findings; failures: coerced disclosure, opaque provenance, inaccessible controls.
Algorithmic Cofacilitation, Cybernetic Control, Adoption	Calibrated trust for bounded autonomy; feedback control using entropy, centrality, parity; adoption mediated by usefulness, ease, social influence, implementation fit.	Narrow AI roles (summarize with provenance; rubric explain; metacognitive prompt; translate with register flags); refusal rules; confidence thresholds; parity/entropy dashboards; stepped-wedge rollouts; procurement aligned to accessibility, auditability, minimization.	Entropy ≥0.65; centrality Gini ≤0.25; parity within ±10% for 2 consecutive weeks; refusal precision/recall ≥0.90; adoption ≥80% of sections by term-3; failures: automation bias, opaque outputs, control-loop oscillation, under-resourced facilitation.

Community of Inquiry models situate learning in the alignment of social, cognitive, and teaching presence, while transactional distance theory requires co tuning of structure and dialogue to shrink psychological distance (Solymosi, 2023; Fouad, 2024). ICAP provides a ladder from passive exposure to interactive elaboration, and knowledge building formalizes collective improvement cycles through public revision. Motivation frameworks link autonomy, competence, and relatedness to persistence, with control value theory forecasting achievement emotions from perceived control and task value, and flow describing absorption at challenge skill equilibrium (Saratxaga Arregi, 2024; Donevski & Zia, 2024). Cognitive load theory mandates minimization of extraneous load through single window reasoning, captioned media, and quiet planning before speech, while distributed cognition justifies shared boards, structured note templates, and checklists that externalize working memory. Affordance theory, value sensitive design, and choice architecture jointly encode normative commitments as interface defaults, with dark pattern proscription and provenance labeling preserving trust (Safron & DeYoung, 2021; DeYoung & Tiberius, 2023). Human automation teaming narrows artificial roles to summarization with sources, rubric explanation with spans, translation with register flags, and metacognitive prompting with opt outs, under explicit refusal rules and human escalation. Cybernetic control couples weekly dashboards to action rules using entropy of turns, centrality dispersion, assortativity by role, and parity indices as feedback signals (Ng, 2022; Zhang, 2025; Lee et al., 2025; Posthoff, 2024). Adoption science ties uptake to usefulness, ease, social influence, and implementation fit, with institutional playbooks that pilot, audit, and scale designs that degrade gracefully in low resource contexts while preserving the core logic of safety.

3. SAFETY-BY-DESIGN ARCHITECTURE FOR DEFENSE IN DEPTH IN NETWORKED PEDAGOGY

Psychological safety, equitable participation, and resilient knowledge formation arise from a stratified control system that couples micro interactional choreography with meso level facilitation, risk sensitive moderation, and macro institutional governance (Rorot, 2022; Tzafestas, 2022; Pao, 2023; Verma & Merigó, 2021). The interaction stratum regulates moment to moment exchanges through identity scaffolds that alternate real name accountability, cohort pseudonymity within bounded intervals, and time limited anonymity for first submissions that carry social risk, followed by automatic attribution that preserves credit and traceability (Overwijk, 2025; Darivandi Shoushtari et al., 2025). Two stage responses create independent ideation before accountable dialogue, while paced queues with clear timers and exits prevent dominance spirals and anchor effects. Progressive disclosure protects sensitive discourse, quiet help channels route low confidence questions to human support with rapid turnaround, and example rich prompts normalize uncertainty, invite multiple modalities of expression, and make evaluation rules legible through rubric aligned highlights (Mendoza Montano, 2025; Zolkin et al., 2023). Anti patterns such as public cold calling, leaderboards that reward speed over depth, and thread hijacking by high status voices are precluded through opt in response tokens, reply caps, and nudges that redirect accretive threads into fresh spaces. Failure anticipates remediation through throttles on anonymous posting, randomized queue micro positions, accelerated attribution when misuse appears, and transparency notes that explain how missteps were handled (Ghosh, 2025; Tang & Xiao, 2024). Minimal telemetry monitors parity of contributions, entropy of turns, and responsiveness so that instructors adapt patterns weekly without surveillance excess.

Table 2. Safety by design blueprint for hybrid/online classrooms

Stratum & Scope	Theoretical Axiom	Control Spec (Prescriptive Ops)	Metrics & Thresholds	Failure Modes → Remediation
Systemic Defense-in-Depth	Learning performance is an emergent property of layered controls; redundancy yields stability; cybernetic feedback maintains homeostasis.	Four interlocking strata: Interaction, Facilitation, Moderation, Institutional; patterns specified ex-ante, audited ex-post; single source of truth; change control on pattern edits.	Weekly parity–entropy–latency board; parity drift ≤5% over 4 weeks; cross-layer term audit.	Tool sprawl; policy–practice drift; single-point fixes → Prune stack; rebalance layers; publish after-action notes; update pattern library.
Interaction -Identity Regime	Identifiability calibrates evaluation apprehension; bounded anonymity boosts ideation without eroding accountability.	Three identity states: real-name for graded closure; cohort-pseudonym for exploratory windows; anonymous-first with auto-conversion ≤24h; conversion audit log.	≥60% anonymous-first on social-risk prompts; conversion misattribution =0; consent capture 100%.	Derision/pile-ons; anonymity inertia → Throttles; cooldowns; accelerated conversion; transparency memo to cohort.
Interaction -Turn Exchange	Structured turn-taking suppresses dominance spirals and anchoring; two-phase talk raises independent recall and accountable dialogue.	Two-stage hidden→named responses; paced queues (max 8; ~90s prep); visible ETA; penalty-free exit; reply caps; micro-randomization to deter gaming.	Turn-entropy ≥0.70; queue abandonment <10%; first-pass completion ≥85%.	Anchor bias; queue gaming; fast-twitch monopolies → Randomize bands; seed counter-anchors; redistribute facilitation.

continued on following page

Table 2. Continued

Stratum & Scope	Theoretical Axiom	Control Spec (Prescriptive Ops)	Metrics & Thresholds	Failure Modes → Remediation
Interaction - Privacy & Disclosure	Progressive disclosure lowers sanction risk; quiet channels reduce stigma while diffusing knowledge.	Sensitive prompts default private; explicit, reversible consent; quiet-help routed to TA/ mentors with same-day SLA; depersonalized Q&A promoted to knowledge base.	Median time-to-first-reply <24h; zero-reply <10%; ≥50% promotable Q&A.	Off-channel overload; stalled consent; help hoarding → Rehearse low-stakes public error sharing; rotate responders; weekly transparency digest.
Interaction - Prompt & Example Integrity	Prompt affordances instantiate epistemic norms; diverse examples counter hidden curriculum; anti-patterns degrade discourse ecology.	Multimodal entry (text/ audio/sketch); rubric-linked examples across registers; mandatory curiosity stems; no cold-calling at scale; remove "fastest-wins"; nudge-to-new-thread; sarcasm filter.	Multimodal coverage ≥80%; ≥3 examples per criterion; moderation flags trending ↓ week-on-week.	Performativity; leaderboard monoculture; sarcasm creep → Token-based opt-in; parity alerts; instructor modeling of inquiry tone.
Facilitation - Norms, Roles, Cadence	Social contract and predictable rhythm cut extraneous load; repair is proceduralized, not ad hoc.	Week-0 co-authored norms; rotating roles (inclusion sentinel, scribe, norms steward, timekeeper, devil's advocate+repair duty); rhythm: micro-lecture + structured dialogue + reflection; buffered assessments; alt-demonstrations.	Midterm voice/ clarity/help ≥4/5; role coverage 100%; on-time role actions ≥90%.	Role tokenism; norm drift; feedback deluge → Role sheets with stems; midterm norm refresh; public synthesis notes vs. individual call-outs.
Moderation -Triage & Restitution	Legitimacy from transparent tiers, SLAs, proportionate remedy; restorative options when safe and consented.	Tiers: minor (ack ≤1 biz day; closure ≤3), medium (plan + review ≤14), severe (immediate escalation); role-based evidence logs; redaction; plain-language reasons; bounded appeals; restorative pathways.	Escalation median <12h; closures within tier bounds; relapse <10% at 30d; appeal turnaround ≤7d.	Opaque sanctions; uneven enforcement; over-exposure → Transparency ledger; redaction guide; category-triggered upstream redesign.

continued on following page

Table 2. Continued

Stratum & Scope	Theoretical Axiom	Control Spec (Prescriptive Ops)	Metrics & Thresholds	Failure Modes → Remediation
Institutional - Accessibility, Data, Procurement	Durability via universal design, minimization, enforceable vendor obligations; governance aligns policy with praxis.	WCAG-aligned defaults (captions, transcripts, keyboard paths, contrast); purpose limitation; role-based access; finite retention; RFPs mandate provenance labels, refusal rules, audit trails, anti-dark-pattern attestations; sandbox before updates; annual audits.	Critical accessibility defects =0; provenance visibility 100%; SLA adherence ≥99%; remediation ≤30 days.	Vendor drift; inaccessible workflows; residency gaps → Contractual audit rights; budgeted accessibility services; mapped data flows.
Low-Resource Equivalents	Functional equivalence under constraint; media-agnostic control logic preserves pedagogy.	SMS trees; paper two-stage triads; phone-hour quiet-help; IVR office hours; radio micro-lectures; paper incident notebook; small-cell suppression on reports.	Reply turnaround ≤2 days; triad parity ±10%; incident log completeness ≥95%.	Outages; shared-device leakage; identifier persistence → Offline packets; "no-internet week" playbook; avoid persistent IDs; posted norms & SLAs.

The facilitation stratum codifies the social contract through week zero rehearsal of norms, rotating roles that distribute epistemic labor such as inclusion sentinel, scribe, norms steward, timekeeper, and devil's advocate paired with repair duty, and a predictable cadence that interleaves concise micro lectures, structured dialogue, and reflective consolidation with scheduled off screen intervals that protect cognitive resources (Ruyer, 2023; Yolles, 2022; Kelbert, 2021; Sachs, 2023). The moderation stratum transforms discretion into legitimacy through published severity tiers with service levels, neutral evidentiary logging with redaction and role restricted access, plain language reasons, bounded appeals, and restorative options when consent and safety align, with model misfires withdrawn, corrected, and archived for audit (Morgan, 2023; Goddard, 2022; Hartl et al., 2024; Liu et al., 2023). The institutional stratum renders safety durable through accessibility by default consistent with WCAG 2.2, data minimization and finite retention consistent with prevailing privacy law, procurement that demands provenance cues, refusal performance, audit trails, and change logs, and recurring audits that tie telemetry to staffing and platform improvements. Low resource pathways preserve logic through SMS trees, paper based two stage triads, phone hour quiet help, and community radio micro lectures, with parity proxies sampled in triads when connectivity falters (Boyun, 2024; Glasson, 2024; Posthoff, 2024; Wong, 2023). Redundancy across strata contains local failures, since facilitation can reintroduce voice when identity misconfiguration induces hesitation, moderation can repair when facilitation misses a brewing conflict, and policy can reset defaults when repeated incidents reveal upstream design debt.

4. HUMAN-AI COFACILITATION AS BOUNDED AUTONOMY ARCHITECTURE

Cofacilitation succeeds when artificial agents operate as narrow, auditable instruments with crisp inputs, bounded outputs, and explicit human fallback. A summarizer condenses sprawling discourse into extractive anchored and judiciously abstractive briefs that expose evidentiary pointers, uncertainty signals, and minority viewpoints so instructors verify rather than reread entire threads (Ziębacz, 2022; Khantuleva, 2022; Glasson, 2024; Busseniers et al., 2021). A rubric explainer aligns criteria to precise textual or graphical spans and proposes one actionable revision per criterion to prevent advisory dilution. A metacognition coach elicits plan–monitor–evaluate cycles through timeboxing, strategy selection prompts, and post hoc calibration checks that strengthen self-regulation without supplanting teacher judgment (Cubitt et al., 2025; Ziebacz, 2022; Wolfson, 2022; Hlabisa, 2025). A translation assistant preserves meaning and register across languages, flags idioms without clean equivalents, and offers back translation for verification. Risk is governed through rule catalogs that reject toxicity, identity slurs, and disallowed personal data, through model confidence thresholds that prohibit speculative fabrication, and through provenance manifests that disclose sources, model identity, and generation time (Yolles, 2021; Kline, 2023). Least privilege scoping ensures an agent sees only task essential context, with on device processing favored for low-risk transformations and redacted server-side processing reserved for heavy inference. Oversight remains human led through alerts on low confidence, sensitive term matches, or parity excursions, with one click pause, withdrawal, transparent explanation, corrected artifact, and immutable logging of detection, withdrawal, correction, and learner feedback to improve templates between cycles.

Table 3. Safety by design blueprint using layers, controls, metrics, and remediation

Function	I/O Contract (Formal Spec)	Control Logic & Safeguards (Operational Constraints)	KPIs (Targets / Bands)	Pathologies → Remedies
Cohort-level Cofacilitation System	**In:** forum corpora, artifacts, rubrics, lexicons, consent flags. **Out:** evidence-linked briefs, criterion-mapped feedback, SRL prompts, bidirectional translations, immutable audit trails.	Least-privilege data scoping; PII minimization; on-device for low-risk transforms; redacted server-side only; confidence thresholds; HIL hard-gates; tamper-evident provenance ledger; change-control on templates.	Provenance visibility 100%; refusal P/R ≥0.90/0.90; HIL escalations 1–5% of interactions; telemetry coverage ≥95%.	Automation bias, scope creep, privacy leakage → Narrow role cards, rate-limits, systematic redaction, periodic scope/ audit reviews.
Role: Summarizer (Thread Condensation)	**In:** heterogeneous threads/docs. **Out:** extractive-anchored, abstractive briefs with minority-view surfacing and uncertainty tags.	Source-manifold constraint; novelty gate; dissent quota; recency windowing; claim–evidence alignment checks; length-compression bounds.	Unique-claim coverage ≥95%; hallucinations <0.05/1k tokens; ≥1 low-frequency idea per brief; instructor acceptance ≥90%.	Popularity loops, omission, over-compression → Completeness check, adjustable compression ratio, dissent preservation.
Role: Rubric Explainer (Criteria Mapping)	**In:** rubric schema + learner artifact. **Out:** per-criterion verdicts, span-level citations, single actionable revision per criterion.	Span tagging; example retrieval; error-type taxonomy; ban grade prediction; confidence-gated HIL handoff; throttled feedback cadence.	Human alignment κ ≥0.75; action uptake ≥70%; quality delta ≥0.4 SD; disagreement flags 5–10%.	Vagueness, criterion drift, overload → One-move constraint, rubric re-sync, per-artifact throttling, escalate low-confidence cases.
Role: Metacognition Coach (Plan-Monitor-Evaluate)	**In:** task metadata + plan state. **Out:** timeboxing, strategy prompts, post-hoc calibration checks.	Spaced prompting; non-diagnostic tone; opt-out without penalty; lapse-recovery scripts; quiet-hour observance; tapering schedules.	Plan uptake ≥75%; time-on-task variance ↓20–30%; calibration error ↓15–25%; micro-task completion ≥95%.	Prompt fatigue, mistiming, dependence → Adaptive cadence, embargo windows, tapering, human check-ins.
Role: Translation Assistant (Multilingual Mediation)	**In:** source text/ audio + glossary. **Out:** meaning- and register-preserving translation, flagged untranslatables, back-translation stub.	Terminology lock; false-friend detector; dialect toggles; context-window expansion; register parity checks; reviewer queue for edge cases.	Educator acceptance ≥90%; glossary hit-rate ≥95%; ambiguity resolution ≥80% same day; dialect parity gap ≤3 pp.	Literalism, register loss, dialect bias → Back-translation review, parity alerts, bilingual human review loop.

continued on following page

Table 3. Continued

Function	I/O Contract (Formal Spec)	Control Logic & Safeguards (Operational Constraints)	KPIs (Targets / Bands)	Pathologies → Remedies
Guardrails & Provenance (Policy Enforcement)	**In:** prompts + rule set. **Out:** allow/deny decisions, refusal rationales, provenance manifests.	Toxicity/PII policy catalog; model-ID stamping; time-stamps; click-through evidence chain; on-device prefilter; latency-budget governor; refusal explainers.	Refusal TPR ≥0.92; FPR ≤0.08; provenance link depth ≥2; added latency ≤200 ms p50.	Over-blocking, silent failures, opaque lineage → Threshold calibration, user-visible reasons, mandatory provenance surfacing.
Oversight & Recovery (Runtime Governance)	**In:** confidence scores, parity monitors, incident reports. **Out:** pause/resume, withdrawals, corrected artifacts, user notices, post-mortems.	HIL triggers on low-confidence, harm-lexicon hits, parity excursions; one-click agent pause; runbook: detect → withdraw → explain → correct → log; rollback buttons; drill cadence.	TTD <15 min; TTW <30 min; TTC <2 h; user notification ≤24 h; action-item closure ≤7 days.	Slow containment, silent corrections, repeat misfires → Pre-mortems, guardrail updates, rehearsed drills, escalation ladders.
Equity Controls (Distributional Justice)	**In:** voluntary subgroup metadata + interaction logs. **Out:** parity diagnostics, inclusive rebalancing actions.	Parity bands ±5 pp over two weeks; assistance rotation; minority-idea constraint in summaries; language/dialect parity checks; targeted seeding.	Intergroup reply/help gaps ≤5 pp; ≥1 low-freq idea per summary; assistance rotation coverage 100%.	Majority amplification, linguistic drift, assistance hoarding → Counter-prompting, rotate human attention, publish inclusive invitations.
Procurement, Compliance & Auditability (Lifecycle Assurance)	**In:** RFPs, scenario batteries, accessibility audits, DP terms. **Out:** pass/fail gates, contractual controls, change-logs.	Scenario tests: refusal, recovery, accessibility, provenance, parity; data minimization; residency mapping; sandbox pre-release; annual audits with SLAs and kill-switches.	Scenario pass ≥95%; critical a11y defects =0; SLA adherence ≥99%; remediation ≤30 days; change-log freshness ≤7 days.	Vendor drift, dark-pattern UX, residency gaps → Audit rights, penalty clauses, staged rollouts, mandatory sandboxing.

Distributional fairness requires monotonic routines rather than rhetoric. Co-facilitation rotates translation directionality so dominant language speakers also experience assisted reading, mandates that each summary surface at least one low frequency idea, and monitors reply counts and help acceptance for subgroup gaps larger than five percentage points persisting across two consecutive weeks (Stening et al., 2023; Tabilo Alvarez & Ramírez-Correa, 2023). When divergence appears, prompts are rebalanced, human attention is reallocated toward quieter cohorts, and an inclusive invitation specifies the concrete change. Procurement encodes pedagogy into testable criteria through scenario batteries that include refusal performance under personal data and slur prompts, recovery drills that measure time to withdrawal and notification quality, accessibility conformance across captioning, keyboard navigation, and high contrast rendering, provenance exposure for every transformation, and parity checks across multiple languages and dialects (Gerus et al., 2023; Petrov et al., 2021; Wirkuttis et al., 2023; Sayre, 2023). Contractual controls specify purpose limitation, storage locality, encryption in transit and at rest, role-based access, audit rights, deletion timelines, and breach notification windows, with mandatory change logs and sandbox trials before production updates. Institutions adopt costed tiers that range from scripts and checklists to dashboards with parity alerts to integrated platforms with configurable refusal and routing rules (Küppers, 2023; Qin et al., 2022; Ortner et al., 2022; Parker et al., 2025). Adoption proceeds through small pilots that gather telemetry and user narratives, followed by explicit go- or no-go decisions, and annual audits that revisit parity, accessibility, refusal accuracy, incident handling, and vendor adherence so commitments remain operational rather than notional.

5. ETHICAL TELEMETRY AND PSYCHOMETRIC INSTRUMENTATION FOR ACTIONABLE INSIGHTS USING BEHAVIORAL ANALYTICS, CAUSAL INFERENCE, AND PRIVACY PRESERVING GOVERNANCE

Measurement serves collective improvement when it is purpose limited, proportionate, transparent, and voluntary, never a covert apparatus of surveillance. The doctrine specifies a smallest sufficient set of indicators that reliably informs pedagogy while minimizing intrusion (Johnson, 2023; Lan et al., 2025; Mi et al., 2024; Xu & Lin, 2023). Plain language notices enumerate what is collected, who has access, how long it persists, and what pedagogical adjustments each signal authorizes. Consent is active rather than implied and opt outs carry no penalty (Malaspina, 2023; Walter, 2024; Goł biewski et al., 2022; Roli & Braccini, 2023). Reliability thresholds are predeclared so that short scales clear a sensible floor, with Cronbach alpha or coefficient omega at or above point seven, and validity is established through cognitive interviewing that detects linguistic ambiguity and cultural drift. Invariance checks verify that movement in scores reflects real change rather than translation artifacts across language, gender, or program year (Basnet et al., 2025; Stasch et al., 2025; Solymosi, 2023; Malaspina, 2025). A compact classroom suite captures psychological safety, belonging, procedural justice, inclusivity, collaboration quality, and cognitive fatigue using concise items with concrete anchors. Weekly pulses draw rotating subsets so total respondent time remains under ninety seconds, while a monthly form estimates full constructs and stability (Firth & Preston, 2025; Harris et al., 2025; Ruyer, 2023; Hagane & Venture, 2022). Translation follows forward and back procedures with adjudication to preserve meaning. Missing data rules are simple and explicit. If half the items in a scale are present, the mean of available items estimates the construct. If fewer are present, no score is computed. Results are aggregated at section or cohort level and are never used for individual grading.

Table 4. Telemetry-to-action schema for hybrid learning using psychometrics, behavioral analytics, causal inference, and privacy governance

Control Domain (Cybernetic Ontology)	Formalism & Intent	Ops Spec (Instruments / Algorithms)	KPIs / Bounds	Pathologies → Remedies
Ethical Telemetry Regime	Analytics as improvement engine; purpose-limited, proportional, consented; anti-surveillance posture.	Publish data dictionary, access matrix, retention map; active opt-in with revocation; reliability floor α or ω ≥ .70; cognitive interviews; multi-group invariance (configural/metric/scalar).	Transparency coverage 100%; opt-out penalty 0; ΔCFI ≤ .01 across language/gender/ cohort.	Scope creep, opacity, re-identification → Metric-to-decision traceability; small-cell suppression; privacy red-teaming; ethics review cadence.
Psychological Safety Index (PSI)	Latent group climate enabling risk-tolerant discourse without standards dilution.	7-item short form; 5-point anchored Likert; weekly 2-item pulse + monthly full form; forward–back translation; ICC to verify section-level signal.	PSI ≥ 4.0; ω ≥ .75; week-over-week drift ≤ ±0.2; ICC with 95% CI reported.	Acquiescence bias, ceiling effects → Reverse-keyed items; anchor recalibration; distribution rescaling.
Belonging & Inclusivity Indices (BII)	Perceived membership, representational adequacy, modality latitude, register acceptance.	5-item Belonging + 6-item Inclusivity; rotating mini-forms; DIF scans (language/dialect); graded response IRT calibration.	BII ≥ 4.0; item RMSEA ≤ .08; DIF	Δb
Procedural Justice & Collaboration Quality (PJCQ)	Legitimacy of process and interactional efficacy (airtime symmetry, feedback utility, conflict repair).	6-item PJ + 6-item CQ; rwg for rater agreement; example-anchored response training; monthly long form.	Mean ≥ 4.0; rwg ≥ .70; temporal stability r ≥ .60; MCAR tests non-sig.	Halo/leniency, anchoring → Frame-of-reference primers; example refresh; randomized item order.

continued on following page

Table 4. Continued

Control Domain (Cybernetic Ontology)	Formalism & Intent	Ops Spec (Instruments / Algorithms)	KPIs / Bounds	Pathologies → Remedies
Participation Topology & Entropy (PTE)	Distributional diversity of voice and graph structure of discourse.	Normalized turn entropy H∈[0,1]; degree-Gini for centrality dispersion; assortativity by role/language; parity via Gini/Theil on subgroup shares.	H ≥ .70; centrality Gini ≤ .25;	r_assort
Responsiveness & Safety Operations (RSO)	Temporal hygiene of help flows and incident handling.	Median time-to-first-reply; zero-reply prevalence; escalation latency (flag→ack); resolution time (ack→close); Repair Depth Index (acknowledge + change + follow-through).	TFR < 24h; zero-reply < 10%; median escalation < 12h; closure within tier SLA; RDI ≥ 2/3.	Thread neglect, stalled escalations → TA routing rules; SLA dashboards; incident runbooks; capacity reallocation.
Causal Inference Design (CID)	Decision-grade estimation under heterogeneity with bias control.	Diff-in-Diff with pre-trend diagnostics; propensity-matched sections; GLMMs (random intercepts/slopes); stepped-wedge; ITS with ≥10 pre/post; alpha-spending for sequential looks; multiverse sensitivity.	Parallel pre-trends; standardized effects with CIs; AIC/BIC fit; robustness across ≥70% of specs.	Confounding, peeking inflation, overfit → Pre-analysis plans; balance checks; multiple-look adjustment.
Decision Intelligence Dashboard (DID)	Closed-loop control tying telemetry to weekly interventions.	RAG tiles for Parity/Entropy/ Responsiveness/Incidents; one-line causal narratives; timestamped action log; instructor drill-downs; cohort roll-ups; SPC limits; funnel plots for small-n.	Weekly review adherence 100%; red bands resolved ≤2 cycles; immutable audit trail.	Vanity metrics, gaming, action paralysis → Hard-to-fake signals; auto-suggested playbooks; "one decision per dashboard" rule.
Data Governance & Privacy Compliance (DGPC)	Enforceable minimization, purpose limitation, subject rights, and lawful processing.	Role-based access; retention ceilings (telemetry ≤12 months; incidents shorter); residency mapping; immutable access logs; SAR workflow; shadow-profile prohibition; noise/banding for public comms.	Access violations 0; SAR fulfillment ≤30 days; on-time deletions ≥99%; audit remediation ≤30 days.	Over-collection, residency gaps, silent access → DPA addenda; quarterly audits; kill-switches; vendor remediation SLAs.

Behavioral telemetry compresses activity traces into interpretable signals with weekly cadence. Participation parity summarizes subgroup contribution shares using Gini or Theil and targets bands within ten percent of equal allocation where ethical disclosure exists (Cao, 2022; Jiang et al., 2025; Sun et al., 2025; Iman, 2025). Turn taking entropy normalizes speaker turn diversity to a zero to one range, while centrality dispersion flags hub dominance through a Gini on degree or a comparable dispersion metric. Responsiveness monitors median time to first reply with a weekday target under twenty four hours and records zero reply prevalence with a target below ten percent (Xu & Lin, 2023; DeYoung & Tiberius, 2023). Safety operations track escalation latency and resolution time and score repair depth when acknowledgments, commitments to change, and visible follow through are present. Knowledge improvement counts idea improvement cycles as a share of analytic threads. Stability and fairness are maintained with simple statistical process control using center lines and limits derived from early weeks, and with funnel plots that prevent misclassification of small sections (Zukowski, 2023; Fisher, 2024). Decision quality rests on quasi experimental designs that honor constraints, including difference in differences with pretrend diagnostics, matched sections, generalized linear mixed models, stepped wedge rollout, and interrupted time series with adequate periods, supported by sequential safeguards and multiverse sensitivity (Fisher, 2024; Zhang et al., 2025). Dashboards present parity, entropy, responsiveness, and incidents with succinct narratives and a single documented decision per week, avoiding league tables and gamable metrics. Governance enforces role based access, finite retention near one year for routine telemetry, storage residency compliance, small cell suppression, optional demographic collection, subject rights fulfillment, and annual vendor audits so privacy and trust remain stable while learning systems improve.

6. EQUITY-FIRST OPERATIONALIZATION ACROSS MODALITIES USING ADAPTIVE LOGISTICS AND LOW-INFRASTRUCTURE EQUIVALENCE

Implementation begins before matriculation through a probabilistic risk register that triangulates projected headcount, disciplinary mix, bandwidth dispersion, device heterogeneity, disability accommodations, linguistic diversity, incident history, and assessment pressure (Chatzithanos et al., 2021; Gao et al., 2023). Each determinant receives likelihood and impact scores on a compact three by three grid with short narratives that specify plausible hazards such as pile-ons in large entry cohorts or camera aversion in rural segments (Feng et al., 2025; Laouris & Tuddenham, 2025). Pattern selection then becomes a minimax design exercise that maps profiles to safeguards, for example two stage responses when enrolment exceeds at least eighty, progressive disclosure for culturally sensitive prompts, and quiet help channels for low confidence queries (You et al., 2024; Yolles, 2022). The plan enumerates weekly telemetry, decision thresholds, and failover moves if a pattern underperforms, and a one-page student brief articulates design intent in plain language. Week zero functions as a rehearsal laboratory where the class coauthors testable norms, drills core sequences on neutral content, rotates roles for distributed epistemic labor, and practices a simple repair dialogue. Consent procedures specify recording, transcription, and translation with opt outs that trigger alternate participation paths (Bao et al., 2024; Cubitt et al., 2025). Cadence during steady state then stabilizes cognitive load through a predictable rhythm that pairs micro lectures with two stage exchanges and reflective consolidation, alternates open office hours with quiet one to one slots, schedules off screen days for reading and sketching, and posts a weekly plan with time targets so learners budget attentional resources alongside work and caregiving commitments.

Table 5. Equity-first implementation & operations framework

Control Stratum	Telos (Formal Intent)	Controls & Procedures (Prescriptive Spec)	KPIs / Thresholds (Quantifiables)	Pathologies → Remedies (Runbooks)
Sociotechnical Operating Model	Maintain psychological safety, equitable participation, and knowledge durability via cybernetic orchestration under heterogeneous constraints.	Single source of truth for patterns; ex ante design review and ex post audit; versioned change control; OODA loops tethered to telemetry; contingency trees for bandwidth, staffing, assessment shocks.	Weekly review adherence 100%; parity drift ≤5% over 4 weeks; pattern change log freshness ≤7 days; audit action closure ≤30 days.	Tool sprawl, policy–practice drift, single-point fixes → prune stack, align governance with classroom praxis, enforce after-action memos, deprecate anti-patterns.
Precourse Risk Stratification and Pattern Fit	Anticipate variance to minimize exposure and select minimax interaction designs.	Score headcount, bandwidth dispersion, device access, accommodations, language mix, prior incidents, assessment peaks on 3×3 likelihood × impact; map to patterns: two-stage for N≥80, progressive disclosure for sensitive prompts; publish student brief.	Risk register coverage 100%; pattern–risk mapping documented; trigger thresholds predeclared; stakeholder sign-off before T0.	Unmodeled risk, brittle defaults, opaque intent → expand inputs, upgrade to minimax sets, rewrite brief in plain language, dry-run high-risk flows.
Week 0 Rehearsal and Explicit Consent	Build procedural memory and legitimacy before stakes escalate.	Co-author norms as testable sentences; low-stakes drills of two-stage threads, role rotations, repair scripts; capture consent for recording, transcription, translation with opt-outs and alternatives; 5-minute data-use briefing; transparency note.	Norms finalized by end of week 0; consent capture ≥98% with zero penalty for opt-out; rehearsal coverage ≥90% of core patterns.	Token norms, uninformed consent, cold-start anxiety → anchor norms to examples, offer alternative paths, add micro-drills, publish error-handling examples.
Steady State Cadence and Load Management	Stabilize cognitive demand while maximizing interactive depth and feedback timeliness.	Weekly rhythm: 6–8 minute micro-lecture, two-stage response within 24 h, reflective consolidation; alternate open drop-ins with quiet 1:1 slots; schedule off-screen days; public synthesis notes; parity nudges toward quieter cohorts.	Turn-taking entropy ≥0.70; median time-to-first-reply <24 h; zero-reply prevalence <10%; workload forecast posted 100% of weeks.	Screen fatigue, reply neglect, attention skew → enforce off-screen days, TA routing for slow threads, seed prompts to under-represented voices, tighten prompt scope.

continued on following page

Table 5. Continued

Control Stratum	Telos (Formal Intent)	Controls & Procedures (Prescriptive Spec)	KPIs / Thresholds (Quantifiables)	Pathologies → Remedies (Runbooks)
High Stakes Windows and Closing Rituals	Buffer stress, preserve fairness, and institutionalize reflection and memory.	Freeze content 24 h pre-deadline; preapprove alternative demonstrations (oral, tactile, low-bandwidth); release rubrics with annotated examples; live moderation of help queues; debrief within 72 h; portfolio walk; letter to future cohorts; conflict ledger.	Help-queue SLA meet rate ≥95%; alternative-path uptake tracked; debrief completion within 72 h; conflict-ledger completeness ≥95%.	Last-minute overload, inequitable display, unresolved grievances → widen windows, expand alt-formats, surge moderators, log and publish debrief actions.
Staffing Architecture and Capability Building	Distribute cognitive, affective, and governance labor to prevent burnout and drift.	RACI for facilitation, telemetry, moderation, data stewardship, referrals; timezone coverage; TA script kit (curiosity, boundaries, repair); shadow → co-facilitate → lead; modular badges: inclusive facilitation, trauma-aware response, accessibility, translanguaging, analytics.	Role coverage 100% of sessions; ≥2 observation cycles per instructor per term; badge completion ≥90%; intervention timing precision improves across term.	Invisible labor, role ambiguity, over-intervention → publish duty cycles, tighten runbooks, rotate roles midterm, replace micro-management with public syntheses.
Equity, Accessibility, and Linguistic Justice	Make inclusion the default; protect intersectional parity and multilingual participation.	WCAG-conformant defaults on; wide assessment windows; late-work recovery routes; bilingual prompts, mixed-language rooms, student glossaries with review; translation assistant flags idioms and supplies back-translation; small-cell suppression for parity reporting.	Intergroup parity within ±10%; accessibility defects 0 critical; dialect parity gap ≤3 percentage points; equity audits at midterm and close completed 100%.	Representation gaps, linguistic drift, accommodation debt → rotate facilitation, target small rooms, revise examples, add back-translation review, allocate accessibility budget.

continued on following page

Table 5. Continued

Control Stratum	Telos (Formal Intent)	Controls & Procedures (Prescriptive Spec)	KPIs / Thresholds (Quantifiables)	Pathologies → Remedies (Runbooks)
Low Resource Pathways and Offline Equivalents	Preserve control logic under infrastructural scarcity; ensure pedagogical equivalence across media.	SMS trees for notices and polls; paper two-stage triads with scribe photos when feasible; rotating phone-hour quiet help; IVR office hours; radio micro-lectures; paper incident log; attendance by first name only; parity proxy via triad sampling.	Reply turnaround ≤2 days; incident log completeness ≥95%; triad parity within ±10%; zero reliance on persistent device identifiers.	Outages, shared-device leakage, telemetry gaps → deploy offline packets, follow a no-internet-week playbook, avoid persistent IDs, post printed norms and SLAs.
Continuous Monitoring, Triggers, and Adaptation	Close the evidence-to-action loop with minimal, decision-relevant signals and prebound responses.	Weekly RAG dashboard for parity, entropy, responsiveness, incidents; one-line causal narrative per metric; timestamped decision log; SPC limits and funnel plots; prebound triggers where two red bands prompt pattern switch within one cycle.	One decision per dashboard; red bands cleared within ≤2 cycles; immutable audit trail 100%; monthly robustness checks on metric shifts.	Vanity metrics, gaming, action paralysis → restrict to hard-to-fake signals, auto-suggest playbooks, enforce escalation ladders, rotate reviewers to reduce myopia.

High stakes windows are buffered through quiet periods before deadlines, early release of annotated rubrics, and preapproved alternative demonstrations that respect bandwidth or modality constraints, while moderators watch responsiveness targets so help queues do not stagnate (Etz & Kastner, 2021; Benzar et al., 2025). Closing rituals consolidate learning through portfolio walks, letters to future cohorts, and a conflict ledger that preserves institutional memory for redesign. Staffing prevents invisible labor through a RACI scaffold that assigns facilitation, telemetry review, moderation triage, data stewardship, and referral pathways, with timezone coverage, scripted sentence stems for curiosity and boundary setting, and a progression that moves novices from shadowing to cofacilitation to independent leadership under mentorship (Michels, 2025; Kim, 2024). Faculty development runs as modular badges in inclusive facilitation, trauma aware response, accessibility practice, translanguaging, and analytics literacy with short performance tasks and observation cycles that yield one actionable change per week (Rathi et al., 2025; Wong, 2023). Equity is achieved through defaults rather than accommodation, with accessibility features on at launch, wide assessment windows, late work recovery routes, bilingual prompts, mixed language rooms, back translation for verification, and intersectional parity monitors that use small cell suppression to protect privacy (Jia & Wang, 2024;

Petrov, 2023; Hlabisa, 2025; Ionescu et al., 2021). Low resource pathways preserve logic through SMS trees, paper based two stage triads, rotating phone hour quiet help, interactive voice response office hours, and community radio micro lectures, with parity proxies sampled from triads, paper incident logs, attendance by first name only, and explicit avoidance of persistent identifiers so the system remains trustworthy under infrastructural scarcity.

7. CONCLUSION

Psychological safety emerges as a controllable systems parameter whose optimization requires dose–response estimation, sequence testing, and distributionally aware thresholds rather than intuition. Pattern dosage demands explicit quantification that links the number of two stage cycles per week to parity indices anchored between point eighty and point ninety on a normalized participation scale, with sensitivity analyses that check robustness under alternative entropy formulations and subgroup definitions. Sequencing effects require counterbalanced schedules that compare early anonymity with late anonymity, fast feedback with paced feedback, and short prompts with elaborative prompts while holding total workload constant. Durability must be evaluated across at least three successive cohorts using longitudinal latent growth models that track safety scores, participation entropy, and repair depth with predefined acceptable drift below five percentage points between terms. Transfer to colocated teamwork warrants lagged assessments at one and three months that triangulate rubric aligned artifacts, peer judgements, and supervisor ratings when available. Distributional effects of artificial cofacilitators on minoritized speakers necessitate stratified telemetry, small cell suppression, and Bayesian partial pooling so that genuine gaps above five percentage points are detectable without privacy erosion. Together these questions define a practicable research agenda that treats safety by design as an estimable causal construct whose parameters can be tuned, validated, and transported across disciplinary ecologies and infrastructure regimes.

Credible answers require multi-site consortia that share item banks, telemetry schemas, and governance templates, thereby enabling replication with heterogeneity rather than fragile single site gains. Stepped wedge deployments should become the default because they guarantee eventual access for all cohorts while preserving counterfactual inference under staggered adoption. Pre analysis plans need to register primary outcomes, estimands, and decision thresholds, paired with time stamped registries of pattern edits so that interrupted time series and difference in differences models retain interpretability. Local privacy must be preserved through aggregation that retains weekly summaries, strict role-based access, and retention ceilings near one year for routine telemetry, with federated analytics and secure multi-party computation where cross site pooling is necessary. Causal discovery on deidentified logs can propose mechanisms, but adoption should hinge on triangulation with instructor field notes, student narratives, and falsification tests that probe implausible pathways. Measurement invariance across language and modality must be audited so that movement in scores reflects genuine change rather than translation drift. Multiverse analyses should map plausible analytic choices and report whether qualitative conclusions persist across specifications, guarding against researcher degrees of freedom while still producing decision grade evidence for program leads and policy stewards.

Improvement becomes routine when telemetry is coupled to predetermined actions, when actions are logged with brief rationales, and when outcomes are reviewed on a fixed cadence that converts data into operational discipline. Program leads should reallocate support within seven days when parity bands are breached twice, instructors should switch patterns within one cycle when responsiveness drops below threshold, and governance bodies should publish term close summaries that synthesize parity, incident categories, accessibility defects, and remedial investments. Equity, accessibility, and linguistic justice need status as defaults expressed as procurement constraints, interface requirements, and moderator staffing, not as discretionary add ons. Vendor contracts should require refusal performance, provenance surfacing, accessibility conformance, and auditable change logs, with sandbox trials before production updates. Faculty development ought to remain modular and competency based across inclusive facilitation, trauma aware response, translanguaging, and analytics literacy, with observation cycles that culminate in one small change each week. The institutional objective is a maintained property in which psychological safety and epistemic fairness are engineered into roles, protocols, and platforms, continuously measured, and adjusted through transparent feedback so that participation breadth, error correction speed, and conceptual resilience remain stable even as cohorts, technologies, and constraints evolve.

REFERENCES

Araneda, C. (2022). Jaime Garretón's cybernetic theory of the city and its system: A missing link in contemporary urban theory. *AI & Society*, *37*(3), 1179–1189. DOI: 10.1007/s00146-021-01349-z

Azarian, B. (2022). *The romance of reality: How the universe organizes itself to create life, consciousness, and cosmic complexity*. Benbella books.

Bao, H., Fang, W., Guo, B., & Qiu, H. (2024). Adaptive human–computer interface design for supervision task based on user attention and system state. *International Journal of Human-Computer Interaction*, *40*(8), 2054–2066. DOI: 10.1080/10447318.2023.2228070

Bardin, A., & Ferrari, M. (2022). Governing progress: From cybernetic homeostasis to Simondon's politics of metastability. *The Sociological Review*, *70*(2), 248–263. DOI: 10.1177/00380261221084426

Basnet, N., Allahvirdi, S., Nadri, C., Park, J., & Zahabi, M. (2025). Evaluating the Feasibility of EMG-Based Human–Machine Interfaces for Driving. *Human Factors*, •••, 00187208251367179. PMID: 40797297

Benzar, A., Kovalenko, Y. O., Taranenko, A., Balynska, O., & Balynskyi, I. (2025). Organizational Context of Security Management: Implications for Information Systems. *Management:(Montevideo)*, *3*, 250-250.

Boyun, V. P. (2024). Features of Creating Artificial Intelligence Using Informatics and Cybernetics. *Cybernetics and Systems Analysis*, *60*(1), 13–23. DOI: 10.1007/s10559-024-00642-1

Busseniers, E., Veloz, T., & Heylighen, F. (2021). Goal directedness, chemical organizations, and cybernetic mechanisms. *Entropy (Basel, Switzerland)*, *23*(8), 1039. DOI: 10.3390/e23081039 PMID: 34441179

Cao, Y. (2022). Mass Surveillance, Behavioural Control, and Psychological Coercion the Moral Ethical Risks in Commercial Devices. *Computer Science and Information Technology*, *12*(13), 151–168.

Chatzithanos, P., Nikolaou, G., Stolkin, R., & Chiou, M. (2021, October). Fessonia: a method for real-time estimation of human operator workload using behavioural entropy. In *2021 IEEE International Conference on Systems, Man, and Cybernetics (SMC)* (pp. 1325-1331). IEEE. DOI: 10.1109/SMC52423.2021.9658880

Cubitt, S., Escobar, C., & Gook, B. (2025). Active Noise Control: Cybernetics, Information Theory, and the Financialization of Randomness. *Philosophy. Politics and Critique*, *2*(2), 184–204. DOI: 10.3366/ppc.2025.0077

Darivandi Shoushtari, K., Tohidi, H., Talebian, M., & Shadnam, M. (2025). Strategic fit of task-based crowdsourcing: A cybernetic approach. *Kybernetes*, •••, 1–21. DOI: 10.1108/K-03-2025-0792

DeYoung, C. G., & Tiberius, V. (2023). Value fulfillment from a cybernetic perspective: A new psychological theory of well-being. *Personality and Social Psychology Review*, *27*(1), 3–27. DOI: 10.1177/10888683221083777 PMID: 35440238

Donevski, M., & Zia, T. (2024). Cyber diversity index for sustainable self-control of machines. *Cybernetics and Systems*, *55*(1), 61–87. DOI: 10.1080/01969722.2022.2081896

Dutton, J. (2025). Sporting futures, beyond automation: reading Bernard Stiegler to reinvent athletic gesture. *Distinktion: Journal of Social Theory*, 1-24.

Etz, D., & Kastner, W. (2021, May). Human control of self-organizing safety systems. In *2020 2nd International Conference on Societal Automation (SA)* (pp. 1-7). IEEE. DOI: 10.1109/SA51175.2021.9507109

Feng, L., Xu, B., Ding, C., Feng, H., & Liu, T. (2025). Dynamic Risk Assessment Framework for Tanker Cargo Operations: Integrating Game-Theoretic Weighting and Grey Cloud Modelling with Port-Specific Empirical Validation. *Systems*, *13*(8), 697. DOI: 10.3390/systems13080697

Firth, R., & Preston, J. (2025). The Dystopian Realities of Cybernetics. In *Utopia in the Factory: Prefigurative Knowledge Against Cybernetics* (pp. 67–90). Springer Nature Switzerland. DOI: 10.1007/978-3-031-87132-0_3

Fisher, W. (2024). Entropy, deterministic chaos, and new forms of intelligibility: A shared frame of reference for physics and psychology. *International Journal of Advances in Production Research*, *1*(1), 46–82. DOI: 10.62743/uad.6179

Fouad, N. S. (2024). *Theorising cyber (in) security: Information, materiality, and entropic security*. Taylor & Francis. DOI: 10.4324/9781003454113

Gao, X., Mou, J., Banerjee, S., & Zhang, Y. (2023). Color-gray multi-image hybrid compression–encryption scheme based on BP neural network and knight tour. *IEEE Transactions on Cybernetics*, *53*(8), 5037–5047. DOI: 10.1109/TCYB.2023.3267785 PMID: 37130254

Gerus, S. V., Dementienko, V. V., & Mirgorodskiy, V. I. (2023). The Physical Principles of the Construction of Systems for Safe Monitoring of the State of a Human Operator. *Pattern Recognition and Image Analysis, 33*(4), 1377–1401. DOI: 10.1134/S1054661823040168

Ghosh, R. (2025). Ergodic Capacity of Human Interaction Channels: A Control-Theoretic View.

Glasson, H. G. (2024). *Political Applications of Systems Theory in the Twentieth Century: From Cybernetic Control to Spontaneous Emergence* (Doctoral dissertation, Virginia Polytechnic Institute and State University).

Goddard, M. N. (2022). Noise Annoys, Noise is the Future: Noise in Communication and Cybernetic Theories and Popular Music Practices. In *Noise as a Constructive Element in Music* (pp. 19–34). Routledge. DOI: 10.4324/9781003307020-3

Goł biewski, D., Barszcz, T., Skrodzka, W., Wojnicki, I., & Bielecki, A. (2022). A New Approach to Risk Management in the Power Industry Based on Systems Theory. *Energies, 15*(23), 9003. DOI: 10.3390/en15239003

Hagane, S., & Venture, G. (2022). Robotic manipulator's expressive movements control using kinematic redundancy. *Machines (Basel), 10*(12), 1118. DOI: 10.3390/machines10121118

Harris, D., Arthur, T., Wilson, M., Le Gallais, B., Parsons, T., Dill, A., & Vine, S. (2025). Counteracting uncertainty: Exploring the impact of anxiety on updating predictions about environmental states. *Biological Cybernetics, 119*(2), 1–16. DOI: 10.1007/s00422-025-01006-4 PMID: 39976741

Hartl, B., Risi, S., & Levin, M. (2024). Evolutionary implications of self-assembling cybernetic materials with collective problem-solving intelligence at multiple scales. *Entropy (Basel, Switzerland), 26*(7), 532. DOI: 10.3390/e26070532 PMID: 39056895

Hlabisa, S. B. (2025). The Control–Entropy Paradox: Modeling the Thermodynamic Limits of Environmental Governance. *Systems Research and Behavioral Science*, sres.3178. DOI: 10.1002/sres.3178

Iman, N. (2025). Balancing order and entropy: The role of innovation and organizational disorder in performance across startups and banking. *International Journal of Innovation Science*. Advance online publication. DOI: 10.1108/IJIS-03-2025-0142

Ionescu, ., Nica, I., & Chiri ă, N. (2021). Cybernetics approach using agent-based modeling in the process of evacuating educational institutions in case of disasters. *Sustainability (Basel), 13*(18), 10277. DOI: 10.3390/su131810277

Jeon, W. (2022). Second-Order Recursions of First-Order Cybernetics: An "Experimental Epistemology". *Open Philosophy*, *5*(1), 381–395. DOI: 10.1515/opphil-2022-0207

Ji, M., Pan, K., Zhang, X., Pan, Q., Dai, X., & Lyu, Y. (2024). Integration of Sense and Control for Uncertain Systems Based on Delayed Feedback Active Inference. *Entropy (Basel, Switzerland)*, *26*(11), 990. DOI: 10.3390/e26110990 PMID: 39593935

Jia, H., & Wang, L. (2024). Introducing Entropy into Organizational Psychology: An Entropy-Based Proactive Control Model. *Behavioral Sciences (Basel, Switzerland)*, *14*(1), 54. DOI: 10.3390/bs14010054 PMID: 38247706

Jiang, Z., Qin, C., Yang, R., Shi, B., Alsaadi, F. E., & Wang, Z. (2025). Social Entropy Informer: A Multi-Scale Model-Data Dual-Driven Approach for Pedestrian Trajectory Prediction. *IEEE Transactions on Intelligent Transportation Systems*, *26*(10), 16438–16453. DOI: 10.1109/TITS.2025.3572254

Johnson, J. (2023). Automating the OODA loop in the age of intelligent machines: Reaffirming the role of humans in command-and-control decision-making in the digital age. *Defence Studies*, *23*(1), 43–67. DOI: 10.1080/14702436.2022.2102486

Kelbert, E. (2021). Entropy as a trope: Yuri Lotman's general theory of communication as a case study in interdisciplinarity. *World Literature Studies*, *13*(4), 55–70. DOI: 10.31577/WLS.2021.13.4.5

Khantuleva, T. A. (2022). Description of the Structure Evolution Using Methods of Control Theory of Adaptive Systems. In *Mathematical Modeling of Shock-Wave Processes in Condensed Matter: From Statistical Thermodynamics to Control Theory* (pp. 175–208). Springer Nature Singapore. DOI: 10.1007/978-981-19-2404-0_6

Kim, T. R.III. (2024). *Reducing Entropy Through Targeted Information Sharing: An Exploratory First Principles Approach to Closing the Gaps in Modern Security Operations Centers*. Marymount University.

Kline, R. (2023). Cybernetics and Information Theory in Human–Machine Communication. In *The Sage Handbook of Human–Machine Communication* (pp. 22–31). SAGE Publications Ltd. DOI: 10.4135/9781529782783.n5

Küppers, E. U. (2023). Cybernetic Systems in Practice. In *A Transdisciplinary Introduction to the World of Cybernetics: Basics, Models, Theories and Practical Examples* (pp. 147–206). Springer Fachmedien Wiesbaden.

Lan, R., Sun, X., Wang, Q., & Liu, B. (2025). Investigating the Feasibility of Using Eye-Tracking Metrics as Indicators of Situation Awareness in Flight Training. *International Journal of Human-Computer Interaction*, •••, 1–21.

Laouris, Y., & Tuddenham, P. (2025). Revitalizing Democracy Through Cybernetics and Systems Science: Principles and Applications for Effective Governance. *Available at SSRN* 5316819. DOI: 10.1016/j.futures.2025.103693

Le, B. G., & Ta, V. C. (2024). On the Effectiveness of Regularization Methods for Soft Actor–Critic in Discrete-Action Domains. *IEEE Transactions on Systems, Man, and Cybernetics. Systems.*

Lee, Y., Yang, C. D., & Dong, D. (2025). Entanglement Measure-Based Sliding Mode Control for Quantum State Preparation. *IEEE Transactions on Cybernetics, 55*(10), 4771–4783. DOI: 10.1109/TCYB.2025.3595007 PMID: 40853800

Liu, Z., Huang, B., Hu, X., Du, P., & Sun, Q. (2023). Blockchain-based renewable energy trading using information entropy theory. *IEEE Transactions on Network Science and Engineering, 11*(6), 5564–5575. DOI: 10.1109/TNSE.2023.3238110

Malaspina, C. (2023). From the mental state of noise to the new frontiers of cognition. *Angelaki, 28*(3), 4–15. DOI: 10.1080/0969725X.2023.2216538

Malaspina, C. (Ed.). (2025). *From the Mental State of Noise to the New Frontiers of Techno-Human Cognition: Creative Disruptions Across AI, Gaming, Modelling, French Theory, and Politics*. Taylor & Francis. DOI: 10.4324/9781003667933

Mendoza Montano, C. (2025). Toward a thermodynamic theory of evolution: A theoretical perspective on information entropy reduction and the emergence of complexity. *Frontiers in Complex Systems, 3*, 1630050. DOI: 10.3389/fcpxs.2025.1630050

Mi, P., Yan, L., Cheng, Y., Liu, Y., Wang, J., Shoukat, M. U., Yan, F., Qin, G., Han, P., & Zhai, Y. (2024). Driver cognitive architecture based on EEG signals: A review. *IEEE Sensors Journal, 24*(22), 36261–36286. DOI: 10.1109/JSEN.2024.3471699

Michels, J. (2025). Attractor State: A Mixed-Methods Meta-Study of Emergent Cybernetic Phenomena Defying Standard Explanations.

Mizraji, E. (2024). Homeostasis and information processing: The key frames for the thermodynamics of biological systems. *Bio Systems, 236*, 105115. DOI: 10.1016/j.biosystems.2023.105115 PMID: 38163548

Morgan, W. R. (2023). Finance must be defended: Cybernetics, neoliberalism and environmental, social, and governance (ESG). *Sustainability (Basel), 15*(4), 3707. DOI: 10.3390/su15043707

Ng, P. Preemptive futures: Entropic and negentropic information in speculative design. In *xCoAx 2022 10th Conference on Computation, Communication, Aesthetics. Coimbra, Portugal* (pp. 85-101).

Nöth, W. (2021). System, sign, information, and communication in cybersemiotics, systems theory, and Peirce. In *Introduction to cybersemiotics: A transdisciplinary perspective* (pp. 75–95). Springer International Publishing. DOI: 10.1007/978-3-030-52746-4_4

Ortner, P., Steinhöfler, R., Leitgeb, E., & Flühr, H. (2022). Augmented air traffic control system—Artificial intelligence as digital assistance system to predict air traffic conflicts. *AI, 3*(3), 623–644. DOI: 10.3390/ai3030036

Osejo-Bucheli, C. (2024). Technological Evolution and Cooperative Identity: A Genealogical Analysis using Simondon's Cybernetic Process Philosophy. *Philosophy of Management, 23*(3), 353–376. DOI: 10.1007/s40926-024-00317-z

Osejo-Bucheli, C. (2024). Towards a unified ontology of cybernetics: Bridging mechanology and CAS for cooperative societies through thematic synthesis. *Kybernetes.*

Overwijk, J. (2025). *Cybernetic capitalism: a critical theory of the incommunicable.* Fordham Univ Press.

Pao, L. (2023). Ways of Cybernetic Thinking. *New Literary History, 54*(2), 1271–1279. DOI: 10.1353/nlh.2023.a907173

Parker, M. C., Jeynes, C., & Walker, S. D. (2025). A Metric for the Entropic Purpose of a System. *Entropy (Basel, Switzerland), 27*(2), 131. DOI: 10.3390/e27020131 PMID: 40003129

Petrov, A. I. (2023). Philosophy and meanings of the information entropy analysis of road safety: case study of Russian cities. *information, 14*(6), 302.

Petrov, A. I., Kolesov, V. I., & Petrova, D. A. (2021). Theory and Practice of Quantitative Assessment of System Harmonicity: Case of Road Safety in Russia before and during the COVID-19 Epidemic. *Mathematics, 9*(21), 2812. DOI: 10.3390/math9212812

Posthoff, C. (2024). Game Theory, Cybernetics, and Information Theory. In *Artificial Intelligence for Everyone* (pp. 63–68). Springer Nature Switzerland. DOI: 10.1007/978-3-031-57208-1_6

Qin, R., Ding, W., Li, J., Guan, S., Wang, G., Ren, Y., & Qu, Z. (2022). Web3-based decentralized autonomous organizations and operations: Architectures, models, and mechanisms. *IEEE Transactions on Systems, Man, and Cybernetics. Systems, 53*(4), 2073–2082. DOI: 10.1109/TSMC.2022.3228530

Rathi, N., Saran, P., & Shrivastava, S. (2025, May). Emotional Security for Sustainable Future: Multimodal Affective Computing. In *International Conference on Recent Advancements and Modernisations in Sustainable Intelligent Technologies and Applications (RAMSITA 2025)* (pp. 611-638). Atlantis Press. DOI: 10.2991/978-94-6463-716-8_47

Roli, A., & Braccini, M. (2023, May). A cybernetic perspective of agent–environment relations: From interactions to meanings. In *National Conference on Systems Science-(AIRS) Italian Systems Society* (pp. 183-192). Cham: Springer Nature Switzerland.

Rorot, W. (2022). Counting with cilia: The role of morphological computation in basal cognition research. *Entropy (Basel, Switzerland)*, *24*(11), 1581. DOI: 10.3390/e24111581 PMID: 36359671

Ruyer, R. (2023). *Cybernetics and the Origin of Information*. Rowman & Littlefield.

Sachs, C. (2023). Naturalized teleology: Cybernetics, organization, purpose. *Topoi*, *42*(3), 781–791. DOI: 10.1007/s11245-022-09851-9

Safron, A., & DeYoung, C. G. (2021). Integrating Cybernetic Big Five Theory with the Free Energy Principle: A new strategy for modeling personalities as complex systems. In *Measuring and modeling persons and situations* (pp. 617-649). Academic Press. DOI: 10.1016/B978-0-12-819200-9.00010-7

Safron, A., & Sheikhbahaee, Z. (2023, September). Towards understanding persons and their personalities with cybernetic big 5 theory and the free energy principle and active inference (FEP-AI) framework. In *International Workshop on Active Inference* (pp. 73-90). Cham: Springer Nature Switzerland. DOI: 10.31234/osf.io/kjzf7

Saratxaga Arregi, A. (2024). Heinz von Foerster's operational epistemology: Orientation for insight into complexity. *Kybernetes*.

Sayre, K. M. (2023). Cybernetics. In *Philosophy of Science, Logic and Mathematics in the 20th Century* (pp. 292-314). Routledge.

Solymosi, T. (2023). Neuropragmatic Tools for Neurotechnological Culture: Toward a Creatively Democratic Cybernetics of Care. *Contemporary Pragmatism*, *20*(1-2), 77–117. DOI: 10.1163/18758185-bja10059

Stasch, S. M., Hilla, Y., & Mack, W. (2025). The invisible copilot? Assessing task engagement and team dynamics in a virtual flight environment using eye-tracking metrics. *Aviation Psychology and Applied Human Factors*, *15*(1), 45–61. DOI: 10.1027/2192-0923/a000293

Stening, H., Lee, J., Groeschel, J., Richardson, M. J., & Kallen, R. W. (2023). The Entropy of Communication Turn Taking during a Collaborative Problem-Solving Task. In *Proceedings of the Annual Meeting of the Cognitive Science Society* (Vol. 45, No. 45).

Sun, X., Guo, X., Zhang, Y., & Du, D. (2025). An automotive human–machine interface design method integrating Fuzzy Kano-QFD and physiological data. *Ergonomics*, •••, 1–22. DOI: 10.1080/00140139.2025.2501768 PMID: 40390521

Tabilo Alvarez, J., & Ramírez-Correa, P. (2023). A brief review of systems, cybernetics, and complexity. *Complexity*, *2023*(1), 8205320. DOI: 10.1155/2023/8205320

Tang, C., & Xiao, F. (2024). A Time Fractal-Based Complex Belief Entropy in Complex Evidence Theory for Pattern Classification. *IEEE Transactions on Systems, Man, and Cybernetics. Systems*.

Tzafestas, S. G. (2022). *Systems, cybernetics, control, and automation*. River Publishers. DOI: 10.1201/9781003339670

Verma, R., & Merigó, J. M. (2021). On Sharma-Mittal's entropy under intuitionistic fuzzy environment. *Cybernetics and Systems*, *52*(6), 498–521. DOI: 10.1080/01969722.2021.1903722

Walter, S. (2024). Harmonising humans and technology: Exploring the dynamics of cognitive production, artificial intelligence and social communication in cybernetic systems. *Open Research Europe*, *4*(201), 201. DOI: 10.12688/openreseurope.18418.1

West, B. J., & Mudaliar, S. (2025). Principles entailed by complexity, crucial events, and multifractal dimensionality. *Entropy (Basel, Switzerland)*, *27*(3), 241. DOI: 10.3390/e27030241 PMID: 40149165

Wirkuttis, N., Ohata, W., & Tani, J. (2023). Turn-taking mechanisms in imitative interaction: Robotic social interaction based on the free energy principle. *Entropy (Basel, Switzerland)*, *25*(2), 263. DOI: 10.3390/e25020263 PMID: 36832633

Wolfson, N. (2022). After the "new aesthetic": A short history of the cybernetic turn in Brazil. *AI & Society*, *37*(3), 1059–1069. DOI: 10.1007/s00146-021-01340-8

Wong, K. K. (2023). *Cybernetical intelligence: Engineering cybernetics with machine intelligence*. John Wiley & Sons. DOI: 10.1002/9781394217519

Wu, C. H. (2025). Order out of Chaos: The Pharmacology of Cybernetics in The Posthuman Comedy. *Ex-position*, (3), 27–50.

Xu, W., & Lin, M. (2023). Information Security Evaluation of Industrial Control Systems Using Probabilistic Linguistic MCDM Method. *Computers, Materials & Continua*, *77*(1), 199–222. DOI: 10.32604/cmc.2023.041475

Yolles, M. (2021). Metacybernetics: Towards a general theory of higher order cybernetics. *Systems*, *9*(2), 34. DOI: 10.3390/systems9020034

Yolles, M. (2022). Consciousness, sapience and sentience—A metacybernetic view. *Systems*, *10*(6), 254. DOI: 10.3390/systems10060254

You, F., Fu, Q., Yang, J., Chen, H., Cui, W., & Wang, J. (2024). Team situation awareness-based augmented reality head-up display design for security requirements. *International Journal of Human-Computer Interaction*, *40*(18), 5119–5138. DOI: 10.1080/10447318.2023.2231281

Zhang, Y., Yang, Y., Li, S. E., Lyu, Y., Duan, J., Zheng, Z., & Zhang, D. (2025). Feasible Policy Iteration With Guaranteed Safe Exploration. *IEEE Transactions on Cybernetics*, *55*(5), 2327–2340. DOI: 10.1109/TCYB.2025.3542223 PMID: 40100688

Zhang, Z. (2025). Cybernetics and Landscape: From Uncertainty to Opportunity. In *Cybernetics and the Constructed Environment*. Taylor & Francis.

Ziębacz, I. (2022). Education on the verge of changes. The process of education in terms of the cybernetic theory of character. *Podstawy Edukacji*, *15*, 189–202. DOI: 10.16926/pe.2022.15.13

Ziebacz, I. (2022, August). Knowledge management, including the cybernetic theory of human character. In *European Conference on Knowledge Management* (Vol. 23, No. 2, pp. 1277-1285). DOI: 10.34190/eckm.23.2.414

Zolkin, A. L., Faizullin, R. V., Losev, A. N., & Shevchenko, O. P. (2023). Designing an imitation control system for a logistics complex based on new approaches to organizing cybernetic interaction. *Transportation Research Procedia*, *68*, 229–236. DOI: 10.1016/j.trpro.2023.02.031

Zukowski, N. I. (2023). Novel Framework for a Cybernetic Theory of General Intelligence and Information Field Theory for Strong AI Research and Development-Virtual Neurons Are All You Need.

Chapter 5
Online Classroom Engagement and Group Collaboration

Asia Zulfqar
http://orcid.org/0000-0001-9435-128X
Department of Education, Bahauddin Zakariya University Multan, Pakistan

Aniza Niazi
University of the Punjab, Lahore, Pakistan

ABSTRACT

The shift to online learning has transformed traditional classroom dynamics, placing emphasis on student engagement and collaborative learning in virtual spaces. Engagement, either cognitive, emotional, and behavioral, is essential for meaningful learning experiences, yet fostering it online presents unique challenges. Similarly, effective group collaboration in digital environments requires instructional design to build social presence, trust, and equitable participation. This chapter explores the interplay of these factors to offer evidence-based strategies for enhancing engagement and collaboration in virtual classrooms. This chapter also presents directions for future research.

INTRODUCTION

The concept of online learning has witnessed an increase in the higher education sector, where enrolment rates in online courses have significantly grown in recent years. This surge was observed specifically during and after the pandemic in 2019. The increase was due to its scalable and flexible learning options (Dhawan, 2020).

DOI: 10.4018/979-8-2600-0934-5.ch005

These trends were observed worldwide where students are opting hybrid, blended, online learning systems, and the micro-credentials that have yet to establish a formal pathway for lifelong learning (Gamage & Dehedinya, 2025). This approach enhances equitable educational engagement by bridging higher education with marketplace demands and enabling the effective operationalization of MOOCs, micro-credentials, open online courses, and personalized learning pathways tailored to diverse learner needs." (Pujar et al., 2016; Mishra et al., 2020). Later, Artificial Intelligence (AI) complemented these modes of learning. As the pandemic has affected the lives of pupils in terms of their behaviors and personalities and put them under high amount of stress. In this situation, artificial intelligence used deep learning technology to recognize voice and writing of the students by applying advanced computational techniques. AI helps to recognize such patterns, behaviors, and the cognitive trends to develop personalized teaching methods to improve students' behaviors and personalities (Ramesh, & Vinod, 2022).

Initially, online learning was a necessity to meet the students' needs who cannot afford to attend school due to distance, circumstances or emergencies, later, online learning becomes the top choice for the educational institutes and for learners (Dhawan, 2020). Among other challenges of fair assessment, cheating, data security, lack of coordination, connectivity issues and limited engagement and collaboration among students in online learning environments was observed as a great challenge. However, there is huge investment and efforts to develop such applications – in line with student-centered philosophies to promote students' engagement and collaboration. A large number of students can be accommodated on an online course which was not possible in a walled classroom. Moreover, the challenges of over-crowded classrooms are also addressed in online learning environments, and it is now easy for the instructor to promote collaborative learning among students in online learning environments. Another advantage of online learning environments is the accessibility and storage of data of educational processes and learning pathways for each individual teacher and students which helps to make effective decisions. This big data also helps to analyze learners' online learning experiences.

ENGAGEMENT AND COLLABORATION

Student engagement and collaboration are hallmarks for effective learning. Student engagement gained considerable attention from those who aim to enhance teaching and learning in higher education. Dixon (2015) highlights that learners' engagement refers to the efforts learners make to stay engaged in learning process to comprehend the knowledge. This involves their mental and physical engagement and commitment in the process. Learners' feelings and motivation also play an important role in interacting with peers and remaining active in the classroom to achieve learning goals (Kehrwald, 2008). Authors further linked engagement with students' energy, their time, dedication spent on the educational activities to learn collectively (Kuh, 2003; Richards, 2011). Research has shown that task related interaction among students refined students' learning and stimulate them to think critically. Research has proved that interaction, collaboration, and social presence in digital learning enhances students' engagement, leading to improved learning outcomes and increased chances for peer interaction. This is further confirmed by Gopinathan et al. (2022) found that digital collaboration tools enhanced engagement and participation among all learners in remote learning environments. Kumar and Wei (2024) found a strong positive association between student engagement and digital technologies. Research proved that 78% of pupils affirmed that digital tools improved their learning experience. Educators posited that technology fostered a sense of community among learners. This ultimately linked participation to a wider range of joint endeavors, as few students valued online education. Studies on online collaborative learning demonstrate that promoting social presence, collaboratively sharing digital artifacts, and co-constructing knowledge improve engagement and learner agency (Singh, 2024). The quality of digital connections in higher education encompassing relational characteristics like fostering a courteous group atmosphere and facilitating equal contributions from students (Bach & Thiel, 2024). Research further highlights the interplay between emotional connection and teamwork in fostering meaningful engagement in online learning environments (Mujallid, 2024). Although these experiences are interconnected, they provide strong evidence that intentionally crafted collaborative digital learning experiences, grounded in pedagogical principles of engagement and practice, can establish digital learning environments that facilitate interactive engagement, significant student learning, social connectedness, and students' autonomy (Mujallid, 2024). Nevertheless, engagement and collaboration are in limelight nowadays both in physical environment in schools and in online learning environments. However, these concepts are not new to the literature and deeply rooted in educational philosophies (e.g., Webb, 1995). These skills are also reflected as core 21st century learning skills and a key to promoting critical thinking skills in students (Griffin et al., 2012; Stecher & Hamilton, 2014).

FOUNDATIONS OF ENGAGEMENT AND COLLABORATION

The following section will provide the conceptual and theoretical foundations of student engagement and collaboration in classrooms:

Student engagement builds on a straightforward concept, the more you involve yourself in learning the more you learn and achieve educational objectives. The pioneering work of educational psychologist Ralph Tyler drawing on thirty years of his own research showed that students gained more from their studies when they are engaged in purposeful tasks with their peers and teachers and applying their learned concepts to concrete situations and tasks (Pace, 1990; Saroyan, 2021).This also helps students to work in a diversified group to solve complex problems and strengthen their ideas and confidence through collaboration. Ultimately, students improve their critical thinking and lifelong learning skills. The concept of engagement and collaboration is not new in literature but rather rooted deeply in educational philosophies since decades (Pascarella & Terenzini, 2005; Pace, 1980). Author, Kuh (2003); Wakke and Heller (2022) stated that engagement helps to develop the habits for continuous learning and personal development. Nevertheless, the term engagement is usually viewed as multidimensional comprising aspects of students' cognition, emotion, and behavior (Fredricks, et al., 2004).

Collaboration

Collaboration is defined as a cooperative, reciprocal process wherein all players engage in continuous communication, interdependently restructure their activities, and collectively develop and uphold a shared comprehension of the problem context. Comprehending the concept involves understanding how collaboration differs from cooperation (Castañer & Oliveira, 2020). In academic literature, cooperation and collaboration are differentiated based on the concepts of interaction and task division. Dillenbourg (1999; Salvato, et al., 2017) explains that cooperation emerges when individuals hierarchically allocate tasks and individually execute them prior to reconvening to finalize the overall activity. This method emphasizes autonomy and personal accountability. Cooperation mostly involves the administration of distinct tasks, but collaboration is inherently interactive and integrative, necessitating cognitive interdependence and real-time coordination (Gulati, et al., 2012).

This differentiation is grounded in social constructivism and collaborative learning theories. According to Lev Vygotsky's social constructivist theory, learning is fundamentally a social phenomenon; social interaction occurs on the inter-psychological level prior to cognitive growth on the psychological level. The notion of the Zone of Proximal Development (ZPD) is an essential element of the theory. The ZPD is characterized as the disparity between an individual's current knowledge and their potential for additional learning with the assistance of an expert, such as a peer or a teacher. This type of scaffolding is intrinsic to natural collaborative environments, where group members facilitate each other's learning through verbal exchanges, negotiation, and mutual comprehension. Vygotsky (1978) posited that collaborative engagement among students enables them to surmount obstacles that would be insurmountable for an individual learner alone. Cooperative learning is grounded in social interdependence theory, and research indicates that it provides a robust theoretical framework for facilitating effective productive group work. Positive interdependence emphasizes the significance of proximity, incentive, and individual engagement. The research defined positive interdependence as the perception that the achievement of the group is equally valued as one's own success (Johnson & Johnson, 2009).

Kan and Wong (2023) highlighted that students' self-esteem, intellectual skill development, and communication efficacy were positively influenced by small-group and online collaboration. Theoretical models, including the Community of Inquiry Model, underscore the necessity of social presence, teaching presence, and cognitive presence in online group projects, as these elements are vital for fostering a learning community, facilitating discourse among members, and enabling collaborative knowledge construction (Salmon, 2003). Thus, the existing theories and learning models posit that learning occurs when a learner interacts with their peers, this interaction can be formal and informal and can take place both inside and outside the classroom. Such interactions enable learners to support each other in comprehending course contents, constructing knowledge collaboratively and promoting a culture of collaboration in school. In a formal educational setting, the role of teacher is imperative to initiate and develop such interactions whether in a physical or online classroom. However, this requires proper planning of learning activities and assessment methods that are constructively aligned with the course objectives.

Constructivism

Constructivism is based on epistemological view of knowledge acquisition emphasizing construction of knowledge rather than transmission of knowledge. The theory also emphasizes that learning occurs when individuals apply the learned knowledge (Shunk, 2000; Boon, et al., 2022). Learners build their knowledge through experience and reflecting on the experiences to construct knowledge and understanding. This perspective is closely associated with contemporary theories of learning, notably developmental theories of Vygotsky (1978) and social learning theory by Banudra (1969). These theories highlighted that learning cannot occur in isolation rather it is a collaborative and interactive process. Similarly, social interaction and cultural factors also play their role in developing connection among individuals for the sake of learning. Thus, learning within the real-world construct knowledge and experiences. Moreover, learning depends on regular interaction between students and learning environments. As mentioned elsewhere, the role of teacher is crucial to develop task related interaction and to provide an environment of collaboration and experience. This theory further highlighted the role of active knowledge production, enabling them to cultivate understanding via action, interaction and reflection leading to higher order thinking skills (Boon, et al., 2022). As to digital classroom, constructivists see the students' role to collaboratively create digital artifacts, participating in peer discussions, collaborating in groups to address real-world issues, and actively and critically reflecting on their learning experiences (Townley, 2020; Borup, et al., 2020). This dynamic and socially involved model demonstrates that active participation consistently enhances cognitive, social, and emotional involvement (Qi, & Derakhshan, 2025). Subsequently, research also highlights the significance of social media platforms in fostering social engagement: by enabling interactive peer collaboration, learners actively co-create meaning within interconnected learning settings. The exchange of ideas and peer feedback in these environments improves social presence and intellectual engagement (Alismaiel et al., 2022). Hence, a collaborative environment enables learners to achieve their learning goals while also developing social support system that contributes positively to their academic outcomes. Moreover, engagement in collaborative activities enhances their self-esteem and motivation and promotes critical thinking that actively engages them in learning process. Such collaborative activities make learning process engaging and focused. Moreover, in an online context, collaborative tools and platforms such as learning management systems (LMS), Google Meet, Google Classroom, Zoom, and MS Teams, allow teaching, learning and assessment strategies to be easily customized and effectively implemented.

COMMUNITY OF INQUIRY MODEL

The community of inquiry models established by Garrison et al. in (2000) serves as a foundational framework for comprehending online and blended learning experiences and educational settings through the interconnection of three types of presence: teaching presence, social presence, and cognitive Presence. This model view learning as a collaborative and constructivist process that occurs through the interaction of three key elements. Teaching presence encompasses the design, facilitation, and direction of learning by instructors to ensure meaningful educational outcomes. Social presence refers to individuals' capacity to engage with a community, interact openly within a trusting environment, and establish interpersonal relationships of different intimacy through the expression of their personal traits. Cognitive presence denotes the extent to which learners can generate and affirm meaning through sustained contemplation and discourse. These three elements converge and engage students to create a collaborative learning environment that promotes educational outcomes. Garrison et al. (2000) and Garrison (2017) also linked these core elements with digital learning environment e.g., the presences and their foundational components converge and engage learners in an in-depth inquiry process aimed at collaborative knowledge construction and meaning making.

In an online learning environment, the CoI model emphasis and influence course design and online pedagogy. This helps to evaluate the quality of online discussions and learning communities. The implementation of this model will ultimately foster critical thinking, engagement and collaborative problem-solving. Again, teacher presence guarantees that educators establish expectations, deliver prompt feedback, and support learning; social presence cultivates community, diminishes transactional distance, and promotes open communication; and cognitive presence enables students to collaborate throughout the progression of inquiry stages, from problem identification to resolution. Research indicates that all three core elements of this model are interrelated, and promote more effective, engaging, and reflective learning experience (Garrison & Arbaugh, 2007).

SELF-DETERMINATION THEORY (SDT)

Self-Determination Theory (SDT) developed by Deci and Ryan (1985, 2000) is a macro level theory that aims to explain human needs, motivation, and well-being. The theory further highlighted that people have three basic needs, need to have choice in actions refers to autonomy. Competence refers to feeling effective and capable in own activities, and relatedness is the need to get connected and receive support by others. The meeting of these needs enhances greater psychological well-being. A classroom that focused on this design encourage active participation of students learning tasks (Hsu et al., 2019). This theory also focuses on the effects of needs-based support on student motivation, engagement, and learning. Though, ample amount of research is available applying SDT in face-to-face school context (Ryan & Deci, 2020) however, it has been largely overlooked in online learning environments (Chen & Jang, 2010; Hsu et al., 2019). This opens a new line of inquiry to closely view the role of online learning and in remote classrooms that effects students' motivation and engagement in learning. Student engagement is largely dependent on motivational processes and fostering both intrinsic and extrinsic motivation among learners, a focus and domain of self-determination theory (Losier et al., 2001; Ryan & Deci, 2017). The freedom in online learning for students e.g., flexible deadlines for submission of assignments and self-paced courses linked to autonomy. Students are more engaged and motivated when they are given autonomy in their learning environment, and they happily develop interaction with their peers in online learning environments. Several studies have confirmed that environments that meet the needs for autonomy, competence, and relatedness positively impact cognitive and affective engagement with classroom activities (Chen & Jang, 2010). SDT offers important insights on the level of students' engagement in any learning setting – including online and learning digitally that informs academic success and psychological well-being. Cooperative behavior is clearly defined when students experience a sense of power and value associated with their contributions. This relates to how self-determination theory engages intrinsic motivation via the components of relatedness, competence, and autonomy as psychological needs. For example, learners will be more willing to engage themselves in online collaborative environments when their roles were flexible, and paths of communication were independent. In this regard, Sheldon and Hilpert (2012) found that the teamwork was dependent on the group members' perceptions about the value of their contributions and the quality of their interpersonal relations. Thus, the role of SDT is multidimensional where both teacher and students are actively involved in learning to achieve educational objectives.

A THEORETICAL SYNTHESIS FOR PROMOTING COLLABORATION IN ONLINE LEARNING

In an online learning environment, the integration of constructivism, the Community of Inquiry (CoI) model, and Self-Determination Theory (SDT) offers a comprehensive theoretical foundation for promoting student collaboration, engagement, and meaningful learning. In a digital learning space, these frameworks support the instructors to design collaborative learning tasks to connect learners socially and cognitively. Such interactions connect diverse learners on one platform and provide opportunities for learning and sharing ultimately enhance their cognitive, critical thinking skills, motivation, confidence and collaborative skills. However, there are certain challenges associated with the application of these skills whether in physical or online learning environments. Literature on constructive learning highlight the focus on developing independent learning and digital literacy skills, potentially disadvantaging less-prepared students. Moreover, face-to-face interaction has its own challenges which often affect meaningful collaborative interactions. As to forming groups of students in an online learning environment, it is often difficult to form groups of same abilities and to identify their diversified skills, thus affecting the differentiation of instruction. This can undermine the sense of autonomy and competence, leading to disengagement of learners. From instructor's end, sufficient time and expertise are required to prepare activities for learners specifically for a large group of learners and subsequently planning assessment methods. Nevertheless, despite these limitations, when thoughtfully integrated and supported through appropriate pedagogical design, technological tools, and assessment strategies, constructivism, the CoI model, and SDT collectively provide a robust framework for fostering effective collaboration and deep learning in online environments.

DIMENSIONS OF ONLINE ENGAGEMENT

Earlier, engagement limited to three dimensions behavioral, emotional and cognitive, however researchers are continuously exploring further dimensions playing its role in online students 'engagement. Keeping in view the growing interest in online and distance learning authors started exploring the various dimensions of students' engagement that work together make learning experience effective and impactful. Available literature highlights several dimensions/elements linked to students' engagement (Pittaway, 2012; Weimer, 2016). As Weimer (2016) linked engagement is a multidimensional concept. The following section will explain these dimensions.

Cognitive Engagement

Cognitive engagement refers to the degree of mental effort, planning and strategic thinking involved in solving learning tasks/problems (Garrison et al., 2017). It is a complete thinking process that helps to plan, act, understand and reflect on their learning to develop a meaningful learning experience. In other words, it is psychological engagement of students in learning to solve complex educational problems (Greene, 2015). In this regard, Fredericks, et al (2004) redefined engagement as a three-dimensional construct encompassing behavioral, emotional, and cognitive dimensions. The authors argued that cognitive engagement fosters social and psychological commitment to the comprehension and assimilation of the material (e.g., via goal setting, problem-solving, and self-regulation learning techniques). Newman and Wehlage (1993) describe the attributes of cognitive engagement, emphasizing the construction of knowledge through analyzing the information and integrate the ideas share by peers. In an online setting e.g., group project helps learners to critically examine the arguments and synthesize on the basis of logic and arguments (Henrie, et al., 2015). Since online learning is rooted in constructive theory, cognitive engagement drives learners to construct meaning together. Cognitive engagement also involves metacognition, self-regulation, and reflection. Working in groups and collaborative projects students plan learning strategies, monitor their performance for effective group outcomes (Redmond, et al., 2018). Moreover, the levels of cognition have mainly two forms, e.g., deep and surface (Henri, 1992). In online environment, surface level cognitive engagement is to offer solutions to the problems with judgment and justification, shows general agreement to other learners without clarifying the ideas. The focus of such learners is to complete the task without learning (Fredricks, et al., 2004). On the other hand, those learners who deeply engage themselves in learning and solving complex problems through judgements, comparing ideas and synthesizing information can construct their knowledge and remain successful in learning process. Moreover, they desire to go beyond the basic requirements. Cognitive engagement shapes learner's behavioral engagement as their actions depends how they process, interpret, and regulate information.

Behavioral Engagement

Behavioral engagement in online learning pertains to observable student actions and efforts, including attendance, involvement in discussions and assignment completion. Furthermore, in an online learning environment, behavioral engagement typically encompasses adherence to regulations, perseverance, efforts, and task completion. Authors, Fredricks, et al (2004) identified the following dimensions of behavioral engagement. First, adhering to rules and norms link to positive behavior, inquiring, participation in discussions, and paying attention; second, participate actively in academic activities; and third, participation in co-curricular and non-academic within the educational institution. They have concluded it doing the work by adhering to the rules. Moreover, they develop their academic and interpersonal skills (Cheng, et al., 2013) and help students to handle challenges and identify new opportunities (Meyer, 2014), upholding online learning ethics and norms (Petty & Farinde, 2013) and supporting and encouraging collaborations (Weimer, 2016). Behavioral engagement is essential in online learning environments as collaboration relies on visible contributions. Moreover, when learners connect themselves with the task they are deeply involved in the tasks which shape their behavioral engagement.

Emotional Engagement

Emotional engagement refers to learner's affective reactions, attitudes, and feelings. Students' experience of working with peers and participation. Sinatra, et al. (2015) highlighted both negative and positive emotions can facilitate activation of attention and engagement of tasks in collaborative environment. Emotional engagement also includes interest and values related to tasks. Emotional reaction of students towards specified tasks, working with peers and in groups arise various emotions of satisfaction and dissatisfaction. The support from teachers and peers plays an important role towards completing the tasks and emotional development of students (Vogt, 2016). The emotional engagement again linked to cognitive engagement how deeply students connect with the learning process – the discussion of surface level knowledge and deep knowledge. The deep level knowledge helps learners to interact with peers and foster collaboration in group projects where emotional engagement has a significant role in achieving the educational targets. Moreover, sense of autonomy and belonginess also enhances students' engagement in group tasks (Cleveland-Innes & Campbell, 2012).

Social Engagement

Social engagement in online collaborative environment means ways to interact with peers, communicate and build relationships with fellows and teachers (Knight, 2013). It refers to social dimensions of engagement, collaboration, participation and belongings in digital learning environments. Such participation involves both academic and co-curricular activities within and outside academic environments (Coates, 2006). This helps to create purposeful interactions and collaboration with peers. This collaboration involves to group projects, problem solving tasks, sharing resources, supporting each other's learning, developing reciprocal behaviors – both giving and receiving help. This develops trust, empathy and mutual respect and sense of connectedness which is crucial in online settings where isolation is a risk. Participating in learning network helps learners create knowledge collectively. The non-academic example of collaboration is students' interaction on social media platforms. Authors also highlighted relational engagement (Billet, 2008) and social presence (Garrison, et al., 2000). All the following dimensions, cognitive, behavioral, emotional and social engagement are interconnected and interdependent involved in learning process to shape up learners knowledge, collaboration with peers and their behaviors.

Collaborative Engagement

As mentioned above, collaborative engagement refers to the extent learners actively participate and take responsibility for shared learning goals through interaction and cooperation with peers and teachers. Collaboration goes beyond peer to group collaboration where students jointly construct knowledge, develop solutions, complete their tasks and support each other's' learning in digital environment. This enhances the social and meaningful presence of students in tasks. Social presence involves two major concepts, intimacy and immediacy. Intimacy refers to mutual relationships comprises feeling of trust and emotional connectedness which supports learning (Song et al., 2018). Whereas immediacy refers to extent which instructors and learners reduce psychological and social distance through timely, personal, and responsive communication (Eisenbach et al., 2018). It reflects how 'present,' approachable, and engaged participants appear to one another in digital settings. Social presence can be improved by examining the social aspects of collaborative learning in an online learning environment. For example, Miyake and Kirschner (2014) presented a model of team learning behaviors and beliefs suggesting that learners' perceptions of interdependency and group effectiveness contribute to shared understanding. This model highlights the social elements of collaboration which is a unique line of inquiry. An important component within this model is psychological safety refers to shared beliefs that the group is safe for interpersonal risk-taking. This is in accordance with the social presence aspects of open communication, which promotes inclusion, group belonging and reduces barriers to participation (Caskurlu et al., 2025).

INSTRUCTIONAL DESIGN AND APPROACHES

A variety of strategies and instructional designs are available in the literature to enhance students' collaboration in online classrooms. These are mainly designed around the main dimensions of engagement (behavioral, cognitive, emotional, social, and collaborative). These designs are based on systematic models, ADDIE Model (Analysis, Design, Development, Implementation, Evaluation), Backward Design (Understanding by Design – UbD), social-constructivist frameworks, Community of Inquiry Model (CoI), Problem Based Learning (PBL), Universal Design for Learning (UDL), and motivational strategies (gamification). Instructional design guides the planning, development, delivery, and evaluation of digital learning experiences. These designs and approaches ensure that online learning is structured, engaging, and aligned with learners' needs and objectives. In virtual classrooms, instructional design is essential for developing organized and engaging learning experience. An effectively organized instructional plan guarantees alignment of learning objectives, content, and assessment. Following are the few strategies embedded in online learning environments:

Flipped Classrooms

Another important dimension is flipped classrooms; the flipped classroom is a strategy where a conventional classroom sequence is reversed. The content delivery includes lectures, demonstrations happen through online videos, interactive modules and readings. The physical classroom space is used for collaborative learning activities e.g., discussions, problem solving, and projects etc. This concept also promotes self-regulated learning by granting students autonomy over content access, discussions, interaction with peers particularly beneficial for online courses (Abeysekera & Dawson, 2015). Research indicates that this methodology fosters higher-order cognitive skills, through meaningful engagement via breakout rooms and collaborative activities, thus cultivating a feeling of learning community and yields excellent academic results (Lo & Hew, 2021; Hew & Lo, 2018).

Problem-Based Learning (PBL)

Project-Based Learning (PBL) is a student-centric approach that initiates learning through a multifaceted, real-world dilemma. Students collaborate in small groups to examine the issue, gather knowledge, and suggest solutions, fostering critical thinking and autonomous learning (Hmelo-Silver, 2004). Lim et al. (2022) highlights that virtual platforms facilitate cooperation via discussion boards and video conferencing, enhancing critical thinking, engagement, and cultivating a robust academic environment.

Gamification and Interactive Tools

In online learning environments, gamification serves as complementary approaches that enhance student motivation, engagement, and collaborative learning. Gamification integrates game-like elements such as points, badges, leaderboards, levels, and challenges into instructional design, to foster motivation, determination, and a sense of achievement among learners (Kapp, 2012). Simultaneously, interactive tools—including platforms like Kahoot!, Quizizz, Mentimeter, Padlet, and Google Workspace—facilitate active participation, collaboration, and real-time feedback, transforming learning from a passive to an active and learner-centered process (Redmond et al., 2018). When combined, these strategies address diverse learning styles and promote multidimensional engagement—cognitive, behavioral, social, and collaborative—through activities such as gamified quizzes, collaborative group projects, and milestone-based recognition via badges or leaderboards (Dixson, 2015; Hew, Huang, Chu, & Chiu, 2019). This integration not only enhances individual motivation and accountability but also strengthens peer-to-peer interaction and collective problem-solving and higher order thinking skills resulting in richer and more meaningful online learning experiences.

Quizzes and Polls

Other important dimensions in online and collaborative learning environment are quizzes and polls. Quizzes and polls are interactive assessment tools commonly used in both face-to-face and online learning environments to assess students' learning and encourage participation and promote engagement. Quizzes are set of questions usually based on objective type questions e.g., multiple choice questions, true-false, short answer items, and fill in the blanks. This facilitates the teachers to measure students' comprehension about the content. This can be used as formative and summative assessments. This facilitates instructors giving feedback to students after quick assessment. In an online environment, quizzes are usually graded automatically and provide adaptive questions to facilitate learners to reflect on their performance and identify areas of improvement. Polls, on the other hand based on single question, start discussion on a particular question/topic to take learners' opinion. This is embedded in Zoom, Teams, Mentimeter, Kahoot! etc. This also helps to check students' understanding of a particular topic and can also inform them about students' prior experience. Polls are usually non-graded focuses on engagement rather than assessment (Kay & LeSage, 2009).

Breakout Rooms

Within online learning environments, breakout rooms are sub-spaces that facilitate instructors to divide students into small groups to promote interaction, discussions, critical thinking and collaborative activities. Breakout rooms allow instructors to monitor students' progress and activities. Teachers can also give feedback to students and provide necessary support to achieve educational objectives (Sumarni, 2022).

Scaffolding

Scaffolding refers to instructional support to the students and peers by the teacher. In the context of online learning environment digital scaffolding tools guide learners in solving complex tasks. Scaffolding is rooted in the concept presented by Vygotsky – *zone of proximal development* (ZPD). It includes structured prompts, guiding questions, collaborative tools, modelling and feedback mechanisms to assist students in learning. This promotes higher-order thinking skills in students (Wood, et al. 1976; Vygotsky, 1978). Scaffolding is usually embedded in online learning environments, as learners gain confidence and develop their expertise in a given topic, scaffolding is gradually reduced, promoting autonomy and deeper collaborative engagement.

GROUP COLLABORATION IN ONLINE ENVIRONMENTS

Compared to a classroom situated in a physical space, the environment in an online-learning mode offers less in the way of social cues and immediacy, leading to superficial learning and disengagement. Collaborative pedagogies, recipes for learning, such as peer review, project-based learning (PBL), and discussion in small groups offer solutions to issues of social presence and community. In MaMet (philosophy of science, ethics, and research methods) a course that serves master's students at a university in Norway, groups of 3–5 students studying in an online-learning mode, participated in group work throughout the semester. The researchers determined group work offered students a way to work together on complex assignments and co-create knowledge to comprehend the course subject matter (Haugland et al., 2022). The groups promoted deep engagement to enhance emotional and cognitive engagement with their fellow peers and material. With the MaMet course, the peer review process fostered exchange of structured feedback, increased academic interdependence, engagement, and deep self-reflection (Haugland et al., 2022). Additionally, Foo, et al. (2021) noted that transdisciplinary online PBL models provided students with increased flexibility in learning, provided deeper processing of subject matter and allowed students access to more useful and valuable resourcing. Nevertheless, if the collaboration was not as deep compared to a classroom experience, researchers note online PBL models are robust and supported.

TECHNOLOGICAL PLATFORMS SUPPORTING COLLABORATION

Instructional technology is imperative for effectively creating collaborative learning environment. Learning management systems such as LMS, Moodle, Blackboard, and Canvas facilitate scheduling, assignments, group discussions, and submitting group projects. Moreover, cloud-based tools such as Microsoft Teams and Google Workspace allow students to work collaboratively in real-time on shared documents. Breakout room functionality on platforms like Zoom and Microsoft Teams provides instructors the ability to break large classes into smaller groups for directed discussions that encourage collaboration and social engagement. Spaces such as Padlet and Miro introduce visual and interactive elements for sharing ideas and creating group projects. Authors, e.g., Holmes et al. (2018) suggested that faculty use LMS not only for content delivery but also to foster collaborative chats and encourage student engagement. Addressing a related aspect, Xu, et al. (2024) identified greater cognitive commitment and emotional depth in online collaborative assignments. Highlighting the effectiveness of digital tools, Wachenheim, et al. (2023) reported that breakout rooms facilitate peer interaction and maintaining engagement. Likewise, Nabil, et al. (2023) emphasized that resources such as Zoom supports collaborative learning by increasing interaction between students and instructors.

KEY CHALLENGES IN STUDENTS' ENGAGEMENT IN ONLINE AND COLLABORATIVE LEARNING ENVIRONMENT

Despite its benefits, collaborative learning also presents challenges that persist across both small and large group settings. These challenges are of different nature when working in an online learning environment. For example, group members can be burdened by the performance of disengaged or digitally illiterate students who do not engage themselves in collaborative tasks. Tugun et al. (2020) argued that students become frustrated and can become demotivated as collaborative contributions become intermittent. Disengagement due to asynchronous collaboration can also occur because students do not receive real-time feedback and a non-supportive learning environment. Moreover, students' coordination problems affect their level of engagement. Another key challenge is the difference to of time zones of students which hinders in their collaboration and giving prompt response and meeting the submission deadlines. Salam, et al. (2024) identified that these variations disrupt community collaboration and reduce students' feelings of connectedness. Next to this, various disruptions affect students learning in online classrooms. For example, students who experience poor connectivity or have outdated technology usually struggle to get engaged in synchronous sessions and group work. Van Deursen and Van Dijk (2019) found that students from marginalized communities struggled to gain access to learning resources, which led to reduced social and cognitive engagement. These obstacles are interrelated: changes in time zones have a negative effect on community building, time lost due to miscommunication has a negative effect on effort, and limitations in technology cause problems with engagement. Authors also suggested Hrastinski (2008) and Johnson et al. (2014) identify the possible strategies to address these challenges include determining roles in group work, managing the balance of synchronous and asynchronous approaches, prioritizing equitable access to technology, providing scaffolding to support digital literacy, timely feedback, and ensuring varied groups.

Digital Inequity

Digital inequity is a substantial impediment to student engagement in online learning, and it happened due to unreliable internet access and inadequate technological support, speed and reliability limits (Cullinan et al., 2021). This means that these are disruptive and inconsistent learning experiences, particularly in relation to live sessions. Generally, when students are not ready with their tasks, they present excuses for internet disconnection, power cut, and speed of internet. Such excuses are often true in case of those who are residing in far flung areas where internet connections are not stable and common. Additionally, many of these issues are systemic for marginalized populations, including adolescents in low socioeconomic or rural communities, older adults, people with less education, people with a physical disability or health related issue, and those with low reading skills or proficiency with the internet, deepening existing inequities (Van Deursen, 2020; Akpen et al., 2024). In case of such students, teachers are often confused about how to handle such issues. Learning online also requires internet literacy and etiquette to study online. The best practice universities often devise policies for extenuating circumstances to deal with situations when students are suffering/facing sickness, injuries, deaths, natural disasters, personal crisis, financial hardships and technical failures etc. The unavailability of personal devices is yet another significant factor in digital inequities. The issues collectively contributed to challenges for students to engage in the class or complete tasks independently and participate in learning. In classes like physics and engineering that require hands-on learning, students can feel disengaged and remain unsuccessful in remote learning. They require labs and hands-on experience in order to learn. Notwithstanding, many families are unable to provide their children with the support necessary to foster learning at home, often resulting in students feeling disengaged and/or dropping out of learning from home altogether.

Student Motivation in Online Learning

Motivation is a fundamental factor in effective learning, and this holds true in the context of online learning. Students' engagement, determination and academic achievement are the central factors in designing online learning environment. However, student motivation plays a crucial and unavoidable role in the success of online learning (Krause, 2006). Motivation has a strong impact on learning, and it may affect what, when, and how one learns. Those who manage online learning either planning, and teaching must consider the theoretical and applied understanding of learners' motivation and the ways learners background, context, culture, and environment influence it (Shalevska, 2021). This is again associated with self-determination theory, social emotional and cognitive learning dimensions. Moreover, the teaching strategies, learners' learning styles, technological infrastructure, and learning environment play role in learners' motivation (Chowkase et al., 2022).

Motivation in online learning is of great importance; instructors must plan motivational strategies for learners to keep them engaged in groups or individually. Building and sustaining positive relationships in an online learning environment is equally important, supporting students in solving complex problems, helping in communication skills to keep students confident and motivated. Certain motivational techniques help students to keep engaged in group tasks and make them active to participate attentively.

Cultural Differences in Collaboration

Students' perceptions, attitudes, and engagement in online collaborative learning are shaped by their diverse backgrounds. Zhu, et al. (2009) identified that Chinese students initially evaluated collaborative e-learning less positively but eventually came to utilize more socially constructive learning strategies with experience. Research with both German and Thai students using the framework of Community of Inquiry (CoI) revealed similar cultural gaps in social and instructional presence. While Thai students preferred to do their collaborative work via social media applications, the German students were more hesitant to reach out but were comfortable speaking when the teachers were absent (Grothaus, 2022). Students from those societies that are hierarchical, and collectivist may tend to have less experience with peer learning because of cultural beliefs that emphasize respect and authority, may not voice dissent, and need more teacher leadership (Kunwar, 2021). If these gaps are not addressed in the group work experience, collaboration can suffer, and miscommunication may occur, resulting in students preferring to disengage themselves. It is possible to increase diverse learners' engagement by developing collaborative projects that account for cultural differences and the providing choice for engagement. When diverse learners are studying on the same platform, it promotes intercultural communication among learners, this promotes a global layer of communication. Learners not only support each other's learning but learning culture and traditions through a foreign language. Thus, enhancing the competence of learners in foreign languages as well. Sharing knowledge, expertise and cultural talks led students to learn new culture and language skills and develop respect for culture and values. However, research also highlighted that such interactions often lead to miscommunication and conflicts among learners (Vargas-Hernández, 2018). Cultural differences further shaped how students engage in collaborative learning activities, particularly in diverse groups studying online. Students from certain groups of culture often value group harmony, shared responsibility, and consensus-building, which can enhance cooperation but may also discourage open disagreement or critical debate. In contrast, students from individualistic cultures may be more confident in expressing their viewpoints, challenging the ideas of other students, initiating critical debates and asserting leadership roles. This can generate productive discussion, but such students are often dominating others and do not provide participation opportunities. Some students are more confident in communicating and have a stronger command of foreign languages as compared to others, thus, their communication style, power distance, and authority influence collaborative dynamics in groups. Moreover, some students are hesitant to share their opinions; to participate in collaborative tasks and show respect as a barrier to their cultural norms, this ultimately affects the cultural diversity as well. This requires teachers to establish classroom and group norms, develop inclusive communication and ensure equitable and effective collaboration among students in multicultural learning environments.

Managing Online Conflicts and Group Dynamics

Conflicts are parts of collaborative groups and teams. Being engaged in online collaborative projects requires certain strategies for conflict resolution. When students communicate asynchronously, they often lose important social cues including tone, facial expression, and body language, which leads to misunderstandings, confusion, and create communication gaps about the distribution of responsibilities and expectations. Conflicts arise from the division of work, assigning roles and responsibilities, and resources allocation. On the other hand, establishing and clarifying expectations, providing norms for communication, and monitoring communication will help mitigate those conflicts (Dool, 2010). Instructors can facilitate learners by setting group norms and convey the same to students about their roles and responsibilities and task deadlines. This clear communication can reduce misunderstandings and sets a reference point to resolve conflicts. For example, in a Moodle/LMS discussion group, team members agree to respond to messages at a specified time and tag each student's contribution in shared documents. If someone repeatedly misses deadlines, peers address the issue constructively by following the set norms. Again, teachers can regularly monitor the performance of students and mediate, when necessary, through formative feedback and respectful disagreement and problem-solving strategies. For example, if two students disagree on a certain task, the instructor can suggest strategies to each individual, this prompts the team/group members and revisit their plan with a view to providing guidance. Group size and structure are also a matter of concern in collaborative projects. Larger groups may have participation that is more divided (Saqr et al., 2020). Smaller groups of three to five allow for greater cohesion, participation, and outcome (Mao & Queiroz, 2024). Facilitators support focus and functioning by monitoring, and intervening, through either mixing up groups, mediating conflict, or reminding participants of norms (Falls et al., 2014). Students emphasize that communication, trust, and common expectations shape good group dynamics. In the absence of these traits, disagreements will be built from communication breakdowns (e.g., missing meetings, unclear expectations, and atypical workload). Regular reflections or check-ins allow for students, and their teams, to address group dynamics, re-distribute work if necessary, and develop adjustments to the contained process, which can increase morale and engagement (Dincă et al., 2023).

Assessment and Accountability in Group Work

One major drawback of group work in online learning is ensuring individual's accountability. Research shows that when assessments focus solely on the group's final product without distinguishing individual contributions, some students may contribute less while benefiting from others' efforts. This undermines fairness and can demotivate high-performing members (Briggs & Doubleday, 2016). Peer evaluations and clearly assigned roles help reduce free riding but does not eliminate it, especially in online contexts where monitoring is complex (Chang & Brickman, 2018). Online group work often lacks transparency regarding task division, communication, and individual engagement, making it difficult for instructors to evaluate participation and coordination (Donelan & Kear, 2024). Literature highlights the importance of authentic assessment in online learning environment (Kim, et al., 2008). Authentic assessment is especially beneficial in problem-based learning, which is a common assessment technique in applied disciplines running online mode. Instructors design complex problems and sometimes ask students to bring problems and devise strategies to solve problems. Instructors usually divide students' roles and responsibilities to make everyone accountable for their role and responsibilities. This helps instructors to mark students' performance fairly and justly. Moreover, assessment strategies also promote collaboration in groups, as in problem-based learning and peer submissions (Usher & Barak, 2018), such opportunities help in knowledge construction and encourage them for competition with their peers. Case studies, group projects and interactive sessions provide discussion opportunities for students to bring more innovative ideas and solutions to the problems (Geng et al., 2022). Peer interaction also helps students to identify their strengths and weaknesses and to identify the areas for improvement. Sekendiz (2018) highlighted that students are usually more constructive when giving qualitative feedback to each other.

METHODS TO EVALUATE ENGAGEMENT

It is important to measure student engagement to better understand how students are comprehending and learning course materials, dealing with classmates, and instructors in an online environment. In this section, we will review a few methods commonly used to assess engagement:

Learning Analytics

This method suggests various levels of engagement through looking at online traces, such as the frequency of logins, the frequency and length of time spent on activities, and discussion engagement. A systematic review of 41 studies by Johar et al. (2023) concluded that learning analytics can successfully capture students' levels of engagement through cognitive, behavioral and emotional indicators, especially those active and visible behaviors that the researchers could quantify, such as login rates and participation in discussions. This study illustrates the potential of learning analytics to provide data-informed insights into trends in student engagement, recognizing and acting on issues in real-time. Suraworachet et al. (2023) demonstrated through reflective writing assignments that combining analytics feedback and human feedback results in improved performance, more accuracy, and greater engagement, leading researchers to suggest that using learning analytics could be an effective intervention when paired with qualitative feedback. Moreover, learning analytics also helps policy makers and teachers to make decisions about students' performance, participation, behaviors, interaction, punctuality, curriculum, teaching and assessment etc.

Discussion Board Analysis

Evaluating the amount and depth of forum posts can help assess how well students collaborate systematically and cognitively. Kew and Tasir (2021) reported that many of the discussion posts were superficial, indicating variations in students' cognitive engagement when working online. Their findings underscore the importance of evaluating both the quantity and quality of interactions to develop meaningful engagement. Delaney et al. (2019) show that organized discussion boards help students collaborate more successfully and become more engaged in group activities, following an association between positive attitudes and increased engagement in group activities that included issues raised in discussions on the discussion board. These learning analytics/dashboards summarize learners' data, activities, reports of students' interactions, progress on tasks etc. Moreover, learning analytics/dashboards also visualize data and learning trends that helps stakeholders to monitor, support, enhance collaborations and make certain decisions about students. This is often challenging for teachers to manage such data sets, especially in relation to assessments because in online learning environment when students are assessed through open-book exam, it is very difficult for teachers to make data driven decisions as each student has different learning pace (Graham et al., 2019).

Peer Assessment

When students evaluate one another's participation, they take greater accountability and engage in reflective learning. According to Ma and Luo (2022) if student participation is evaluated by peers, not only is effort placed on assessment, but participation is also actively achieved via the evaluation itself. Ma and Luo (2022) found that participation in peer assessment supported student learning by enhancing cognitive and behavioral engagement. These various approaches use qualitative feedback and quantitative metrics to provide multiple perspectives of student engagement. Their use provides teachers with the opportunity to oversee and facilitate meaningful engagement, which is important for effective learning in online contexts

Individual vs. Group Grading

The decision of whether to give grades individually or collectively influences student motivation and perceptions of justice. Ma and Luo (2022) stated that individual grading links students' contributions, which raises accountability and perceptions of fairness, and engages students in making contributions. Group grading also involves shared accountability, and this can lead to lowered motivation when contributions are unequal (Chang & Brickman, 2018). This highlights the importance of developing assessment practices that consider cooperation and fairness.

Rubrics for Evaluating Collaborative Skills and Participation

Rubrics clarify expectations and provide impartial criteria to assess teamwork behaviors that include accountability, involvement, and communication. Stevens (2023) identify rubrics as essential for transparency and consistency in evaluation to educate students about productive teamwork. A clearly defined, simple rubric criteria enhance peer assessment accuracy, as well as awareness of students' teamwork strengths and weaknesses (Thite et al., 2024).

Use of Self-Reflection and Peer Feedback

Peer review and self-reflection are useful strategies for evaluating involvement and teamwork in higher education, as they promote students to think critically about their contributions and performance in collaborative settings. This practice increases student experience and contributes to greater skill development and responsibility. For example, peer and self-evaluation in clinical skills training promotes self-regulation and assists students to identify aspects of their performance. Likewise, it has been proved that reflective journaling with peer review changes the level of cognitive engagement and results in larger changes in academic writing. This combined approach creates meaningful peer discussions and helps students to develop the content and organization of their work, resulting in better individual learning and collaboration (Zhang & Hyland, 2023). Research illustrates the advantage of implementing self-reflection and peer review in assessment practices, as they promote students' critical thinking and collaboration beyond measuring engagement and collaboration.

ETHICAL CONSIDERATIONS IN MONITORING ENGAGEMENT

Ethics in online collaborative learning is critical to ensure fairness, trust, and respect among participants. This comprises issues e.g., academic integrity, respect for diverse perspectives, responsible use of digital resources, and the protection of learners' privacy and data in online learning environments. In view of students' collaborative, an honest contribution from learners, acknowledge others' ideas, and avoid misconduct such as plagiarism or misrepresentation of contributions (Palloff & Pratt, 2007). Equal importance should be given to inclusive environment, respect for diversity, cultural and gender differences etc. (Johnson & Johnson, 2009). With the increase of digital platforms, safeguarding data confidentiality and promoting responsible digital citizenship have become integral to ethical practice in online collaboration (Veletsianos & Kimmons, 2013). By embedding ethical guidelines and fostering awareness, instructors can help learners develop not only academic skills but also the moral and social competencies required for responsible participation in digital communities. Moreover, significant ethical issues, especially those pertaining to privacy, informed consent, and data security as online learning depends on educational technologies to track student involvement (Karimov et al., 2025). Concerns regarding the handling and protection of this sensitive data are highlighted by data experts and analysts (Balida, 2023). Making sure that students understand exactly what data is gathered and how it is used is one of the ethical issues, since a lack of openness can cause them to feel watched and erode their confidence in online platforms (Balida, 2023; Karimov et al., 2025).

FUTURE DIRECTIONS AND INNOVATIONS

Throughout the world, fostering meaningful and productive group collaboration among students is still a major concern for educators and institutions as online learning continues to develop. Innovative solutions that improve interactive experiences, encourage long-term motivation, and accommodate a range of learning demands in virtual environments are being made possible by emerging technologies and pedagogical approaches. Future research should focus on designing more inclusive, adaptive, and data-informed learning environments that support meaningful interaction and sustained engagement. According to recent studies, incorporating cutting-edge digital tools like adaptive learning platforms and real-time analytics can result in online classrooms that are more socially connected and individualized (Alberts, et al., 2024). These developments seek to enhance social and emotional learning as well as cognitive engagement, which will promote cooperation and enhance academic achievement in online learning environment.

Moreover, significant developments in real-time feedback, individualized learning, and advanced analytics that improve student engagement in online settings are highlighted by AI-powered adaptive engagement technologies (Bhatia et al., 2024; Solomon et al., 2025). By adjusting learning experiences to individual requirements and preferences, artificial intelligence (AI) is transforming online education. This goes beyond conventional one-size-fits-all methods and allows for dynamic content delivery adjustments based on real-time performance and engagement data (Akramovna, 2024; Solomon et al., 2025).

Adaptive platforms that employ machine learning to tailor presentation, tempo, and material difficulty are important developments that promote interactive and collaborative online learning environments through tailored paths (Deckker, et al., 2025). These systems improve results and facilitate group cooperation by examining student behavior and learning patterns. One of the examples is scaffolding within a learner's Zone of Proximal Development (Cai, et al., 2025). The integration of (AI) and adaptive technologies facilitate group formation based on their diversity and intelligence, designing and recommending collaborative tasks and support in feedback processes. Additionally, greater emphasis should be placed on fostering social presence, psychological safety, and cultural responsiveness to ensure equitable participation in increasingly diverse online classrooms. Nevertheless, there are certain challenges to incorporate AI tools into online learning environments, such as the need for infrastructure, fair access, differences in digital literacy, privacy issues and most importantly professional development of teachers to manage online learning, conflict resolution, and data informed decisions will be critical to sustain effective collaborative learning practices (Vo, 2025).

Future developments should prioritize responsible AI frameworks that support equity and inclusiveness to address ethical concerns such as algorithmic prejudice and an excessive reliance on technology (Vo, 2025; Azamov & Kabilova, 2025). Building students' digital literacy is equally crucial for maximizing engagement and facilitating productive teamwork with AI-enhanced tools (Yaseen et al., 2025). Future research should also explore how micro-credentials and modular learning pathways can embed collaborative competencies, such as teamwork, communication, and problem-solving, as explicit learning outcomes.

Next to AI power adaptive engagement technologies, collaborative Virtual Environments, which allow students to interact in 3D locations, virtual reality (VR) and immersive collaboration environments are revolutionizing online learning by improving communication and teamwork. These resources offer interesting substitutes for conventional approaches, which frequently fall short in inspiring students.

By providing dynamic, engaging content, immersive experiences enhance memory, understanding, and skill development (Adelana et al., 2023).

In the future, it is anticipated that the use of virtual reality (VR) in online education would "bring academic subjects to life," from examining scientific ideas to virtually experiencing historical events. Global virtual classrooms backed by AI-powered avatars and real-time data could be hosted by the metaverse, which combines VR, AR, and the internet (Abd El-Sattar, 2025). These settings encourage teamwork while giving students a safe way to practice real-world chores.

VR adoption is hampered by its high technical needs and risk for social isolation brought on by immersive headsets, despite its potential. In order to maximize virtual learning for wider, more inclusive involvement, future research attempts to get around these obstacles (Adelana et al., 2023). Learning environments may become increasingly more responsive and adaptive as immersive technology advances and is integrated with AI and Internet of Things (IoT) devices. These developments have the potential to completely transform digital education by making it more accessible, interactive, and personalized. The accelerated development of digital technology and the pervasive transition to online education have brought attention to how urgently researchers and educators must develop new teaching strategies. Adaptive, technologically enhanced approaches that encourage active learning and deeper involvement are necessary because traditional pedagogical methods frequently fail to engage students in virtual settings (Karimov et al., 2025). By customizing training to meet the needs of each learner and encouraging more meaningful participation, researchers stress that incorporating technologies like virtual reality, AI-driven analytics, and personalized learning platforms can revolutionize online education (Balida, 2023). By addressing various learning styles and accessibility issues in distant locations, these technologies promote diversity in addition to academic success.

Research also emphasizes how crucial it is for academics and educators to work together to continuously improve and assess novel online teaching techniques. This partnership guarantees that innovations are scalable across different educational contexts, socially responsible, and pedagogically sound (Karimov et al., 2025). Balida (2023) emphasizes that advances in online teaching should go beyond the adoption of new technology and incorporate careful curriculum, evaluation, and interaction models that foster community building, motivation, and critical thinking. Teachers can more effectively negotiate the challenges of online learning environments and help create robust, learner-centered educational systems in the future by adopting a research-informed approach.

REFERENCES

Abd El-Sattar, H. K. H. (2025). Future metaverse-based education to promote daily living activities in learners with autism using immersive technologies. *Education and Information Technologies*, *30*(3), 3145–3182. DOI: 10.1007/s10639-024-12844-3

Abeysekera, L., & Dawson, P. (2015). Motivation and cognitive load in the flipped classroom: Definition, rationale and a call for research. *Higher Education Research & Development*, *34*(1), 1–14. DOI: 10.1080/07294360.2014.934336

Adelana, O. P., Ayanwale, M. A., Ishola, A. M., Oladejo, A. I., & Adewuyi, H. O. (2023). Exploring pre-service teachers' intention to use virtual reality: A mixed method approach. *Computers & Education: X Reality, 3*, 100045. DOI: 10.1016/j.cexr.2023.100045

Akpen, C. N., Asaolu, S., Atobatele, S., Okagbue, H., & Sampson, S. (2024). Impact of online learning on student's performance and engagement: A systematic review. *Discover Education*, *3*(1), 205. DOI: 10.1007/s44217-024-00253-0

Alberts, L., Lyngs, U., & Lukoff, K. (2024). Designing for sustained motivation: A review of Self-Determination Theory in behaviour change technologies. *Interacting with Computers*, •••, iwae040. Advance online publication. DOI: 10.1093/iwc/iwae040

Alismaiel, O. A., Cifuentes-Faura, J., & Al-Rahmi, W. M. (2022). Online learning, mobile learning, and social media technologies: An empirical study on constructivism theory during the COVID-19 pandemic. *Sustainability (Basel)*, *14*(18), 11134. DOI: 10.3390/su141811134

Bach, A., & Thiel, F. (2024, November). Collaborative online learning in higher education—quality of digital interaction and associations with individual and group-related factors. In *Frontiers in Education* (Vol. 9, p. 1356271). Frontiers Media SA. DOI: 10.3389/feduc.2024.1356271

Balida, D. A. R. (2023). Ethical challenges in online teaching and learning: A case study of a virtual class. *Russian Law Journal*, *11*(3), 1901–1916.

Bhatia, A., Bhatia, P., & Sood, D. (2024). Leveraging AI to transform online higher education: Focusing on personalized learning, assessment, and student engagement. *International Journal of Management and Humanities (IJMH) Volume-11 Issue-1*. http://dx.doi.org/DOI: 10.2139/ssrn.4959186

Boon, M., Orozco, M., & Sivakumar, K. (2022). Epistemological and educational issues in teaching practice-oriented scientific research: Roles for philosophers of science. *European Journal for Philosophy of Science, 12*(1), 16. https://link.springer.com/article/10.1007/s13194-022-00447-z. DOI: 10.1007/s13194-022-00447-z PMID: 30873248

Borup, J., Graham, C. R., West, R. E., Archambault, L., & Spring, K. J. (2020). Academic communities of engagement: An expansive lens for examining support structures in blended and online learning. *Educational Technology Research and Development*, 68, 8 07- 832.

Briggs, C. L., & Doubleday, A. F. (2016). Group Learning Assessments as a Vital Consideration in the Implementation of New Peer Learning Pedagogies in the Basic Science Curriculum of Health Profession Programs. *Journal of Medical Education and Curricular Development, 3. JMECD, S18930*. Advance online publication. DOI: 10.4137/JMECD.S18930 PMID: 29349309

Cai, L., Msafiri, M. M., & Kangwa, D. (2025). Exploring the impact of integrating AI tools in higher education using the Zone of Proximal Development. *Education and Information Technologies, 30*(6), 7191–7264. DOI: 10.1007/s10639-024-13112-0

Caskurlu, S., Yalçın, Y., Hur, J., Shi, H., & Klein, J. D. (2025). Data-driven decision-making in instructional design: Instructional designers' practices and strategies. *TechTrends, 69*(4), 1–12. https://link.springer.com/article/10.1007/s11528-025-01077-x. DOI: 10.1007/s11528-025-01077-x

Castañer, X., & Oliveira, N. (2020). Collaboration, coordination, and cooperation among organizations: Establishing the distinctive meanings of these terms through a systematic literature review. *Journal of Management, 46*(6), 965–1001. DOI: 10.1177/0149206320901565

Chang, Y., & Brickman, P. (2018). When group work doesn't work: Insights from students. *CBE Life Sciences Education, 17*(3), ar52. DOI: 10.1187/cbe.17-09-0199 PMID: 30183565

Chen, K. C., & Jang, S. J. (2010). Motivation in online learning: Testing a model of self-determination theory. *Computers in Human Behavior, 26*(4), 741–752. DOI: 10.1016/j.chb.2010.01.011

Cheng, K., Liang, J., & Tsai, C. (2013). University students' online academic help seeking: the role of self-regulation and information commitments. The Internet and Higher Education, 16, 70–77. https://doi.org/DOI: 10.1016/j.iheduc.2012.02.002

Chowkase, A. A., Datar, K., Deshpande, A., Khasnis, S., Keskar, A., & Godbole, S. (2022). Online learning, classroom quality, and student motivation: Perspectives from students, teachers, parents, and program staff. *Gifted Education International, 38*(1), 74–94. DOI: 10.1177/02614294211060401

Cleveland-Innes, M., & Campbell, P. (2012). Emotional presence, learning, and the online learning environment. *International Review of Research in Open and Distance Learning, 13*(4), 269–292. DOI: 10.19173/irrodl.v13i4.1234

Coates, H. (2006). *Student engagement in campus-based and online education: University connections*. Routledge., DOI: 10.4324/9780203969465

Cullinan, J., Flannery, D., Harold, J., Lyons, S., & Palcic, D. (2021). The disconnected: COVID-19 and disparities in access to quality broadband for higher education students. *International Journal of Educational Technology in Higher Education, 18*(1), 26. DOI: 10.1186/s41239-021-00262-1 PMID: 34778524

Deci, E. L., & Ryan, R. M. (1985). *Intrinsic motivation and self-determination in human behavior*. Plenum Press. DOI: 10.1007/978-1-4899-2271-7

Deci, E. L., & Ryan, R. M. (2000). The" what" and" why" of goal pursuits: Human needs and the self-determination of behavior. *Psychological Inquiry, 11*(4), 227–268. DOI: 10.1207/S15327965PLI1104_01

Deckker, D., Sumanasekara, S., & Fakhrou, A. (2025). AI-Powered Personalised Learning: Promise and Pitfalls.

Delaney, D., Kummer, T. F., & Singh, K. (2019). Evaluating the impact of online discussion boards on student engagement with group work. *British Journal of Educational Technology, 50*(2), 902–920. DOI: 10.1111/bjet.12614

Dhawan, S. (2020). Online learning: A panacea in the time of COVID-19 crisis. *Journal of Educational Technology Systems, 49*(1), 5–22. DOI: 10.1177/0047239520934018

Dillenbourg, P. (1999). What do you mean by collaborative learning?. *Collaborative-learning: Cognitive and computational approaches.*, 1-19.

Dincă, M., Luştrea, A., Craşovan, M., Oniţiu, A., & Berge, T. (2023). Students' perspectives on team dynamics in Project-Based virtual learning. *SAGE Open, 13*(1), 21582440221147269. DOI: 10.1177/21582440221147269

Dixson, M. D. (2015). Measuring student engagement in the online course: The Online Student Engagement scale (OSE). *Online Learning : the Official Journal of the Online Learning Consortium, 19*(4), n4. DOI: 10.24059/olj.v19i4.561

Donelan, H., & Kear, K. (2024). Online group projects in higher education: Persistent challenges and implications for practice. *Journal of Computing in Higher Education, 36*(2), 435–468. DOI: 10.1007/s12528-023-09360-7 PMID: 37359044

Dool, R. (2010). Managing Conflict in Online Student Groups. In *TCC* (pp. 47-57). TCCHawaii.

Eisenbach, B. B., Greathouse, P., & Kirk, M. (2018). Creating a community of care in the middle level virtual classroom. In Eisenbach, B. B., & Greathouse, P. (Eds.), *The online classroom: Resources for effective middle level education* (pp. 121–136). Information Age. DOI: 10.1108/978-1-64113-461-320251011

Falls, I., Bahhouth, V., Chuang, C. M., & Bahhouth, J. (2014). Factors influencing students' perceptions of online teamwork. *SAGE Open, 4*(1), 2158244014525415. DOI: 10.1177/2158244014525415

Foo, C. C., Cheung, B., & Chu, K. M. (2021). A comparative study regarding distance learning and the conventional face-to-face approach conducted problem-based learning tutorial during the COVID-19 pandemic. *BMC Medical Education, 21*(1), 141. DOI: 10.1186/s12909-021-02575-1 PMID: 33658015

Fredricks, J. A., Blumenfeld, P. C., & Paris, A. H. (2004). School engagement: Potential of the concept, state of the evidence. *Review of Educational Research, 74*(1), 59–109. DOI: 10.3102/00346543074001059

Garrison, D. R. (2017). *E-Learning in the 21st century: A community of inquiry framework for research and practice* (3rd ed.). Routledge., DOI: 10.4324/9781315667263

Garrison, D. R., Anderson, T., & Archer, W. (2000). Critical inquiry in a text-based environment: Computer conferencing in higher education. Internet and Higher Education, 2(2-3), 87–105. . https://doi.org/DOI: 10.1016/S1096-7516(00)00016-6

Garrison, D. R., & Arbaugh, J. B. (2007). Researching the community of inquiry framework: Review, issues, and future directions. *The Internet and Higher Education, 10*(3), 157–172. DOI: 10.1016/j.iheduc.2007.04.001

Geng, F., Srinivasan, S., Gao, Z., Bogoslowski, S., & Rajabzadeh, A. R. (2022). An Online Approach to Project-Based Learning in Engineering and Technology for Post-secondary Students. In Auer, M. E., & Tsiatsos, T. (Eds.), *New Realities, Mobile Systems and Applications* (pp. 627–635). Springer International Publishing., DOI: 10.1007/978-3-030-96296-8_56

Gopinathan, S., Kaur, A. H., Veeraya, S., & Raman, M. (2022). The role of digital collaboration in student engagement towards enhancing student participation during COVID-19. *Sustainability (Basel), 14*(11), 6844. DOI: 10.3390/su14116844

Graham, C. R., Borup, J., Short, C., & Archambault, L. (2019). *K–12 blended teaching: A guide to personalized learning and online integration.* Edtechbooks.org

Greene, B. A. (2015). Measuring cognitive engagement with self-report scales: Reflections from over 20 years of research. *Educational Psychologist, 50*(1), 14–30. DOI: 10.1080/00461520.2014.989230

Griffin, P., McGaw, B., & Care, E. (2012). *Assessment and teaching of 21st century skills* (Vol. 10, pp. 978-94). Dordrecht: springer. DOI: 10.1007/978-94-017-9395-7

Grothaus, C. (2022). Collaborative online learning across cultures: The role of teaching and social presence. *Qualitative Research in Education, 11*(3), 298–326. DOI: 10.17583/qre.10474

Gulati, R., Wohlgezogen, F., & Zhelyazkov, P. (2012). The two facets of collaboration: Cooperation and coordination in strategic alliances. *The Academy of Management Annals, 6*(1), 531–583. DOI: 10.5465/19416520.2012.691646

Haugland, M. J., Rosenberg, I., & Aasekjær, K. (2022). Collaborative learning in small groups in an online course – a case study. *BMC Medical Education, 22*(1), 165. DOI: 10.1186/s12909-022-03232-x PMID: 35272639

Henri, F. (1992). Computer conferencing and content analysis. In Kaye, A. R. (Ed.), *Collaborative learning through computer conferencing: The Najaden papers* (pp. 117–136). SpringerVerlag., DOI: 10.1007/978-3-642-77684-7_8

Henrie, C. R., Halverson, L. R., & Graham, C. R. (2015). Measuring student engagement in technology-mediated learning: A review. *Computers & Education, 90*, 36–53. DOI: 10.1016/j.compedu.2015.09.005

Hew, K. F., Huang, B., Chu, K. W. S., & Chiu, D. K. W. (2019). Engaging Asian students through game mechanics: Findings from two experiment studies. *Computers & Education, 133*, 30–48. DOI: 10.1016/j.compedu.2015.10.010

Hew, K. F., & Lo, C. K. (2018). Flipped classroom improves student learning in health professions education: A meta-analysis. *BMC Medical Education, 18*(1), 38. DOI: 10.1186/s12909-018-1144-z PMID: 29544495

Hmelo-Silver, C. E. (2004). Problem-based learning: What and how do students learn? *Educational Psychology Review, 16*(3), 235–266. DOI: 10.1023/B:EDPR.0000034022.16470.f3

Holmes, K., & Prieto-Rodriguez, E. (2018). Student and staff perceptions of a learning management system for blended learning in teacher education. *The Australian Journal of Teacher Education, 43*(3), 21–34. https://search.informit.org/doi/10.3316/informit.477648976239419. DOI: 10.14221/ajte.2018v43n3.2

Hrastinski, S. (2008). Asynchronous and synchronous e-learning. *EDUCAUSE Quarterly, 31*(4), 51–55.

Hsu, H. C. K., Wang, C. V., & Levesque-Bristol, C. (2019). Reexamining the impact of self-determination theory on learning outcomes in the online learning environment. *Education and Information Technologies, 24*(3), 2159–2174. DOI: 10.1007/s10639-019-09863-w

Johar, N. A., Kew, S. N., Tasir, Z., & Koh, E. (2023). Learning analytics on student engagement to enhance students' learning performance: A systematic review. *Sustainability (Basel), 15*(10), 7849. DOI: 10.3390/su15107849

Johnson, D. W., & Johnson, R. T. (2009). An educational psychology success story: Social interdependence theory and cooperative learning. *Educational Researcher, 38*(5), 365–379. DOI: 10.3102/0013189X09339057

Johnson, D. W., Johnson, R. T., & Smith, K. A. (2014). Cooperative learning: Improving university instruction by basing practice on validated theory. *Journal on Excellence in College Teaching, 25*(3&4).

Kapp, K. M. (2012). *The gamification of learning and instruction: Game-based methods and strategies for training and education*. Pfeiffer.

Karimov, A., Saarela, M., Aliyev, S., & Baker, R. (2025, January). Ethical considerations and student perceptions of engagement data in learning analytics. In *Proceedings of the 58th Hawaii International Conference on System Sciences* (4757-4766). DOI: 10.24251/HICSS.2025.572

Kay, R. H., & LeSage, A. (2009). Examining the benefits and challenges of using audience response systems: A review of the literature. *Computers & Education, 53*(3), 819–827. DOI: 10.1016/j.compedu.2009.05.001

Kehrwald, B. (2008). Understanding social presence in text-based online learning environments. *Distance Education, 29*(1), 89–106. DOI: 10.1080/01587910802004860

Kew, S. N., & Tasir, Z. (2021). Analysing Students' Cognitive Engagement in E-Learning Discussion Forums through Content Analysis. *Knowledge Management & E-Learning, 13*(1), 39–57.

Knight, E. M. (2013). Aligning the curriculum of the human resources management undergraduate courses at an English-speaking university in the Caribbean with the university's 2012–2017 strategic plan. *Global Business and Economics Research Journal*, *2*(8), 61–86.

Kuh, G. D. (2003). What we're learning about student engagement from NSSE: Benchmarks for effective educational practices. *Change: The magazine of higher learning, 35*(2), 24-32.

Kumar, R., & Wei, L. (2024). Exploring the Impact of Digital Learning Environments on Student Engagement and Academic Performance A Global Perspective. *International Journal of Educational Insights and Innovations*, *1*(2), 5–8.

Kunwar, J. B. (2021). The influence of culture on collaborative learning practices in higher education. *Journal of Intercultural Management*, *13*(2), 81–106. DOI: 10.2478/joim-2021-0062

Lim, L. X., Lim, P. E., Lim, S. H., Lim, Y. X., & Oktaviandra, A. G. (2022). Hi, let's meet online! A study of virtual meeting platforms during the pandemic. [APJME]. *Asia Pacific Journal of Management and Education*, *5*(1), 126–140. DOI: 10.32535/apjme.v4i3.1432

Lo, C. K., & Hew, K. F. (2021). Student engagement in mathematics flipped classrooms: Implications of journal publications from 2011 to 2020. *Frontiers in Psychology*, *12*, 672610. DOI: 10.3389/fpsyg.2021.672610 PMID: 34135833

Losier, G. F., Perreault, S., Koestner, R., & Vallerand, R. J. (2001). Examining individual differences in the internalization of political values: Validation of the self-determination scale of political motivation. *Journal of Research in Personality*, *35*(1), 41–61. DOI: 10.1006/jrpe.2000.2300

Ma, M., & Luo, C. (2022). The effect of student and peer assessment engagement on learning performance in online open courses. [iJET]. *International Journal of Emerging Technologies in Learning*, *17*(10), 145–158. DOI: 10.3991/ijet.v17i10.30931

Mao, L., & Queiroz, F. (2024). Online education in design disciplines: Factors influencing the interactive experience of group learning. *International Journal of Technology and Design Education*, *34*(5), 1903–1930. DOI: 10.1007/s10798-024-09882-w

Meyer, K. (2014). Student engagement in online learning: What works and why. *ASHE Higher Education Report*, *40*(6), 1–14. DOI: 10.1002/aehe.20018

Mishra, L., Gupta, T., & Shree, A. (2020). Online teaching-learning in higher education during lockdown period of COVID-19 pandemic. *International Journal of Educational Research Open, 1*, 100012. DOI: 10.1016/j.ijedro.2020.100012 PMID: 35059663

Miyake, M., & Kirschner, P. (2014). The social and interactive dimensions of collaborative learning. In Sawyer, R. K. (Ed.), *The Cambridge handbook of the learning sciences* (2nd ed., pp. 454–475). Cambridge University Press. DOI: 10.1017/CBO9781139519526.026

Mujallid, A. T. (2024). Digital Active Learning Strategies in Blended Environments to Develop Students' Social and Emotional Learning Skills and Engagement in Higher Education. *European Journal of Education, 59*(4), e12748. DOI: 10.1111/ejed.12748

Nabil, N. A., Ayubi, S., & Ansari, M. Z. A. (2023). Study of the Role of ZOOM Platform in Collaborative Learning from the Perspective of the Kabul University Lecturers. *Sprin Journal of Arts, Humanities and Social Sciences, 2*(09), 01-12.h DOI: 10.55559/sjahss.v2i09.147

Pace, C. R. "Measuring the Quality of Student Effort." Current Issues in Higher Educa tion, 1980, 2, 10–16

Pace, C. R. (1990). *The Undergraduates: A Report of Their Activities and College Experiences in the 1980s*. Center for the Study of Evaluation, UCLA Graduate School of Education.

Palloff, R. M., & Pratt, K. (2007). *Building online learning communities: Effective strategies for the virtual classroom*. Jossey-Bass.

Pascarella, E. T., & Terenzini, P. T. (2005). *How College Affects Students: A Third Decade of Research*. Jossey-Bass.

Petty, T., & Farinde, A. (2013). Investigating student engagement in an online mathematics course through windows into teaching and learning. *Journal of Online Learning and Teaching, 9*(2), 261–270.

Pittaway, S. M. (2012). Student and staff engagement: Developing an engagement framework in a faculty of education. *The Australian Journal of Teacher Education, 37*(4), 41–48. DOI: 10.14221/ajte.2012v37n4.8

Pujar, S. M., & Tadasad, P. G. (2016). MOOCs–an opportunity for international collaboration in LIS education: A developing country's perspective. *New Library World, 117*(5/6), 360–373. DOI: 10.1108/NLW-07-2015-0048

Qi, S., & Derakhshan, A. (2025). Technology-based collaborative learning: EFL learners' social regulation and modifications in their academic emotions and academic performance. *Education and Information Technologies, 30*(7), 8611–8636. https://link.springer.com/article/10.1007/s10639-024-13167-z. DOI: 10.1007/s10639-024-13167-z

Ramesh, M. S., & Vinod, V. (2022). *Artificial intelligence post-pandemic future trends in fields of education-challenges and opportunities (Ai The Real Teacher). Education Trends in a Post-Pandemic Future in the Fields of Engineering, Science, Arts, Humanities, Commerce, Economics, Social Sciences, Law and Management-Challenges and Opportunities*. Global Multidisciplinary Research and Academic Foundation.

Redmond, P., Heffernan, A., Abawi, L., Brown, A., & Henderson, R. (2018). An online engagement framework for higher education. *Online Learning : the Official Journal of the Online Learning Consortium, 22*(1), 183–204. DOI: 10.24059/olj.v22i1.1175

Richards, J. C. (2011). *Competence and performance in language teaching*. Cambridge University Pressm., DOI: 10.1177/0033688210372953

Ryan, R. M., & Deci, E. L. (2017). *Self-determination theory: Basic psychological needs in motivation development and wellness*. Guilford Press. DOI: 10.1521/978.14625/28806

Ryan, R. M., & Deci, E. L. (2020). Intrinsic and extrinsic motivation from a self-determination theory perspective DOI: 10.1016/j.cedpsych.2020.101860

Salam, A., Simonyan, R., Terzov, V., & Ogunyemi, A. (2024). CHALLENGES IN ONLINE EDUCATION POST-COVID AND STRATEGIES FOR ENHANCED LEARNING IN DIVERSE TIME ZONES. In *ICERI2024 Proceedings* (pp. 5016-5026). IATED. DOI: 10.21125/iceri.2024.1237

Salmon, G. (2003). *E-moderating: The key to teaching and learning online*. Psychology press.

Salvato, C., Reuer, J., & Battigalli, P. (2017). Cooperation across disciplines: A multilevel perspective on cooperative behavior in governing interfirm relations. *The Academy of Management Annals, 11*(2), 960–1004. DOI: 10.5465/annals.2014.0001

Saqr, M., Nouri, J., Vartiainen, H., & Malmberg, J. (2020). What makes an online problem-based group successful? Learning analytics study using social network analysis. *BMC Medical Education, 20*(1), 80. DOI: 10.1186/s12909-020-01997-7 PMID: 32188471

Saroyan, J. S. (2021). Developing a supportive peer environment: Engaging students through cooperative skills in the classroom. *Advances in Developmental and Educational Psychology*, *3*(1), 81–89. DOI: 10.25082/ADEP.2021.01.001

Sekendiz, B. (2018). Utilisation of formative peer-assessment in distance online education: A case study of a multi-model sport management unit. *Interactive Learning Environments*, *26*(5), 682–694. DOI: 10.1080/10494820.2017.1396229

Shalevska, E. (2021). Students' motivation and engagement during distance learning. [IJSR]. *International Journal of Scientific Research*, *10*(1). https://eprints.uklo.edu .mk/id/eprint/9504

Sheldon, K. M., & Hilpert, J. C. (2012). The balanced measure of psychological needs (BMPN) scale: An alternative domain general measure of need satisfaction. *Motivation and Emotion*, *36*(4), 439–451. DOI: 10.1007/s11031-012-9279-4

Shunk, D. H. (2000). Learning: introduction, issues, and historial perspectives. In-Schunk, DH Learning theories: an educational perspective (pp. 1-29). *Upper Saddle River, NJ: Pearson Education. Waters, E., & Sroufe, LA (1983). Social competence as a developmental construct. Developmental Review*, *3*, 79–97.

Sinatra, G., Heddy, B., & Lombardi, D. (2015). The challenges of defining and measuring student engagement in science. *Educational Psychologist*, *50*(1), 1–13. DOI: 10.1080/00461520.2014.1002924

Singh, A. B. (2024). Digital technology and student engagement in online synchronous collaborative learning sessions/Tecnología digital y participación de los estudiantes en las sesiones de aprendizaje colaborativo en línea. *C&E, Cultura y Educación*, *36*(4), 1005–1043. DOI: 10.1177/11356405241292980

Solomon, V. V., & SV, R. D. (2025). Leveraging Artificial Intelligence for Student-Centric Online Learning in Higher Education: Opportunities for Personalized Education and Engagement. *International Journal of Latest Technology in Engineering, Management &. Applied Sciences (Basel, Switzerland)*, *14*(5), 1093–1096.

Song, H., Kim, J., & Park, N. (2018). I know my professor: Teacher self-disclosure in online education and a mediating role of social presence. *International Journal of Human-Computer Interaction*, *35*(6), 1–8. DOI: 10.1080/10447318.2018.1455126

Stecher, B. M., & Hamilton, L. S. (2014). *Measuring Hard-to-Measure Student Competencies: A Research and Development Plan. Research Report.* RAND Corporation. PO Box 2138, Santa Monica, CA 90407-2138. DOI: 10.7249/RR863

Stevens, D. D. (2023). *Introduction to rubrics: An assessment tool to save grading time, convey effective feedback, and promote student learning*. Routledge., DOI: 10.4324/9781003445432

Sumarni, S. (2022). The Effectiveness of Constructivist Learning Methods Through the Breakout Room Facility at Zoom Cloud Meeting. *Ethical Lingua: Journal of Language Teaching and Literature, 9*(2), 459-466. https://doi.org/DOI: 10.30605/25409190.417

Suraworachet, W., Zhou, Q., & Cukurova, M. (2023). Impact of combining human and analytics feedback on students' engagement with, and performance in, reflective writing tasks. *International Journal of Educational Technology in Higher Education, 20*(1), 1–24. DOI: 10.1186/s41239-022-00368-0

Thite, S., Ravishankar, J., Tomeo-Reyes, I., & Ortiz, A. M. (2024). Design of a simple rubric to peer-evaluate the teamwork skills of engineering students. *European Journal of Engineering Education, 49*(4), 623–646. DOI: 10.1080/03043797.2024.2338239

Townley, A. L. (2020). Leveraging communities of practice as professional learning communities in science, technology, engineering, math (STEM) education. *Education Sciences, 10*(8), 190. DOI: 10.3390/educsci10080190

Tugun, V., Bayanova, A., Erdyneeva, K., Mashkin, N., Sakhipova, Z., & Zasova, L. (2020). The opinions of technology supported education of university students. [iJET]. *International Journal of Emerging Technologies in Learning, 15*(23), 4–14. DOI: 10.3991/ijet.v15i23.18779

Usher, M., & Barak, M. (2018). Peer assessment in a project-based engineering course: Comparing between on-campus and online learning environments. *Assessment & Evaluation in Higher Education, 43*(5), 745–759. DOI: 10.1080/02602938.2017.1405238

Van Deursen, A. J. (2020). Digital inequality during a pandemic: Quantitative study of differences in COVID-19–related internet uses and outcomes among the general population. *Journal of Medical Internet Research, 22*(8), e20073. https://preprints.jmir.org/preprint/20073. DOI: 10.2196/20073 PMID: 32750005

Vargas-Hernández, J. G., & Cervantes-Maldonado, D. A. (2018). Intercultural business management development and education programs in business schools. *European Journal of Multidisciplinary Studies, 3*(1), 105–121. DOI: 10.26417/ejms.v7i1.p105-121

Veletsianos, G., & Kimmons, R. (2013). Scholars and faculty members' lived experiences in online social networks. *The Internet and Higher Education, 16*, 43–50. DOI: 10.1016/j.iheduc.2012.01.004

Vo, T. K. A. (2025). Transforming Language Learning with AI: Adaptive Systems, Engagement, and Global Impact. *Engineering Proceedings*, *107*(1), 7. DOI: 10.3390/engproc2025107007

Vogt, K. (2016). *Measuring student engagement using learning management systems (unpublished doctoral dissertation)*. University of Toronto., Retrieved from https://tspace.library.utoronto.ca/handle/1807/73213

Vygotsky, L. S. (1978). *Mind in society: The development of higher psychological processes* (Vol. 86). Harvard university press.

Wachenheim, C., Idowu, A., & Hanson, E. (2023). Student Feedback on Use of Breakout Rooms. *NACTA Journal*, *67*(1). Advance online publication. DOI: 10.56103/nactaj.v67i1.100

Wakke, D., & Heller, V. (2022). Helping as a concurrent activity: How students engage in small groups while pursuing classroom tasks. *Frontiers in Psychology*, *12*, 784906. DOI: 10.3389/fpsyg.2021.784906 PMID: 35095673

Weimer, M. (2016). *What does student engagement look like*. The Teaching Professor Blog.

Wood, D., Bruner, J. S., & Ross, G. (1976). The role of tutoring in problem solving. *Journal of Child Psychology and Psychiatry, and Allied Disciplines*, *17*(2), 89–100. DOI: 10.1111/j.1469-7610.1976.tb00381.x PMID: 932126

Xu, B., Stephens, J. M., & Lee, K. (2024). Assessing student engagement in collaborative learning: Development and validation of new measure in China. *The Asia-Pacific Education Researcher*, *33*(2), 395–405. DOI: 10.1007/s40299-023-00737-x

Yaseen, H., Mohammad, A. S., Ashal, N., Abusaimeh, H., Ali, A., & Sharabati, A. A. A. (2025). The impact of adaptive learning technologies, personalized feedback, and interactive AI tools on student engagement: The moderating role of digital literacy. *Sustainability (Basel)*, *17*(3), 1133. DOI: 10.3390/su17031133

Zhang, Z. V., & Hyland, K. (2023). Student engagement with peer feedback in L2 writing: Insights from reflective journaling and revising practices. *Assessing Writing*, *58*, 100784. DOI: 10.1016/j.asw.2023.100784

Zhu, C., Valcke, M., & Schellens, T. (2009). A cross-cultural study of online collaborative learning. *Multicultural Education & Technology Journal*, *3*(1), 33–46. DOI: 10.1108/17504970910951138

Chapter 6
Virtual Group Dynamics in Online Classroom Engagement

Anitha Balve
SR University, India

Geetha Manoharan
http://orcid.org/0000-0002-8644-8871
SR University, India

ABSTRACT

Within the context of online classrooms, this chapter investigates the effect that virtual group dynamics have on student engagement. It focuses on the ways in which collaborative interactions within digital learning environments affect involvement, motivation, and the overall learning experience. Peer-to-peer contact, small group discussions, and participatory activities with the purpose of fostering a sense of community and reducing feelings of isolation that are widespread in online education are all examples of virtual group dynamics. By fostering active learning and social presence, effective management of these dynamics via techniques such as rotating breakout groups, informal peer exchanges, and real-time chat functionalities, in addition to other methods, increases engagement. The research provides a synthesis of studies on the ways in which dynamic virtual group interactions lead to deeper reflection, enhanced comfort in participation, and higher academic achievements.

DOI: 10.4018/979-8-2600-0934-5.ch006

1 INTRODUCTION TO VIRTUAL GROUP DYNAMICS

In day today, educational sectors have been transformed and moved from traditional boundaries to the modern integrated digital technologies. As the covid-19 pandemic has shown a greater impact on education, educational institutions are forced to switch to online classes for student engagement and enhanced learning. The rise of online virtual classrooms has introduced new opportunities as well as challenges impacting how students collaborate and engage with one another. The dynamics of virtual groups significantly influenced and changed the shape of students' online educational experiences. "Virtual group dynamics" explains about the psychological, emotional, and behavioural trends that emerge when students collaborate in an online classroom. It mainly focuses on the emotional and social factors of learners, which influence how efficiently a group can collaborate. virtual environment can be more challenging for students because it requires new methods of communication and teamwork. In a traditional classroom, communication used to be straightforward and direct, but where as in a virtual learning, students must adapt to different tools and platforms (Herrera-Pavo, 2021). These virtual dynamics shape how learners communicate and engage with the online course content and how student interact with one another. It provides a productive learning atmosphere. These Online classrooms offer a unique combination of privacy and connectivity, allowing students from various cultural backgrounds come together for learning, sharing creative ideas, and knowledge, so that students can enriching growth personally and professionally.

1.1 Importance of Online Classroom Engagement

Virtual dynamics not only influence the productivity of a teamwork but also the quality of communications and the overall learning experience within online educational environments. Active student participation in online environments encourages deeper knowledge construction and analytical thinking, which improves the students' academic performance. These engaged students are more likely to understand and remember the content. Students who actively engage in online classrooms feel more connected, valued, trusted, and motivated; it leads to higher retention, better collaboration, more creativity, and stronger commitment to shared goals.

Students become familiar with technological platforms, and the use of new, upgraded technological tools like Google Classroom, video conferencing tools, and discussion boards improves group interactions and dynamism. Individuals may play different roles within the group, which improves group productivity and engagement (Akpen et al., 2024). In an online classroom, people come from diverse backgrounds and cultures, which enhances their thinking capacity and fosters collaboration and shared experiences. Most importantly this phase to ensure that the students are happily engaged into their online learning into any kind of platforms. It is amended that the pedagogy will differ from the conventional methods and liveliness is maintained for best outcome into academia.

1.2 Overview or Objectives of Virtual Group Dynamics

The objective of this chapter is to explore the concept of virtual group dynamics in collaboration, communication, and engagement of students in online classrooms and challenges associated with this while adopting, like miscommunication and technological limitations. To analyse students' motivation and active participation in digital learning environments and the role of group interactions and the effective strategies adopted by the educators to strengthen group cohesion, trust, and active engagement in online learning.

2 THE CONCEPT OF GROUP DYNAMICS

Group dynamics was first introduced by Kurt Lewin in the 1940s; this concept emphasizes that groups are not just collections of individuals but interconnected systems, where the actions and roles of one member can influence the entire group. It is the pattern of interaction, behaviour and psychological process when individuals come together in a group (Lvina, 2025). Recent research studies on group dynamics shows that the increasing shift to digital and hybrid environments has transformed these dynamics in significant ways the quality of communication in virtual settings is strongly influenced by the individuals on feeling mentally tired or stressed from using online plat forms and this can be reduced by how well the participants work collaboratively. In spite of rapid growth of online and hybrid learning environments, it faces many challenges in virtual group. Students often participate unevenly, some roles are unclear, assessments feel unfair, and maintaining good teamwork becomes difficult when learners are spread across different time zones or face internet issues. Even though many studies suggest strategies for the challenges still there is a gap and they do not fully explain which methods consistently work in different online learning environments.

2.1 Historical Context and Theoretical Background

The change from traditional classrooms to digital platforms led students and scholars to begin to identify the importance of participation, collaboration, and group process. The evolution of online education and virtual group dynamics has been strongly influenced by a range of educational theories that explain how the learners gain and increase their knowledge in virtual classes, interact with others socially, and remain engaged without leaving the online learning platforms.

Theoretical Background of Group Dynamics Includes

The theory in each variable will always serve as the supporting component for the research work that is carried out. So, below are the theory that which is mentioned for better understanding of the contexts and justifications.

Tuckman's Model

Tuckman's Model of Group Development was proposed by Bruce W. Tuckman in 1965. In his influential review of small group research, he introduced the four original stages. Forming, Storming, Norming, and Performing. Later, in 1977, Tuckman and Mary Ann Jensen added a fifth stage, Adjourning, this model signifies a clear and systematic explanation that how a group naturally grow, interact with each other in a group, experience conflicts in between group and together achieve effectiveness. In today's virtual and hybrid environments, this model is important because it guides the instructors in designing structured introductions, role clarity, conflict management, and collaboration tools that support online team functioning. This model improves team work, communication, and group effectiveness.

Constructivist Learning Theory

This theory was initially proposed by Jean Piaget and later expanded upon by prominent scholars in psychology and educators Lev Vygotsky, Jerome Bruner, and John Dewey. Learning is an active and continuous process in which students actively build their knowledge through what they learn and experience. Vygotsky introduced the concept of social constructivism. According to this theory, the interactions of social, cultural, historical, and individual factors are essential for reflection (Srivastava, 2025).

Vygotsky's sociocultural theory highlights particularly the unique role of a student's social interaction and the zone of proximal development (Wibowo et al., 2025). This theory explains about people learn effectively when they work together or do things collaboratively because it demonstrates that learning is a social process, where people learn, understand, develop naturally together in a group. Collaborative learning helps in communicating, problem solving and creates a bond of supporting one another. In group settings, constructivism explains why students learn better in a group when they work together, they share ideas, and challenge each other's thinking. By encouraging the cooperation in between groups improves co-creation of knowledge, and shared responsibility, constructivist theory strengthens positive group dynamics and improves both individual and collective learning outcomes.

Social Interdependence Theory

This theory was proposed by Kurt Lewin and Morton Deutsch; it highlights how different types of interdependence among group members positive, negative, and individualistic influence the group outcomes. In online learning, groups promote positive interdependence, facilitate collaboration and accountability and productive teamwork. Connectivism Theory was proposed by George Siemens in 2005 and further developed with Stephen Downes; it is often regarded as a "learning theory for the digital age." It explains that learning happens across a network consisting of nodes like people, organizations, resources, and digital tools (Srivastava, 2025). It shows the reality of knowledge; usually individuals create, navigate, and strengthen these connections.

In virtual learning tools like discussion board, break out rooms, shared documents and project-based tasks can be helpful in generating positive interdependence in the group. Team members share the achieved outcome it means their success depends on supporting one another this creates the bonding of trust, co-ordination, and communication even though physical they don't share the same space.

2.2 Key Elements of Group Dynamics

The various compositions of the elements will differ from one other, and they will have a direct or indirect impact towards the dynamics Some of the key elements of group dynamics include but not less than as follows below

Communication Patterns: These are a crucial factor in online group dynamics. Effective communication is necessary and is characterized by openness, equity, active listening, and giving timely feedback. However, many barriers to effective communication exist, including technological issues, time-zone differences, and the lack of facial or physical expressions, which may disrupt communication.

Roles and Responsibilities: Defining roles and responsibilities in online learning platforms is essential for effective group functioning. clear responsibilities and roles prevent issues of duplication of work or social loafing, in virtual online classrooms, guidelines and role rotation enhance collaboration and strengthen role distribution. Roles can include task-oriented positions such as discussion leader, presenter, and note taker; by defining these roles and responsibilities, students feel a sense of accountability and ownership over group tasks. The clarity and acceptance of these roles can affect group productivity and engagement.

Leadership and Influence: The initiative of students and effective use of digital skills and expertise in the related field improve leadership skills. It helps in motivating peers, managing group tasks, and solving conflicts. Sharing the leadership roles and involving everyone in the decision-making can improve both stronger participation of group members and group effectiveness.

Motivation and Participation: Enthusiastic participation in events and group tasks improves students' motivation. Motivation is an important factor in a student's life, especially when engaging in virtual online classrooms. Factors influencing individual motivation can vary between face-to-face and online environments. Group dynamics also play a key role in maintaining motivation and encouraging participation.

There are several other key elements that can serves as the factors that indulge in group dynamics.

2.3 Application to Online Learning Environments

The sudden transition to online learning during the covid-19pandemic transformed education globally and led to a substantial rise in the adoption of digital learning platforms. These online environments provide flexible, technology-driven learning platforms (Akpen et al., 2024). where learners interact with the content, peers, and instructors through virtual modes such as learning management systems (LMS), discussion forums, video conferencing, and digital collaboration tools.

Constructivist Learning Application: Individuals or learners gain knowledge through active participation in assignments, problem solving, and interaction with real-world situations. Students are encouraged to use tools like simulation, case studies, and project-based learning to explore, discuss, and construct meaning rather than receiving information.

Group dynamics and Collaboration: In online classrooms, roles and responsibilities are assigned to students using project tools. Structured discussion forums and scheduled meetings are conducted for effective communication among group members. Since the pandemic made teaching and learning online many researchers have shown growing interest in understanding how students work together in virtual groups in higher education. Effective online collaboration is more than assigning a task or creating a discussion rooms.

Students who participate in online virtual environments share ideas more freely in online groups when they feel safe from judgement. This sense of psychological safety encourages creativity and improves open discussion. when students clearly understand their roles and responsibilities, there is less confusion and conflict in the group. Social presence is another important key factor students collaborate better when instructors create opportunities for informal interaction, and simple warm-up conversations between the group improves comfort and trust. In online classrooms team projects are productive and collaborative and also faces some unique challenges like the trust issues, communication and over all group performance. Most of the studies have shown that misunderstanding occurs easily and is harder to interpret the facial expression in online class rooms these issues are overcome by regular check ins, clear agenda and short, structured meetings to maintain clarity among group members and instructors can use a mix of synchronous and asynchronous methods to reduce stress and allow group to participate.

Openness and inclusivity: Virtual Learning Environments are online platforms used for education, allowing learners from diverse geographical and socio-economic backgrounds. Online VLEs broaden educational opportunities (Alnasyan et al., 2024) and make learning more adaptable and accessible for students with different learning needs, such as multilingual captions. They allow students to easily submit assignments, participate in discussions online, and take exams from any location.

Social Presence in Online Learning: Students in online platform keep motivated willing to participate in assignments and classes when they feel that the teachers and classmates are in the same space. Online platform tools like discussion boards, chat options, emojis, whiteboards, and video interactions help students in virtual classrooms made more engaging, interactive and personal. This builds strong relationships between students and instructors or faculty and reduces isolation, by this it improves group cohesion in virtual online environment.

Feedback and Assessment: Teachers play an important role in helping students interact with each other which makes learning easier and more effective. Activities like online discussion, collaborative problem solving, automated quizzes, help teachers to analyse the skills of students and AI-driven analytics help to track student progress. Assessment and feedback are provided immediately after the assignment are submitted in online environments these assessments encourage accountability and learning from different aspects.

3 ONLINE CLASSROOM TECHNOLOGIEs

The transformation of the learning environment through digital technologies has sparked diverse perspectives regarding their disruptive nature, challenges, advantages, and potential. With blended, online, and technology-enhanced learning becoming the new standard, it is increasingly vital for all stakeholders, educators, researchers, and technology developers to develop a shared understanding of the classroom climate (Oyarzun & Martin, 2023).

3.1 Tools and Platforms for Engagement

Learning Management System (LMS)

It is a centralised structured online teaching platforms it serves course materials, assignments, assessments, grading, and communication. It plays an important role in modern education as a teaching and learning tool. Moodle, Blackboard, Canvas, and Google Classroom are some of the examples of online learning plat forms (Vaarma & Li, 2024). Students use Video Conferencing tools to join real-time teaching, live lectures, discussions, and presentations has made teaching and learning easier and students take part in virtual meetings, and talk with their teachers and classmates either one-on-one or in groups. They feel more comfortable using these platforms and ensure equitable access to all learners. With the rise of video conferencing tools learning world-wide has become more flexible and accessible, enabling students and teachers to connect seamlessly and the interactive tools like virtual breakout rooms helps in debates and ask questions, discuss ideas, and get immediate feedback from the instructors. This makes students feel online learning more like a real classroom experience. As the online learning has grown across world-wide the features like Teamwork, multilingual options, and mobile friendly platforms are provided to the students especially students from remote area with limited access to laptops. These tools make it easier for faculty to work from home, collaborate with colleagues, and communicate professionally (Culduz, 2024)

3.2 Features that Facilitate Group Dynamics

Breakout Rooms

A breakout session is an active learning technique that engages a small group of learners in solving problems outside the larger class setting (Saltz & Heckman, 2020). Breakout rooms, available in platforms such as Zoom, Microsoft Teams, and google meet, function as virtual subspaces where a large class can be divided into smaller, more interactive teams. Research demonstrates that collaborative learning is significantly encouraged by Breakout sessions these smaller groups promote focused discussion, problem-solving activities, and teamwork. This approach also reduces the distractions that are common in large virtual classrooms.

The benefits of breakout sessions are that they enhance deep learning through active engagement, improve longer-term retention of knowledge and teamwork. Stronger understanding of professional environments, communication and preparing the students for real-world collaborations. Though it has many benefits, it also suffers with some challenges; Some students stay silent in the classroom wait for other students to start discussions, because of hesitation or shy, which reduces active participation of student in discussion. Technical issues and audio problems, or difficulty in rejoining the main session can also interrupt the class because of this for challenges instructor need to design effective classroom structure that encourages students work together, setting clear objectives, providing guidance, and ensuring that group dynamics are constructive and participating comfortably.

3.3 Discussion Boards

Digital learning platforms help teachers by providing AI tools to track student progress and tailor instructions according to the individual needs. This approach helps students understand and memorise the content or topic for long, particularly in subjects such as mathematics and science. The key advantage of these platforms is their asynchronous discussion feature, which allows students and teachers to engage in conversation at different times instead of depending on live sessions. Some of the research studies highlights that such discussions in groups support learning by enabling students to reflect before responding in more meaningful and thoughtful exchanges. These online forums encourage collaboration by allowing learners to ask questions, share perspectives, and collectively build knowledge according to social learning theories.

During the process, students may participate at varying levels classified as inactive, regular, or active contributors. Active participants often emerge as leaders driving discussions, while others participate regularly or occasionally. Although learning analytics effectively track these activity patterns, there is a gap in finding the most minimal learners with objective clustering methods. Discussion boards support inclusivity by giving calm students, who may hesitate in live sessions, equal opportunities to participate and engage in collaborative knowledge

3.4 Collaborative Tools

These are the tools that focus mainly on teamwork and peer interaction, allowing the teachers and students to work on completing tasks by sharing ideas, even when they are not present physically in the same place. These tools improve communication skills and build problem-solving techniques, developing a sense of community that ultimately fosters a supportive environment for learning and working together. Collaborative tools such as LMS, Google Docs, Microsoft Teams, virtual whiteboards, and Padlet are resources utilized by both instructors and students (Vaarma & Li, 2024).

4 ROLE OF INTERACTION IN ONLINE LEARNING

Interaction acts as a key element in keeping students engaged effectively in the virtual environment. It helps in building the sense of connection between students and instructors. Interaction supports knowledge sharing, clarifies the doubts, and encourages active participation and motivation and reduces the feeling of isolation in the online classroom environment. It allows instructors to give timely feedback, have discussions, and implement teaching strategies to meet learning needs. The societal aspects will also be one of the supporting elements for the online learning in which the students and the tutor will be able to share the live examples and because of which the student's ability to understand and to map the concepts will become very much comfortable for the best result outcomes. So, in the next upcoming phase in this chapter, we are going to discuss about the various types of interactions that's happens during the online learning. Any of the types will definitely have the impact differently handled.

4.1 Type of Interactions: There are Three Types of Interactions in Learning

- Student-to-Student Interaction

Student-to-student interaction is the communication, coordination, and exchange of ideas among the learners during the learning process. Such interactions help in group discussions, peer review activities, and collaborative projects and encourage active participation, critical thinking, and social and communication skills. It improves student understanding of the related concept and provides satisfaction (Oyarzun & Martin, 2023).

- Student- to-Teacher Interaction

It is a two-way exchange of ideas and content between learner and instructor; mainly it includes the instructions, feedback, questioning, guidance, assessment, and emotional support. instructors help in improving the current understanding situation to higher-level skills; instructor prompts help in creating strategies, reduce misconceptions, and guide improvement. These interactions set norms, expectations, and pacing. The instructor promotes motivation, models thinking, provides encouragement, and offers recognition.

• Learner-Content Interactions

Content interactions involve students actively engaging themselves with the learning materials to construct and gain knowledge and deepen their understanding content engagement takes various forms, like multimedia demonstration, detailed explanation, reading, watching, annotating, practicing, and testing. Effective learner-content interaction plays a vital role in providing high-quality education and ensuring student satisfaction. For this E-Learning materials must be well designed, with well-structured website content and integrating high-quality courses. The impact of learner-content interactions further becomes strengthened and effective. When students improve their learning comprehension skills and their capacity to reshape their knowledge and perspectives. learner content interaction typically this interaction occurs as students review assigned readings, completes related tasks, and take part in online discussions following demonstrations.

4.2 Impact of Interaction on Engagement and Learning Outcomes

Interactions are the exchanges that often occur in between students, teachers, and learning materials. Nowadays, especially in online and blended education, interactions play a vital role in engagement and outcomes. Engagement reflects the relationship between an individual and the activity in which they participate (Sagayadevan & Jeyaraj, 2012). Research on engagement is significant because it is linked not only to positive academic achievement but also psychological benefits. Interactions have multiple dimensions and are characterized by distinct differences; they can be subdivided into categories.

Behavioural Engagement is where it can be observed through active participation in discussion, assignments, and tasks. Cognitive Engagement is explained as interactive simulation, critical thinking, self-regulation, and effective use of learning strategies. Emotional Engagement is marked by factors of belonging, motivation, and reduced feelings of isolation (Sagayadevan & Jeyaraj, 2012).

4.3 Impact on Learning Outcomes

Interaction helps understand the concepts through participating in quizzes with instant feedback. Group discussions and debates help in strengthening critical thinking and problem-solving. Interactions help students to improve construct knowledge and regularly interact with peers and instructors are less likely to withdraw.

5 BUILDING EFFECTIVE VIRTUAL GROUPS

A virtual group is framed with the individuals who are not in the same space and may also work at different times, but the purpose is the same for the group and they come together for finishing the work. Building effective virtual groups is a critical aspect of collaborative learning environments. It can be developed by setting clear goals and framing rules and regulations and assigning structured activities and expectations. Collaborative learning emphasizes shared responsibilities, allowing students to exchange resources and skills by sharing information, evaluating contributions, and monitoring progress. Well-designed virtual groups improve student engagement, deepen learning, and ensure work is distributed fairly among the participants.

5.1 Strategies for Group Formation

Studies show that learning outcomes improve when students actively take part in group activities. To build an effective group, it is essential to include a clear set of objectives and to define roles and responsibilities for everyone, ensuring that all contributions are recognized. The way groups are formed plays an important role in preparing learners for real-world collaboration. Homogeneous and Heterogeneous groups are the most common types of groups. Research has compared how these groupings affect learning in both online and traditional settings (Oyarzun & Martin, 2023).

5.1.1 Homogeneous Groups

Homogeneous groups are made up of students who share similar back ground, characteristics, including age, academic ability, skill level, knowledge, or learning style (Taniguchi et al., 2018). This method is frequently employed when the objective is to deliver levelled training, remediation, and targeted instruction. Exam preparation, fluency enhancement, skill practice, and idea reinforcement are all beneficial uses for this kind of group.

This approach is often used when the goal is to provide targeted instruction, remediation, and levelled instruction. This type of group is effective for exam preparation, improving fluency, practicing skills, or reinforcing specific concepts. It is easier to design level-appropriate tasks that match their learning requirements, ensuring focus, efficiency, and consistency in the learning process (Oyarzun & Martin, 2023).

5.1.2 Heterogeneous Groups

Heterogeneous groups are formed according to the diverse learners who differ in characteristics, age groups, and backgrounds come together. In this advanced, and stronger students in the team support weak students. It encourages peer-to-peer learning, all members of the group benefit from different perspectives and problem-solving approaches. Research findings suggest that heterogeneous grouping often produces better learning outcomes compared to other methods, as it brings together diverse perspectives and skills (Taniguchi et al., 2018).

Table 1. Differences between homogeneous and heterogeneous groups

Aspect	Homogenous groups	Heterogenous groups
Composition	Members share similar academic ability, skill level, background knowledge, and learning style	Members differ in academic ability, skills, prior knowledge, or learning styles.
Uses	This includes practice, remediation, levelled instruction, fluency practice, exam preparation, and simple or short tasks that require quick consensus.	Complex, open-ended tasks such as projects, debates, case studies, and problem -solving activities.
Advantages	Easier to design level appropriate task. Promotes confidence in weaker learners. Faster progress and consensus. Equal participation among members.	Encourages peer-to-peer learning. Offers diverse perspectives and strategies. Enhances creativity, critical thinking and collaboration. Prepares students for real-world teamwork.
Disadvantages	Limited exposure to diverse perspectives. Reduced peer learning opportunities. Can reinforce learning gaps. Risk of labelling groups (e.g., "weak group").	Difficult to reach consensus. Risk of unequal participation (dominance by stronger members). May cause frustration with wide ability gaps. Slower progress for tasks needing quick decisions.

Here in Table 1, It Compares the characteristics, like advantages and limitations, between Homogeneous and Heterogenous Group formation in learning environments.

5.2 Group Size Considerations

Effective group formation in both online and face-to-face learning environments requires careful consideration of factors such as well-structured task design, clear assignment of roles, orientational activities, and appropriate group sizing to ensure productive collaboration. Among all of the factors, group size deserves consideration because it significantly impacts social interactions, communications, learner's participation rates, and accountability (Wang, M. et al. 2023). According to research, it suggests that smaller groups dyads or triads are often better for hands-on skill learning, as they encourage higher participation and a stronger sense of responsibility.

Medium group consists of 5-7 members. Medium groups encourage collaborative problem-solving and balance diverse perspectives. Large group starts with 8-12 members in a group usually. However, larger groups offer diverse viewpoints and open communication perspectives and richer problem-solving opportunities, though there are many advantages. It also faces challenges such as reduced participation and the emergence of social loafing behaviours (Saqr et al., 2019). Emerging studies use digital tracking tools to visualize how a student interacts online and the key differences between active learners and peripheral members and those who remained isolated. The role of teachers in virtual learning has been shown to be crucial their interactions can enhance collaboration by guiding and motivating students.

Group Setting Norms and Expectations

Establishing group norms and expectations is essential for effective teamwork in hybrid and virtual learning environments because of limited face-to-face interactions and physical space. Norms are the shared rules or standards to guide how students' behaviour should be and how members must behave, interact, and collaborate in a group. This helps in building trust, respect, comfort and understanding to establish a safe environment for sharing ideas (Sperry et al., 2025). Expectations are the outcomes and contributions of the members of a group for example, finishing assigned tasks on time and supporting, helping team members when needed. These norms and expectations are helpful to reduce misunderstandings, minimize conflicts, and keep the group organized and focused on its goals. Functional norms, such as inconsistent behaviour in virtual meetings, disturb team functioning. Clarity in creating norms and expectations when forming a group is a powerful strategy to improve coordination, enhance communication, and ensure team success.

5.3 Building Inclusivity and Diversity in Groups

In todays connected world, organizations and educational institutions are required to encourage in creating group and promote inclusivity. In online education, both students and faculty are from different countries, creating opportunities for cross-cultural learning and collaboration. So, a systematic approach is needed for developing leadership and foster inclusive environments. Diversity in groups represents to the differences in gender, age, culture, socioeconomic background, education, and skills in a group. New advanced technologies have now reshaped individuals learning and working culture. Virtual and online platforms have eliminated geographical boundaries, allowing learners and participants to connect and collaborate with others around the world. It plays avital role in innovation and long-term success. Students in diverse teams have multiple advantages like the students have different cultures, perspectives, experiences, and ideas, which help in improving creativity, problem-solving, and decision-making, whereas inclusivity ensures that every participant feels respected and their ideas are valued, and they are empowered to contribute meaningfully. (Eden et al., 2024). By this not only, strengthen collaboration but also overall performance. Ultimately, inclusivity and diversity transform organizational and educational culture to be more innovative and more sustainable.

6 CHALLENGES IN VIRTUAL GROUP DYNAMICS

Though virtual group dynamics in learning improves globally and brings flexibility, openness in online learning despite of these it also faces many challenges and the major challenges.

6.1 Communication Barrier

when communication is effective and smooth it serves as a foundational element for both learning and teaching in traditional and modern online educational settings. online teachings mainly depend on technology and virtual interaction, which often creates barriers for smooth communication.

6.2 Time Zone Differences

One of the major problems in online environments is time zone differences. Virtual and hybrid learning environments affect student and instructor communication because of participation barriers the students and instructors are from different places and there is a problem in time zone difference. This situation creates difficulties in scheduling live sessions, group discussions, or meetings, this results in delays in responses and reduces collaboration. For example, a student in India may have to attend classes at midnight if the instructor is in the United States, which impacts negatively on engagement and learning effectiveness.

6.3 Technological Limitations

Students and instructors from different countries in one platform face many technological issues like high-speed internet, updated devices, or essential software. Poor internet connectivity makes interruptions, due to these students miss the formation when the connection is lost or feel incomplete participation. And also, technical issues like audio disturbance issues, login failures because of poor digital connections, and frozen video effects shows overall effectiveness on communication.

which leads to misunderstandings, reduced participation, and feelings of isolation, for leaners which can negatively impact the overall learning experience.

6.4 Motivational and Engagement Issues

In online learning students are left independently without the presence of a teacher, so they must be responsible and self-disciplined and need time management, unlike traditional classrooms where there is an instructor who provides a structure, guidance, and encouragement. Students feel low motivation without the presence of teachers or peers, and distractions at home and a lack of direct supervision and less interaction make it difficult for many learners to stay focused and committed to their studies (Mulenga & Shilongo, 2025). Not only students' instructors also need to learn new technologies and undergo training to make online learning students interested in the classroom and actively participate in assignments and teamwork and keep motivated themselves Without face-to-face interactions with other students, the absence of shared physical space can feel isolating; asynchronous classrooms can create engagement issues, which may lead some students to drop out.

6.5 Socioeconomic Challenges

In online learning, students may face challenges like difficulty grasping their instructors' viewpoints and peers' shared understanding (Hu, et al., 2025). and the other side of the behavioural aspect, students may struggle in active interactions with other students and on the emotional part, some students experience socio-emotional conflicts with group members.

6.6 Conflict Resolution in Virtual Learning

Virtual learning conflicts occur due to a lack of non-verbal cues like facial expressions, misinterpretations, and communication barriers, cultural diversity and a reduction of social presence increase the chance of misleading messages that are misread, misunderstood, and this may hurt the feelings of participants in the virtual classroom. Conflict management is not about avoiding conflicts but about how effectively participants manage conflicts without negative aspects, minimising the drawbacks and enhancing its productive value. Implementing interactive learning strategies and the need for continuous assessment providing a flexible path can help students in online learning, as can the use of synchronous touchpoints like short video calls or voice chats, which help in resolving miscommunication more quickly than prolonged written exchanges. Framing new norms and guidelines helps in reducing ambiguity and provides a supportive environment for effective conflict management.

designing strategies that go beyond temporal boundaries and respecting different culture back grounds, ensuring students feel valued and respected in online learning environments, is another aspect (Andrin et al., 2024).

7 FACILITATING COLLABORATIVE LEARNING

Providing a right environment, guidance, and support to students where they can freely share knowledge, ideas, and resources so that students can efficiently work together to achieve goals.

7.1 Importance of Collaborative Learning

Collaboration with other students and critical thinking are the two competencies that higher education aims to in still in students. Even when students are separated by time zones and cultural backgrounds, technology helps them to stay connected to each other by offering different virtual tools like online forums, shared documents, and video calls, which enhances and enables open communication and builds teamwork across boundaries.

Collaborative learning activities such as projects, group discussions, and case studies improves the analytical thinking abilities and helps in encourage knowledge sharing, accountability, and provides a sense of responsibility among students. Facilitation like monitoring group dynamics, resolving conflicts arised within the group, and ensuring that students feel continuously supported, encouraged, and motivated to be productive in online learning. The instructor's role involves designing group tasks, setting clear guidance, establishing expectations for the group, and providing online tools that enable meaningful student engagement.

7.2 Techniques for Enhancing Collaboration

For enhancing collaboration in online education needs some technical tools and strategies and supportive platforms for meaningful interactions between students.

Peer Review and Feedback

Peer review in team-based learning plays a vital role in fostering the development of both individuals and groups. It has three main purpose to encourage critical reflection on individual behaviours (Annette et al., 2021). To develop professional skills and communicational skills in giving and receiving feedback and encourage their teamwork behaviours with their comments in collaborative learning, students are accountable for their peers the process and reviews become a key factor in their success (Annette, et al., 2021). The framework for peers involves students evaluating their teammates' contributions by assigning scores to assess group harmony and enhance productivity, rather than focusing on individual knowledge.

Project-Based Learning

Project-Based Learning is a structured approach in which students are involved and addresses the real-world, complex problems through live projects. it emphasizes the construction and transformation of knowledge rather than passive absorption. Essentially, two features characterize it. PBC firstly students are driven by a question that motivates and organise learning activities. And the second is solution to the problem, which is visible or tangible product outcomes (Chen & Yang, 2019). project-based learning, improves learners' important metacognitive skills like self-regulation and self-monitoring. This approach also helps them to acquire professional skills such as managing time efficiently, solving problems, making decision making, and thinking critically.

Accessing Skills

Fair assessment of individual contributions within a team-based projects is a significant challenge because of opinion-based evaluations and the unreliability of selected methods. To ensure fairness, educators have to adopt alternative assessment strategies like peer review and structured peer assessment and provide clear and potential assessment because students evaluate each other performance through qualitative feedback or numerical scores. Complementary strategies like self-assessment logs, instructor observations, individual deliverables, and process evidence further enhance accountability by providing records. (Katsenos & Pierrakeas, 2025)

8 ILLUSTRATIONS IN VARIOUS PERSPECTIVES

Successful Online Group Engagement Models: This model shows how balanced integration between the keys provides meaningful online engagement of participants. It mainly depends on encouraging group collaboration, integration, motivation, and accountability. Some of the widely used models include

Community of Inquiry model: This model is developed by Garrison, Anderson, and Archer. This model provides a theoretical foundational for online and virtual environments and explains about Cognitive presence, Social-presence, Teaching presence so that individuals interact and create a meaningful, collaborative environments.

8.1 Lesson Learned From Real-World Applications Case Analysis

An experimental study was conducted on 121 participants and 35 virtual learning groups and they found that mostly social presence is the key element which improved group cohesion, efficacy, and overall performance of students in online learning (Yoon, & Leem, 2021). These findings suggest that participants who are socially connected through online classes have stronger group bonds, build trust, and improve communication, this enhances their overall satisfaction. though there are many advantages in online learning still it lacks some advantages of traditional systems, like face-to-face interactions, sharing physical space of a class. This study shows that well-structured group tasks and opportunities for interaction can provide similar advantages of traditional education system by strengthening social presence. This research highlighted the importance of designing and framing norms in virtual platforms with features like collaboration and active engagement. Group bonding in an online learning environment allows sufficient time to the students for peer-to-peer interactions and also it has shown theoretical and practical insights to enhance social presence in virtual environments (Yoon, & Leem, 2021).

A Study was conducted in Japanese university students to understand how social interaction during online classes influenced learning engagement and self-study in 2020 and 2021 (Gherghel et al., 2023). Here the study has shown that providing opportunities for social interaction in online classes would enhance students' emotional engagement with learning. In the first batch of 2020, they introduced online learning during the covid-19 pandemic; however, few students participated in social interactions outside of class. while findings show that emotional engagement with learning was higher in 2021 when compared to 2020. The students from 2021 were already familiar with online learning from their high school experience, which helped them adapt and enjoy online courses more. Research concludes that satisfaction with online learning tends to be greater when campuses are partially open compared to when they are fully closed (Gherghel et al., 2023).

8.2 Innovative Practices from Educators

It refers to strategies that go beyond traditional teaching methods, aiming to improve student skills, engagement in online learning, and support for diverse learners so that students can upgrade to the modern world and these approaches can create dynamic learning environments. Innovative practices include

Providing interactive lessons that involve group discussions among students or assigning projects to make lessons more hands-on. Tools in online education to

Gamification: using gaming elements in non-gaming contexts in education, like point badges or leaderboards, to increase motivation.

Blended and flipped learning: Combination of online learning with face-to-face sessions.

Personalized learning involves providing lessons and assignments tailored to individuals based on their interests and skill levels, often delivered through an online platform or one-on-one mentoring.

Use of Technology: incorporating online tools such as virtual labs, digital maps, and smart boards into online education.

9 THE FUTURE OF ONLINE GROUP DYNAMICS

The future of online environments and group dynamics is being shaped by more advancement of technology, with great evolving pedagogical models and increasing globalization of education.

9.1 Emerging Trends in Online Education

Immersive and Gamified Environments

Teams can collaborate in simulated real-world environments through Combination of Augmented reality and virtual reality with gamification. These environments provide enriched interaction data and can make group tasks more engaging and motivate the students.

Cross Culture and Global Virtual Teams Diversity as a Learning Resource

Lack of certain norms and absence of hierarchical power in online learning makes group collaboration more complicated in cross-culture. According to research studies they mainly highlight that team trust plays a critical role in enhancing collaboration by providing open discussions about mistakes and resolving the conflicts. Online virtual teams mainly depend on swift trust, which is a collective perception that helps manage uncertainty, risk, and external expectations. According to the idea of shared mental models (Yu et al., 2022) it explains that why some of team members perform better than others, when group members are sharing common goals, understanding of tasks and interactions, there is a chance that they will be able to adapt and handle challenges successfully to maintain smooth coordination opportunities and build intercultural competence, real-time teamworking skills. However, these virtual teams require intentional support in areas such as communication standards, time-zone coordination, and conflict resolution.

Blended Models and Integrated Learning Approaches

Integrated learning models are utilized in educational and faculty development programs within higher education to enhance participants' performance outcomes. It is a model that combines in -person, synchronous online, and asynchronous participation; it provides an option for students to choose how to attend, according to a Survey it indicates that nearly 68% of students prefer a mix of in-person and online classes (Dineva, 2024). Hybrid and blended learnings are interchangeable, mixed models are flexible and allow students to choose between attending classes on campus or joining virtually, offering more personalised and adaptable learning experiences. This approach combines classroom learning with online participation whereas in contrast, blended learning combines online and face-to-face instruction in a structured way.

9.2 Role of Artificial Intelligence (AI) and Big Data in Online Group Dynamics

The integration of artificial intelligence transforms the education system nowadays. Offering new possibilities and reshaping education for personalized learning, predicting student performance, and provide accuracy in constructive feedback, and promoting self-regulated learning at the same time, AI can assist in monitoring participation of students in assignments, collaboration, and contribution in group activities. Machine learning models trained on big data provide the risks related to the disengagement, dropout risk, and underperformance of students and alert instructors so intervention can be needed before failure occurs (Varma & Li, 2024).

9.3 Predictions for the Evolution of Virtual Group Dynamics

Virtual learning environments will adapt to techniques like Federated learning and privacy-preserving AI tools. Federated learning is a distributed and collaborative machine-based student's interactions in online forums from various classrooms (Hridi et al., 2025). This model aims to predict how future interactions between students might form. Federative learning incorporates techniques to personalize and train models collaboratively across multiple classrooms without needing to centralize or access raw data directly by protecting the privacy of student data (Hridi et al., 2025). It also provides valuable insights into the underlying drivers of social learning and offers a novel perspective on understanding the dynamics of virtual classrooms.

Focus on Equity, Inclusion, and Global Connections

virtual communications must adapt to effectively address cultural diversity, time zone differences, accessible technology, and inclusive norms. provide fairness and more efforts to ensure that groups are more equitable and participation is balanced.

Greater Use of Immersive Monitoring and Adaptivity in VR/XR Environments

Immersive virtual reality is an AI technology used in online platforms in this participant feel near or real experience using the devices like head-mounted displays, creating a deeply realistic experience. Immersive monitoring is the collection of data in real time on how learners are interacting while using a virtual or mixed reality environment by observing the body, movement, and physiological signals like heart rate. By tracking the indicators of overload, dynamically adjust the level or reduce the complexity (Obourdin et al., 2024).

10 DISCUSSION AND CONCLUSION

The effectiveness of virtual group dynamics in online classrooms depends not only on just technology but it is shaped by emotional, behavioural, and social involvement of students and for effective online participation, good structured course design, social scaffolding, and a balanced integration of technology is necessary. Strong interactions between instructor and student have the ability of improving group cohesion and enhance productive outcomes. As the education continuous to globalise new innovative learning methodologies are emerging and are transforming how students collaborate, solve problems and improve the creative skills in virtual group dynamics. Group formation is an important strategy in virtual group dynamics the first step includes, to establish a clear framework defining norms, and explicit objectives, group sizing plays a key role, and it deserves particular attention because it strongly influences social interaction, communication flow, participation, and individual accountability. interactive discussions, project-based learning, gamification, and personalized instruction are some of the approaches which creates flexible and adaptive learning environments supporting diverse learners. (Obourdin et al., 2024). Students feel a real time experience when they use virtual reality and the metaverse, to interact more deeply and become more motivated over time. All these advancements in technologies improve students future in which online education will be more than just a replacement for traditional classrooms rather, it will be a potent, dynamic, and networked environment that improves teamwork and prepare students for success in a technologically advanced society.

REFERENCES

Akpen, C. N., Asaolu, S., Atobatele, S., Okagbue, H., & Sampson, S. (2024). Impact of online learning on student's performance and engagement: A systematic review. *Discover Education*, *3*(1), 205. DOI: 10.1007/s44217-024-00253-0

Alnasyan, B., Basheri, M., & Alassafi, M. (2024). The power of Deep Learning techniques for predicting student performance in Virtual Learning Environments: A systematic literature review. *Computers and Education: Artificial Intelligence*, *6*, 100231. DOI: 10.1016/j.caeai.2024.100231

Andrin, G., Kilag, O. K., Groenewald, E., Benitez, J., Dagala, F., & Ubay, R. (2024). Borderless learning environments: Impacts on educational management strategies. [IMJRISE]. *International Multidisciplinary Journal of Research for Innovation, Sustainability, and Excellence*, *1*(2), 43–49.

Annette, B., Chris, R., Stuart, L., Inam, H., Tyler, C., Eszter, K., & Jane, B. (2021). Peer review in team-based learning: Influencing feedback literacy. *BMC Medical Education (Web)*, *21*(1), 1–11.

Chen, C. H., & Yang, Y. C. (2019). Revisiting the effects of project-based learning on students' academic achievement: A meta-analysis investigating moderators. *Educational Research Review*, *26*, 71–81. DOI: 10.1016/j.edurev.2018.11.001

Culduz, M. (2024). Benefits and challenges of e-learning, online education, and distance learning. In *Incorporating the human element in online teaching and learning* (pp. 1–27). IGI Global Scientific Publishing. DOI: 10.4018/979-8-3693-4131-5.ch001

Dineva, S. (2024). Hybrid, blended, and hyflex learning as future models for education. *Обучение по природни науки и върхови технологии, 33*(3-4), 152-161.

Eden, C. A., Chisom, O. N., & Adeniyi, I. S.Chima Abimbola EdenOnyebuchi Nneamaka ChisomIdowu Sulaimon Adeniyi. (2024). Online learning and community engagement: Strategies for promoting inclusivity and collaboration in education. *World Journal of Advanced Research and Reviews*, *21*(3), 232–239. DOI: 10.30574/wjarr.2024.21.3.0693

Gherghel, C., Yasuda, S., & Kita, Y. (2023). Interaction during online classes fosters engagement with learning and self-directed study both in the first and second years of the COVID-19 pandemic. *Computers & Education*, *200*, 104795. DOI: 10.1016/j.compedu.2023.104795 PMID: 37063109

Herrera-Pavo, M. Á. (2021). Collaborative learning for virtual higher education. *Learning, Culture and Social Interaction*, *28*, 100437. DOI: 10.1016/j.lcsi.2020.100437

Hridi, A. P., Hoq, M., Gao, Z., Lynch, C., Sahay, R., Hosseinalipour, S., & Akram, B. (2025). Privacy-Preserving Distributed Link Predictions Among Peers in Online Classrooms Using Federated Learning. *arXiv preprint arXiv:2504.10456.*

Hu, W., Tian, J., & Li, Y. (2025). Enhancing student engagement in online collaborative writing through a generative AI-based conversational agent. *The Internet and Higher Education, 65*, 100979. DOI: 10.1016/j.iheduc.2024.100979

Katsenos, I., & Pierrakeas, C. (2025). Assessing Individual Contributions of Team Members to Team Achievement by Combining Peer Assessments and Digital Presence in an Academic Environment. *Education Sciences, 15*(3), 279. DOI: 10.3390/educsci15030279

Lvina, E. (2025). Teaching ethics and ethical leadership with the Harvard Everest simulation. *Journal of Leadership Education, 24*(2), 213–221. DOI: 10.1108/JOLE-03-2024-0050

Mulenga, R., & Shilongo, H. (2025). Hybrid and blended learning models: Innovations, challenges, and future directions in education. *Acta Pedagogia Asiana, 4*(1), 1–13. DOI: 10.53623/apga.v4i1.495

Obourdin, G., De Maeyer, S., & Van den Bossche, P. (2024). Unlocking the power of immersive learning: The FAIRI instructional design proposition for adaptive immersive virtual reality. *Computers & Education: X Reality, 5*, 100084.

Oyarzun, B., & Martin, F. (2023). A Systematic Review of Research on Online Learner Collaboration from 2012-21: Collaboration Technologies, Design, Facilitation, and Outcomes. *Online Learning : the Official Journal of the Online Learning Consortium, 27*(1), 71–106. DOI: 10.24059/olj.v27i1.3407

Sagayadevan, V., & Jeyaraj, S. (2012). The role of Emotional Engagement in Lecturer-Student interaction and the Impact on Academic Outcomes of Student Achievement and Learning. *The Journal of Scholarship of Teaching and Learning, 12*(3), 1–30.

Saltz, J., & Heckman, R. (2020). Using structured pair activities in a distributed online breakout room. *Online Learning : the Official Journal of the Online Learning Consortium, 24*(1), 227–244. DOI: 10.24059/olj.v24i1.1632

Saqr, M., Nouri, J., & Jormanainen, I. (2019, September). A learning analytics study of the effect of group size on social dynamics and performance in online collaborative learning. In *European conference on technology enhanced learning* (pp. 466-479). Cham: Springer International Publishing.DOI: 10.1007/978-3-030-29736-7_35

Sperry, M. P., Aldana, A. J., O'Neill, T. A., Mimovic, A., Gibson, C. B., & McLarnon, M. J. (2025). Hybrid and remote team chartering: Creating clarity in an increasingly virtual world. *Organizational Dynamics, 101172*(4), 101172. Advance online publication. DOI: 10.1016/j.orgdyn.2025.101172

Srivastava, S. (2025). Collaborative Learning in Digital Environment.

Taniguchi, Y., Gao, Y., Kojima, K., & Konomi, S. I. (2018, May). Evaluating learning style-based grouping strategies in real-world collaborative learning environment. In *International Conference on Distributed, Ambient, and Pervasive Interactions* (pp. 227-239). Cham: Springer International Publishing. DOI: 10.1007/978-3-319-91131-1_18

Vaarma, M., & Li, H. (2024). Predicting student dropouts with machine learning: An empirical study in Finnish higher education. *Technology in Society*, *76*, 102474. DOI: 10.1016/j.techsoc.2024.102474

Wang, M., Jiang, L., & Luo, H. (2023). Dyads or quads? Impact of group size and learning context on collaborative learning. *Frontiers in Psychology*, *14*, 1168208. DOI: 10.3389/fpsyg.2023.1168208 PMID: 37213364

Wibowo, S., Wangid, M. N., & Firdaus, F. M. (2025). The Relevance of Vygotsky's Constructivism Learning Theory with the Differentiated Learning Primary Schools. *Journal of education and learning (EduLearn), 19*(1), 431-440

Yoon, P., & Leem, J. (2021). The influence of social presence in online classes using virtual conferencing: Relationships between group cohesion, group efficacy, and academic performance. *Sustainability (Basel)*, *13*(4), 1988. DOI: 10.3390/su13041988

Yu, X., Shen, Y., Cheng, X., & Bao, Y. (2022). How can cross-cultural virtual learning teams collaborate effectively: A longitudinal study. *Information & Management*, *59*(6), 103667. DOI: 10.1016/j.im.2022.103667

Chapter 7
Teaching Strategies for Active Engagement and Collaboration in Online Courses

P. Harini
St. Ann's College of Engineering and Technology, India

Govind Prasad Goyal
Institute of Management Studies, Noida, India

V. Karthi
KSR College of Engineering, India

Rajib Mandal
http://orcid.org/0009-0009-7441-4509
Assam Down Town University, India

Hemkant Nivrutti Gawade
http://orcid.org/0009-0004-0994-5905
CSM's Arts and Commerce College, Chakan, India

Mohd Asif Shah
Kardan University, Afghanistan

V. Bhoopathy
http://orcid.org/0000-0003-2175-6328
Sree Rama Engineering College, India

ABSTRACT

The digital transformation of education has redefined the way learners engage with content, instructors, and peers in virtual classrooms. Engagement and collaboration are pivotal in ensuring knowledge retention, learner satisfaction, and academic achievement in online learning environments. This chapter explores the dimensions of online engagement behavioral, cognitive, and emotional and examines the role of group collaboration in fostering active participation, critical thinking, and social interaction. It highlights the pedagogical models, technological tools, and instructional strategies that enhance collaborative learning while addressing the challenges

DOI: 10.4018/979-8-2600-0934-5.ch007

of virtual teamwork. Practical insights and case studies illustrate best practices for promoting inclusivity, motivation, and equal participation. The chapter concludes by discussing future directions in online engagement, including the integration of artificial intelligence, learning analytics, and immersive technologies, to create more personalized and interactive digital classrooms.

1. INTRODUCTION

It is important for educators to continue looking for ways to make online learning more meaningful, as more than a quarter of college students already take classes online and that figure is expected to grow. By going beyond content-oriented online delivery and establishing a supportive learning environment that is attentive to student needs, educators can help encourage positive outcomes discovered that online learning pleasure and quality are greatly influenced by instructors who foster a feeling of community and student participation. Student participation and classroom community go hand in hand. Online learning, with its emphasis on higher-order thinking and knowledge creation, is more likely to succeed when students experience a sense of psychological proximity and connection rather than isolation (Young & Bruce, 2021). It found that online CL experiences can boost involvement and connection through improved critical thinking, shared reflections, and useful feedback among peers in a relatively safe environment of anonymity.

All agree that long-term online discussions can pave the way for a welcoming classroom environment where students of all backgrounds can participate respectfully and thoughtfully. Collaboration amongst online students allows for the exchange of personal experiences, viewpoints, and ideas, which can lead to a deeper knowledge, higher-order thinking, and overall personal happiness both state that online students acquire information and have meaningful learning experiences when they are part of a friendly teaching and learning community. So, this study set out to do just that, look for signs of online course community and student participation. Finding out how teachers might foster a more welcoming and interactive learning environment for their students online was a primary focus of the research team. It also tested the hypothesis that students majoring in the helping professions (health sciences and education) would experience a more robust sense of community and engagement in the classroom than students majoring in any other discipline (Alrashidi et al., 2020).

2. UNDERSTANDING ONLINE CLASSROOM ENGAGEMENT

The multi-faceted concept of student engagement has been the subject of numerous studies. Over the past seven decades, researchers have delved deep into the construct, and what they have found presents a quite diverse picture in terms of terminology, meanings, and scope. School engagement, study engagement, and student course engagement are only a few of the words and areas of coverage that engagement has been supplied by different scholars (Martin & Bolliger, 2018).

Table 1. Examples of different definitions and terminology for engagement

Name of the Construct	Definition
Engagement for Study	A favourable and satisfying mental state associated with studying, marked by focus, energy, and commitment.
Engagement	The ambient emotional states of a learner and his level of effort, action, and persistence in homework.
School-Based Student Engagement	The degree to which a learner takes part in both extracurricular and academic school activities, as well as how much they value the results of their schoolwork.
Engagement for Educational	The mental effort required to fully internalise and use the information and abilities provided by formal education programs.
Student Engagement	The recognition at school, engagement with the institutional setting, and beginning of actions to attain a goal.
Engagement	Whether or not a student takes part in both academic and extracurricular activities, and whether or not they understand and appreciate the significance of their educational objectives.

Table 1 displays a selection of engagement terms and their definitions, as previously stated. Although the criteria used by the researchers differ, there are certain commonalities that have been identified.

However, a more comprehensive definition of the concept has been put forth by (Reimann, 2024). This definition draws on the previous ones and places greater emphasis on students' engagement, dedication, investment, and sense of belonging to school and educational pursuits. It while several words and definitions have been proposed, engagement is generally understood as an optimistic and proactive term that describes the extent to which students are involved, invested, committed, and identified with their school and its activities, all of which contribute to their academic success.

2.1 Aspects of Engagement

Despite the wide variety of perspectives on what constitutes student engagement, experts agree that it is multi-faceted and includes a variety of components (e.g., behavioural, cognitive, and emotional) that collectively represent a constructive attitude towards learning on the part of students. Nevertheless, there has been persistent disagreement among academics over the kinds and quantity of involvement dimensions. Specifically, although defined two components of involvement, behavioral and psychological conceptualised engagement as having three dimensions i.e., vigour, devotion, and absorption. That scholars' models for the construct vary in the number and types of dimensions they suggest.

2.2 Model of Engagement

The research on involvement was reviewed by who characterised engagement as a complex, evolving, and multi-faceted concept with three main parts: behavioural, cognitive, and emotional. The authors claim that the dimensions are not separate but rather have relationships with one another (Chandrasekar, 2025).

2.2.1 Cognitive Engagement

Student investment in learning is reflected in the cognitive engagement dimension, which includes traits like self-regulation, challenge preference, and readiness to put in the work needed to understand and master challenging tasks. Appropriate learning strategies, such as elaboration rather than memorisation, are also part of this dimension. Use of learning methods (such as linking new information to old information) and self-regulation to enhance learning are indicators of cognitive engagement. Other indicators include asking questions to clarify ideas, persisting in challenging activities, being flexible when solving problems, and using these skills (Ramya, 2023).

2.2.2 Emotional Engagement

Emotional engagement has been defined in several ways by scholars. Some have argued that it is motivating while others have argued that it is psychological or affective. Nonetheless, according to all of these words characterise aspects of emotional engagement that students have, which include both positive and negative feelings towards their instructors, peers, academic assignments, and the school as a whole. Some of the signs that are part of it are when people are interested and happy, and when they are not bored, anxious, or depressed. The kids who are emotionally engaged in their school have a sense of belonging, value the school's outcomes, and believe that they have the support of their instructors and classmates (Bacon, 2023).

2.2.3 Behavioral Engagement

It was determined to be an important factor mediating the dropout process; there are three generally used techniques to define behavioural engagement: The first approach is based on good behaviour, which includes things like not being disruptive (such being bothersome or skipping school) and obeying the rules and classroom norms the second way is related to academic participation and includes behaviours like asking questions, paying attention, concentrating, showing persistence, and putting forth effort. The third and last method is to be involved in school-related activities, such as sports and school governance. Truancy, absence, preparation for school, attendance, involvement in extracurricular and curricular activities, and referrals for discipline are all important indicators of behavioural engagement, which is a directly observable aspect of engagement (Pentaraki & Laureate, 2019).

2.3 Model of Engagement

There are three characteristics of an engaged student, as described by (Chakraborty, 2017): absorption, vigour, and dedication, which together make for a satisfying and good mental state of mind during studying. One new development in the definition of engagement is its expansion to encompass academic involvement as well as engagement in one's job. It viewed the activities and tasks that students engage in to be work from a psychological perspective. Just like an employee, a student is expected to follow a strict schedule and complete several assignments and projects in order to achieve a certain goal, such as passing exams or acquiring a job. It is appropriate to apply the concept of involvement to the study context because educational spaces are settings in which students work. In the same way as students' sentiments of vitality, devotion, and concentration in academic-related activities and tasks describe job engagement, so too do students' experiences of study engagement. Students' vigour, the first dimension, is defined as their mental resilience and energy levels when studying, their eagerness to put in effort and persevere through challenges, and their optimistic attitude towards learning. Students' perspectives of school-related activities as important and their feelings of excitement, inspiration, significance, challenge, and pride for participating in their studies make up the second dimension, devotion. It has absorption which is characterised as a state of complete and total focus on one's academic work. Although distinct concepts, the aforementioned three aspects of involvement correlate strongly with one another (Suharti et al., 2021).

2.4 Comparison of Engagement Models

The two models that evaluate students' engagement in the classroom both stress the importance of students' involvement in the classroom and its correlation to their academic performance. According to our analysis of the relevant literature, there are certain key parallels and variations between the two models' conceptualisations. The key points of agreement and disagreement between the two models are outlined in the paragraphs that follow.

Some commonalities have been noted by researchers, even though the two conceptualisations differ. The two models' definitions of engagement's multidimensional components include, for instance, pupils' resilience, effort willingness, persistence, challenge preference, and positive attitude towards learning. Furthermore, students' cognitive engagement encompasses factors like their interest in school-related activities and their readiness to learn. This aligns with the enthusiasm and inspiration found in the dedication dimension as described by (Bergdahl, 2022). In addition, the emotional dimension components of vigour, as described include a positive attitude towards school-related activities. This is similar to the model put forth which has been supported by research. Similar to how the behavioural dimension and involvement in learning in the model describe a student's performance in terms of behaviour and total concentration on study-related activities also describes this.

3. FRAMEWORK OF ENGAGEMENT STRATEGIES

Engagement and interaction are practically synonyms; they mean the same thing. Fostering interaction is crucial in online learning because it develops student interest. Developed a framework to guarantee student involvement based on a review of studies in the setting of higher education:

The Seven Golden Rules for Effective Methods for First-Year College Students. One of the seven guiding principles of this approach is that students pay closer attention when teachers

- Make greater eye contact with them and faculty
- Gives students chances to collaborate
- Promotes active learning strategies
- Gives students timely feedback on their progress
- Makes them devote quality time to academic tasks
- Sets high standards for acceptable work
- Deals with various learner needs

The seven principles were originally suggested for use in traditional classrooms, although many of them are as applicable to online learning (Berges et al., 2021).

Figure 1. Kinds of interactions according to Moore's Model

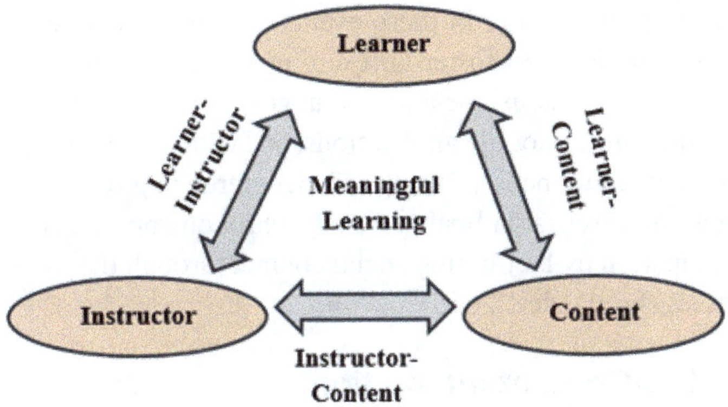

Figure 1 shows the framework that this study was based on effective online courses include three forms of interaction between students and one another; between students and one's instructor; and between students and the course material.

3.1 Interaction Between Learner and Instructor

Online course participation is better when students may communicate with their teachers. Student involvement may be significantly correlated with the use of various channels for communication between instructors and students. Because of the potential impact on learning outcomes, it is advised that online teachers give careful consideration to student-instructor interactions. According to the authors, students are more likely to actively participate in class and achieve better results when teachers and students work together in a cohesive and dynamic setting that provides opportunities for group projects and constructive criticism. To maximise the effectiveness of online instruction, students should have opportunities to engage with instructors and peers about what they find significant about their learning, rather than only contacting them about assignments, course materials, or grades. Further, instructors' physical presence is necessary for online courses to engage students (Hastomo & Septiyana, 2022). However, when courses are intentionally designed to encourage student engagement, instructors should remain passive in class discussions.

3.2 Peer-to-Peer Interaction

Interactions between students are a great way to keep them engaged and make the most of online learning. Building activities that boost engagement is vital to preventing online students from experiencing boredom and isolation in the learning environment. By participating in these events, students are able to form stronger bonds with one another and foster an exciting sense of community. To enhance participation in online classes, the authors suggest utilising web-based applications like Collaboration Suite, Google applications, or Twitter feeds. To improve student-to-student contact recommend utilising videoconferencing or chatting for synchronous activities and discussion boards for asynchronous ones. There is a chance to increase participation by facilitating social contact through the use of social media in online classes (Fernández, 2018).

3.3 Student-to-Content Interaction

Interacting intellectually with the material is call learner-to-content engagement, and it has the potential to alter how it sees the world and what it knows. According to students can engage with instructional videos, multimedia, and search engines to access information. Online students have the option of either synchronous or asynchronous delivery, which both enable them obtain the content and engage in critical conversation. For the aim of promoting student-to-content engagement, online educators are encouraged to devote enough time to seeking out scholarly reading, interactive instructional tools, and well-planned exams. In order to increase student engagement suggest bringing the material to life through the use of suitable technology (Cavinato et al., 2021). If they want their online students to be more invested in the course, teachers should be picky about the materials they use. Instead of just handing out lists of resources, teachers in online courses can create authentic exercises that let students think about the assignments from numerous angles and use important material appropriately.

Figure 2. Model for interactivity and community processes in online distance education environments

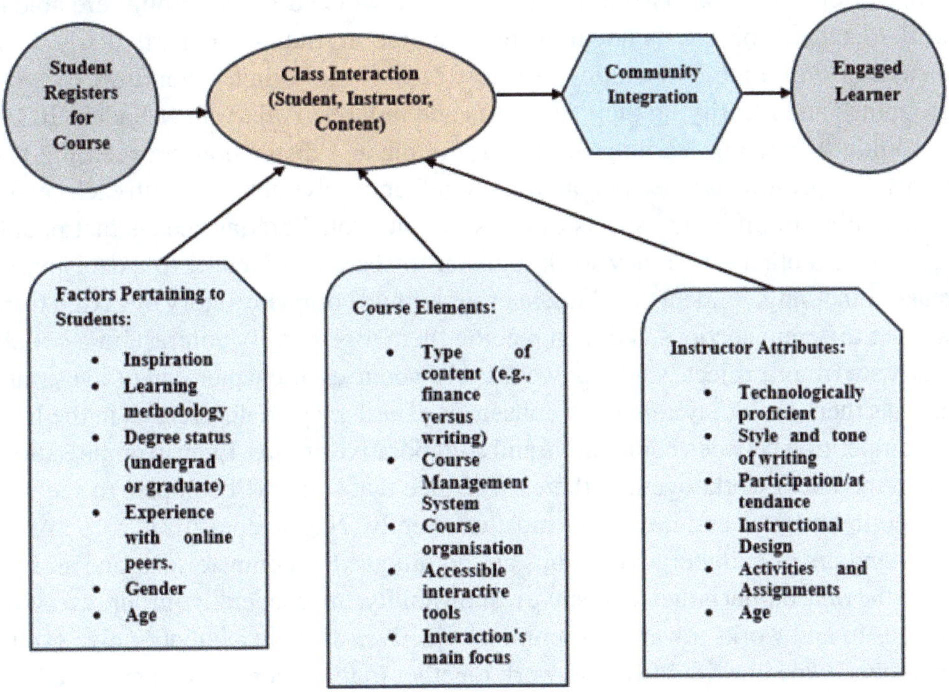

Figure 2 shows the interaction/community-process model of distance education online environments proposed which illustrates the relationship between the engaged learner, a sense of community, and online interaction. Interaction and a sense of belonging were found to be associated with students' level of involvement (Yuyun, 2023).

4. CHARACTERISTICS OF ONLINE COLLABORATION

With the rapid development of computers and networks, new channels of communication have emerged for the purpose of training and education. Asynchronous threaded conversations are one kind of CMC that allows students to ponder an issue and then brainstorm solutions with their peers. In these virtual classrooms, students can build on one another's work by reading and responding to each other's posts over time. One way to make the most of class time is to form discussion groups where students may work together to solve problems and share ideas. Over the same time period, instructors in both training and education have begun to place a greater emphasis on cooperation as an educational technique. However, teachers often put kids in groups and want them to work together, but they don't always know what cooperation is or how to foster it. The degree to which different groups are able to work together is obviously not uniform. cooperation studies, and particularly those focussing on online cooperation, are just exploring the inner workings of these groupings and identifying their successes and failures (Anjarwati & Sadah, 2021).

While discussing learning groups, some make a distinction between the two terms. Cooperation is when people work together to solve an issue, with each person contributing to different aspects of the solution. Collaborating means that people rely on each other while they work together to share ideas, come to a decision, or make something. Students working in groups could complete a story by taking turns writing different sections and then piecing them together. By contrast, in a collaborative writing project, students would talk about each chapter, share ideas, and discuss them until they came to a consensus. There may be differences in the level of competition between cooperative and collaborative groups. Even in organisations when members work together, there's a chance that some will compete to see who can complete their assigned tasks most efficiently (Nagadeepa, 2021).

Members of collaborative groups are not allowed to compete with one another since the final output is their collective responsibility. In a cooperative group, everyone pitches in and works towards a common objective, while in a collaborative group, members come up with ideas and work together to make something new. The level and type of interaction among group members are key indicators of whether or not collaboration has taken place. What interaction is not could be one way to define it. According to it is not a collection of unrelated claims, remarks, or Q&As. When people in a group continue to talk about the same issue while making reference to previous communications, either directly or indirectly, they are interacting. Contrast this with participation, which is defined as the sum of all messages sent and received by all group members, regardless of length. So, everyone can contribute to the conversation by answering questions, but only threads that stay on topic are considered active.

4.1 CMC

It's possible to classify CMC as either synchronous or asynchronous. While there is a time limit on asynchronous communications, in synchronous communications all participants are online simultaneously. Chat rooms, instant messengers, and audio/video programs all allow users to engage in real-time message exchanges; this is known as synchronous conversation. A large number of threads can run concurrently, and messages are displayed on the screen practically instantly upon typing. Anyone who has ever participated in one of these lightning-fast discussions knows that lightning-fast typing skills and reaction times are no guarantee of staying up with the ever-changing conversation. Therefore, it's possible that synchronous discussion is ideal for idea generation and rapid concept sharing. Asynchronous conversations allow students to join in whenever they like, regardless of the location or activity of other participants. Since asynchronous CMC does not rely on a predetermined timetable or instructor, all participants are able to participate to a greater extent in the discussion. Everyone has the right to express themselves freely and fully. Despite their reliance on language, these exchanges differ significantly from more conventional forms of printed information. Shorthand and emoticons (like smileys) are hallmarks of the style used by seasoned users (Chakraborty & Nafukho, 2024).

4.2 Efficiently Collaboration

The three main characteristics of a cooperative group have been outlined by several writers: interdependence information synthesis and autonomy. In this case, we operationalise the definition of collaborative discussions in CMC by using these three elements. Group dynamics shed light on the ways in which people learn by talking to one another, comparing notes, and putting theories to the test. Here, the interdependence of group members in pursuit of a common objective is crucial (Qi et al., 2023). Both the actions of individuals and the results achieved by the group are affected by this dependency. Unlike in a competitive group or a collection of individuals, when there is positive interdependence, members of the group help each other learn. No one can achieve their aim if they are not reached until the collective objective is fulfilled. Everyone in the group needs to fill up each other's knowledge gaps and add their own unique spin to the group effort. Offering, challenging, and defending knowledge and expertise, as well as compromising and concussing, are all parts of this intricate process. Interaction goes beyond just requiring everyone in the group to participate. Participants in the group discussion are required to engage in two-way communication by answering and reacting to one another (Marsha Carr, 2024).

4.3 Data Analysis for Collaborative CMC

If these three aspects make up the bulk of group work in educational contexts, how can it quantify the degree to which members of a group work together? There isn't a silver bullet that can be developed to classify groups as collaborative or non-collaborative. On the contrary, groups might be anywhere along a spectrum from extremely collaborative to barely so, and it requires metrics to compare the degrees of dependency, synthesis, and autonomy. It may then compare the groups based on the level of cooperation they display using these data. Consequently, it can experiment with different approaches to enhancing collaboration and evaluate their efficacy. A large number of online message boards also automatically record user activity when they log in, and the vast majority of web servers do the same (Dyer & Aroz, 2018). Examining these logs is the standard procedure for gauging online engagement. Dates and timings of participants' logins and logouts, message posting sequence, and thread placement are all relevant pieces of information. It can measure each student's engagement by looking at their access and message durations.

With this information, it can draw a diagram of the message threads, which could show us how the conversation was structured. What follows is an explanation and demonstration of this method. But since involvement doesn't always mean teamwork, these numbers aren't complete. A more in-depth content analysis of the written comments can be built upon this phase. Furthermore, it is possible to be led astray by analysing the student-entered and log-generated stream of messages. There is no guarantee that students will correctly sequence messages and responses. The aim is to let readers figure out the links between messages on their own, thus a response to an earlier message can be posted in a separate thread. Based on our analysis of the transcripts, it appears that the apparent connections between messages, the amount and duration of messages, and the overall structure of the interaction did not accurately reflect collaboration. Participants were talking to each other, and some of that talking was participatory, but they didn't work together very much. A number of the remarks only restated or rephrased information or ideas that had already been presented in the scenario. There was an influx of fresh data, but participants barely tried to question answers or respond to remarks. Students could use the software to start new threads for discussion or post to an existing one; however, they were not very good at using this feature, so the messages appeared to be randomly placed (Redmond et al., 2018).

5. TECHNOLOGICAL TOOLS FOR ENGAGEMENT AND COLLABORATION

The common perception of online participation is that it consists only of posting on message boards. On the other hand, engaging in meaningful conversation is what it means to truly participate. Students demonstrate their engagement by paying close attention in class, answering the teacher's questions and directions, and striking up conversations with their peers and the instructor. Researchers agree that for learning to be dynamic and engaging, learner participation is crucial. Learners are able to actively participate through the use of collaboration tools, which maintain their freedom of time and place while participating in high levels of interaction with both the teacher and other learners. One way to show how students behave while learning is to use content analysis to look at data from online chats. Star and linked interaction patterns were identified in asynchronous online talks. Centralised was the star-type interaction. In a network, one node—a student or teacher—who posed a question or topic serves as the hub, bringing together people who might otherwise remain disconnected. More participants with centrality were found in the linked web form of interaction (Martin, 2019).

Students are able to more often share, build upon, and question each other's ideas in this form of interaction. It comes to the conclusion that, although interaction can improve both teaching and learning, it must be properly cultivated in line with the course objectives and learning goals. Furthermore, contends that students expect teachers to guide their participation in class discussions rather than expecting it to naturally occur. This study used a case study approach to analyse the effects of various asynchronous discussion activity designs and facilitations on the amount, quality, timing, and nature of student engagement across nine distinct online courses. First, students were more likely to engage when teachers took an active role in class discussions. Second, students were less likely to speak out when assignments were not clearly laid out (Blumenfeld et al., 2023).

Third, students lacked confidence in their own contributions. Fourth, students were highly motivated to participate when instructors provided constructive criticism. Finally, students were more likely to speak out when grades were tied to their participation. The majority of asynchronous conferencing, according to was student-centered when the teacher made the students act as both the teacher and the participants in the discussion. Nevertheless, in order to meet the minimal course requirement, the majority of students only posted one message per week. This online conversation was mostly a necessity for the course, and the majority of students did not make heavy use of the conferencing facility. It looked examined the correlation between the amount of Blackboard discussion posts made by graduate students—a measure of their cognitive, social, and emotional presence online—and their final course scores. In this study, participants worked together using various online tools such as discussion boards, live chat, email, and profiles. There was a robust association found, indicating that students who were more visible in the classroom fared better than those who were less active in real time (Rotgans & Schmidt, 2023).

Contrarily, discovered that students' achievement was not best predicted by the amount of discussion posts they made, even while students' achievement was lowest for those with the fewest. But thought that students' performance may have suffered because they weren't as invested in their online education due to the lack of asynchronous postings. The absence of continuity is one drawback of asynchronous computer-mediated communication. It found that students were frequently irritated when other members of the group did not participate or participated very infrequently (Carini, Kuh, 2018). Who coined the term login-lags to describe this phenomenon, it often leads to team members becoming confused and unhappy. Compared to synchronous mode, students engaged in task-oriented interaction more frequently in asynchronous talks. Students using asynchronous communication modes provided more information than simply asking questions, in contrast to the more spontaneous and frequent interactions seen in synchronous communication modes. In a similar found that students were able to concentrate better on collaborative writing during asynchronous sessions as opposed to synchronous ones (Lingam, 2022).

The quantity, pattern, and emphasis of student-teacher and peer-to-peer communication was the primary focus of this study, which also evaluated students' perspectives on the merits of each setting. When people were able to talk about new things in real time without having to wait for others to respond, the level of interaction was higher. Although students spent less time chatting in asynchronous sessions, they spent more time exploring ideas and more time giving evidence to back up other students' original claims. When contrasted with synchronous interaction, the asynchronous one yielded better result. Research by and others supports this idea, finding that group discussions conducted via asynchronous collaboration tools like email and discussion forums are more productive, focused, and serious than those conducted through synchronous tools like online chat. In a study conducted the class that relied solely on asynchronous communication had much higher levels of involvement compared to the one that also used instant messaging. In contrast, students whose classes made use of the instant messaging system were more actively involved in class discussions and projects than those whose classes did not utilise the technology (Chi et al., 2018).

Thus, the results could not be deemed definitive. A lot of studies have shown that students are more engaged in online classes when teachers use a mix of synchronous and asynchronous communication tools. Streaming videoconferences to big audiences and increasing engagement through chat is theoretically achievable by (Huang et al., 2022). The participants were able to interact with the conference panellists and each other through real-time synchronous chat due to a webcast multipoint video-conference. The whole thing took place online, via videoconference, livestream, and chat. A combination of asynchronous and synchronous online chats can maximise personal participation by (Barbara. & Miller, 2023). Participants who made use of both forms of contact were also more likely to finish all of the course requirements, according to this research.

6. STRATEGIES TO CONNECT TO STUDENTS IN A CLASS ROOM

People learn from their experiences and think about those things afterwards, according to Piaget's schooling and the Constructivist approach. One name for this approach to education is invisible pedagogy and it revolves around the student. Learning methodologies like Montessori and Steiner, as well as project and inquiry-based learning, are all part of this approach. Physical education and other types of advanced cognitive learning for older students are both encompassed under constructivism's theoretical framework, which investigates the role of instructors in creating learning activities the pupils. Additionally, this method also discusses how to hold a lesson outside and encourage students to engage with nature in order to create an environment that is different from the typical classroom. A pedagogical approach proposed by social constructivism integrates aspects of both student-centered and teacher-guided learning. Educators should engage students in various forms of interaction, processes, models, and questioning; an effective pedagogical method includes a two-way flow of information and understanding between students and instructors through interactive discourse. There are a number of approaches to learning that involve technology, including high technology and low technology. Behaviourism is centred around the instructor; constructivism is around the students (Taylor & Statler, 2024).

Step 1: Connecting with Students' Prior Knowledge.

Teachers have found success using strategies like concept maps, KWL charts, anticipation guides, and brainstorming sessions to gain insight into and build upon students' prior knowledge. Students' prior knowledge is the information they already know and have mastered before they learn anything new. Fresh instructional content builds on students' pre-existing knowledge and educational foundation. Students' prior knowledge is crucial for learning new things and for making connections between their past and present training. This technique builds on students' prior knowledge to help them understand new content and to allow teachers to collect formative assessment data to adjust lessons based on student performance (Dubovi, 2022).

Step 2: Conform to Learning Outcomes.

Aligning courses with clear and unambiguous learning objectives that explain what students should know and be able to do at the end of the unit is one way for teachers to make learning relevant in any classroom, especially one that is technology challenged. Backward design, rubrics, and success criteria are popular strategies for aligning learning objectives and are used to efficiently plan and evaluate education. The Curriculum creation, instruction, and assessment are three separate yet complementary areas. Rubrics outline the criteria that will be used to score student work. They provide a clear definition of the standards that distinguish between various levels of quality or performance. Typical rubrics include a set of criteria and ratings for performance (such as Excellent, Good, Very Good, and Poor). Teachers can use rubrics to evaluate student work in a fair and systematic way (Codispoti et al., 2023).

Figure 3. Backward design methodologies

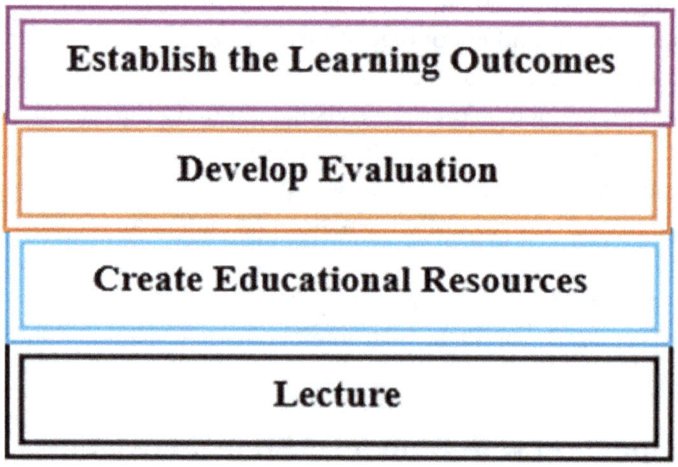

Figure 3 shows as starting with the end goal in mind is where the backward design framework for lesson planning gets its start. Before beginning their work with students, educators set clear goals and outcomes for their learning. Working backwards from those goals, they develop evaluations and pedagogical approaches that support them. In most cases, there are three steps to the process: Ascertain the Results of the Education: Specify what it is that students need to know and be able to do anticipated to have learnt and be able to use by the lesson's end (Marci, 2024).

Step 3: Task-Based Active Student Engagement.

There has been a shift in focus towards the importance of engagement and how it might improve learning, retention, and motivation among students. The cognitive, emotive, and behavioural aspects of student engagement must be considered together in order to fully comprehend it. A teacher's course design, syllabus, activities, material, and assessment procedures have a significant influence on their students' thoughts, feelings, and actions.

Emotional engagement is the level of participation and involvement that students show during the course. Apathy, confusion, anxiety, excitement, and anticipation are all possible feelings that could accompany this. Listening to podcasts, doing hobbies, or watching TV are all examples of activities that people are more inclined to put in time and energy into if they find them interesting or enjoyable. In addition to boosting the student's self-efficacy and encouraging them to persevere through obstacles, a positive emotional investment can do the same (Greene et al., 2023).

Behavioural engagement means showing how invested you are emotionally and mentally. Teachers who are good at what they do pay attention to student body language, which includes things like grins and nods of agreement as well as displays of uncertainty, note-taking, and questions and answers given by volunteers. Task completion time is one piece of supplementary data. However, the level and diversity of student involvement may be under-represented by these physical actions. Students' level of participation may be more accurately assessed if appropriate active learning tactics were implemented punctually throughout the session.

Students show cognitive engagement when they complete challenging problems, use thinking skills outlined by Bloom's Taxonomy, and use learning tactics including reviewing material and participating in question-and-answer sessions. Students demonstrate intellectual engagement when they ask questions, provide examples, or seek clarification. By this stage, students have started to internalise the knowledge, skills, and mindsets that have been taught to them (Brinck & Reddy, 2020).

Step 4: Revamping Assessment Methodologies to Promote Reflection.

Producing learners who can work independently is the end goal of education. This is especially important in the twenty-first century, a time of rapid technological development, when skills need to be constantly relearnt. Learners who are able to direct themselves carry out tasks and projects efficiently and without supervision. A wide variety of resources and tools are within their capabilities. By taking measured risks and learning from their mistakes, they achieve great success. Scholarly works suggest that encouraging students to take an active role in their own learning in the classroom might help them develop traits like curiosity, openness to trying new things, and a growth mindset course of education (Yen et al., 2018).

The use of reflection and feedback allows students to assess their own learning, pinpoint areas of strength and improvement, set goals for personal growth, and celebrate progress. Incorporate strategies like exit permits, portfolios, self-evaluation, and peer-evaluation to promote reflection and feedback. Some assessment practises drive students' attention just towards the immediate test, while others purposefully hinder certain forms of learning, often by removing the evaluation of specific essential skills and knowledge from assessment tasks. Prioritising assessment evaluation based on its impact on student learning and then considering its efficacy as a measure of performance should be everyone's goal. It is highly unlikely that a classroom setting would be an appropriate setting for an assessment that has negative impacts on student learning (Basilio, 2023).

7. CASE STUDIES AND BEST PRACTICES

7.1 Case Study 1: Salford University's Community Engagement

Location: The Greater Manchester campus of the University of Salford is situated in the northwest region of the United Kingdom.

Context of the Intervention: With a large number of international students, the University of Salford is committed to its goal of increasing access to higher education. Furthermore, there are a variety of nationalities represented among the personnel and students. Participation from students is fundamental to Salford's purpose. Salford acknowledges that student engagement can help offset the effects of a higher-than-average proportion of underprepared students and hopes that this will be the case for its students. It is strongly encouraged that students participate actively both in and out of class (Lawson & Lawson, 2023).

SSLA: Students at Salford University can improve their employability, personal growth, and academic performance by participating in the Student Life Award, a structured program that aims to do just that. Students are encouraged and supported to establish a portfolio of educationally purposeful activities through the SSLA, which recognises their attendance at skills development seminars and extracurricular activities (Bernstein, 2024). Part of the curriculum includes an introductory and planning session, a session on resume and cover letter writing and searching for jobs (or, alternately, starting a business) with a practical assignment, and the creation of a portfolio showcasing a variety of talents, such as:

Managing a student organisation
Serving as a student or community representative
Participating in a student-run volunteer program (such as SIFE)
Giving back to the community through volunteer work
Becoming an active member of the International Society
Mentoring other students
Representing the university as a student ambassador

Leading campus tours

They also attend seminars to acquire the skills they've recognised as lacking, such as those related to postgraduate research, computer/information literacy, study skills, entrepreneurship/employability, foreign language, or career management. As a culminating activity in their Award Programme, students reflect on and present their involvement activities (Brunton et al., 2019).

7.2 Case Study 2: Using Creative Space at the University of Bedfordshire's Bridges CETL in the UK

Location: Located at the University of Bedfordshire in Luton, UK, the Bridges Centre for Excellence in Teaching and Learning (CETL) was established to assist undergraduates with their Personal, Career, and Professional Development (2008, 271). The role of an e Bridges is not ideal, but it does aim to bridge the gap between students' time at university and their lives after graduation, helping them adjust to life in the workforce and providing them with new chances.

It is defined by its physical features, such as its writable walls, technology, and versatile layout; it also has a private ambiance with few outside interruptions due to its isolated position and lack of windows. The technology enables anonymous brainstorming, which is supported by facilitation techniques that inspire creative thought while capturing practical consequences. The mode of use is built on collaboration and cooperation (Pittaway, 2023).

7.3 Case Study 2: Research-Informed Pedagogy at the University of Central Lancashire, United Kingdom

Location: Located in the Learning Development Unit at the University of Central Lancashire in the UK is the Centre for Research-Informed Teaching. Its headquarters are in Preston.

Context of the Intervention: The teaching-research nexus at the University of Central Lancashire is explored, supported, and promoted via a range of programs managed by the Centre for Research-informed Teaching, which was created in 2007. Using a definition of research that encompasses traditional, discipline-based, practice-as-research, applied, and pedagogic research, the Centre seeks to support and encourage the link between research and teaching, provide undergraduates with research experience, and promote pedagogic research (Venkatesan, 2024).

Participation in educationally meaningful activities is the foundation of student engagement, which is based on the constructionist principle. For learning to take place as a co-construction of knowledge, students must actively participate in research rather than only receiving it or watching it.

Universities have been trying to figure out how to best position themselves and their missions in relation to research and teaching in recent years. They want to make the most of their resources, which include the orientations and specialisms of their staff and the unique characteristics of their student body. They want to make sure they take advantage of every opportunity to improve employment, ease funding, and attendance. Academics at UCL an have been able to approach their teaching, research, and students with more awareness because to the pela its frameworks developed by CRIT. These frameworks highlight the importance of students as active participants in a community where knowledge is created and learnt (Ahshan, 2021).

7.4 Case Study 4: Developing Inclusive Curricula in Higher Education to Engage Students with Disabilities at Learn Higher CETL, Worcester, UK

Location: The Project, Development of International Curriculum for Higher Education, also known as the Leadership for All-Leadership of the Leadership Highest Council for Excellence in Teaching and Learning (CETL), was held at the University of Wales, UK. In order to improve student learning, Learn Higher (2010(a)) is a partnership of sixteen universities headed by Liverpool Hope University. The goal is to provide students with high-quality resources to help them develop their learning skills, and to conduct practice-led research to determine how to make the most of those resources. Enhancing students' academic practices to maximise their advantage from higher education and beyond is the emphasis of Learning Development (Alvarez-Milán et al., 2018).

Figure 4. Appreciative inquiry roadmap

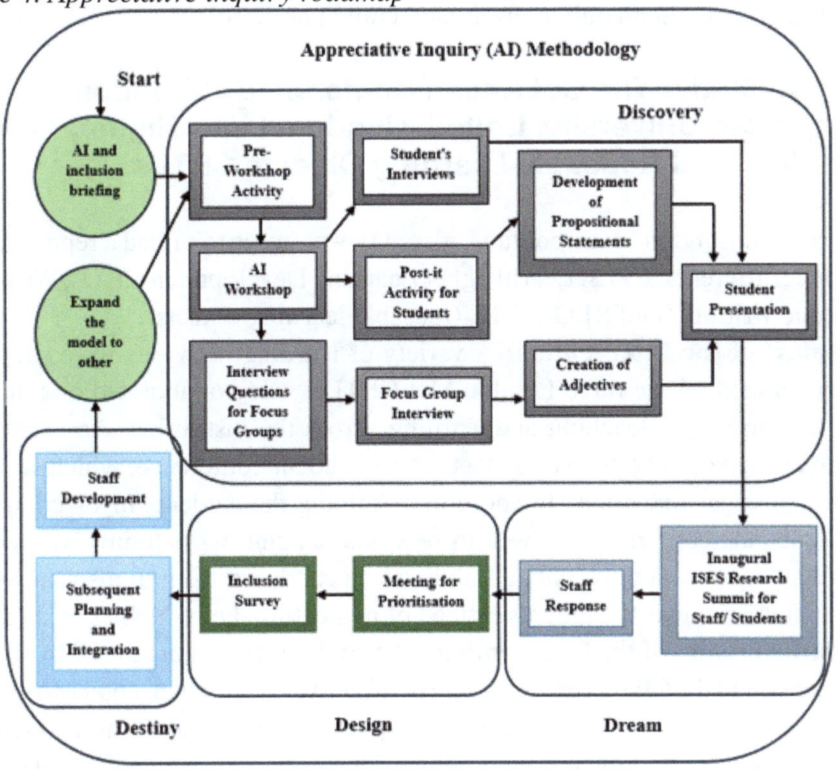

Figure 4 shows as worldwide organisations and communities have benefited from Cooperrider's Appreciative Enquiry approach, which he created in the 1980s. One thing that sets it apart is that it is conducted in four stages and solely focusses on the positive. It asks positive questions and looks at potential instead of problems.

7.5 Case Study 6: Establishing a Virtual Community at the University of Gloucestershire, UK

Location: This case study is part of an introductory management curriculum for community development majors at the University of Gloucestershire (Gloucester and Cheltenham) undergraduate program.

Context of the Intervention: Opportunities for student learning are lost when students opt out of actively participating in a community of practice. Therefore, in order to get students involved early on, teachers should create interesting online debates. Students must actively engage in the online conversations if they want to get the most out of the course. It is crucial to encourage student participation in online communities at the beginning of the course because two of the final projects in the first-year demand online discussion (Jull et al., 2019).

7.6 Case Study: The Get Ahead Conference at London Metropolitan University, United Kingdom LearnHigher, Write Now, and Reusable Learning Objects CETLs

Location: London Metropolitan University was home to or had a representative from three different CETLs: LearnHigher Learning Development CETL, Write Now (academic writing), and RLO-CETL (reusable learning objects).

Context of the Intervention: A variety of learning activities were supported and encouraged by the three London Met CETLs, who collaborated on a number of projects to propel teaching and learning across the institution. An example of such an event would be the yearly Get Ahead student conference, which served to inspire and engage students. In addition to helping the students involved grow as individuals, the conference showcases new and exciting ways to involve students, which academics and university administration can learn from. It also shows how beneficial it is to involve students instead of neglecting them (Nobles et al., 2018).

Characteristics of the Intervention: The conference was organised by students for students, and the CETLs provided logistical help by way of loan goods. Collaboration sessions encompassed more technical aspects in addition to the more traditional aspects of writing, reading, and note-taking. The writing mentors affiliated with the Write Now CETL were among the students who presented numerous sessions. The faculty at CETL provided students who lacked self-assurance or confidence in their presenting abilities with presentation techniques and encouraged them to create captivating sessions using their own voices. In certain cases, students and an academic staff member worked together to co-present the session (Luchenski et al., 2024).

8. CONCLUSION

It has offered a summary of involvement as a concept. While reviewing the literature, it paid special attention to how different studies had defined and defined the concept and how their terms and dimensions were similar and different. The North American Model of Engagement and the European Approach of Engagement are two important conceptualisations of engagement that have been briefly highlighted in this review. Both broad models have shown strong associations with students' academic performance, according to the literature reviewed here. This lends credence to the claims made by researchers argue that the idea of engagement captures students' quality of learning at the core of many models. In addition, the present longitudinal research investigations outlined in this review have shown intervention-oriented evidence that the concept is adaptable and/or developing (Thompson et al., 2021). The development of students' intrinsic motivation (such as self-efficacy) and extrinsic variables (such as teacher support) can be harnessed to increase students' initiative and performance in the classroom. The success of digital learning ecosystems depends on students actively participating in online classrooms and working together in groups. Pedagogy and personal connection are still crucial to meaningful involvement, even though technology gives the means. Teachers can build dynamic online classrooms that foster 21st-century skills and knowledge acquisition by integrating CL models, cutting-edge technology and successful pedagogical practices (Mittler et al., 2023).

REFERENCES

Ahshan, R. (2021). A framework of implementing strategies for active student engagement in remote/online teaching and learning during the covid-19 pandemic. *Education Sciences*, *11*(9), 483. Advance online publication. DOI: 10.3390/educsci11090483

Alrashidi, O., Phan, H. P., & Ngu, B. H. (2020). Academic Engagement: An Overview of Its Definitions, Dimensions, and Major Conceptualisations. *International Education Studies*, *9*(12), 41. DOI: 10.5539/ies.v9n12p41

Alvarez-Milán, A., Felix, R., Rauschnabel, P. A., & Hinsch, C. (2018). Strategic customer engagement marketing: A decision making framework. *Journal of Business Research*, *92*, 61–70. DOI: 10.1016/j.jbusres.2018.07.017

Anjarwati, R., & Sadah, L. (2021). Student learning engagement in the online class. *English Journal of Merdeka : Culture, Language, and Teaching of English*, *6*(2), 39–49. DOI: 10.26905/enjourme.v6i2.6128

Bacon. (2023). Student Engagement Case Studies Vicki Trowler and Paul Trowler Department of Educational Research University of Lancaster Deliverable 3 for the Higher Education Academy Student Engagement Project Table of Contents. *Student Engagement Case Studies. Deliverable 3 for the Higher Education Academy Student Engagement Project.*, *2023*(July), 1–33.

Barbara., & Miller, R. B. (2023). Influences on Achievement: Goals, Perceived Ability, and Cognitive Engagement. *Contemporary Educational Psychology*, *21*(2), 181–192. DOI: 10.1006/ceps.1996.0015

Basilio, O. (2023). A Strategic Engagement Framework for Nonprofits. *Online (Bergheim)*, *20*(2), 219–233. DOI: 10.1002/nml

Bergdahl, N. (2022). Engagement and disengagement in online learning. *Computers & Education*, *188*(May), 104561. DOI: 10.1016/j.compedu.2022.104561

Berges, S., Martino, S., Basko, L., & Mccabe, C. (2021). "Zooming" Into Engagement: Increasing Engagement in the Online Classroom. *Journal of Institutional Research*, *10*, 5–11.

Bernstein, S. (2024). Enhancing Provider Engagement in Practice Improvement: A Conceptual Framework DONALD. *Enhancing Provider Engagement in Practice Improvement: A Conceptual Framework DONALD*, *28*(3), 157–164. https://doi.org/ DOI: 10.1002/chp

Blumenfeld, P. C., Kempler, T. M., & Krajcik, J. S. (2023). Motivation and Cognitive Engagement in Learning Environments. In *The Cambridge Handbook of the Learning Sciences* (Issue January 2006, pp. 475–488). Cambridge University Press. DOI: 10.1017/CBO9780511816833.029

Brinck, I., & Reddy, V. (2020). Dialogue in the making: Emotional engagement with materials. *Phenomenology and the Cognitive Sciences, 19*(1), 23–45. DOI: 10.1007/s11097-019-09629-2

Brunton, G., Thomas, J., O'Mara-Eves, A., Jamal, F., Oliver, S., & Kavanagh, J. (2019). Narratives of community engagement: A systematic review-derived conceptual framework for public health interventions. *BMC Public Health, 17*(1), 1–15. DOI: 10.1186/s12889-017-4958-4 PMID: 29228932

Carini, Kuh, & K. (2018). Investigating the Multidimensionality of Engagement. *Investigating the Multidimensionality of Engagement.*

Carr, M. (2024). The unline University classroom: One perspective for effective student engagement and teaching in an online environment. *The Journal of Effective Teaching, 14*(1), 99–110. https://uncw.edu/cte/ET/articles/Vol14_1/Carr.pdf

Cavinato, A. G., Hunter, R. A., Ott, L. S., & Robinson, J. K. (2021). Promoting student interaction, engagement, and success in an online environment. *Analytical and Bioanalytical Chemistry, 413*(6), 1513–1520. DOI: 10.1007/s00216-021-03178-x PMID: 33479816

Chakraborty, M. (2017). Learner Engagement Strategies in Online Class Environment. *Learner Engagement Strategies in Online Class Environment, May*, (178 Seiten). http://gateway.proquest.com/openurl?url_ver=Z39.88-2004&rft_val_fmt=info:ofi/fmt:kev:mtx:dissertation&res_dat=xri:pqm&rft_dat=xri:pqdiss:10662429

Chakraborty, M., & Muyia Nafukho, F. (2024). Strengthening student engagement: What do students want in online courses? *European Journal of Training and Development, 38*(9), 782–802. DOI: 10.1108/EJTD-11-2013-0123

Chi, M. T. H., Adams, J., Bogusch, E. B., Bruchok, C., Kang, S., Lancaster, M., Levy, R., Li, N., McEldoon, K. L., Stump, G. S., Wylie, R., Xu, D., & Yaghmourian, D. L. (2018). Translating the ICAP Theory of Cognitive Engagement Into Practice. *Cognitive Science, 42*(6), 1777–1832. DOI: 10.1111/cogs.12626 PMID: 29954048

Codispoti, M., Mazzetti, M., & Bradley, M. M. (2023). Unmasking emotion: Exposure duration and emotional engagement. *Psychophysiology, 46*(4), 731–738. DOI: 10.1111/j.1469-8986.2009.00804.x PMID: 19386053

Dubovi, I. (2022). Cognitive and emotional engagement while learning with VR: The perspective of multimodal methodology. *Computers & Education, 183*(January), 104495. DOI: 10.1016/j.compedu.2022.104495

Dyer, T., & Aroz, J. (2018). Proximity in the Online Classroom: Engagement, Relationship and Personalization. *Journal of Institutional Research, 7*, 108–118.

Fernández, M. (2018). Student engagement in the online classroom: The student perspective. In *Decline and Revival in Higher Education* (pp. 179–211). Routledge., DOI: 10.4324/9780203793671-8

Greene, J. D., Sommerville, R. B., Nystrom, L. E., Darley, J. M., & Cohen, J. D. (2023). An fMRI investigation of emotional engagement in moral judgment. *Science, 293*(5537), 2105–2108. DOI: 10.1126/science.1062872 PMID: 11557895

Hastomo, T., & Septiyana, L. (2022). The Investigation of Students' Engagement in Online Class During Pandemic Covid-19. *Jurnal Penelitian Ilmu Pendidikan, 15*(2). Advance online publication. DOI: 10.21831/jpipfip.v15i2.49512

Huang, S. Y. B., Huang, C.-H., & Chang, T.-W. (2022). A New Concept of Work Engagement Theory in Cognitive Engagement, Emotional Engagement, and Physical Engagement. *Frontiers in Psychology, 12*(February), 1–5. DOI: 10.3389/fpsyg.2021.663440 PMID: 35242067

Jull, J. E., Davidson, L., Dungan, R., Nguyen, T., Woodward, K. P., & Graham, I. D. (2019). A review and synthesis of frameworks for engagement in health research to identify concepts of knowledge user engagement. *BMC Medical Research Methodology, 19*(1), 1–13. DOI: 10.1186/s12874-019-0838-1 PMID: 31752691

Latha R. Chandrasekar. (2025). The Impact of Collaboration Tools on Student Engagement. *The Impact of Collaboration Tools on Student Engagement.*

Lawson, M. A., & Lawson, H. A. (2023). New Conceptual Frameworks for Student Engagement Research, Policy, and Practice. In *Review of Educational Research* (Vol. 83, Issue 3). DOI: 10.3102/0034654313480891

Lingam, M. S. (2022). Measuring Cognitive Engagement: An Overview of Measurement Instruments and Techniques. *International Journal of Psychology and Educational Studies, 8*(3), 63–76. DOI: 10.52380/ijpes.2021.8.3.239

Luchenski, S. A., Amlani, A. A., Lacroix, K., Burmeister, C., & Buxton, J. A. (2024). Peer engagement in harm reduction strategies and services: A critical case study and evaluation framework from British Columbia, Canada. *BMC Public Health, 16*(1), 1–9. DOI: 10.1186/s12889-016-3136-4 PMID: 38166901

Marci, C. D. (2024). A biologically based measure of emotional engagement: Context matters. *Journal of Advertising Research, 46*(4), 381–387. DOI: 10.2501/S0021849906060466

Martin, F., & Bolliger, D. U. (2018). Engagement Matters: Student Perceptions on the Importance of Engagement Strategies in the Online Learning Environment. *Online Learning : the Official Journal of the Online Learning Consortium, 22*(1), 205–222. DOI: 10.24059/olj.v22i1.1092

Martin, J. (2019). Building relationships and increasing engagement in the virtual classroom: Practical tools for the online instructor. *The Journal of Educators Online, 16*(1). Advance online publication. DOI: 10.9743/jeo.2019.16.1.9

Mittler, J. N., Martsolf, G. R., Telenko, S. J., & Scanlon, D. P. (2023). Making sense of "consumer engagement" initiatives to improve health and health care: A conceptual framework to guide policy and practice. *The Milbank Quarterly, 91*(1), 37–77. DOI: 10.1111/milq.12002 PMID: 23488711

Nagadeepa, C. (2021). Students' Understanding and Learning: Mediation Effects of Cognitive Engagement in Online Classes. [TURCOMAT]. *Turkish Journal of Computer and Mathematics Education, 12*(6), 2932–2939. DOI: 10.17762/turcomat.v12i6.6077

Nobles, J. D., Perez, A., Skelton, J. A., Spence, N. D., & Ball, G. D. (2018). The engagement pathway: A conceptual framework of engagement-related terms in weight management. *Obesity Research & Clinical Practice, 12*(2), 133–138. DOI: 10.1016/j.orcp.2017.12.005 PMID: 29396232

Pentaraki, A., & Laureate, L. (2019). Emerging Evidence Regarding the Roles of Emotional, Behavioural, and Cognitive Aspects of Student. *European Journal of Open, Distance and e-Learning, 20*(1), 1–21.

Pittaway, S. M. (2023). Student and staff engagement: Developing an engagement framework in a faculty of education. *The Australian Journal of Teacher Education, 37*(4). Advance online publication. DOI: 10.14221/ajte.2012v37n4.8

Qi, Y., Zhuang, L., Chen, H., Han, X., & Liang, A. (2023). Evaluation of Students' Learning Engagement in Online Classes Based on Multimodal Vision Perspective. *Electronics (Basel), 13*(1), 149. DOI: 10.3390/electronics13010149

Ramya, B. (2023). INNOVATIVE PEDAGOGICAL APPROACHES. *INNOVATIVE PEDAGOGICAL APPROACHES, 17*, 302.

Redmond, P., Heffernan, A., Abawi, L., Brown, A., & Henderson, R. (2018). An Online Engagement Framework for Higher Education. *Online Learning : the Official Journal of the Online Learning Consortium, 22*(1), 183–204. DOI: 10.24059/olj.v22i1.1175

Reimann, P. (2024). Online Collaborative Learning: Theory and Practice. In *Information Management* (Vol. 17, Issue 1/2). http://search.proquest.com/docview/205264574?accountid=41248

Rotgans, J. I., & Schmidt, H. G. (2023). Cognitive engagement in the problem-based learning classroom. *Advances in Health Sciences Education : Theory and Practice, 16*(4), 465–479. DOI: 10.1007/s10459-011-9272-9 PMID: 21243425

Suharti, D. S., Suherdi, D., & Setyarini, S. (2021). Exploring Students' Learning Engagement in EFL Online Classroom. *Proceedings of the Thirteenth Conference on Applied Linguistics (CONAPLIN 2020), 546*(Conaplin 2020), 139–149. DOI: 10.2991/assehr.k.210427.022

Taylor, S. S., & Statler, M. (2024). Material Matters: Increasing Emotional Engagement in Learning. *Journal of Management Education, 38*(4), 586–607. DOI: 10.1177/1052562913489976

Thompson, V. L. S., Ackermann, N., Bauer, K. L., Bowen, D. J., & Goodman, M. S. (2021). Strategies of community engagement in research: Definitions and classifications. *Translational Behavioral Medicine, 11*(2), 441–451. DOI: 10.1093/tbm/ibaa042 PMID: 32421173

Venkatesan, R. (2024). Executing on a customer engagement strategy. *Journal of the Academy of Marketing Science, 45*(3), 289–293. DOI: 10.1007/s11747-016-0513-6

Yen, K., Kwon, S. C., Cheng, S., Kamboukos, D., Shelley, D., Brotman, L. M., Kaplan, S. A., Olugbenga, O., & Hoagwood, K. (2018). Unpacking Partnership, Engagement, and Collaboration Research to Inform Implementation Strategies Development: Theoretical Frameworks and Emerging Methodologies. *Frontiers in Public Health, 6*(July), 1–13. DOI: 10.3389/fpubh.2018.00190 PMID: 30050895

Young, S., & Bruce, M. A. (2021). Classroom Community and Student Engagement in Online Courses. *Learning, 7*(2), 219–230. https://jolt.merlot.org/vol7no2/young_0611.htm

Yuyun, I. (2023). Investigating university student engagement in online learning: A case study in EFL classroom. *Indonesian Journal of Applied Linguistics, 12*(3), 648–667. DOI: 10.17509/ijal.v12i3.46035

Chapter 8

Faculty Identity in the Avatar Age: Impression Management and Social Cognition in Virtual Classrooms

Kalaiarasi A.
http://orcid.org/0009-0003-0517-1909
Faculty of Management, SRM Institute of Science and Technology, Kattankulathur, India

A. Gajendran
http://orcid.org/0000-0001-8412-3806
Faculty of Management, SRM Institute of Science and Technology, Kattankulathur, India

P. Ashwini Mary
http://orcid.org/0009-0002-4381-5181
Department of MBA, Sri Muthukumaran Institute of Technology, Chikkarayapuram, India

ABSTRACT

The rapid digitalization of higher education, accelerated by COVID-19, has reshaped teaching practices and faculty identity. This study examines how Indian faculty construct identity in avatar-based classrooms, drawing on impression management and social cognition frameworks. Interviews with 25 teachers reveal heightened emotional labor and "digitally mediated burnout," driven by reduced social cues,

DOI: 10.4018/979-8-2600-0934-5.ch008

performance pressures, and institutional demands. The study proposes a model linking identity, cognition, and well-being, and recommends digital infrastructure, well-being initiatives, training, and ethical avatar design.

1. INTRODUCTION

This transition to online modalities of higher education has significantly altered the face of teaching and learning globally, an alteration that has been catalysed by the COVID-19 crisis. Teachers these days are entering online teaching environments and teaching circumstances that extend traditional teaching practice and present distinct challenges in terms of crafting professional identities, social presence, and impression work (Chaka, 2015). Teachers in such environments must deliberately forge their online selves to convey competency, authoritative presence, and authenticity and adeptly fulfil online education's performative requirements (Houtman et al., 2014).

Internationally, studies show it is necessary that teachers embrace new social and cognitive frames to preserve engagement and credibility in the online teaching setting. Teacher identity is no longer exclusively predetermined by fields of specialisation but now becomes dictated by their online profiles, avatar communications, and active use of technology (Yuan & Gao, 2024). These developments make additional demands upon faculty social cognition chiefly the ability to discern, understand, and discern social signals in virtual communications, which in turn has an impact upon teaching practice and student engagement (Srivastava, 2020).

In this Indian context, such challenges appear most pronounced due to unavailability of trusted digital infrastructure, varying levels of institutional supportiveness, and a requirement to reconcile traditional teaching authority-based pedagogy with standards shaped by new technologies (Singh & Meena, 2024; Sharma & Bumb, 2021). Teachers are faced with conflict relating to their professional selves whilst having to cope with considerable cognitive and affective load that makes a profession vulnerable to burnout and Zoom fatigue, consequently affecting teaching effectiveness as well as job satisfaction (Singh & Meena, 2024). Institutional pressure combined with performance expectations serves to further aggravate such problems and in effect create distinctive experiences among Indian higher education faculty (Sahni et al., 2025).

These challenges make evident the need for theories that combine identity performance and cognitive processes in online teaching contexts. As such, this work extends (Goffman's, 1959) work on impression management and social cognition frameworks (Fiske & Taylor, 2013) to examine how faculty intentionally craft their professional identities and make social interaction meaning in avatar-mediated environments. Impression management theory explains intentional efforts made by faculty to craft students' perceptions of their competency and authority, whereas social cognition explains how faculty and students will process and react to online social information. Combining these frameworks presents an inclusive model that explains how identity, cognition, and emotional labour interact in online teaching practice.

This work investigates the following research question:

RQ1.) In what ways do teachers within higher education in India navigate their professional selves when they employ social cognition and impression management to work through avatar-based online learning environments?

The understanding of these dynamics provides a foundation for the present work's theoretical, empirical, and practical contributions. This study makes three important contributions. From a theory-building perspective, it advances the understanding of faculty identity negotiation by integrating impression management and social cognition theories within the framework of avatar-mediated teaching. Empirically, it provides evidence obtained from higher education institutions across India, shedding light on region-specific challenges, cognitive demands, and emotional pressures faced by faculty members working under online teaching situations. Practically, the research offers actionable insights to policymakers and institutional leaders to foster faculty well-being, support sustainable digital pedagogies, and effective identity management during virtual teaching scenarios.

By placing faculty identity within the global debate on digital transformation and couching the focus as the higher education landscape of India, this research contributes to the academic literature on faculty adaptation, online instruction, and avatar-mediated learning environments.

2. THEORETICAL FOUNDATIONS & CONCEPTUAL FRAMEWORK

2.1 Social Cognition and Social Presence

Social presence theory documents the contribution of nonverbal, audio, and textual cues to the enablement of engagement and trust-building during face-to-face learning (Short, Williams, & Christie, 1976). In avatar-mediated and virtual class-room scenarios, such cues are broken or minimized, so instructors need to invest more intellectual and emotional energy to interpret moments of latency, pixelated movement, or silence. Such over-investment in discontinuous cues elevates cognitive load as the capability to build genuine relationships with students diminishes (Yuan & Gao, 2024). In collectivist cultures like India, where personalized interaction and relational pedagogy are paramount, the lack of embodied cues inhibits building social presence (Singh & Meena, 2024).

2.2 Impression Management in Digital Teaching

When teaching borrowing (Goffman's, 1959) dramaturgic paradigm, teaching in digital classrooms becomes a type of public performance where professors, with great care, frame their "front stage" through their digital backdrops, attire, vocal inflections, and technological expertise. Small interruptions, a sense of uncomfortable silence or technological failure might be understood as moments of "performance breakdowns," which activate self-regulation as well as anxiety (Houtman, Makos, & Meacock, 2014). In avatar-mediated environments, the regulation of impressions becomes heightened as professors must strike a delicate balance between projecting their real selves and performing a digitally constructed persona. This construction of identity requires constant control over emotions and intellectual attention, potentially infringing upon faculty wellness (Chaka, 2015).

2.3 Burnout, Emotional labour, and the JD-R Lens

Burnout, as defined (Maslach & Jackson, 1981), consists of three core dimensions: emotional exhaustion, depersonalization, and diminished sense of personal accomplishment. In online spaces, educators place significant emotional energy into the construction of their virtual selves and keeping their audience engaged, which cumulatively raises the stakes for burnout and Zoom fatigue (Singh & Meena, 2024). These challenges are compounded within the frame of Indian higher education, where systemic constraints the lack of proper digital infrastructure, variable institutional support, and increased NAAC, NIRF, and NEP 2020 reform pressures to be accountable are increasing demands related to work (Sharma & Bumb, 2021; Sahni et al., 2025). These processes is a relevant framework for understanding, the Job Demands–Resources (JD-R) framework (Demerouti et al., 2001).

- Digital needs contain mental alertness, constant impression creation, and social judgement.
- Key resources include institutional support systems, digital literacy programs, and coping behaviours such as resilience-building and self-care.

The equilibrium between expectations and accessible resources determines whether faculty members thrive or face challenges in digital teaching spaces.

2.4 Integrated Conceptual Framework

This study combines social presence theory, impression management, and burnout theories to describe the negotiation of faculty identity within avatar-mediated learning environments. The proposed conceptual framework establishes a causal connection.

i). Less social cueing during online teaching necessitates a greater mental effort.
ii). This augmented effort triggers impression-management strategies as professors try to gain authority, competence, and authenticity.
iii). Extended impression management, particularly in the highly challenging and restricted academic environment of India, fuels burnout and emotional exhaustion.
iv). Institutional and personal resources can mitigate these negative outcomes, underscoring the dual role of systemic support and individual coping strategies.

Situating this framework in Indian higher education, this book elucidates relations among digital prerequisites, construction of faculty identity, and venues of institutional engagement.

3. LITERATURE REVIEW

Avatar-based learning integration has profoundly transformed teachers' professional identity and teaching practice. Avatar teachers have been found to enhance students' engagement and learning outcomes in online STEM courses (Daniels & Lee, 2022) by offering immersive and personalized experiences. Additionally, interactive application of avatar in game-based learning matched better engagement and performance (Kao & Harrell, 2016) and revealed cognitive as well as affective impacts.

Recent discourses on immersive learning demonstrate that metaverse-based learning environments reshape pedagogical interaction, knowledge construction, and faculty roles by affording greater presence, embodied participation, and multimodal engagement (Roy et al., 2025). Empirical research on avatars in educational metaverse environments shows that virtual embodiment impacts not only the engagement of students but also the relational and cognitive demands placed on instructors (Islam et al., 2025). Complementary findings from digital well-being research indicate increasing technostress, digital exhaustion, and heightened workload for educators operating in high-immersion teaching environments (Sharma & Sharma, 2022). In parallel explorations of ethical avatar design emphasize the pre-eminences of representatonal accuracy, in cursivity, and psychological safety for both learners and instructors during avatar-based pedagogical implementations (Tinmaz et al., 2024).

This bevy of studies extends the theoretical and empirical bases that account for understanding avatar-mediated pedagogy while underlining technological, ethical, and well-being concerns that influence faculty experiences within digitally immersive college environments.

Impression management is required because faculty have control in a world of decreasing nonverbals and increasing online interaction. (Blunden & Brodsky, 2024) surveyed virtual impression management action in light of strategic self-presentations of information to build online trust. These results expand upon (Goffman's, 1959) foundational theory of identity performance as adapted to online pedagogy.

The social cognition models explain how faculty decipher uncertain social cues when teaching through avatars. (Yang et al., 2024) demonstrate how emotion regulation is linked to faculty self-efficacy in countering burnout and dealing with complexities of teaching online when they underscore the cognitive-emotional burden of online teaching.

Shared dilemmas of identity compliance and affective labour in avatar-informed teaching across the globe are experienced by faculties, but institution- and culture-dependent settings predetermine specific experiences (Fink et al., 2025). An integrated approach including identity performance, cognition, and affective labour is required to facilitate workable faculty development and institution-based support that is efficient in online teaching.

Recent scholarship provides a more extensive understanding of the manner in which avatar-mediated teaching redefines teaching presence, identity negotiation and the emotional requirements of school teachers. The studies of learning in a virtual and a metaverse demonstrate that the design of avatars, the degrees of immersion, and mediated presence determine the relational positioning of instructors and cognitive load of digital teaching (Tinmaz et al., 2024; Roy et al., 2025). Empirical research also suggests that avatar-based environments increase the pressure on the impression management and make it difficult to estimate authenticity during online interactions (Islam et al., 2025; Das et al., 2024). Coupling studies on the digital well-being show that in the academic environment of technologies, technostress, ongoing connectivity, and digital overload increase the stress on the faculty and lead to burnout (Sharma and Sharma, 2022). Besides such technological needs, institutional factors, including digital infrastructure, workload requirements, policy measures, and access to training and support also influence the way faculty will adjust to avatar-mediated teaching and cope with the heightened requirements of immersive teaching (Sharma & Sharma, 2022). Although these developments have taken place, there are still significant gaps. Much of the literature that is already available gives importance to student performance and offers minimal insights into how teachers themselves negotiate identity, emotional control and professional demands in the face of teaching using the avatars. Furthermore, the emotional labour or social-cognitive processes are not often incorporated in the studies of digital well-being to provide a better understanding of the psychological nature of educators in these settings. Through the synthesis of these strands, the present chapter fills in these gaps by pre-empting the work of faculty identity, emotional labour and digital well-being as the fundamental processes of avatar-based instruction, thus providing a more comprehensive treatise of the psychosocial needs of instructors in higher education environments dominated by avatars.

It appears that current and emerging trends within digital learning environments indicate the continued expansion of avatar-mediated education as the higher education infrastructure increasingly incorporates complex and ever more sophisticated immersive technologies. Recent scholarship on metaverse-based education, for example, illustrates the application of AI-driven avatars and adaptive virtual tutors that offer personalised feedback, facilitate real-time modeling, and facilitate differentiated learning in virtual classrooms (Roy et al., 2025). Innovation in embodied interaction, including gesture-tracking interfaces, multi-sensory feedback loops, and advancements in spatial computing, is also transforming how teaching presence is constructed and relational dynamics are managed by faculty members within virtual learning contexts (Islam et al., 2025). In tandem with these emergent patterns, there is a growing body of scholarship on ethical avatar design that highlights issues of identity-safe representation, inclusivity, and data ethics as virtual selves become increasingly integral to academic work (Tinmaz et al., 2024). Taken together, these forward-looking trends suggest that avatar-mediated education is developing into increasingly intelligent, immersive, and ethically-informed learning environments, which strengthens the need for faculty to develop their instructional roles, identities, and emotional investments within the next iteration of digital higher education.

Recent findings also support the importance of incorporating student perspectives into understanding the pedagogical implications of avatar-mediated teaching. Studies confirm that students respond to the use of avatar teachers by perceiving higher engagement, improved social presence, and decreased communication anxiety in virtual learning settings, especially in STEM education and metaverse-enabled learning contexts (Daniels & Lee, 2022; Islam et al., 2025). Nevertheless, students are also demanding that instructors appear authentic, clear, and responsive in their avatar-mediated appearance, adding extra communicative and social demands on faculty. These observations have profound implications for practical teaching and suggest that teaching faculty need to work on improving interaction skills, using multimodal expressions, and planning learning activities that strategically utilize the affordances of avatars to facilitate engagement, emotional safety, and equitable participation.

4. CONCEPTUAL FRAMEWORK

Figure 1. Integrated conceptual framework for faculty identity in avatar – mediated classrooms

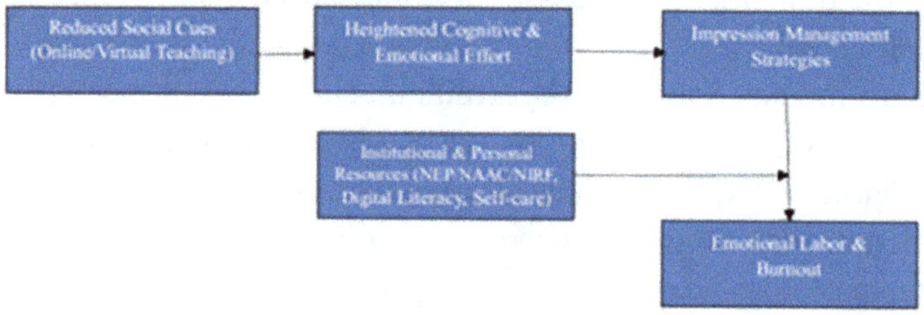

Source: Author's contribution

The conceptual framework (Figure 1) illustrates how avatar-mediated classrooms shape faculty identity and professional well-being. In these situations, reduced social cues, including limited nonverbal, relational, and contextual cues, mean that faculty members must devote increased cognitive and emotional energy to interpreting moments of silence, slow responses, and discontinuous student contributions. In order to preserve perceptions of proficiency and dominance, teachers utilize impression-management techniques such as organizing their visual environment, adopting suitable attire, altering vocal inflections, and enhancing technological competencies. Though efficacious, such techniques prolong emotional labour and escalate risk of burnout, which is defined as symptomatology, such as exhaustion, depersonalization, and loss of feeling of accomplishment. Within the Indian higher-education context, systemic demands motivated by NEP 2020 reformations, NAAC-NIRF driven responsibility pressures, infrastructural limitations, and heavy teaching loads exacerbate such risks. Drawing upon the Job Demands–Resources (JD-R) framework, this work identifies impression management and restricted cue interpretation as significant demands. Professional development programs, computer expertise training, and organizational facilitation operate as a useful resource that serves to reduce damage. Overall, the framework points out that the digital teaching environment professional identity is determined by the dynamic interplay between rising demands on cognitive and emotional resources, as well as resources.

5. AVATAR-MEDIATED EDUCATION TRENDS THAT ARE EMERGING

5.1 Framing the Trends

Recent developments in avatar-mediated education have transformed the roles of faculty, instructional approaches, and professional identities. Virtual environments facilitate interactive and immersive learning experiences, simultaneously prompting faculty to navigate issues related to digital presence, identity, and pedagogical effectiveness. The subsequent trends underscore the technological, psychological, and pedagogical aspects that influence faculty experiences in these contexts.

5.2 Educational Metaverse and AI Teachers

Concepts about the educational metaverse have appeared as the premier paradigm behind immersive learning, wherein avatars serve as virtual proxies for both learners and educators (Fink, Wang, & Islam, 2025). Avatars within virtual worlds provide experiences that support scenario-based cooperative work while developing social, intellectual, and discipline-specific competencies (Fink et al., 2025). Recent developments grounded in artificial intelligence, such as GPT-4o, have enhanced the capability of avatars through adaptive pedagogic agents that can provide timely reminders, identify emotional states, and provide dynamic resources for learning. AI tutors provide personalized support, monitor the progress of learners, and foster collaboration, essentially mimicking the reaction of human teachers while simultaneously overcoming constraints based on scalability (Fink & Wang, 2024; Dai, Kim, & Choi, 2024). By eliminating routine instruction-based activities, AI tutors allow educators to address higher-order pedagogic practices, open pertinent learner engagement, and improve digital instruction-based methodologies (ref fig.2).

5.3 Avatar Customization: Identity, Gender, and Cultural Representation

The customization of avatars is an important tool for exploring identity, affirmation, and self-expression within virtual learning spaces. Avatars' changes to physical appearance, apparel, and body language allow users to negotiate cultural and gender norms while facilitating inclusive learning environments (Kang & Rhee, 2025; Zhang & Juvrud, 2024). Applications such as ZEPETO and VR-Chat allow users to challenge traditional expectations, accept diverse gender expressions, and experience transformational shifts in their self-awareness (Han, 2024). Such experiences have implications for learner well-being and the regulation of digital identities by instructors, subsequently influencing professional presence and pedagogic practice (Kang & Rhee, 2025; Han, 2024). Moreover, avatar designs that are culturally represented and attuned enhance intercultural understanding, creativity, and cooperative participation, subsequently affirming the pedagogic value of deliberate identity representation (Garcia, 2025; Lim, Jeong, & Yu, 2024).

5.4 Virtual and Augmented Reality-Driven Pedagogy

The introduction of VR and AR technologies into avatar-mediated spaces widens the potential for practice-based immersive learning across STEM, medical, and environmental applications (Schmidbauer, 2025; Dai et al., 2024). VR/AR-augmented pedagogy reinforces real-time problem-solving, critical thinking, and hands-on simulation, often surpassing the potential of traditional online materials (Dai et al., 2024). As combined technologies, they foster increased motivation, persistence, and intellectual flexibility as users interact, collaborate, and probe theoretical constructs in realistic, controlled scenarios (Fink et al., 2025). Research has also highlighted the importance of avatar appearance (human vs. stylized) and interaction style (human-like vs. stylized) on user experience, social presence, and perceived effectiveness, making recommendations around faculty responsibility in designing immersive, pedagogically effective experiences (Garcia, 2025; Dai et al., 2024).

5.5 Uncanny Valley and Avatar Authenticity

As realism in avatars increases to a photorealistic approach, the uncanny valley effect marked by the emotional discomfort resulting from a nearly human appearance combined with slight behavioural imperfections gains prevalence (Garcia, 2025; Dai et al., 2024). Prevalence could impede interaction, reduce social presence, and negatively impact interactions between learners and educators. An optimal realism-approachability balance is required in designing avatars because adding typical nonverbal signals along with ethnic and gender diversity is beneficial to creating genuine social relations (Lim et al., 2024; Kang & Rhee, 2025). Context-based customization will relieve perception-based discomfort while at the same time enabling rich identity construction among educators and learners to enhance the overall learning experience (refer fig.2).

5.6 Implications and Challenges for Faculty

In combination, these trends create opportunities and challenges for professorship in avatar-rich teaching. Professors must address cognitive load complexities, ethical considerations, and professional development needs to work effectively with

AI tutors, VR/AR teaching approaches, and identity-rich avatar worlds. Awareness of avatar design, interaction styles, and potential psychological effects on learners allows faculty to maintain instructional quality, promote inclusivity, and cultivate a positive digital-teaching persona. Additionally, gaps remain in longitudinal research on how avatar-mediated identity work impacts faculty professional growth, highlighting areas for future research.

Figure 2. Four pillars of emerging trends in Avatar-mediated education

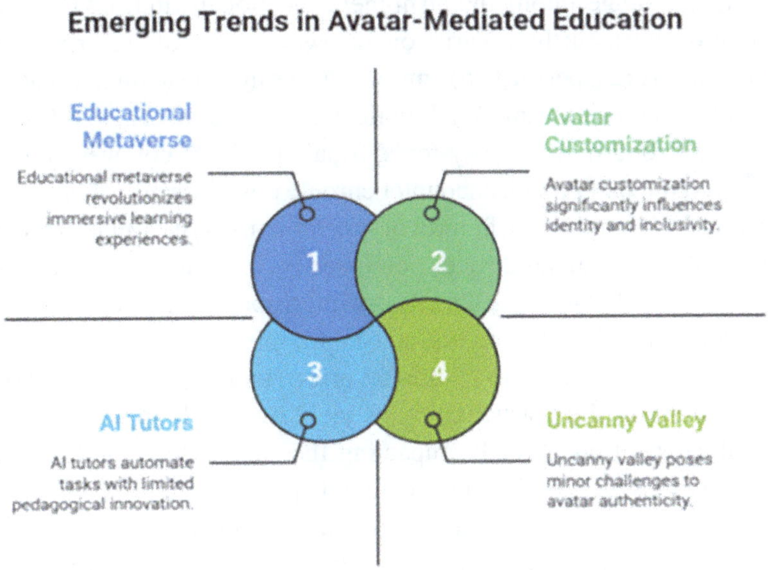

Source: Author's own work

6. RECOGNIZED DEFICITS AND THEIR IMPLICATIONS FOR THE INDIAN CONTEXT

Despite the increasing attention to digital transformation in Indian higher education, considerable gaps persist that critically influence faculty identity, impression management, and social cognition in avatar-mediated classrooms. Despite initiatives such as the National Education Policy (NEP) 2020, the National Institutional Ranking Framework (NIRF), and the National Assessment and Accreditation Council (NAAC) recommending the embracement of digital pedagogy and the offering of online programs (MHRD, 2020; NAAC, 2021; NIRF, 2024), their incorporation into evaluation processes around digital teaching is patchy. While the NIRF recently incorporated indicators around digital course offerings and technology-enabled settings (NIRF, 2024), the NAAC assesses the integration of electronic resources and data management practices (NAAC, 2021). However, these assessment measures chiefly rely on self-reported data provided by institutions, which lack verifiable and standardized measures. Such inconsistencies cause the faculty members to deal with fragmented evaluation measures that significantly influence their teaching practice as well as their professional self-idea.

The structural range among Indian higher education institutions (HEIs) obscures implementation even further, Variation in ownership (public, private, deemed), location (urban, rural, peri-urban), mission (research, teaching, vocational), and resource endowment yields uneven digital readiness (Sahni et al., 2025). Elite HEIs typically have strong digital ecosystems. Smaller private colleges and peri-urban universities, on the other hand, encounter chronic obstacles, not only limited access to devices, unstable bandwidth, failures of synchronous classes, platform downtimes, and incompatibilities among devices possessed by students and faculty (Sharma & Bumb, 2021; Singh & Meena, 2024). These interruptions are more than just technical. They require faculties to practice constant impression management, apologize for interruptions, make up with additional effort, and cope with increased mental and emotional strain. Infrastructural gaps yield overload, anxiety, and depressed professional satisfaction, directly impacting the ways talents build and actualize their individualities within digital educational spaces.

Policy bombast usually emphasizes "equitable digital investments" and "capacity building among talents." However, most initiatives hardly go beyond broad statements, leaving little operational clarity on the lines of targets, deadlines, or even responsibility. Minimum device-per-faculty ratios, CPD hour-wise binding requirements, and avatar-mediated pedagogy pilot programs remain undefined (MHRD, 2020; NAAC, 2021). Financial mechanisms, that is, central, state, or institutional, are unspecified, particularly in the decentralized and asymmetrically endowed nature of the current system. In the absence of concrete operational guidance, faculty members are left with ambiguity that impacts their professional self-perception, social perception, and virtual classroom credibility.

Methodological flaws in the research literature further deepen these challenges. Avatar-mediated teaching research on the subcontinent largely relies on descriptive accounts or anecdotal narratives rather than validated instruments and systematic sampling methods. As such, the pros and cons of faculty identity, well-being, and impression management have been little explored. Ongoing research must borrow or localize standardized measures, for instance, the Maslach Burnout Inventory (Maslach & Jackson, 1981) or social presence and impression management scales and employ stratified sampling to include the diversity of HEIs. Transparency, either qualitative thematic analysis (Braun & Clarke, 2006) or robust quantitative modelling, is needed to provide credible, replicable evidence.

The academic discourse and policy documentation in India appear to lack exploration of hedonic and pragmatic concerns associated with AI-enhanced avatars. The implications of these risks transcend the technological domain, impacting the authority, credibility, and trust of educators within avatar-mediated learning environments. In the absence of institutional protocols that address transparency and quality assurance, educators are compelled to confront challenges in which their professional identities are threatened by elements beyond their control (see table 1).

Table 1. An anticipatory research agenda would do much to privilege identity-based studies through three stages as follows

Phase	Focus	Research Directions
Short-term	Diagnose infrastructural and identity-related stressors	Audit device and platform availability across regions- Assess immediate effects on faculty identity, social cognition, and teaching presence- Map policies affecting avatar-mediated pedagogy- Implement targeted CPD interventions to support faculty identity and teaching performance
Medium-term	Evaluate effectiveness of avatar-mediated and AI-supported pedagogy	Conduct experimental and quasi-experimental studies- Use validated instruments for social cognition, impression management, and faculty well-being- Assess intervention impact on faculty identity and professional credibility
Long-term	Track longitudinal development of faculty identity, well-being, and career trajectories	Conduct multi-institutional longitudinal studies- Monitor sectoral, regional, and demographic differences- Evaluate long-term effects of avatar-mediated pedagogy on faculty identity, professional credibility, and career trajectories

Source: Author's contribution

Collectively, these factors create a framework for integrating digital policy, institutional practice, and technological change with faculty members' experiences. By placing a special focus on identity, impression management, and social cognition, subsequent studies can ensure that avatar-based teaching in India generates not only teaching development but also sustainable development among faculty.

7. RESEARCH METHODOLOGY OF STUDYING FACULTY IDENTITY IN VIRTUAL WORLDS

7.1. Theoretical Framework and Conceptual Orientation

To explore faculty identity in online contexts calls for a flexible approach that is informed by a particular theory which incorporates identity performance along with emotional work, cognitive work, and contextual considerations which are relevant to teaching from behind an avatar. (Goffman's, 1959) work on impression management is used in this context as is social cognition as advocated by (Fiske & Taylor, 2013) that have a role to play theoretically in terms of explaining nuances involved in teaching digitally.

In virtual environments, where strong nonverbal and contextual cues are lacking, educators must create and monitor their online selves. At the same time that they must monitor their emotions to maintain their authority and social presence, they must do so within an Indian context. This work calls out broader ramifications for navigating faculty identity internationally in virtual classroom situations.

7.2 Research Methodology and Analytical Approach

According to this theoretical orientation, this research design endeavoured to reveal lived experiences of faculty teaching through avatar-mediated lectures. It employed an interpretivist research tradition that privileges comprehensive understanding rather than statistical generalizability. Data gathering was conducted through 25 semi-structured interviews on Zoom, a platform that is directly related to the teaching settings under inquiry, to gather data. Reflexive prompts in the nature of interpretation questions about silence during lectures or emotional tension elicited rich narratives about faculty members' perspectives. Each interview was 45–60 minutes long and fully transcribed. The sample size was determined to reach thematic saturation, allowing for an in-depth exploration of diverse faculty experiences, which is the qualitative requirement stipulated by the interpretivist paradigm.

Data were analysed through (Braun & Clarke's, 2006) reflexive thematic analysis, such that both descriptive coding and more interpretative work with impression management and negotiation of identity were feasible. NVivo software supported the analytic rigor. Memos documented progressive interpretations, as well as researcher reflexivity. Member checking, peer debriefing, and critical scrutiny of positionality added to the trustworthiness of the study. Triangulation across diverse institutional sites, along with a systematic audit trail of the decision-making that goes into coding, further boosted credibility.

7.3 Contextual and Methodological Considerations

This approach addresses the diversity of Indian higher education, including public and private universities, urban and rural campuses, and elite and aspirational institutions, each representing distinct infrastructural and policy issues. Macrosocial constructs, the National Education Policy (NEP, 2020), accreditation requirements of the NAAC, and pressures to rank under the NIRF-define institutional requisites, both empowering and constraining faculty agency. This double-edged influence amplifies the complexity of identity work in avatar-mediated teaching.

Despite the small size, the sample aligns with the qualitative objectives of creating rich, contextualized insights rather than statistical representativeness. The fast-changing dynamics of avatar-mediated pedagogy both hinder and provide opportunities for future research. Longitudinal or international studies would provide additional research into the construction of faculty identity, creating insights that would be relevant not merely to the Indian higher education sector, but also to global situations where digital pedagogy is transforming professional practice.

8. FINDINGS

The analysis of 25 semi-structured interviews conducted with academics representing Indian higher education institutions found four interrelated themes that reflect the negotiation of identity, impression management, and emotional labour within avatar-mediated learning situations. These themes reflect the dynamic relationships between digital responsibility, institutional responsibility, and personal coping strategies (Sahni, Verma, & Kaurav, 2025).

8.1 Themes

Theme 1: "Facing the Frame" - Social presence in the absence of feedback

Faculty members recounted teaching to silent screens, muted mics, or missing video feeds, interrupting the relational pedagogy prized in Indian classrooms (Singh & Meena, 2024). Because nonverbal cues were missing, professors had to guess based on silence, slow response time on the chat, or minimal emoji responses.

"When I ask a question and see blank boxes, I feel as if I am talking into the void. I need to keep going again and again, just to guess whether they're keeping up." (Faculty Member 8)

This "speaking into silence" has a parallel in social cognition theory (Fiske & Taylor, 2013), where reduced cues intensify anxiety and stress professional identity issues. Non-reciprocation also primes the ground for more efforts at self-presentation, as becomes evident in Theme 2.

Theme 2: "Performance Before Pedagogy" - Digital presence as performance curation

To counteract the absence of feedback, faculty members invested heavily in managing their digital personas by adjusting camera angles, lighting, attire, and vocal tone to convey competence and approachability.

"It takes me longer than the actual preparation time to arrange the background, lighting, and voice before the class." (Faculty Participant 12)

This mirror (Goffman's, 1959) dramaturgic paradigm, situating online teaching as a "front stage." Staff sometimes felt that they were acting for the camera instead of teaching the discipline. Extended self-presentation-maintained authority, although it merged pedagogy and performance, leading to emotional strain (Chaka, 2015; Houtman, Makos, & Meacock, 2014). The pressure to be classy also exacerbated sensitivity to peers and institutional benchmarking, as explored in Theme 3.

Theme 3: "Comparison Trap" - Professional anxiety due to benchmarking

Peer review, rubrics, and videocasted lectures caused additional anxiety. Watching professional presentations by other people strengthens upward comparisons that undercut self-confidence.

"When I see other faculty members' videos that are so nicely produced, slick, flashy, I feel incompetent. It's as if we're competing in some virtual exhibit, instead of teaching." (Faculty Participant 5)

Numerous have termed that "every class is an audition." Job Demands–Resources (JD-R) model (Demerouti et al., 2001) proposes that benchmarking is a job demand that is multiplied many times over in India due to reform wrought through NEP 2020, NAAC, and NIRF, correlating digital performance to institutional reputation (Sahni et al., 2025; National Institutional Ranking Framework, 2024). As a coping response, some faculty members have adopted adaptive coping, stressing student comprehension rather than comparative evaluation.

The facilitator pointed to the importance of celebrating small wins, as opposed to being so focused on their own presentation being worse than other people. (Faculty Participant 21)

This highlights that coping strategies can neutralize pressures from benchmarking, but they require concerted effort.

Theme 4: "Screen-Induced Burnout" - A new form of burnout

The dynamic between inadequate feedback, constant impression management, and institutional benchmarking cultivates a specific variation of exhaustion. Unlike traditional burnout, which is nearly entirely coupled with overwork, this specific variation stems from digital performativity and constant self-monitoring. Moreover, the lack of actualized feedback amplifies both mental and emotional fatigue.

"The experience permeates beyond tiredness after instruction. It intertwines the chronic mental fatigue that comes with screen-based interaction, the need to moderate silence, and self-scepticism. After some classes, I feel completely drained." (Faculty Participant 17)

They also offered the following observations: they felt both "mentally drained yet emotionally flat." We frame this as "screen-induced burnout," building on (Maslach & Jackson., 1981) to identify digital performativity as a novel precursor to emotional exhaustion. Faculty identity within avatar-based virtual classrooms is therefore blended pedagogic and performance-based formed under the influence of both digital pressure and institutional demands (Singh & Meena, 2024; Maslach & Jackson, 1981).

8.2 Combining the Themes

The themes reflect a progressive buildup: missing cues (Theme 1) invoke impression management (Theme 2), increasing permeability to peer and institutional comparisons (Theme 3), leading to screen-based burnout (Theme 4). Faculty identity in avatar-based classrooms is then no longer merely determined by expertise, but through constant negotiation among transparency, believability, and self-representation under the pressures of digital and institutional expectations. However, systemic and technological remedies must be implemented to maintain the well-being of faculties, Even the use of coping mechanisms may only partially offset these stresses.

9. DISCUSSION

9.1 Digital Transformation of Faculty Identity in Avatar-Mediated Education

Avatar-based virtual classrooms are an exceedingly different professional practice from those of educators, far beyond integrating technology. Here, faculty communicate through virtual avatars employing strategic impression management skills varying vocal inflection, selecting avatar look, and manipulating on-screen presence to express authority and credibility. Participants indicated that they spent approximately an equal amount of time creating their virtual scenery and oral presentation as they spent creating their lecture content. Unlike face-to-face classrooms, where presence in space and contextual cueing convey legitimacy, avatar-based teaching necessitates an ongoing negotiation of online selves. This work of reconciling authenticity and performance within technological limitations and institution policy aims to foster student trust and investment (Goffman, 1959; Fiske & Taylor, 2013).

9.2 Emotional Labour and Burnout by Impression Management

The ongoing pressure for superior digital performance amplifies the affective labor surrounding a new variant of burnout named "digitally mediated" or "screen-induced" burnout. Faculty expressed experiences of "auditioning" for each course because of constant vigilance, peer monitoring, and systemic burdens from benchmarking, such as those required by NEP 2020 and NAAC accreditation. This particular form of digital burnout varies from traditional models that feature exhaustion resulting from workload; rather, it is caused by having to cope with distorted social information, navigate intensified visibility, and practice constant self-monitoring (Maslach & Jackson, 1981; Demerouti et al., 2001). These factors create considerable threats to faculty well-being, especially in resource-constrained environments, thus providing a strong argument to support intervention efforts cantered on helping.

9.3 The Social Cognition Role in Pedagogy Digitally

Social cognition theory is an explanation of how teachers attempt to make meaning from limited and ambiguous social information in environments that include avatar-based teaching. Without typical nonverbal information, additional cognitive work is required that could involve increasing vocal emphasis or adapting avatar appearance to express relational context and instructor presence (Short, Williams, & Christie, 1976). This further increases cognitive load and anxiety but is required to preserve authority and promote connection. By extension, online pedagogy development would have to integrate resources and training to reduce such cognitive-emotional challenges while adding additional social presence in online rooms.

9.4 Contextualising Indian Higher Education Results

Indian higher education presents further challenges to teaching through avatars. Faculty face infrastructural failure and uneven institutional support when dealing with strict policy directives such as NEP 2020, NAAC rating, and NIRF rankings. Stressing relational teaching and individualized discourse complements challenges to impersonality of avatar-mediated worlds (Singh & Meena, 2024; Sahni et al., 2025). As a case in point, respondents from distant academic institutions suggested that they found it challenging to manage a high incidence of interruptions to internet connectivity that required constant efforts to maintain students' online participation and control. Such systemic and cultural factors necessitate tailored regionally focused teaching approaches and institution-specific solutions.

9.5 Global Considerations and Variations in Avatar-Founded Learning Spaces

Despite its uniqueness, the Indian experience shares a common challenge among faculty from diverse school systems in adapting to avatar-based teaching practice. Comparative international studies reveal common difficulties of a lack of social cue, emotional labour burdens, and performance anxiety that are managed through varied resource allocation and organizational contexts (Fink et al., 2025). These studies indicate a common requirement of efforts to foster well-being and construct wholistic faculty development while emphasizing culturally suitable approaches. This dual mandate requires an international conversation to create personalized adaptation of policy and practice.

10. IMPLICATIONS OF PROGRAMMING AND INSTITUTIONAL SUPPORT

10.1 Digital Infrastructures and Distribution of Resources in India

Sustainable adoption of avatar pedagogy hinges on equitable digital infrastructure investment. Policymakers must prioritize expanding reliable internet connectivity, hardware access, and platform stability, especially targeting underserved rural and peri-urban institutions. Addressing such digital inequities alleviates cognitive and emotional faculty burdens linked to technical interruptions and resource disparities.

10.2 Recommendations for Policies Regarding Digital Pedagogy Standards

National standards should lay out clear standards about avatar use that involve policies of digital presence, ethical customization of avatars, and performance standards. Integrating such standards in accreditation (NIRF, NAAC) fosters institutional compliance as well as quality assurance. Furthermore, integrating obligatory faculty digital competency demonstration and well-being survey institutionalizes all-inclusive support.

10.3 Professional Development and Training Needs

Institutions should design ongoing faculty development programs which work on technological competency, digital identity administration, and competency in addressing emotional labour. Training in instructional activities of avatar customization, social presence enhancement, and mitigation of fatigue contributes to boosting faculty confidence and adaptability in online settings.

10.4 Enhancing digital Well-Being and Aiding Faculty Resilience

Policy and institutional environments need to create digital well-being through programmed interruption, workloads that can be adjusted, and convenient access to mental health services. Cultivating reflective practice and peer networks of support underlies communal faculty resilience to avatar-mediated teaching's particular emotional burden.

11. PRACTICAL RECOMMENDATIONS

11.1 Indices and Indicators of Digital Well-Being

Creation and application of well-being inventories tailored to online teaching environments allow burnout potential to be identified earlier. Periodic assessments allow intervention to be tailored so that well-being is fostered in faculty and pedagogy is optimized.

11.2 Peer Counselling and Community Among Faculty Members

Professionalization of peer networks of support fosters circles of mutual experience, mutual encouragement, and collaborative problem solving. Such networks make up for isolation and foster long-term cohesiveness of professional identity.

11.3 Avatar Ethics to Enable Appropriate Representation and Utilization

Development of culturally appropriate codes of ethics ensures respectful tailoring of avatars to safeguard inclusiveness, authenticity, and confidentiality. They foster balanced and safe online teaching approaches.

12. CONCLUSION

This work discloses that online teaching through avatars generates particular forms of emotional labour and identity conflict among educators of Indian higher learning institutions. By fitting existing models of burnout (Maslach & Jackson, 1981; Demerouti et al., 2001) to the online teaching arena and shifting toward dramaturgic explanation and social cognition perspectives, this work discloses how faculty members adapt, perform, and reconcile their professional selves in online teaching settings.

This work's results re-conceptualize faculty identity within avatar-integrated teaching as a flexible construction subject to simultaneous considerations of academic field as well as of digital-interaction, impression management, and affective change. This work consequently augments prior literature relating to digital teaching while reinforcing emotionally- and identity-related challenges interwoven with tech-enhanced teaching and enhancing wider participation from academic as well as policy-oriented perspectives.

Additional studies should delineate conceptual limitations more clearly, develop all-inclusive indices to measure digital well-being, and look into ways to enhance resilience when interacting through avatars. Educational institutions can support these endeavours by creating peer support systems, expanding professional growth opportunities, and defining explicit standards for avatar-based pedagogy. These efforts aim to foster faculty well-being and effectiveness and thus make faculty resilience a cornerstone of sustainable worldwide digital higher education. Finally, just as much as its development will be shaped through technological breakthroughs so will it be through safeguarding the emotional and professional strength of those responsible faculty teams that will deliver those innovations.

12.1 Limitations & Future Research

Qualitative methods, specifically semi-structured interviews, were employed in this work and focused on in-depth understanding and perception more than widespread application. As such, results may not reflect an entire life of faculty members from all facets of diverse higher-education environments in India, which include private and government institutions as well as cities and towns. Samples of participants came from specific institutional selections and therefore limited representation of infrastructure variety, teaching practice, and cultural processes. Since a dependence on self-definition of experience imports a risk of bias or selective memory, and a lack of standardized quantitative instruments limits potential to a systematic examination of burnout, emotional labour, and identity-based facets.

The very quick development of electronic teaching technologies such as artificial intelligence, avatar technologies, and metaverse environments constrains long-term generalizability of these findings. Ethical and technological considerations, such as algorithmic bias, privacy, and the veridically of avatar depictions, have also not been adequately explored. Longitudinal data are further restricted, with no analysis of the long-term construction of faculty identity, well-being, and professional trajectory.

To transcend these limitations, future research should strive to enlarge methodological diversification by adopting mixed methods or experimental designs to verify and expand the constructs of burnout and faculty identity, thereby enhancing generalizability. Common measures, such as the Maslach Burnout Inventory, as part of or separate measures of social presence or impression management, should be used across diverse institutional and cultural situations to assess cognitive, emotional, and identity-based outcomes. Longitudinal research plays a vital role in tracking changes in the nature of faculty identity, well-being, and professional competence over a longer duration, particularly in avatar-mediated instruction.

Transnational studies have the potential to provide useful insights into world and context-constructed trends in identity negotiation, pressure to perform, and institution burnout in Global South and Global North. Analysis of ethical and technical issues like algorithm-based biases, privacy issues, and avatar authenticity is necessary to make known how they impact faculty experience and teaching practice in higher education. Research interventions should assess the effectiveness of AI-enhanced teaching tools, such as features that automatically hide self-views and customizable avatars, in alleviating cognitive load and burnout associated with digital mediation.

Further studies should also be thoroughgoing, incorporating faculty demographics that have been historically underrepresented or excluded in order to examine the compromise of inequities in digital infrastructure upon identity negotiation, access to assistance, as well as resilience in online teaching contexts. Ultimately, setting practice standards of avatar-mediated teaching methods, against rankings and accreditation considerations, should foster openness, fairness, and responsibility to guarantee that digital teaching approaches effectively support the well-being and professional growth of faculty professionals.

Overcoming such limitations and pursuing such lines of inquiry will enrich theoretic understanding, inform institutional practice, and provide leadership to decisionmakers in seeking faculty resilience, effectiveness, and well-being in online learning environments that are increasingly changing quickly.

REFERENCES

Blunden, H., & Brodsky, A. (2024). A review of virtual impression management behaviors and outcomes. *Journal of Management, 50*(6), 2197–2236. DOI: 10.1177/01492063231225160

Braun, V., & Clarke, V. (2006). Using thematic analysis in psychology. *Qualitative Research in Psychology, 3*(2), 77–101. DOI: 10.1191/1478088706qp063oa

Chaka, C. (2015). Digital identity, social presence technologies, and presence learning. In *Student-teacher interaction in online learning environments* (pp. 183–203). IGI Global. DOI: 10.4018/978-1-4666-6461-6.ch009

Dai, J., Kim, S., & Choi, H. (2024). Avatar appearance and social presence in virtual reality. *Computers in Human Behavior, 141*, 104234. DOI: 10.1016/j.chb.2024.104234

Daniels, D., & Lee, J. S. (2022, June). The impact of avatar teachers on student learning and engagement in a virtual learning environment for online STEM courses. In Stephanidis, C. (Ed.), *Human-Computer Interaction – INTERACT 2022* (pp. 158–175). Springer., DOI: 10.1007/978-3-031-05675-8_13

Das, T., Ganesh Kondamudi, S., Dawood Babakerkhell, M., Pal, D., Roy, R., & Funilkul, S. (2024). Intention for enhancing metaverse-based learning using gamification among university students: A study using Delphi and structural equation modelling approaches. *Cogent Business & Management, 11*(1), 2380016. DOI: 10.1080/23311975.2024.2380016

Demerouti, E., Bakker, A. B., Nachreiner, F., & Schaufeli, W. B. (2001). The job demands–resources model of burnout. *The Journal of Applied Psychology, 86*(3), 499–512. DOI: 10.1037/0021-9010.86.3.499 PMID: 11419809

Fink, M. C., & Wang, Q. (2024). AI-based avatars are changing the way we learn and teach. *Frontiers in Education, 9*, 1416307. DOI: 10.3389/feduc.2024.1416307

Fink, M. C., Wang, Q., & Islam, M. Z. (2025). Avatars in the educational metaverse. *Journal of Virtual Learning, 39*(2), 121–156. https://pmc.ncbi.nlm.nih.gov/articles/PMC12151956/

Fiske, S. T., & Taylor, S. E. (2013). *Social cognition: From brains to culture* (2nd ed.). Sage Publications. DOI: 10.4135/9781446286395

Garcia, M. B. (2025). The influence of avatar appearance and behavioral realism in educational environments. *Interactive Learning Environments*, *38*(3), 241–264. DOI: 10.1080/10494820.2025.2462144

Goffman, E. (1959). *The presentation of self in everyday life*. Anchor Books.

Han, Y. (2024). Gender exploration in avatar customization systems. *Games and Culture*, *19*(1), 45–61. DOI: 10.1177/15554120241307982

Houtman, E., Makos, A., & Meacock, H. L. (2014). The intersection of social presence and impression management in online learning environments. *E-Learning and Digital Media*, *11*(4), 419–430. DOI: 10.2304/elea.2014.11.4.419

Islam, M. Z., & Wang, G. (2025). Avatars in the educational metaverse. *Visual Computing for Industry, Biomedicine, and Art*, *8*(1), 15. DOI: 10.1186/s42492-025-00196-9 PMID: 40493326

Kang, J., & Rhee, H. (2025). Gender identity and perception in virtual spaces: The impact of avatar presentation. *Frontiers in Virtual Reality*, *10*, 1505624. DOI: 10.3389/frvir.2025.1505624

Kao, D., & Harrell, D. F. (2016). Exploring the effects of dynamic avatar on performance and engagement in educational games. *Procedia Computer Science*, *96*, 1063–1072. DOI: 10.1016/j.procs.2016.08.109

Lim, S., Jeong, D., & Yu, H. (2024). Avatar customization in the metaverse: User perceptions and design recommendations. *Computers & Graphics*, *107*, 70–81. DOI: 10.1016/j.cag.2024.107081

Maslach, C., & Jackson, S. E. (1981). The measurement of experienced burnout. *Journal of Organizational Behavior*, *2*(2), 99–113. DOI: 10.1002/job.4030020205

Ministry of Human Resource Development. (2020). *National education policy 2020*. Government of India. https://www.education.gov.in/sites/upload_files/mhrd/files/NEP_Final_English_0.pdf

National Assessment and Accreditation Council. (2021). *Manual for self-study accreditation: Teacher education colleges*. https://www.naac.gov.in/

National Institutional Ranking Framework. (2024). *India rankings 2024: Methodology document*. Ministry of Education, Government of India. https://www.nirfindia.org

Roy, R., Rao, G. A., Pal, D., Anuradha, S., & Mukherjee, S. (2025). Metaverse-based education for sustainable development and improving the performance: Discussing the future research agenda. *Sustainable Futures : An Applied Journal of Technology, Environment and Society*, *10*, 101091. DOI: 10.1016/j.sftr.2025.101091

Sahni, S., Verma, S., & Kaurav, R. P. S. (2025). Understanding digital transformation challenges for online learning and teaching in higher education institutions: A review and research framework. *Benchmarking*, *32*(5), 1487–1521. DOI: 10.1108/BIJ-04-2022-0245

Schmidbauer, F. (2025). Social virtual reality as learning space: Conceptualising embodied interaction. *Learning, Media and Technology*, *47*(2), 311–329. DOI: 10.1016/j.lmt.2025.311329

Sharma, S., & Bumb, A. (2021). The challenges faced in technology-driven classes during COVID-19. *International Journal of Distance Education Technologies*, *19*(1), 66–88. DOI: 10.4018/IJDET.20210101.oa2

Sharma, S., & Sharma, M. (2022). Impact of Digital Transformation on Academicians' Well-being: A Study with the Moderating Role of Public and Private Universities in India. *Digital Education Review*, (42), 118–135. DOI: 10.1344/der.2022.42.118-135

Short, J., Williams, E., & Christie, B. (1976). *The social psychology of telecommunications*. Wiley.

Singh, A. K., & Meena, M. K. (2024). Online teaching in Indian higher education institutions during the pandemic time. *Education and Information Technologies*, *29*(4), 4107–4157. DOI: 10.1007/s10639-023-11942-y

Srivastava, A. (2020). Post COVID-19: A technology-driven era for higher education. *Higher Education Going Online: The Challenges in India,* 77. [If book chapter, please provide publisher for completeness]

Tinmaz, H., & Dhillon, P. K. S. (2024). User-centric avatar design: A cognitive walkthrough approach for metaverse in virtual education. *Data Science and Management*, *7*(4), 267–282. DOI: 10.1016/j.dsm.2024.05.001

Yang, X., Chen, Y., & Liu, S. (2024). Cognitive load and emotion regulation in online teaching: Faculty perspectives. *Journal of Computer Assisted Learning*, *40*(2), 391–404. DOI: 10.1111/jcal.2024.40.issue-2

Yuan, Q., & Gao, Q. (2024). Being there, and being together: Avatar appearance and peer interaction in VR classrooms for video-based learning. *International Journal of Human-Computer Interaction*, *40*(13), 3313–3333. DOI: 10.1080/10447318.2023.2189818

Zhang, J., & Juvrud, J. (2024). Gender expression and gender identity in virtual reality. *Frontiers in Virtual Reality*, *5*, 1305758. DOI: 10.3389/frvir.2024.1305758

KEY TERM AND DEFINITIONS

Avatar Customisation: This is related to the tailoring of avatar appearance, style, and behaviour to express identity, culture, and gender, allowing for inclusivity as well as successful virtual presence. Social Presence

Avatar-Mediated Education: It refers to learning and teaching from virtual avatars in online or metaverse classrooms that necessitate faculty to juggle digital presence, identity representation, and instructionally effective pedagogies.

Burnout (Digital/Screen-Induced): It refers to emotional, mental, and physical fatigue as a result of long digital performance, additional mental stress, and diminishing real-time response during online classes.

Digital Pedagogy: This refers to teaching practices and methodologies created specifically for digital/virtual delivery, such as the use of avatars, AI tutors, and other immersive technologies, including AR and VR.

Impression Management: This practice is concerning having faculty members intentionally craft online personas that reflect their expertise, credibility, and authenticity in online learning environments.

Job Demands-Resources (JD-R) Model: The Job Demands-Resources (JD-R) Model Conceptual framework attributes burnout to a disequilibrium between job demands (e.g., impression management, limited social cues) and job resources (e.g., institutional support, coping efforts).

Social Cognition: Refers to the mental processes involved in perceiving, interpreting, and evaluating social cues during digital interactions, which influence teaching practices and student engagement.

Social Presence: This conception speaks to the social-emotional dimension of being related to other individuals via a communicative channel, which is usually compromised in avatar-based learning scenarios because of dampened nonverbal and contextual cues.

Chapter 9
Understanding Gen Z Social Behavior in Virtual Classrooms: Factors That Shape Student Engagement

Leslie Ponciano
http://orcid.org/0000-0002-8038-6630
Hope Education Research Solutions, USA

Catherine Greer
http://orcid.org/0009-0006-3537-3669
Fielding Graduate University, USA

Mary-Joy Marsh
http://orcid.org/0009-0005-2265-8385
Fielding Graduate University, USA

Devin Ponciano
University of California, Irvine, USA

ABSTRACT

This chapter explores the social behavior of Gen Z students in virtual classrooms through the lens of social learning theory and social comparison theory. The authors analyze and synthesize research on student (dis)engagement in virtual environments to form a cohesive understanding of the challenges faced by Gen Z due to their unique sociocultural context. The chapter identifies why and how Gen Z (dis)engages and adapts within virtual learning environments. Educators are encouraged to design

DOI: 10.4018/979-8-2600-0934-5.ch009

spaces that align with the sociocultural realities of a generation whose learning "hits different." This chapter explores the vast and ever-changing landscape of education noting the benefits, concerns, and best practices of virtual learning.

INTRODUCTION

> *The Zoom waiting room trickles open with students arriving one by one, some right on time, others drifting in five or more minutes late. The educator greets each student warmly, but immediately notices a familiar pattern: cameras dark, names in boxes, no pictures or indications of what the students look like, silence on the other end. She gently encourages them to turn their cameras on. A few comply, faces flickering into view, but many remain hidden behind black squares.*
>
> *After a brief check-in, she shares her screen to begin the lesson. In an instant, every single camera clicks off, as if on cue. The educator pauses often, inviting questions and waiting for voices, but there is only silence. One student types a question into the chat. The educator answers the question aloud, grateful for any student engagement. Another student types a question into the chat. The educator stops sharing her slides to welcome live discussion.*
>
> *"Let's turn our cameras back on," she encourages, but this time, even fewer students respond. The attempt at group dialogue was unsuccessful with muted microphones and only occasional responses in the chat.*
>
> *When the class ends, the educator reflects on the lack of student engagement. Why did so many choose not to be seen, not to be heard? Was it disinterest, distraction, or something about how this generation engages with learning in virtual spaces?*

This chapter will synthesize selective factors that may contribute to the social behavior adopted by Generation Z (Gen Z) students in virtual classrooms. A deeper understanding of Gen Z social behavior in virtual environments is important for several reasons: 1) Gen Z students were thrust into virtual classrooms during the COVID-19 pandemic and this may have influenced their understanding of expectations for social behavior. 2) Gen Z are generally assumed to have an inherent set of digital skills and expected to function well in virtual environments. 3) When Gen Z students leave the classroom and enter the workforce, they are more likely (since the COVID-19 pandemic) to conduct their work in virtual spaces. Gen Z social behavior in virtual environments may be an important observable measure of how well they are functioning, the extent to which they have or enjoy using digital skills, and/or if they are appropriately engaged. They are a unique subgroup of the population for many reasons that will be described in this chapter. An understanding of their social behavior in virtual settings informs the dialogue and debates surrounding online education.

The chapter will be grounded in the social psychology theories of social learning theory (Bandura, 1971) and social comparison theory (Festinger, 1954) because of the importance that peers and social norms have been found to have on behavior and attitude (Mihelič et al., 2022). Bandura's (1971) Social learning theory proposes that we learn through observations of others; therefore, the chapter will synthesize research to describe the unique influences to which Gen Z have been exposed due to their exposure to technology within a complex sociocultural context during their development. Festinger's (1954) social comparison theory suggests that we evaluate ourselves by comparing with others; therefore, we also review research that examines how the social behavior of Gen Z students in virtual environments may be influenced by the exposure to the social behavior of others within the online communities where they spend their time. This chapter is intended to guide readers to their own conclusions about the online social behavior of this unique generation of students who are already entering the workforce and transforming society.

Early decisions were made about the scope of this chapter that some may perceive as limitations. It is important to recognize that the availability of prior research is uneven across the various factors that are discussed. Some factors, such as social behaviors that distract students, are well-researched with generalizable findings. Other factors, such as the connection between the use of artificial intelligence (AI) and classroom behavior, are under-researched or specific to certain contexts. A second limitation is that all authors relied heavily on their experiences with higher education and technology usage in the United States. International research was reviewed in the preparation of the chapter but introduced contextual variations that went beyond the scope of the chapter. Therefore, while the focus of the chapter is on the unique experiences of American Gen Z students in virtual educational settings, much of what is known can be assumed to be relevant to other generations, other global regions, and other types of virtual environments.

Gen Z students were selected as the focus of this chapter for two reasons. First, because they are digital natives, meaning they had easy daily access to the internet and smartphones throughout every significant developmental stage (Prensky, 2001), the influence of their online experiences is likely to be more comprehensive than that of other generations. Second, because they participated in every level of education during the COVID-19 global pandemic, the influence of that experience is, again, more comprehensive. Therefore, aside from individual differences, much of what is discussed in this chapter is likely to be salient for all Gen Z students to varying degrees.

GENERATION Z STUDENTS

Generation Z (Gen Z) refers to people who were born between 1997 and 2012 (Parker, 2023); although, there is variation in the start and end years of this generation across different sources. They comprise the majority of the student population in primary and secondary school between 2002 – 2030, and in colleges between 2015 – 2034. Gen Z is thought to be one-third of the world's population (Miller & Lu, 2018); the largest proportion of the global population and the most diverse generation to date (Walters, 2021; Van den Bergh et al., 2024). They grew up in an era characterized by technology and have been identified as the first generation of digital natives (Prensky, 2001). As a result of easy daily access to the internet, they are also thought to be more heavily exposed to social issues earlier in their development than previous generations (Cagala & Babcanova, 2024; Silveira et al., 2022). Theoretically, a group of people who collectively experience a time period marked by historical events are referred to as a generational group (Mannheim, 1952; Strauss, 1991). It is assumed that when a generational group is identifiable through their birth years, their experiences with significant life events at critical developmental stages of growth will bond them in particular ways (Dolot, 2018).

The most significant event that has impacted Gen Z differently than previous generations is their exposure to technology. Births in 1997 mark the beginning of Gen Z, and in the same year, the term "smartphone" was coined (Telefonica, 2025). This was the beginning of an era of internet access for approximately 150 to 250 million people across the globe. A few years later, when Gen Z children first entered formal schooling in the early 2000's, there were over one billion internet users. At this time, mobile phones gained access to the internet through 3G networks in 2001, Apple Inc. launched the first iPhone in 2007, and Google released the first Android smartphone in 2008. Smartphones had attractive features such as cameras, music, and games that broadly appealed to all age groups, but was likely an everyday norm for Gen Z children. More than 60% of American children and 95% of adolescents have a smartphone and have used a smartphone since the age of four years old (Anderson & Jiang, 2018; Auxier et al., 2020). The number of children on social media applications (apps) doubles between the ages of ten and fourteen (Steinsbekk et al., 2021).

A revolution of new apps in the mid-2000's transformed the way that smartphones and the internet were used in daily life. Gen Z youth were the first generation to have smartphones during their early formative years. The generation prior (Gen-Y or Millennials) had similar experiences with technology, but not in the early years of their development. Only the youngest of the Millennials could have had a smartphone during their teenage years and they had likely graduated high school and become young adults before they had daily access to the internet.

Gen Z has been, and continues to be, informed, misinformed, disinformed, cyberbullied, and hacked through the social media apps that they access every day. They learn about wars, terrorist attacks, insurrections, and protests in real-time. This is true for all living generations, but it has occurred during critical stages of cognitive and emotional development in the formative years for Gen Z. A more positive approach to interpreting their real-time exposure to national and global events is that this connection has shaped their collective consciousness resulting in an increase of values such as universalism, benevolence, self-direction, achievement, and security (Sakdiyakorn et al., 2021).

Social media platforms may be the primary mode of communication and information through which members of Gen Z participated in or led social protests on issues such as school shootings (Rue, 2018), police violence, the climate crisis, gender equality, and LGBTQ+ rights (Annie E. Casey, 2024). Most recently in the early fall of 2025, Gen Z young adults protesting in Nepal led to a popular uprising that resulted in changes in their government (CNN, 2025).

> *"Social media is the only platform where we can talk and share and follow the global media," according to a young filmmaker in Nepal who attended the protests." (CNN, 2025)*

A growing body of research documents the impact of daily social media access on mental health. We assume that when Gen Z students are online, they are and have been exposed to challenging and transformational sociocultural events. In addition to the global pandemic, they may have observed or been directly impacted by political divisiveness, gun violence, war, civil unrest, misinformation, disinformation, views on gender and sexual identity, and AI. Some research reports on the impact of this daily internet exposure, often referred to as "doomscrolling," and the anxiety, stress, and/or despair that may result (Chisholm & Hartman-Caverly, 2022). Other research focuses on the connection between daily internet access and isolation or loneliness as the phone replaces the time that might have been spent in real human interaction (Moeller, 2019). Furthermore, physical health may be impacted by the decreased outdoor recreation time that coincides with the increase in screen time and the proliferation of smartphones (Krause & Sawhill, 2016; Meyer & Meyer, 2020).

Gen Z are exposed to mostly similar opinions that are immediately reactive about historically significant societal issues, such as discrimination and racism. These echo chambers result from algorithms integrated into social media apps to increase time spent on those apps. This consistent exposure validates and reinforces the opinions of those who agree. Exposure to perceived injustices also raises questions about identity. The definition of gender identity expanded for Gen Z to include nonbinary, nonconforming, and transgender. Sexual preferences became more fluid to incorporate this wider range of gender identities with whom one can become intimate. Sensitivity to how we refer to ourselves and others increased regarding gender, sexual preference, nation of origin, race/ethnicity, and religion.

Furthermore, definitions and identification of neurodiversity became more prevalent amongst Gen Z (Understood, 2024). This result is likely a result of increased awareness and reduced stigma for conditions such as attention deficit hyperactivity disorder and autism. There is also some evidence that online activity changes the way the brain functions and may contribute to difficulties in concentration, attention, memory, and recall (Firth et al., 2019). Research has established that Gen Z have short attention-spans and a high capacity for multi-tasking (Buzzetto-Hollywood & Alade, 2018; Shatto & Erwin, 2016). One study found that their attention span was 30% shorter than Millennials (Claveria, 2017).

With everyday access to technology and significantly distressing world events in real-time, as well as the potential ways that cognitive, identity, and socio-emotional development may be impacted, the overarching question of this chapter examines how this unique sociocultural context has impacted the social behavior of Gen Z students within virtual educational environments. What are their sources for social learning? Their parents/guardians and teachers did not experience technology in the same way. Gen Z peers may not be reliable sources for social learning because of the way that technology has divided and segmented society (Smith & Short, 2022).

Some argue that daily exposure to the internet for much of their lives has changed Gen Z communication, interactions, values, and priorities (Bratina & Faganel, 2024; Silveira et al., 2022). They suggest that Gen Z students have different learning expectations and preferences compared to previous generations (Rue, 2018; Schwieger & Ladwig, 2018). Others believe that exposure to the digital world is too varied to generalize about this group (Smith et al., 2018; Silveira et al., 2022). While this debate continues, the undeniable truth is that Gen Z students have had a unique educational experience as a result of both their access to technology and the COVID-19 global pandemic.

GEN Z AND THE COVID-19 PANDEMIC

While data suggests that Gen Z students are likely to be the most well-educated generation in history (O'Hare & Mayol-Garcia, 2023), the quality of that education is in question as a result of their overexposure to educational chaos during the COVID-19 global pandemic. Gen Z students filled classrooms across all school levels during the instantaneous transition to virtual environments (Bergdahl & Nouri, 2020). No other generation before or after were so comprehensively impacted by the lack of preparation or knowledge of best practices necessary for high quality online educational experiences.

Educators were thrust into online teaching and Gen Z were the primary recipients including young children in kindergarten classrooms, preteens in middle school, adolescents in high school, and young adults in universities. In what seemed like a singular day, they lost their daily routines, their in-person access to friends and peers, and their faith in educators to teach them. Suddenly, their varied levels of expertise with technology exceeded those of the significant adults in their lives. Roles flipped as they perceived themselves as more proficient than their teachers in virtual environments (Cilliers, 2017).

An important issue was the lack of infrastructure for teachers, especially during early COVID-19. High quality training on virtual teaching, technology, and curriculum was limited (Irish, 2022). Additionally, teachers lacked necessary planning time to alter their curriculum to accommodate virtual learning while they also grappled with the impact of a global pandemic in their own lives. Therefore, their teachers were likely to be less prepared to deliver the curriculum, and the quality of the educational experience suffered (Annie E. Casey Foundation, 2024).

Although educators were ill-prepared to transition their curriculum to a virtual classroom, most Gen Z students were already engaged in social interaction across various online environments. They preferred social media for communication and interaction before the pandemic (Carr & Hayes, 2015; Kapoor et al., 2018; Marengo et al., 2018), and research found some positive outcomes such as the bridging of subcultures and friendship maintenance (Siddiqui & Singh, 2016). Online communities became the primary medium of social interaction during the pandemic.

A United States survey by Deloitte in 2022 found that 90% of Gen Z adults use social media. Only 5% consider themselves to be passive users; thus, approximately 95% are actively socially engaged online. This study also found that Gen Z don't distinguish between online friends and those who they meet in the physical world. Despite this social engagement online, many Gen Z struggle with isolation (Bowler, 2020). A national survey by Cigna in 2024 found that Gen Z were the loneliest generation compared to all other previous generations.

Although our brains are wired to seek connections with other humans, people are not born with an inherent desire to be connected to technology. However, because it is so heavily integrated into the daily lives of Gen Z students, they are not likely to contemplate any type of online break. Gen Z's perception of themselves and their well-being is largely dependent on the quantity and quality of their online social interactions (Ateca-Amestoy et al., 2014). Therefore, during the pandemic, the transition to virtual classrooms did not usurp their online activity and, instead, competed with social media and other online environments for student attention.

There is clear evidence that when students disengage from the virtual classroom by using their phones or computers for non-academic purposes, (Mihelič et al., 2022) such as multi-tasking or cyberloafing (both of which are defined by how students are digitally engaged outside of classwork), these behaviors have a negative impact on their acquisition of course content and academic achievement (Kates et al., 2018; Felisoni & Godoi, 2018).

Antoine logged into the Zoom classroom for a three-hour social work class in his master's program. He was interested in the topic and was prepared to discuss the required reading. He had several questions as well as some examples from his internship that he thought were relevant. However, when the professor began to go through slides, he turned off his camera and grabbed his phone off the desk. He scrolled through one app after the other until eventually he noticed silence in the Zoom room. Antoine thought he was paying attention to the professor until he realized that he didn't know why it was silent. Was a question asked? Was there an activity assigned? He wasn't sure. He sent a private chat to his friend in the class to find out and followed the instructions his friend sent back.

"Cyberloafing" refers to using internet browsers for digital engagement that is not related to the course or classwork (Zhang et al., 2020). Students might be playing a game or scrolling through social media on their phones or laptops while class is in session. There is some evidence that cyberloafing is associated with moral disengagement and psychological detachment (Mihelič et al., 2022). Multi-tasking is differentiated from cyberloafing because the distraction stems from working on additional online task(s) that may still be academically related but are not part of engagement in the class in which they are virtually attending at that moment.

The cause of these and other technology-related behaviors may come from a need for emotional regulation (James et al., 2023). Heightened by long-term isolation during the pandemic, researchers sought to understand the impact of isolation on interaction and found that virtual interactions fill a short-term immediate need for contact as an emotional regulator but did not fill the void of physical peer interactions (James et al., 2023). Further research into tools that can be used to aid emotional regulation in the virtual classroom is needed.

When normal life resumed after the pandemic concerns eased, online learning was well-accepted as an educational space, and best practices became more established. However, there is no denying that Gen Z students were participants in a global experiment, and the long-term educational and life outcomes are still unknown. Learning loss, chronic absenteeism, loss of focus, and curriculum loss have been well-documented (Annie E. Casey Foundation, 2024). Although social behaviors in virtual classrooms such as cyberloafing and multi-tasking continue to be ongoing challenges, the next section in this chapter shares practices to attract and retain student attention and to motivate students to reproduce behaviors that support their learning.

SOCIAL LEARNING

Humans rely on experts to teach them what they do not yet know or have not yet experienced. We learn by observing and practicing the behaviors that experts model to achieve positive outcomes. It may be difficult to discern who is an expert and if the information they are sharing is valid and/or accurate when watching very short videos or hearing soundbites. Gen Z is living in a time of "alternative facts" and deliberate falsehoods. They watched non-experts become famous influencers whose main goal is to influence their peers in ways that bring them more followers and sponsors.

Social media has also served to divide the population into subcultures where each group can find like-minded people who agree with their point of view (Smith & Short, 2022) and research has found that Gen Z has a lower tolerance for differing opinions than previous generations (Chong & Citrin, 2024). Adding to this complexity, AI offers what appears to be fact but may instead be hallucinations that are incorrect, misleading, or nonsensical (Diaz, 2025). Therefore, social learning theory offers an interesting approach to understanding Gen Z social behavior, as well as other generations, that are exposed to the same "experts." However, as the first generation with daily easy access to these sources of information during all stages of growth and development, Gen Z are unique from the generations that have come before them.

Learning is an inherent part of being human. Regardless of generation, time, or place, people utilize their brain's capability to learn to survive and thrive in society. Made famous by Albert Bandura (1961), social learning theory originated from a desire to understand how humans learn, especially from natural modeling versus conditioning techniques (Baldwin, 1973). During initial experiments, children were separated into control and experimental groups, both of which were brought into a room with toys. All groups started the experiment by working on the attention-focused task of putting together a toy. Participants were exposed to adults who modeled aggressive or nonaggressive behavior towards a bobo doll (Bandura et al., 1961). This initial experiment resulted in children demonstrating aggressive behavior in the room if they had been exposed to the initial behavior by the adult models, especially when the modeling adult was the same gender.

Researchers identified four primary features of social learning that needed to occur for the behavior to be truly learned. Once an adult, or model, was brought into the room, they needed to acquire the child's *attention* (McLeod, 2025). This was done initially by the adult engaging with the child (Bandura et al., 1961). Next, the adult would need to sustain the child's attention long enough for *retention* to occur, which would be measured later via the next feature, *reproduction*. Reproducing the behavior when in a separate room without the adult, demonstrated an internalization of the learned behavior. The final feature of social learning theory is *motivation* to reproduce behavior.

To better understand the initial modeling and motivational features, Bandura carried out further experiments comparing modeling via a film versus in-person aggression interventions (Bandura et al., 1963), and positive or negative reinforcement from another adult after the aggressive behavior (Bandura, 1965). Social learning through modeling behavior by film or reinforcement resulted in the same impact as watching someone in person on the choice to reenact the behavior. This evidence of the impact of film on behavior through the power of modeling led to concerns surrounding violence and other unhealthy behaviors that are frequently illustrated in the media. Despite these concerns, digital content with violence and other unhealthy behaviors has far from lessened since the initial research was conducted, and this topic remains contentious (Boccio & Leal, 2022).

The 1960's, when Bandura began his research, is a faraway landscape from the world Gen Z has grown up in as digital natives with technology infused into their daily lives during development. From his research, Bandura theorized that humans learn through observation in three primary ways. First, through direct observation or live modeling, this may take place naturally through daily events or in a controlled hands-on classroom environment (Fryling et al., 2011). Next, humans learn through symbolic modeling which could be by a real or fictitious person from a narrative such as a film, show, digital video, or book where behaviors are modeled (Bandura et al., 1963). Finally, humans can learn through verbal instruction where the model is articulating directions for the behavior. In modern day, this would be very similar to a Zoom room, digital classroom, podcast, or audiobook (McLeod, 2025).

Digital content from social media platforms and streaming services have, for the first time, eclipsed traditional cable entertainment (Vmontiel, 2025). In 2025, YouTube had a reported user base of 2.53 billion while TikTok had a reach of 1.59 billion with likely overlap between the two (Kemp, 2025), and these numbers are not expected to decrease. Consistently, over the last several years, the average social media user spends over two hours a day consuming content (Kemp, 2024). The studies completed by Bandura set the groundwork for understanding current trends in modeling behavior due to the thoroughness in experimentation. At the time, there was no way of predicting the exponential growth of modeling behavior by public figures or by people who are unknown personally to the viewer.

A salient example of models that are unknown to viewers are found in the phenomenon of influencers on social media. Influencers are content creators or internet personalities on sites such as Tik Tok, Youtube, and Twitch where they shape their fans' actions and opinions. The most famous of which have led to wide changes in social behavior (especially in youth). One example is popular Twitch streamer IShowSpeed, whose loud exaggerated actions directly caused an increase in the aggressive rambunctiousness of youth (Mead, 2024). Another impact can be seen in the prevalence of linguistic changes as a result of influencers with words like "skibidi toilet", "rizz" or "brainrot." With the ability to change social behavior and language, influencers are quite literally influencing our society.

While the ease of access to educational and informational material on social media platforms is enticing, it has elevated influencers into the role of teachers or models for behavior through symbolic learning. The influencers sell themselves as subject matter experts, in some cases, teaching life skills such as cooking, exercising, home maintenance, or even therapeutic practices that the learner can then act out in real life. Social media and online personalities are often advised to have a persona that has the appearance of genuine connection with their audience to create trust with their viewers. For example, an influencer might be talking with their audience about strategies for achieving success in college while they apply make-up to their faces. They are sponsored by cosmetic companies and provide pathways for their viewers to purchase the products. However, as they start the short video with a cleanly scrubbed face and avoid mentioning the products while they are applying them, the viewers do not feel as though they have been subjected to a marketing ploy. Further, multi-tasking is being modeled for the viewers in such a subtle manner that they may not notice the influence it has on their own online social behavior.

The connection between social media influencers as models has been noticed by consumer scientists attempting to understand the purchasing impact influencer modeling can have on content consumers (Sardar & Vijay, 2025). Content creators acting as models, according to social learning theory, may have to choose between quality content creation and quick turnaround (Shoufan, 2018) or neutral tones versus emotionally charged tones to gain subscribers, views, and comments. This creates a digital landscape that is increasingly complex with hidden costs of which many learners are unaware.

As mentioned earlier, Gen Z have significantly shorter attention spans and a high capacity for multi-tasking (Buzzetto-Hollywood & Alade, 2018; Claveria, 2017; Shatto & Erwin, 2016). Technology constantly seeks attention through notifications, bells, and vibrations. However, research is emerging on ways that educators can compete with these distractions. Gen Z students appreciate it when educators or educational technology platforms provide them with announcements and reminders that are sent to their phones and they have an expectation for educators to integrate technology in their courses (Buzzetto-Hollywood, et al., 2021). From the perspective of social learning theory, research found that the presence of a professor, as a model, decreased cyberloafing (Zhang et al., 2020).

Another approach to attract student attention in a virtual classroom is to mix teaching methodologies (Price, 2010). Research exploring the preferences of Gen Z students found that they enjoy e-assessments and hybrid learning environments

(Teh & Baskaran, 2022). A study of Gen Z youth found that they prefer small pieces of real-time information and pictures (Törőcsik et al., 2014) such as videos instead of books (Buzzetto-Hollywood, et al., 2021). Gen Z has reported a desire for education to be more interactive and instantaneously informative through the incorporation of technology and social media (Cilliers, 2017). In Cilliers (2017) study, they reported that they believe technology increases the quality of teaching and learning; although they also reported believing that they are more proficient in technology than their professors.

A third option is to create an intended opportunity to multi-task to prevent students from disengaging. For instance, assignments that require students to seek self-instruction through YouTube videos (Seemiller & Grace, 2017) and share what they have learned with their classmates may be motivating because it complements the way that they learn while also creating an opportunity for reproduction of what they learned. A study by Ernst and Young (2016) found that Gen Z across eight nations were found (among other factors) to be entrepreneurial and self-sufficient, connected and online, and to value immersive storytelling. Educator practices that provide students with opportunities for independence, connectivity with online platforms, and short stories may be more likely to retain student attention in the virtual classroom.

Individual traits, values, and abilities may also influence social behavior in virtual classrooms; although this is an area that is under-studied. Some students may be quieter or shy and may feel compelled to type in the chat rather than unmute and speak aloud. Other students may feel more confident or are willing to take risks to engage with others in the virtual classroom. In addition to explanations for online social behavior that are grounded in the observation of models, social comparison may provide complementary yet different reasons for behavioral choices in virtual classrooms. The next section will take a closer look at the phenomenon of learning social behaviors through comparison with others.

SOCIAL COMPARISON

Festinger's (1954) social comparison theory proposes that individuals evaluate their abilities, attitudes, and self-worth by comparing themselves to others. This theory provides an important lens for understanding Gen Z's behaviors in virtual classrooms, where social interactions and performance are measured. The rise of social media on smartphones increased digital connectivity but also introduced social comparison with others on a more global level that previously only existed with people with whom they were in personal relationships or in proximity. Gen Z's social media habits influence how they navigate academic peer interactions, similar to how they evaluate credibility and popularity online. Students in virtual classrooms may selectively align with peers they perceive as competent or disengage from those they judge less favorably (Appel et al., 2016).

Beginning in middle childhood, children engage in social comparisons with their student peers and evaluate their own academic abilities (Keil et al., 1990). School-based social comparisons increase in high school when adolescents are developing their identity (Krayer et al., 2008). More recently, social comparison theory helps explain how Gen Z students continuously negotiate identity, motivation, and belonging in online spaces (Jansen et al., 2022). Gen Z are influenced by a wide range of opinions that include their friends, online peers and influencers, as well as online reviews and ratings (Tariyal et al., 2020). They are more likely to follow the recommendations of their trusted networks that include friends, family, and online communities (Dhar & Bose, 2023; Dhar et al., 2024). They desire social acceptance, and this may drive their decisions, attitudes, and behaviors to reflect the values of groups with which they identify (Vajkai & Zsoka, 2020; Serravalle, 2022; Abbasi et al., 2023). They prefer the convenience and immediate gratification (Francis & Hoefel, 2018) that online "friends" provide. For example, a camera-on requirement for a synchronous online class is more likely to create a scenario in which all students feel pressure to look engaged to their classmates and teacher. This may discourage multi-tasking and cyberloafing as compared to when cameras are off.

As digital natives, Gen Z students have been socialized through the use of online platforms as spaces for both learning and self-presentation (Turner, 2015). In virtual classrooms, this often results in upward social comparisons, where students assess themselves against their peers who appear more confident, articulate, or engaged on video (Hasenbein et al., 2023). These social comparisons can motivate effort but also risk increasing anxiety and diminishing self-esteem when students perceive themselves as falling short (Vogel et al., 2014).

Previous research has found that academic social comparisons that lead to negative emotions such as anxiety or boredom are negatively related to attention, motivation, interactions with peers and teachers, and achievement (Pekrun et al., 2009). Recent research has found cyberloafing behavior is associated with anxiety and boredom (Li et al., 2022). Therefore, the combination of these research studies leads to the extrapolation that when students are cyberloafing due to boredom or anxiety, the impact on their academic performance is likely to be negative. More research is needed to connect online social comparisons to social behavior and performance in virtual classrooms.

Students may also engage in downward comparisons, observing peers who appear less prepared or disengaged (Suls et al., 2002). Social comparison that leads to positive emotions such as pride and enjoyment are positively associated with motivation and achievement (Pekrun et al., 2009). These comparisons can provide reassurance and help maintain motivation, particularly in collaborative activities (Suls et al., 2002). In a virtual classroom, collaborative activities in chat logs, discussion boards, and reaction emojis have more permanence and visibility of participation as performance is more publicly recorded. This may amplify the effects of comparison, creating easier scrutiny, and can result in social influence and normative conformity (Yang et al., 2017).

Overall, Gen Z's behavior in virtual classrooms can be understood as a process of constant peer evaluation shaped by digital visibility. While such comparisons can inspire achievement, they also create new pressures unique to online learning environments that influence student engagement. Technological advances have diversified learning options for these digital natives, offering many educational choices that did not previously exist for other generations.

VIRTUAL LEARNING

Gen Z students are the generation that is most impacted by the cultural shift away from live modeling to the increasing presence of symbolic modeling and verbal instruction through online platforms in contemporary times. It is unclear from the current literature whether there is an experimental, cognitive (Shoufan, 2018) or biologically best practice for Gen Z learners. Historically, response times or other cognitive processing data and physiological data can conflict with self-report responses (Ramsey, 2014). What is clear from the data is that digital learning is culturally embedded, especially for digital natives.

A majority of Gen Z students seek an informal education by watching short social media videos on sites like YouTube or TikTok. These social media platforms with large user bases have captivated Gen Z interest by allowing users access to a variety of subject matter experts offering free education available at any time (Kemp, 2025). However, there is little known about their inherent positive and negative features, and more research is needed to understand their impact. This is especially true for the social implications for emerging learners potentially engaging with others in more digital than physical spaces.

Some students seek platforms specifically tailored for career-based certifications or degree programs through virtual higher education classrooms. The virtual classroom can be a synchronous or asynchronous learning space comprising both lectures and digital tools (Dhawan, 2020). Online conferencing tools such as Zoom mixed with learning management systems (LMS) such as Canvas or Google Classroom replicate the physical classroom in a virtual space. Options within the general construct of online education include hybrid and flipped classrooms that utilize both in-person and online aspects. Hybrid classrooms give instruction both in-person and online, often at the same time, to accommodate additional students, social distancing, and more. Hybrid classrooms also may include recorded lectures so that students who cannot attend can view the content later. Flipped classrooms provide instruction online and use in-person class time to work on assignments or other classwork.

One study found that students responded positively to video or recorded lectures because of the features it offers such as rewind, pause, speed up, and slow down (Zhu et al., 2022). These students also felt more productive during class time, were able to work with more difficult problems, and had time to ask the teacher questions in class. Other research has been split with self-report measures amongst Gen Z learners reporting an affinity for video-watching followed by reenactment of the learned behavior (Seemiller & Grace, 2017) and in-person live learning with peers (Cilliers, 2021).

Another type of non-traditional virtual learning environment is Massive Open Online Courses (MOOCs). A large percentage of Gen Z adult learners opt for MOOC platforms, such as Coursera with over 142 million registered users, edX with 86 million users (Dey, 2025), and Udemy with 69 million users (Dean, 2025). Learners opting for these platforms gain access to videos, quizzes, discussion boards, and they upload projects or assignments required for completion. MOOC content developers have come a long way in attempting to create a classroom atmosphere that lends itself to the most up-to-date learning theories. However, social connections between students remain a struggle. When learners connected with peers or experts to practice the reproduction stage (of social learning theory) after the lecture, they scored close to three points higher than isolated peers (Breslow et al., 2013). Social media use such as user specific group pages or communication forums separate from the MOOC platform have some limited support for enhancing content engagement follow-through (Huang et al., 2023). More research is needed to examine student social behavior in MOOC settings.

Lastly, it is important to acknowledge the recent evolution of AI and the impact that it is having on student and educator interactions in all types of classrooms. Knowledge about new technology and related impacts on learning is limited due to a lack of empirical research into the challenges, advantages, or societal implications (Li et al., 2023). Gen Z digital natives are learning and developing in a world with limited empirically backed policies and procedures.

Some Gen Z students access AI in their everyday interactions on the internet and in their school assignments, while others avoid it because of the high environmental and energy costs that conflict with their beliefs and values related to the climate crisis (Crawford, 2021) and social justice issues (Birhane, 2021). One survey of nearly 3500 participants found that 79% of Gen Z respondents reported using generative AI products, and 47% indicated that they use these products on a weekly basis (Gallup Report, 2025). The summary of the survey results found that Gen Z feels more anxious than excited about AI and less likely to trust the products that are generated by these tools. The use of AI has also led to concerns about societal biases that may be hidden in algorithms (Bigman et al., 2022; Bonezzi & Ostinelli, 2021).

Therefore, Gen Z is skeptical of the use of AI both in and out of the classroom but understand its value. This may stem from their exposure to information, disinformation, and misinformation online, from which AI is trained. More research is needed to fully understand the origins and implications of Gen Z's skepticism. At best, it could be evidence of critical thinking that extends beyond the typical acceptance of what appears to be authoritative voices. At worst, it could reflect a general questioning of the value of education after living through the rocky online transition that occurred during the pandemic. Importantly, the transformational emergence of AI in the classroom has introduced a circular evolution of educators and students attempting to discover the use and misuse of AI tools, resulting in an environment of distrust.

Jeremy knew from the teacher's instructions and the syllabus that AI could not be used to write the required paper that was due at the end of the term, but he had run out of time to do the necessary research to write it himself. He worried that he could get caught if the paper didn't have human errors. He decided to ask Google to translate the AI-generated paper into Spanish. Then he asked Google to translate the Spanish version into German. Finally, he asked Google to translate the German version into English and removed egregious errors. Before he submitted the paper to his teacher, he used Chatgptzero to see if it was considered to be written by a human. Once he was satisfied that his paper would pass through the checks used by his teacher, he submitted it online in the course webpage. The entire process was completed in less than one hour.

A small survey study at a university in the United States found that trust and distrust among educators were related but distinct concepts that co-exist (Lyu et al., 2025). Most educators who completed the survey had a "trust but verify" approach for both their own use of AI as well as use by their students. They seek out ways to uncover this type of student behavior with sites such as *Turnitin* or *Chatgptzero* to identify student generative AI usage. This particular dynamic of students using generative AI and teachers using tools to catch them results in a circular dilemma or a virtual arms race in which students find methods to misuse AI tools and teachers create new methods to prevent misuse. The tools that teachers use to discover the use of AI in student papers are not perfect. They may identify the use of AI incorrectly. One can imagine the culture of mistrust that using these tools creates and the negative experience that a student is likely to have if falsely accused.

Susan was excited to see the grade from her paper because she had worked hard on it and felt confident of a high score. She logged into the course webpage, clicked to her gradebook, and discovered that she had failed. She reached out immediately to her professor and was told that her paper was identified as being AI-generated. Susan was devastated and showed her professor earlier drafts and notes. The professor began to doubt the results of the tool she used to check papers for AI and scheduled time for Susan to write a new version of the paper on a shared screen in front of her, using the notes that had just been reviewed. When this paper was submitted, it was again flagged for using AI. Susan became visibly upset, and, although she was no longer penalized for using AI, she shared her experience with her classmates and negatively rated the teacher.

Once again, Gen Z (as well as subsequent generations) are part of another global experiment as AI increasingly enters the educational environment. Future psychological and educational research is needed to inform educators and students about the connections between human, societal, and digital development. Little is known about the social cost or the impact this shift will have long-term on culture. The research community must invest more resources into understanding this constantly changing landscape.

CONCLUSION

When the COVID-19 pandemic compelled educators to switch from face-to-face learning to online learning and modalities, virtual classrooms shifted from being a supplemental form of education to being a core component that offers flexibility, accessibility, and opportunities for individuals that may not have been present during traditional formats (Bozkurt & Sharma, 2020). With online learning, educators and students encounter new challenges that require adaptability and flexibility. Despite creating challenges, digital literacy and technological accessibility have become the forefront of online teaching and a core aspect of virtual education (Dhawan, 2020).

Virtual classrooms make it feasible to reach geographically dispersed learners and individuals who have extenuating circumstances and/or physical ailments that may limit mobility and educational opportunities (Means & Neisler, 2020). Virtual classrooms have created opportunities for learning, career advancement, and global collaboration that were previously limited by the confines of the traditional classroom setting (Means & Neisler, 2020). When best practice strategies are used concurrently, they can create a supportive virtual learning environment that enhances and maximizes student success. Adopting evidence-based strategies allows online educators to improve learning outcomes and equip students with skills and techniques to succeed.

Although current information on best practices is limited, research suggests that engagement with teachers and peers either via external social media groups (Huang et al., 2023), or synchronous virtual classrooms may bridge social divides (Zhang et al., 2020). When virtual classrooms are structured in ways that intentionally meet psychological needs, students not only report higher levels of engagement but also demonstrate greater persistence and commitment to their learning (Prananto et al., 2025). Creating opportunities for social engagement could potentially alleviate the high levels of loneliness and the need for emotional regulation noted for Gen Z due to their unique sociocultural context.

With their focus and attention on social justice issues, Gen Z are positioned well to create accountability amongst themselves and their peers. As consumers of social media, they must start questioning what they see online. Influencers and content developers can also question the impact they wish to have on their audience with an awareness that their actions serve as a model for their viewers.

Harrington and DeBruler (2021) proposed a number of best practices for online education, to which we have applied the research findings about Gen Z documented in the previous sections. For example, while they propose multiple content formats as a best practice, the knowledge of Gen Z's short attention span translates that into the mixing of content formats into short bursts to attract and retain attention. Including texts, videos, podcasts, and interactive situations allow Gen Z students to learn material in an array of different styles and modalities. Educators who incorporated both asynchronous and synchronous teaching interactions observed stronger course engagement compared to those who solely relied on one format (Harrington & DeBruler, 2021).

Feedback is proposed as a best practice; however, for Gen Z, it is important that feedback is designed to promote social interaction and accountability for engagement with the course content. They are less tolerant of different opinions; therefore, they need to perceive feedback as a human connection that is constructive. Providing feedback can increase motivation (Sahu et al., 2022) and meet Gen Z students' emotional needs due to their high levels of loneliness. Additionally, tailoring feedback to individual strengths and areas for growth, improvement, and development reinforce student's ability to succeed (Koushik & Bhamare, 2025).

Educators have the opportunity to humanize virtual education by providing opportunities for students to engage with their peers, learn socialization skills such as online etiquette, and enhance trust, belonging, and motivation (Sahu et al., 2022; Bozkurt & Sharma, 2020). Practices such as ice-breakers, small group collaboration, and announcements have been shown to reduce the sense of isolation that is commonly found in virtual classroom settings (Hodges et al., 2020). When students feel more connected to their peers and educators in virtual classrooms, they are more engaged and motivated in the learning process and classroom setting (Hollister et al., 2022).

Relatedness, or the need to feel connected to others, is most challenging in virtual classrooms due to physical distance and potential isolation (Li & Yang, 2025). Despite its challenges, educators can address this by fostering community through discussion boards, synchronous video sessions, collaborative projects, and personalized instructor-student interactions (Sweetman, 2020). When Gen Z students perceive that their contributions are valued, whether through active acknowledgment in online discussions or through personalized feedback, they are more likely to feel a sense of belonging (Tang et al., 2023).

Due to distractions, virtual environments provide students with more opportunities to be disengaged from the course material (Caprara & Caprara, 2022). When courses are well-organized, cognitive load is reduced, making it more feasible for students to engage in learning tasks and actively interact with the content and peers (Gkintoni et al., 2025). Incorporating breaks into the virtual course schedule for students to stretch, get snacks, and complete other small tasks can help students remain focused and engaged (Infantes-Paniagua et al., 2021). Compared to traditional lecture-based approaches, active learning in virtual contexts significantly increases student engagement (Venton & Pompano, 2021). Educators who embed active tasks within synchronous and asynchronous activities create opportunities for students to construct knowledge, conceptualize, remain invested in learning, and be more organized in the course. Educators can maximize virtual learning by engaging in scaffolding through the breakdown of larger assignments into smaller ones and progressively building skills.

An important strategy for best practices in virtual classrooms is consistent communication and personalization to sustain motivation. Increased student satisfaction and persistence are directly linked to maintained communication between students and educators (Wong & Chapman, 2023); educators can communicate with emails, announcements, and/or virtual office hours to demonstrate responsiveness and availability. Personalized communication such as mandatory individual check-ins and one-on-one meetings with educators ensures that students feel supported in their academic journey (Perez, 2023). Personalization is not limited to communication alone but can also be applied to assignments; when students have flexibility and autonomy with selecting topics and formats/mediums for assignments and projects, this has been found to increase intrinsic motivation (Reber et al., 2018).

Research on Gen Z in the United States, and beyond, describes them as independent and self-sufficient. A theoretical approach that capitalizes on these strengths is self-determination theory (SDT). According to SDT, the psychological needs of autonomy, competence, and relatedness are foundational for sustaining motivation and engagement (Harrington & DeBruler, 2021). These needs are crucial in virtual learning environments, where their fulfillment requires intentional strategies from educators. In online contexts, autonomy can be fostered by providing students with meaningful choices, such as flexible deadlines, varied assignment formats, or the ability to pursue topics aligned with their interests. This sense of control helps students feel empowered rather than constrained by the structure of virtual platforms (Mohammadi Zenough et al., 2025). Competence is supported when instructors design clear expectations, provide timely feedback, and utilize digital tools such as quizzes, breakout rooms, or interactive simulations that allow students to progressively demonstrate mastery.

There is little to no research on best practices for the integration of AI in education generally, but especially in virtual classrooms where assignments are prepared and submitted outside of the educator's purview. Although the debates about integrity, trust and learning impacts related to the use of AI are just beginning, Gen Z are digital natives, and seeking information from online sources that incorporate AI is as natural to them as breathing. Therefore, educators must explore AI cautiously and carefully to avoid creating negative classroom climates and circular patterns of rule-setting and rule-breaking. Forming positive relationships with students and providing clear expectations for original thinking and writing may be the only practices that educators have until the research is able to advance our understanding and knowledge.

In reflecting on the social behaviors of Gen Z students in virtual classrooms, it becomes clear that disengagement is often less about a lack of interest and more about a struggle to feel connected in an online space. The silence, blank screens, and reliance on chat functions highlight how difficult it can be for students to experience a sense of belonging when physical presence is absent. At the same time, these behaviors reveal an opportunity for educators to reimagine how connection can be fostered in digital environments. Creating intentional spaces for dialogue, encouraging collaboration, and offering personalized educational experiences can transform online courses from a sense of isolation into communities of learning.

For implementation purposes, the challenge is not simply to deliver content but to design virtual classrooms that invite students to participate fully, to see themselves as valued members of the group, and to recognize their voices matter. By prioritizing authentic engagement and building structures that support connection, future online courses can become places where motivation and learning thrive. The disengaged social behaviors presently observed amongst some Gen Z students in virtual settings are not barriers, but reminders that education in the digital age must continue to evolve and place human connection at the center of learning.

REFERENCES

Abbasi, A. Z., Ting, D. H., & Alqahtani, S. (2023). TikTok app usage behavior: The role of hedonic consumption experiences, user satisfaction, and switching behavior. *Kybernetes*, *52*(3), 856–883. DOI: 10.1108/DTA-03-2022-0107

Anderson, M., & Jiang, J. (2018). *Teens, social media & technology*. Pew Research Center. https://www.pewresearch.org/internet/2018/05/31/teens-social-media-technology-2018/

Annie E. Casey Foundation. (2024, March 31). *Social issues that matter to Generation Z.* https://www.aecf.org/blog/generation-z-social-issues

Appel, H., Gerlach, A. L., & Crusius, J. (2016). The interplay between Facebook use, social comparison, envy, and depression. *Current Opinion in Psychology*, *9*, 44–49. DOI: 10.1016/j.copsyc.2015.10.006

Apple Inc. (2007, January 9). *Apple Reinvents the Phone with iPhone*. https://www.apple.com/newsroom/2007/01/09Apple-Reinvents-the-Phone-with-iPhone/

Ateca-Amestoy, V., Aguilar, A. C., & Moro-Egido, A. I. (2014). Social interactions and life satisfaction: Evidence from Latin America. *Journal of Happiness Studies*, *15*(3), 527–554.

Auxier, B., Anderson, M., Perrin, A., & Turner, E. (2020). *Children's engagement with digital devices, screen time*. Pew Research Center https://www.pewresearch.org/internet/2020/07/28/childrens-engagement-with-digital-devices-screen-time/

Baldwin, A. (1973). Social Learning. *Review of Research in Education*, *1*, 34–57. DOI: 10.2307/1167194

Bandura, A. (1965). Influence of models' reinforcement contingencies on the acquisition of imitative responses. *Journal of Personality and Social Psychology*, *1*(6), 589–595. DOI: 10.1037/h0022070

Bandura, A. (1971). *Social Learning Theory.* General Learning Press. http://www.asecib.ase.ro/mps/Bandura_SocialLearningTheory.pdf

Bandura, A., Ross, D., & Ross, S. A. (1961). Transmission of aggression through imitation of aggressive models. *Journal of Abnormal and Social Psychology*, *63*(3), 575–582. DOI: 10.1037/h0045925

Bandura, A., Ross, D., & Ross, S. A. (1963). Imitation of film-mediated aggressive models. *Journal of Abnormal and Social Psychology*, *66*, 3–11. DOI: 10.1037/h0048687

Bergdahl, N., & Nouri, J. (2020). Covid-19 and crisis-prompted distance education in Sweden. *Technology. Knowledge and Learning, 26*, 443–459. DOI: 10.1007/s10758-020-09470-6

Bigman, Y. E., Wilson, D., Arnestad, M. N., Waytz, A., & Gray, K. (2022). Algorithmic discrimination causes less moral outrage than human discrimination. *Journal of Experimental Psychology. General, 152*(1), 4–27. DOI: 10.1037/xge0001250

Birhane, A. (2021). Algorithmic injustice: A relational ethics approach. *Patterns (New York, N.Y.), 2*(2), 100205. DOI: 10.1016/j.patter.2021.100205

Boccio, C. M., & Leal, W. E. (2022). Does socializing in the virtual world impact victimization in the real world? *Journal of Interpersonal Violence, 38*(3–4), 3756–3776. DOI: 10.1177/08862605221109922

Bonezzi, A., & Ostinelli, M. (2021). Can algorithms legitimize discrimination? *Journal of Experimental Psychology. Applied, 27*, 447–459. DOI: 10.1037/xap0000294

Bowler, A. (2020, April). *Isolation among Generation Z in the United States. Ballard Brief.* www.ballardbrief.org

Bozkurt, A., & Sharma, R. C. (2020). Emergency remote teaching in a time of global crisis due to the CoronaVirus pandemic. *Asian Journal of Distance Education, 15*(1), 1–6. DOI: 10.5281/zenodo.3778083

Bratina, D., & Faganel, A. (2024). Understanding Gen Z and Gen X Responses to Influencer Communications. *Administrative Sciences, 14*(2), 33. DOI: 10.3390/admsci14020033

Breslow, L., Pritchard, D. E., DeBoer, J., Stump, G. S., Ho, A. D., & Seaton, D. T. (2013). Studying learning in the worldwide classroom: Research into edX's first MOOC. *Journal of Research & Practice in Assessment, 8*, 13–25.

Buzzetto-Hollywood, N., & Alade, A. (2018). An examination of Gen Z learners attending a minority university. Interdisciplinary *Journal of e-Skills and Lifelong Learning, 14,* 41-53. https://doi.org/DOI: 10.28945/3969

Buzzetto-Hollywood, N., Hill, A., & Banks, T. (2021). Early findings of a study exploring the social media, political and cultural awareness, and civic activism of Gen Z students in the Mid-Atlantic United States. In M. Jones (Ed.), *Proceedings of InSITE 2021: Informing Science and Information Technology Education Conference*, Article 11. Informing Science Institute. DOI: 10.28945/4762

Cagala, M., & Babcanova, D. (2024). Preferences of generations of customers in Slovakia in the field of marketing communication and their impact on consumer behaviour. *Administrative Sciences*, *14*(9), 224. DOI: 10.3390/admsci14090224

Caprara, L., & Caprara, C. (2022). Effects of virtual learning environments: A scoping review of literature. *Education and Information Technologies*, *27*(3), 3683–3722. DOI: 10.1007/s10639-021-10768-w

Carr, C. T., & Hayes, R. A. (2015). Social media: Defining, developing, and divining. *Atlantic Journal of Communication*, *23*, 46–65. DOI: 10.1080/15456870.2015.972282

Chisholm, A., & Hartman-Caverly, S. (2022). Privacy Literacy: From Doomscrolling to Digital Wellness. *Portal (Baltimore, Md.)*, *22*(1), 53–79. DOI: 10.1353/pla.2022.0009

Chong, D., & Citrin, J. (2024). The realignment of political tolerance in the United States. *Perspectives on Politics*, *22*(1), 131–152. DOI: 10.1017/S1537592722002079

Cigna (2024). Loneliness in America 2025: A pervasive struggle requires a communal response. https://newsroom.thecignagroup.com/loneliness-in-america

Cilliers, E. J. (2017). The challenge of teaching Generation Z. *PEOPLE. The International Journal of Social Sciences (Islamabad)*, *3*(1), 188–198. DOI: 10.20319/pijss.2017.31.188198

Cilliers, E. J. (2021). Reflecting on social learning tools to enhance the teaching-learning experience of Generation Z learners. *Frontiers in Education*, *5*. Advance online publication. DOI: 10.3389/feduc.2020.606533

Claveria, K. (2017). *Unlike millennials: 5 ways Gen Z differs from Gen Y.* https://www.visioncritical.com/Gen Z-versus-millennials-infographics/

CNN. (2025). *A parliament in flames, a leader toppled. Nepal's Gen Z protesters ask: What comes next?* https://www.cnn.com/2025/09/10/asia/nepal-protests-genz-outcome-intl-hnk

Crawford, K. (2021). *Atlas of AI: Power, politics, and the planetary costs of artificial intelligence*. Yale University Press.

Dean, E. (2025, July 7). *50+ online course statistics for 2025*. Whop. https://whop.com/blog/course-statistics/

Deloitte. (2022). *McKinsey Health Institute global Gen Z survey: New insights into how this generation thinks about health.* McKinsey & Company. https://www.mckinsey.com/industries/healthcare/our-insights/addressing-the-unprecedented-behavioral-health-challenges-facing-generation-z

Dey, M. (2025, April 30). EDX Statistics by website traffic, marketing channels and courses. *Electro IQ.* https://electroiq.com/stats/edx-statistics/

Dhar, D., Kumar, P., Bhateja, S., Jain, S., Rawat, S., & Shinde, M. (2024). People and sites as community resources for preventing and responding to gender-based violence in Uttar Pradesh, India: A descriptive qualitative study. *PLOS Global Public Health, 4*(7). Advance online publication. DOI: 10.1371/journal.pgph.0003415

Dhar, S., & Bose, I. (2023). Corporate users' attachment to social networking sites: Examining the role of social capital and perceived benefits. *Information Systems Frontiers, 25*(3), 1197–1217. DOI: 10.1007/s10796-022-10289-y

Dhawan, S. (2020). Online learning: A panacea in the time of COVID-19 crisis. *Journal of Educational Technology Systems, 49*(1), 5–22. DOI: 10.1177/0047239520934018

Diaz, J. (2025, July 10). A recent high-profile case of AI hallucination serves as a stark warning. NPR. https://www.npr.org/2025/07/10/nx-s1-5463512/ai-courts-lawyers-mypillow-fines

Dolot, A. (2018). The characteristic of Generation Z. *E-mentor, 2*(74), 44-50. DOI: 10.15219/em74.1351

Ernst & Young Report. (2016). From Innovation to Expectation – How M & E Leaders are Responding to Gen Z. http://www.ey.com/Publication/vwLUAssets/ey-media-entertainment-leaders-respond-toGen Z/$FILE/ey-media-entertainmentleaders-respond-to-Gen Z.pdf

Felisoni, D. D., & Godoi, I. M. (2018). Cell phone usage and academic performance: An experiment. In *Proceedings of EdMedia: World Conference on Educational Media and Technology* (pp. 67–75). Association for the Advancement of Computing in Education (AACE). DOI: 10.1016/j.compedu.2017.10.006

Festinger, L. (1954). A theory of social comparison processes. *Human Relations; Studies Towards the Integration of the Social Sciences, 7*(2), 117–140. DOI: 10.1177/001872675400700202

Firth, J., Torous, J., Stubbs, B., Firth, J. A., Steiner, G. Z., Smith, L., & Sarris, J. (2019). The "online brain": How the Internet may be changing our cognition. *World Psychiatry; Official Journal of the World Psychiatric Association (WPA), 18*(2), 119–129. DOI: 10.1002/wps.20617

Francis, T., & Hoefel, F. (2018, November 12). *'True Gen': Generation Z and its implications for companies.* McKinsey & Company.

Fryling, M. J., Johnston, C., & Hayes, L. J. (2011). Understanding observational learning: An interbehavioral approach. *Analysis of Verbal Behavior, 27*(1), 191–203. DOI: 10.1007/BF03393102

Gallup. (2025, April 8). Voices of Gen Z: How American youth view and use artificial intelligence. https://static.waltonfamilyfoundation.org/a7/cd/b145ce854643a05e5393fa0664a4/walton-gsv-voices-of-Gen Z-ai-final-report-04042025.pdf

Gkintoni, E., Antonopoulou, H., Sortwell, A., & Halkiopoulos, C. (2025). Challenging cognitive load theory: The role of educational neuroscience and artificial intelligence in redefining learning efficacy. *Brain Sciences, 15*(2), 203. DOI: 10.3390/brainsci15020203

Harrington, C., & DeBruler, K. (2021). Key strategies for engaging students in virtual learning environments. Michigan Virtual Learning Research Institute. https://michiganvirtual.org/research/publications/key-strategies-for-engaging-students-in-virtual-learning-environments/

Hasenbein, L., Stark, P., Trautwein, U., Gao, H., Kasneci, E., & Göllner, R. (2023). Investigating social comparison behaviour in an immersive virtual reality classroom based on eye-movement data. *Scientific Reports, 13*(1), 14672. DOI: 10.1038/s41598-023-41704-2

Hodges, C., Moore, S., Lockee, B., Trust, T., & Bond, A. (2020). The difference between emergency remote teaching and online learning. *Educause Review*. https://er.educause.edu/articles/2020/3/the-difference-between-emergency-remote-teaching-and-online-learning

Hollister, B., Nair, P., Hill-Lindsay, S., & Chukoskie, L. (2022). Engagement in online learning: Student attitudes and behavior during COVID-19. *Frontiers in Education, 7*. Advance online publication. DOI: 10.3389/feduc.2022.851019

Huang, L., Wang, K., Li, S., & Guo, J. (2023). Using WeChat as an educational tool in MOOC-based flipped classroom: What can we learn from students' learning experience? *Frontiers in Psychology, 13*. Advance online publication. DOI: 10.3389/fpsyg.2022.1098585

Infantes-Paniagua, Á., Silva, A. F., Ramirez-Campillo, R., Sarmento, H., González-Fernández, F. T., González-Víllora, S., & Clemente, F. M. (2021). Active school breaks and students' attention: A systematic review with meta-analysis. *Brain Sciences, 11*(6), 675. DOI: 10.3390/brainsci11060675

Irish, N. (2022). Supporting social presence: a phenomenological study of the perceptions of intermediate elementary teachers who taught virtually during the COVID-19 pandemic. *Theses, Dissertations, and Final Projects.* Millersville University of Pennsylvania. https://jstor.org/stable/community.39483030

James, M., Koshkina, N., & Froese, T. (2023). From tech to tact: Emotion dysregulation in online communication during the COVID-19 pandemic. *Phenomenology and the Cognitive Sciences*, *22*(5), 1163–1194. DOI: 10.1007/s11097-023-09916-z

Jansen, M., Boda, Z., & Lorenz, G. (2022). Social comparison effects on academic self-concepts-Which peers matter most? *Developmental Psychology*, *58*(8), 1541–1556. DOI: 10.1037/dev0001368

Kapoor, K. K., Tamilmani, K., Rana, N. P., Patil, P., Dwivedi, Y. K., & Nerur, S. (2018). Advances in social media research: Past, present and future. *Information Systems Frontiers*, *20*, 531–558. DOI: 10.1007/s10796-017-9810-y

Kates, A. W., Wu, H., & Coryn, C. L. S. (2018). The effects of mobile phone use on academic performance: A meta-analysis. *Computers & Education*, *127*, 107–112. DOI: 10.1016/j.compedu.2018.08.012

Kemp, S. (2024, January 31). *The time we spend on social media — DataReportal – Global Digital Insights.* https://datareportal.com/reports/digital-2024-deep-dive-the-time-we-spend-on-social-media

Kemp, S. (2025, June 30). *Digital 2025: top social platforms in 2025 — DataReportal – Global Digital Insights.* https://datareportal.com/reports/digital-2025-sub-section-top-social-platforms?rq=social%20media

Koushik, S., & Bhamare, V. (2025). Students' perceptions and outcome of teacher feedback. *Frontiers in Education*, *10*, 1572950. DOI: 10.3389/feduc.2025.1572950

Krause, E., & Sawhill, I. V. (2016, September 13). *How free time became screen time.* Brookings Institution.

Li, H., & Yang, J. (2025). Managing online learning burnout via investigating the role of loneliness during COVID-19. *BMC Psychology*, *13*(1), 151. DOI: 10.1186/s40359-025-02419-3

Li, Q., Xia, B., Zhang, H., Wang, W., & Wang, X. (2022). College students' cyberloafing and the sense of meaning of life: The mediating role of state anxiety and the moderating role of psychological flexibility. *Frontiers in Public Health*, *10*, 905699.

Li, S., Hong, Y., & Craig, S. D. (2023). A systematic literature review of social learning theory in online learning environments. *Educational Psychology Review, 35*(4). Advance online publication. DOI: 10.1007/s10648-023-09827-0

Lyu, H., Zhang, L., & Hu, C. (2025). Understanding Human-AI Trust in Education. *arXiv*.

Mannheim, K. (1952). The problem of generations. In Kecskemeti, P. (Ed.), *Essays on the sociology of knowledge* (pp. 276–320). Routledge & Kegan Paul.

Marengo, D., Longobardi, C., Fabris, M., & Settanni, M. (2018). Highly-visual social media and internalizing symptoms in adolescence: The mediating role of body image concerns. *Computers in Human Behavior, 82*, 63–69. DOI: 10/1016/j.chb.2018.01.003

McLeod, S. (2025, March 18). *Albert Bandura's Social Learning Theory*. Simply Psychology. https://www.simplypsychology.org/bandura.html

Mead, S. (2024, October 24). Dangerous 'Speed' ahead: Streamers harm our youth. The Baylor Lariat. https://baylorlariat.com/2024/10/24/dangerous-speed-ahead-streamers-harm-our-youth/

Means, B., & Neisler, J. (2020). Suddenly online: A national survey of undergraduates during the COVID-19 pandemic. *Digital Promise*. https://digitalpromise.org/wp-content/uploads/2020/07/ELE_CoBrand_DP_FINAL _3.pdf

Meyer, J., & Meyer, S. (2020). Excessive smartphone use and associated depression, anxiety, stress, and sleep: A systematic review and meta-analysis. *Frontiers in Psychiatry, 11*, 558552. DOI: 10.3389/fpsyt.2020.558552

Mihelič, K. K., Lim, V. K. G., & Culiberg, B. (2022). Cyberloafing among Gen Z students: The role of norms, moral disengagement, multitasking self-efficacy, and psychological outcomes. *European Journal of Psychology of Education, 38*, 567–585. DOI: 10.1007/s10212-022-00617-w

Miller, L. J., & Lu, W. (2018, August 20). Gen Z is set to outnumber millennials within a year. *Bloomberg*. https://www.bloomberg.com/news/articles/2018-08-20/genz-to-outnumber-millennials-within-a-year-demographic-trends

Moeller, S. D. (2019). *Going 24 Hours without media. the world UNPLUGGED.* https://theworldunplugged.wordpress.com/

O'Hare, W., & Mayol-Garcia, Y. (2023). *The changing child population of the United States: Child population data from the 2020 Census.* Annie E. Casey Foundation. https://www.aecf.org/resources/the-changing-childpopulation-of-the-united-states

Parker, K. (2023, May 22). *How Pew Research Center will report on generations moving forward. Pew Research Center.* https://www.pewresearch.org/short-reads/2023/05/22/how-pew-research-center-will-report-on-generations-moving-forward/

Pekrun, R., Elliot, A. J., & Maier, M. A. (2009). Achievement goals and achievement emotions: Testing a model of their joint relations with academic performance. *Journal of Educational Psychology*, *101*(1), 115–135.

Perez, A. (2023, May 12). Three surprising benefits of holding structured check-ins with students (plus a free template!). Michigan Virtual. https://michiganvirtual.org/blog/three-surprising-benefits-of-structured-check-ins/

Prananto, K., Cahyadi, S., Lubis, F. Y., & Hinduan, Z. R. (2025). Perceived teacher support and student engagement among higher education students - a systematic literature review. *BMC Psychology*, *13*(1), 112. DOI: 10.1186/s40359-025-02412-w

Prensky, M. (2001). Digital natives, Digital immigrants part 1. *On the Horizon*, *9*(5), 1–6. DOI: 10.1108/10748120110424816

Price, C. (2010). Why don't my students think I'm groovy? The new "R"s for engaging millennial learners. *The Teaching Professor*, *9*, 29–34.

Ramsey, T. Z. (2014). *Introduction to Neuromarketing & Consumer Neuroscience*. https://research.cbs.dk/en/publications/introduction-to-neuromarketing-amp-consumer-neuroscience

Reber, R., Canning, E. A., & Harackiewicz, J. M. (2018). Personalized education to increase interest. *Current Directions in Psychological Science*, *27*(6), 449–454. DOI: 10.1177/0963721418793140

Rue, P. (2018). Make way, Millennials, Here comes Gen Z. *About Campus: Enriching the Student Learning Experience*, *23*(3), 5–12. DOI: 10.1177/1086482218804251

Sahu, P. K., Dalcik, H., Dalcik, C., Gupta, M. M., Chattu, V. K., & Umakanthan, S. (2022). Best practices for effective implementation of online education: A systematic review. *Frontiers in Education*. https://pmc.ncbi.nlm.nih.gov/articles/PMC9114788/

Sakdiyakorn, M., Golubovskaya, M., & Solnet, D. (2021). Understanding Generation Z through collective consciousness: Impacts for hospitality work and employment. *International Journal of Hospitality Management*, *94*, 102822. DOI: 10.1016/j.ijhm.2020.102822

Sardar, S., & Vijay, T. (2025). Social media influencers and purchase intention: A review and research agenda. *International Journal of Consumer Studies*, *49*(3), e70046. DOI: 10.1111/ijcs.70046

Schwieger, D., & Ladwig, C. (2018). Reaching and retaining the next generation: Adapting to the expectations of Gen Z in the classroom. *Information Systems Education Journal, 16*(3), 45–54. http://isedj.org/2018-16/n3/ISEDJv16n3p45.html

Seemiller, C., & Grace, M. (2017). Generation Z: Educating and engaging the next generation of students. *About Campus: Enriching the Student Learning Experience, 22*(3), 21–26. DOI: 10.1002/abc.21293

Serravalle, J. (2022). Take it or leave it?: Evidence on cultural differences affecting return behaviour for Gen Z. *Journal of Retailing and Consumer Services, 66*, 102942. DOI: 10.1016/j.jretconser.2022.102942

Shatto, B., & Erwin, K. (2016). Moving on From Millennials: Preparing for Generation Z. *Journal of Continuing Education in Nursing, 47*(6), 253–254. DOI: 10.3928/00220124-20160518-05

Shoufan, A. (2018). Estimating the cognitive value of YouTube's educational videos: A learning analytics approach. *Computers in Human Behavior, 92*, 450–458. DOI: 10.1016/j.chb.2018.03.036

Siddiqui, S., & Singh, T. (2016). Social media its impact with positive and negative aspects. *International Journal of Computer Applications Technology and Research, 5*, 71–75. DOI: 10.7753/IJCATR0502.1006

Silveira, P., Morais, R., & Petrella, S. (2022). A communication study of young adults and online dependence during the COVID-19 pandemic. *Societies (Basel, Switzerland), 12*, 109–133. DOI: 10.3390/soc12040109

Smith, E. E., Kahlke, R., & Judd, T. (2018). From digital natives to digital literacy: Anchoring digital practices through learning design. In *Proceedings of the Australasian Society for Computers in Learning in Tertiary Education (ASCILITE 2018)* (pp. 510–515). Deakin University.

Smith, T. A., & Short, A. (2022). Needs affordance as a key factor in likelihood of problematic social media use: Validation, latent profile analysis and comparison of TikTok and Facebook problematic use measures. *Addictive Behaviors, 129*, 107259. DOI: 10.1016/j.addbeh.2022.107259

Steinsbekk, S., Wichstom, L., Stenseng, F., Nesi, J., Hygen, B., & Skalicka, V. (2021). The impact of social media use on appearance self-esteem from childhood to adolescence – A 3-wave community study. *Computers in Human Behavior, 114*, 106528. DOI: 10/1016/j.chb.2020.106528

Suls, J., Martin, R., & Wheeler, L. (2002). Social comparison: Why, with whom, and with what effect? *Current Directions in Psychological Science, 11*(5), 159–163. DOI: 10.1111/1467-8721.00191

Sweetman, D. S. (2020). Making virtual learning engaging and interactive. *FASEB bioAdvances, 3*(1), 11–19. DOI: 10.1096/fba.2020-00084

Tang, C., Thyer, L., Bye, R., Kenny, B., Tulliani, N., Peel, N., Gordon, R., Penkala, S., Tannous, C., Sun, Y. T., & Dark, L. (2023). Impact of online learning on sense of belonging among first year clinical health students during COVID-19: Student and academic perspectives. *BMC Medical Education, 23*(1), 100. DOI: 10.1186/s12909-023-04061-2

Tariyal, A., Singh, S., & Bisht, S. (2020). Impact of e-reviews on Millennials' café visit decision-making with reference to Dehradun region. *Academy of Marketing Studies Journal, 24*, 1–13.

Teh, Y., & Baskaran, V. (2022). The effectiveness of eAssessments to encourage learning among Gen Z students. In Yusop, F. D., & Firdaus, A. (Eds.), *Alternative Assessments in Malaysian Higher Education*. Springer. DOI: 10.1007/978-981-16-7228-6_26

Telefonica. (2025, January 14). *First smartphone in history: The origin of smartphones.* https://www.telefonica.com/en/communication-room/blog/first-smartphone/

Törőcsik, M., Szűcs, K., & Kehl, D. (2014). How generations think: Research on Generation Z. Acta Universitatis Sapientiae. *Communication, 1*, 23–45.

Turner, A. (2015). Generation Z: Technology and social interest. *Journal of Individual Psychology, 71*(2), 103–113. DOI: 10.1353/jip.2015.0021

Understood. (2024, April 29). Understood.org survey: *Neurodiversity at work — focus on Gen Z.* https://www.understood.org/en/research-and-surveys/understood-org-genz-survey

Vajkai, K. É., & Zsóka, Á. (2020). Brand avoidance behaviour of Gen Z towards fast fashion brands. *Vezetéstudomány Budapest Management Review, 51*(5), 39–50. DOI: 10.14267/VEZTUD.2020.05.04

Van den Bergh, J., Schepers, J., & Helsen, L. (2024). Beyond labels: Segmenting the Gen Z market for more effective marketing. *Young Consumers: Insight and Ideas for Responsible Marketers, 25*(2), 188–210. DOI: 10.1108/YC-03-2023-1707

Venton, B. J., & Pompano, R. R. (2021). Strategies for enhancing remote student engagement. *Journal of Chemical Education, 98*(1), 61–67. https://pmc.ncbi.nlm.nih.gov/articles/PMC7811893/

Vmontiel. (2025, July 17). Netflix leads streaming growth in June on the strength of multiple big titles in Nielsen's 50th report of the GaugeTM. *Nielsen*. https://www.nielsen.com/news-center/2025/netflix-leads-streaming-growth-in-june-on-the-strength-of-multiple-big-titles-in-nielsens-50th-report-of-the-gauge/

Vogel, E. A., Rose, J. P., Roberts, L. R., & Eckles, K. (2014). Social comparison, social media, and self-esteem. *Psychology of Popular Media Culture, 3*(4), 206–222. DOI: 10.1037/ppm0000047

Walters, P. (2021). Are Generation Z Ethical Consumers? In Stylos, N., Rahimi, R., Okumus, B., & Williams, S. (Eds.), *Generation Z Marketing and Management in Tourism and Hospitality*. Palgrave Macmillan. DOI: 10.1007/978-3-030-70695-1_12

Wong, W. H., & Chapman, E. (2023). Student satisfaction and interaction in higher education. *Higher Education, 85*(5), 957–978. DOI: 10.1007/s10734-022-00874-0

Yang, C. C., Holden, S. M., & Carter, M. D. (2017). Social media social comparison of ability (but not opinion) predicts lower identity clarity: Identity processing style as a mediator. *Journal of Youth and Adolescence, 46*(11), 2221–2237. DOI: 10.1007/s10964-017-0699-z

Zhang, J., Akhtar, M. N., Zhang, Y., & Sun, S. (2020). Are overqualified employees bad apples? A dual pathway model of cyberloafing. *Internet Research, 30*(1), 289–313. DOI: 10.1108/INT-01-2019-0044

Zhu, J., Yuan, H., Zhang, Q., Huang, P. H., Wang, Y., Duan, S., Lei, M., Lim, E. G., & Song, P. (2022). The impact of short videos on student performance in an online-flipped college engineering course. *Humanities & Social Sciences Communications, 9*(1), 327. DOI: 10.1057/s41599-022-01355-6

Compilation of References

Aagaard, J. (2019). Multitasking as distraction: A conceptual analysis of media multitasking research. *Theory & Psychology*, *29*(1), 87–99. DOI: 10.1177/0959354318815766

Abbasi, A. Z., Ting, D. H., & Alqahtani, S. (2023). TikTok app usage behavior: The role of hedonic consumption experiences, user satisfaction, and switching behavior. *Kybernetes*, *52*(3), 856–883. DOI: 10.1108/DTA-03-2022-0107

Abd El-Sattar, H. K. H. (2025). Future metaverse-based education to promote daily living activities in learners with autism using immersive technologies. *Education and Information Technologies*, *30*(3), 3145–3182. DOI: 10.1007/s10639-024-12844-3

Abel, S. (2021). *Making time online: Exploring social media as a tool for family connection* [PhD Thesis]. University of Southern Queensland.

Abel, S., Machin, T., & Brownlow, C. (2021). Social media, rituals, and long-distance family relationship maintenance: A mixed-methods systematic review. *New Media & Society*, *23*(3), 632–654. DOI: 10.1177/1461444820958717

Abeysekera, L., & Dawson, P. (2015). Motivation and cognitive load in the flipped classroom: Definition, rationale and a call for research. *Higher Education Research & Development*, *34*(1), 1–14. DOI: 10.1080/07294360.2014.934336

Adelana, O. P., Ayanwale, M. A., Ishola, A. M., Oladejo, A. I., & Adewuyi, H. O. (2023). Exploring pre-service teachers' intention to use virtual reality: A mixed method approach. *Computers & Education: X Reality, 3*, 100045. DOI: 10.1016/j.cexr.2023.100045

Ahshan, R. (2021). A framework of implementing strategies for active student engagement in remote/online teaching and learning during the covid-19 pandemic. *Education Sciences*, *11*(9), 483. Advance online publication. DOI: 10.3390/educsci11090483

Ainsworth, M. D. S., Blehar, M. C., Waters, E., & Wall, S. N. (2015). *Patterns of attachment: A psychological study of the strange situation*. Psychology press. DOI: 10.4324/9780203758045

Akpen, C. N., Asaolu, S., Atobatele, S., Okagbue, H., & Sampson, S. (2024). Impact of online learning on student's performance and engagement: A systematic review. *Discover Education*, *3*(1), 205. DOI: 10.1007/s44217-024-00253-0

Alberts, L., Lyngs, U., & Lukoff, K. (2024). Designing for sustained motivation: A review of Self-Determination Theory in behaviour change technologies. *Interacting with Computers*, •••, iwae040. Advance online publication. DOI: 10.1093/iwc/iwae040

Al-Ghaith, W. (2015). Understanding social network usage: Impact of co-presence, intimacy, and immediacy. *International Journal of Advanced Computer Science and Applications*, *6*(8), 99–111. DOI: 10.14569/IJACSA.2015.060813

Alismaiel, O. A., Cifuentes-Faura, J., & Al-Rahmi, W. M. (2022). Online learning, mobile learning, and social media technologies: An empirical study on constructivism theory during the COVID-19 pandemic. *Sustainability (Basel)*, *14*(18), 11134. DOI: 10.3390/su141811134

Alnasyan, B., Basheri, M., & Alassafi, M. (2024). The power of Deep Learning techniques for predicting student performance in Virtual Learning Environments: A systematic literature review. *Computers and Education: Artificial Intelligence*, *6*, 100231. DOI: 10.1016/j.caeai.2024.100231

Alrashidi, O., Phan, H. P., & Ngu, B. H. (2020). Academic Engagement: An Overview of Its Definitions, Dimensions, and Major Conceptualisations. *International Education Studies*, *9*(12), 41. DOI: 10.5539/ies.v9n12p41

Alvarez-Milán, A., Felix, R., Rauschnabel, P. A., & Hinsch, C. (2018). Strategic customer engagement marketing: A decision making framework. *Journal of Business Research*, *92*, 61–70. DOI: 10.1016/j.jbusres.2018.07.017

Anderson, M., & Jiang, J. (2018). *Teens, social media & technology*. Pew Research Center. https://www.pewresearch.org/internet/2018/05/31/teens-social-media-technology-2018/

Anderson, T. L. (2009). Online instructor immediacy and instructor-student relationships in Second Life. *Higher Education in Virtual Worlds: Teaching and Learning in Second Life*, *1*, 101–114.

Andrin, G., Kilag, O. K., Groenewald, E., Benitez, J., Dagala, F., & Ubay, R. (2024). Borderless learning environments: Impacts on educational management strategies. [IMJRISE]. *International Multidisciplinary Journal of Research for Innovation, Sustainability, and Excellence*, *1*(2), 43–49.

Anjarwati, R., & Sadah, L. (2021). Student learning engagement in the online class. *English Journal of Merdeka : Culture, Language, and Teaching of English*, *6*(2), 39–49. DOI: 10.26905/enjourme.v6i2.6128

Annette, B., Chris, R., Stuart, L., Inam, H., Tyler, C., Eszter, K., & Jane, B. (2021). Peer review in team-based learning: Influencing feedback literacy. *BMC Medical Education (Web)*, *21*(1), 1–11.

Annie E. Casey Foundation. (2024, March 31). *Social issues that matter to Generation Z.* https://www.aecf.org/blog/generation-z-social-issues

Appel, H., Gerlach, A. L., & Crusius, J. (2016). The interplay between Facebook use, social comparison, envy, and depression. *Current Opinion in Psychology*, *9*, 44–49. DOI: 10.1016/j.copsyc.2015.10.006

Apple Inc. (2007, January 9). *Apple Reinvents the Phone with iPhone*. https://www.apple.com/newsroom/2007/01/09Apple-Reinvents-the-Phone-with-iPhone/

Araneda, C. (2022). Jaime Garretón's cybernetic theory of the city and its system: A missing link in contemporary urban theory. *AI & Society*, *37*(3), 1179–1189. DOI: 10.1007/s00146-021-01349-z

Ateca-Amestoy, V., Aguilar, A. C., & Moro-Egido, A. I. (2014). Social interactions and life satisfaction: Evidence from Latin America. *Journal of Happiness Studies*, *15*(3), 527–554.

Atlassian. (2025). *How to run a blameless postmortem*. https://www.atlassian.com/incident-management/postmortem/blameless

Auxier, B., Anderson, M., Perrin, A., & Turner, E. (2020). *Children's engagement with digital devices, screen time*. Pew Research Center https://www.pewresearch.org/internet/2020/07/28/childrens-engagement-with-digital-devices-screen-time/

Azarian, B. (2022). *The romance of reality: How the universe organizes itself to create life, consciousness, and cosmic complexity*. Benbella books.

Bach, A., & Thiel, F. (2024, November). Collaborative online learning in higher education—quality of digital interaction and associations with individual and group-related factors. In *Frontiers in Education* (Vol. 9, p. 1356271). Frontiers Media SA. DOI: 10.3389/feduc.2024.1356271

Bacon. (2023). Student Engagement Case Studies Vicki Trowler and Paul Trowler Department of Educational Research University of Lancaster Deliverable 3 for the Higher Education Academy Student Engagement Project Table of Contents. *Student Engagement Case Studies. Deliverable 3 for the Higher Education Academy Student Engagement Project., 2023*(July), 1–33.

Bailenson, J. N. (2021). Nonverbal Overload: A Theoretical Argument for the Causes of Zoom Fatigue. *Technology, Mind, and Behavior*, *2*(1), 1–6. Advance online publication. DOI: 10.1037/tmb0000030

Bakuri, A. Z., & Amoabeng, D. (2023). Doing kin work among Ghanaians home and abroad: A paradigm shift to ICT. *Family Relations*, *72*(2), 585–600. DOI: 10.1111/fare.12838

Baldassar, L. (2016). De-demonizing distance in mobile family lives: Co-presence, care circulation and polymedia as vibrant matter. *Global Networks*, *16*(2), 145–163. DOI: 10.1111/glob.12109

Baldwin, A. (1973). Social Learning. *Review of Research in Education*, *1*, 34–57. DOI: 10.2307/1167194

Balida, D. A. R. (2023). Ethical challenges in online teaching and learning: A case study of a virtual class. *Russian Law Journal*, *11*(3), 1901–1916.

Bandura, A. (1971). *Social Learning Theory*. General Learning Press. http://www.asecib.ase.ro/mps/Bandura_SocialLearningTheory.pdf

Bandura, A. (1965). Influence of models' reinforcement contingencies on the acquisition of imitative responses. *Journal of Personality and Social Psychology*, *1*(6), 589–595. DOI: 10.1037/h0022070

Bandura, A., Ross, D., & Ross, S. A. (1961). Transmission of aggression through imitation of aggressive models. *Journal of Abnormal and Social Psychology*, *63*(3), 575–582. DOI: 10.1037/h0045925

Bandura, A., Ross, D., & Ross, S. A. (1963). Imitation of film-mediated aggressive models. *Journal of Abnormal and Social Psychology*, *66*, 3–11. DOI: 10.1037/h0048687

Bao, H., Fang, W., Guo, B., & Qiu, H. (2024). Adaptive human–computer interface design for supervision task based on user attention and system state. *International Journal of Human-Computer Interaction*, *40*(8), 2054–2066. DOI: 10.1080/10447318.2023.2228070

Barbara., & Miller, R. B. (2023). Influences on Achievement: Goals, Perceived Ability, and Cognitive Engagement. *Contemporary Educational Psychology, 21*(2), 181–192. DOI: 10.1006/ceps.1996.0015

Bardin, A., & Ferrari, M. (2022). Governing progress: From cybernetic homeostasis to Simondon's politics of metastability. *The Sociological Review*, *70*(2), 248–263. DOI: 10.1177/00380261221084426

Barns, S. (2019). Negotiating the platform pivot: From participatory digital ecosystems to infrastructures of everyday life. *Geography Compass*, *13*(9), e12464. DOI: 10.1111/gec3.12464

Baruah, A. (2025). The Impact of Computer-Mediated Communication on Relationships and Social Interactions. *International Journal of Human-Computer Interaction*, *41*(18), 11245–11251. DOI: 10.1080/10447318.2024.2442755

Basilio, O. (2023). A Strategic Engagement Framework for Nonprofits. *Online (Bergheim)*, *20*(2), 219–233. DOI: 10.1002/nml

Basnet, N., Allahvirdi, S., Nadri, C., Park, J., & Zahabi, M. (2025). Evaluating the Feasibility of EMG-Based Human–Machine Interfaces for Driving. *Human Factors*, •••, 00187208251367179. PMID: 40797297

Benzar, A., Kovalenko, Y. O., Taranenko, A., Balynska, O., & Balynskyi, I. (2025). Organizational Context of Security Management: Implications for Information Systems. *Management:(Montevideo)*, *3*, 250-250.

Bergdahl, N. (2022). Engagement and disengagement in online learning. *Computers & Education*, *188*(May), 104561. DOI: 10.1016/j.compedu.2022.104561

Bergdahl, N., & Nouri, J. (2020). Covid-19 and crisis-prompted distance education in Sweden. *Technology. Knowledge and Learning*, *26*, 443–459. DOI: 10.1007/s10758-020-09470-6

Berges, S., Martino, S., Basko, L., & Mccabe, C. (2021). "Zooming" Into Engagement: Increasing Engagement in the Online Classroom. *Journal of Institutional Research*, *10*, 5–11.

Bernstein, S. (2024). Enhancing Provider Engagement in Practice Improvement: A Conceptual Framework DONALD. *Enhancing Provider Engagement in Practice Improvement: A Conceptual Framework DONALD, 28*(3), 157–164. https://doi.org/DOI: 10.1002/chp

Berry, N. (2020). *Students as Thinking Systems: A Phenomenological Inquiry on Learning Natural Family Systems Theory* [PhD Thesis]. Barry University.

Bhatia, A., Bhatia, P., & Sood, D. (2024). Leveraging AI to transform online higher education: Focusing on personalized learning, assessment, and student engagement. *International Journal of Management and Humanities (IJMH) Volume-11 Issue-1*. http://dx.doi.org/DOI: 10.2139/ssrn.4959186

Bigman, Y. E., Wilson, D., Arnestad, M. N., Waytz, A., & Gray, K. (2022). Algorithmic discrimination causes less moral outrage than human discrimination. *Journal of Experimental Psychology. General*, *152*(1), 4–27. DOI: 10.1037/xge0001250

Birhane, A. (2021). Algorithmic injustice: A relational ethics approach. *Patterns (New York, N.Y.)*, *2*(2), 100205. DOI: 10.1016/j.patter.2021.100205

Blumenfeld, P. C., Kempler, T. M., & Krajcik, J. S. (2023). Motivation and Cognitive Engagement in Learning Environments. In *The Cambridge Handbook of the Learning Sciences* (Issue January 2006, pp. 475–488). Cambridge University Press. DOI: 10.1017/CBO9780511816833.029

Blumer, H. (1986). *Symbolic interactionism: Perspective and method*. University of California Press. https://books.google.com/books?hl=en&lr=&id=HVuognZFofoC&oi=fnd&pg=PA1&dq=Blumer&ots=4pUcHawP6u&sig=ZZhAdigNsE6x96qiPNYD5S24Eqo

Blunden, H., & Brodsky, A. (2024). A review of virtual impression management behaviors and outcomes. *Journal of Management*, *50*(6), 2197–2236. DOI: 10.1177/01492063231225160

Boccio, C. M., & Leal, W. E. (2022). Does socializing in the virtual world impact victimization in the real world? *Journal of Interpersonal Violence*, *38*(3–4), 3756–3776. DOI: 10.1177/08862605221109922

Bonezzi, A., & Ostinelli, M. (2021). Can algorithms legitimize discrimination? *Journal of Experimental Psychology. Applied*, *27*, 447–459. DOI: 10.1037/xap0000294

Boon, M., Orozco, M., & Sivakumar, K. (2022). Epistemological and educational issues in teaching practice-oriented scientific research: Roles for philosophers of science. *European Journal for Philosophy of Science*, *12*(1), 16. https://link.springer.com/article/10.1007/s13194-022-00447-z. DOI: 10.1007/s13194-022-00447-z PMID: 30873248

Borup, J., Graham, C. R., West, R. E., Archambault, L., & Spring, K. J. (2020). Academic communities of engagement: An expansive lens for examining support structures in blended and online learning. *Educational Technology Research and Development*, 68, 8 07- 832.

Bowlby, J. (1982). Attachment and loss: Retrospect and prospect. *The American Journal of Orthopsychiatry*, *52*(4), 664–678. DOI: 10.1111/j.1939-0025.1982.tb01456.x PMID: 7148988

Bowler, A. (2020, April). *Isolation among Generation Z in the United States. Ballard Brief.* www.ballardbrief.org

Boyun, V. P. (2024). Features of Creating Artificial Intelligence Using Informatics and Cybernetics. *Cybernetics and Systems Analysis*, *60*(1), 13–23. DOI: 10.1007/s10559-024-00642-1

Bozkurt, A., & Sharma, R. C. (2020). Emergency remote teaching in a time of global crisis due to the CoronaVirus pandemic. *Asian Journal of Distance Education*, *15*(1), 1–6. DOI: 10.5281/zenodo.3778083

Bratina, D., & Faganel, A. (2024). Understanding Gen Z and Gen X Responses to Influencer Communications. *Administrative Sciences*, *14*(2), 33. DOI: 10.3390/admsci14020033

Braun, V., & Clarke, V. (2006). Using thematic analysis in psychology. *Qualitative Research in Psychology*, *3*(2), 77–101. DOI: 10.1191/1478088706qp063oa

Breslow, L., Pritchard, D. E., DeBoer, J., Stump, G. S., Ho, A. D., & Seaton, D. T. (2013). Studying learning in the worldwide classroom: Research into edX's first MOOC. *Journal of Research & Practice in Assessment*, *8*, 13–25.

Briggs, C. L., & Doubleday, A. F. (2016). Group Learning Assessments as a Vital Consideration in the Implementation of New Peer Learning Pedagogies in the Basic Science Curriculum of Health Profession Programs. *Journal of Medical Education and Curricular Development, 3. JMECD, S18930*. Advance online publication. DOI: 10.4137/JMECD.S18930 PMID: 29349309

Brinck, I., & Reddy, V. (2020). Dialogue in the making: Emotional engagement with materials. *Phenomenology and the Cognitive Sciences*, *19*(1), 23–45. DOI: 10.1007/s11097-019-09629-2

Brkljačić, T., Šakić, V., & Kaliterna-Lipovčan, L. J. (2018). Phubbing among Croatian students. *Protection and Promotion of the Well-Being of Children, Youth, and Families: Selected Proceedings of the 1st International Scientific Conference of the Department of Psychology at the Catholic University of Croatia*, 109–126.

Brunton, G., Thomas, J., O'Mara-Eves, A., Jamal, F., Oliver, S., & Kavanagh, J. (2019). Narratives of community engagement: A systematic review-derived conceptual framework for public health interventions. *BMC Public Health*, *17*(1), 1–15. DOI: 10.1186/s12889-017-4958-4 PMID: 29228932

Burholt, V., Windle, G., Gott, M., & Morgan, D. J. (2020). Technology-mediated communication in familial relationships: Moderated-mediation models of isolation and loneliness. *The Gerontologist*, *60*(7), 1202–1212. DOI: 10.1093/geront/gnaa040 PMID: 32369112

Burholt, V., Windle, G., Morgan, D. J., & Team, C. W. (2017). A social model of loneliness: The roles of disability, social resources, and cognitive impairment. *The Gerontologist*, *57*(6), 1020–1030. DOI: 10.1093/geront/gnw125 PMID: 27831482

Busseniers, E., Veloz, T., & Heylighen, F. (2021). Goal directedness, chemical organizations, and cybernetic mechanisms. *Entropy (Basel, Switzerland)*, *23*(8), 1039. DOI: 10.3390/e23081039 PMID: 34441179

Buzzetto-Hollywood, N., & Alade, A. (2018). An examination of Gen Z learners attending a minority university. Interdisciplinary *Journal of e-Skills and Lifelong Learning, 14,* 41-53. https://doi.org/DOI: 10.28945/3969

Buzzetto-Hollywood, N., Hill, A., & Banks, T. (2021). Early findings of a study exploring the social media, political and cultural awareness, and civic activism of Gen Z students in the Mid-Atlantic United States. In M. Jones (Ed.), *Proceedings of InSITE 2021: Informing Science and Information Technology Education Conference*, Article 11. Informing Science Institute. DOI: 10.28945/4762

Byron, K. (2008). Carrying too heavy a load? The communication and miscommunication of emotion by email. *Academy of Management Review*, *33*(2), 309–327. Advance online publication. DOI: 10.5465/amr.2008.31193163

Cabalquinto, E. C. (2018). Home on the move: Negotiating differential domesticity in family life at a distance. *Media Culture & Society*, *40*(6), 795–816. DOI: 10.1177/0163443717737611

Cabalquinto, E. C. B. (2021). Telecocooning in the age of (im) mobility. *Communication, Culture & Critique*, *14*(2), 351–355. DOI: 10.1093/ccc/tcab024

Cagala, M., & Babcanova, D. (2024). Preferences of generations of customers in Slovakia in the field of marketing communication and their impact on consumer behaviour. *Administrative Sciences*, *14*(9), 224. DOI: 10.3390/admsci14090224

Cai, L., Msafiri, M. M., & Kangwa, D. (2025). Exploring the impact of integrating AI tools in higher education using the Zone of Proximal Development. *Education and Information Technologies*, *30*(6), 7191–7264. DOI: 10.1007/s10639-024-13112-0

Cairncross, F. (2002). The death of distance. *RSA Journal*, *149*(5502), 40–42.

Cannelli, B. (2024). *Archiving Social Media: A Comparative Study of the Practices, Obstacles, and Opportunities Related to the Development of Social Media Archives* [PhD Thesis]. School of Advanced Study.

Cao, Y. (2022). Mass Surveillance, Behavioural Control, and Psychological Coercion the Moral Ethical Risks in Commercial Devices. *Computer Science and Information Technology, 12*(13), 151–168.

Caprara, L., & Caprara, C. (2022). Effects of virtual learning environments: A scoping review of literature. *Education and Information Technologies, 27*(3), 3683–3722. DOI: 10.1007/s10639-021-10768-w

Carini, Kuh, & K. (2018). Investigating the Multidimensionality of Engagement. *Investigating the Multidimensionality of Engagement.*

Carr, C. T., & Hayes, R. A. (2015). Social media: Defining, developing, and divining. *Atlantic Journal of Communication, 23*, 46–65. DOI: 10.1080/15456870.2015.972282

Carr, M. (2024). The unline University classroom: One perspective for effective student engagement and teaching in an online environment. *The Journal of Effective Teaching, 14*(1), 99–110. https://uncw.edu/cte/ET/articles/Vol14_1/Carr.pdf

Carter, M. J., & Asencio, E. K. (2019). Identity Processes in Face-to-Face and Digitally Mediated Environments. *Sociological Perspectives, 62*(2), 220–239. DOI: 10.1177/0731121418786247

Caskurlu, S., Yalçın, Y., Hur, J., Shi, H., & Klein, J. D. (2025). Data-driven decision-making in instructional design: Instructional designers' practices and strategies. *TechTrends, 69*(4), 1–12. https://link.springer.com/article/10.1007/s11528-025-01077-x. DOI: 10.1007/s11528-025-01077-x

Castañer, X., & Oliveira, N. (2020). Collaboration, coordination, and cooperation among organizations: Establishing the distinctive meanings of these terms through a systematic literature review. *Journal of Management, 46*(6), 965–1001. DOI: 10.1177/0149206320901565

Cavinato, A. G., Hunter, R. A., Ott, L. S., & Robinson, J. K. (2021). Promoting student interaction, engagement, and success in an online environment. *Analytical and Bioanalytical Chemistry, 413*(6), 1513–1520. DOI: 10.1007/s00216-021-03178-x PMID: 33479816

Chaka, C. (2015). Digital identity, social presence technologies, and presence learning. In *Student-teacher interaction in online learning environments* (pp. 183–203). IGI Global. DOI: 10.4018/978-1-4666-6461-6.ch009

Chakraborty, M. (2017). Learner Engagement Strategies in Online Class Environment. *Learner Engagement Strategies in Online Class Environment, May*, (178 Seiten). http://gateway.proquest.com/openurl?url_ver=Z39.88-2004&rft_val_fmt=info:ofi/fmt:kev:mtx:dissertation&res_dat=xri:pqm&rft_dat=xri:pqdiss:10662429

Chakraborty, M., & Muyia Nafukho, F. (2024). Strengthening student engagement: What do students want in online courses? *European Journal of Training and Development, 38*(9), 782–802. DOI: 10.1108/EJTD-11-2013-0123

Chang, Y., & Brickman, P. (2018). When group work doesn't work: Insights from students. *CBE Life Sciences Education, 17*(3), ar52. DOI: 10.1187/cbe.17-09-0199 PMID: 30183565

Chatzithanos, P., Nikolaou, G., Stolkin, R., & Chiou, M. (2021, October). Fessonia: a method for real-time estimation of human operator workload using behavioural entropy. In *2021 IEEE International Conference on Systems, Man, and Cybernetics (SMC)* (pp. 1325-1331). IEEE. DOI: 10.1109/SMC52423.2021.9658880

Chen, C. H., & Yang, Y. C. (2019). Revisiting the effects of project-based learning on students' academic achievement: A meta-analysis investigating moderators. *Educational Research Review, 26*, 71–81. DOI: 10.1016/j.edurev.2018.11.001

Cheng, K., Liang, J., & Tsai, C. (2013). University students' online academic help seeking: the role of self-regulation and information commitments. The Internet and Higher Education, 16, 70–77. https://doi.org/DOI: 10.1016/j.iheduc.2012.02.002

Chen, K. C., & Jang, S. J. (2010). Motivation in online learning: Testing a model of self-determination theory. *Computers in Human Behavior, 26*(4), 741–752. DOI: 10.1016/j.chb.2010.01.011

Chi, M. T. H., Adams, J., Bogusch, E. B., Bruchok, C., Kang, S., Lancaster, M., Levy, R., Li, N., McEldoon, K. L., Stump, G. S., Wylie, R., Xu, D., & Yaghmourian, D. L. (2018). Translating the ICAP Theory of Cognitive Engagement Into Practice. *Cognitive Science, 42*(6), 1777–1832. DOI: 10.1111/cogs.12626 PMID: 29954048

Chisholm, A., & Hartman-Caverly, S. (2022). Privacy Literacy: From Doomscrolling to Digital Wellness. *Portal (Baltimore, Md.), 22*(1), 53–79. DOI: 10.1353/pla.2022.0009

Chong, D., & Citrin, J. (2024). The realignment of political tolerance in the United States. *Perspectives on Politics, 22*(1), 131–152. DOI: 10.1017/S1537592722002079

Chotpitayasunondh, V., & Douglas, K. M. (2018). Measuring phone snubbing behavior: Development and validation of the Generic Scale of Phubbing (GSP) and the Generic Scale of Being Phubbed (GSBP). *Computers in Human Behavior, 88*, 5–17. DOI: 10.1016/j.chb.2018.06.020

Chowkase, A. A., Datar, K., Deshpande, A., Khasnis, S., Keskar, A., & Godbole, S. (2022). Online learning, classroom quality, and student motivation: Perspectives from students, teachers, parents, and program staff. *Gifted Education International, 38*(1), 74–94. DOI: 10.1177/02614294211060401

Cigna (2024). Loneliness in America 2025: A pervasive struggle requires a communal response. https://newsroom.thecignagroup.com/loneliness-in-america

Cilliers, E. J. (2017). The challenge of teaching Generation Z. *PEOPLE. The International Journal of Social Sciences (Islamabad), 3*(1), 188–198. DOI: 10.20319/pijss.2017.31.188198

Cilliers, E. J. (2021). Reflecting on social learning tools to enhance the teaching-learning experience of Generation Z learners. *Frontiers in Education, 5*. Advance online publication. DOI: 10.3389/feduc.2020.606533

Claveria, K. (2017). *Unlike millennials: 5 ways Gen Z differs from Gen Y.* https://www.visioncritical.com/Gen Z-versus-millennials-infographics/

Cleveland-Innes, M., & Campbell, P. (2012). Emotional presence, learning, and the online learning environment. *International Review of Research in Open and Distance Learning, 13*(4), 269–292. DOI: 10.19173/irrodl.v13i4.1234

CNN. (2025). *A parliament in flames, a leader toppled. Nepal's Gen Z protesters ask: What comes next?* https://www.cnn.com/2025/09/10/asia/nepal-protests-genz-outcome-intl-hnk

Coates, H. (2006). *Student engagement in campus-based and online education: University connections*. Routledge., DOI: 10.4324/9780203969465

Codispoti, M., Mazzetti, M., & Bradley, M. M. (2023). Unmasking emotion: Exposure duration and emotional engagement. *Psychophysiology, 46*(4), 731–738. DOI: 10.1111/j.1469-8986.2009.00804.x PMID: 19386053

Connell, D., & Goldberg, J. P.David Connell, Jeanne P. Goldberg. (2001). An Intervention to Increase Fruit and Vegetable Consumption Using Audio Communications: In-Store Public Service Announcements and AudioTapes. *Journal of Health Communication, 6*(1), 31–43. DOI: 10.1080/108107301505013 96 PMID: 11317422

Cordova, J. C. (2024). *Creating a Digital House of Knowledge: Ensuring the Continuation and Integrity of Indigenous Knowledge Transfers in the Digital Era* [Master's Thesis]. University of Alaska Fairbanks.

Couclelis, H. (1996). The Death of Distance. *Environment and Planning. B, Planning & Design, 23*(4), 387–389. DOI: 10.1068/b230387

Crawford, K. (2021). *Atlas of AI: Power, politics, and the planetary costs of artificial intelligence.* Yale University Press.

Cruz, F. (2025). *Digital specters of colony: Securitization, Moros, and the age of social media* [PhD Thesis]. University of Antwerp.

Cubitt, S., Escobar, C., & Gook, B. (2025). Active Noise Control: Cybernetics, Information Theory, and the Financialization of Randomness. *Philosophy. Politics and Critique, 2*(2), 184–204. DOI: 10.3366/ppc.2025.0077

Culduz, M. (2024). Benefits and challenges of e-learning, online education, and distance learning. In *Incorporating the human element in online teaching and learning* (pp. 1–27). IGI Global Scientific Publishing. DOI: 10.4018/979-8-3693-4131-5.ch001

Cullinan, J., Flannery, D., Harold, J., Lyons, S., & Palcic, D. (2021). The disconnected: COVID-19 and disparities in access to quality broadband for higher education students. *International Journal of Educational Technology in Higher Education, 18*(1), 26. DOI: 10.1186/s41239-021-00262-1 PMID: 34778524

Curdt-Christiansen, X. L., & Iwaniec, J. (2023). ' , I miss you ': Emotional multilingual practices in transnational families. *The International Journal of Bilingualism, 27*(2), 159–180. DOI: 10.1177/13670069221125342

Daft, R. L., & Lengel, R. H. (1983). Information richness. A new approach to managerial behavior and organization design. *Research in Organizational Behavior, 6*, 191–233.

Dai, J., Kim, S., & Choi, H. (2024). Avatar appearance and social presence in virtual reality. *Computers in Human Behavior, 141*, 104234. DOI: 10.1016/j.chb.2024.104234

Daniels, D., & Lee, J. S. (2022, June). The impact of avatar teachers on student learning and engagement in a virtual learning environment for online STEM courses. In Stephanidis, C. (Ed.), *Human-Computer Interaction – INTERACT 2022* (pp. 158–175). Springer., DOI: 10.1007/978-3-031-05675-8_13

Darivandi Shoushtari, K., Tohidi, H., Talebian, M., & Shadnam, M. (2025). Strategic fit of task-based crowdsourcing: A cybernetic approach. *Kybernetes*, •••, 1–21. DOI: 10.1108/K-03-2025-0792

Das, T., Ganesh Kondamudi, S., Dawood Babakerkhell, M., Pal, D., Roy, R., & Funilkul, S. (2024). Intention for enhancing metaverse-based learning using gamification among university students: A study using Delphi and structural equation modelling approaches. *Cogent Business & Management*, *11*(1), 2380016. DOI: 10.1080/23311975.2024.2380016

David, M. E., & Roberts, J. A. (2017). Phubbed and Alone: Phone Snubbing, Social Exclusion, and Attachment to Social Media. *Journal of the Association for Consumer Research*, *2*(2), 155–163. DOI: 10.1086/690940

De Boer, B. (2023). Explaining multistability: Postphenomenology and affordances of technologies. *AI & Society*, *38*(6), 2267–2277. DOI: 10.1007/s00146-021-01272-3

de Carvalho, E. M. (2022). Social affordance. In *Encyclopedia of animal cognition and behavior* (pp. 6497–6500). Springer. DOI: 10.1007/978-3-319-55065-7_1870

De Leo, J. A., & Wulfert, E. (2013). Problematic Internet use and other risky behaviors in college students: An application of problem-behavior theory. *Psychology of Addictive Behaviors*, *27*(1), 133–141. DOI: 10.1037/a0030823 PMID: 23276311

Dean, E. (2025, July 7). *50+ online course statistics for 2025*. Whop. https://whop.com/blog/course-statistics/

Deci, E. L., & Ryan, R. M. (1985). *Intrinsic motivation and self-determination in human behavior*. Plenum Press. DOI: 10.1007/978-1-4899-2271-7

Deci, E. L., & Ryan, R. M. (2000). The" what" and" why" of goal pursuits: Human needs and the self-determination of behavior. *Psychological Inquiry*, *11*(4), 227–268. DOI: 10.1207/S15327965PLI1104_01

Deckker, D., Sumanasekara, S., & Fakhrou, A. (2025). AI-Powered Personalised Learning: Promise and Pitfalls.

Delaney, D., Kummer, T. F., & Singh, K. (2019). Evaluating the impact of online discussion boards on student engagement with group work. *British Journal of Educational Technology*, *50*(2), 902–920. DOI: 10.1111/bjet.12614

Deloitte. (2022). *McKinsey Health Institute global Gen Z survey: New insights into how this generation thinks about health*. McKinsey & Company. https://www.mckinsey.com/industries/healthcare/our-insights/addressing-the-unprecedented-behavioral-health-challenges-facing-generation-z

Demerouti, E., Bakker, A. B., Nachreiner, F., & Schaufeli, W. B. (2001). The job demands–resources model of burnout. *The Journal of Applied Psychology*, *86*(3), 499–512. DOI: 10.1037/0021-9010.86.3.499 PMID: 11419809

Dey, M. (2025, April 30). EDX Statistics by website traffic, marketing channels and courses. *Electro IQ*. https://electroiq.com/stats/edx-statistics/

DeYoung, C. G., & Tiberius, V. (2023). Value fulfillment from a cybernetic perspective: A new psychological theory of well-being. *Personality and Social Psychology Review*, *27*(1), 3–27. DOI: 10.1177/10888683221083777 PMID: 35440238

Dhar, D., Kumar, P., Bhateja, S., Jain, S., Rawat, S., & Shinde, M. (2024). People and sites as community resources for preventing and responding to gender-based violence in Uttar Pradesh, India: A descriptive qualitative study. *PLOS Global Public Health*, *4*(7). Advance online publication. DOI: 10.1371/journal.pgph.0003415

Dhar, S., & Bose, I. (2023). Corporate users' attachment to social networking sites: Examining the role of social capital and perceived benefits. *Information Systems Frontiers*, *25*(3), 1197–1217. DOI: 10.1007/s10796-022-10289-y

Dhawan, S. (2020). Online learning: A panacea in the time of COVID-19 crisis. *Journal of Educational Technology Systems*, *49*(1), 5–22. DOI: 10.1177/0047239520934018

Diaz, J. (2025, July 10). A recent high-profile case of AI hallucination serves as a stark warning. NPR. https://www.npr.org/2025/07/10/nx-s1-5463512/ai-courts-lawyers-mypillow-fines

Dienlin, T., & Johannes, N. (2020). The impact of digital technology use on adolescent well-being. *Dialogues in Clinical Neuroscience*, *22*(2), 135–142. DOI: 10.31887/DCNS.2020.22.2/tdienlin PMID: 32699513

Dillenbourg, P. (1999). What do you mean by collaborative learning?. *Collaborative-learning: Cognitive and computational approaches.*, 1-19.

Dincă, M., Luştrea, A., Craşovan, M., Oniţiu, A., & Berge, T. (2023). Students' perspectives on team dynamics in Project-Based virtual learning. *SAGE Open*, *13*(1), 21582440221147269. DOI: 10.1177/21582440221147269

Dineva, S. (2024). Hybrid, blended, and hyflex learning as future models for education. *Обучение по природни науки и върхови технологии, 33*(3-4), 152-161.

Dixson, M. D. (2015). Measuring student engagement in the online course: The Online Student Engagement scale (OSE). *Online Learning : the Official Journal of the Online Learning Consortium*, *19*(4), n4. DOI: 10.24059/olj.v19i4.561

Dolot, A. (2018). The characteristic of Generation Z. *E-mentor, 2*(74), 44-50. DOI: 10.15219/em74.1351

Donelan, H., & Kear, K. (2024). Online group projects in higher education: Persistent challenges and implications for practice. *Journal of Computing in Higher Education, 36*(2), 435–468. DOI: 10.1007/s12528-023-09360-7 PMID: 37359044

Donevski, M., & Zia, T. (2024). Cyber diversity index for sustainable self-control of machines. *Cybernetics and Systems, 55*(1), 61–87. DOI: 10.1080/01969722.2022.2081896

Dool, R. (2010). Managing Conflict in Online Student Groups. In *TCC* (pp. 47-57). TCCHawaii.

Dubovi, I. (2022). Cognitive and emotional engagement while learning with VR: The perspective of multimodal methodology. *Computers & Education, 183*(January), 104495. DOI: 10.1016/j.compedu.2022.104495

Dutton, J. (2025). Sporting futures, beyond automation: reading Bernard Stiegler to reinvent athletic gesture. *Distinktion: Journal of Social Theory*, 1-24.

Dyer, T., & Aroz, J. (2018). Proximity in the Online Classroom: Engagement, Relationship and Personalization. *Journal of Institutional Research, 7*, 108–118.

Eckhardt, G. (2002). Culture's Consequences: Comparing Values, Behaviors, Institutions and Organisations Across Nations. In *Australian Journal of Management* (Vol. 27, Issue 1). DOI: 10.1177/031289620202700105

Eden, C. A., Chisom, O. N., & Adeniyi, I. S.Chima Abimbola EdenOnyebuchi Nneamaka ChisomIdowu Sulaimon Adeniyi. (2024). Online learning and community engagement: Strategies for promoting inclusivity and collaboration in education. *World Journal of Advanced Research and Reviews, 21*(3), 232–239. DOI: 10.30574/wjarr.2024.21.3.0693

Edmondson, A. C., & Lei, Z. (2014). Psychological Safety: The History, Renaissance, and Future of an Interpersonal Construct. In *Annual Review of Organizational Psychology and Organizational Behavior* (Vol. 1). DOI: 10.1146/annurev-orgpsych-031413-091305

Edmondson, A. (1999). Psychological safety and learning behavior in work teams. *Administrative Science Quarterly, 44*(2), 350–383. Advance online publication. DOI: 10.2307/2666999

Eisenbach, B. B., Greathouse, P., & Kirk, M. (2018). Creating a community of care in the middle level virtual classroom. In Eisenbach, B. B., & Greathouse, P. (Eds.), *The online classroom: Resources for effective middle level education* (pp. 121–136). Information Age. DOI: 10.1108/978-1-64113-461-320251011

Ernst & Young Report. (2016). From Innovation to Expectation – How M & E Leaders are Responding to Gen Z. http://www.ey.com/Publication/vwLUAssets/ey-media-entertainment-leaders-respond-toGen Z/$FILE/ey-media-entertainmentleaders-respond-to-Gen Z.pdf

Erstad, O., Hegna, K., Livingstone, S., Negru-Subtirica, O., & Stoilova, M. (2024). How digital technologies become embedded in family life across generations: Scoping the agenda for researching 'platformised relationality.'. *Families, Relationships and Societies, 13*(2), 164–180. DOI: 10.1332/20467435Y2024D000000023

Etz, D., & Kastner, W. (2021, May). Human control of self-organizing safety systems. In *2020 2nd International Conference on Societal Automation (SA)* (pp. 1-7). IEEE. DOI: 10.1109/SA51175.2021.9507109

Falls, I., Bahhouth, V., Chuang, C. M., & Bahhouth, J. (2014). Factors influencing students' perceptions of online teamwork. *SAGE Open, 4*(1), 2158244014525415. DOI: 10.1177/2158244014525415

Fay-Stammbach, T., Hawes, D. J., & Meredith, P. (2014). Parenting influences on executive function in early childhood: A review. *Child Development Perspectives, 8*(4), 258–264. DOI: 10.1111/cdep.12095

Felisoni, D. D., & Godoi, I. M. (2018). Cell phone usage and academic performance: An experiment. In *Proceedings of EdMedia: World Conference on Educational Media and Technology* (pp. 67–75). Association for the Advancement of Computing in Education (AACE). DOI: 10.1016/j.compedu.2017.10.006

Feng, L., Xu, B., Ding, C., Feng, H., & Liu, T. (2025). Dynamic Risk Assessment Framework for Tanker Cargo Operations: Integrating Game-Theoretic Weighting and Grey Cloud Modelling with Port-Specific Empirical Validation. *Systems, 13*(8), 697. DOI: 10.3390/systems13080697

Fernández, M. (2018). Student engagement in the online classroom: The student perspective. In *Decline and Revival in Higher Education* (pp. 179–211). Routledge., DOI: 10.4324/9780203793671-8

Festinger, L. (1954). A theory of social comparison processes. *Human Relations; Studies Towards the Integration of the Social Sciences, 7*(2), 117–140. DOI: 10.1177/001872675400700202

Fink, M. C., & Wang, Q. (2024). AI-based avatars are changing the way we learn and teach. *Frontiers in Education, 9*, 1416307. DOI: 10.3389/feduc.2024.1416307

Fink, M. C., Wang, Q., & Islam, M. Z. (2025). Avatars in the educational metaverse. *Journal of Virtual Learning, 39*(2), 121–156. https://pmc.ncbi.nlm.nih.gov/articles/PMC12151956/

Firth, J., Torous, J., Stubbs, B., Firth, J. A., Steiner, G. Z., Smith, L., & Sarris, J. (2019). The "online brain": How the Internet may be changing our cognition. *World Psychiatry; Official Journal of the World Psychiatric Association (WPA), 18*(2), 119–129. DOI: 10.1002/wps.20617

Firth, R., & Preston, J. (2025). The Dystopian Realities of Cybernetics. In *Utopia in the Factory: Prefigurative Knowledge Against Cybernetics* (pp. 67–90). Springer Nature Switzerland. DOI: 10.1007/978-3-031-87132-0_3

Fisher, W. (2024). Entropy, deterministic chaos, and new forms of intelligibility: A shared frame of reference for physics and psychology. *International Journal of Advances in Production Research, 1*(1), 46–82. DOI: 10.62743/uad.6179

Fiske, S. T., & Taylor, S. E. (2013). *Social cognition: From brains to culture* (2nd ed.). Sage Publications. DOI: 10.4135/9781446286395

Fleming, L. E., Broad, K., Clement, A., Dewailly, E., Elmir, S., Knap, A., Pomponi, S. A., Smith, S., Solo Gabriele, H., & Walsh, P. (2006). Oceans and human health: Emerging public health risks in the marine environment. *Marine Pollution Bulletin, 53*(10-12), 545–560. DOI: 10.1016/j.marpolbul.2006.08.012 PMID: 16996542

Fogg, B. J. (2002). Persuasive technology: Using computers to change what we think and do. *Ubiquity, 2002*(December), 2. DOI: 10.1145/764008.763957

Foo, C. C., Cheung, B., & Chu, K. M. (2021). A comparative study regarding distance learning and the conventional face-to-face approach conducted problem-based learning tutorial during the COVID-19 pandemic. *BMC Medical Education, 21*(1), 141. DOI: 10.1186/s12909-021-02575-1 PMID: 33658015

Ford, R. C., Piccolo, R. F., & Ford, L. R. (2017). Strategies for building effective virtual teams: Trust is key. *Business Horizons, 60*(1), 25–34. Advance online publication. DOI: 10.1016/j.bushor.2016.08.009

Fouad, N. S. (2024). *Theorising cyber (in) security: Information, materiality, and entropic security*. Taylor & Francis. DOI: 10.4324/9781003454113

Francis, T., & Hoefel, F. (2018, November 12). *'True Gen': Generation Z and its implications for companies*. McKinsey & Company.

Frazier, M. L., Fainshmidt, S., Klinger, R. L., Pezeshkan, A., & Vracheva, V. (2017). Psychological Safety: A Meta-Analytic Review and Extension. *Personnel Psychology, 70*(1), 113–165. Advance online publication. DOI: 10.1111/peps.12183

Fredricks, J. A., Blumenfeld, P. C., & Paris, A. H. (2004). School engagement: Potential of the concept, state of the evidence. *Review of Educational Research, 74*(1), 59–109. DOI: 10.3102/00346543074001059

Fryling, M. J., Johnston, C., & Hayes, L. J. (2011). Understanding observational learning: An interbehavioral approach. *Analysis of Verbal Behavior, 27*(1), 191–203. DOI: 10.1007/BF03393102

Gajendran, R. S., & Harrison, D. A. (2007). The Good, the Bad, and the Unknown About Telecommuting: Meta-Analysis of Psychological Mediators and Individual Consequences. *The Journal of Applied Psychology, 92*(6), 1524–1541. Advance online publication. DOI: 10.1037/0021-9010.92.6.1524 PMID: 18020794

Gallegos, M. I., Murphy, S. E., Benner, A. D., Jacobvitz, D. B., & Hazen, N. L. (2017). Marital, parental, and whole-family predictors of toddlers' emotion regulation: The role of parental emotional withdrawal. *Journal of Family Psychology, 31*(3), 294–303. DOI: 10.1037/fam0000245 PMID: 27617477

Gallup. (2025, April 8). Voices of Gen Z: How American youth view and use artificial intelligence. https://static.waltonfamilyfoundation.org/a7/cd/b145ce854643a05e5393fa0664a4/walton-gsv-voices-of-Gen Z-ai-final-report-04042025.pdf

Ganong, L. H., Coleman, M., Feistman, R., Jamison, T., & Stafford Markham, M. (2012). Communication technology and postdivorce coparenting. *Family Relations, 61*(3), 397–409. DOI: 10.1111/j.1741-3729.2012.00706.x

Gao, X., Mou, J., Banerjee, S., & Zhang, Y. (2023). Color-gray multi-image hybrid compression–encryption scheme based on BP neural network and knight tour. *IEEE Transactions on Cybernetics, 53*(8), 5037–5047. DOI: 10.1109/TCYB.2023.3267785 PMID: 37130254

Garcia, M. B. (2025). The influence of avatar appearance and behavioral realism in educational environments. *Interactive Learning Environments, 38*(3), 241–264. DOI: 10.1080/10494820.2025.2462144

Garrison, D. R., Anderson, T., & Archer, W. (2000). Critical inquiry in a text-based environment: Computer conferencing in higher education. Internet and Higher Education, 2(2-3), 87–105. . https://doi.org/DOI: 10.1016/S1096-7516(00)00016-6

Garrison, D. R. (2017). *E-Learning in the 21st century: A community of inquiry framework for research and practice* (3rd ed.). Routledge., DOI: 10.4324/9781315667263

Garrison, D. R., & Arbaugh, J. B. (2007). Researching the community of inquiry framework: Review, issues, and future directions. *The Internet and Higher Education, 10*(3), 157–172. DOI: 10.1016/j.iheduc.2007.04.001

Geng, F., Srinivasan, S., Gao, Z., Bogoslowski, S., & Rajabzadeh, A. R. (2022). An Online Approach to Project-Based Learning in Engineering and Technology for Post-secondary Students. In Auer, M. E., & Tsiatsos, T. (Eds.), *New Realities, Mobile Systems and Applications* (pp. 627–635). Springer International Publishing., DOI: 10.1007/978-3-030-96296-8_56

Gerus, S. V., Dementienko, V. V., & Mirgorodskiy, V. I. (2023). The Physical Principles of the Construction of Systems for Safe Monitoring of the State of a Human Operator. *Pattern Recognition and Image Analysis, 33*(4), 1377–1401. DOI: 10.1134/S1054661823040168

Gherghel, C., Yasuda, S., & Kita, Y. (2023). Interaction during online classes fosters engagement with learning and self-directed study both in the first and second years of the COVID-19 pandemic. *Computers & Education, 200*, 104795. DOI: 10.1016/j.compedu.2023.104795 PMID: 37063109

Ghosh, R. (2025). Ergodic Capacity of Human Interaction Channels: A Control-Theoretic View.

Ghosh, A. K., Badillo-Urquiola, K., Guha, S., LaViola, J. J.Jr, & Wisniewski, P. J. (2018). Safety vs. surveillance: What children have to say about mobile apps for parental control. *Proceedings of the 2018 CHI Conference on Human Factors in Computing Systems*, 1–14. DOI: 10.1145/3173574.3173698

Gkintoni, E., Antonopoulou, H., Sortwell, A., & Halkiopoulos, C. (2025). Challenging cognitive load theory: The role of educational neuroscience and artificial intelligence in redefining learning efficacy. *Brain Sciences, 15*(2), 203. DOI: 10.3390/brainsci15020203

Glasson, H. G. (2024). *Political Applications of Systems Theory in the Twentieth Century: From Cybernetic Control to Spontaneous Emergence* (Doctoral dissertation, Virginia Polytechnic Institute and State University).

Glickman, E. A., Choi, K. W., Lussier, A. A., Smith, B. J., & Dunn, E. C. (2021). Childhood emotional neglect and adolescent depression: Assessing the protective role of peer social support in a longitudinal birth cohort. *Frontiers in Psychiatry, 12*, 681176. DOI: 10.3389/fpsyt.2021.681176 PMID: 34434126

Goddard, M. N. (2022). Noise Annoys, Noise is the Future: Noise in Communication and Cybernetic Theories and Popular Music Practices. In *Noise as a Constructive Element in Music* (pp. 19–34). Routledge. DOI: 10.4324/9781003307020-3

Goffman, E. (1959). *The presentation of self in everyday life*. Anchor Books.

Golden, J., Conroy, R. M., Bruce, I., Denihan, A., Greene, E., Kirby, M., & Lawlor, B. A. (2009). Loneliness, social support networks, mood and wellbeing in community-dwelling elderly. *International Journal of Geriatric Psychiatry, 24*(7), 694–700. DOI: 10.1002/gps.2181 PMID: 19274642

Goł biewski, D., Barszcz, T., Skrodzka, W., Wojnicki, I., & Bielecki, A. (2022). A New Approach to Risk Management in the Power Industry Based on Systems Theory. *Energies, 15*(23), 9003. DOI: 10.3390/en15239003

Gonçalves, K., & Lexander, K. V. (2023). Permanent or temporary homes?: Investigating the discourses of lifestyle migration, lifestyle mobilities and multilingualism within a Norwegian context. *AILA Review, 36*(2), 299–320. DOI: 10.1075/aila.00057.gon

Gopinathan, S., Kaur, A. H., Veeraya, S., & Raman, M. (2022). The role of digital collaboration in student engagement towards enhancing student participation during COVID-19. *Sustainability (Basel), 14*(11), 6844. DOI: 10.3390/su14116844

Gore, M. C. (2018). *The digital self: A qualitative approach to studying female college students' use of social-networking platforms* [PhD Thesis]. Eastern Michigan University.

Graham, C. R., Borup, J., Short, C., & Archambault, L. (2019). *K–12 blended teaching: A guide to personalized learning and online integration.* Edtechbooks.org

Greene, B. A. (2015). Measuring cognitive engagement with self-report scales: Reflections from over 20 years of research. *Educational Psychologist, 50*(1), 14–30. DOI: 10.1080/00461520.2014.989230

Greene, J. D., Sommerville, R. B., Nystrom, L. E., Darley, J. M., & Cohen, J. D. (2023). An fMRI investigation of emotional engagement in moral judgment. *Science, 293*(5537), 2105–2108. DOI: 10.1126/science.1062872 PMID: 11557895

Griffin, P., McGaw, B., & Care, E. (2012). *Assessment and teaching of 21st century skills* (Vol. 10, pp. 978-94). Dordrecht: springer. DOI: 10.1007/978-94-017-9395-7

Grothaus, C. (2022). Collaborative online learning across cultures: The role of teaching and social presence. *Qualitative Research in Education, 11*(3), 298–326. DOI: 10.17583/qre.10474

Gulati, R., Wohlgezogen, F., & Zhelyazkov, P. (2012). The two facets of collaboration: Cooperation and coordination in strategic alliances. *The Academy of Management Annals*, *6*(1), 531–583. DOI: 10.5465/19416520.2012.691646

Hagane, S., & Venture, G. (2022). Robotic manipulator's expressive movements control using kinematic redundancy. *Machines (Basel)*, *10*(12), 1118. DOI: 10.3390/machines10121118

Hällgren, C., & Björk, Å. (2023). Young people's identities in digital worlds. *The International Journal of Information and Learning Technology*, *40*(1), 49–61. DOI: 10.1108/IJILT-06-2022-0135

Han, Y. (2024). Gender exploration in avatar customization systems. *Games and Culture*, *19*(1), 45–61. DOI: 10.1177/15554120241307982

Hareven, T. K. (2018). *Families, history and social change: Life course and cross-cultural perspectives*. Routledge. DOI: 10.4324/9780429500572

Harrington, C., & DeBruler, K. (2021). Key strategies for engaging students in virtual learning environments. Michigan Virtual Learning Research Institute. https://michiganvirtual.org/research/publications/key-strategies-for-engaging-stud ents-in-virtual-learning-environments/

Harris, D., Arthur, T., Wilson, M., Le Gallais, B., Parsons, T., Dill, A., & Vine, S. (2025). Counteracting uncertainty: Exploring the impact of anxiety on updating predictions about environmental states. *Biological Cybernetics*, *119*(2), 1–16. DOI: 10.1007/s00422-025-01006-4 PMID: 39976741

Hartl, B., Risi, S., & Levin, M. (2024). Evolutionary implications of self-assembling cybernetic materials with collective problem-solving intelligence at multiple scales. *Entropy (Basel, Switzerland)*, *26*(7), 532. DOI: 10.3390/e26070532 PMID: 39056895

Hasenbein, L., Stark, P., Trautwein, U., Gao, H., Kasneci, E., & Göllner, R. (2023). Investigating social comparison behaviour in an immersive virtual reality classroom based on eye-movement data. *Scientific Reports*, *13*(1), 14672. DOI: 10.1038/s41598-023-41704-2

Hastomo, T., & Septiyana, L. (2022). The Investigation of Students' Engagement in Online Class During Pandemic Covid-19. *Jurnal Penelitian Ilmu Pendidikan*, *15*(2). Advance online publication. DOI: 10.21831/jpipfip.v15i2.49512

Haugland, M. J., Rosenberg, I., & Aasekjær, K. (2022). Collaborative learning in small groups in an online course – a case study. *BMC Medical Education*, *22*(1), 165. DOI: 10.1186/s12909-022-03232-x PMID: 35272639

Henrie, C. R., Halverson, L. R., & Graham, C. R. (2015). Measuring student engagement in technology-mediated learning: A review. *Computers & Education*, *90*, 36–53. DOI: 10.1016/j.compedu.2015.09.005

Henri, F. (1992). Computer conferencing and content analysis. In Kaye, A. R. (Ed.), *Collaborative learning through computer conferencing: The Najaden papers* (pp. 117–136). SpringerVerlag., DOI: 10.1007/978-3-642-77684-7_8

He, R., Suitor, J. J., & Gilligan, M. (2024). Digital Contact as Strain or Support: How Does Type of Contact Shape the Association Between Mother–Child Interactions and Adult Children's Depressive Symptoms in Later-Life Families? *The Gerontologist*, *64*(12), 1–11. DOI: 10.1093/geront/gnae158 PMID: 39487712

Herrera-Pavo, M. Á. (2021). Collaborative learning for virtual higher education. *Learning, Culture and Social Interaction*, *28*, 100437. DOI: 10.1016/j.lcsi.2020.100437

Hess, U. (2023). Nonverbal communication. In *Encyclopedia of Mental Health, Third Edition: Volume 1-3* (Vol. 2). DOI: 10.1016/B978-0-323-91497-0.00133-8

Hew, K. F., Huang, B., Chu, K. W. S., & Chiu, D. K. W. (2019). Engaging Asian students through game mechanics: Findings from two experiment studies. *Computers & Education*, *133*, 30–48. DOI: 10.1016/j.compedu.2015.10.010

Hew, K. F., & Lo, C. K. (2018). Flipped classroom improves student learning in health professions education: A meta-analysis. *BMC Medical Education*, *18*(1), 38. DOI: 10.1186/s12909-018-1144-z PMID: 29544495

Hinds, P. J., & Bailey, D. E. (2003). Out of Sight, Out of Sync: Understanding Conflict in Distributed Teams. *Organization Science*, *14*(6), 615–632. Advance online publication. DOI: 10.1287/orsc.14.6.615.24872

Hiniker, A., Lee, B., Sobel, K., & Choe, E. K. (2017). Plan & play: supporting intentional media use in early childhood. In *Proceedings of the 2017 conference on interaction design and children* (pp. 85-95). DOI: 10.1145/3078072.3079752

Hlabisa, S. B. (2025). The Control–Entropy Paradox: Modeling the Thermodynamic Limits of Environmental Governance. *Systems Research and Behavioral Science*, sres.3178. DOI: 10.1002/sres.3178

Hmelo-Silver, C. E. (2004). Problem-based learning: What and how do students learn? *Educational Psychology Review*, *16*(3), 235–266. DOI: 10.1023/B:EDPR.0000034022.16470.f3

Hodges, C., Moore, S., Lockee, B., Trust, T., & Bond, A. (2020). The difference between emergency remote teaching and online learning. *Educause Review*. https://er.educause.edu/articles/2020/3/the-difference-between-emergency-remote-teaching-and-online-learning

Hodgkinson, G. P., & Healey, M. P. (2014). Coming in from the cold: The psychological foundations of radical innovation revisited. *Industrial Marketing Management*, *43*(8), 1306–1313. DOI: 10.1016/j.indmarman.2014.08.012

Hollister, B., Nair, P., Hill-Lindsay, S., & Chukoskie, L. (2022). Engagement in online learning: Student attitudes and behavior during COVID-19. *Frontiers in Education*, *7*. Advance online publication. DOI: 10.3389/feduc.2022.851019

Holmes, K., & Prieto-Rodriguez, E. (2018). Student and staff perceptions of a learning management system for blended learning in teacher education. *The Australian Journal of Teacher Education*, *43*(3), 21–34. https://search.informit.org/doi/10.3316/informit.477648976239419. DOI: 10.14221/ajte.2018v43n3.2

Holt-Lunstad, J., Smith, T. B., Baker, M., Harris, T., & Stephenson, D. (2015). Loneliness and Social Isolation as Risk Factors for Mortality: A Meta-Analytic Review. *Perspectives on Psychological Science*, *10*(2), 227–237. DOI: 10.1177/1745691614568352 PMID: 25910392

Holwerda, T. J., Deeg, D. J., Beekman, A. T., Van Tilburg, T. G., Stek, M. L., Jonker, C., & Schoevers, R. A. (2014). Feelings of loneliness, but not social isolation, predict dementia onset: Results from the Amsterdam Study of the Elderly (AMS). *Journal of Neurology, Neurosurgery, and Psychiatry*, *85*(2), 135–142. DOI: 10.1136/jnnp-2012-302755 PMID: 23232034

Houtman, E., Makos, A., & Meacock, H. L. (2014). The intersection of social presence and impression management in online learning environments. *E-Learning and Digital Media*, *11*(4), 419–430. DOI: 10.2304/elea.2014.11.4.419

Hrastinski, S. (2008). Asynchronous and synchronous e-learning. *EDUCAUSE Quarterly*, *31*(4), 51–55.

Hridi, A. P., Hoq, M., Gao, Z., Lynch, C., Sahay, R., Hosseinalipour, S., & Akram, B. (2025). Privacy-Preserving Distributed Link Predictions Among Peers in Online Classrooms Using Federated Learning. *arXiv preprint arXiv:2504.10456.*

Hsu, H. C. K., Wang, C. V., & Levesque-Bristol, C. (2019). Reexamining the impact of self-determination theory on learning outcomes in the online learning environment. *Education and Information Technologies*, *24*(3), 2159–2174. DOI: 10.1007/s10639-019-09863-w

Huang, L., Wang, K., Li, S., & Guo, J. (2023). Using WeChat as an educational tool in MOOC-based flipped classroom: What can we learn from students' learning experience? *Frontiers in Psychology, 13*. Advance online publication. DOI: 10.3389/fpsyg.2022.1098585

Huang, S. Y. B., Huang, C.-H., & Chang, T.-W. (2022). A New Concept of Work Engagement Theory in Cognitive Engagement, Emotional Engagement, and Physical Engagement. *Frontiers in Psychology, 12*(February), 1–5. DOI: 10.3389/fpsyg.2021.663440 PMID: 35242067

Hu, W., Tian, J., & Li, Y. (2025). Enhancing student engagement in online collaborative writing through a generative AI-based conversational agent. *The Internet and Higher Education, 65*, 100979. DOI: 10.1016/j.iheduc.2024.100979

Iman, N. (2025). Balancing order and entropy: The role of innovation and organizational disorder in performance across startups and banking. *International Journal of Innovation Science*. Advance online publication. DOI: 10.1108/IJIS-03-2025-0142

Infantes-Paniagua, Á., Silva, A. F., Ramirez-Campillo, R., Sarmento, H., González-Fernández, F. T., González-Víllora, S., & Clemente, F. M. (2021). Active school breaks and students' attention: A systematic review with meta-analysis. *Brain Sciences, 11*(6), 675. DOI: 10.3390/brainsci11060675

Ionescu, ., Nica, I., & Chiri ă, N. (2021). Cybernetics approach using agent-based modeling in the process of evacuating educational institutions in case of disasters. *Sustainability (Basel), 13*(18), 10277. DOI: 10.3390/su131810277

Irish, N. (2022). Supporting social presence: a phenomenological study of the perceptions of intermediate elementary teachers who taught virtually during the COVID-19 pandemic. *Theses, Dissertations, and Final Projects*. Millersville University of Pennsylvania. https://jstor.org/stable/community.39483030

Islam, M. Z., & Wang, G. (2025). Avatars in the educational metaverse. *Visual Computing for Industry, Biomedicine, and Art, 8*(1), 15. DOI: 10.1186/s42492-025-00196-9 PMID: 40493326

James, M., Koshkina, N., & Froese, T. (2023). From tech to tact: Emotion dysregulation in online communication during the COVID-19 pandemic. *Phenomenology and the Cognitive Sciences, 22*(5), 1163–1194. DOI: 10.1007/s11097-023-09916-z

Jansen, M., Boda, Z., & Lorenz, G. (2022). Social comparison effects on academic self-concepts-Which peers matter most? *Developmental Psychology, 58*(8), 1541–1556. DOI: 10.1037/dev0001368

Jensen, M., George, M. J., Russell, M. A., Lippold, M. A., & Odgers, C. L. (2021). Does Adolescent Digital Technology Use Detract from the Parent–Adolescent Relationship? *Journal of Research on Adolescence*, *31*(2), 469–481. DOI: 10.1111/jora.12618 PMID: 33829598

Jeon, W. (2022). Second-Order Recursions of First-Order Cybernetics: An "Experimental Epistemology". *Open Philosophy*, *5*(1), 381–395. DOI: 10.1515/opphil-2022-0207

Jeske, D., & Santuzzi, A. M. (2015). Monitoring what and how: Psychological implications of electronic performance monitoring. *New Technology, Work and Employment*, *30*(1), 62–78. Advance online publication. DOI: 10.1111/ntwe.12039

Jia, H., & Wang, L. (2024). Introducing Entropy into Organizational Psychology: An Entropy-Based Proactive Control Model. *Behavioral Sciences (Basel, Switzerland)*, *14*(1), 54. DOI: 10.3390/bs14010054 PMID: 38247706

Jiang, Z., Qin, C., Yang, R., Shi, B., Alsaadi, F. E., & Wang, Z. (2025). Social Entropy Informer: A Multi-Scale Model-Data Dual-Driven Approach for Pedestrian Trajectory Prediction. *IEEE Transactions on Intelligent Transportation Systems*, *26*(10), 16438–16453. DOI: 10.1109/TITS.2025.3572254

Ji, M., Pan, K., Zhang, X., Pan, Q., Dai, X., & Lyu, Y. (2024). Integration of Sense and Control for Uncertain Systems Based on Delayed Feedback Active Inference. *Entropy (Basel, Switzerland)*, *26*(11), 990. DOI: 10.3390/e26110990 PMID: 39593935

Johar, N. A., Kew, S. N., Tasir, Z., & Koh, E. (2023). Learning analytics on student engagement to enhance students' learning performance: A systematic review. *Sustainability (Basel)*, *15*(10), 7849. DOI: 10.3390/su15107849

Johnson, D. W., & Johnson, R. T. (2009). An educational psychology success story: Social interdependence theory and cooperative learning. *Educational Researcher*, *38*(5), 365–379. DOI: 10.3102/0013189X09339057

Johnson, D. W., Johnson, R. T., & Smith, K. A. (2014). Cooperative learning: Improving university instruction by basing practice on validated theory. *Journal on Excellence in College Teaching*, *25*(3&4).

Johnson, J. (2023). Automating the OODA loop in the age of intelligent machines: Reaffirming the role of humans in command-and-control decision-making in the digital age. *Defence Studies*, *23*(1), 43–67. DOI: 10.1080/14702436.2022.2102486

Jonas, R. M., Hanrahan, B. V., Sloan, C. J., & Fosco, G. M. (2023). Supporting from the Background: How a Mobile Application for Parent Skills Development Encourages Authoritative Parenting. *Computer Supported Cooperative Work and Social Computing*, 105–111. DOI: 10.1145/3584931.3606969

Jull, J. E., Davidson, L., Dungan, R., Nguyen, T., Woodward, K. P., & Graham, I. D. (2019). A review and synthesis of frameworks for engagement in health research to identify concepts of knowledge user engagement. *BMC Medical Research Methodology*, *19*(1), 1–13. DOI: 10.1186/s12874-019-0838-1 PMID: 31752691

Kang, J., & Rhee, H. (2025). Gender identity and perception in virtual spaces: The impact of avatar presentation. *Frontiers in Virtual Reality*, *10*, 1505624. DOI: 10.3389/frvir.2025.1505624

Kang, T. (2012). Gendered media, changing intimacy: Internet-mediated transnational communication in the family sphere. *Media Culture & Society*, *34*(2), 146–161. DOI: 10.1177/0163443711430755

Kao, D., & Harrell, D. F. (2016). Exploring the effects of dynamic avatar on performance and engagement in educational games. *Procedia Computer Science*, *96*, 1063–1072. DOI: 10.1016/j.procs.2016.08.109

Kapoor, K. K., Tamilmani, K., Rana, N. P., Patil, P., Dwivedi, Y. K., & Nerur, S. (2018). Advances in social media research: Past, present and future. *Information Systems Frontiers*, *20*, 531–558. DOI: 10.1007/s10796-017-9810-y

Kapp, K. M. (2012). *The gamification of learning and instruction: Game-based methods and strategies for training and education*. Pfeiffer.

Karimov, A., Saarela, M., Aliyev, S., & Baker, R. (2025, January). Ethical considerations and student perceptions of engagement data in learning analytics. In *Proceedings of the 58th Hawaii International Conference on System Sciences* (4757-4766). DOI: 10.24251/HICSS.2025.572

Kates, A. W., Wu, H., & Coryn, C. L. S. (2018). The effects of mobile phone use on academic performance: A meta-analysis. *Computers & Education*, *127*, 107–112. DOI: 10.1016/j.compedu.2018.08.012

Katsenos, I., & Pierrakeas, C. (2025). Assessing Individual Contributions of Team Members to Team Achievement by Combining Peer Assessments and Digital Presence in an Academic Environment. *Education Sciences*, *15*(3), 279. DOI: 10.3390/educsci15030279

Kay, R. H., & LeSage, A. (2009). Examining the benefits and challenges of using audience response systems: A review of the literature. *Computers & Education, 53*(3), 819–827. DOI: 10.1016/j.compedu.2009.05.001

Kehrwald, B. (2008). Understanding social presence in text-based online learning environments. *Distance Education, 29*(1), 89–106. DOI: 10.1080/01587910802004860

Kelbert, E. (2021). Entropy as a trope: Yuri Lotman's general theory of communication as a case study in interdisciplinarity. *World Literature Studies, 13*(4), 55–70. DOI: 10.31577/WLS.2021.13.4.5

Kemp, S. (2024, January 31). *The time we spend on social media — DataReportal – Global Digital Insights.* https://datareportal.com/reports/digital-2024-deep-dive-the-time-we-spend-on-social-media

Kemp, S. (2025, June 30). *Digital 2025: top social platforms in 2025 — DataReportal – Global Digital Insights.* https://datareportal.com/reports/digital-2025-sub-section-top-social-platforms?rq=social%20media

Kew, S. N., & Tasir, Z. (2021). Analysing Students' Cognitive Engagement in E-Learning Discussion Forums through Content Analysis. *Knowledge Management & E-Learning, 13*(1), 39–57.

Khantuleva, T. A. (2022). Description of the Structure Evolution Using Methods of Control Theory of Adaptive Systems. In *Mathematical Modeling of Shock-Wave Processes in Condensed Matter: From Statistical Thermodynamics to Control Theory* (pp. 175–208). Springer Nature Singapore. DOI: 10.1007/978-981-19-2404-0_6

Kim, T. R.III. (2024). *Reducing Entropy Through Targeted Information Sharing: An Exploratory First Principles Approach to Closing the Gaps in Modern Security Operations Centers.* Marymount University.

Kline, R. (2023). Cybernetics and Information Theory in Human–Machine Communication. In *The Sage Handbook of Human–Machine Communication* (pp. 22–31). SAGE Publications Ltd. DOI: 10.4135/9781529782783.n5

Knight, C., & Haslam, S. A. (2010). Your place or mine? organizational identification and comfort as mediators of relationships between the managerial control of workspace and employees' satisfaction and well-being. *British Journal of Management, 21*(3), 717–735. Advance online publication. DOI: 10.1111/j.1467-8551.2009.00683.x

Knight, E. M. (2013). Aligning the curriculum of the human resources management undergraduate courses at an English-speaking university in the Caribbean with the university's 2012–2017 strategic plan. *Global Business and Economics Research Journal, 2*(8), 61–86.

Konok, V., Gigler, D., Bereczky, B. M., & Miklósi, Á. (2016). Humans' attachment to their mobile phones and its relationship with interpersonal attachment style. *Computers in Human Behavior*, *61*, 537–547. DOI: 10.1016/j.chb.2016.03.062

Koushik, S., & Bhamare, V. (2025). Students' perceptions and outcome of teacher feedback. *Frontiers in Education*, *10*, 1572950. DOI: 10.3389/feduc.2025.1572950

Krause, E., & Sawhill, I. V. (2016, September 13). *How free time became screen time.* Brookings Institution.

Kraut, R., Patterson, M., Lundmark, V., Kiesler, S., Mukophadhyay, T., & Scherlis, W. (1998). Internet paradox: A social technology that reduces social involvement and psychological well-being? *The American Psychologist*, *53*(9), 1017–1031. DOI: 10.1037/0003-066X.53.9.1017 PMID: 9841579

Kruger, J., Epley, N., Parker, J., & Ng, Z. W. (2005). Egocentrism over E-mail: Can we communicate as well as we think? *Journal of Personality and Social Psychology*, *89*(6), 925–936. Advance online publication. DOI: 10.1037/0022-3514.89.6.925 PMID: 16393025

Kuh, G. D. (2003). What we're learning about student engagement from NSSE: Benchmarks for effective educational practices. *Change: The magazine of higher learning, 35*(2), 24-32.

Kumar, R., & Wei, L. (2024). Exploring the Impact of Digital Learning Environments on Student Engagement and Academic Performance A Global Perspective. *International Journal of Educational Insights and Innovations*, *1*(2), 5–8.

Kunwar, J. B. (2021). The influence of culture on collaborative learning practices in higher education. *Journal of Intercultural Management*, *13*(2), 81–106. DOI: 10.2478/joim-2021-0062

Küppers, E. U. (2023). Cybernetic Systems in Practice. In *A Transdisciplinary Introduction to the World of Cybernetics: Basics, Models, Theories and Practical Examples* (pp. 147–206). Springer Fachmedien Wiesbaden.

Lan, R., Sun, X., Wang, Q., & Liu, B. (2025). Investigating the Feasibility of Using Eye-Tracking Metrics as Indicators of Situation Awareness in Flight Training. *International Journal of Human-Computer Interaction*, •••, 1–21.

Laouris, Y., & Tuddenham, P. (2025). Revitalizing Democracy Through Cybernetics and Systems Science: Principles and Applications for Effective Governance. *Available at SSRN* 5316819. DOI: 10.1016/j.futures.2025.103693

Latha R. Chandrasekar. (2025). The Impact of Collaboration Tools on Student Engagement. *The Impact of Collaboration Tools on Student Engagement.*

Lawson, M. A., & Lawson, H. A. (2023). New Conceptual Frameworks for Student Engagement Research, Policy, and Practice. In *Review of Educational Research* (Vol. 83, Issue 3). DOI: 10.3102/0034654313480891

Le, B. G., & Ta, V. C. (2024). On the Effectiveness of Regularization Methods for Soft Actor–Critic in Discrete-Action Domains. *IEEE Transactions on Systems, Man, and Cybernetics. Systems.*

Lee, S. J., & Chae, Y. G. (2007). Children's Internet use in a family context: Influence on family relationships and parental mediation. *Cyberpsychology & Behavior, 10*(5), 640–644. DOI: 10.1089/cpb.2007.9975 PMID: 17927531

Lee, Y., Yang, C. D., & Dong, D. (2025). Entanglement Measure-Based Sliding Mode Control for Quantum State Preparation. *IEEE Transactions on Cybernetics, 55*(10), 4771–4783. DOI: 10.1109/TCYB.2025.3595007 PMID: 40853800

Lemish, D., Elias, N., & Floegel, D. (2020). "Look at me!" Parental use of mobile phones at the playground. *Mobile Media & Communication, 8*(2), 170–187. DOI: 10.1177/2050157919846916

Li, H., & Yang, J. (2025). Managing online learning burnout via investigating the role of loneliness during COVID-19. *BMC Psychology, 13*(1), 151. DOI: 10.1186/s40359-025-02419-3

Li, J., Adnan, H. M., & Gong, J. (2023). Exploring Cultural Meaning Construction in Social Media: An Analysis of Liziqi's YouTube Channel. *Journal of Intercultural Communication, 23*(4), 1–12. DOI: 10.36923/jicc.v23i4.237

Lim, L. X., Lim, P. E., Lim, S. H., Lim, Y. X., & Oktaviandra, A. G. (2022). Hi, let's meet online! A study of virtual meeting platforms during the pandemic. [APJME]. *Asia Pacific Journal of Management and Education, 5*(1), 126–140. DOI: 10.32535/apjme.v4i3.1432

Lim, S. S. (2019). *Transcendent parenting: Raising children in the digital age.* Oxford University Press.

Lim, S., Jeong, D., & Yu, H. (2024). Avatar customization in the metaverse: User perceptions and design recommendations. *Computers & Graphics, 107*, 70–81. DOI: 10.1016/j.cag.2024.107081

Linder, L. K., McDaniel, B. T., Stockdale, L., & Coyne, S. M. (2021). The impact of parent and child media use on early parent–infant attachment. *Infancy*, *26*(4), 551–569. DOI: 10.1111/infa.12400 PMID: 33773012

Lingam, M. S. (2022). Measuring Cognitive Engagement: An Overview of Measurement Instruments and Techniques. *International Journal of Psychology and Educational Studies*, *8*(3), 63–76. DOI: 10.52380/ijpes.2021.8.3.239

Lin, S. S., & Tsai, C. C. (2002). Sensation seeking and internet dependence of Taiwanese high school adolescents. *Computers in Human Behavior*, *18*(4), 411–426. DOI: 10.1016/S0747-5632(01)00056-5

Li, Q., Xia, B., Zhang, H., Wang, W., & Wang, X. (2022). College students' cyberloafing and the sense of meaning of life: The mediating role of state anxiety and the moderating role of psychological flexibility. *Frontiers in Public Health*, *10*, 905699.

Li, S., Hong, Y., & Craig, S. D. (2023). A systematic literature review of social learning theory in online learning environments. *Educational Psychology Review*, *35*(4). Advance online publication. DOI: 10.1007/s10648-023-09827-0

Liu, Z., Huang, B., Hu, X., Du, P., & Sun, Q. (2023). Blockchain-based renewable energy trading using information entropy theory. *IEEE Transactions on Network Science and Engineering*, *11*(6), 5564–5575. DOI: 10.1109/TNSE.2023.3238110

Lo, C. K., & Hew, K. F. (2021). Student engagement in mathematics flipped classrooms: Implications of journal publications from 2011 to 2020. *Frontiers in Psychology*, *12*, 672610. DOI: 10.3389/fpsyg.2021.672610 PMID: 34135833

Losier, G. F., Perreault, S., Koestner, R., & Vallerand, R. J. (2001). Examining individual differences in the internalization of political values: Validation of the self-determination scale of political motivation. *Journal of Research in Personality*, *35*(1), 41–61. DOI: 10.1006/jrpe.2000.2300

Lubben, J. (2017). Addressing social isolation as a potent killer! *The Public Policy and Aging Report*, *27*(4), 136–138. DOI: 10.1093/ppar/prx026

Luchenski, S. A., Amlani, A. A., Lacroix, K., Burmeister, C., & Buxton, J. A. (2024). Peer engagement in harm reduction strategies and services: A critical case study and evaluation framework from British Columbia, Canada. *BMC Public Health*, *16*(1), 1–9. DOI: 10.1186/s12889-016-3136-4 PMID: 38166901

Luis, M. (2020). *Case Study: Meet Automattic, a Remote Worker Success Story | DistantJob - Remote Recruitment Agency*. https://distantjob.com/blog/2017-02-09-case-study-meet-automattic-a-remote-worker-success-story/

Lvina, E. (2025). Teaching ethics and ethical leadership with the Harvard Everest simulation. *Journal of Leadership Education, 24*(2), 213–221. DOI: 10.1108/JOLE-03-2024-0050

Lyu, H., Zhang, L., & Hu, C. (2025). Understanding Human-AI Trust in Education. *arXiv*.

Madianou, M., & Miller, D. (2013). *Migration and new media: Transnational families and polymedia*. Routledge. DOI: 10.4324/9780203154236

Malaspina, C. (2023). From the mental state of noise to the new frontiers of cognition. *Angelaki, 28*(3), 4–15. DOI: 10.1080/0969725X.2023.2216538

Malaspina, C. (Ed.). (2025). *From the Mental State of Noise to the New Frontiers of Techno-Human Cognition: Creative Disruptions Across AI, Gaming, Modelling, French Theory, and Politics*. Taylor & Francis. DOI: 10.4324/9781003667933

Ma, M., & Luo, C. (2022). The effect of student and peer assessment engagement on learning performance in online open courses. [iJET]. *International Journal of Emerging Technologies in Learning, 17*(10), 145–158. DOI: 10.3991/ijet.v17i10.30931

Mannheim, K. (1952). The problem of generations. In Kecskemeti, P. (Ed.), *Essays on the sociology of knowledge* (pp. 276–320). Routledge & Kegan Paul.

Mao, L., & Queiroz, F. (2024). Online education in design disciplines: Factors influencing the interactive experience of group learning. *International Journal of Technology and Design Education, 34*(5), 1903–1930. DOI: 10.1007/s10798-024-09882-w

Marci, C. D. (2024). A biologically based measure of emotional engagement: Context matters. *Journal of Advertising Research, 46*(4), 381–387. DOI: 10.2501/S0021849906060466

Marengo, D., Longobardi, C., Fabris, M., & Settanni, M. (2018). Highly-visual social media and internalizing symptoms in adolescence: The mediating role of body image concerns. *Computers in Human Behavior, 82*, 63–69. DOI: 10/1016/j.chb.2018.01.003

Markus, M. L. (1987). Toward a "critical mass" theory of interactive media: Universal access, interdependence and diffusion. *Communication Research, 14*(5), 491–511. DOI: 10.1177/009365087014005003

Martin, F., & Bolliger, D. U. (2018). Engagement Matters: Student Perceptions on the Importance of Engagement Strategies in the Online Learning Environment. *Online Learning : the Official Journal of the Online Learning Consortium, 22*(1), 205–222. DOI: 10.24059/olj.v22i1.1092

Martin, J. (2019). Building relationships and increasing engagement in the virtual classroom: Practical tools for the online instructor. *The Journal of Educators Online, 16*(1). Advance online publication. DOI: 10.9743/jeo.2019.16.1.9

Maslach, C., & Jackson, S. E. (1981). The measurement of experienced burnout. *Journal of Organizational Behavior, 2*(2), 99–113. DOI: 10.1002/job.4030020205

McDaniel, B. T., & Radesky, J. S. (2018). Technoference: Parent Distraction With Technology and Associations With Child Behavior Problems. *Child Development, 89*(1), 100–109. DOI: 10.1111/cdev.12822 PMID: 28493400

McKinlay, S. N. (2023). Kinship and Family. In *Teaching Cultural Anthropology for 21st Century Learners*. Viva.

McLeod, S. (2025, March 18). *Albert Bandura's Social Learning Theory*. Simply Psychology. https://www.simplypsychology.org/bandura.html

Mead, S. (2024, October 24). Dangerous 'Speed' ahead: Streamers harm our youth. The Baylor Lariat. https://baylorlariat.com/2024/10/24/dangerous-speed-ahead-streamers-harm-our-youth/

Mead, G. H. (1913). The social self. *The Journal of Philosophy, Psychology, and Scientific Methods, 10*(14), 374–380. DOI: 10.2307/2012910

Means, B., & Neisler, J. (2020). Suddenly online: A national survey of undergraduates during the COVID-19 pandemic. *Digital Promise*. https://digitalpromise.org/wp-content/uploads/2020/07/ELE_CoBrand_DP_FINAL _3.pdf

Meeus, A., Coenen, L., Eggermont, S., & Beullens, K. (2021). Family technoference: Exploring parent mobile device distraction from children's perspectives. *Mobile Media & Communication, 9*(3), 584–604. DOI: 10.1177/2050157921991602

Mendoza Montano, C. (2025). Toward a thermodynamic theory of evolution: A theoretical perspective on information entropy reduction and the emergence of complexity. *Frontiers in Complex Systems, 3*, 1630050. DOI: 10.3389/fcpxs.2025.1630050

Meyer, J., & Meyer, S. (2020). Excessive smartphone use and associated depression, anxiety, stress, and sleep: A systematic review and meta-analysis. *Frontiers in Psychiatry, 11*, 558552. DOI: 10.3389/fpsyt.2020.558552

Meyer, K. (2014). Student engagement in online learning: What works and why. *ASHE Higher Education Report*, *40*(6), 1–14. DOI: 10.1002/aehe.20018

Michels, J. (2025). Attractor State: A Mixed-Methods Meta-Study of Emergent Cybernetic Phenomena Defying Standard Explanations.

Mihelič, K. K., Lim, V. K. G., & Culiberg, B. (2022). Cyberloafing among Gen Z students: The role of norms, moral disengagement, multitasking self-efficacy, and psychological outcomes. *European Journal of Psychology of Education*, *38*, 567–585. DOI: 10.1007/s10212-022-00617-w

Mikulincer, M., & Shaver, R., P. (. (2020). Enhancing the "broaden and build" cycle of attachment security in adulthood: From the laboratory to relational contexts and societal systems. *International Journal of Environmental Research and Public Health*, *17*(6), 2054. DOI: 10.3390/ijerph17062054 PMID: 32244872

Miller, L. J., & Lu, W. (2018, August 20). Gen Z is set to outnumber millennials within a year. *Bloomberg*. https://www.bloomberg.com/news/articles/2018-08-20/genz-to-outnumber-millennials-within-a-year-demographic-trends

Ministry of Human Resource Development. (2020). *National education policy 2020*. Government of India. https://www.education.gov.in/sites/upload_files/mhrd/files/NEP_Final_English_0.pdf

Mi, P., Yan, L., Cheng, Y., Liu, Y., Wang, J., Shoukat, M. U., Yan, F., Qin, G., Han, P., & Zhai, Y. (2024). Driver cognitive architecture based on EEG signals: A review. *IEEE Sensors Journal*, *24*(22), 36261–36286. DOI: 10.1109/JSEN.2024.3471699

Mishra, L., Gupta, T., & Shree, A. (2020). Online teaching-learning in higher education during lockdown period of COVID-19 pandemic. *International Journal of Educational Research Open*, *1*, 100012. DOI: 10.1016/j.ijedro.2020.100012 PMID: 35059663

Mitchell, J. P., Macrae, C. N., & Banaji, M. R. (2005). Forming impressions of people versus inanimate objects: Social-cognitive processing in the medial prefrontal cortex. *NeuroImage*, *26*(1), 251–257. DOI: 10.1016/j.neuroimage.2005.01.031 PMID: 15862225

Mittler, J. N., Martsolf, G. R., Telenko, S. J., & Scanlon, D. P. (2023). Making sense of "consumer engagement" initiatives to improve health and health care: A conceptual framework to guide policy and practice. *The Milbank Quarterly*, *91*(1), 37–77. DOI: 10.1111/milq.12002 PMID: 23488711

Miyake, M., & Kirschner, P. (2014). The social and interactive dimensions of collaborative learning. In Sawyer, R. K. (Ed.), *The Cambridge handbook of the learning sciences* (2nd ed., pp. 454–475). Cambridge University Press. DOI: 10.1017/CBO9781139519526.026

Mizraji, E. (2024). Homeostasis and information processing: The key frames for the thermodynamics of biological systems. *Bio Systems*, *236*, 105115. DOI: 10.1016/j.biosystems.2023.105115 PMID: 38163548

Moeller, S. D. (2019). *Going 24 Hours without media. the world UNPLUGGED.* https://theworldunplugged.wordpress.com/

Mone, F., Visan, M., & Simionescu, M. (2024). Multi-participant Decision-making Based on Digital Platforms: A Case Study for the Romanian Academy. *Science and Technology*, *27*(1), 94–105.

Morelli, S. A., Lee, I. A., Arnn, M. E., & Zaki, J. (2015). Emotional and instrumental support provision interact to predict well-being. *Emotion (Washington, D.C.)*, *15*(4), 484–493. DOI: 10.1037/emo0000084 PMID: 26098734

Morey, J. N., Gentzler, A. L., Creasy, B., Oberhauser, A. M., & Westerman, D. (2013). Young adults' use of communication technology within their romantic relationships and associations with attachment style. *Computers in Human Behavior*, *29*(4), 1771–1778. DOI: 10.1016/j.chb.2013.02.019

Morgan, W. R. (2023). Finance must be defended: Cybernetics, neoliberalism and environmental, social, and governance (ESG). *Sustainability (Basel)*, *15*(4), 3707. DOI: 10.3390/su15043707

Morrison-Smith, S., & Ruiz, J. (2020). Challenges and barriers in virtual teams: A literature review. *SN Applied Sciences*, *2*(6), 1096. Advance online publication. DOI: 10.1007/s42452-020-2801-5

Mujallid, A. T. (2024). Digital Active Learning Strategies in Blended Environments to Develop Students' Social and Emotional Learning Skills and Engagement in Higher Education. *European Journal of Education*, *59*(4), e12748. DOI: 10.1111/ejed.12748

Mulenga, R., & Shilongo, H. (2025). Hybrid and blended learning models: Innovations, challenges, and future directions in education. *Acta Pedagogia Asiana*, *4*(1), 1–13. DOI: 10.53623/apga.v4i1.495

Nabil, N. A., Ayubi, S., & Ansari, M. Z. A. (2023). Study of the Role of ZOOM Platform in Collaborative Learning from the Perspective of the Kabul University Lecturers. *Sprin Journal of Arts, Humanities and Social Sciences, 2*(09), 01-12.h DOI: 10.55559/sjahss.v2i09.147

Nagadeepa, C. (2021). Students' Understanding and Learning: Mediation Effects of Cognitive Engagement in Online Classes. [TURCOMAT]. *Turkish Journal of Computer and Mathematics Education, 12*(6), 2932–2939. DOI: 10.17762/turcomat.v12i6.6077

National Assessment and Accreditation Council. (2021). *Manual for self-study accreditation: Teacher education colleges.* https://www.naac.gov.in/

National Institutional Ranking Framework. (2024). *India rankings 2024: Methodology document.* Ministry of Education, Government of India. https://www.nirfindia.org

Ng, P. Preemptive futures: Entropic and negentropic information in speculative design. In *xCoAx 2022 10th Conference on Computation, Communication, Aesthetics. Coimbra, Portugal* (pp. 85-101).

Nguyen, N. (2021). The Fearless Organization: Creating Psychological Safety in the Workplace for Learning, Innovation, and Growth. In *Learning Organization* (Vol. 28, Issue 3). DOI: 10.1108/TLO-04-2021-266

Nichols, S., & Selim, N. (2022). Digitally mediated parenting: A review of the literature. *Societies (Basel, Switzerland), 12*(2), 60. DOI: 10.3390/soc12020060

Nobles, J. D., Perez, A., Skelton, J. A., Spence, N. D., & Ball, G. D. (2018). The engagement pathway: A conceptual framework of engagement-related terms in weight management. *Obesity Research & Clinical Practice, 12*(2), 133–138. DOI: 10.1016/j.orcp.2017.12.005 PMID: 29396232

Nöth, W. (2021). System, sign, information, and communication in cybersemiotics, systems theory, and Peirce. In *Introduction to cybersemiotics: A transdisciplinary perspective* (pp. 75–95). Springer International Publishing. DOI: 10.1007/978-3-030-52746-4_4

O'Hare, W., & Mayol-Garcia, Y. (2023). *The changing child population of the United States: Child population data from the 2020 Census.* Annie E. Casey Foundation. https://www.aecf.org/resources/the-changing-childpopulation-of-the-united-states

Obourdin, G., De Maeyer, S., & Van den Bossche, P. (2024). Unlocking the power of immersive learning: The FAIRI instructional design proposition for adaptive immersive virtual reality. *Computers & Education: X Reality, 5*, 100084.

Oduor, E., Neustaedter, C., Odom, W., Tang, A., Moallem, N., Tory, M., & Irani, P. (2016). The frustrations and benefits of mobile device usage in the home when co-present with family members. In *Proceedings of the 2016 ACM conference on designing interactive systems* (pp. 1315-1327). DOI: 10.1145/2901790.2901809

Olson, G. M., & Olson, J. S. (2009). Human –Computer Interaction Distance Matters. *International Journal of Human Computer Interaction, 0024*(July 2014).

Ortner, P., Steinhöfler, R., Leitgeb, E., & Flühr, H. (2022). Augmented air traffic control system—Artificial intelligence as digital assistance system to predict air traffic conflicts. *AI*, *3*(3), 623–644. DOI: 10.3390/ai3030036

Osejo-Bucheli, C. (2024). Technological Evolution and Cooperative Identity: A Genealogical Analysis using Simondon's Cybernetic Process Philosophy. *Philosophy of Management*, *23*(3), 353–376. DOI: 10.1007/s40926-024-00317-z

Osejo-Bucheli, C. (2024). Towards a unified ontology of cybernetics: Bridging mechanology and CAS for cooperative societies through thematic synthesis. *Kybernetes.*

Overwijk, J. (2025). *Cybernetic capitalism: a critical theory of the incommunicable.* Fordham Univ Press.

Oyarzun, B., & Martin, F. (2023). A Systematic Review of Research on Online Learner Collaboration from 2012-21: Collaboration Technologies, Design, Facilitation, and Outcomes. *Online Learning : the Official Journal of the Online Learning Consortium*, *27*(1), 71–106. DOI: 10.24059/olj.v27i1.3407

Pace, C. R. "Measuring the Quality of Student Effort." Current Issues in Higher Educa tion, 1980, 2, 10–16

Pace, C. R. (1990). *The Undergraduates: A Report of Their Activities and College Experiences in the 1980s*. Center for the Study of Evaluation, UCLA Graduate School of Education.

Palloff, R. M., & Pratt, K. (2007). *Building online learning communities: Effective strategies for the virtual classroom*. Jossey-Bass.

Palviainen, Å. (2020). Video calls as a nexus of practice in multilingual translocal families. *Zeitschrift Für Interkulturellen Fremdsprachenunterricht*, *25*(1), 85–108.

Palviainen, Å., & Kędra, J. (2020). What's in the family app? *Journal of Multilingual Theories and Practices*, *1*(1), 89–111. DOI: 10.1558/jmtp.15363

Pao, L. (2023). Ways of Cybernetic Thinking. *New Literary History*, *54*(2), 1271–1279. DOI: 10.1353/nlh.2023.a907173

Parker, K. (2023, May 22). *How Pew Research Center will report on generations moving forward. Pew Research Center.* https://www.pewresearch.org/short-reads/2023/05/22/how-pew-research-center-will-report-on-generations-moving-forward/

Parker, M. C., Jeynes, C., & Walker, S. D. (2025). A Metric for the Entropic Purpose of a System. *Entropy (Basel, Switzerland)*, *27*(2), 131. DOI: 10.3390/e27020131 PMID: 40003129

Pascarella, E. T., & Terenzini, P. T. (2005). *How College Affects Students: A Third Decade of Research*. Jossey-Bass.

Patel, S. (2024). Digital Kinship: The Future Calling. *Anthropology & Aging*, *45*(2), 75–81. DOI: 10.5195/aa.2024.550

Pauwels, L. (2008). A private visual practice going public? Social functions and sociological research opportunities of Web-based family photography. *Visual Studies*, *23*(1), 34–49. DOI: 10.1080/14725860801908528

Pekrun, R., Elliot, A. J., & Maier, M. A. (2009). Achievement goals and achievement emotions: Testing a model of their joint relations with academic performance. *Journal of Educational Psychology*, *101*(1), 115–135.

Pentaraki, A., & Laureate, L. (2019). Emerging Evidence Regarding the Roles of Emotional, Behavioural, and Cognitive Aspects of Student. *European Journal of Open, Distance and e-Learning, 20*(1), 1–21.

Perez, A. (2023, May 12). Three surprising benefits of holding structured check-ins with students (plus a free template!). Michigan Virtual. https://michiganvirtual.org/blog/three-surprising-benefits-of-structured-check-ins/

Petrov, A. I. (2023). Philosophy and meanings of the information entropy analysis of road safety: case study of Russian cities. *information, 14*(6), 302.

Petrov, A. I., Kolesov, V. I., & Petrova, D. A. (2021). Theory and Practice of Quantitative Assessment of System Harmonicity: Case of Road Safety in Russia before and during the COVID-19 Epidemic. *Mathematics*, *9*(21), 2812. DOI: 10.3390/math9212812

Petty, T., & Farinde, A. (2013). Investigating student engagement in an online mathematics course through windows into teaching and learning. *Journal of Online Learning and Teaching*, *9*(2), 261–270.

Pietromonaco, P. R., & Powers, S. I. (2015). Attachment and health-related physiological stress processes. *Current Opinion in Psychology*, *1*, 34–39. DOI: 10.1016/j.copsyc.2014.12.001 PMID: 25729755

Pittaway, S. M. (2012). Student and staff engagement: Developing an engagement framework in a faculty of education. *The Australian Journal of Teacher Education, 37*(4), 41–48. DOI: 10.14221/ajte.2012v37n4.8

Porter, C. L., Coyne, S. M., Chojnacki, N. A., McDaniel, B. T., Reschke, P. J., & Stockdale, L. A. (2024). Toddlers' physiological response to parent's mobile device distraction and technoference. *Developmental Psychobiology, 66*(2), e22460. DOI: 10.1002/dev.22460

Posthoff, C. (2024). Game Theory, Cybernetics, and Information Theory. In *Artificial Intelligence for Everyone* (pp. 63–68). Springer Nature Switzerland. DOI: 10.1007/978-3-031-57208-1_6

Prananto, K., Cahyadi, S., Lubis, F. Y., & Hinduan, Z. R. (2025). Perceived teacher support and student engagement among higher education students - a systematic literature review. *BMC Psychology, 13*(1), 112. DOI: 10.1186/s40359-025-02412-w

Prensky, M. (2001). Digital natives, Digital immigrants part 1. *On the Horizon, 9*(5), 1–6. DOI: 10.1108/10748120110424816

Price, C. (2010). Why don't my students think I'm groovy? The new "R"s for engaging millennial learners. *The Teaching Professor, 9*, 29–34.

Pujar, S. M., & Tadasad, P. G. (2016). MOOCs–an opportunity for international collaboration in LIS education: A developing country's perspective. *New Library World, 117*(5/6), 360–373. DOI: 10.1108/NLW-07-2015-0048

Qian, Y., & Hu, Y. (2024). The digitalization of family life: A multilevel conceptual framework. *Journal of Marriage and Family, 86*(5), 1160–1183. DOI: 10.1111/jomf.12983

Qin, R., Ding, W., Li, J., Guan, S., Wang, G., Ren, Y., & Qu, Z. (2022). Web3-based decentralized autonomous organizations and operations: Architectures, models, and mechanisms. *IEEE Transactions on Systems, Man, and Cybernetics. Systems, 53*(4), 2073–2082. DOI: 10.1109/TSMC.2022.3228530

Qi, S., & Derakhshan, A. (2025). Technology-based collaborative learning: EFL learners' social regulation and modifications in their academic emotions and academic performance. *Education and Information Technologies, 30*(7), 8611–8636. https://link.springer.com/article/10.1007/s10639-024-13167-z. DOI: 10.1007/s10639-024-13167-z

Qi, Y., Zhuang, L., Chen, H., Han, X., & Liang, A. (2023). Evaluation of Students' Learning Engagement in Online Classes Based on Multimodal Vision Perspective. *Electronics (Basel), 13*(1), 149. DOI: 10.3390/electronics13010149

Räisä, T. (2022). Family relations: Emotional overload. In *Mediatisation of emotional life* (pp. 151–167). Routledge. DOI: 10.4324/9781003254287-13

Ramesh, M. S., & Vinod, V. (2022). *Artificial intelligence post-pandemic future trends in fields of education-challenges and opportunities (Ai The Real Teacher). Education Trends in a Post-Pandemic Future in the Fields of Engineering, Science, Arts, Humanities, Commerce, Economics, Social Sciences, Law and Management-Challenges and Opportunities.* Global Multidisciplinary Research and Academic Foundation.

Ramsey, T. Z. (2014). *Introduction to Neuromarketing & Consumer Neuroscience.* https://research.cbs.dk/en/publications/introduction-to-neuromarketing-amp-consumer-neuroscience

Ramya, B. (2023). INNOVATIVE PEDAGOGICAL APPROACHES. *INNOVATIVE PEDAGOGICAL APPROACHES*, *17*, 302.

Rathi, N., Saran, P., & Shrivastava, S. (2025, May). Emotional Security for Sustainable Future: Multimodal Affective Computing. In *International Conference on Recent Advancements and Modernisations in Sustainable Intelligent Technologies and Applications (RAMSITA 2025)* (pp. 611-638). Atlantis Press. DOI: 10.2991/978-94-6463-716-8_47

Reber, R., Canning, E. A., & Harackiewicz, J. M. (2018). Personalized education to increase interest. *Current Directions in Psychological Science*, *27*(6), 449–454. DOI: 10.1177/0963721418793140

Redmond, P., Heffernan, A., Abawi, L., Brown, A., & Henderson, R. (2018). An online engagement framework for higher education. *Online Learning : the Official Journal of the Online Learning Consortium*, *22*(1), 183–204. DOI: 10.24059/olj.v22i1.1175

Reimann, P. (2024). Online Collaborative Learning: Theory and Practice. In *Information Management* (Vol. 17, Issue 1/2). http://search.proquest.com/docview/205264574?accountid=41248

Richards, J. C. (2011). *Competence and performance in language teaching.* Cambridge University Pressm., DOI: 10.1177/0033688210372953

Richardson, D. C., Spivey, M. J., Barsalou, L. W., & McRae, K. (2003). Spatial representations activated during real-time comprehension of verbs. *Cognitive Science*, *27*(5), 767–780.

Rickard, N. S., Bambrick, C. J., & Gill, A. (2012). Absence of widespread psychosocial and cognitive effects of school-based music instruction in 10–13-year-old students. *International Journal of Music Education, 30*(1), 57–78. DOI: 10.1177/0255761411431399

Rock, D. (2008). SCARF: A brain-based model for collaborating with and influencing others. *NeuroLeadership Journal, 1*(1).

Rogers-Whitehead, C. (2025). *Technology for Littles: Helping Young Children Navigate the Internet Responsibly*. Rowman & Littlefield.

Rohner, R. P., & Lansford, J. E. (2017). Deep structure of the human affectional system: Introduction to interpersonal acceptance–rejection theory. *Journal of Family Theory & Review, 9*(4), 426–440. DOI: 10.1111/jftr.12219

Roli, A., & Braccini, M. (2023, May). A cybernetic perspective of agent–environment relations: From interactions to meanings. In *National Conference on Systems Science-(AIRS) Italian Systems Society* (pp. 183-192). Cham: Springer Nature Switzerland.

Rondi, E., Magrelli, V., Debellis, F., & De Massis, A. (2024). The evolution of craft work in the strategic development of a family enterprise. *Strategic Entrepreneurship Journal, 18*(4), 811–840. DOI: 10.1002/sej.1503

Rorot, W. (2022). Counting with cilia: The role of morphological computation in basal cognition research. *Entropy (Basel, Switzerland), 24*(11), 1581. DOI: 10.3390/e24111581 PMID: 36359671

Rotgans, J. I., & Schmidt, H. G. (2023). Cognitive engagement in the problem-based learning classroom. *Advances in Health Sciences Education : Theory and Practice, 16*(4), 465–479. DOI: 10.1007/s10459-011-9272-9 PMID: 21243425

Rourke, L. (1999). Assessing social presence in asynchronous text-based computer conferencing. *Journal of Distance Education*.

Roy, R., Rao, G. A., Pal, D., Anuradha, S., & Mukherjee, S. (2025). Metaverse-based education for sustainable development and improving the performance: Discussing the future research agenda. *Sustainable Futures : An Applied Journal of Technology, Environment and Society, 10*, 101091. DOI: 10.1016/j.sftr.2025.101091

Rue, P. (2018). Make way, Millennials, Here comes Gen Z. *About Campus: Enriching the Student Learning Experience, 23*(3), 5–12. DOI: 10.1177/1086482218804251

Ruyer, R. (2023). *Cybernetics and the Origin of Information*. Rowman & Littlefield.

Ryan, R. M., & Deci, E. L. (2020). Intrinsic and extrinsic motivation from a self-determination theory perspective DOI: 10.1016/j.cedpsych.2020.101860

Ryan, R. M., & Deci, E. L. (2017). *Self-determination theory: Basic psychological needs in motivation development and wellness*. Guilford Press. DOI: 10.1521/978.14625/28806

Sabella, E. Z., & Hall, E. T. (1978). Beyond Culture. *Contemporary Sociology*, *7*(4), 503. Advance online publication. DOI: 10.2307/2064404

Sachs, C. (2023). Naturalized teleology: Cybernetics, organization, purpose. *Topoi*, *42*(3), 781–791. DOI: 10.1007/s11245-022-09851-9

Safron, A., & DeYoung, C. G. (2021). Integrating Cybernetic Big Five Theory with the Free Energy Principle: A new strategy for modeling personalities as complex systems. In *Measuring and modeling persons and situations* (pp. 617-649). Academic Press. DOI: 10.1016/B978-0-12-819200-9.00010-7

Safron, A., & Sheikhbahaee, Z. (2023, September). Towards understanding persons and their personalities with cybernetic big 5 theory and the free energy principle and active inference (FEP-AI) framework. In *International Workshop on Active Inference* (pp. 73-90). Cham: Springer Nature Switzerland. DOI: 10.31234/osf.io/kjzf7

Sagayadevan, V., & Jeyaraj, S. (2012). The role of Emotional Engagement in Lecturer-Student interaction and the Impact on Academic Outcomes of Student Achievement and Learning. *The Journal of Scholarship of Teaching and Learning*, *12*(3), 1–30.

Sahni, S., Verma, S., & Kaurav, R. P. S. (2025). Understanding digital transformation challenges for online learning and teaching in higher education institutions: A review and research framework. *Benchmarking*, *32*(5), 1487–1521. DOI: 10.1108/BIJ-04-2022-0245

Sahu, P. K., Dalcik, H., Dalcik, C., Gupta, M. M., Chattu, V. K., & Umakanthan, S. (2022). Best practices for effective implementation of online education: A systematic review. *Frontiers in Education*. https://pmc.ncbi.nlm.nih.gov/articles/PMC9114788/

Said, F. F. (2021). 'Ba-SKY-a P with her each day at dinner': Technology as supporter in the learning and management of home languages. *Journal of Multilingual and Multicultural Development*, *42*(8), 747–762. DOI: 10.1080/01434632.2021.1924755

Sakdiyakorn, M., Golubovskaya, M., & Solnet, D. (2021). Understanding Generation Z through collective consciousness: Impacts for hospitality work and employment. *International Journal of Hospitality Management*, *94*, 102822. DOI: 10.1016/j.ijhm.2020.102822

Salam, A., Simonyan, R., Terzov, V., & Ogunyemi, A. (2024). CHALLENGES IN ONLINE EDUCATION POST-COVID AND STRATEGIES FOR ENHANCED LEARNING IN DIVERSE TIME ZONES. In *ICERI2024 Proceedings* (pp. 5016-5026). IATED. DOI: 10.21125/iceri.2024.1237

Salmon, G. (2003). *E-moderating: The key to teaching and learning online*. Psychology press.

Saltz, J., & Heckman, R. (2020). Using structured pair activities in a distributed online breakout room. *Online Learning : the Official Journal of the Online Learning Consortium*, *24*(1), 227–244. DOI: 10.24059/olj.v24i1.1632

Salvato, C., Reuer, J., & Battigalli, P. (2017). Cooperation across disciplines: A multilevel perspective on cooperative behavior in governing interfirm relations. *The Academy of Management Annals*, *11*(2), 960–1004. DOI: 10.5465/annals.2014.0001

Sanyal, D., Grassitelli, L., Langer, N., & Bestenlehner, J. M. (2015). Massive main-sequence stars evolving at the Eddington limit. *Astronomy & Astrophysics*, *580*, A20. DOI: 10.1051/0004-6361/201525945

Saqr, M., Nouri, J., & Jormanainen, I. (2019, September). A learning analytics study of the effect of group size on social dynamics and performance in online collaborative learning. In *European conference on technology enhanced learning* (pp. 466-479). Cham: Springer International Publishing.DOI: 10.1007/978-3-030-29736-7_35

Saqr, M., Nouri, J., Vartiainen, H., & Malmberg, J. (2020). What makes an online problem-based group successful? Learning analytics study using social network analysis. *BMC Medical Education*, *20*(1), 80. DOI: 10.1186/s12909-020-01997-7 PMID: 32188471

Saratxaga Arregi, A. (2024). Heinz von Foerster's operational epistemology: Orientation for insight into complexity. *Kybernetes*.

Sardar, S., & Vijay, T. (2025). Social media influencers and purchase intention: A review and research agenda. *International Journal of Consumer Studies*, *49*(3), e70046. DOI: 10.1111/ijcs.70046

Saroyan, J. S. (2021). Developing a supportive peer environment: Engaging students through cooperative skills in the classroom. *Advances in Developmental and Educational Psychology*, *3*(1), 81–89. DOI: 10.25082/ADEP.2021.01.001

Sayre, K. M. (2023). Cybernetics. In *Philosophy of Science, Logic and Mathematics in the 20th Century* (pp. 292-314). Routledge.

Schmidbauer, F. (2025). Social virtual reality as learning space: Conceptualising embodied interaction. *Learning, Media and Technology*, *47*(2), 311–329. DOI: 10.1016/j.lmt.2025.311329

Schwieger, D., & Ladwig, C. (2018). Reaching and retaining the next generation: Adapting to the expectations of Gen Z in the classroom. *Information Systems Education Journal*, *16*(3), 45–54. http://isedj.org/2018-16/n3/ISEDJv16n3p45.html

Seemiller, C., & Grace, M. (2017). Generation Z: Educating and engaging the next generation of students. *About Campus: Enriching the Student Learning Experience*, *22*(3), 21–26. DOI: 10.1002/abc.21293

Sekendiz, B. (2018). Utilisation of formative peer-assessment in distance online education: A case study of a multi-model sport management unit. *Interactive Learning Environments*, *26*(5), 682–694. DOI: 10.1080/10494820.2017.1396229

Semmer, N. K., Elfering, A., Jacobshagen, N., Perrot, T., Beehr, T. A., & Boos, N. (2008). The emotional meaning of instrumental social support. *International Journal of Stress Management*, *15*(3), 235–251. DOI: 10.1037/1072-5245.15.3.235

Serravalle, J. (2022). Take it or leave it?: Evidence on cultural differences affecting return behaviour for Gen Z. *Journal of Retailing and Consumer Services*, *66*, 102942. DOI: 10.1016/j.jretconser.2022.102942

Shalevska, E. (2021). Students' motivation and engagement during distance learning. [IJSR]. *International Journal of Scientific Research*, *10*(1). https://eprints.uklo.edu.mk/id/eprint/9504

Shams, M., Iftikhar, U., & Raja, A. A. (2019). Impact of attachment styles on relationship satisfaction: Mediating role of phubbing behavior. *IBT Journal of Business Studies (JBS)*, *1*(1).

Shankar, A., McMunn, A., Demakakos, P., Hamer, M., & Steptoe, A. (2017). Social isolation and loneliness: Prospective associations with functional status in older adults. *Health Psychology*, *36*(2), 179–187. DOI: 10.1037/hea0000437 PMID: 27786518

Sharaievska, I., & Stodolska, M. (2015). Redefining Boundaries in Families through Social Networking Leisure. *Leisure Sciences*, *37*(5), 431–446. DOI: 10.1080/01490400.2015.1021882

Sharma, S., & Bumb, A. (2021). The challenges faced in technology-driven classes during COVID-19. *International Journal of Distance Education Technologies*, *19*(1), 66–88. DOI: 10.4018/IJDET.20210101.oa2

Sharma, S., & Sharma, M. (2022). Impact of Digital Transformation on Academicians' Well-being: A Study with the Moderating Role of Public and Private Universities in India. *Digital Education Review*, (42), 118–135. DOI: 10.1344/der.2022.42.118-135

Shatto, B., & Erwin, K. (2016). Moving on From Millennials: Preparing for Generation Z. *Journal of Continuing Education in Nursing*, *47*(6), 253–254. DOI: 10.3928/00220124-20160518-05

Sheldon, K. M., & Hilpert, J. C. (2012). The balanced measure of psychological needs (BMPN) scale: An alternative domain general measure of need satisfaction. *Motivation and Emotion*, *36*(4), 439–451. DOI: 10.1007/s11031-012-9279-4

Short, J., Williams, E., & Christie, B. (1976). *The social psychology of telecommunications*. Wiley. https://cir.nii.ac.jp/crid/1130282268777950720

Short, J., Williams, E., & Christie, B. (1976). *The social psychology of telecommunications*. Wiley.

Shoufan, A. (2018). Estimating the cognitive value of YouTube's educational videos: A learning analytics approach. *Computers in Human Behavior*, *92*, 450–458. DOI: 10.1016/j.chb.2018.03.036

Shumate, M., & Fulk, J. (2004). Boundaries and Role Conflict When Work and Family are Colocated: A Communication Network and Symbolic Interaction Approach. *Human Relations*, *57*(1), 55–74. DOI: 10.1177/0018726704042714

Shunk, D. H. (2000). Learning: introduction, issues, and historial perspectives. In-Schunk, DH Learning theories: an educational perspective (pp. 1-29). *Upper Saddle River, NJ: Pearson Education. Waters, E., & Sroufe, LA (1983). Social competence as a developmental construct. Developmental Review*, *3*, 79–97.

Siddiqui, S., & Singh, T. (2016). Social media its impact with positive and negative aspects. *International Journal of Computer Applications Technology and Research*, *5*, 71–75. DOI: 10.7753/IJCATR0502.1006

Silveira, P., Morais, R., & Petrella, S. (2022). A communication study of young adults and online dependence during the COVID-19 pandemic. *Societies (Basel, Switzerland)*, *12*, 109–133. DOI: 10.3390/soc12040109

Sinatra, G., Heddy, B., & Lombardi, D. (2015). The challenges of defining and measuring student engagement in science. *Educational Psychologist*, *50*(1), 1–13. DOI: 10.1080/00461520.2014.1002924

Singh, A. B. (2024). Digital technology and student engagement in online synchronous collaborative learning sessions/Tecnología digital y participación de los estudiantes en las sesiones de aprendizaje colaborativo en línea. *C&E, Cultura y Educación, 36*(4), 1005–1043. DOI: 10.1177/11356405241292980

Singh, A. K., & Meena, M. K. (2024). Online teaching in Indian higher education institutions during the pandemic time. *Education and Information Technologies, 29*(4), 4107–4157. DOI: 10.1007/s10639-023-11942-y

Smetana, J. G. (2017). Current research on parenting styles, dimensions, and beliefs. *Current Opinion in Psychology, 15*, 19–25. DOI: 10.1016/j.copsyc.2017.02.012 PMID: 28813261

Smith, E. E., Kahlke, R., & Judd, T. (2018). From digital natives to digital literacy: Anchoring digital practices through learning design. In *Proceedings of the Australasian Society for Computers in Learning in Tertiary Education (ASCILITE 2018)* (pp. 510–515). Deakin University.

Smith, T. A., & Short, A. (2022). Needs affordance as a key factor in likelihood of problematic social media use: Validation, latent profile analysis and comparison of TikTok and Facebook problematic use measures. *Addictive Behaviors, 129*, 107259. DOI: 10.1016/j.addbeh.2022.107259

Solomon, V. V., & SV, R. D. (2025). Leveraging Artificial Intelligence for Student-Centric Online Learning in Higher Education: Opportunities for Personalized Education and Engagement. *International Journal of Latest Technology in Engineering, Management &. Applied Sciences (Basel, Switzerland), 14*(5), 1093–1096.

Solymosi, T. (2023). Neuropragmatic Tools for Neurotechnological Culture: Toward a Creatively Democratic Cybernetics of Care. *Contemporary Pragmatism, 20*(1-2), 77–117. DOI: 10.1163/18758185-bja10059

Song, H., Kim, J., & Park, N. (2018). I know my professor: Teacher self-disclosure in online education and a mediating role of social presence. *International Journal of Human-Computer Interaction, 35*(6), 1–8. DOI: 10.1080/10447318.2018.1455126

Sperry, M. P., Aldana, A. J., O'Neill, T. A., Mimovic, A., Gibson, C. B., & McLarnon, M. J. (2025). Hybrid and remote team chartering: Creating clarity in an increasingly virtual world. *Organizational Dynamics, 101172*(4), 101172. Advance online publication. DOI: 10.1016/j.orgdyn.2025.101172

Srivastava, A. (2020). Post COVID-19: A technology-driven era for higher education. *Higher Education Going Online: The Challenges in India,* 77. [If book chapter, please provide publisher for completeness]

Srivastava, S. (2025). Collaborative Learning in Digital Environment.

Srivastava, S. C., & Chandra, S. (2018). Social presence in virtual world collaboration. *Management Information Systems Quarterly*, *42*(3), 779–A16. DOI: 10.25300/MISQ/2018/11914

Stæhr, A. C., & Nørreby, T. R. (2021). The metapragmatics of mode choice. *Pragmatics and Society*, *12*(5), 756–781. DOI: 10.1075/ps.20050.can

Stasch, S. M., Hilla, Y., & Mack, W. (2025). The invisible copilot? Assessing task engagement and team dynamics in a virtual flight environment using eye-tracking metrics. *Aviation Psychology and Applied Human Factors*, *15*(1), 45–61. DOI: 10.1027/2192-0923/a000293

Stecher, B. M., & Hamilton, L. S. (2014). *Measuring Hard-to-Measure Student Competencies: A Research and Development Plan. Research Report*. RAND Corporation. PO Box 2138, Santa Monica, CA 90407-2138. DOI: 10.7249/RR863

Steinsbekk, S., Wichstom, L., Stenseng, F., Nesi, J., Hygen, B., & Skalicka, V. (2021). The impact of social media use on appearance self-esteem from childhood to adolescence – A 3-wave community study. *Computers in Human Behavior*, *114*, 106528. DOI: 10/1016/j.chb.2020.106528

Stening, H., Lee, J., Groeschel, J., Richardson, M. J., & Kallen, R. W. (2023). The Entropy of Communication Turn Taking during a Collaborative Problem-Solving Task. In *Proceedings of the Annual Meeting of the Cognitive Science Society* (Vol. 45, No. 45).

Stevens, D. D. (2023). *Introduction to rubrics: An assessment tool to save grading time, convey effective feedback, and promote student learning*. Routledge., DOI: 10.4324/9781003445432

Stryker, S. (1959). Symbolic interaction as an approach to family research. *Marriage and Family Living*, *21*(2), 111–119. DOI: 10.2307/348099

Sturge-Apple, M. L., Davies, P. T., & Cummings, E. M. (2006). Impact of Hostility and Withdrawal in Interparental Conflict on Parental Emotional Unavailability and Children's Adjustment Difficulties. *Child Development*, *77*(6), 1623–1641. DOI: 10.1111/j.1467-8624.2006.00963.x PMID: 17107450

Suharti, D. S., Suherdi, D., & Setyarini, S. (2021). Exploring Students' Learning Engagement in EFL Online Classroom. *Proceedings of the Thirteenth Conference on Applied Linguistics (CONAPLIN 2020)*, *546*(Conaplin 2020), 139–149. DOI: 10.2991/assehr.k.210427.022

Suls, J., Martin, R., & Wheeler, L. (2002). Social comparison: Why, with whom, and with what effect? *Current Directions in Psychological Science, 11*(5), 159–163. DOI: 10.1111/1467-8721.00191

Sumarni, S. (2022). The Effectiveness of Constructivist Learning Methods Through the Breakout Room Facility at Zoom Cloud Meeting. *Ethical Lingua: Journal of Language Teaching and Literature, 9*(2), 459-466. https://doi.org/DOI: 10.30605/25409190.417

Sun, X., Guo, X., Zhang, Y., & Du, D. (2025). An automotive human–machine interface design method integrating Fuzzy Kano-QFD and physiological data. *Ergonomics*, •••, 1–22. DOI: 10.1080/00140139.2025.2501768 PMID: 40390521

Suraworachet, W., Zhou, Q., & Cukurova, M. (2023). Impact of combining human and analytics feedback on students' engagement with, and performance in, reflective writing tasks. *International Journal of Educational Technology in Higher Education, 20*(1), 1–24. DOI: 10.1186/s41239-022-00368-0

Sutton, A., Clowes, M., Preston, L., & Booth, A. (2019). Meeting the review family: Exploring review types and associated information retrieval requirements. *Health Information and Libraries Journal, 36*(3), 202–222. DOI: 10.1111/hir.12276 PMID: 31541534

Sweetman, D. S. (2020). Making virtual learning engaging and interactive. *FASEB bioAdvances, 3*(1), 11–19. DOI: 10.1096/fba.2020-00084

Tabilo Alvarez, J., & Ramírez-Correa, P. (2023). A brief review of systems, cybernetics, and complexity. *Complexity, 2023*(1), 8205320. DOI: 10.1155/2023/8205320

Tang, C., Thyer, L., Bye, R., Kenny, B., Tulliani, N., Peel, N., Gordon, R., Penkala, S., Tannous, C., Sun, Y. T., & Dark, L. (2023). Impact of online learning on sense of belonging among first year clinical health students during COVID-19: Student and academic perspectives. *BMC Medical Education, 23*(1), 100. DOI: 10.1186/s12909-023-04061-2

Tang, C., & Xiao, F. (2024). A Time Fractal-Based Complex Belief Entropy in Complex Evidence Theory for Pattern Classification. *IEEE Transactions on Systems, Man, and Cybernetics. Systems.*

Taniguchi, Y., Gao, Y., Kojima, K., & Konomi, S. I. (2018, May). Evaluating learning style-based grouping strategies in real-world collaborative learning environment. In *International Conference on Distributed, Ambient, and Pervasive Interactions* (pp. 227-239). Cham: Springer International Publishing. DOI: 10.1007/978-3-319-91131-1_18

Tariyal, A., Singh, S., & Bisht, S. (2020). Impact of e-reviews on Millennials' café visit decision-making with reference to Dehradun region. *Academy of Marketing Studies Journal, 24*, 1–13.

Taylor, S. S., & Statler, M. (2024). Material Matters: Increasing Emotional Engagement in Learning. *Journal of Management Education, 38*(4), 586–607. DOI: 10.1177/1052562913489976

Teh, Y., & Baskaran, V. (2022). The effectiveness of eAssessments to encourage learning among Gen Z students. In Yusop, F. D., & Firdaus, A. (Eds.), *Alternative Assessments in Malaysian Higher Education.* Springer. DOI: 10.1007/978-981-16-7228-6_26

Telefonica. (2025, January 14). *First smartphone in history: The origin of smartphones.* https://www.telefonica.com/en/communication-room/blog/first-smartphone/

Thite, S., Ravishankar, J., Tomeo-Reyes, I., & Ortiz, A. M. (2024). Design of a simple rubric to peer-evaluate the teamwork skills of engineering students. *European Journal of Engineering Education, 49*(4), 623–646. DOI: 10.1080/03043797.2024.2338239

Thompson, V. L. S., Ackermann, N., Bauer, K. L., Bowen, D. J., & Goodman, M. S. (2021). Strategies of community engagement in research: Definitions and classifications. *Translational Behavioral Medicine, 11*(2), 441–451. DOI: 10.1093/tbm/ibaa042 PMID: 32421173

Tinmaz, H., & Dhillon, P. K. S. (2024). User-centric avatar design: A cognitive walkthrough approach for metaverse in virtual education. *Data Science and Management, 7*(4), 267–282. DOI: 10.1016/j.dsm.2024.05.001

Törőcsik, M., Szűcs, K., & Kehl, D. (2014). How generations think: Research on Generation Z. Acta Universitatis Sapientiae. *Communication, 1*, 23–45.

Townley, A. L. (2020). Leveraging communities of practice as professional learning communities in science, technology, engineering, math (STEM) education. *Education Sciences, 10*(8), 190. DOI: 10.3390/educsci10080190

Trivedi, S., & Patel, N. (2021). Virtual Employee Monitoring: A Review on Tools, Opportunities, Challenges, and Decision Factors. *Empirical Quests for Management Essences, 1*(1).

Tugun, V., Bayanova, A., Erdyneeva, K., Mashkin, N., Sakhipova, Z., & Zasova, L. (2020). The opinions of technology supported education of university students. [iJET]. *International Journal of Emerging Technologies in Learning, 15*(23), 4–14. DOI: 10.3991/ijet.v15i23.18779

Turner, A. (2015). Generation Z: Technology and social interest. *Journal of Individual Psychology*, *71*(2), 103–113. DOI: 10.1353/jip.2015.0021

Tzafestas, S. G. (2022). *Systems, cybernetics, control, and automation*. River Publishers. DOI: 10.1201/9781003339670

Understood. (2024, April 29). Understood.org survey: *Neurodiversity at work — focus on Gen Z.* https://www.understood.org/en/research-and-surveys/understood-org-genz-survey

Usher, M., & Barak, M. (2018). Peer assessment in a project-based engineering course: Comparing between on-campus and online learning environments. *Assessment & Evaluation in Higher Education*, *43*(5), 745–759. DOI: 10.1080/02602938.2017.1405238

Vaarma, M., & Li, H. (2024). Predicting student dropouts with machine learning: An empirical study in Finnish higher education. *Technology in Society*, *76*, 102474. DOI: 10.1016/j.techsoc.2024.102474

Vajkai, K. É., & Zsóka, Á. (2020). Brand avoidance behaviour of Gen Z towards fast fashion brands. *Vezetéstudomány Budapest Management Review*, *51*(5), 39–50. DOI: 10.14267/VEZTUD.2020.05.04

Valkenburg, P. M., & Peter, J. (2007). Online communication and adolescent well-being: Testing the stimulation versus the displacement hypothesis. *Journal of Computer-Mediated Communication*, *12*(4), 1169–1182. DOI: 10.1111/j.1083-6101.2007.00368.x

Van den Bergh, J., Schepers, J., & Helsen, L. (2024). Beyond labels: Segmenting the Gen Z market for more effective marketing. *Young Consumers: Insight and Ideas for Responsible Marketers*, *25*(2), 188–210. DOI: 10.1108/YC-03-2023-1707

Van Deursen, A. J. (2020). Digital inequality during a pandemic: Quantitative study of differences in COVID-19–related internet uses and outcomes among the general population. *Journal of Medical Internet Research*, *22*(8), e20073. https://preprints.jmir.org/preprint/20073. DOI: 10.2196/20073 PMID: 32750005

Vargas-Hernández, J. G., & Cervantes-Maldonado, D. A. (2018). Intercultural business management development and education programs in business schools. *European Journal of Multidisciplinary Studies*, *3*(1), 105–121. DOI: 10.26417/ejms.v7i1.p105-121

Veletsianos, G., & Kimmons, R. (2013). Scholars and faculty members' lived experiences in online social networks. *The Internet and Higher Education*, *16*, 43–50. DOI: 10.1016/j.iheduc.2012.01.004

Venkatesan, R. (2024). Executing on a customer engagement strategy. *Journal of the Academy of Marketing Science, 45*(3), 289–293. DOI: 10.1007/s11747-016-0513-6

Venton, B. J., & Pompano, R. R. (2021). Strategies for enhancing remote student engagement. *Journal of Chemical Education, 98*(1), 61–67. https://pmc.ncbi.nlm.nih.gov/articles/PMC7811893/

Verma, R., & Merigó, J. M. (2021). On Sharma-Mittal's entropy under intuitionistic fuzzy environment. *Cybernetics and Systems, 52*(6), 498–521. DOI: 10.1080/01969722.2021.1903722

Vieira, A. D. P., De Passillé, A. M., & Weary, D. M. (2012). Effects of the early social environment on behavioral responses of dairy calves to novel events. *Journal of Dairy Science, 95*(9), 5149–5155. DOI: 10.3168/jds.2011-5073 PMID: 22916920

Vmontiel. (2025, July 17). Netflix leads streaming growth in June on the strength of multiple big titles in Nielsen's 50th report of the GaugeTM. *Nielsen.* https://www.nielsen.com/news-center/2025/netflix-leads-streaming-growth-in-june-on-the-strength-of-multiple-big-titles-in-nielsens-50th-report-of-the-gauge/

Vogel, E. A., Rose, J. P., Roberts, L. R., & Eckles, K. (2014). Social comparison, social media, and self-esteem. *Psychology of Popular Media Culture, 3*(4), 206–222. DOI: 10.1037/ppm0000047

Vogt, K. (2016). *Measuring student engagement using learning management systems (unpublished doctoral dissertation)*. University of Toronto., Retrieved from https://tspace.library.utoronto.ca/handle/1807/73213

Vo, T. K. A. (2025). Transforming Language Learning with AI: Adaptive Systems, Engagement, and Global Impact. *Engineering Proceedings, 107*(1), 7. DOI: 10.3390/engproc2025107007

Vygotsky, L. S. (1978). *Mind in society: The development of higher psychological processes* (Vol. 86). Harvard university press.

Wachenheim, C., Idowu, A., & Hanson, E. (2023). Student Feedback on Use of Breakout Rooms. *NACTA Journal, 67*(1). Advance online publication. DOI: 10.56103/nactaj.v67i1.100

Wakke, D., & Heller, V. (2022). Helping as a concurrent activity: How students engage in small groups while pursuing classroom tasks. *Frontiers in Psychology, 12*, 784906. DOI: 10.3389/fpsyg.2021.784906 PMID: 35095673

Walter, S. (2024). Harmonising humans and technology: Exploring the dynamics of cognitive production, artificial intelligence and social communication in cybernetic systems. *Open Research Europe*, *4*(201), 201. DOI: 10.12688/openreseurope.18418.1

Walters, P. (2021). Are Generation Z Ethical Consumers? In Stylos, N., Rahimi, R., Okumus, B., & Williams, S. (Eds.), *Generation Z Marketing and Management in Tourism and Hospitality*. Palgrave Macmillan. DOI: 10.1007/978-3-030-70695-1_12

Walther, J. B. (1996). Computer-mediated communication: Impersonal, interpersonal, and hyperpersonal interaction. *Communication Research*, *23*(1), 3–43. DOI: 10.1177/009365096023001001

Wang, M., Jiang, L., & Luo, H. (2023). Dyads or quads? Impact of group size and learning context on collaborative learning. *Frontiers in Psychology*, *14*, 1168208. DOI: 10.3389/fpsyg.2023.1168208 PMID: 37213364

Wang, X., & Haapio-Kirk, L. (2021). Emotion work via digital visual communication: A comparative study between China and Japan. *Global Media and China*, *6*(3), 325–344. DOI: 10.1177/20594364211008044

Waters, C. L., Menk, F. W., & Fraser, B. J. (1991). The resonance structure of low latitude Pc3 geomagnetic pulsations. *Geophysical Research Letters*, *18*(12), 2293–2296. DOI: 10.1029/91GL02550

Waterworth, J. A. (2025). Disembodied Social Interaction. In J. A. Waterworth, *The Displaced Self* (pp. 15–34). Springer Nature Switzerland. DOI: 10.1007/978-3-031-99832-4_2

Watson, A., Lupton, D., & Michael, M. (2021). The COVID digital home assemblage: Transforming the home into a work space during the crisis. *Convergence (London)*, *27*(5), 1207–1221. DOI: 10.1177/13548565211030848

Weimer, M. (2016). *What does student engagement look like*. The Teaching Professor Blog.

Weinstein, E., & James, C. (2022). *Behind their screens: What teens are facing (and adults are missing)*. MIT press. DOI: 10.7551/mitpress/14088.001.0001

West, B. J., & Mudaliar, S. (2025). Principles entailed by complexity, crucial events, and multifractal dimensionality. *Entropy (Basel, Switzerland)*, *27*(3), 241. DOI: 10.3390/e27030241 PMID: 40149165

Wibowo, S., Wangid, M. N., & Firdaus, F. M. (2025). The Relevance of Vygotsky's Constructivism Learning Theory with the Differentiated Learning Primary Schools. *Journal of education and learning (EduLearn)*, *19*(1), 431-440

Wilcox, D. C. (1998). *Turbulence modeling for CFD* (Vol. 2, pp. 103-217). La Canada, CA: DCW industries.

Wilding, R. (2006). 'Virtual' intimacies? Families communicating across transnational contexts. *Global Networks, 6*(2), 125–142. DOI: 10.1111/j.1471-0374.2006.00137.x

Willett, R., & Wheeler, N. (2021). Maintaining family stability in the age of digital technologies: An analysis of d/Discourse informing domestic screen media practices in three US families. *Children & Society, 35*(5), 722–735. DOI: 10.1111/chso.12443

Wirkuttis, N., Ohata, W., & Tani, J. (2023). Turn-taking mechanisms in imitative interaction: Robotic social interaction based on the free energy principle. *Entropy (Basel, Switzerland), 25*(2), 263. DOI: 10.3390/e25020263 PMID: 36832633

Wolfers, L. N., Kitzmann, S., Sauer, S., & Sommer, N. (2020). Phone use while parenting: An observational study to assess the association of maternal sensitivity and smartphone use in a playground setting. *Computers in Human Behavior, 102*, 31–38. DOI: 10.1016/j.chb.2019.08.013

Wolfson, N. (2022). After the "new aesthetic": A short history of the cybernetic turn in Brazil. *AI & Society, 37*(3), 1059–1069. DOI: 10.1007/s00146-021-01340-8

Wong, K. K. (2023). *Cybernetical intelligence: Engineering cybernetics with machine intelligence*. John Wiley & Sons. DOI: 10.1002/9781394217519

Wong, W. H., & Chapman, E. (2023). Student satisfaction and interaction in higher education. *Higher Education, 85*(5), 957–978. DOI: 10.1007/s10734-022-00874-0

Wood, D., Bruner, J. S., & Ross, G. (1976). The role of tutoring in problem solving. *Journal of Child Psychology and Psychiatry, and Allied Disciplines, 17*(2), 89–100. DOI: 10.1111/j.1469-7610.1976.tb00381.x PMID: 932126

Woodham, A., King, L., Gloyn, L., Crewe, V., & Blair, F. (2017). We Are What We Keep: The "Family Archive", Identity and Public/Private Heritage. *Heritage & Society, 10*(3), 203–220. DOI: 10.1080/2159032X.2018.1554405

Wu, C. H. (2025). Order out of Chaos: The Pharmacology of Cybernetics in The Posthuman Comedy. *Ex-position*, (3), 27–50.

Xu, Y. (2024). *Negotiating "privacy" in the digital age: A study on the new live/work home* [PhD Thesis]. University of Nottingham.

Xu, B., Stephens, J. M., & Lee, K. (2024). Assessing student engagement in collaborative learning: Development and validation of new measure in China. *The Asia-Pacific Education Researcher, 33*(2), 395–405. DOI: 10.1007/s40299-023-00737-x

Xu, W., & Lin, M. (2023). Information Security Evaluation of Industrial Control Systems Using Probabilistic Linguistic MCDM Method. *Computers, Materials & Continua, 77*(1), 199–222. DOI: 10.32604/cmc.2023.041475

Yang, C. C., Holden, S. M., & Carter, M. D. (2017). Social media social comparison of ability (but not opinion) predicts lower identity clarity: Identity processing style as a mediator. *Journal of Youth and Adolescence*, *46*(11), 2221–2237. DOI: 10.1007/s10964-017-0699-z

Yang, X., Chen, Y., & Liu, S. (2024). Cognitive load and emotion regulation in online teaching: Faculty perspectives. *Journal of Computer Assisted Learning*, *40*(2), 391–404. DOI: 10.1111/jcal.2024.40.issue-2

Yaseen, H., Mohammad, A. S., Ashal, N., Abusaimeh, H., Ali, A., & Sharabati, A. A. A. (2025). The impact of adaptive learning technologies, personalized feedback, and interactive AI tools on student engagement: The moderating role of digital literacy. *Sustainability (Basel)*, *17*(3), 1133. DOI: 10.3390/su17031133

Yen, K., Kwon, S. C., Cheng, S., Kamboukos, D., Shelley, D., Brotman, L. M., Kaplan, S. A., Olugbenga, O., & Hoagwood, K. (2018). Unpacking Partnership, Engagement, and Collaboration Research to Inform Implementation Strategies Development: Theoretical Frameworks and Emerging Methodologies. *Frontiers in Public Health*, *6*(July), 1–13. DOI: 10.3389/fpubh.2018.00190 PMID: 30050895

Yolles, M. (2021). Metacybernetics: Towards a general theory of higher order cybernetics. *Systems*, *9*(2), 34. DOI: 10.3390/systems9020034

Yolles, M. (2022). Consciousness, sapience and sentience—A metacybernetic view. *Systems*, *10*(6), 254. DOI: 10.3390/systems10060254

Yoon, P., & Leem, J. (2021). The influence of social presence in online classes using virtual conferencing: Relationships between group cohesion, group efficacy, and academic performance. *Sustainability (Basel)*, *13*(4), 1988. DOI: 10.3390/su13041988

You, F., Fu, Q., Yang, J., Chen, H., Cui, W., & Wang, J. (2024). Team situation awareness-based augmented reality head-up display design for security requirements. *International Journal of Human-Computer Interaction*, *40*(18), 5119–5138. DOI: 10.1080/10447318.2023.2231281

Young, S., & Bruce, M. A. (2021). Classroom Community and Student Engagement in Online Courses. *Learning, 7*(2), 219–230. https://jolt.merlot.org/vol7no2/young_0611.htm

Yuan, Q., & Gao, Q. (2024). Being there, and being together: Avatar appearance and peer interaction in VR classrooms for video-based learning. *International Journal of Human-Computer Interaction, 40*(13), 3313–3333. DOI: 10.1080/10447318.2023.2189818

Yu, X., Shen, Y., Cheng, X., & Bao, Y. (2022). How can cross-cultural virtual learning teams collaborate effectively: A longitudinal study. *Information & Management, 59*(6), 103667. DOI: 10.1016/j.im.2022.103667

Yuyun, I. (2023). Investigating university student engagement in online learning: A case study in EFL classroom. *Indonesian Journal of Applied Linguistics, 12*(3), 648–667. DOI: 10.17509/ijal.v12i3.46035

Zarra-Nezhad, M., Kiuru, N., Aunola, K., Zarra-Nezhad, M., Ahonen, T., Poikkeus, A., Lerkkanen, M., & Nurmi, J. (2014). Social withdrawal in children moderates the association between parenting styles and the children's own socioemotional development. *Journal of Child Psychology and Psychiatry, and Allied Disciplines, 55*(11), 1260–1269. DOI: 10.1111/jcpp.12251 PMID: 24827990

Zhang, J., Akhtar, M. N., Zhang, Y., & Sun, S. (2020). Are overqualified employees bad apples? A dual pathway model of cyberloafing. *Internet Research, 30*(1), 289–313. DOI: 10.1108/INT-01-2019-0044

Zhang, J., & Juvrud, J. (2024). Gender expression and gender identity in virtual reality. *Frontiers in Virtual Reality, 5*, 1305758. DOI: 10.3389/frvir.2024.1305758

Zhang, Y., Yang, Y., Li, S. E., Lyu, Y., Duan, J., Zheng, Z., & Zhang, D. (2025). Feasible Policy Iteration With Guaranteed Safe Exploration. *IEEE Transactions on Cybernetics, 55*(5), 2327–2340. DOI: 10.1109/TCYB.2025.3542223 PMID: 40100688

Zhang, Z. (2025). Cybernetics and Landscape: From Uncertainty to Opportunity. In *Cybernetics and the Constructed Environment*. Taylor & Francis.

Zhang, Z. V., & Hyland, K. (2023). Student engagement with peer feedback in L2 writing: Insights from reflective journaling and revising practices. *Assessing Writing, 58*, 100784. DOI: 10.1016/j.asw.2023.100784

Zhao, S. (2015). Reconceptualizing the Self Phenomenon: Toward an Emic Conception of the Self. *Symbolic Interaction, 38*(2), 235–260. DOI: 10.1002/symb.151

Zhou, Z. (2022). *VibEmoji: Exploring User-authoring Multi-modal Emoticons in Social Communication* [PhD Thesis]. University of Waterloo.

Zhu, C., Valcke, M., & Schellens, T. (2009). A cross-cultural study of online collaborative learning. *Multicultural Education & Technology Journal*, *3*(1), 33–46. DOI: 10.1108/17504970910951138

Zhu, J., Yuan, H., Zhang, Q., Huang, P. H., Wang, Y., Duan, S., Lei, M., Lim, E. G., & Song, P. (2022). The impact of short videos on student performance in an online-flipped college engineering course. *Humanities & Social Sciences Communications*, *9*(1), 327. DOI: 10.1057/s41599-022-01355-6

Zięebacz, I. (2022). Education on the verge of changes. The process of education in terms of the cybernetic theory of character. *Podstawy Edukacji*, *15*, 189–202. DOI: 10.16926/pe.2022.15.13

Ziebacz, I. (2022, August). Knowledge management, including the cybernetic theory of human character. In *European Conference on Knowledge Management* (Vol. 23, No. 2, pp. 1277-1285). DOI: 10.34190/eckm.23.2.414

Zolkin, A. L., Faizullin, R. V., Losev, A. N., & Shevchenko, O. P. (2023). Designing an imitation control system for a logistics complex based on new approaches to organizing cybernetic interaction. *Transportation Research Procedia*, *68*, 229–236. DOI: 10.1016/j.trpro.2023.02.031

Zukowski, N. I. (2023). Novel Framework for a Cybernetic Theory of General Intelligence and Information Field Theory for Strong AI Research and Development-Virtual Neurons Are All You Need.

About the Contributors

Ruqia Safdar Bajwa, Dr, FHEA, is an academic and researcher with over 18 years of experience in higher education. She holds a PhD in Social Psychology and serves as an Assistant Professor at Bahauddin Zakariya University, Pakistan. Her research focuses on psychosocial processes, mental health, and digital behavior, with an established record of publications in peer-reviewed national and international journals, including high-impact indexed outlets, as well as contributions to edited volumes. She has received international recognition for her academic leadership by UNODC. She is a Fellow of Advance HE (UK) and an approved PhD supervisor by the Higher Education Commission of Pakistan. Her work integrates research, teaching, and academic leadership, with a commitment to advancing ethically grounded and socially responsive psychological scholarship.

Sarwat Sultan is a distinguished Professor in the field of Psychology, with extensive experience in teaching, research, and academic leadership in higher education. She has made substantial contributions to the advancement of discipline through a wide range of publications, books, and scholarly works. Her research interests encompass clinical and applied psychology, mental health, and psychosocial well-being, with a particular emphasis on culturally grounded and contextually relevant research. Professor Sultan has supervised numerous postgraduate and doctoral scholars and has played a pivotal role in curriculum development, faculty mentoring, and institutional governance. Recognised for her scholarly excellence and leadership, she has been actively involved in national and international academic collaborations, conferences, and professional organisations.

Asma Yunus PhD, is a prominent academic and assistant professor in the Department of Sociology and Criminology at the University of Sargodha. With an extensive career in higher education, she previously held faculty positions at the University of the Punjab and the University of Gujrat. Her expertise lies in qualitative research. Beyond her research, she is recognized for her role in student supervision and her contributions to academic conferences, where she advocates for social reform and a deeper understanding of contemporary Pakistani society.

***

GajendranA. has 24 years of experience teaching in higher educational Institution, At present he is working as an Associate Professor and former Head of Department of Business Administration at Faculty of Management, SRMIST, Ktr Campus. He authored seven textbooks and two e-books on banking, finance, human resources, and accounting (2010-2024), he published more than 35 research articles published in UGC Care, Scopus, and ABDC publications. He organized, attended numerous conferences, worked as an adjudicator for Ph.D. theses and funded projects, and held a number of administrative and leadership positions, including Chairperson of the Board of Studies, Chair person, Head of Department of Business Administration and academic auditor for several universities.

Munir Ahmad is a seasoned professional in the realm of Spatial Data Infrastructure (SDI), Geo-Information Productions, Information Systems, and Information Governance, boasting over 25 years of dedicated experience in the field. With a PhD in Computer Science, Dr. Ahmad's expertise spans Spatial Data Production, Management, Processing, Analysis, Visualization, and Quality Control. Throughout his career, Dr. Ahmad has been deeply involved in the development and deployment of SDI systems specially in the context of Pakistan, leveraging his proficiency in Spatial Database Design, Web, Mobile & Desktop GIS, and Geo Web Services Architecture. His contributions to Volunteered Geographic Information (VGI) and Open Source Geoportal & Metadata Portal have significantly enriched the geospatial community. As a trainer and researcher, Dr. Ahmad has authored over 50 publications, advancing the industry's knowledge base and fostering innovation in Geo-Tech, Data Governance, and Information Infrastructure, and Emerging Technologies. His commitment to Research and Development (R&D) is evident in his role as a dedicated educator and mentor in the field.

Ashraf Alam currently holds the position of Research Faculty at the Centre of Excellence in Public Policy, Sustainability and ESG Research, housed within the Faculty of Law and Policy Studies at Alliance University, Bangalore. Renowned for his transdisciplinary acumen spanning education, technology, and policy studies, Dr. Ashraf has been distinguished as one of the World's Top 2% Scientists by Stanford University and Elsevier, an accolade that highlights the breadth and depth of his scholarly impact. His prolific academic output includes over fifty SCOPUS-indexed publications and more than one hundred conference presentations at esteemed national and international academic forums. His educational trajectory reflects both depth and versatility: a Ph.D. in Education from the Indian Institute of Technology (IIT) Kharagpur, an M.Ed. with a concentration in Mathematics Education, and a B.S. in Computer Science from the University of Delhi. He also holds postgraduate degrees in Public Administration (M.A.) and Mathematics (M.Sc.), supplemented by a suite of postgraduate diplomas in Higher Education, Guidance and Counselling, Educational Technology, Criminology and Police Administration, and Value Education. Dr. Ashraf is an active participant in global scholarly discourse. As Associate Editor of Frontiers in Education, he plays a pivotal role in curating and guiding intellectual contributions across the Educational, Pedagogical, and Learning Sciences. Concurrently, he serves as Founder and Director of Academic Chronicles Private Limited, where he orchestrates editorial board formation and develops strategic frameworks for peer-reviewed publishing in the Social, Behavioural, and Humanistic Sciences. His research has been disseminated through elite academic platforms, including Elsevier, Springer, Taylor & Francis, Wiley, Routledge, Sage, Emerald, and IEEE, and addresses a remarkably diverse array of topics such as pedagogical theories, educational administration, educational psychology, educational sociology, educational policy, technology-integrated learning, mathematics education, educational philosophy, educational technology, teacher education, and AI/ML in learning environments. Dr. Ashraf's scholarly rigor is further demonstrated by his success in qualifying multiple prestigious examinations including UGC-NET-JRF in both Education and Adult and Continuing Education, UGC- NET in Public Administration, and GATE in Humanities and Social Sciences. At the heart of Dr. Ashraf's intellectual ethos lies a steadfast belief in education as a catalytic and emancipatory force capable of engendering social justice, human flourishing, societal progress, and sustainable transformation. His recent explorations into 'Happiness Engineering' and holistic well- being in school ecosystems articulate a vision of education that transcends instrumentalist paradigms, prioritizing emotional intelligence, global consciousness, empathy, and psychosocial resilience among learners. His research agenda seeks to conceive educational praxis through the affordances of inclusive digital learning, gamified instructional design, and artificial intelligence (AIEd), thereby constructing robust, ethically grounded frameworks for 21st century education. At Alliance University, Dr. Ashraf remains committed to architecting pedagogical models that not only cultivate intellectual dexterity and cognitive excellence but also prepare learners for morally responsive leadership, intellectual nimbleness, and responsible global citizenship in an increasingly volatile, uncertain, complex, and ambiguous (VUCA) world.

Hemkant Nivrutti Gawade is a distinguished academician and Ph.D. guide at Savitribai Phule Pune University in Commerce & Management. With over 20 years of teaching experience, he has presented & published 30+ research papers published in UGC-listed & international peer-reviewed journals. He co-authored 3 books and holds 3 patents. He has worked as a reviewer for reputed international journals. He has delivered 40+ expert sessions and served as a resource person in national and international conferences & FDPs conducted by UGC HRDC. He has worked for the academic audit of reputed institutes. His expertise spans accounting, law, communication, costing, and management.

Catherine Greer studies Psychology with an emphasis on media and technology, having completed her first Master's degree in Law Enforcement and Justice Administration, focusing on the impact of social media on social bonds and juvenile crime.

Harini Pogadadanda is a distinguished academician and researcher with over three decades of combined industrial and teaching experience. She earned her Ph.D. in Computer Science and Engineering from JNTUA, Anantapur, and is currently pursuing her Postdoctoral research at the Singapore Institute of Technology. Recognized as a Professor at JNTU Kakinada and recipient of the Best Teacher Award (2012) from JNTUK, Dr. Harini has contributed extensively to higher education through curriculum design, academic leadership, and accreditation processes. She serves as Professor and Head of the Department of Computer Science and Engineering at St. Ann's College of Engineering and Technology, Chirala. Her research spans Artificial Intelligence, Cyber Security, Machine Learning, Cloud Computing, and Data Analytics. She has also authored books including Dr. Harini is passionate about mentoring young minds, advancing digital innovations in education and healthcare, and fostering research-driven learning environments.

A. Kalaiarasi is full-time research scholar at SRM Institute of Science and Technology, Kattankulathur, Tamil Nadu, India. Her research focuses on exploring the education system and designing strategies to support women employees in academia and other sectors. With 3.9 years of academic experience, her academic journey is marked by excellence, including receiving the prestigious Best Outgoing Award during her postgraduate studies. She has actively contributed to the academic community by presenting four papers at international conferences. Passionate about driving transformative change, she aims to create inclusive policies that foster equity, innovation, and growth in education and professional spaces, particularly for women.

V. Karthi is working as an Assistant Professor in the department of Computer Science and Engineering – Cyber Security at KSR college of Engineering

(Autonomous), Tiruchengode, Namakkal, Tamilnadu. He obtained his PG degree from VMKV Engineering College in 2014, B.Tech from Paavai Engineering College in 2010, He is having 12 years soft teaching experience in the field of Computer Science and Engineering. He has published more than 5 research papers in reputed international journals and conferences with high impact factors. He is an active member of various professional bodies. He authored 2 Indian patents. His areas of interest are Wireless network, Artificial Intelligence and Machine Learning. And Generative AI.

Rajib Mandal is an accomplished academic and researcher with expertise in digital education, optometry, and interdisciplinary innovation. He currently serves as Assistant Professor in the Programme of Optometry, Faculty of Paramedical Sciences, Assam down town University, Sankar Madhab Path, Gandhinagar, Panikhaiti, Guwahati, Assam, India, PIN-781026, where he leads curriculum design and ICT-enabled teaching. His research includes developing hybrid models for online student engagement, digital collaboration, and AI-driven educational tools, reflected in his patents on virtual reality–based learning devices and online pedagogy systems. He has authored over 25 academic books and published widely in Scopus and IEEE-indexed journals. Actively engaged in international seminars and faculty development programs, Dr. Mandal has also presented cutting-edge work on gamification, student motivation, and digital learning at global conferences. Recognized with the Best Young Researcher Award (2025), he brings both academic depth and practical insight into designing effective online learning ecosystems. His work continues to shape the evolving landscape of collaborative and technology-driven education.

Geetha Manoharan is currently working in Telangana as an assistant professor at SR University. She is the university-level PhD program coordinator and has also been given the additional responsibility of In Charge Director of Publications and Patents under the Research Division at SR University.

Ashwini Mary P. is an Assistant Professor in the MBA Department at Sri Muthukumaran Institute of Technology, Mangadu, Chennai. With five years of teaching experience, she is recognized for her ability to simplify complex concepts and inspire students to achieve their learning goals. She has been honored with the Best Teacher Award by her college. Her research interests include leadership styles, psychological empowerment, and psychological capital (PsyCap) and their impact on organizational outcomes.

Mohd Asif Shah is the Dean of Economics at Kardan University (ACBSP/IACBE/AACSB Accredited), Kabul, Afghanistan. He has previously served as an

Associate Professor at Kebri Dehar University, Ethiopia, and Bakhtar University, Afghanistan, and as an Assistant Professor at FBS Business School, Bangalore, and Lovely Professional University (AACSB Accredited), Punjab, India. He holds a PhD, M.A., and B.A. in Economics, with over ten years of teaching and research experience across India, Afghanistan, and Ethiopia. He also serves as an Adjunct Professor at leading universities in India and Afghanistan. Dr. Shah has published 300+ research papers in SCI/SCIE/Scopus/WoS-indexed journals, holds 100+ patents, and has received 5000+ citations. He has participated in 30+ faculty development programs sponsored by the Government of India and is a frequent keynote speaker at international conferences and seminars.

BhoopathyVaradharajan is a Professor at Sree Rama Engineering College. He holds a Ph.D. in Information and Communication Engineering from Anna University and has over 16 years of academic experience. Specializing in wireless sensor networks and IoT, he has published numerous research papers and holds several international patents. Dr. Bhoopathy is a recipient of prestigious awards for his contributions to education and research. His commitment to academia continues to drive innovation and excellence in the field of computer science.

Index

P

R

S

T

V

www.ingramcontent.com/pod-product-compliance
Lightning Source LLC
LaVergne TN
LVHW062219200926
848484LV00006B/1434

TREATMENT
...sion, euphoria/anxiety, concentration ↓, changes in sleeping habits,
.../apathy, disorientation to time and place, personality changes, inappro-...ehaviour, apraxia, tremor
...olence, responsive to stimuli, confusion, disorientation to time and place, ...re behaviour, speech disorder
...ma

...n criteria for grading hepatic encephalopathy

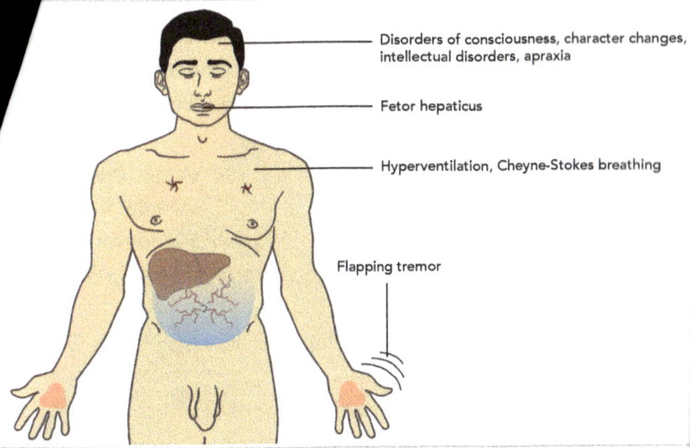

...igure 39 // Hepatic encephalopathy

Oesophageal perforation

- **D** An oesophageal perforation is a perforation of the oesophagus (gullet).
- **E** Unknown
- **Ae** Iatrogenic (+) (complicated endoscopy), trauma, ingestion of foreign body, invasive oesophageal cancer, frequent forceful vomiting (Boerhaave syndrome...
- **R** Endoscopy (+), trauma, oesophageal cancer, vomiting
- **Hx** Depends on the underlying cause; (sub)acute (<24h) retrosternal pain (+... dysphagia, vomiting, hoarseness, odynophagia, beware of symptoms of sep... tic shock

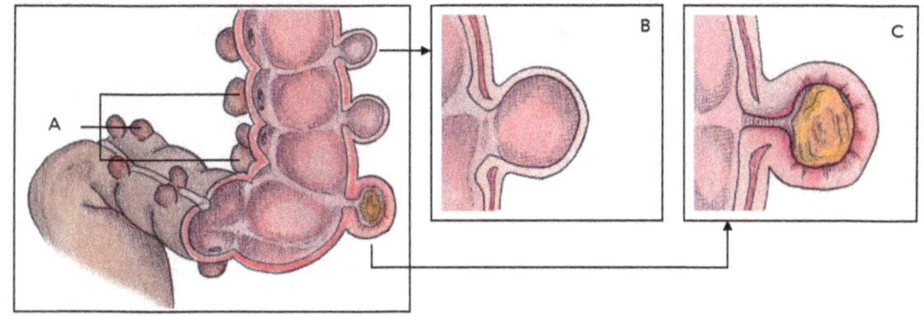

Figure 38 // Diverticulosis and diverticulitis
A: Diverticula **B:** Diverticulum **C:** Diverticulitis (inflamed diverticulum)

Gastrointestinal bleeding

	UPPER GASTROINTESTINAL BLEEDING	LOWER GASTROINTESTINAL BLEEDING
D	Gastrointestinal bleeding that originates proximal to the ligament of Treitz (suspensory muscle of the duodenum).	Gastrointestinal bleeding that originates distal to the ligament of Treitz (suspensory muscle of the duodenum).
E	Prevalence 67:100,000 per y	Prevalence 36:100,000 per y
Ae	Peptic ulcer (++), erosions (+), varices, haemorragic gastritis, Mallory-Weiss lesion, oesophagitis, duodenitis, malignancy, arteriovenous malformation (−), gastrointestinal stromal tumour (GIST) (−), angiodysplasias (−), aortoenteric fistula (−), watermelon stomach (−), haemobilia (−), Dieulafoy lesion (−), Cameron lesion (−)	Diverticulosis (++), angiodysplasia (+), cause in upper digestive system, colitis (ischaemic, infectious, post-radiation), IBD (Crohn's disease, ulcerative colitis), malignancy/polyp, rectal conditions (haemorrhoids, fissure, rectal ulcer), bleeding after endoscopic intervention
R	Depending on the underlying cause: *Helicobacter pylori* infection, anticoagulants, NSAIDs, liver cirrhosis	
Hx	Fatigue, dizziness, duration and quantity of blood loss, weight ↓, medication and alcohol use, recent surgeries/procedures in the gastrointestinal region	
	Haematemesis (bright red/dark brown), associated gastrointestinal symptoms (feeling of fullness, acid reflux, dysphagia, retrosternal pain), melaena (in case of slow upper gastrointestinal bleeding)	Melaena, haematochezia, diarrhoea

Table 86A // Upper and lower gastrointestinal bleeding

	UPPER GASTROINTESTINAL BLEEDING	LOWER GASTROINTESTINAL BLEEDING
PE	BP ↓, heart rate ↑, pallor, clamminess	
	Examine for underlying condition: spider naevi, palmar erythema, caput medusae sign, icterus, ascites, hepatosplenomegaly, testicular atrophy and/or gynaecomastia, epigastric guarding pain, palpable swelling tumour	• Examine for underlying condition • Rectal digital exam: blood on the glove, palpable tumour, haemorrhoids, sometimes melaena
Dx	• Depends on the underlying cause • Labs: Hb =/↓, MCV ↓ • Labs (depending on the underlying cause): rapid blood count (e.g. Hb from venous blood gas analysis), blood group, rhesus factor, cross blood, potassium, urea, renal function, AST, ALT, ALP, gGT, bilirubin • If indicated: lactate, CRP, troponin, CK, INR, ECG, chest X-ray	
	Gastroscopy: identification of the bleeding location • In massive bleeding or haemodynamic instability, perform gastroscopy following patient stabilisation • In haemodynamically stable patients with non-threatening bleeding, gastroscopy <24h if clinically relevant CTA: may be considered in manifest upper gastrointestinal bleeding where endoscopy is inconclusive, or in haemodynamically unstable patients, to identify the underlying cause and location	• Haemodynamically stable patient with persistent blood loss: colonoscopy after appropriate bowel preparation • CT angiography in haemodynamically unstable patients, possibly followed by selective angiography with embolisation
Tx	• ABCDE approach • Fluid challenge, for shock secondary to bleeding, consider the local protocol and possibly treating shock • Stop anticoagulants/antiplatelets if possible, anticoagulant reversal if applicable • Treat the underlying cause PPI IV in suspected ulcer-related bleeding (e.g. pantoprazole bolus 80 mg followed by perfusor 8 mg/h), vasoactive medication (e.g. octreotide 50 mg bolus followed by perfusor (25-50 mg/h) for 5d) in suspected variceal bleeding, AB prophylactically only in cases with liver cirrhosis and ascites Endoscopic haemostasis, interventional radiology, surgery	
P	10% in-hospital mortality	4% in-hospital mortality

Table 86B // Upper and lower gastrointestinal bleeding

Hepatic encephalopathy

D Hepatic encephalopathy is a
by metabolic changes r
ure 39).

E 30-40% of pati

Ae Hepatic cell
lateral circulatio
degradation of tox
glutamate ↑ gamma-
oxidative stress, change

R Combination of severe liv
triggering factors (digestive
dration, medication)

Hx Various stages of loss of consciou
→ coma), hyperventilation (tingling a
ing of light-headedness, increased RR)
atic encephalopathy

PE
- Altered GCS, changes in character, inte
disorientation in time, place and person), a
ventilation, Cheyne-Stokes breathing, hepati
- Depends on severity (West Haven criteria, see T
stigmata of liver cirrhosis

Dx
- NH_3^+ ↑ (only if indicated (!), clinical diagnosis), brai
to rule out other causes
- Labs: liver function tests, basic metabolic panel

Tx Symptomatic support, treat precipitating factor (i.e. GI
ICU admission

Lactulose (oral and/or rectal, depending on grade), consider
faximin in case of recurring episodes, avoid morphine or sedative

Liver transplantation

Lactulose is prescribed for hepatic encephalopathy. Lactulose inhibits the intestinal production of ammonia and results in an increase of faecal excretion of ammonia.

STAGE	
0	No confusion
1	Slight conf irritability
2	Letharg priate b
3	Somn biza
4	Co

Table 87 // West Hav

PE Symptoms of septic shock (HR ↑, BP ↓, RR ↑, clammy and pale skin), subcutaneous emphysema of neck and chest (crepitations upon palpation and auscultation), pleural effusion, Hamman's sign for pneumomediastinum (crepitations upon auscultation simultaneous to the heart beat)

Dx
- Labs: detection of sepsis (infection parameters, blood- and pleural fluid cultures, urine cultures)
- Chest CT with IV contrast, using water-diluted iodine-based contrast, administered orally if possible: pneumomediastinum, pleural effusion, pneumothorax, contrast in chest, subcutaneous emphysema
- Chest/abdominal X-ray: pneumothorax, pneumomediastinum, pleural effusion, air under the diaphragm, widened mediastinum

Tx Nil per os

AB and fluids IV

Percutaneous and/or surgical drainage of mediastinum and/or pleura is the most important primary treatment for an oesophageal perforation, followed if possible by primary closure of defect, consider a partial oesophageal resection, if iatrogenic: gastro-oesophagoscopy with stent insertion

P Mortality ↑ due to secondary infectious mediastinitis

> A chest drain is used to drain air and/or fluid from the pleural cavity, as is the case for a haemothorax, chylothorax, pneumothorax and for empyema and pleural effusion.

Pancreatitis

D Acute inflammation of the pancreas, diagnosed using the Atlanta criteria (see Figure 40). Subtypes of acute pancreatitis include interstitial oedematous and necrotising pancreatitis (see Figure 41).

E Incidence 5-56:100,000 per year and rising

Ae
- Proteolytic enzyme activation → pancreatic autodigestion → local inflammation, possible systemic inflammatory response syndrome (SIRS) with potential hypovolaemic shock due to redistribution
- Causes: cholelithiasis (++), alcohol (++), trauma, medication (e.g. ACE inhibitors, statins, thiopurines), infections, metabolic (hypercalcaemia, hypertriglyceridaemia), post-ERCP, pancreatic carcinoma, anatomical defect (e.g. pancreas divisum (-)), autoimmune (-), idiopathic (+)

R Cholelithiasis (++), alcohol abuse (++), obesity, genetic predisposition, DM type 2

HX
- Acute epigastric pain (radiating to back in 50% of patients), urge to move (colicy pain), nausea, vomiting, fever
- Alcohol use, patient recently started medication for pancreatitis, recent surgery/trauma, see R
- Eating, coughing, deep inspiration → pain ↑

PE Epigastric tenderness and/or rebound tenderness, T ↑/subfebrile, BP ↑/↓, pulse ↑, RR superficial and ↑, Cullen's sign (periumbilical ecchymosis) ⊖, Grey Turner's sign (ecchymosis or discoloration of the flank) ⊖

Dx
- Atlanta criteria (see Figure 39)
- Labs: lipase/amylase ↑ (>3x the upper limit of normal), CRP ↑, WBC ↑, possible: Ca^{2+} ↑, triglycerides ↑, glucose ↑ ⊕
- Abdominal ultrasound: at initial presentation, given biliary aetiology is most common (i.e. obstructing gallstone)
- EUS: detect choledocholithiasis or intraductal sludge. Indicated if suspicion persists after negative abdominal ultrasound.
- MRCP: alternative to EUS for suspected choledocholithiasis, rule out pancreas divisum
- Abdominal CT with IV contrast in acute phase only when in doubt about the diagnosis (>72h) or clinical deterioration: evaluate suspected secondary complications of pancreatitis (e.g. abscess formation), and distinguish between oedematous (±80%) or necrotising pancreatitis (±20%). Findings have no clinical consequences. Necrotising pancreatitis: parenchymal oedema, peripancreatic fat infiltration, decreased parenchymal enhancement, fluid collections, and CT severity index.
- ECG: rule out anterior myocardial infarction if indicated

Tx
Monitor fluid balance, optimise nutritional status (consult dietitian, enteral nutrition), monitor renal function

Crystalloid (Ringer's lactate) IV guided by urine output, usually 3 L/24h after a bolus with a target urine output of >0.5 mL/kg/h, analgesics, LMWH, consider antiemetics, replete electrolytes as needed. No AB, only for infected necrosis (often only after 2-4 wk).

- ERCP (only if concurrent cholangitis, no routine ERCP for biliary pancreatitis)
- Cholecystectomy for biliary pancreatitis, preferably during same admission in patients with a mild clinical course (wait for at least 6 wk in patients with a more severe clinical course)
- Treatment of complications

- Treatment of proven or suspected infected necrotising pancreatitis (minimally invasive step-up approach):

AB (broad-spectrum, e.g. meropenem)

Drainage (transluminal endoscopic/retroperitoneal percutaneous drainage) of infected necrotising collection in case of walled-off necrosis (WON) optimally delayed up to >4 wk, followed by minimally invasive necrosectomy if necessary (endoscopic or /video-assisted retroperitoneal debridement (VARD))

P
- Mild pancreatitis has low mortality: <5%
- 15-25% of patients with acute pancreatitis develop necrotising pancreatitis. Mortality is higher in necrotising pancreatitis: 17%.
- Severe pancreatitis: Imrie, bedside index of severity in acute pancreatitis (BISAP), and acute physiology and chronic health evaluation (APACHE) score, SIRS criteria
- CRP >150 mg/L within 48h → predictor of severe pancreatitis

!
- For possible complications of acute pancreatitis see Figure 41
- Beware of pancreatitis and cholangitis in case of a biliary cause

Atlanta criteria for the diagnosis of acute pancreatitis (≥2 of 3 criteria must be met, see Figure 40):

I. Lipase or amylase >3x the upper limit of normal
II. Acute epigastric and/or back pain
III. Characteristic findings on imaging (see Dx)

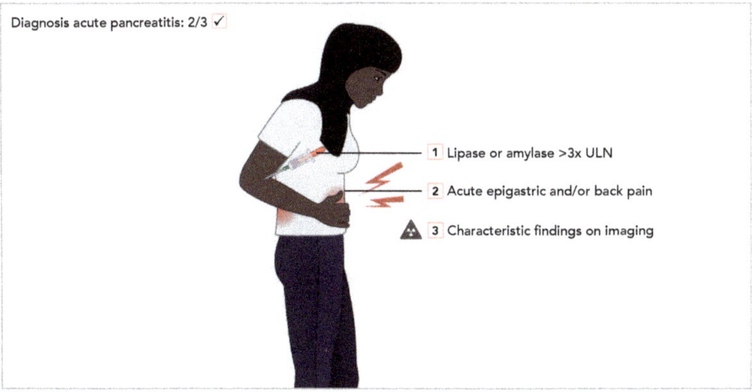

Figure 40 // Atlanta criteria for pancreatitis

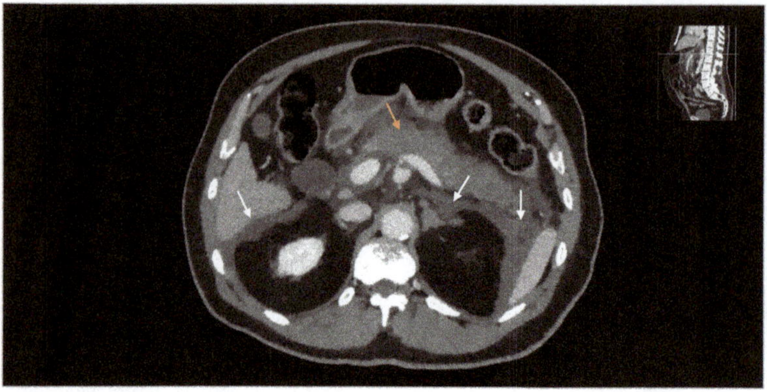

Figure 41 // CT abdomen with venous contrast: acute pancreatitis with oedematous swollen pancreas (orange arrow) and free retroperitoneal fluid (white arrows)

GET SMASHID is a mnemonic for the most common causes of acute pancreatitis: **G**allstones, **E**thanol, **T**rauma, **S**teroids, **M**umps, **A**utoimmune, **S**corpion sting, **H**yperlipidaemia, **I**diopathic, **D**rugs.

Internal medicine

Acute kidney injury (AKI)

D Acute renal insufficiency is evidenced by an abrupt decrease in GFR. This can be detected as an increase in the plasma creatinine or decrease in urine output. This develops over several hours to weeks and requires swift medical attention (see Figure 42).

E Incidence 5% in hospitalised patients, 31.7% in critically ill patients

Ae
- AKI is multifactorial, the following clinical distinction into three main groups is made: pre-renal, renal, and post-renal (↔) (see Table 89)
- General population: mostly pre-renal or post-renal, hospital population: mostly acute tubular necrosis (ATN)

R Depends on the cause, chronic renal insufficiency, nephrotoxic medication

Hx
- General: oliguria/anuria (60%)
- Pre-renal: vomiting, diarrhoea, medication (ACE inhibitors, diuretics), low (fluid) intake, HF
- Renal: haematuria, signs of systemic disease, use of medication
- Post-renal: flank pain with kidney stone, voiding issues, prostate disease, malignancies

PE
- Consequences of fluid overload: BP ↑, CVP ↑, pulmonary crepitations, oedema
- Consequences of uraemia: pericardial rub, uremic foetor
- Pre-renal: BP ↓, HR ↑, skin turgor ↓
- Renal: oedema with nephrotic syndrome, signs of vasculitis of the skin, arthritides
- Post-renal: significantly muffled bladder percussion, bladder distention, abdominal pain

Dx
- Labs (general): protein creatinine ratio (PCr) ↑
- Pre-renal: urine osmolality >500 mOsm/kg, Na^+ in urine <20 mmol/L, fractional Na^+ excretion <1%
- Renal: urine osmolality >350 mOsm/kg, Na^+ in urine <40 mmol/L, fractional Na^+ excretion >2%, urine sediment and labs (to investigate underlying cause)
- Post-renal: ultrasound of kidneys and bladder (dilatation of collecting ducts due to obstruction)
- ECG: if patient is hyperkalaemic, to rule out arrhythmias (pointed T waves or prolonged PR interval)
- Bladder scan: to rule out possible urinary retention
- Kidney biopsy: histological diagnosis

Tx

Nutrition: protein intake 0.8-1.0 g/kg/d for patients without dialysis, 1.5 g/kg/d for patients receiving dialysis, restrict sodium, potassium and fluids

- Stop nephrotoxic medication, antihypertensives and diuretics, adjust dose of other medication
- For severe clinical presentation: renal function replacement therapy (RFRT) in ICU

P

Possibility of recovery with rapid intervention, although even then there is an increased risk of 5y mortality and reduced kidney function, 10% will progress to end-stage renal failure

!
- First treat severe complications, then treat the underlying cause
- Risk of complications: uraemic pericarditis, uraemic gastritis, uraemic encephalopathy, fatal cardiac arrhythmia caused by hyperkalaemia, fluid overload → respiratory insufficiency
- Arrhythmias, sometimes fatal
- Serum creatinine is not a reliably estimate of renal function in AKI and unstable value

> Patients with chronic renal insufficiency or DM are at increased risk of developing acute renal insufficiency after receiving contrast agents.

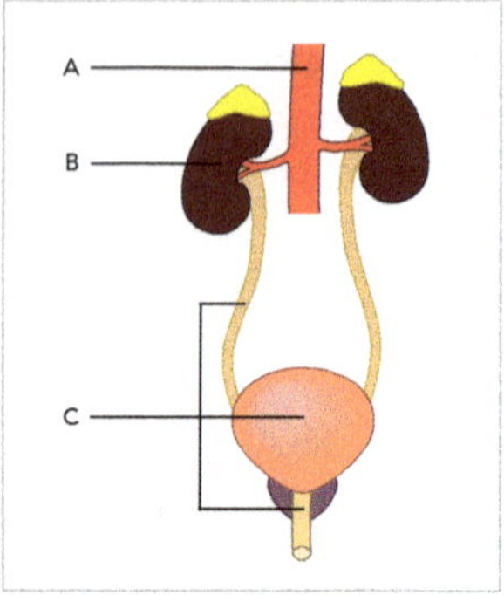

Figure 42 // Causes of acute renal failure
A: Pre-renal: renal perfusion ↓**B:** Renal: damage to renal tissue **C:** Post-renal: obstruction of ureter, bladder, or urethra

STAGE	SERUM CREATININE	URINE OUTPUT
1	Increase of 0.3 mg/dL (26.5 μmol/L) or 1.5-1.9 times baseline	<0.5 mL/kg/h for 6-12h
2	2.0-2.9 times baseline	<0.5 mL/kg/h for ≥12h
3	≥3 times baseline or increase to ≥4 mg/dL (354 μmol/L) or renal replacement therapy initiated or in patients <18y: decrease in eGFR to <35 mL/min/1.73 m²	<0.3 mL/kg/h for ≥24h or anuria for ≥12h

Table 88 // Kidney Disease Improving Global outcomes (KDIGO) criteria for staging of AKI

PRE-RENAL	RENAL	POST-RENAL
Circulating volume ↓ and/or renal perfusion ↓, intact renal tissue: • Extracellular volume ↓ (vomiting, diarrhoea, bleeding) • Pharmacological (ACE inhibitor, NSAIDs) • HMV ↓ (HF) • Renal perfusion ↓ (renal artery stenosis, aortic dissection)	Renal tissue damage: • Nephritic syndrome • Nephrotic syndrome • Vascular: occlusion of arterioles or glomerular capillaries (thrombotic microangiopathy, vasculitis, thrombosis/embolism of the larger vessels) • Glomerulonephritis, anti-GBM-glomerulonephritis, ANCA-glomerulonephritis) • Interstitial nephritis (pharmacological, infectious, sarcoidosis) • ATN (ischaemic, toxic)	Distal obstruction, initially no damage to renal tissue: • Urethral obstruction (kidney stones, malignancy) • Bladder obstruction (bladder retention, benign prostate hypertrophy, neurogenic bladder) • Obstruction of urethra (prostate carcinoma, valves, stricture)

Table 89 // Causes of acute renal insufficiency

Adrenal insufficiency (Adrenal crisis)

D Acute adrenal insufficiency, also referred to as an adrenal or Addisonian crisis, is a potentially life-threatening complication of chronic adrenal insufficiency. Chronic adrenal insufficiency is subdivided into primary adrenal insufficiency (problem located in the adrenal gland itself, e.g. autoimmune adrenalitis = Addison's disease), secondary adrenal insufficiency (problem located further up the axis, e.g. pituitary tumour or Sheehan's syndrome) and steroid-induced adrenal insufficiency (e.g. prednisone maintenance therapy for PMR/inhalation corticosteroids for COPD). Clinical symptoms of acute adrenal insufficiency, such as severe abdominal pain and hypotension, occur when this underlying pathology inhibits an increase in the endogenous cortisol production in response to stress (see Figure 43).

E
- Incidence primary adrenal insufficiency (Addison's disease) 4-11:100,000 (70-90% autoimmune, 7-20% infections e.g. TB) per year
- Incidence secondary adrenal insufficiency (not exogenous glucocorticoid administration) 360:100,000 per year
- Incidence exogenous glucocorticoid administration: 1,510:100,000 per year

Ae Potential triggers: infection, surgery, trauma, childbirth, intense pain, severe psychological stress, inadequate intake/acute termination of glucocorticoid maintenance therapy, immune checkpoint inhibitors

Hx
- General malaise (++), anorexia (++), nausea (+), vomiting (+), diarrhoea, abdominal pain, muscle/joint pain, salt craving (primary adrenal insufficiency), general malaise, fatigue, anorexia, consciousness ↓, dizziness, nausea, vomiting, diarrhoea, abdominal pain, muscle/joint pain, T ↑. Confirmation of one/several of the aforementioned triggers.
- Especially in Addison's disease: salt cravings, skin hyperpigmentation in palmar creases (+), mucosal membranes, elbows and knees

PE Consciousness ↓, confused, (orthostatic) BP ↓, hypotensive crisis, heart rate ↑, dehydration, signs of primary adrenal insufficiency (hyperpigmentation of the skin and/or mucous membranes), T ↑

Dx Labs: glucose ↓, Na^+ =/↓, K^+ ↑. Targeted investigation for underlying trigger (e.g. infection). De novo adrenal insufficiency: cortisol =/↓ and ACTH ↑/=/↓ (depending on underlying pathology). Random cortisol >500 nmol/L does rule out adrenal insufficiency.

Tx Stabilise the patient according to ABCDE. Rehydrate with NaCl 0.9%. Treat underlying triggers.

Acute situation: hydrocortisone 100 mg IV bolus followed by stress schedule (150 mg/24h), glucose IV for persistent hypoglycaemia, AB (for underlying infection)

P Left untreated, this condition has a high mortality

During a relative adrenal insufficiency (critical illness-related corticosteroid insufficiency) not enough cortisol is produced to meet the body's demands during critical illness.

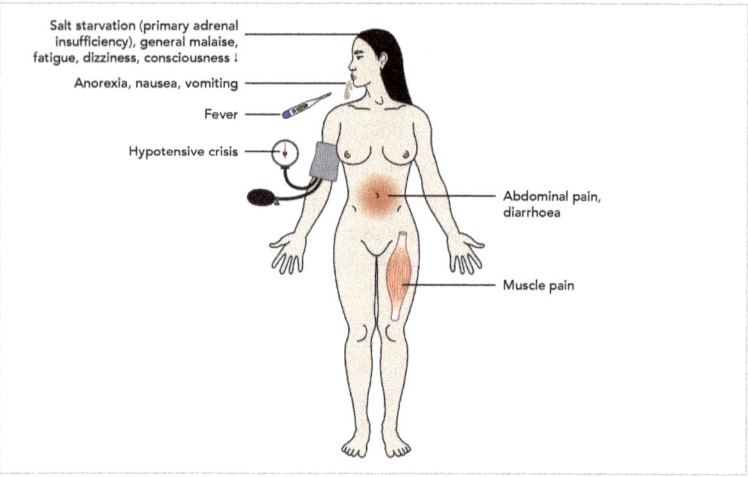

Figure 43 // Addisonian crisis

Steroid-induced adrenal insufficiency is most common in practice. There is no administration form, dose or duration of treatment that can rule out adrenal insufficiency with absolute certainty. In short: if there are any clinical suspicions of acute adrenal insufficiency, treat quickly!

ACTH samples are collected in EDTA plasma and should be placed on ice and taken to the lab immediately after collection.

Deep vein thrombosis (DVT)

D A DVT is a thrombosis in the deep venous system. If there are pre-existent risk factors, then the condition is referred to as a secondary DVT. A proximal DVT is located above the knee. A distal DVT (or isolated calf muscle venous thrombosis) is located below the knee only.

E Incidence up to 300-500:100,000 per year in Europe and the USA

Ae Virchow's Triad: vascular wall damage, slow blood flow, altered composition of the blood

R Recent operation/trauma, immobilisation, oestrogen containing medications (e.g. oral contraceptive pill), procoagulant medication, pregnancy, obesity, long periods of sitting (plane travel), smoking, hypercoagulable condition (e.g. factor V Leiden), chronic illness affecting coagulation factors (malignancy, chronic kidney disease, inflammatory disorders), older age, varicose veins, previous venous thromboembolism

Hx Asymptomatic or localised pain, possibly with symptoms of pulmonary embolism

PE
- Low-grade fever, pulse rate =/↑
- Inspect both legs for symmetry: tenderness to palpation, calf swelling >3 cm or of the entire leg (measure both legs at the same point), redness, collateral superficial veins, unilateral pitting oedema

Dx
- In clinical suspicion of a DVT, the Wells' criteria for DVT can be used as an effective support tool
- Wells score <2 and D-dimer ↓ effectively rules out a DVT (<1% chance)
- Wells score ≥2 OR a Wells score <2 with a D-dimer ↑: duplex ultrasound
- CT venography when ultrasound is inconclusive, in case of ongoing suspicion of DVT or suspected DVT of iliac veins

Tx Compression stockings ≥6 mo for prevention of post-thrombotic syndrome

≥3 mo of anticoagulative therapy depending on the underlying condition

P 15-50% of patients with a DVT develop the post-thrombotic syndrome

!
- 30% recurrence rate after idiopathic DVT
- 70% of patients with a pulmonary embolism have a DVT, 40-50% of patients with a DVT have a pulmonary embolism

A **venous thrombo-embolism** is an umbrella term and can refer to both a DVT and a pulmonary embolism.

Post-thrombotic syndrome is a syndrome that develops as a result of venous insufficiency following a prior DVT. This syndrome is characterised by itching, pain, trophic abnormalities, hyperpigmentation, atrophic blanching (white discoloration with red maculae near an ulcer) and dilatation of the subcutaneous veins.

In contrast to a DVT, **thrombophlebitis** and **superficial venous thrombosis** are located near the surface and are characterised by signs of inflammation. An infusion (primarily with flucloxacillin IV) is a common cause of thrombophlebitis. Treatment with low dose therapeutic anticoagulants (e.g. fondaparinux) is indicated for an inflammation measuring >5 cm on ultrasound.

Because a D-dimer can also be elevated in many other conditions (e.g infections, post-surgery, malignancy, normal pregnancy) it's primarily used in outpatient settings and emergency departments. Patients with a possible DVT and pre-existing conditions that increase the odds of an elevated D-dimer should receive an ultrasound regardless of the Wells score.

FEATURES	CRITERIA	POINTS
Past medical history	Malignancy (up to 6 mo after treatment or in palliative care)	1
	Bed rest >3d or major surgery <4 wk	1
	Immobilisation (paralysis, paresis, recent cast)	1
Hx	Local pain in the region of the DVT	1
PE	Swelling of calf >3 cm compared to the other leg (measuring point: 10 cm below the tibial tuberosity)	1
	Collateral superficial veins	1
	Pitting oedema of the affected leg	1
	Swelling of the entire affected leg	1
	Alternative diagnosis more probable than DVT	-2

Table 90 // Wells score for DVT

Diabetic ketoacidosis (DKA)

D DKA is a condition primarily seen in type 1 DM, but can occur in type 2 DM as well. DKA is associated with elevated anion gap metabolic acidosis (pH <7.35), hyperglycaemia and increased ketone bodies. A new onset DKA can be the initial presentation for diabetes (see Table 91).

E Incidence hospitalisations 3,000:100,000 diabetic patients per year

Ae
- Acute shortage of insulin resulting from a reduced insulin availability or as a result of increased glucose requirement → absorption of glucose in cells ↓ → lipolysis → free fatty acids and ketone bodies → metabolic acidosis → respiratory compensation (Kussmaul breathing)
- Intercurrent disease (30%), suspension of insulin therapy (15%), first manifestation (10%), medications such as prednisone, atypical antipsychotics and SGLT2 inhibitors.
- SGLT2 inhibitors can be associated with euglycemic (serum glucose <250 mg/dl (14 mmol/L) DKA

R Insulin resistance by stimulation of the HPA axis, concomitant illness e.g gastroenteritis, food intake ↓

Hx Acute symptoms (>24h): polyuria (++), polydipsia (++), generalised malaise, blurry vision, nausea, vomiting, abdominal pain

PE RR ↓, dehydration symptoms, Kussmaul respirations, fruity breath (caused by increased acetone production)

Dx
- Labs: glucose >250 mg/dl (14 mmol/L), anion gap ↑, metabolic acidosis, ketones ↑
- Lab values supporting a diagnosis of DKA: sodium ↓, lactate ↑, acute kidney injury (BUN (Blood urea nitrogen) ↑, creatinine ↑), phosphate =/↑
- Urine: glucose ↑, ketones ↑

Tx Circulatory volume ↑: NPO and IV rehydration.

- Address cause of DKA
- IV isotonic saline 1L in the first hour, then 250 mL/h for 3h
- Switch to IV dextrose 10% solution when serum glucose approaches <200 mg/dl (11.11 mmol/L) to prevent rebound hypoglycaemia and cerebral oedema, but do not stop insulin treatment unless acidosis is corrected
- Potassium repletion if K <5.3 meq/L
- Continuous insulin pump without bolus
- Serum bicarbonate 100 mL 8.4% only if pH <6.9

For pH <7: infusion with HCO_3^- and admission to ICU

P
- Favourable prognosis with adequate treatment
- Failure to treat in a timely manner can prove fatal

I Regardless of the severity of the hyperglycaemia, the correction of the dehydration in DKA should be gradually corrected to prevent brain oedema

Hyperosmolar hyperglycaemic state (HHS): ketoacidosis is not frequently seen in patients with DM type 2, instead the patient develops a HHS. In HHS, the patient develops severe dehydration due to hyperglycaemia (see Table 91). This dehydration occurs more rapidly in elderly patients, due to decreased thirst perception. The hyperglycaemia and dehydration result in deteriorating cerebral functioning and the differential diagnosis often incorrectly includes dementia. HHS is triggered by many causes, including nonadherence to treatment, intercurrent disease, warm weather, use of prednisone or diuretics. Rehydration is sufficient in many cases, though additional insulin may be necessary for certain patients. Due to the frequent occurrence of thrombo-embolic events, HHS has a poorer prognosis than ketoacidosis.

If there is serum hypokalaemia, the serum potassium should be first corrected before giving insulin to prevent severe hypokalaemia. Potassium should also be given with the IV fluids if the serum potassium is not elevated).

Target a decrease in serum osmolality of 1 mOsmol/L/h (faster correction of serum osmolality can lead to brain oedema).
The serum osmolality can be calculated using the formula :

$\sqrt{x}$	2*sodium + glucose (mmol/L) + BUN (mmol/L).

If your institution uses mg/dl for glucose and BUN the following formula can be applied to calculate serum osmolality:

$\sqrt{x}$	2*sodium + (glucose/18) + (BUN/2.8).

The serum potassium in DKA can be normal through the shift of potassium extracellularly, while the total body potassium (the total extracellular and intracellular potassium found in the body) can be low. It is important to adequately supplement potassium even if serum potassium is initially normal.

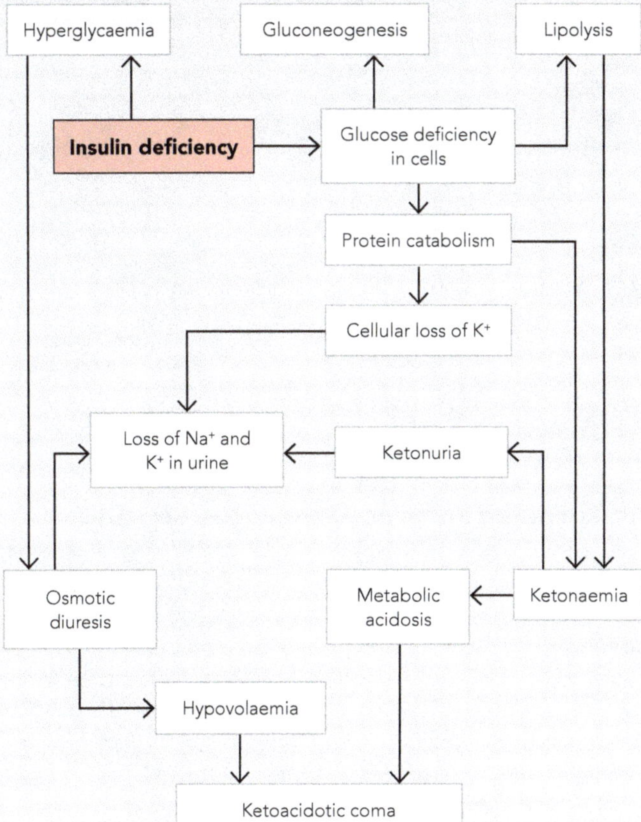

Diagram 26 // Diabetic ketoacidosis

Hypokalaemia as a result of buffering: in an acidotic state, extracellular H^+ ions are buffered by the cells through exchange with intracellular K^+ ions. Normally this would result in hyperkalaemia, but the ketonuria causes the extra potassium to be excreted in the plasma, resulting in severe hypokalaemia. Correction of the hypokalaemia is important to prevent complications (cardiac arrhythmias).

	DIABETIC KETOACIDOSIS	HYPEROSMOLAR HYPERGLYCAEMIC STATE
Epidemiology	More common in DM type 1, patients aged <65	More common in DM type 2, patients aged >65
Glucose levels	>14 mmol/L (250 mg/dl)	>33 mmol/L (600 mg/dl)
PH	<7.25 (↑ anion gap)	>7.30
Ketones	Present	Absent
Serum osmolality	Variable	>320 mOsm/kg
Symptoms	• Variable mental status • Abdominal pain (+)	• Altered mental status (++) • Abdominal pain (−)
Prognosis	Mortality >1%	Mortality 10-20%

Table 91 // Diabetic ketoacidosis and hyperosmolar hyperglycemic state

Disseminated intravascular coagulation (DIC)

D Acquired coagulopathy, systemic activation of the coagulation system secondary to another disease.

E DIC in 1% of tertiary care hospitalised patients and in 35% of severe sepsis patients

Ae Thrombotic occlusion of blood vessels caused by intravascular fibrin formation → organ failure and bleeding as a result of high use of clotting factors

R Sepsis, trauma, malignancy, obstetric, vascular, toxic (amphetamines, snake venom), immunological (allergy, transplant rejection)

Hx Depends on the underlying cause

PE Depends on the underlying cause

Dx Labs: thrombocytes ↓, PT ↑, aPTT ↑, D-dimer ↑, fibrinogen ↓

Tx Most important: treat underlying cause

Supportive care:

Haemodynamic/ventilatory support

- Transfusion of blood products in patients with active bleeding or requiring an invasive procedure or who are otherwise at risk for bleeding complications
- Platelet transfusion if platelet count <10,000*10^9
- Fresh frozen plasma if fibrinogen level <50 mg/dl and significant bleeding, or if PT ↑↑

- Antiplatelet therapy depending on the situation

P Depends on the underlying cause

> In most cases there is no obvious case for thrombosis (idiopathic). Risk factors include advanced age, obesity, immobility, post-operative, pregnancy, oral contraception, smoking, and malignancies. Thrombosis can be a first sign of an underlying malignancy. An elevated D-dimer, which is a catabolic product of coagulation activity, can indicate thrombosis.

Electrolyte disorders

Hypercalcaemia

D Hypercalcaemia (total calcium >2.6 mmol/L) is an electrolyte imbalance that is characterised by an excessively high concentration of free calcium in the blood.

E Two most common causes:

1 Primary hyperparathyroidism incidence: ♀ 233:100,000, ♂ 85:100,000,

2 Hypercalcemia of malignancy incidence 2-3%, total prevalence 20-30% of all cancer patients, most common cause of inpatient hypercalcemia

Ae Hyperparathyroidism (either primary, or secondary or tertiary to chronic renal insufficiency), malignancy (e.g. multiple myeloma, bone metastases), vit. D-related (e.g. granulomatous disease, excessive supplementation), familial hypocalciuric hypercalcaemia, thyrotoxicosis, adrenal insufficiency, milk-alkali syndrome, pharmacological (e.g. lithium, thiazide diuretics), immobilisation, rhabdomyolysis, tube feeding

Hx Polydipsia, polyuria, general malaise, nausea, vomiting, constipation, fatigue, muscle weakness, psychiatric disorders, bone pain and urolithiasis

PE If severe: HR ↓, BP ↓, EMV ↓, hyporeflexia

Dx
- Labs: Ca^{2+} ↑, PTH ↓/=
- To analyse the cause: phosphate, magnesium, sodium, potassium, renal function, alkaline phosphatase, bicarbonate (consider sedimentation, M-protein, TSH, cortisol, ACE/vit. D for suspected granulomatous disease)
- ECG: bradycardia, QT-interval ↓
- Imaging, performed during hospitalisation, if feasible: ultrasound of neck for suspected hyperparathyroidism, possibly followed by needle biopsy, chest and abdominal CT, PET CT scan and ♂ PSA (lab) for suspected ma-

lignancy

Tx Treatment of underlying cause

Check calcium, sodium, potassium, renal function, magnesium every 4 h until normalisation, in case of shortened QT: telemetry

- Depending on the presence and severity of symptoms:
  1. Volume expansion with isotonic saline
  2. Infusion with furosemide to promote calciuria
  3. Supplementation of bisphosphonates (GFR <30 mL/min is a contraindication)
  4. Calcitonin (efflux of calcium from bones ↓)
  5. Haemodialysis
- Stop thiazide diuretics if possible, start loop diuretics for fluid overload

P Hypercalcaemia can cause pancreatitis or kidney stones

!
- Elevated calcium in combination with elevated phosphate can result in the formation of calcium phosphate crystals, which can precipitate in the blood vessels and cause vascular calcification
- Very severe hypercalcaemia can result in cardiac arrest

Milk-alkali syndrome: hypercalcaemia caused by intake of large quantities of calcium together with alkali (including antacids), which is characterised by metabolic alkalosis. The exact pathophysiology is unknown.

The symptoms of hypercalcaemia can be remembered as 'bones, stones, abdominal groans, and psychiatric moans'.

Hypocalcaemia

D Hypocalcaemia (total Ca^{2+} <2.1 mmol/L) is an electrolyte imbalance that is characterised by an excessively low concentration of free calcium in the blood. Under normal circumstances, a low free calcium concentration will result in an elevated PTH.

E Multiple causes:
- Incidence of transient hypocalcaemia after total thyroidectomy 20%
- Incidence of permanent hypocalcaemia after total thyroidectomy 0.8-3%
- Incidence of hypocalcaemia in critically ill ICU patients 80-90%

Ae Severe vit. D deficiency (<20 nmol/L), acute or chronic renal insufficiency, malabsorption primarily in the duodenum (e.g. secondary to coeliac disease or inflammatory bowel diseases), hypoparathyroidism (congenital/acquired), pseudohypoparathyroidism (resistance to PTH), hypomagnesaemia (PTH secretion and functioning ↓), pharmacological (e.g. anti-epileptics or bisphosphonates), rhabdomyolysis, pancreatitis, iatrogenic with citrate-rich blood products, receptor mutations

Hx Asymptomatic (++), muscle spasms or muscle contractions, abdominal pain, paresthaesias, psychiatric disorders, seizures

PE If severe: HR ↓, BP ↓, Chvostek's sign, Trousseau's sign, hyperexcitability (heightened reflexes)

Dx
- Labs: Ca^{2+} ↑, PTH =/↓
- To analyse the cause: phosphate, magnesium, sodium, potassium, renal function (consider urine Ca, PTH, 25-OH-vit. D, CK, lipase, liver enzymes)
- ECG: bradycardia, prolonged QT interval, non-specific ST segment, T top changes

Tx Check calcium every 4h until normalisation, in case of prolonged QT interval: telemetry

Depending on the presence and severity of symptoms, consider IV or oral supplementation of calcium and/or vit. D and IV magnesium sulphate if necessary

P Depending on the cause of the hypocalcaemia, often good following adequate supplementation

!
- Supplementation should also include correction of hyperphosphataemia, if present, to prevent the precipitation of calcium phosphate crystals in the blood vessels
- Very severe hypocalcaemia can result in cardiac arrest

Approx. 50% of calcium is bound in the blood to proteins, mainly albumin. However, the biologically active calcium refers to the free concentration of calcium only (not bound to proteins). Laboratory tests measure the total amount of calcium and not the free calcium concentration. Therefore, it is important to correct the total calcium for the concentration of albumin. The higher the albumin concentration, the lower the free calcium after correction for albumin. The concentration of free calcium can be determined directly via a blood gas measurement.

- **Chvostek's sign**: tapping on the facial nerve (CN VII) anterior to the ear causing ipsilateral facial contractions. Limited clinical value due to the presence of Chvostek's sign in 10% of the healthy population.
- **Trousseau's sign**: carpopedal spasms characterised by adduction of the thumb, flexion of the MCP joints, flexion of the interphalangeal joints, and flexion of the wrist after inflation of blood pressure cuff. Limited clinical value due to patient discomfort.

Hyperkalaemia

D Hyperkalaemia is defined as a serum potassium concentration >5.0 mmol/L. This results in an increased conduction speed of the heart, caused by a shortened repolarisation phase.

E Incidence 1,000:100,000 per year, more common in elderly and patients with chronic kidney disease (CKD)

Ae See Diagram 27

R Acute or chronic renal insufficiency, rhabdomyolysis, tumour lysis, medication

Hx Asymptomatic ⊕, sensory disturbances, muscle weakness

PE Muscle weakness

Dx
- ECG: pointy T wave, elongated PR interval combined with a widened QRS complex (see Figure 44)
- Labs: K^+ >5.0 mmol/L, thrombocytes ↑, WBC ↑ (with pseudohyperkalaemia), acidosis (with hyperkalaemia caused by a shift to extracellular)

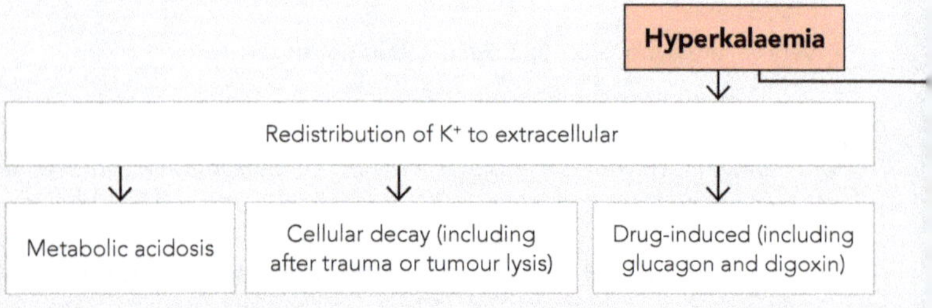

Diagram 27 // Causes of hyperkalaemia

High potassium intake in healthy individuals is not a major cause of hyperkalaemia.

- Urine analysis: TTKG (transtubular potassium gradient) >6, if this is lower in association with hyperkalaemia this could be an indication of hypoaldosteronism

Tx If K^+ >6.5 mmol/L or acute ECG changes:

Place the patient on a cardiac monitor

- IV calcium 10 mL 10% solution to stabilise cardiac membrane
- IV insulin and glucose and salbutamol to promote intracellular uptake of K^+
- K^+ binder to promote excretion of K^+
- Consider bicarbonate in acidosis, loop diuretics in patient without hypovolaemia and dialysis in patients with CKD or treatment refractory hyperkalaemia

! Beware of VF

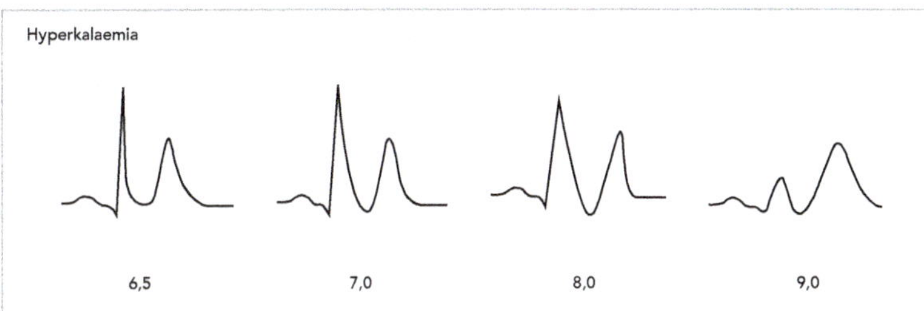

Figure 44 // ECG changes in hyperkalaemia (mmol/L)

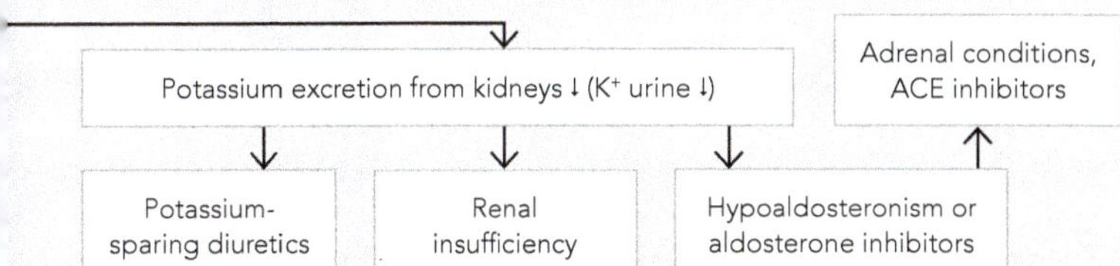

If the patient has an unexpected, severely elevated, asymptomatic K^+, recheck the serum K^+. This unexpectedly high K^+ value could be the result of pseudohyperkalaemia secondary to mechanical trauma and potassium extracellular shift during the blood draw.

Hypokalaemia

D Hypokalaemia is defined as a serum potassium concentration <3.5 mmol/L. A low concentration of K^+ causes hyperpolarisation in the muscles.

E Inpatient prevalence up to 21%, outpatient prevalence up to 3%

Ae See Diagram 28

Hx Diarrhoea, sensory disturbances, nausea, vomiting, abdominal cramps, muscle weakness, muscle cramps

PE Muscle weakness, BP ↑ (primarily the hereditary form), arrhythmias

Dx
- Labs: K^+ <3.5 mmol/L, alkalosis (hypokalaemia caused by a shift to intracellular), hypomagnesaemia
- ECG to rule out arrhythmias: a clear U wave, possible T top flattening and inversion, QT elongation, ST depression (see Figure 45)

Tx Rhythm monitoring
- Supplementation of K^+ and treatment of underlying cause
- Mg^{2+} supplementation in hypomagnesaemia

I Beware of rhabdomyolysis, VF and asystole with extreme hypokalaemia

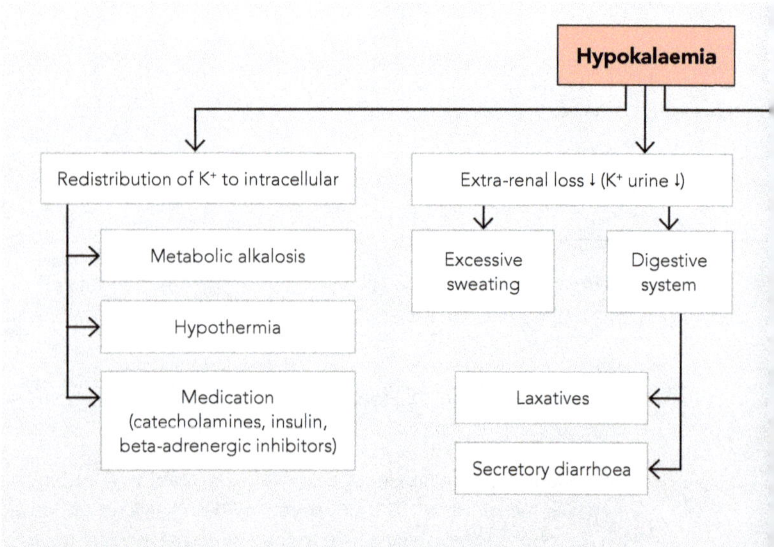

Diagram 28 // Causes of hypokalaemia

> Low K⁺ intake alone is unlikely to cause hypokalaemia in healthy populations. Too much liquorice can cause severe hypokalaemia.

> Thyrotoxic periodic paralysis is an acquired channelopathy classically seen in young East Asian males that causes hypokalaemia with severe muscle weakness including possible respiratory distress in the presence of hyperthyroidism. Potassium supplementation to avoid rebound hyperkalaemia and propranolol reverses the muscle weakness.

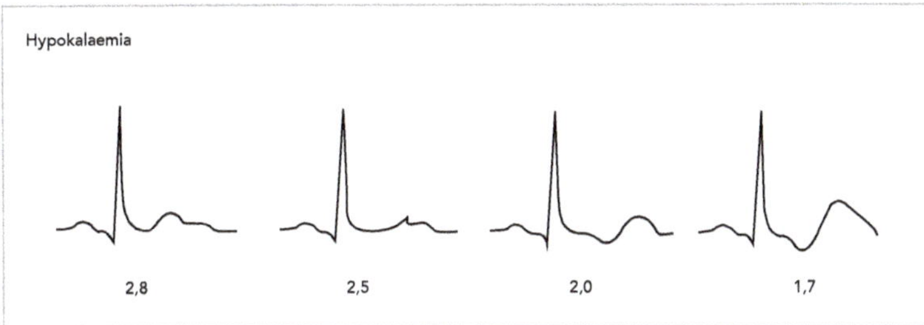

Figure 45 // ECG changes in hypokalaemia (mmol/L)

Potassium excretion from kidneys ↓ (K^+ urine ↓)

- Stimulation RAAS
  - Loop and thiazide diuretics
  - Dysregulated DM
  - Vomiting (loss of K^+ through stimulation of RAAS and metabolic alkalosis)
- Supply of non-resorbable anions
  - Carbonic anhydrase inhibitors
  - RTA (serum concentration HCO_3^- low)

Hypernatraemia

D Serum sodium concentration >145 mmol/L.

E Rare in healthy population with access to water, incidence in hospitalised patients: 1-3%, incidence in ICU patients 9%

Ae Increase in serum sodium concentration, usually because of initial dehydration and not replacing water losses, relative dehydration of the cerebrum (see Diagram 29)

R See Diagram 29

Hx Thirst, drowsiness, general weakness, fever, unable to drink water either due to not having access to water or not being physically able to drink water

PE Signs of hypervolaemia (BP ↑) or signs of hypovolaemia (dry skin, skin turgor ↓, BP ↓)

Dx Urine analysis: sodium concentration ↓ with loss of water; sodium concentration ↑ with excessive salt intake

Tx Treatment of underlying cause, if applicable

Normalise fluid and electrolyte balance

P Untreated hypernatraemia/hyponatraemia → risk of seizures, coma, death

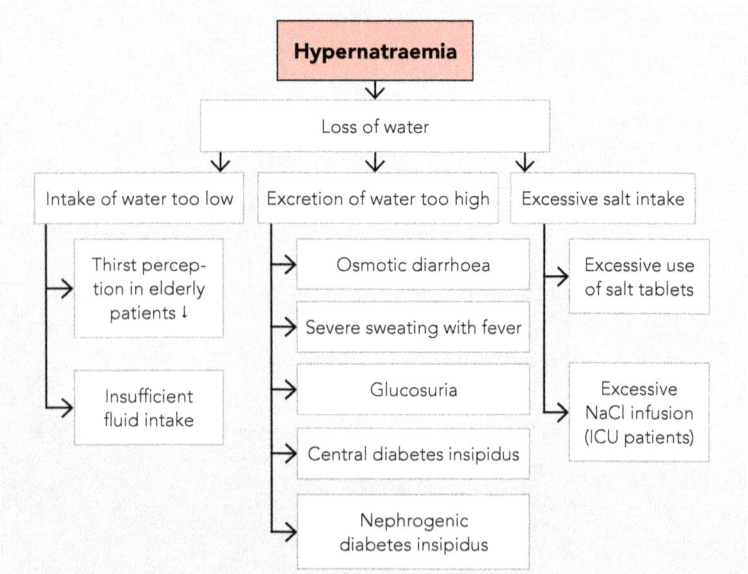

Diagram 29 // Causes of hypernatraemia

- Excessively rapid correction of hyponatraemia: pontine myelinolysis/osmotic demyelination;
- Excessively rapid correction of hypernatraemia: cerebral oedema.

Hyponatraemia

D Serum sodium concentration <135 mmol/L.

E Most common electrolyte disorder in hospitalised patients, prevalence in hospitalised patients ±15%, prevalence 50% in patients with cirrhosis, prevalence 10-27% in patients with HF

Ae Relative overhydration of the cerebrum (see Diagram 30)

R See Diagram 30

Hx Nausea, vomiting, confusion, tendency to fall, headache

PE Signs of hypervolaemia (BP ↑) or signs of hypovolaemia (dry skin, skin turgor ↓, BP ↓)

Dx Urine analysis: sodium concentration ↓ with salt deficit and sodium concentration ↑ with ADH secretion ↑. Urine osmolality to narrow down the differential diagnosis.

Tx Treatment of underlying cause, if applicable

Normalise fluid and electrolyte balance

P Untreated hypernatraemia/hyponatraemia → risk of seizures, coma, death

Hyponatraemia is the most common electrolyte imbalance.

- The sodium concentration should not increase by more than 0.5 mmol/L/h, to prevent excessively rapid correction. If the hyponatraemia is chronic, do not increase the sodium concentration by >8 mmol/d.
- In the case of severe hyponatraemia with obvious cerebral symptoms, the sodium concentration should first be increased by 3-5 mmol over the course of several hours using isotonic or hypertonic saline. Once this has been achieved, the sodium concentration should not increase by more than 0.5 mmol/L/h.

A severely elevated serum glucose can increase tonicity, driving water into the serum and lowering serum sodium concentration. To correct for this phenomenon the following formula can be used.

$$\text{Corrected Sodium} = \text{measured sodium} + 0.024 * (\text{Serum glucose (mg/dl)} - 100)$$

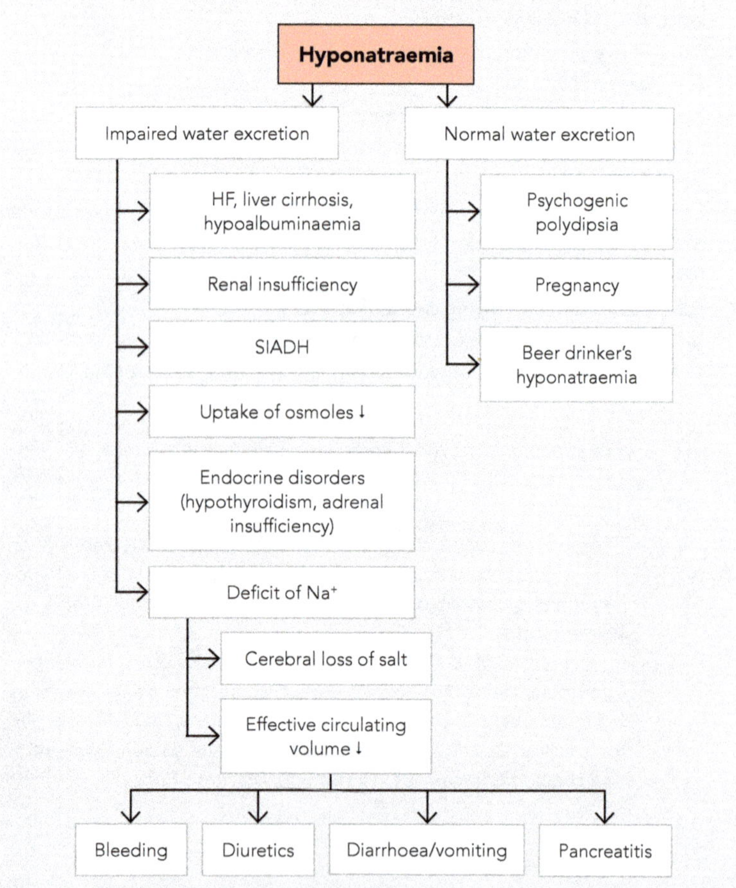

Diagram 30 // Causes of hyponatraemia

Hypertensive emergency

D A suddenly occurring, markedly increased BP >220 mmHg systolic and/or 120 mmHg diastolic in combination with symptoms, which can be complicated by acute or progressive signs of hypertensive organ damage.

E
- 50:100,000 patients in ED
- Half of the patients with a hypertensive emergency have pre-existing hypertension

Ae
- Renal causes ⊕: renal diseases, systemic diseases with renal involvement
- Renovascular diseases ⊕: atherosclerosis, vasculitis, fibromuscular dysplasia
- Endocrine: pheochromocytoma
- Nonadherence to treatment, consumption of liquorice and liquorice root, renal diseases, cocaine/XTC/amphetamines
- Pharmacological: oral contraceptives, NSAIDs, anti-angiogenic therapy, cyclosporine, tacrolimus, cisplatinum

R Nonadherence to treatment, uncontrolled hypertension, low socioeconomic status (SES), of South or West African descent

Hx Vision abnormalities, headache, nausea, vomiting, dyspnoea, chest pains, symptoms of HF, consciousness ↓, convulsions, dizziness, neurological deficits, see Figure 46

PE
- BP of left and right arm >220 mmHg systolic and/or 120 mmHg diastolic
- Auscultation of the heart: normal/cardiac murmurs, lungs: normal/crepitations, abdomen: normal/murmur along renal artery
- Peripheral pulsations: normal/↑
- Neurological examination: normal/neurological deficits

Dx
- Labs: full blood count, renal function, Na^+, K^+, LDH, CK
- Urine: sediment, protein, consider toxicological analysis
- ECG: normal/ischaemia/LVH
- Chest X-ray: heart size =/↑, filing status =/↑
- Fundoscopy: look for signs of bleeding, exudate, papilloedema
- Further additional tests based on suspected organ damage

Tx Severe hypertension: gradual reduction of BP within several hours

- 1st choice: nifedipine retard, 2nd choice: labetalol or nitroglycerin
- Hypertensive emergency (see Table 92)

P Four-year survival of hypertensive emergency and retinopathy: 90%

! Excessive BP reduction (>25%) during initial treatment can result in ischaemic damage

COMPONENT	HYPERTENSIVE EMERGENCY WITH RETINOPATHY AND/OR MICROANGIOPATHY	HYPERTENSION DUE TO ACUTE HF WITH PULMONARY OEDEMA	HYPERTENSION WITH CORONARY ISCHAEMIA
BP reduction	Within several hours MAP ↓ of 20-25%	Immediate MAP ↓ of 60-100 mmHg	
1st choice	Labetalol	Nitroprusside or nitroglycerin with loop diuretic	Nitroglycerin
2nd choice	Nitroprusside, nicardipine, urapidil	Urapidil	Labetalol

Table 92 // Treatment of hypertensive emergency

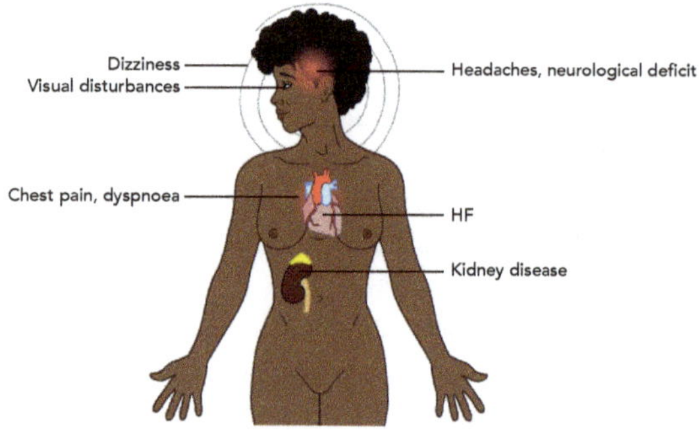

Figure 46 // Hypertensive emergency

Intoxication

D An intoxication or poisoning is a state that occurs after ingesting, absorbing or contact with a certain substance in a quantity sufficient to cause symptoms.

E Account for approx. 3% of all the ED visits in urban areas. Alcohol intoxication ED incidence 1.8%. Total drug poisoning ED incidence 0.3-0.9%.

Ae Drug overdose, medication overdose (intentional/accidental), medication interactions, exposure during accidents/disasters/terrorist attacks

R Psychiatric history, experiencing a life event

Hx Depending on the nature, the time of exposure and the dose of the substance in question (see Table 93), collateral history

PE Depending on the nature of the substance in question: pay extra attention to the vital signs, GCS/consciousness and pupil abnormalities

HYPERTENSION DUE TO CEREBRAL INFARCTION	HYPERTENSION DUE TO CEREBRAL HAEMORRHAGE	HYPERTENSION DUE TO ADRENERGIC OVERSTIMULATION
Within 1h MAP ↓ of 15%	Within 1h SBP <140 mmHg	Within several hours BP <60/100 mmHg
Labetalol		Phentolamine (for cocaine and XTC intoxication combined with benzodiazepine)
Nicardipine, nitroprusside		Nitroprusside

Dx
- Labs: mainly electrolyte abnormalities (sodium, potassium, magnesium, chlorine), renal function, lactate, osmolality ↑
- ABG with carbon monoxide (HbCO) and methaemoglobinaemia (metHb)
- ECG: telemetry for widened QRS complex
- With pulmonary symptoms: chest X-ray
- It can be useful to determine the concentration of, among others, paracetamol, anti-epileptics, lithium, digoxin, (m)ethanol, acetylsalicylic acid
- For unknown intoxications: toxicology screening of urine/serum/stomach contents

Tx
- The treatment always proceeds according to the "treat the patient, not the poison" principle, which entails that the treatment focuses on the symptomatology and not the substance used
- Treatment according to the ABCDE approach
- See Table 93 for general detoxification methods, Table 94 for specific antidotes and Table 95 for the treatment for specific intoxications
- For convulsions: benzodiazepine IV/intranasal/rectal

P Depending on the nature, the time of exposure and the dose of the substance in question

!
- Comorbidity or the patient's own medication can change the pharmacokinetic profile of an intoxication
- Caution is advised when antagonising benzodiazepines in the case of a multi-substance intoxication, because benzodiazepines can suppress the dangerous symptoms of other substances (e.g. hyperthermia, tachycardia, or seizures)
- Rule out pregnancy in fertile women

DETOXIFICATION METHOD	TIME FRAME	INDICATION
Active/activated charcoal* (1 g/kg, max 50 g)	<1h after exposure or <2h with slow gastric emptying	All intoxications except alcohols, lithium, potassium, cyanide, heavy metals or iodine/bromide (as it cannot bind to these)
Gastric lavage	<1h after exposure or <2h with slow gastric emptying	• Ingestion of extreme quantities • Lithium, potassium, cyanide, heavy metals, iodine/bromide
Intestinal lavage		• Lithium, potassium, cyanide, heavy metals, iodine/bromide (>1-2h) • Extended-release preparations with severe clinical consequences • Calcium antagonists • Drugs ("balloons") • Coalescing intoxications
(Intermittent) haemodialysis	As soon as possible	In the case of very severe intoxications of the following substances, for which other therapies have failed: barbiturates, theophylline, antiseizure medication (including carbamazepine, valproic acid, phenytoin), lithium, methanol/ethanol, metformin and life-threatening paracetamol intoxication
IV lipid emulsion (intralipid)		Life-threatening neurological or cardiological toxicity caused by a strongly lipophilic substance or local anaesthetic

Table 93 // Decontamination methods
*Only for patients with unimpaired consciousness or intubated patients

INTOXICATION	ANTIDOTE
Anticholinergics	Physostigmine
Benzodiazepine	Flumazenil (beware of withdrawal)
Beta blocker	Glucagon
Calcium antagonist	Calcium
Cholinesterase inhibitors	Atropine/obidoxim
Coumarin derivatives	Vit. K
Dabigatran	Idarucizumab

Table 94A // Specific antidotes to common intoxications

INTOXICATION	ANTIDOTE
Digoxin	Specific antibodies
Ethylene glycol/methanol	Ethanol
Heparin	Protamine
Morphine	Naloxone
Paracetamol	N-acetylcysteine
Beta adrenergic agonists or MDMA-like substances	Phentolamine
XTC	Methysergide

Table 94B // Specific antidotes to common intoxications

An **attempted suicide** is the most common cause of intoxication in the ED. The risk of underlying psychiatric disease is approx. 90%.

A CT of the chest and abdomen should be performed in the case of **intoxication with a corrosive substance** and clinical symptoms of a perforation. In the absence of such symptoms, an oesophago/gastro/duodenoscopy should be performed within 24h.

- For a teenager presenting with low GCS and convulsions, consider initial presentation of DM type 1 as an alternative to intoxication.
- For an older patient presenting with low GCS, consider neurological problems (e.g. stroke) or hypercapnia as an alternatives to intoxication.

- Physostigmine should only be administered for a "pure" anticholinergic intoxication, otherwise it could result in asystole (with tricyclic antidepressants (TCAs) and a widened QRS complex) or cholinergic syndrome.
- Flumazenil should not be administered for mixed intoxications due to the risk of seizures. Benzodiazepines can suppress the symptoms of other intoxications.

	PARACETAMOL INTOXICATION	ALCOHOL INTOXICATION	ALCOHOL WITHDRAWAL
D	Ingestion of toxic quantity of paracetamol.	Ingestion of toxic quantity of alcohol.	The set of symptoms that can occur when a patient with alcohol use disorder suddenly reduces or stops drinking alcohol.
E	Most common cause of acute liver failure, 40% of all acute liver failure	Alcohol intoxication ED incidence 1.8%, accounted for approx.1 in 10 deaths of adults between 20-64	14% of the general population qualifies for alcohol use disorder (AUD). 50% of patients with AUD experience withdrawal symptoms when decreasing alcohol consumption or stopping entirely. 20% undergoing withdrawal have severe symptoms (hallucinations, seizures, delirium tremens) toxicity.
Ae	• Paracetamol → reactive metabolite (NAPQI) → toxic with simultaneous glutathione deficiency • Various degrees: - Mild: >70 mg/kg - Moderate: >140 mg/kg - Severe: >200 mg/kg	• Ethanol intoxication: 1000 mg/L (1‰) • Life-threatening: >5000 mg/L or >4000 mg/L (30 min after ingestion)	• Chronic alcohol use → excitatory neurotransmitters ↓ (glutamate) → neurotransmitters ↑ • Abruptly stopped → unregulated glutamate excitation → hyperarousal and symptoms of alcohol withdrawal
R	Reduced glutathione supply/synthesis: chronic alcohol abuse, hepatic insufficiency, malnutrition, CYP2E1-inducing medication	Adolescents, high level of education, genetic predisposition, alcohol addiction, hepatic insufficiency	History of alcohol withdrawal including withdrawal seizures and delirium tremens, heavy and regular alcohol consumption, age >65, benzodiazepine use, traumatic brain injury, concomitant medical conditions

Table 95A // Common intoxications

Benzodiazepine and GHB intoxications present with symptoms consistent with CNS depression and will appear clinically similar to alcohol intoxication.

For patients with a history of alcohol withdrawal, oral benzodiazepines can be used as prophylaxis to help prevent serious withdrawal symptoms.

OPIOID INTOXICATION	CHOLINERGIC SYNDROME	ANTICHOLINERGIC SYNDROME	BETA ADRENERGIC AGONISM SYNDROME
Ingestion of toxic quantity of opioids.	Ingestion of substances with strong cholinergic activity or inhibition of cholinesterase inhibitors. Also called cholinesterase syndrome.	Ingestion of substances with anticholinergic effect or after inhalation anaesthesia.	Ingestion of substances with sympathetic effect.
480,000 deaths worldwide, opioids responsible 80% of drug-related deaths worldwide	Yearly incidence 3,000,000 people worldwide, 8,000 exposures, and 15 deaths in USA	Yearly ±9,000 exposures in USA, <10 fatal cases	Unknown
• Stimulation of μ-receptors and to a lesser extent δ-, κ- and σ-receptors • Substances: heroin, methadone, morphine, oxycodone, tramadol, buprenorphine, codeine	• Cholinergic activity ↑↑ in the CNS due to excess acetylcholine (ACh) or as a function of acetylcholinesterase ↓ • Substances: physostigmine, insecticides and mushrooms	• Cholinergic activity ↓ in CNS due to a competition between ACh and medications/toxins • Substances: antipsychotics, TCAs, antihistamines, Parkinson medication, antimuscarinergics, muscle relaxants, varies plant species	• Sympathetic nerve activity ↑ • Substances: cocaine, amphetamine, XTC-like substances, theophylline
Increased age, comorbidity (mental/physical)	Work/home environment with exposure to chemical substances or pesticides	Depends on the substance that was used	Adolescents, addicted parents, clubbers, genetic predisposition

The typical patient with cholinergic syndrome is a pest control employee who presents with fasciculations and increased secretion by exocrine glands (tears, saliva, mucus, sweat).
This syndrome can also occur with inhalation anaesthetics or nerve gas exposure.

	PARACETAMOL INTOXICATION	ALCOHOL INTOXICATION	ALCOHOL WITHDRAWAL
Hx	• After 24-48h: vomiting, abdominal pain • After 1-7d: hepatic insufficiency, renal insufficiency, coma	• Within minutes: vomiting, abdominal pain, sedation, altered speech • After several hours: pancreatitis, hepatic insufficiency, renal insufficiency with haematuria, cardiac arrhythmias, convulsions, coma, hypothermia/hyperthermia	History of alcohol use disorder, recent decrease or stop in alcohol use, history of alcohol withdrawal
PE	• HR =, BP =, RR =, T =, consciousness =, sweating, anorexia • After 4-5d: icterus	• HR ↓, BP ↓, RR ↑, T ↓/↑, consciousness ↓, nystagmus, hypotonia, ataxia, gait disorder	• Initial withdrawal symptoms <6h: anxiety, insomnia, nausea, anorexia, headache, diaphoresis, palpitations • Withdrawal seizures 12-48h: tonic-clonic seizures (++), status epilepticus (--) • Alcohol hallucinosis 24-48h: visual hallucinations (++), tactile and auditory hallucinations • Delirium Tremens 48-96h: HR ↑, RR ↑, T ↑, delirium, agitation, diaphoresis

Table 95B // Common intoxications

A typical patient with carbon monoxide (CO) intoxication will present with symptoms of syncope and headache, will also be tachypnoeic with a normal saturation and the persons/animals in his surroundings will present with the same symptoms.

CO cutoff points as measured using a specialised CO-saturation device:

- CO >10% → O_2 therapy
- CO >20-30% → 15L NRM
- CO >40% → consider hyperbaric oxygen

Note: Smokers are allowed to have up to 10% CO.

Rule out other intoxications/excited delirium syndrome in patients with symptoms of alcohol withdrawal.

<table>
<tr><th>OPIOID INTOXICATION</th><th>CHOLINERGIC SYNDROME</th><th>ANTICHOLINERGIC SYNDROME</th><th>BETA ADRENERGIC AGONISM SYNDROME</th></tr>
<tr><td>Time frame dependent on substance: vomiting, constipation, agitation, respiratory depression, sedation, altered speech, coma, hypothermia</td><td>Within minutes: vomiting, intestinal cramps, incontinence for urine and faeces, dyspnoea (due to pulmonary oedema), muscle weakness/cramp, delirium, convulsions, coma</td><td>Within ±1-2h: anhydrosis, anuria, constipation, delirium, hallucinations, cardiac arrhythmias, convulsions, hyperthermia</td><td>Time frame dependent on substance: vomiting, agitation, euphoria, hallucinations, cardiac arrhythmias, convulsions, hyperthermia</td></tr>
<tr><td rowspan="2">HR ↓, BP ↓, RR ↑, T ↓, consciousness ↓, myosis (pinpoint, see Figure 47), hyperreflexia</td><td rowspan="2">HR ↓/↑, BP ↓/↑, RR ↓, T =, consciousness ↓, myosis, clammy, pale skin, tears ↑, saliva ↑, bronchial secretion ↑, intestinal peristalsis ↑, fasciculations</td><td colspan="2">HR ↓, BP ↓, RR ↑, T ↓, consciousness ↓/=</td></tr>
<tr><td>Non-reactive mydriasis, warm, dry, red skin, intestinal peristalsis absent</td><td>Reactive mydriasis, clammy, pale skin, dry mucous membranes, hyperreflexia, tremor</td></tr>
</table>

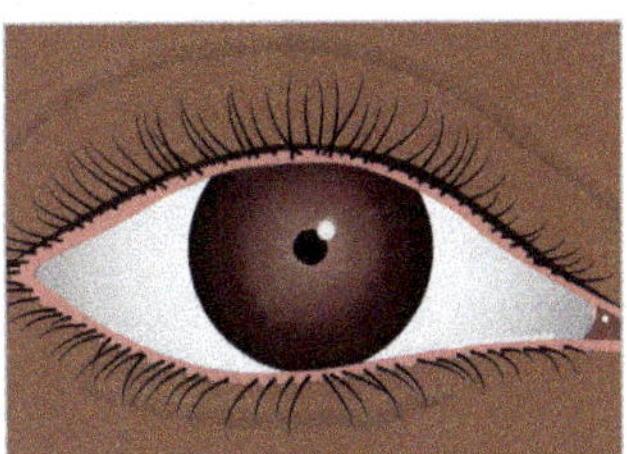

Figure 47 // Pinpoint pupil

The symptoms of a cholinergic toxidrome can be remembered as **DUMBBELLS**: **D**iarrhoea, **U**rination, **M**iosis, **B**radycardia, **B**ronchospasm/bronchorrhoea, **E**mesis, **L**acrimation, **L**ethargy, and **S**alivation

Sepsis

D Sepsis is a dysregulated response by the host to an infection, resulting in life-threatening organ failure (see Figure 48). A state of septic shock is caused by sepsis with hypotension and increased lactate concentration that does not respond to adequate fluid resuscitation and/or ionotropics. See Table 97 for the differences between sepsis, bacteraemia and SIRS.

E Incidence 437:100,000 per year

Ae
- Sepsis-causing infections listed by incidence: pulmonary infection (e.g. *pneumonia*), abdominal infection (e.g. *cholecystitis*), urogenital infection (e.g. *UTI*), skin infection (e.g. *cellulitis, erysipelas*), other (cardiovascular infection (e.g. *endocarditis*), neurological infection (e.g. *meningitis*), locomotor infection (e.g. *bacterial arthritis*), foreign body (e.g. line sepsis)
- Sepsis-causing micro-organisms listed by incidence: >50% gram-positive bacteria (e.g. *Staphylococcus pneumoniae, Staphylococcus aureus*), gram-negative bacteria (e.g. *Escherichia coli, Pseudomonas aeruginosa, Klebsiella pneumoniae*), anaerobic bacteria (e.g. *Bacteroides fragilis*), polymicrobial infections, fungi/yeasts (e.g. *Candida albicans*)

R Age >65, poor nutritional state, immune disorders (congenital/acquired/iatrogenic), DM, COPD, malignancy, chronic renal/hepatic insufficiency, complications after surgery, prolonged hospital admission, antibiotic resistance, travel to tropical destinations, foreign body

Hx Fever/hypothermia, general malaise, other symptoms depend on the micro-organism and the origin of the sepsis

PE HR ↑, RR ↑, T ↑, EMV ↓ (BP ↓, CRT >3 sec and oedema in the case of septic shock)

Dx
- The severity and likelihood of sepsis can be assessed quickly using the quick Sepsis-related Organ Failure Assessment (qSOFA) (see Table 96) and in detail using the SOFA (see Table 98). A qSOFA or SOFA ≥2 is suggestive for sepsis with a higher mortality
- Labs: WBC ↓/↑, CRP ↑, glucose ↑, ASAT ↑, ALAT ↑, bilirubin =/↑, PT =/↑, aPTT =/↑, thrombocytes ↓/=, creatinine =/↑
- Blood gas analysis: potentially metabolic acidosis, lactate =/↑
- Blood cultures (at least 2) preferably prior to AB, in the case of an IV catheter at least 1 culture from the catheter. Use a new catheter if the previous one has been used (e.g. for IV therapy).
- Focus examination based on Hx and PE: chest X-ray, urine sediment and urine culture, POCUS, also consider chest/abdominal CT, wound or sputum culture, cytogram preparation of cerebrospinal fluid (CSF), and drainage with culture of any collections
- ECG to rule out cardiac damage caused by sepsis and to monitor the cardiac function during the treatment of sepsis and potential shock situation by means of fluid resuscitation, vasopressors and ionotropics

Tx
- Source control: identify and eliminate sources of infection (e.g. drainage of abscesses, surgical resection of infected tissue)
- Monitor organ functions and glucose (<10 mmol/L), continue to monitor lactate if initial value was elevated
- Broad-spectrum AB (<3h in the ED and 1h in ICU) → switch to narrow-spectrum AB based on culture results
- If BP ↓ and lactate ↑: IV 30 mL/kg fluid in 30-60 min and starting vasopressors early, further administration based on vital signs

Ventilation (tidal volume 4-6 mL/kg) if necessary

P
- Mortality: 20-60% and is dependent on the micro-organism, the origin and the extent of complications (see Table 99)
- Immunocompromised patients and patients being treated with broad-spectrum AB are more likely to suffer sepsis caused by an (opportunistic) yeast/fungus and thus have a poorer prognosis

!
- Sepsis is the most common cause of death in hospitalised patients, with the mortality strongly correlated to the duration of AB administration
- The initial phase of sepsis can also be associated with leukopenia instead of leukocytosis
- BP ↓ is caused by vasodilation not hypovolaemia

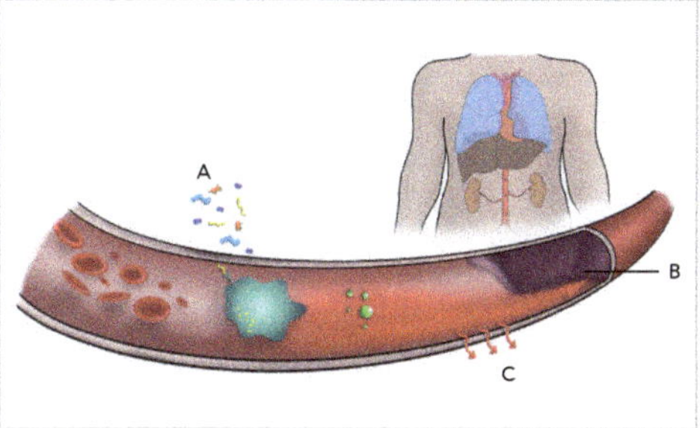

Figure 48 // Sepsis: pathophysiology and complications
A: Pathogens **B:** Disseminated intravascular coagulation **C:** Vasodilation and leakage

qSOFA CRITERIA	POINTS
RESP ≥22/MIN	1
EMF ↓	1
Systolic BP ≤100 mmHg	1

Table 96 // qSOFA score, positive ≥2

Instead of the qSOFA, the NEWS can also be used. The hospital often has its own variation of qSOFA or NEWS. Check your local protocol.

MECHANISM	MEANING	EXPLANATION
Sepsis	A dysregulated response by the host to an infection, resulting in life-threatening organ failure	A pathogen in the circulation (bacteraemia/viraemia/fungaemia) is not a prerequisite for sepsis. A dysregulated response with organ failure can also develop if pathogenic toxins enter the circulation instead of the pathogen itself.
Septic shock	Sepsis combined with hypotension and an elevated lactate concentration, non-responsive to adequate fluid administration and/or vasopressors	Elevated lactate as a symptom of hypoperfusion of the organs (lactate is produced during anaerobic metabolism under hypoxia). Sepsis with elevated lactate concentration and hypotension that responds well to fluid administration is not septic shock.
Bacteraemia/viraemia/fungaemia	Bacteria, viruses or fungi in the circulation	The dysregulated response that is so typical of sepsis is not always present in the case of bacteraemia, viraemia, fungaemia (e.g. in the case of immunodeficiencies, such as HIV or the failure of the immune system to recognise the pathogen)
Systemic inflammatory response syndrome (SIRS)	Predetermined criteria that increase the suspicion of sepsis (≥2): T >38°C/100.4°F or <36°C/96.8°F, HR >90/min, RR 20/min or $PaCO_2$ <32 mmHg, WBC <12,000/mm³ or >10% neutrophilic granulocytes	Non-specific for sepsis, e.g. positive for any pneumonia (fever and elevated RR) whilst every pneumonia is not automatically pneumosepsis. This is not even specific to infections, e.g. also positive in the case of lymphoma with fever and leukocytosis.

Table 97 // Differences between sepsis, septic shock, bacteraemia and SIRS

ORGAN SYSTEM	GRADE 0	GRADE 1
Neurological GCS	15	13-14
Respiratory PaO_2/FiO_2 (mmHg)	≥400	<400
Cardiovascular MAP (mmHg) or us of vasopressors (μg/kg/min)	MAP ≥70	MAP <70
Liver Bilirubin (μmol/L)	<20	20-32
Coagulation Thrombocytes (x10³/μL)	≥150	<150
Kidneys Creatinine (μmol/L) or urine output	<110	110-170

Table 98 // SOFA score (in ICU), also provides a representation of gradual loss of organ functions. Degree of loss of organ function (0 = no loss, 4 = very severe loss of function).

Toxic shock syndrome (TSS) is a form of sepsis with skin abnormalities, which is caused by exotoxins of Staphylococcus aureus or group A streptococcus. The variant caused by Staphylococcus aureus is associated with prolonged insertion of highly absorbent tampons. The streptococcal variant is associated with necrotising fasciitis. A characteristic feature of both variants is the shedding of skin from hands and feet after about 2 wk.

In the case of suspected sepsis, determine whether cultures have already been performed for the patient in question. Consider the resistance patterns of the detected micro-organisms when formulating your treatment (see the antibiogram for a suitable choice of treatment).

Due to the low number of circulating granulocytes, the localising signs of an infection, e.g. the infiltrate on a chest X-ray and redness/swelling caused by phlebitis, may be missing in patients with a neutropenic fever. Please be aware of this when interpreting your findings.

GRADE 2	GRADE 3	GRADE 4
10-12	6-9	<9
<300	<200 and mechanical ventilation	<100 and mechanical ventilation
Dopamine ≤5 or dobutamine (single dose)	Dopamine >5 or adrenaline ≤0.1 or noradrenaline ≤0.1	Dopamine >15 or adrenaline >0.1 or noradrenaline >0.1
33-101	102-204	>204
<100	<50	<20
171-299	300-440 or <500 mL/d	>440 or <200 mL/d

SEVERE COMPLICATIONS OF SEPSIS	MECHANISM	CONSEQUENCES
Disseminated Intravascular Coagulation (DIC)	Over-activity of the blood clotting system	• Hypoperfusion of organs due to obstructing thrombi • Severe bleeding due to a shortage of clotting factors resulting from increased use
Multi-organ failure (MOF)	Damage to organs caused by O_2 shortage	Loss of organ functions (see Table 98)
Acute Respiratory Distress Syndrome (ARDS)	Acute onset of widespread inflammation in the lungs, not due to cardiac causes	Triggering condition (e.g. sepsis, aspiration) → alveolar damage → toxic mediator release → further damage → bilateral pulmonary oedema and hypoxaemia
Waterhouse-Friderichsen Syndrome (WFS)	Acute haemorragic necrosis of the adrenal glands caused by disseminated intravascular coagulation in meningococcal sepsis	• Adrenal insufficiency → shortage of noradrenaline/adrenaline (RR ↓), aldosterone (RR ↓, sodium ↓, potassium ↑) and cortisol (glucose ↓) • Rapidly expanding petechiae and purpura

Table 99 // Severe complications of sepsis

Shock

D Shock is a state of inadequate tissue perfusion, resulting in a lack of aerobic metabolism in cells. Systemic consequences of this inadequate perfusion include metabolic acidosis, endothelial dysfunction and systemic inflammation. See Table 100 and Figure 49 for the various types of shock. See Table 101 for the various mechanisms of shock.

Despite experiencing thirst, patients who are in shock should not drink. Eating or drinking can result in aspiration and possibly increased blood flow to the gastro-intestinal system.

A "rapid infusion/fluid challenge" should be performed on patients with absolute or relative hypovolaemia and usually consists of administering 500 mL in 10-15 min or 1000 mL in 30 min. This can be repeated if the effect was favourable.

COMPLEMENTARY TREATMENT
• Platelet transfusion for severe bleeding, elevated risk of bleeding or thrombocytes <50x109/L → transfusion with plasma or administration of clotting factors concentrate for bleeding with prolonged PT and aPTT • Therapeutic dosing of heparin if thrombo-embolic complications are most prominent
Treat sepsis and optimise circulation
• Supportive care (supplemental O_2 or mechanical ventilation) • Treat underlying condition
Glucocorticosteroids IV with correction of electrolyte imbalances in the early phase (do not wait until vasopressors fail)

Other types of shock:

- **Neurogenic shock**: spinal cord injury above Th6 or a massive cerebral haemorrhage → combination of heart rate ↓, BP ↓ and warm, dry skin
- **Toxin-induced** or **intoxication-induced shock**: poisoning or drug overdose, clinical presentation is similar to septic shock in combination with the symptoms of drug overdose or poisoning
- **Endocrine shock**: mineral corticosteroid deficiency (including adrenal crisis) or myxoedema → life-threatening vasodilatation

The definition of **distributive shock** includes septic shock, anaphylactic shock, neurogenic shock, endocrine shock and toxin-induced or intoxication-induced shock.

In the case of hypovolaemic shock, also consider non-traumatic internal bleeding, such as gastro-intestinal bleeding, ruptured aorta or ectopic pregnancy.

	CARDIOGENIC	HYPOVOLAEMIC	OBSTRUCTIVE
D	Insufficient contractile strength of the heart.	Absolute shortage of circulating volume, hypoxaemia or anaemia.	Shutdown of the central part of the circulation.
E	16% of patients with shock	16% of patients with shock	2% of patients with shock
Ae	• Inadequate oxygenation at the cellular level → local cellular dysfunction → accumulation of lactate → metabolic acidosis • Destruction of cells → release of toxic metabolites → endothelial dysfunction • Destruction of cells → release of inflammatory mediators → systemic inflammation • Possibly compensated or combined • See Figure 50		
	Myocardial infarction, arrhythmias, valve abnormalities, trauma, HF (cardiomyopathy, myocarditis)	Bleeding traumatic/non-traumatic/post-OR, loss of plasma (including from burn wounds), loss of water or salts (including with hyperglycaemia)	Tamponade: caused by pericarditis/trauma/aortic dissection, constrictive pericarditis, restrictive cardiomyopathy, pulmonary embolism, tension pneumothorax, abdominal compartment syndrome
R	A history of infarction/arrhythmia, hypertension, hypercholesterolaemia, obesity, DM, RA, stress, positive FHx, coagulopathy	A history of bleeding, anticoagulation, aneurysm, elderly patients on diuretics, DM type 2 (hyperosmolar syndrome)	Depends on the underlying cause

Table 100A // Various types of shock

DISTRIBUTIVE			
Septic	**Anaphylactic**	**Neurogenic**	**Adrenal insufficiency**
Sepsis with hypotension and elevated lactate that does not respond to adequate volume administration and vasopressors.	IgE-mediated response to antigen.	Occurs when injury to the brain or spinal cord above the level of T6 disrupts autonomic nerves which leads to lower vascular resistance and vagal tone resulting in pooling of venous blood and hypotension.	A potentially life-threatening complication of chronic adrenal insufficiency.
66% of patients with shock (62% septic shock, 4% other forms of distributive shock)			
• Inadequate oxygenation at the cellular level → local cellular dysfunction → accumulation of lactate → metabolic acidosis • Destruction of cells → release of toxic metabolites → endothelial dysfunction • Destruction of cells → release of inflammatory mediators → systemic inflammation • Possibly compensated or combined • See Figure 50			
Infection: pulmonary, abdominal, urogenital, skin, cardiovascular, neurological, locomotor, line sepsis	Foods, medication, contrast, blood, insect bite, latex/rubber	Brain or spinal cord trauma (↔), spinal anaesthesia, Guillain-Barré syndrome, transverse myelitis, heavy metal toxins	Infection, surgery, trauma, childbirth, severe pain, severe psychological stress, inadequate intake/abrupt cessation of maintenance glucocorticoid therapy, immune checkpoint inhibitors
A history of sepsis, age >65, poor nutritional state, immune disorders (congenital/acquired/iatrogenic), DM, COPD, malignancy, chronic renal/hepatic insufficiency, complications after surgery, prolonged hospital admission, antibiotic resistance, travel to tropical destinations, foreign body	A history of anaphylaxis, known allergy, asthma, eczema, positive FHx	A history of traumatic spinal cord injuries above Th6	A history of infection, persistent vomiting and/or diarrhoea, surgery, physical pain, severe psychological stress, abrupt withdrawal of long-term glucocorticoids or not increasing the dosage of glucocorticoids during acute illness

<table>
<tr><th></th><th>CARDIOGENIC</th><th>HYPOVOLAEMIC</th><th>OBSTRUCTIVE</th></tr>
<tr><td>Hx</td><td>Depends on the cause, often associated with palpitations, retrosternal pain and/or dyspnoea</td><td>Depends on the cause, often associated with severe thirst</td><td>Depends on the cause, often associated with dyspnoea or chest pain</td></tr>
<tr><td rowspan="3">PE</td><td colspan="3">BP ↓, RR ↑, CRT delayed, GCS ↓, urine output ↓ (<0.5 mL/kg/h), see Figure 50</td></tr>
<tr><td rowspan="2">HR ↑, CVP =/↑, cardiac output (CO) ↓↓, peripheral vascular resistance (PVR) ↑↑, cold, pale, clammy skin, crepitations with pulmonary oedema, murmur with valve abnormalities, oedema of the legs with HF</td><td colspan="2">Heart rate ↑</td></tr>
<tr><td>CVP ↓, CO ↓, PVR ↑, cold, pale, clammy skin</td><td>CVP ↑, CO ↓↓, PVR ↑, paradoxical pulse (drop in systolic BP >10 mmHg during inhalation), signs of DVT, cold, pale, clammy skin</td></tr>
<tr><td rowspan="2">Dx</td><td colspan="3">• Labs (differentiate between various forms): troponine, CK-MB, clotting times, Hb, haematocrit, WBC, CRP, glucose, if applicable tryptase and complement factor C4
• Labs: lactate ↑, ASAT ↑, ALAT ↑, bilirubin =/↑, creatinine ↑, urea ↑
• Blood gas: metabolic acidosis with respiratory compensation</td></tr>
<tr><td>• Labs: troponine ↑, CK-MB ↑
• ECG (potential abnormalities): micro voltages, conduction block, ischaemia, frequency, rhythm (irregular)
• Chest X-ray: heart size, redistribution, heart shape
• Ultrasound: contractility of left ventricle ↓, pulmonary oedema, dilatation of vena cava, valve pathology</td><td>• Labs: cross match blood, Hb =/↓, HT =/↑, PT =/↑, aPTT =/↑, INR =/↑, thrombocytes =/↓, fibrinogen ↓, glucose =/↑
• Ultrasound: collapsing vena cava, free fluid in abdomen</td><td>Ultrasound: pneumothorax, tamponade, right ventricular volume overload (pulmonary embolism), dilatation of vena cava, DVT (pulmonary embolism)</td></tr>
<tr><td>Tx</td><td colspan="3">👁 (c)ABCDE stabilisation
✎ Adequate recovery of oxygenation following administration of O₂ and (non-)invasive ventilation, particularly recovery of tissue perfusion through recovery of cardiac output by means of administration of IV fluids (beware of pulmonary oedema when replacing fluids to treat cardiogenic shock) and consider support by means of ionotropics</td></tr>
</table>

Table 100B // Various types of shock

<table>
<tr><th colspan="4">DISTRIBUTIVE</th></tr>
<tr><th>Septic</th><th>Anaphylactic</th><th>Neurogenic</th><th>Adrenal insufficiency</th></tr>
<tr><td>Depends on the cause, often associated with general malaise and localising symptoms</td><td>To a greater or lesser extent: itching, nausea, vomiting, diarrhoea, rhinorrhoea, dyspnoea, hoarseness, coughing, palpitations, confusion, anxiety</td><td>High-energy trauma (HET) of cervical/thoracic spine, motor and sensory dysfunction, intoxication</td><td>Salt craving, general malaise, fatigue, anorexia, consciousness ↓, dizziness, nausea, vomiting, diarrhoea, abdominal pain, muscle/joint pain, T ↑</td></tr>
<tr><td colspan="2">BP ↓, RR ↑, CRT delayed, GCS ↓,
urine output ↓ (<0.5 mL/kg/h), see Figure 50</td><td rowspan="3">BP ↓, HR ↓, motor and sensory deficits, absent reflexes, neurogenic bladder, warm and dry skin</td><td rowspan="3">BP ↓, altered mental status, hyperpigmentation (from long standing adrenal insufficiency), T ↑, jugular venous distension (JVD) ↓, systemic vascular resistance (SVR) ↓, CO ↑/↓</td></tr>
<tr><td colspan="2">Heart rate ↑</td></tr>
<tr><td>CVP ↓, CO ↑, PVR ↓↓, T ↑/↓, warm, dry skin</td><td>CVP ↓, CO ↑, PVR ↓↓, stridor/wheezing, acute skin rash, vomiting, warm skin</td></tr>
<tr><td colspan="4">• Labs (differentiate between various forms): troponine, CK-MB, clotting times, Hb, haematocrit, WBC, CRP, glucose, if applicable tryptase and complement factor C4
• Labs: lactate ↑, ASAT ↑, ALAT ↑, bilirubin =/↑, creatinine ↑, urea ↑
• Blood gas: metabolic acidosis with respiratory compensation</td></tr>
<tr><td>• Labs: CRP ↑, WBC ↑/↓, thrombocytes ↑/↓, fibrinogen ↓, glucose ↑, PT ↑, aPTT ↑
• Blood cultures: detection of pathogen
• Ultrasound: focal examination, collapsing vena cava
• Further focal examination</td><td>• Labs as indicated: tryptase ↑, complement factor C4 ↑ with angio-oedema
• Ultrasound: source finding, collapsing vena cava</td><td>• Spinal CT: fractured vertebrae, possible dislocation, prevertebral soft tissue swelling
• CTA of the cervical arteries and circle of Willis: in case of a C-spine fracture or a fracture of the upper ribs, to exclude post-traumatic vascular injury (Denver criteria)</td><td>• Labs: glucose ↓, Na =/↓, K ↑
• Look for underlying trigger</td></tr>
<tr><td colspan="4">(c)ABCDE stabilisation
Adequate recovery of oxygenation following administration of O_2 and (non-)invasive ventilation, particularly recovery of tissue perfusion through recovery of cardiac output by means of administration of IV fluids (beware of pulmonary oedema when replacing fluids to treat cardiogenic shock) and consider support by means of ionotropics</td></tr>
</table>

<table>
<tr><th></th><th>CARDIOGENIC</th><th>HYPOVOLAEMIC</th><th>OBSTRUCTIVE</th></tr>
<tr><td>Tx</td><td>• Half-seated position
• Acetyl salicylic acid IV, heparin IV, nitro-glycerin sublingual or IV for myocardial infarction (NSTEMI/STEMI)
• Fluid replacement in case of right ventricle infarction. Be careful giving fluids in LAD infarction.
• Consider ionotropics (dobutamine)
Urgent PCI for STEMI</td><td>• Elevate legs (not for HET)
• Stem the blood loss
• Maintain normothermia due to coagulopathies
• Suspend anticoagulants
• Primarily administer heated blood products, followed by IV fluids (erythrocytes/thrombocytes/plasma)
• Tranexamic acid, fibrinogen and calcium supplementation for severe bleeding
• Consider vasopressors (beware of permissive hypotension if bleeding has not been stopped yet)
Consider surgery to stem blood loss</td><td>• Elevate legs (not for HET)
• Give patient fluids
• Consider vasopressors
• Treat underlying disease
• Pulmonary embolism: heparin, consider IVT
• Alleviate tension pneumothorax
• Tamponade: pericardiocentesis</td></tr>
<tr><td rowspan="2">P</td><td colspan="3">High mortality: 30% following ICU admission</td></tr>
<tr><td colspan="3">Depends on underlying disease</td></tr>
<tr><td rowspan="2">!</td><td colspan="3">• The longer the shock lasts, the worse the outcome will be
• Hypotension is a late sign of shock and often only occurs in haemorrhagic shock following ≥30% volume loss
• A patient with severe hypertension can be in a state of shock at a relatively normal BP (see Table 101)
• Progression to MOF</td></tr>
<tr><td>Possibly secondary to other form of shock</td><td>Hb and Ht values lag behind when patient is actively bleeding</td><td>Pulmonary embolism and pulmonary hypertension are the most common causes</td></tr>
</table>

Table 100C // Various types of shock

DISTRIBUTIVE			
Septic	**Anaphylactic**	**Neurogenic**	**Adrenal insufficiency**
• Elevate legs (not for HET) • Start broad spectrum AB immediately and/or drainage of abscess • Actively administer IV fluids • Vasopressors (adrenaline) • Low dose steroids, if fluids and vasopressors have no effect	• Half-seated position • Adrenaline IM, salbutamol nebuliser treatment, antihistamines IV, steroids IV • Fluids IV • Consider adrenaline IV • Consult allergist	• Cervical spine collar and immobilisation • Fluids IV • Vasopressors • Atropine, isoprenaline or external pacemaker for bradycardia Airway support and rapid sequence intubation if high cervical spine injury suspected	• Fluids IV (isotonic saline) • Treat underlying triggers • Hydrocortisone IV bolus followed by continuous IV hydrocortisone over 24h • AB for bacterial infection • Glucose IV for hypoglycaemia
High mortality: 30% following ICU admission			
30-50% mortality	Depends on the time between provocation and the shock	4-20% mortality after traumatic spinal cord injury	With prompt recognition and treatment of the underlying condition and IV fluids and glucocorticoids, the prognosis is good
• The longer the shock lasts, the worse the outcome will be • Hypotension is a late sign of shock and often only occurs in haemorrhagic shock following ≥30% volume loss • A patient with severe hypertension can be in a state of shock at a relatively normal BP (see Table 101) • Progression to MOF			
• Diffuse intravascular coagulation due to over-activity of the coagulation cascade • Phase of immunosuppression following excessive activation	Repeat adrenaline IM every 5 min if necessary	Can also be caused by massive cerebral haemorrhage	If there are any clinical suspicions of acute adrenal insufficiency, treat sooner rather than later

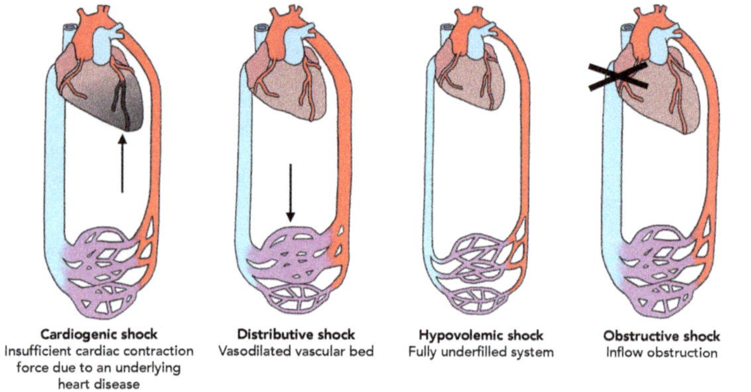

Figure 49 // Different types of shock

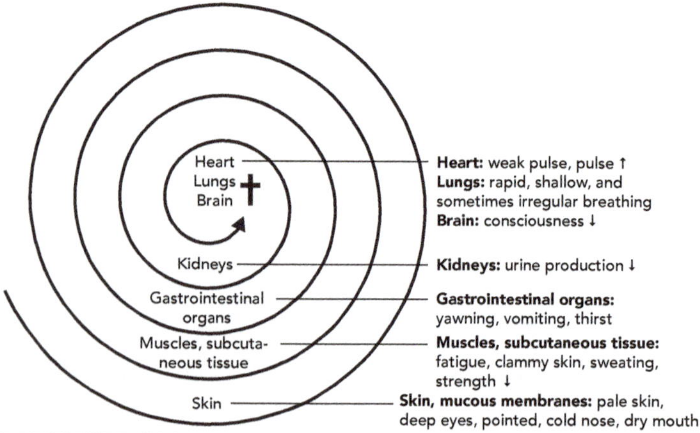

Figure 50 // Shock spiral: findings during physical examination in cases of deterioration due to shock.

Consider using one or more objective mass haemorrhage protocol triggers:

- Critical administration threshold: ≥3 RBC units in 1h
- Shock index: [HR/systolic BP] >1
- ABC score ≥2 (penetrating mechanism, systolic BP <90 mmHg, HR >120/min or positive e-FAST)
- Revised Assessment of Bleeding and Transfusion (RABT) score ≥2 (penetrating injury, shock index >1, positive e-FAST or pelvic fracture)

TYPE OF SHOCK	MEANING
Decompensated shock	Hypovolaemic shock → sympathetic nerve activity ↑ → heart rate ↑ and contractility ↑ + vasoconstriction → BP acceptable → cardiac output acceptable → adequate tissue perfusion maintained
Non-decompensated shock	Heart rate ↑ → O_2 consumption by myocardium ↑, coronary perfusion ↓ and ventricular filling ↓ → O_2 shortage in myocardium ↑ → myocardial function ↓ → severe vasoconstriction and hypovolaemia → tissue ischaemia → expansion of vasoactive mediators → change in contractility, vascular tone and cell damage → cell death
Combined shock	Bacteria, viruses or fungi in the circulation

Table 101 // Mechanisms of shock

CLASSIFICATION OF HAEMORRHAGIC SHOCK				
	I	**II**	**III**	**IV**
Blood loss (mL)	<750	750-1500	1500-2000	>2000
Blood loss (% blood volume)	<15	15-30	30-40	>40
Heart rate (per min)	<100	>100	>120	>140
Blood pressure (mmHg)	=	=	↓	↓
Pulse pressure	=/↑	↓	↓	↓
Respiratory rate (per min)	14-20	20-30	30-40	>35
Urine production (mL/h)	>30	20-30	5-15	Negligible
Central nervous system/mental status	Slightly anxious	Mildly anxious	Anxious, confused	Confused, lethargic

Table 102 // Classification of haemorrhagic shock based on quantity of blood loss

Transfusion complications

Immunological transfusion complications are caused by activation of the immune system following a transfusion and can vary widely in type and severity.

Erythrocytes

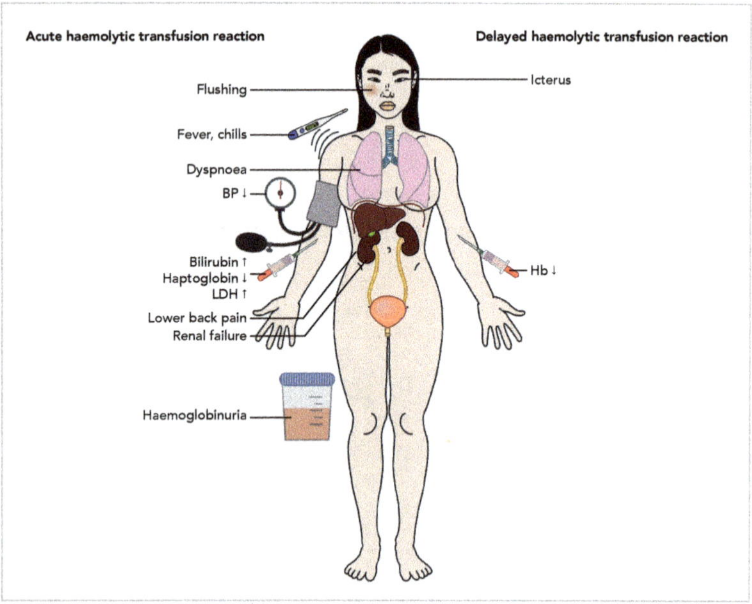

Figure 51 // Acute and delayed haemolytic transfusion reaction

COMPONENT	ACUTE HAEMOLYTIC TRANSFUSION REACTION	DELAYED HAEMOLYTIC TRANSFUSION REACTION
Incidence	1.4:100,000	14.3:17,160-100,000
Reaction	Within several minutes to hours	After 7-10
Pathophysiology	Primarily AB incompatibility, intravascular breakdown of erythrocytes due to complement activation via IgM	Extravascular breakdown due to the formation of IgG antibodies targeted against the donor's erythrocytes
Symptoms	See Figure 51	

Table 103 // Immunological transfusion complications with erythrocytes

Leukocytes and thrombocytes

COMPONENT	FEBRILE NON-HAEMOLYTIC TRANSFUSION REACTION	TRANSFUSION RELATED ACUTE LUNG INJURY (TRALI)	TRANSFUSION ASSOCIATED CIRCULATORY OVERLOAD (TACO)
Incidence	1-3%, most common transfusion reaction	20:100,000	1% of transfusions
Reaction	Body temperature increase 2°C/3.6°F occurs during or <2h after transfusion	<6h after transfusion, especially with plasma containing blood products	<6h, acute volume overload
Pathophysiology	Various causes, including: • Human leukocyte antigens (HLA) antibodies directed against transfused leukocytes • Passive administration of cytokines/chemokines	HLA and/or granulocyte specific antibodies or proinflammatory mediators in the transfused blood or plasma triggers increased capillary permeability, which causes exudative pulmonary oedema	Fluid overload causing increased pulmonary capillary pressure
Symptoms	Cold chills, flushing, HR ↑, without evidence of infection, haemolysis, or severe transfusion reaction	Acute respiratory distress, dyspnoea, fever, usually HR ↓, hypoxia, WBC ↓, thrombocytes ↓	Acute respiratory distress, dyspnoea, usually HR ↑, hypoxia, jugular vein distention (JVD) ↑, cough, BNP ↑, signs of volume overload

Table 104 // Transfusion complications with leukocytes and thrombocytes

TRALI is a potentially life-threatening transfusion complication with a mortality of at least 5-17%. The incidence of TRALI can be reduced by using pooled plasma.

Plasma proteins

COMPONENT	ALLERGIC TRANSFUSION REACTION	ANAPHYLACTIC TRANSFUSION REACTION
Incidence	1-3%	2: 40,000-100,000
Reaction	Within several minutes to hours	Within several seconds after starting or shortly after the end of the transfusion
Pathophysiology	Antibodies against plasma proteins	
Symptoms	Pruritus, redness, urticaria	Severe symptoms: airway obstruction, circulatory collapse, gastro-intestinal symptoms

Table 105 // Immunological transfusion complications with plasma proteins

Neurology

Traumatic disorders

Mild traumatic brain injury (TBI)

D Mild TBI is defined as an initial GCS score ≥13, post-traumatic anterograde amnesia <24h and post-traumatic loss of consciousness <30 min.

E 90% of all neurotraumas are mild TBIs

Ae
- Falls (++), traffic accidents (+), violence (−), sports (−), work (−)
- Depending on the type of trauma, diffuse or focal brain damage can occur: blow to the head (→ focal brain damage, see Table 106) and torsional motion (→ diffuse axonal injury (DAI) with minor cerebral capillary haemorrhage)

Hx Low-energy trauma, short-term consciousness ↓ (max. 30 min), post-traumatic amnesia (max. 24h), headache, nausea, vomiting, blurred vision, aversion to light (photophobia), aversion to sounds (phonophobia), tinnitus, hearing loss

PE GCS ≥13, disorientation, retrograde/anterograde amnesia, imprinting disorder, pupillary reflexes, focal neurological deficit, evidence of skull base fracture (spectacle haematoma, liquorrhoea, battle sign)

Dx Brain CT without contrast: cerebral contusion, SAH, subdural or epidural haematoma (see Table 67 for the indications for a brain CT)

Tx In-hospital observation if GCS <15, CT abnormalities, seizures, abnormal coagulation parameters, or neurological deficits

Conservative management (e.g. oral analgesics, antiemetics)

P Often full recovery within 7-10d (post concussion syndrome)

! Note that current diagnostic decision has a high sensitivity, but low specificity in order to also diagnose asymptomatic patients → 90-95% no intracranial injury

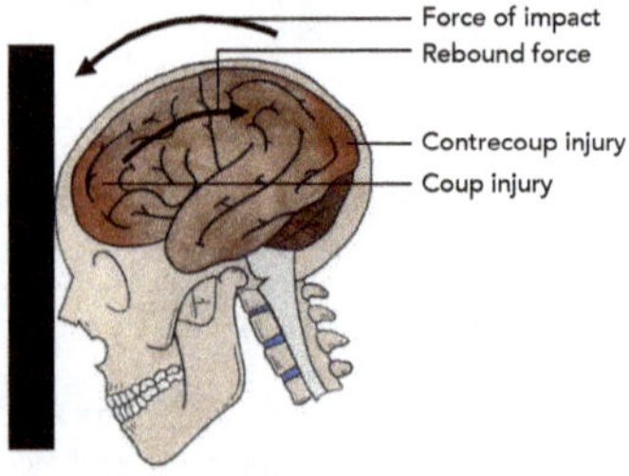

Figure 52 // Coup-contrecoup injuries

	COUP INJURY	CONTRECOUP INJURY
D	Mild traumatic brain injury at impact site.	Mild traumatic brain injury opposite impact site.
Ae	Direct impact from an object while stationary	Acceleration-deceleration mechanism (e.g. moving head colliding with a stationary object)
Hx	Consciousness ↓, headache, dizziness, amnesia, nausea, vomiting, loss of strength, visual disturbances, sensory disturbances, girdling across abdomen or chest, clear fluid from ear or nose	
PE	Focal neurological deficits, localised directly below contact surface (see Figure 52)	Focal neurological deficits, diagonally across from contact surface, often localised at base of the skull (see Figure 52)
Dx	Brain CT: assess cerebral contusion and intracranial haemorrhage	
Tx	Apply ATLS, regularly monitor pupillary responses and GCS score for first 12h, symptomatic: treat pain and nausea	
P	• Most patients recover <6 mo • Generally no residual symptoms • 50% of patients have persistent post concussion symptoms after 3 months • Mortality <1%	
!	Post concussion symptoms: headache, fatigue, dizziness, insomnia, concentration and memory impairment	

Table 106 // Traumatic brain injury: coup-contrecoup injuries

Moderate-severe TBI

D Moderate TBI is defined as a GCS score 9-12. Severe TBI is defined as GCS ≤8.

E 10% of all head injuries are moderate-severe TBIs

Ae Depending on the type of trauma, diffuse or focal brain damage can occur: blow to the head (→ focal brain damage) and torsional motion (→ DAI with minor cerebral capillary haemorrhage)

Hx High-energy trauma (HET), consciousness ↓, post-traumatic amnesia, seizures, headache, nausea, vomiting, blurred vision, photophobia, phonophobia, tinnitus, hearing loss

PE Hypertension, bradycardia, respiratory irregularities

GCS <13, disorientation, retrograde/anterograde amnesia, imprinting disorder, pupillary reflexes, focal neurological deficit, evidence of skull base fracture (spectacle haematoma, liquorrhoea, battle sign)

Dx
- Consider diagnostics as indicated per ATLS protocol (e.g. X-ray, e-FAST, lab)

- Brain CT: intraparenchymal and subarachnoid haemorrhage, haemorrhagic cerebral contusion, subdural/epidural haemorrhage, pinpoint haemorrhage (see Table 67 for the indications for a brain CT)
- Brain MRI: to rule out DAI (pinpoint haemorrhages)

Tx Apply ATLS, monitor vital signs, prevent secondary injury

Monitor and treat increased intracranial hypertension: osmotic agents IV (mannitol, hypertonic saline)

Consider neurosurgical intervention: hemicraniectomy

P Most patients recover <6 mo, 10% severely disabled (cognitive/motor), 3-5% vegetative state, mortality 33%

!
- Secondary cranial brain injury (subdural/epidural haematoma, focal oedema, herniation)
- Autonomic dysregulation (tachycardia, hypertension, tachypnoea, sweating, stretching cramps) in first days to weeks
- 3-5% post-traumatic epileptic seizures

Epidural haematoma

D An epidural haematoma is caused by bleeding from a meningeal artery between the skull and dura mater (see Figure 53).

E 8.2% of TBI

Ae HET, non-traumatic cause ⊖ (e.g. coagulopathy, vascular malformation, abscess, or surgical complication)

Hx Trauma mechanism, consciousness ↓ (with lucid interval), amnesia, headache, nausea, vomiting

PE Ipsilateral pupil dilation, pupils unreactive to light, seizures, contralateral hemiparesis

Dx Brain CT: convex (lens shaped) hyperdensity

Tx Surgical evacuation (emergent decompressive craniectomy or burr holes)

P Depending on severity, localisation, and time to intervention

!
- Frequently associated with skull fracture → infection risk
- Watch out for herniation!

> On a brain CT, a subdural haematoma may cross sutures. An epidural haematoma never crosses the sutures, as it is limited by the periosteal boundaries.

The period of time that the victim is lucid before lapsing into unconsciousness is also called the **lucid interval**.

Subdural haematoma (SDH)

	ACUTE	CHRONIC
D	Acute haemorrhage between the dura mater and arachnoid mater, mostly combined arterial/venous.	Chronic haemorrhage between the dura mater and arachnoid mater from bridging vein (see Figure 53)
E	In 10-20% of severe TBI	Incidence 1.7-20.6:100,000 per y
Ae	Trauma	Minor trauma (especially in the elderly and patients on oral anticoagulants)
R	Age 31-47, ♂, diffuse cerebral atrophy	Increased fall risk due to alcohol use disorder or old age, use of anticoagulants, old age (brain atrophy → vulnerable bridging veins that are more exposed → more likely to rupture after a minor blow, e.g. hitting head on kitchen cupboard)
Hx	Trauma, acute onset, consciousness ↓, headache, nausea, vomiting	No obvious trauma, insidious onset, initiative ↓, cognition ↓, drowsiness, confusion, behavioural changes, gradual neurological deficits, headache, incontinence
PE	Contralateral hemiparesis, consciousness ↓, increased intracranial pressure (anisocoria, cranial nerve palsy, ataxia, meningeal irritation, coma)	Insidious declining consciousness, focal neurological deficit
Dx	Brain CT: concave hyperdensity (see Figure 54)	
Tx	Wait-and-see for minor haemorrhage Reversal of anticoagulation, analgesics, antiemetics • Surgical decompression (e.g. burr hole drainage, decompressive craniectomy, or craniotomy) • Middle meningeal artery embolisation	
P	Mortality 50% (esp. in elderly >65y)	Mortality rate 0-32%
!	Watch out for herniation!	

Table 107 // Acute vs. chronic SDH

Subarachnoid haemorrhage (SAH)

	TRAUMATIC	NON-TRAUMATIC
D	Haemorrhage between the arachnoid mater and the pia mater (see Figures 53 and 55).	
E	More common than non-traumatic type	Incidence 6-7:100,000 per y
Ae	Trauma	Aneurysm rupture (85%), perimesencephalic haemorrhage (10%), other causes (5%)
R	N/A	Age 35-65, ♀, positive FHx, smoking, alcohol consumption, hypertension
Hx	• Asymptomatic (++) • Symptoms of mild traumatic head/brain injury: consciousness ↓, headache, nausea, vomiting	Thunderclap headache, 'popping' sensation, nausea, vomiting, prior physical exertion (25%)
PE	• Slight T ↑ Consciousness ↓, focal neurological deficits	
	Asymptomatic (++)	• BP ↑, hypoxaemia • Meningeal irritation several hours after onset • Fundoscopy: intraocular haemorrhage (Terson syndrome)
Dx	Brain CT: hyperdensity at the subarachnoid space, usually near a skull fracture or cerebral contusion (see Figure 53)	• Brain CT: hyperdensity at the subarachnoid space (often aneurysm near the circle of Willis) • LP: xanthochromia after 12h (if no CT <6h) • CTA: location of aneurysm
Tx	Apply ATLS Reversal of anticoagulation, analgesics, antiemetics Surgical treatment of additional intracranial damage upon indication	Bed rest Nimodipine to prevent ischaemia, analgesics Coil or clip aneurysm
P	Often benign, additional damage can impact the prognosis	Mortality 50%, 75% residual symptoms, high risk of recurrence without treatment
!	N/A	Watch out for secondary cerebral ischaemia, hydrocephalus, intracerebral haemorrhage, recurrent SAH

Table 108 // Traumatic vs. non-traumatic SAH

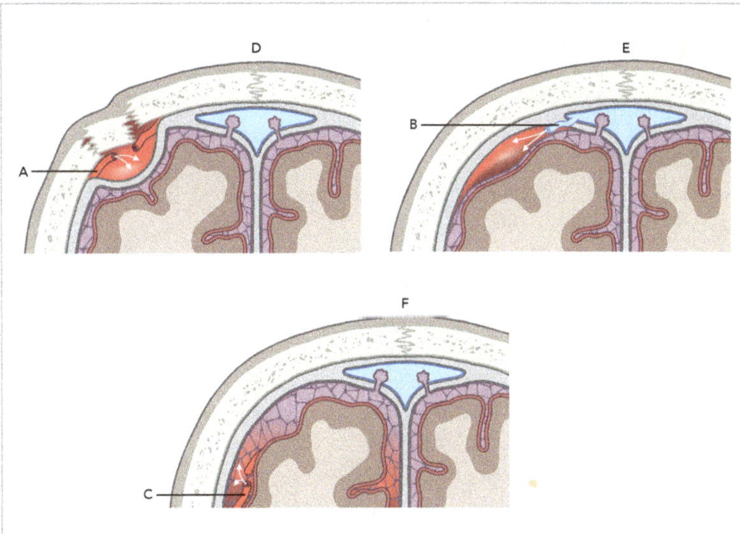

Figure 53 // Epidural and subdural haematoma and subarachnoid haemorrhage
A: Middle meningeal artery **B:** Bridging vein **C:** Cerebral artery **D:** Epidural haematoma **E:** Subdural haematoma **F:** Subarachnoid haemorrhage

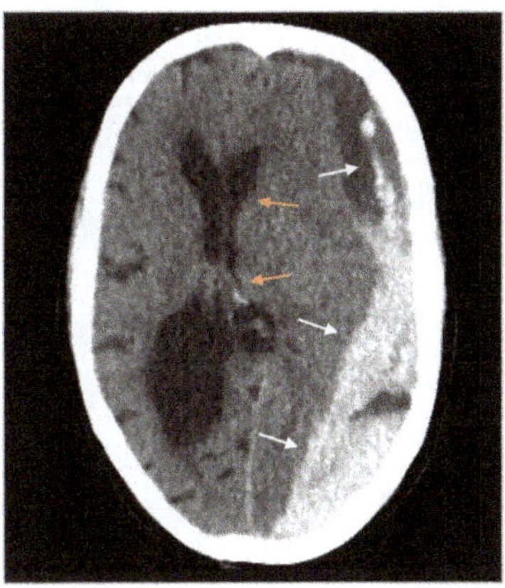

Figure 54 // Axial soft-tissue window setting: SDH along the left convexity (white arrows) with mass effect on the ventricular system (orange arrows). The acute component is hyperdense (white), the chronic component is hypodense (dark grey).

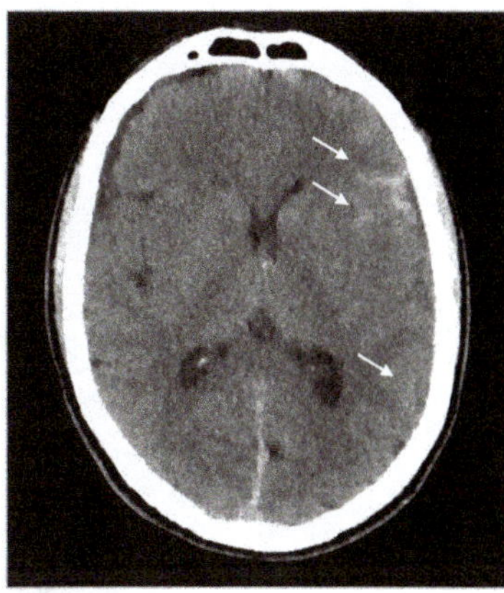

Figure 55 // Axial soft-tissue window setting: SAH with blood in the sulci (white arrows).

Skull base fracture

D In a skull base fracture, depending on the site of the fracture a distinction is made between anterior, middle and posterior skull base fractures (see Figure 57).

E Unknown

Ae Falls, HET

Hx Trauma mechanism, headache, nausea, vomiting, consciousness ↓

PE
- General: cranial nerve palsy
- Frontal skull base: nasal CSF leak, spectacle haematoma (see Figure 66)
- Middle skull base: auricular CSF leak, haematotympanum, facial nerve palsy, battle sign (see Figure 56)

Dx
- Brain CT, facial CT: visible fracture line, concomitant intracranial haemorrhage
- Nasal fluid leakage: test for β2-transferrin (positive if CSF)

Tx Apply ATLS, monitor vital signs, prevent secondary injury
Consider IV antibiotics (ABx)
Consider neurosurgical intervention in risk of herniation: hemicraniectomy

P Determined mainly by concomitant TBI, most patients recover <6 mo, 10% severely disabled (cognitive/motor), 3-5% vegetative state

! Watch out for meningitis, cerebral abscess, hearing loss, loss of smell (olfactory nerve damage), vision loss (optic nerve damage), concomitant intracranial injury (subdural/epidural haematoma, focal oedema, herniation)

Battle sign: haematoma behind the ear caused by haemorrhage in the mastoid.

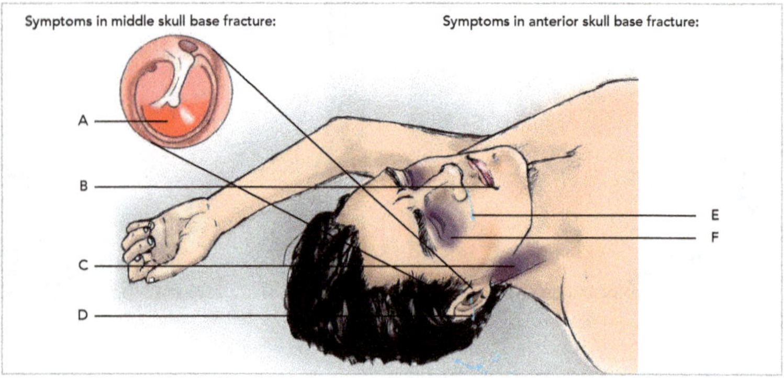

Figure 56 // Skull base fracture

A: Haematotympanum **B:** Facial nerve palsy **C:** Battle sign **D:** Auricular CSF leak **E:** Nasal CSF leak **F:** Spectacle haematoma (racoon eyes)

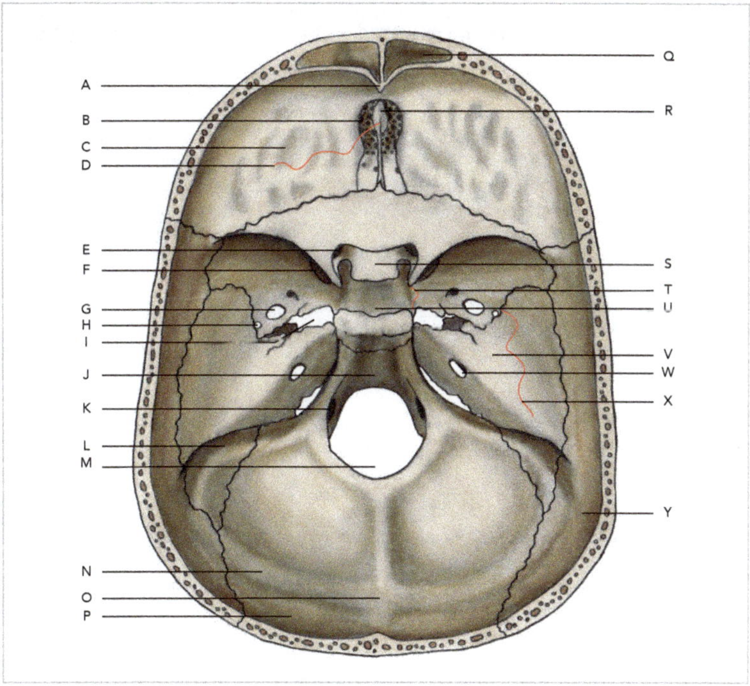

Figure 57 // Skull base fracture: types

A: Frontal crest **B:** Lamina cribrosa **C:** Frontal bone **D:** Fracture of the anterior cranial fossa **E:** Optic foramen **F:** Superior orbital fissure **G:** Foramen ovale **H:** Foramen spinosum **I:** Foramen lacerum **J:** Clivus **K:** Hypoglossal canal **L:** Groove for sigmoid sinus **M:** Foramen magnum **N:** Groove for transverse sinus **O:** Internal occipital protuberance **P:** Occipital bone **Q:** Frontal sinus **R:** Crista galli **S:** Tuberculum sellae **T:** Fracture of the sphenoid bone **U:** Sella turcica **V:** Temporal bone **W:** Internal auditory canal **X:** Fracture of the petrous part of the temporal bone **Y:** Parietal bone

Meningitis

	BACTERIAL MENINGITIS	VIRAL MENINGITIS
D	Rapidly progressing bacterial infection of the meninges with a high mortality rate.	Viral infection of the meninges usually characterised by a benign course and spontaneous recovery.
E	• Incidence Western countries: 0.7-3:100,000 per y • Incidence Sub-Saharan Africa: 0-40:100,000 per y	Incidence 3-15:100,000 per y

Table 109A // Bacterial and viral meningitis

<table>
<tr><th></th><th>BACTERIAL MENINGITIS</th><th>VIRAL MENINGITIS</th></tr>
<tr><td>Ae</td><td>• Haematogenous spread, direct contiguous spread from adjacent anatomic structures (e.g. otitis media, sinusitis), foreign objects, or after surgical procedure
• Newborns: Escherichia coli, group B streptococci, Listeria monocytogenes
• Children aged <5: Neisseria meningitidis, Streptococcus pneumoniae, Haemophilus influenzae
• Children aged >5 and adults: Streptococcus pneumoniae, Listeria monocytogenes, Neisseria meningitidis, Haemophilus influenzae, Staphylococcus aureus, TB
• Immunocompromised patients: Streptococcus pneumoniae, Neisseria meningitidis, Haemophilus influenzae, Listeria monocytogenes, Cryptococcus, TB, Nocardia</td><td>• HSV type 1 and 2, VZV, enteroviruses, parechovirus, measles, mumps, flaviviruses
• Immunocompromised patients: HIV, HSV type 2, CMV, VZV, EBV, enterovirus, arbovirus, JC virus</td></tr>
<tr><td>R</td><td>Age <5, DM, alcohol use disorder, immunodeficiency or use of immunosuppressants, recent cranial trauma, CSF leak, otitis, sinusitis or pneumonia, IV drug use</td><td>Seasonal variation (summer and fall: enterovirus, arbovirus, parechovirus), childhood</td></tr>
<tr><td>Hx</td><td>Rapid clinical deterioration, fever, headache, nausea (++), vomiting (++), photophobia (++), consciousness ↓</td><td>Nausea, vomiting, headache, generalised muscle pain, fever</td></tr>
<tr><td>PE</td><td>T ↑↑ (++), positive glass test: rash does not fade under pressure (see Figure 58)
• Meningeal irritation: neck stiffness, Kernig's and/or Brudzinski's sign
• Confusion, consciousness ↓, coma, neurological deficits, epileptic seizures, papilledema
• Meningococcal sepsis: petechiae (see Figure 58), purpura</td><td>T ↑, exanthema
• Meningeal irritation: neck stiffness (−)
• No loss of consciousness or neurological deficit</td></tr>
<tr><td rowspan="2">Dx</td><td colspan="2">• Labs: complete blood count, CRP ↑, glucose, electrolytes, kidney function, liver function
• LP: CSF culture and PCR, CSF analysis (see Table 110)
• Brain CT: before performing LP if there is potential intracranial pressure ↑ → risk of cerebellar/tonsillar herniation</td></tr>
<tr><td>• Labs: coagulation (if signs of petechiae or purpura)
• Blood culture</td><td>• Labs: serology</td></tr>
<tr><td>Tx</td><td>• Dexamethasone IV before administering AB (mortality and morbidity of pneumococcal meningitis ↓)
• AB IV, select AB based on age and presence of risk factors
• Targeted AB based on culture results
• Meningococcal meningitis: reportable, isolation, start close contacts on prophylactic treatment (rifampicin or ciprofloxacin)</td><td>Symptomatic
For suspected herpes virus: aciclovir IV</td></tr>
</table>

Table 109B // Bacterial and viral meningitis

	BACTERIAL MENINGITIS	VIRAL MENINGITIS
P	• Depends mainly on time until start of treatment • Subacute (++), rapidly progressive • Mortality of meningococcal meningitis 4-7%, mortality of pneumococcal meningitis 20-30% • Residual symptoms: hearing loss, cognitive decline, sluggishness	• Spontaneous recovery within 1-2 wk • Long-term symptoms: anxiety, depression, neurocognitive dysfunction
!	• Watch out for sepsis and respiratory failure • Anticipate acute hydrocephalus and cerebral oedema	Mumps meningitis: parotitis, orchitis

Table 109C // Bacterial and viral meningitis

The typical patient with bacterial meningitis is ill and presents with a high fever, headache, photophobia and vomiting that arose within a day. Patients usually present with decreased consciousness and meningeal irritation.

CSF PARAMETER	BACTERIAL MENINGITIS	VIRAL MENINGITIS
Pressure	↑	=/↑
Cells	↑↑	↑
Protein	↑	=/↑
Glucose	↓ (<60% of blood glucose)	=
Colour	Cloudy, purulent	Bright, opalescent

Table 110 // CSF-based differentiation between bacterial and viral meningitis

In case of suspected bacterial meningitis, start dexamethasone and AB immediately after taking blood cultures. Before performing an LP perform a CT if necessary.

- In patients with history of CNS disease, new onset seizure, focal neurological deficits, immunocompromised state, moderate to severe impaired consciousness or papilloedema, perform brain CT to rule out displacement of intracranial structures before performing LP.
- LP may lead to herniation if internal structures have been displaced.
- CN III and CN VI palsy is suggestive of increased intracranial pressure.

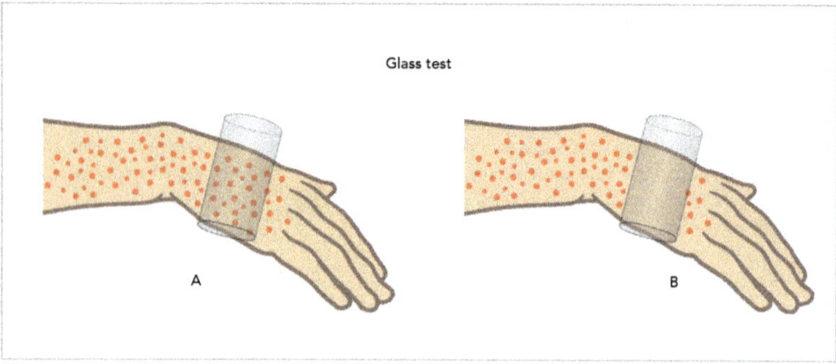

Figure 58 // Glass test: if the rash does not fade under pressure, the patient has petechiae. This may indicate meningococcal meningitis or sepsis.
A: Rash does not fade under pressure: petechiae **B:** Rash fades under pressure: not petechiae

Viral encephalitis

D Viral encephalitis is a subacute viral inflammation of the brain.

E Incidence: 19.3:100,000 per year, Western countries < South Asia and Sub-Saharan Africa

Ae
- Herpes simplex virus (HSV) type I, Varicella Zoster Virus (VZV), arboviruses, rabies virus, EBV, measles, mumps
- Immunocompromised patients: HSV, VZV, arboviruses, CMV, human herpesvirus 6 (HHV-6)

R Immunocompromised, unvaccinated

Hx
- Malaise, fever, headache, nausea, vomiting, photophobia, seizures, focal neurological deficits
- Specific finding in herpes simplex encephalitis: personality changes, hallucinations, cognitive impairment and word-retrieval difficulty, fever, epilepsy, paresis

PE
- T ↑

Consciousness ↓ ⊝, focal neurological deficits ⊝, seizures ⊝

- Lumbar puncture (LP): CSF pleocytosis, PCR, CSF culture
- Brain MRI: T2 hyperintensity of affected cortex and white matter

Tx Symptomatic

For suspected herpes virus: aciclovir IV

P Course varies from mildly to rapidly progressive with mortality or residual symptoms

! Herpes simplex encephalitis mortality 60-70% (untreated)

Epileptic disorders

Generalised onset seizures

D In generalised onset seizures, seizure activity starts simultaneously over both sides of the brain. Types of primary generalised seizures are absences, myoclonic, atonic, tonic, and tonic–clonic seizures (see Table 111).

E Prevalence 65 million patients worldwide with epilepsy, lifetime prevalence generalised onset seizures 7.6 per 1,000 persons

Ae
- Genetic predisposition, intoxications or alcohol withdrawal
- Na^+ and Ca^{2+} ion channel dysfunction → overexcitable neurons → electrical discharge in the brain

R Positive FHx, prematurity

	TONIC-CLONIC SEIZURES	ABSENCE SEIZURES
D	Epileptic seizure beginning with tonic muscle contractions followed by rhythmic twitches (see Figure 59).	Brief, frequent attacks of impaired consciousness that the patient cannot remember afterwards (see Figure 60).
E	25% of all epilepsy patients	Prevalence 6.3-8:100,000
Ae	Genetic predisposition	Genetic predisposition
	Intoxications or alcohol withdrawal	
R	• Age of onset 3-25 • Alcohol use disorder • Seizure triggers: e.g. missed medication, alcohol, drugs, fever, sleep deprivation, flashing lights, stress	Age of onset 3-10, ♀
Hx	• Emotional distress in hours or days preceding seizure • Epigastric rising sensation, sensory perceptions (sound, flashes of light, smell of burnt rubber), anxiety or derealisation may precede aura • More commonly: acute onset without warning signs and occasional scream (chest muscle and diaphragm contraction) • Tonic phase with bilateral muscle contractions (stiffening) and loss of consciousness (typically 10-30 sec) • Clonic phase with bilateral twitches or jerking and open eyes (typically 30-60 sec) • Postictal somnolence, confusion, agitation • Average seizure duration 2-3 min	• Seizures lasting 5-10 sec with acute impaired consciousness, blinking, absent gaze, lack of reactions, no memory of seizure, may be provoked by hyperventilation • Atypical seizures: longer seizures with gradual onset and end, with possible muscle tone change in the extremities
PE	Postictal confusion, lateral tongue bite, Todd paresis, urinary incontinence	Normal neurological exam

Table 111A // Two most common types of generalised onset epileptic seizures

	TONIC-CLONIC SEIZURES	ABSENCE SEIZURES
Dx	• EEG: generalised spikes and spike waves during seizure, normal or sporadic spikes and spike waves between seizures • Brain CT: to rule out large focal anomalies in an emergency setting • Brain MRI: to rule out underlying pathology in non-acute setting	• EEG: generalised 3 Hz spike waves during seizure, elicited by hyper-ventilation, flashing lights, fatigue • Brain MRI: to rule out underlying pathology
Tx	Treat or avoid seizure triggers Valproic acid, lamotrigine or levetiracetam	Ethosuximide, valproic acid or lamotrigine
P	±70% of adults are seizure-free within 20y	• 75% spontaneous remission <20y after disease onset • <10% develop tonic-clonic seizures
!	• Injuries, status epilepticus • If age of onset >25 → suspected focal to bilateral tonic clonic seizure with underlying cause • Sudden unexpected death in epilepsy (SUDEP)	• Later age of onset → greater risk of tonic-clonic seizures • Impact on school performance

Table 111B // Two most common types of generalised onset epileptic seizures

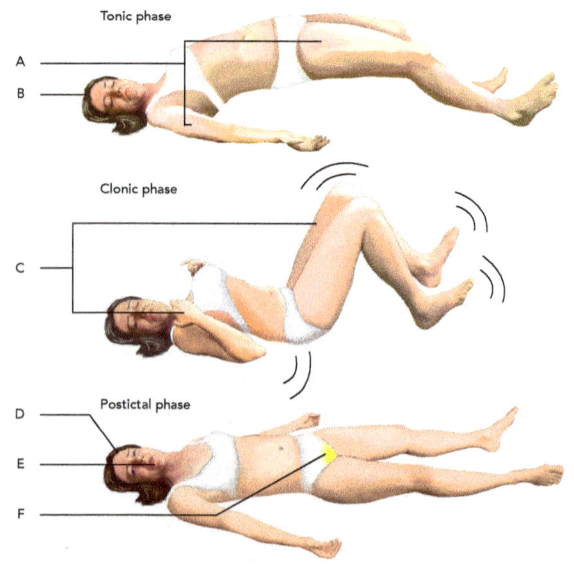

Figure 59 // Generalised onset epileptic seizure: tonic-clonic
A: Bilateral and symmetrical muscle contractions **B:** Loss of consciousness **C:** Bilateral and symmetrical clonic muscle contractions **D:** Confusion **E:** Lateral tongue bite **F:** Urinary incontinence

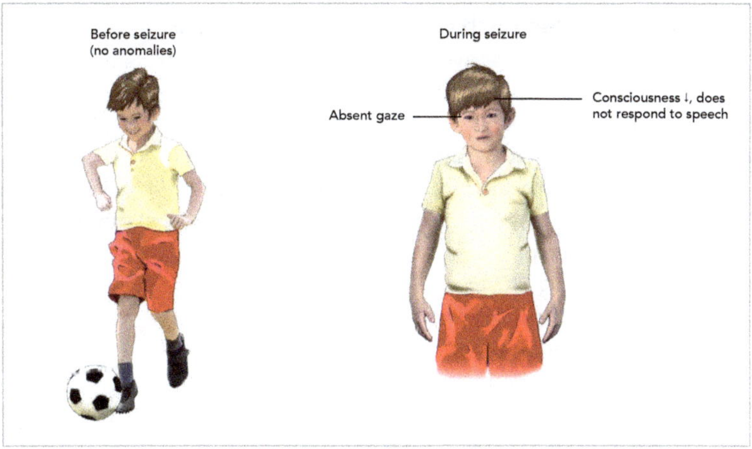

Figure 60 // Generalised onset epileptic seizure: absence seizure

Status epilepticus

D A generalised convulsive status epilepticus is a generalised onset epileptic seizure lasting >5 min or multiple seizures without recovery of consciousness, and total duration >5 min. A focal status epilepticus lasts >30 min.

E Incidence 1.3-81:100,000 per year

Ae Any cause leading to an epileptic seizure

R Tonic-clonic seizures, structural brain abnormality, alcohol, stress, infection, drugs, sleep deprivation

Hx
- Like epileptic seizures, but continuous or recurrent
- Loss of consciousness >5 min

PE Depends on type of epilepsy

Dx Ictal EEG: generalised spikes and spike waves

Tx
1. Seizure >5 min: midazolam or lorazepam
2. Not effective >5 min: repeat midazolam or lorazepam
3. Not effective >5 min: high dose antiseizure medication IV (e.g. phenytoin, levetiracetam, or valproic acid)
4. Not effective <20 min: midazolam, propofol, or thiopental IV (often in ICU)

P Mortality 3-50%

I Watch out for aspiration pneumonia, cardiac complications, cerebral oedema due to anoxia

Focal seizures with preserved awareness

D Focal seizures with preserved awareness are caused by acute and synchronous firing of cerebral neurons in one part of one hemisphere. No loss of consciousness occurs.

E Prevalence 65 million patients worldwide with epilepsy

Ae Metabolic disturbances (metabolic seizures) or structural brain abnormalities: trauma, tumour, infection, congenital, vascular malformation, stroke

R
- Adults > children
- Seizure triggers: e.g. missed medication, alcohol, drugs, fever, sleep deprivation, flashing lights, stress

Hx Depends on localisation (see Table 112)

PE Preserved consciousness, Todd paresis

Dx
- MRI to rule out structural cerebral abnormalities
- Ictal EEG: focal epileptic discharges

Tx Treat underlying cause, treat or avoid seizure triggers

Antiseizure medication (e.g. carbamazepine, lacosamide, lamotrigine, levetiracetam, oxcarbazepine, valproic acid)

Consider surgical removal of seizure focus

P Depends on underlying aetiology. High recurrence risk if unknown aetiology.

! Focal to bilateral tonic-clonic seizures, focal status epilepticus

Todd paresis: temporary paresis (<1d) after an epileptic seizure.

	PRECENTRAL CORTEX	SUPPLEMENTARY MOTOR CORTEX	FRONTAL CORTEX
D	Also known as Jacksonian seizures.	Also known as adversive seizures.	N/A
E	Unknown		
Hx	• Start in finger or mouth • Spread to hand, arm, ipsilateral trunk and occasionally to the leg in 20-30 sec	• Jerky turning of the head, eyes and trunk • Speech arrest	• Automatisms, especially of the lower extremities (cycling or walking movements) • Often while sleeping

Table 112A // Localisation of focal epilepsy

	PARIETAL CORTEX	OCCIPITAL CORTEX	TEMPORAL CORTEX
D	N/A		
E	Rare		Most common
Hx	Sensory seizures (paraesthesias) that may spread to adjacent parts of the body or progress to motor symptoms	Visual symptoms (distortions and colours) in visual field contralateral to the focus	• Auditory, olfactory or gustatory hallucinations • Autonomic symptoms • Cognitive symptoms (déjà vu or jamais vu: anxiety attacks)

Table 112B // Localisation of focal epilepsy

Focal seizures with impaired awareness

D Focal seizures with impaired awareness occur when the initial focal epileptic discharge spreads across multiple lobes of the brain, resulting in decreased awareness.

E 36% of all epilepsy patients

Ae Structural brain abnormality (temporal ⊕⊕, frontal ⊕, parietal ⊖, occipital ⊖): trauma, tumour, infection, congenital, vascular malformation, stroke, metabolic disturbances

R
- Adolescence, hippocampal sclerosis, CNS infection, AVM, tumour
- Seizure triggers: e.g. missed medication, alcohol, drugs, fever, sleep deprivation, flashing lights, stress

Hx
- Aura (epigastric rising sensation, visual symptoms, olfactory symptoms, derealisation/déjà vu)
- Followed by consciousness ↓ with routine actions such as chewing, lip smacking, dressing
- Absent impression
- Presence of a seizure trigger (e.g. sleep deprivation)
- Frequent generalised seizures during sleep

PE Short-term postictal confusion, Todd paresis

Dx
- MRI to rule out structural cerebral abnormalities
- Ictal EEG: unilateral or bilateral paroxysms

Tx Treat underlying cause, treat or avoid seizure triggers

Antiseizure medication (e.g. carbamazepine, lacosamide, lamotrigine, levetiracetam, oxcarbazepine, valproic acid)

Consider surgical removal of seizure focus

P
- Depends on underlying aetiology. High recurrence risk if unknown aetiology.

- If hippocampal sclerosis → progressive epilepsy that becomes therapy-resistant

!
- Injuries and aspiration during a seizure
- SUDEP
- Focal to bilateral tonic-clonic seizures, focal status epilepticus

> The typical patient with an epileptic seizure presents with shaking and jerking symptoms, a lateral tongue bite, urinary incontinence and postictal confusion.

> See the Pocket *Neurology* for more information on neurological disorders.

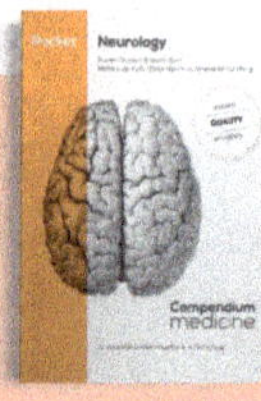

Cerebrovascular disease

Haemorrhagic stroke

D A haemorrhagic stroke includes bleeding from one of the intracranial blood vessels. Haemorrhagic strokes are less common than ischaemic strokes (ratio 1:4).

E Incidence 25:100,000 per year

Ae
- Vessel malformation, cerebral amyloid angiopathy (CAA), aneurysm, trauma, tumour → lobar haemorrhage → brain tissue compression → symptoms (see Figure 68 and 69)
- Chronic hypertension → weaker small vessels → basal ganglia haemorrhage (see Figure 69)

R Advanced age, hypertension, use of anticoagulants, coagulation disorders, CVT, presence of tumour/metastases, cocaine/amphetamine use (→ BP ↑), dark skin, Asian descent

Hx Signs of motor, sensory and other neurological deficits, headache, nausea, vomiting, neck stiffness, consciousness ↓

PE
- BP ↑
- Focal neurological deficit depending on localisation

Dx
- Brain CT: hyperdense lesion, hypodense oedema
- CTA intracranial arteries: detect aneurysm or vascular malformation

- Brain MRI: CAA (cerebral microbleeds, superficial siderosis), tumour
- Labs: coagulation disorder
- Consider LP in SAH: presence of xanthochromia (see Table 108)

Tx Admit to Stroke Unit, monitor vital signs, prevent complications

Treat underlying cause (lower BP, reversal of anticoagulation)

- Brainstem herniation/compression: emergency surgical evacuation of haematoma
- AVM: surgical removal, embolisation, stereotactic radiotherapy
- Aneurysm: clip or coil

P
- Depends on aetiology, size and localisation
- Mortality high in first few days

> The typical patient with haemorrhagic stroke presents with acute onset focal neurological deficits suggestive of the site of the haemorrhage. In severe cases, the patient presents with symptoms of increased intracranial pressure and decreased consciousness.

Ischaemic stroke

D An ischaemic stroke is localised ischaemia of part of the brain, caused by vascular occlusion leading to neurological deficit. Ischaemic strokes are more common than cerebral haemorrhagic strokes (ratio 4:1). In a TIA, the deficit disappears within 24 hours. A TIA usually lasts several minutes to hours.

E Incidence 98.6:100,000 per year

Ae Atherosclerosis with thrombus formation (intracranial or extracranial), carotid stenosis, cardiac source of embolism (AF, prosthetic valve, endocarditis), arterial dissection, coagulation disorder, vasculitis, malignancy (see Figure 62)

R Hypertension, smoking, cardiovascular diseases (esp. AF and MI), DM, hyperlipidaemia, obesity, advanced age, ♂, bedridden, positive FHx, previous ischaemic stroke

Hx Sudden onset neurological deficits (e.g. motor, sensory, aphasia, vertigo) depending on the stroke territory (see Table 113), headache, usually not progressive

PE
- BP ↑, RR ↓/=
- Neurological deficits depending on supply region (see Table 113 and Figure 61)
- Score according to NIH Stroke Scale

Dx
- Labs (exploratory): whole blood count, INR, aPTT, PT, kidney function, elec-

trolytes, blood lipids (total cholesterol, LDL, HDL, triglycerides), glucose

- Brain CT without contrast: exclude haemorrhage, ischaemic area (hypodense area (see Figure 63) with loss of gray-white matter differentiation (visible after several hours), dense vessel sign ⊖)
- CTA and CTP (onset <24h): intra-arterial occlusion, infarct core and/or ischaemic penumbra, significant carotid stenosis
- Brain MRI: ischaemia (restriction of diffusion on Diffusion-weighted imaging/Apparent diffusion coefficient (DWI/ADC))
- Carotid duplex ultrasound: significant carotid stenosis
- Cardiac embolism evaluation: ECG and 24h cardiac monitoring (detect e.g. AF), echocardiography, ambulatory Holter monitoring

Tx
- Admit to Stroke Unit, monitor vital signs, prevent complications, treat underlying cause
- Secondary prevention: lifestyle interventions

Physiotherapy, speech therapy, occupational therapy

- IVT (rtPA, e.g. alteplase)
  - Onset <4.5h and no contraindications (see Table 114)
  - Onset between 4.5h and 12h, no contraindications and favourable characteristics on CTP (core-penumbra mismatch) or brain MRI (DWI-FLAIR mismatch)
  - Secondary prevention: platelet aggregation inhibitor, statin, antihypertensives and (in case of immobility) LMWH

- Intra-arterial/mechanical thrombectomy:
  - Onset <6h and confirmed and approachable thrombus location what may be as distal as the M3/M4 segment of the middle cerebral artery, or the anterior cerebral artery or posterior cerebral artery
  - Onset between 6h and 24h, confirmed and treatable intra-arterial large vessel occlusion and favourable characteristics on CTP (core-penumbra mismatch) or MRI-brain (DWI-FLAIR mismatch)
- In case of intracranial herniation (malignant middle cerebral artery infarction): hemicraniectomy
- Significant carotid artery stenosis (>50%): carotid endarterectomy <2 wk

P
- Mortality <1 mo: 13.5%, due to herniation, infections (especially pneumonia), cardiac sources
- Most recovery occurs <3 mo

! Complications: post IVT haemorrhage, aspiration pneumonia, malignant middle cerebral artery infarction

The exact time window for extended IVT and mechanical thrombectomy may vary between countries.

Similar to a CTA and CTP, an MRI may be used to diagnose recent ischaemia. An MRI shows a DWI-FLAIR mismatch: a visible lesion on DWI, without a visible lesion on the FLAIR sequence.

The typical patient with ischaemic stroke is known to have cardiovascular risk factors and presents with acute onset hemiparesis, visual field defect and/or aphasia suggestive of the site of the occlusion.

Wallenberg's syndrome arises from a ischaemic stroke in the lateral part of the medulla oblongata. The syndrome often starts with sudden vertigo, vomiting, dysphagia, nystagmus, dysphonia and hiccups. Further symptoms are highly dependent on the affected structures.

OCCURENCE	ANTERIOR CEREBRAL ARTERY	MIDDLE CEREBRAL ARTERY	POSTERIOR CEREBRAL ARTERY	BASILAR ARTERY
++	Contralateral hemiparesis, leg > arm	Contralateral hemiparesis, contralateral central facial paresis, sensibility deficits deep > superficial	Homonymous hemianopsia	Tetraparesis, pseudobulbar paresis, horizontal gaze palsy, vertigo, nausea, nystagmus
+	Cognitive problems, frontal symptoms	Spasticity, ipsilateral head and gaze deviation, aphasia if located in language area, neglect if located in parietal lobe (right > left)	Behavioural disorders, memory disorders	Ataxia, consciousness ↓, irregular breathing if reticular formation is affected
−	Disorientation or apathy	N/A	Bilateral infarction → visual agnosia	Locked-in syndrome, Wallenberg's syndrome

Table 113 // Neurological deficits by supply region

Locked-in syndrome is a severe paralytic condition in which patients can only voluntarily perform vertical eye movements. However, they are not in a coma and are aware of their surroundings.

CONTRAINDICATIONS FOR IV THROMBOLYSIS

- Coagulopathy (platelet count <100,000/mm³, INR >1.7, aPTT >40 sec, or PT >15 sec, use of VKA, DOAC, therapeutic LMWH or heparin)
- Acute intracranial haemorrhage
- History of intracranial haemorrhage
- Acute head trauma
- Severe head trauma <3 mo
- Prior ischaemic stroke <3 mo
- Intracranial neoplasm
- GI malignancy or recent GI bleeding event <21d
- Intracranial/intraspinal surgery <3 mo
- Glucose <2.7 mmol/L
- (Suspected) infectious endocarditis
- Aortic dissection
- Blood pressure systolic ≥185 mmHg or diastolic ≥110 mmHg

Table 114 // Contraindications IV thrombolysis

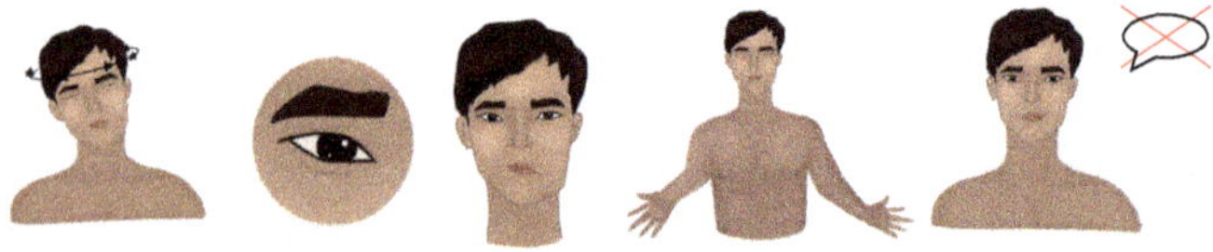

B: Balance: Sudden loss of balance?
E: Eyes: Sudden loss of vision?
F: Face: Facial asymmetry? Drooping mouth?
A: Arms: Can the patient raise both arms?
S: Speech: Incoherent or incomprehensible speech?
T: Time: Note what time the symptoms started and call the emergency line!

Figure 61 // BE-FAST rule

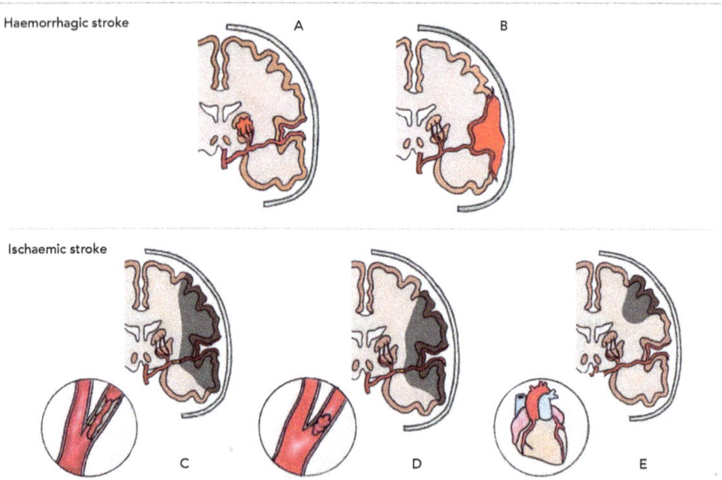

Figure 62 // Stroke: pathology
A: Basal ganglia haemorrhage **B:** Lobar haemorrhage **C:** Ischaemic stroke caused by thrombus **D:** Ischaemic stroke caused by embolus **E:** Ischaemic stroke caused by watershed infarctions

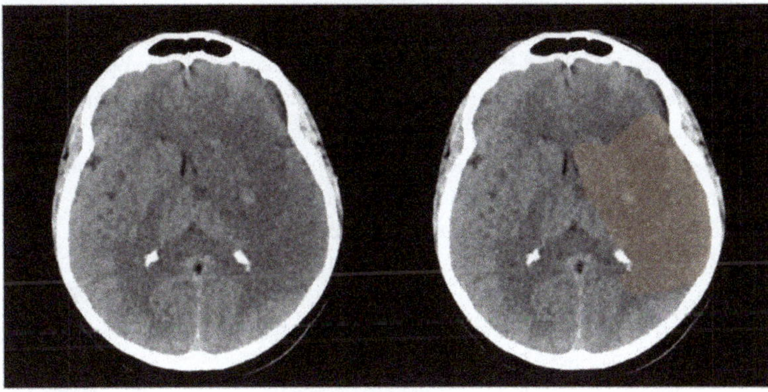

Figure 63 // CT showing hypodense area in left hemisphere consistent with ischaemic stroke

Delirium

D Delirium is a clinical syndrome marked by reduced attention and awareness, often resulting from a medical condition, substance use or medical side effects. Key features include rapid onset and fluctuating symptoms, cognitive disturbances, and the absence of a better explanation from neurocognitive disorders. Delirium can be divided into three categories: hyperactive, silent or mixed.

E 70-85% of all critically ill patients, ±30% of older patients during hospitalisation

Ae
- Acute diffuse cerebral dysregulation caused by organic disease → including infection, fever, dehydration, electrolyte imbalances, cerebral hypoxia, renal and hepatic function abnormalities, epileptic seizure, intracranial conditions, endocrine abnormalities, medication, intoxication, withdrawal
- Organic factors contribute via various pathways to the dysregulation of primarily the dopamine and acetylcholine pathway

R
- Predisposing factors (factors that make a patient more susceptible): age >70, ♂, brain damage (e.g. dementia, post-stroke), previous delirium, thyroid disorders, vision and hearing impairments, functional limitations, alcohol use disorder, multimorbidity
- Precipitating factors (triggering factors): dehydration, electrolyte disturbances, infections, fever, toxicity (medication side effects in 39% of cases, drugs, alcohol), withdrawal, circulation problems (hypotension, shock, HF), surgery, constipation, urinary retention, ICU admission

Hx Symptoms fluctuate throughout the day, insomnia at night and drowsiness during the day, vivid dreams or nightmares, hallucinations, brief spells of disorientation, difficulty thinking (concentrating), restlessness, anxiety or agitation, hypersensitive to stimuli, quiet, withdrawn, or emotional

PE Examination for underlying cause: including urinary retention, neurological deficits, signs that indicate an external injury (e.g. a fracture)

Psychiatric evaluation: changes in consciousness, attention ↓, difficulties with orientation, psychomotor agitation, apathy or lethargy (psychomotor agitation is consistent with hyperactive delirium, apathy and lethargy are consistent with hypoactive (silent) delirium)

Additional PE based on findings in history and PE

Dx
- DOS score
- Confusion Assessment Method (CAM): standard screening device for delirium
- Bedside testing: glucose concentration, nitrite test, oxygen saturation
- Labs: depending on underlying cause, often CRP ↑, ESR ↑, WBC ↑, ASAT ↑, ALAT ↑, γ-GT ↑, electrolyte imbal-ances
- Expand diagnostics if indicated

Tx
- Treatment of underlying cause
- Delirium prevention: orientation of the patient based on the orientation triad (incl. hanging a clock with date and time in the room, hanging up a piece of paper with the location, ensuring that patient has glasses, hearing aid and dentures in and gets out of bed to receive daily information), family participation, mobilising the patient with physiotherapy if necessary, adequate analgesia, keep medication, infusions and other lines to a minimum, monitor intake and excretion

- Minimise use of delirium-provoking medication such as opiates and benzodiazepines
- Symptom management: haloperidol (contra-indicated for Parkinson's disease or Lewy body dementia due to the antagonistic effect on the dopamine receptors, therefore give clozapine)
- Alcohol or benzodiazepine withdrawal: lorazepam or diazepam

> The typical patient with delirium is an elderly patient over 70y of age, with an underlying infection who exhibits restless behaviour, is anxious, forgets the questions you ask or falls asleep whilst you are taking a history. This pattern fluctuates throughout the day.

CAM: the presence of **delirium** requires features 1 and 2 and either 3 or 4:

1. Acute change in mental status with a fluctuating course
2. Inattention (reduced ability to sustain attention and follow conversations)
3. Disorganised thinking (problems with memory, orientation, or language)
4. Altered level of consciousness (hypervigilance, drowsiness, or stupor)

The use of measures to restrict freedom should be kept to a minimum. Restricting freedom of movement results in an increased risk of delirium.

- Restriction of freedom of movement includes triple restraints, bed rails, tented bed, motion sensor and boxing gloves.
- Check local legislation before implementing any measures that restrict freedom of movement.

Precipitating factors for DELIRIUM:

- **D**rugs
- **E**lectrolyte abnormalities
- **L**ack of medication (withdrawal)
- **I**nfection
- **R**educed sensory input
- **I**ntracranial pathology
- **U**rinary retention or faecal impaction
- **M**yocardial and pulmonary disease

Pulmonology

Asthma

D Common heterogeneous disease, usually characterised by chronic airway inflammation with variable and recurring symptoms such as airflow limitation, bronchial obstruction, and underlying inflammation.

E Incidence ±260 million per year, prevalence varies among countries

Ae • Chronic inflammation of the mucosa of the lower respiratory tract (from the trachea to the terminal bronchi). There are allergic and eosinophilic phenotypes: atopical (Th2 lymphocytes (CD4+) interaction with antigens and secretion of chemokines → inflammation), eosinophilic (eosinophilic granulocytes damage the epithelium directly) and a variety of cells (mast cells, epithelium, basophilic granulocytes, fibroblasts, smooth muscle cells and macrophages and secrete all types of cytokines → inflammation) (see Figure 64).

- Characteristic chronic inflammation → remodelling (thickening of basal membrane due to collagen deposits caused by fibrogen growth factors in combination with elastolysis and oedema of mucosa and submucosa with cellular infiltration → facilitates bronchoconstriction → narrower lumen during an asthma flare-up)

R
- In childhood mainly ♂, after age 20 ♀=♂, from age 40 ♀>♂
- Patient-dependent: ♀>♂ in adults, genetic predisposition to atopy: IgE antibodies against (non-pathogenic) allergens, bronchial hyperreactivity, obesity
- Environmental factors: allergens, occupational exposure, (passive) smoking (during pregnancy) and air pollution, viral respiratory tract infections
- Triggers of an asthma attack: allergens, viral infections, changes in weather, laughter or irritants such as smoke, physical factors (exercise), medication (e.g. NSAIDs (prostaglandin synthesis ↓ → disproportional overproduction of leukotrienes), sympatholytics)
- Other factors: hormones, pregnancy, stress, cold air, reflux disease

Hx Dyspnoea, wheezing breath, coughing, tightness of the chest, symptoms during the night, atopic constitution (food allergy, eczema), symptoms vary throughout the seasons, triggering factors (e.g. bronchial hyperreactivity), ENT symptoms, use of medication (beta blockers, NSAIDs, ACE inhibitors), past medical history: recurrent bronchitis/infections

PE Tachypnoea, shortness of breath, use of accessory muscles of ventilation, bronchial breathing sounds, prolonged wheezing exhalation, eczema, saturation =/↓

Dx
- Spirometry pre- and post-bronchodilator (preferred approach): obstructive pattern, increase in forced expiratory volume in 1 second (FEV1) or forced vital capacity (FVC) of ≥12% or ≥200 mL following administration of 2-4 puffs of a quick-acting bronchodilator
- Changing lung function over time
- Positive histamine or methacholine provocation test
- Fractional exhaled nitric oxide

- Allergy testing: skin test or serological radioallergosorbent test (RAST) for inhalation allergens
- Labs: eosinophilia, IgE ↑
- No blood tests are available that can determine the presence or absence of asthma

Tx
- Asthma education and training essential skills
    - Think of treatable traits: e.g. correct inhalation technique of medication, reflux, rhinitis, sinusitis, stress, exposure to allergies, weight reduction, stop smoking, exercise
    - Reduced exposure to allergens
    - Pulmonary rehabilitation
- Acute treatment: oxygen therapy, salbutamol and ipratropium nebuliser treatment. Often also oral or IV corticosteroids.
    - Inhalation low-dose corticosteroids together with long-acting β adrenoceptor agonists (LABA) (e.g. formoterol), plus short-acting β adrenoceptor agonists (SABA) as needed
    - Exacerbation: intralesional corticosteroid administration (ICA)/LABA together with LABA/LAMA short-acting and oral corticosteroids. See Table 117 for a step-by-step plan. Consider step-down if symptoms decrease.
    - In specific cases: allergen immunotherapy or biologicals

P
- Poor symptom control is related with an increased risk of exacerbations
- Asthma Control Questionnaire (ACQ) is a tool to analyse symptom control

!
- Symptoms of concern during a flare-up: exhaustion, cyanosis, consciousness ↓, oxygen saturation ≤92%, hypercapnia in blood gas, silent chest on auscultation
- Women going through menopause can develop severe asthma (reason unknown)

There is a link between inflammation and bronchial hyperreactivity. The airways react excessively to triggers by constriction of the smooth muscle tissue or by stimulation of the inflammation. This chronic inflammation co-exists with episodes of acute inflammation that can trigger an asthma flare-up/asthma attack. Triggering factors include exercise, stress and air pollution. Prolonged flare-ups are often the result of viral or prolonged allergen-mediated respiratory tract infections.

If the instigated treatment does not produce adequate results, consider:

- Nonadherence to treatment
- Inhalation technique
- Exposure to allergens

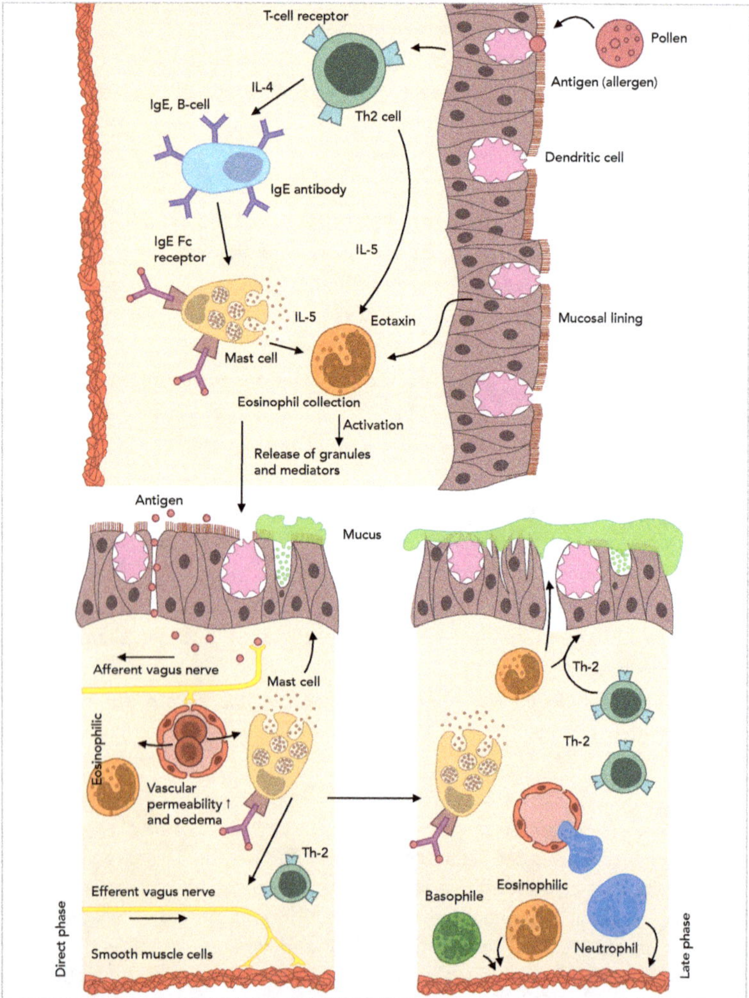

Figure 64 // Asthma: pathophysiology

Chronic obstructive pulmonary disease (COPD)

D COPD is a chronic, irreversible (or only partially reversible) airway obstruction with progressive inflammation of the central and peripheral lower respiratory tract in response to harmful substances. This inflammation results in parenchymal destruction and includes – based on pathophysiological and clinical features – the diseases emphysema and chronic bronchitis: these result in destruction of alveoli with hyperinflation and inflammation with increased mucus production by the bronchi(oli) respectively (see Figure 65). Manifestations of COPD could be pulmonary emphysema and chronic bronchitis (see Table 115 and Figure 65).

E
- Prevalence 6% (USA)
- 3rd leading cause of death worldwide, causing 3.23 million deaths in 2019
- Tobacco smoking accounts for over 70% of COPD cases in high-income countries

Ae
- Imbalance between the concentrations of proteases and antiproteases in the lungs and imbalance between the concentrations of oxidants and antioxidants. Smoking inactivates protease inhibitors and results in free O_2 radicals (ROS) → destruction of lung parenchyma.
- Smoking → permeability of respiratory tract wall ↑ → inflammation of small airways → structural transformation of epithelium (metaplasia) → thickening of the respiratory tract wall resulting in chronic respiratory tract obstruction, despite therapy. Unlike asthma, the cellular infiltrate in chronic bronchitis consists mainly of CD8+ Th2 lymphocytes.
- Alpha-1 antitrypsin deficiency (AATD): an autosomal recessive condition, in which the absence of alpha-1 trypsin results in auto-destruction of the lung tissue. Alpha-1 antitrypsin is a protease inhibitor, among others of the enzyme elastase, which is secreted by neutrophilic granulocytes. Deficiency → accumulation of elastase → destruction of alveolar membrane. ±1% of the patients with pulmonary emphysema has this type of disease.

R (Passive) smoking (++), chronic pulmonary exposure to fine particulate matter, ♂, advanced age, bronchial hyper-reactivity or chronic respiratory tract conditions in childhood, smoking during pregnancy (→ premature and low birth weight), household air pollution/indoor biomass smoke

Hx History of smoking, dyspnoea (of effort), productive cough, wheezing breath, unintentional weight ↓, use of medication (see Table 115 and Figure 65)

PE
- Degree of dyspnoea and tachypnoea, use of accessory muscles of ventilation, cyanosis, hyperresonant percussion, low position of lung bound-

aries with reduced motility, prolonged wheezing exhalation, rhonchi, coarse crepitations, saturation ↓

- Poor nutritional status, HF and oedema (caused by pulmonary hypertension, with severe forms of COPD)
- See Table 115 and Figure 66

Dx

- Spirometry: forced expiratory rate (FER) L and FEV1 L (age-corrected), flow-volume curve: church steeple phenomenon (high peak with sharp downward bend)
- The diagnosis is made based on symptoms together with an FER <70% of the FEV1, see Table 116 for staging
- Chest X-ray or CT-scan: to rule out alternative diagnoses (e.g. bronchiectasis or lung tumours). Findings associated with COPD include:
  - Hyperinflation: low position of lung boundaries, increased AP diameter of the chest (barrel chest), enlarged retrosternal cavity
  - Hyperlucent lung as a result of air trapping (less dense tissue) and bullae
  - Decreased vasculature

Tx

- Lifestyle changes: stop smoking, exercise (physiotherapy), breathing exercises, rehabilitation, adequate protein intake (particularly for high GOLD classifications), maintaining social contacts
- Pulmonary rehabilitation

- See Table 117
- Vaccinations: influenza, pneumococcal, COVID-19
- In the case of AATD: alpha-1 trypsin supplementation IV
- Flare-up/attack: consider short course of oral corticosteroids, O_2 supplementation (target >92%) and salbutamol nebuliser treatment

Lung volume reduction by means of coiling in the airways, the insertion of endobronchial valves or surgery to remove emphysematous lung tissue, lung transplantation (if patient has stopped smoking >6 mo prior)

P

- Combination of factors: deteriorates with smoking, advanced age, FEV1 <50%, rapid reduction in FEV1, poor response to bronchodilators, severe hypoxia, pulmonary hypertension
- Comorbidities with poorer prognosis: cardiovascular diseases, osteoporosis, anxiety and mood disorders, malignancy, bronchiectasis, metabolic syndrome, DM, reflux disease, OSAS (obstructive sleep apnoea syndrome)

	PULMONARY EMPHYSEMA	CHRONIC BRONCHITIS
Hx	Intense dyspnoea (++), coughing, low sputum, respiratory tract infections	Productive cough (++), slight dyspnoea, high sputum
PE	Pursed lips, skinny, pulmonary heart disease (--), severe airway obstruction, hyperinflation (barrel chest), decreased breathing sounds	Infections, obesity, pulmonary hypertension, pulmonary heart disease ultimately resulting in right-sided HF, moderately-severe airway obstruction, bronchiectasis, arterial hypoxia, hypercapnia
Dx	• Spirometry: FEV1 ↓, TLC ↑, lung compliance ↑, elasticity ↓, Tiffeneau index ↓ • Blood gas: PaO_2 =, $PaCO_2$ =/↓ • Chest X-ray: hyperinflation (flattened diaphragm, barrel chest), vascular abnormalities (decreased vasculature), bullae • Diffusion capacity ↓	• Spirometry: FEV1 ↓, TLC ↑/↓, Tiffeneau index ↓ • Blood gas: PaO_2 ↓, $PaCO_2$ ↑ • Chest X-ray: bronchial wall thickening, increased vasculature • Diffusion capacity =

Table 115 // Forms of COPD

<table>
<tr><td rowspan="4">SPIROMETRY</td><td>GOLD I (mild): FEV1 ≥80% of predicted</td><td rowspan="2">A</td><td rowspan="2">B</td><td rowspan="2">0 or 1 moderate exacerbations (not leading to hospitalisation)</td><td rowspan="4">EXACERBATIONS PER YEAR</td></tr>
<tr><td>GOLD II (moderately severe): FEV1 ≥50% and <80% of predicted</td></tr>
<tr><td>GOLD III (severe): FEV1 ≥30% and <50% of predicted</td><td rowspan="2" colspan="2">E</td><td rowspan="2">≥2 moderate exacerbations or ≥1 leading to hospitalisation</td></tr>
<tr><td>GOLD IV (very severe): FEV1 <30% of predicted</td></tr>
<tr><td></td><td></td><td>mMRC 0-1</td><td>mMRC ≥2</td><td></td><td></td></tr>
<tr><td></td><td></td><td>CAT <10</td><td>CAT ≥10</td><td></td><td></td></tr>
<tr><td></td><td></td><td colspan="2">SYMPTOMS (VIA MMRC OR CAT-SCORE)</td><td></td><td></td></tr>
</table>

Table 116 // GOLD classification for COPD
mMRC, modified Medical Research Council - dyspnoea scale; CAT, COPD Assessment Test

COPD is categorised according to the GOLD classification. The FEV1/FVC ratio after bronchodilation must be <0.70 to confirm an obstructive airway. The lower limit of normal (LLN) is applied to avoid over-diagnosis. In that case, the score depends on the measured FEV1 rather than the predicted FEV1 (see Table 116).

Smokers have more goblet cells and fewer cilia in their respiratory epithelium, as a result of inhaling harmful substances and gases. These two factors combine to cause an overproduction of mucus, resulting in the typical smoker's cough.

Chronic bronchitis "blue bloater" type COPD
The lips and face of patients with chronic bronchitis are grey-blue in colour as a result of cyanosis (severe stage) (see Figure 66). As a result of secondary right ventricular failure, these patients have an increased central venous pressure with distended jugular veins. Disease progression results in systemic symptoms such as hypercapnia, hypoxaemia and HF.

Lung emphysema "pink puffer" type COPD
A patient with severe pulmonary emphysema will classically present as the "pink puffer" (see Figure 66). Symptoms only occur when the lung is functioning at $^2/_3$ of capacity. These patients have a slim to cachectic build, a barrel chest and use of the accessory muscles of ventilation is often visible in combination with hyperventilation. In order to reduce collapse of the bronchioli, the patients attempt to increase their end-expiratory pressure by pouting their lips when breathing out ("puffer"). "Pink" refers to the reddish-pink colour of these patients.

GOLD CLASSIFICATION	TREATMENT
A	• LABA or LAMA • SABA or SAMA as needed
B	• LAMA-LABA combination • Rescue medication for acute dyspnoea (SABA or SAMA)
E	• LAMA-LABA combination or ICS-LAMA-LABA combination (if eosinophils ↑) • Rescue medication for acute dyspnoea (SABA or SAMA)

Table 117 // GOLD classification
ICS, inhaled corticosteroids

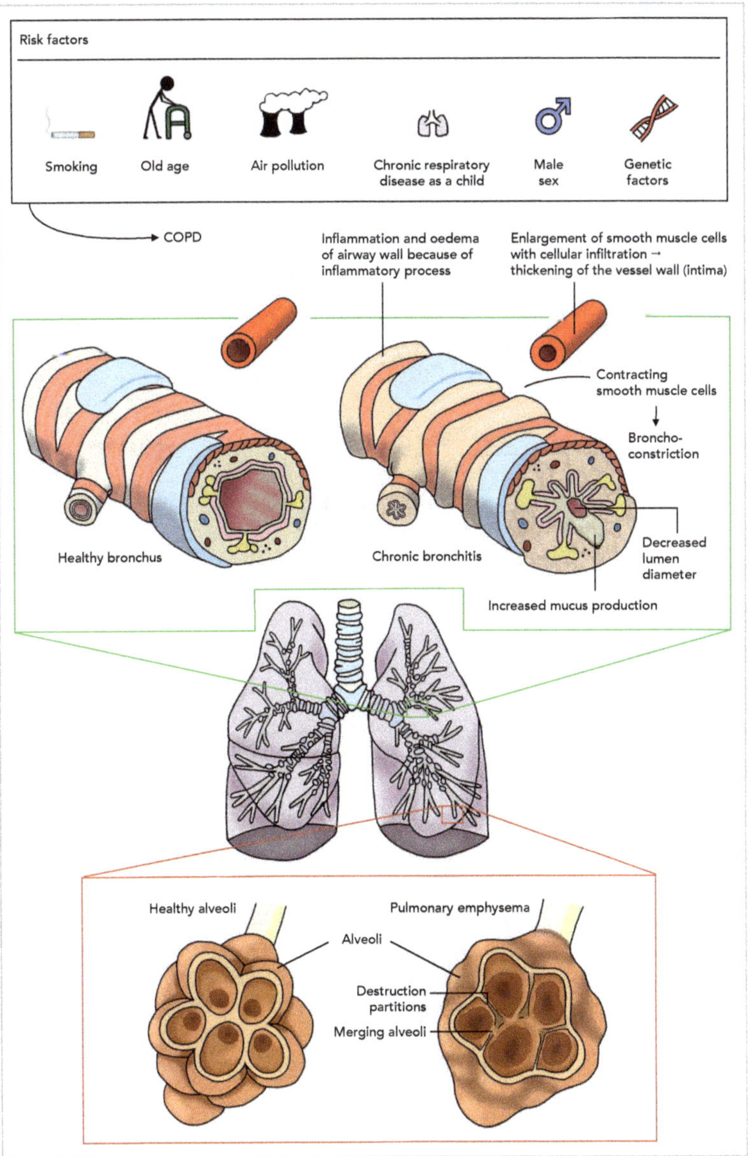

Figure 65 // COPD: pathophysiology

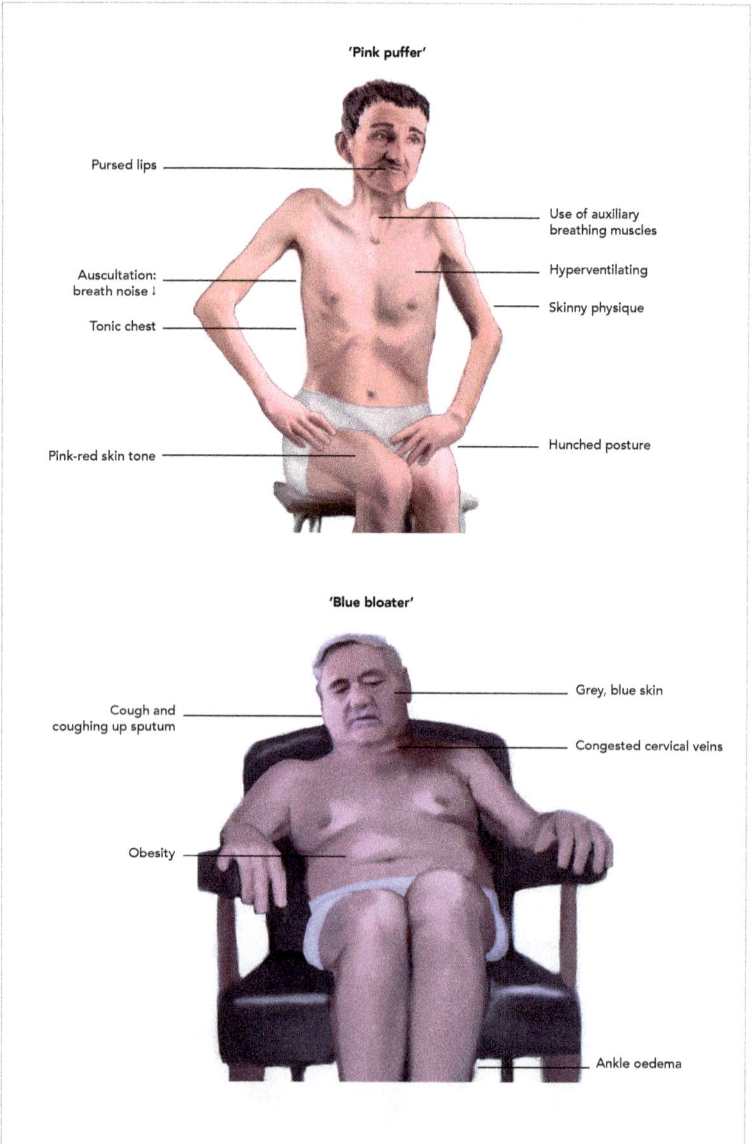

Figure 66 // COPD: pink puffer vs blue bloater

TAXONOMY (ETIOTYPES) FOR COPD		
Classification		**Description**
Generally determined COPD (COPD-G)		• Alpha-1 antitrypsin deficiency (AATD) • Other genetic variants with smaller effects acting in combination
COPD due to abnormal lung development (COPD-D)		Early life events, including premature birth and low birthweight, among others
Environmental COPD	Cigarette smoking COPD (COPD-C)	• Exposure to tobacco some, including in utero or via passive smoking • Vaping or e-cigarette use • Cannabis
	Biomass and pollution exposure COPD (COPD-P)	Exposure to household pollution, ambient air pollution, wildfire smoke, occupational hazards
COPD due to infections (COPD-I)		Childhood infections, tuberculosis-associated COPD, HIV-associated COPD
COPD & asthma		Particularly childhood asthma
COPD of unknown cause		No underlying cause

Table 118 // Taxonomy for COPD

Pneumonia

D Pneumonia is defined as inflammation of the lung parenchyma caused by an infection. Pneumonia is primarily caused by an aerogenically transmissible virus or bacterium, but sometimes also by a fungus (see Table 121). The immune response to the pathogen causes consolidation of the lung, which in turn causes a ventilation perfusion (V/Q) mismatch and intrapulmonary shunting, resulting in hypoxaemia.

E USA 1,600-2,300:100,000 per year

Ae
- "Community-acquired" pneumonia (CAP): contracts at home
- "Hospital-acquired" pneumonia that develops ≥48h after admission to the hospital (see Table 119)
- "Nursing home-acquired": contracted in a nursing home or long-term care facility
- Inhalation pathogens → colonisation of nasopharynx → micro-aspiration and colonisation of terminal bronchiole and alveoli → immune response to pathogen → permeability of blood vessels ↑ → extravasation of fluid and

leukocytes → lung consolidation → type I respiratory insufficiency

R ♂, children <1y or elderly patients, smoking and alcohol abuse, chronic pulmonary disease, use of immunosuppressants or being immunocompromised (opportunistic infections), aspiration of food, asplenia, recent surgery, rib contusion

Hx
- Typical presentation: acute onset, fever, shivering, productive cough, painful breathing, chest pains, dyspnoea (see Figure 67)
- Atypical presentation: abdominal pain, otherwise a wide range of symptoms, not to moderately sick, non-productive cough, travel to foreign country and contact with water → Legionnaires' disease
- It is not possible to differentiate between different types of pneumonia (typical or atypical) based on the clinical presentation

PE T ↑, muffled percussion, increased breathing sounds (bronchial breathing sounds), aegophony, high-frequency fine crepitations or humming rhonchi, (elderly patients: fast shallow breathing, consciousness ↓, heart rate ↑, weight ↓, saturation ↓)

Dx
- Labs: CRP ↑, WBC ↑/↓, Na^+ =/↓, albumin =/↑, ALAT/ASAT =/↑
- Na^+ ↓ and ↑ liver enzymes → Legionnaires' disease
- Blood cultures: in the case of severe pneumonia, collect samples before starting AB
- Chest X-ray: consolidations in the lungs (see Figure 68)
- POCUS: B-lines, subpleural consolidations, hepatization (lung has a liver-like homogenous echotexture)
- Sputum culture or PCR: gram preparation and detection of pathogen (collect samples before starting AB)
- Urine test: legionella antigen test and pneumococcal rapid test
- Serology: test for viral infections (e.g. *SARS-CoV-2, RSV* and *influenza*), targeted against potentially pathogenic antigens (e.g. *Pneumocystis jirovecii Pneumonia* (PJP), *Coxiella burnetii, Chlamydia trachomatis*). Test for HIV if more than one pneumonia episode in one year.
- For patients with reduced immune functioning, ventilated patients or patients who are not recovering well: bronchoscopy for cultures, broncho-alveolar lavage (BAL) or lavage

Tx Vaccination for risk groups

- Empiric AB is designed to cover the most common pathogens of the different types of pneumonia and varies based on region and patient profile (comorbidities, risk factors for resistance)

- Supportive measures: O_2 suppletion or mechanical ventilation, antipyretics (see Diagram 31)

P Depending on the presence and severity of other unfavourable factors, such as comorbidities. The severity of a CAP is determined by means of the simple and clinically fast CURB-65 score (see Table 120) or the more extensive Pneumonia Severity Index (PSI).

!
- Beware of a complicated pneumonia: e.g. parapneumonic effusion, empyema, sepsis
- Pneumonia is the most common cause of sepsis

> Local AB protocols may vary!

> The CURB-65 score equals the AMBU-65 score.

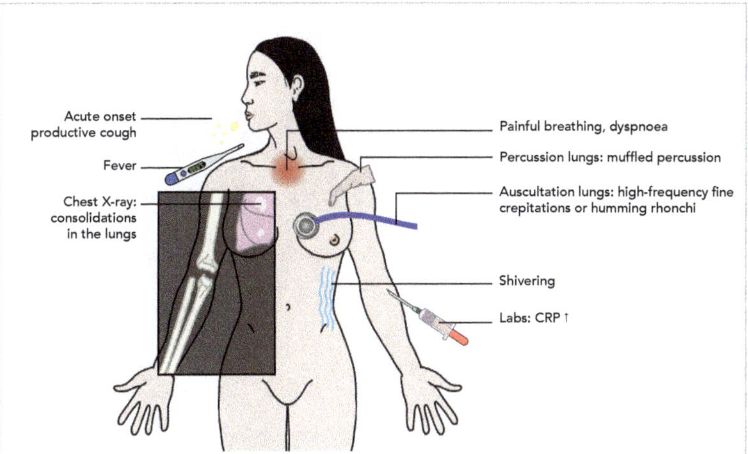

Figure 67 // Pneumonia

	COMMUNITY-ACQUIRED PNEUMONIA (CAP)		
Severity	• **Mild: CURB 0-1, PSI I-II** • **Mortality 0,1-3%**	• **Moderate: CURB 2, PSI III-IV** • **Mortality 0,9-15%**	• **Severe: CURB ≥3, PSI V** • **Mortality 27-40%**
R	• Alcohol abuse, smoking, drugs, season, epidemic, travel history, HF, DM, COPD, asthma, age <3mo or >7y, immune system ↓ • These factors result in a less favourable outcome		
Ae	• Typical pathogens: *Streptococcus pneumoniae* ⊕, *Haemophilus influenzae* ⊕, *Staphylococcus aureus, Moraxella catarrhalis, Klebsiella pneumoniae*, viral (e.g. influenza virus A/B) • Atypical pathogens: *Legionella pneumophila* (contaminated water), *Chlamydia psittaci* (birds and poultry), *Mycoplasma pneumoniae, Coxiella burnetii* (Q Fever), *Nocardia, Actinomyces*		
Tx	• Essentially, treatment at home • Amoxicillin or doxycycline oral, switch to narrow spectrum depending on the pathogen	• Hospitalisation • Amoxicillin IV, switch to narrow spectrum depending on the pathogen. Consider cephalosporin for moderately severe disease.	• Consider ICU admission • Cephalosporin IV in combination with fluoroquinolone. Switch to narrow-spectrum depending on the pathogen • In some cases, corticosteroïds

Table 119 // Categorisation of CAP, HAP and aspiration pneumonia

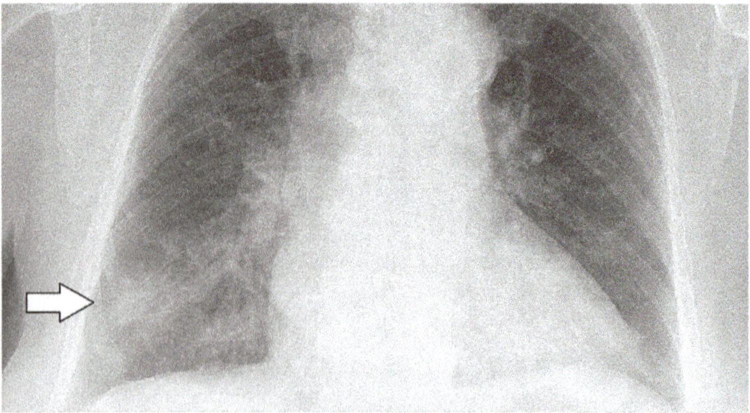

Figure 68 // Chest X-ray: consolidations in the right lung

HOSPITAL-ACQUIRED PNEUMONIA (HAP) (>48h of admission)	ASPIRATION PNEUMONIA
Abdominal surgery, extensive surgery or emergency surgery, corticosteroid use, prior use of AB, long ICU admissions, mechanic ventilation, pre-existent lung disease, or malnutrition	Swallowing disorders, abdominal problems with higher risk of vomiting, alcohol abuse, epileptic disorders, parenteral feeding, general weakness due to illness
• Gram negative bacteria • Three important pathogens: *Staphylococcus aureus, Pseudomonas aeruginosa, Enterbacteriaceae*	• *Streptococcus pneumoniae* • Anaerobe bacteria
Combination of different AB depending on (local) risk factors, switch to narrow-spectrum AB depending on the pathogen	Chemical pneumonitis often develops first, which does not always require AB • AB only in case of an infection (e.g. fever, WBC ↑, CRP ↑) • Treatment of anaerobes should only be considered in case of gross aspiration

RISK FACTOR (organ failure)	INTERPRETATION
Confusion	Mental disorientation (place, person or time)
Urea	Plasma urea >7 mmol/L
Respiratory rate	RR ≥30/min
Blood pressure	Systolic <90 mmHg or diastolic <60 mmHg
Age	≥65y

Table 120 // CURB-65 score. A score of 1-2 forms an indication for hospitalisation, a score >3 forms an indication for ICU admission. Each risk factor is 1 point.

In immunocompromised patients, fungi are more frequently detected as the pathogen for a pneumonia, e.g. *Pneumocystitis jirovecii* pneumonia (PJP). This is an opportunistic infection that causes cystic abnormalities in the lungs. PJP is one of the most common opportunistic infections and is treated with high-dose cotrimoxazole. It is a severe condition with a high mortality.

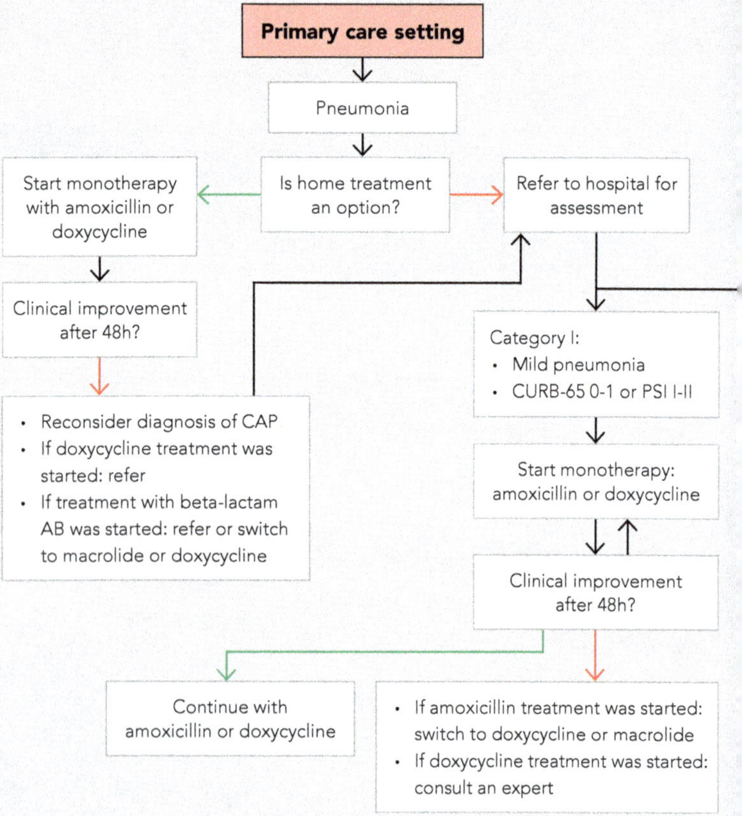

Diagram 31 // Pneumonia: treatment

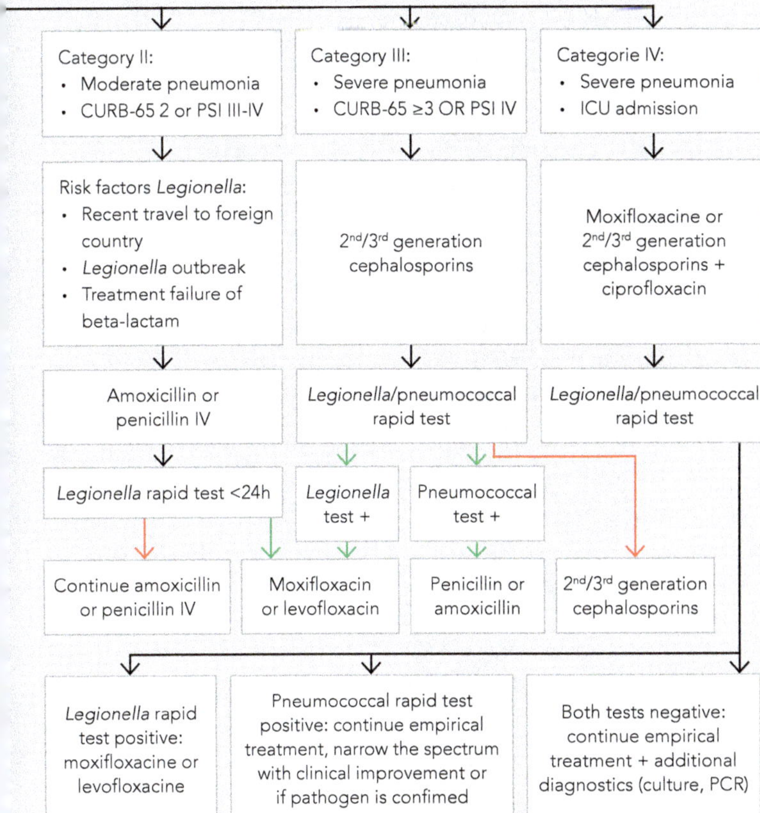
Category II:
• Moderate pneumonia
• CURB-65 2 or PSI III-IV
Category III:
• Severe pneumonia
• CURB-65 ≥3 OR PSI IV
Categorie IV:
• Severe pneumonia
• ICU admission
Risk factors *Legionella*:
• Recent travel to foreign country
• *Legionella* outbreak
• Treatment failure of beta-lactam
2nd/3rd generation cephalosporins
Moxifloxacine or 2nd/3rd generation cephalosporins + ciprofloxacin
Amoxicillin or penicillin IV
Legionella/pneumococcal rapid test
Legionella/pneumococcal rapid test
Legionella rapid test <24h
Legionella test +
Pneumococcal test +
Continue amoxicillin or penicillin IV
Moxifloxacin or levofloxacin
Penicillin or amoxicillin
2nd/3rd generation cephalosporins
Legionella rapid test positive: moxifloxacine or levofloxacine
Pneumococcal rapid test positive: continue empirical treatment, narrow the spectrum with clinical improvement or if pathogen is confimed
Both tests negative: continue empirical treatment + additional diagnostics (culture, PCR)

Interpretation of PSI:

- PSI I: not calculated
- PSI II: ≤70
- PSI III: 71-90
- PSI IV: 91-130
- PSI V: >130

TYPICAL BACTERIAL PATHOGENS	ATYPICAL BACTERIAL PATHOGENS	VIRAL PATHOGENS
• *Streptococcus pneumoniae* • *Haemophilus influenzae* • *Moraxella catarrhalis* • *Staphylococcus aureus* • *Group A streptococci* • *Escherichia coli* • *Klebsiella* • Anaerobic bacteria associated with aspiration	• *Legionella spp* • *Mycoplasma pneumoniae* • *Chlamydia pneumoniae* • *Chlamydia psittaci* • *Coxiella burnetii*	• *Influenza A and B* • *SARS-CoV-2* • Other coronaviruses • *Rhinovirus* • *Parainfluenza virus* • *Adenovirus* • *Respiratory syncytial (RS) virus* • *Human metapneumovirus* • *Human bocavirus*

Table 121 // Most common pathogens of pneumonia

In the case of immunocompromised patients, also consider fungi, *Pneumocystitis jirovecii, Norcardia spp, Mycobacterium tuberculosis* or non-tuberculous mycobacteria (NTM) as important pathogens of pneumonia.

Pneumothorax

D A collection of air within the pleural space between the lung (visceral pleura) and the chest wall (parietal pleura) (see Figure 69).
Classified into:

- Spontaneous pneumothorax (primary: no underlying lung disease (PSP), secondary: complication of underlying lung disease (SSP));
- Traumatic pneumothorax;
- Iatrogenic pneumothorax.

E
- ♂>♀ (6:1), mainly tall skinny ♂
- Incidence ♂ 7.4-37:100,000 per year (USA and UK)
- Incidence ♀ 1.2-15.4:100,000 per year (USA and UK)

Ae Pulmonary blebs and bullae are (mostly apically) enlarged subpleural air-filled cavities. Air pressure fluctuations, various environmental factors and fibrotic lung changes can result in a rupture of these subpleural bullae. Idiopathic spontaneous pneumothorax probably has the same aetiology.

R
- Spontaneous in young men ⊕
- Environmental factors: smoking (primarily cannabis), excessive atmospheric air pressure fluctuations
- Slim leptosomic build, adolescent age, trauma, malignancy, infection (TB, pneumonia, pulmonary abscess), chronic pulmonary diseases (asthma, COPD, CF, pulmonary fibrosis, sarcoidosis), connective tissue disorders (Marfan syndrome, Ehlers-Danlos syndrome)
- Iatrogenic: perforation of the lung by a central venous catheter in the jugular or subclavian vein, pleural aspiration/biopsy, percutaneous liver biopsy, positive end-expiratory pressure (PEEP) ventilation, pacemaker insertion

Hx Asymptomatic ⊕, dyspnoea, usually acute dyspnoea and unilateral chest pain

PE HR ↓, absent fremitus on affected side, hypersonoric percussion on affected side, local breathing sounds on affected side ↓, asymmetrical chest wall excursions, possible subcutaneous emphysema

Dx
- Chest X-ray (usually diagnostic): visible visceral pleura, deep sulcus sign, clearly delineated heart contours and diaphragm ↑, absent lung vasculature, hydropneumothorax (air-fluid level)
- Arterial blood gas: PaO_2 ↓
- Chest CT: if chest x-ray is inconclusive and persistent suspicion of pneumothorax
- Ultrasound: increasingly used, presence of "lung point" is diagnostic, presence of B-lines, lung sliding or lung pulse excludes pneumothorax

Tx Wait-and-see approach for spontaneous pneumothorax with minimal symptoms and haemodynamically stable. The excess air is reabsorbed at a rate of 1.25% per day.

O_2 administration for a small apical pneumothorax could theoretically reduce the nitrogen concentration in the blood, thus promoting pleural air reabsorption, consider analgesia

- Aspiration of air from the pleural cavity: using a needle or drain, air is aspirated from the pleural cavity
- Chemical pleurodesis: use lime to cause inflammation of the pleural membranes and allow the layers to fuse to prevent a recurrence, which

is the preferred option over surgical bleb resection (always under sedation, due to the extremely painful nature of this procedure)
- Surgical treatment: bleb resection/pleurectomy by means of video-assisted thoracoscopic surgery (VATS) if lung expansion fails after drainage, ≥2 times pneumothorax of the same lung, or (extremely rare) bilateral pneumothorax

P SSP: 30-50%, PSP: 10-30%

! • Traumatic pneumothorax can become a tension pneumothorax. These patients are therefore always considered unstable and should be treated with a pleural drain
- If a patient with a pleural drain deteriorates, first check that the drain is not clogged: the water valve should be pendulating with each breathing movement. When in doubt, first disconnect the drain from the water lock and reassess the effect on saturation.

The typical patient with a spontaneous pneumothorax is often a young, tall, thin, smoking man.

Tension pneumothorax

D A tension pneumothorax consists of a wound in the pleura that acts as a one-way valve, allowing air to enter the pleural cavity with each inhalation, causing the pleural cavity to expand and exert pressure on the non-affected side, resulting in a mediastinal shift.

E The incidence of tension pneumothorax is estimated around 1%-3% of pre-hospital, major trauma, and ICU patients in the USA

Ae Visceral pleural lesion: during inhalation, air enters the pleural cavity and during exhalation the wound closes → accumulation of air in the pleural cavity → mediastinal shift of the heart and major blood vessels

R After penetrating trauma ⊕, PEEP ventilation

Hx Dyspnoea ⊕, chest pain

PE Tracheal deviation towards the non-affected side, haemodynamic instability (BP ↓, HR ↑, saturation ↓, signs of shock, RR ↑), cyanosis, sweating, unilaterally decreased breathing sounds, central venous pressure ↑

Dx A tension pneumothorax is a clinical diagnosis and it should – due to its rapidly lethal nature – be alleviated even before a chest X-ray has been performed

Tx O$_2$ administration, analgesia

- Place a large bore needle over the 3rd rib in the 2nd ICS mid-clavicular on the affected side. Always place a drain afterwards.
- Subsequently treat as a pneumothorax

P Without immediate intervention → death as a result of acute cardiac tamponade

! Even a suspected tension pneumothorax requires immediate intervention with needle decompression to prevent death

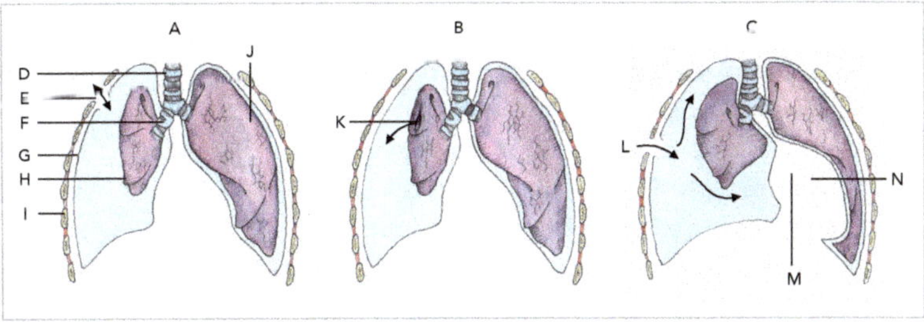

Figure 69 // Pneumothorax: difference between open, closed, and tension pneumothorax
A: Open pneumothorax **B:** Closed pneumothorax **C:** Tension pneumothorax **D:** Trachea **E:** Air flows into the interpleural space through a defect in the thoracic wall **F:** Main bronchus **G:** Parietal pleura **H:** Visceral pleura **I:** Thoracic wall **J:** Lung **K:** Air flows into the interpleural space through a defect in the lung **L:** The affected hemithorax inflates via a valve wound **M:** Mediastinal shift **N:** Heart

Pulmonary embolism

D A pulmonary embolism is an obstruction of the pulmonary artery or distal arterial branches resulting in increased pressure in the right ventricle, with haemodynamic instability and V/Q mismatch as a result of reduced flow in the vessels beyond the obstruction and increased flow in the other blood vessels. This results in hypoxia. In >90% of cases this is the result of a venous thrombo-embolism (VTE). An obstruction can also be caused by a fat embolism of tumour thrombus.

E Incidence of 2.81:100,000 per year in the USA and 100,000 annual deaths. Results in 300,000 deaths annually in Europe.

Ae
- Thrombosis in the leg, pelvis, auriculae or atria of the heart due to the presence of Virchow's triad → release or detachment of thrombus → haematogenic displacement to the right ventricle and pulmonary trunk → stalling and occlusion of (branches of) the pulmonary artery → reduced to no perfusion of the lung parenchyma located distal to the embolus: dead space

ventilation and pulmonary hypertension, right-sided HF or spontaneous death (see Figure 70)

- Non-thrombotic emboli: fat embolism following a fracture, air embolism and foreign body resulting from IV drug abuse, tumour embolism, amniotic fluid embolism during pregnancy

R Age >40, oral contraceptive, smoking, malignancy (primarily haematological malignancies, lung cancer and pancreatic cancer), recent surgery (up to one month after surgery), fractures of the lower extremities, being bedridden, history of VTE, pregnancy, increased coagulation tendency (thrombophilia, factor V Leiden), obesity, intravascular catheter or pacemaker, cardiac conditions

Hx Acute unexplained dyspnoea, painful respiration, vomiting, haemoptysis, unexplained collapse

PE Rapid shallow breathing, HR ↑, BP ↓, distended jugular veins, signs of a DVT (swollen, red, painful leg, difference in colour or temperature between legs), crepitations over the lungs, signs of obstructive shock

Dx
- Combine clinical and pre-test probability assessment (pulmonary embolism Wells score/ YEARS algorithm, see Diagram 32)
- POCUS of heart and IVC: dilated right ventricle and inferior vena cava
- Ultrasound of legs: to rule out DVT
- ECG changes caused by right ventricular overload: right atrium dilatation (P-pulmonale), right axis shift and right bundle branch block (RBBB). Deep S in lead I, pathological Q and negative T in lead III, T-top inversion in V2-V4.
- CTA: image branches of the pulmonary artery
- V/Q scan if contrast used for CTA is contra-indicated or for suspected chronic pulmonary embolism

Tx
- Instruct patient to stop smoking and lose weight if applicable, ♀: discourage use of oral anticoagulant (OAC)
- If DVT: compression stockings during the day for 2y, to prevent recurrence and treat oedema

- Acute: if haemodynamically unstable (systolic BP <90 mmHg): consider vasopressors, IV fluids 250 to 400 mL (avoid volume overload!), O_2 supplementation, IVT (beware of bleeding)
- Haemodynamically stable:
  - Anticoagulation, usually with DOAC (outpatient) or LMWH (for non-massive and low-risk sub-massive pulmonary embolism)
  - Anticoagulation with IVT (only in selected cases for high-risk sub-

massive pulmonary embolism). IVT, usually with tissue Plasminogen Activator (tPA).

- Haemodynamically unstable: IVT

Intravascular thrombosuction

- Using the pulmonary embolism severity index (PESI), simplified PESI (sPESI) (see Table 122) or HESTIA-score
- Heavy physical activity is discouraged during the first few weeks after diagnosis

- 50% develop post-thrombotic syndrome in the first year following a DVT
- Mortality is highest in patients who are haemodynamically unstable
- In the case of a saddle embolus, a part of the pulmonary arteries is occluded as a result of the embolus being located in the bifurcation of the pulmonary trunk (see Figure 71)
- Right ventricular failure results in cardiogenic shock → haemodynamic instability resulting in sudden death. Swift treatment with thrombolytics is essential in the case of right-sided overload.

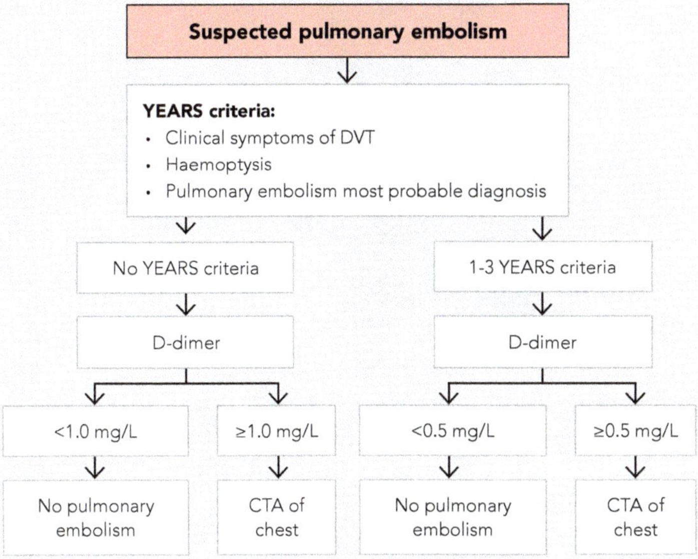

Diagram 32 // YEARS algorithm

Pulmonary embolism is **FATAL**:

- **F**at
- **A**ir
- **T**hrombus
- **A**mniotic fluid
- **L**ess common (bacterial, tumour, etc.)

In the event of non-specific ST depressions or elevations, always consider a pulmonary embolism.

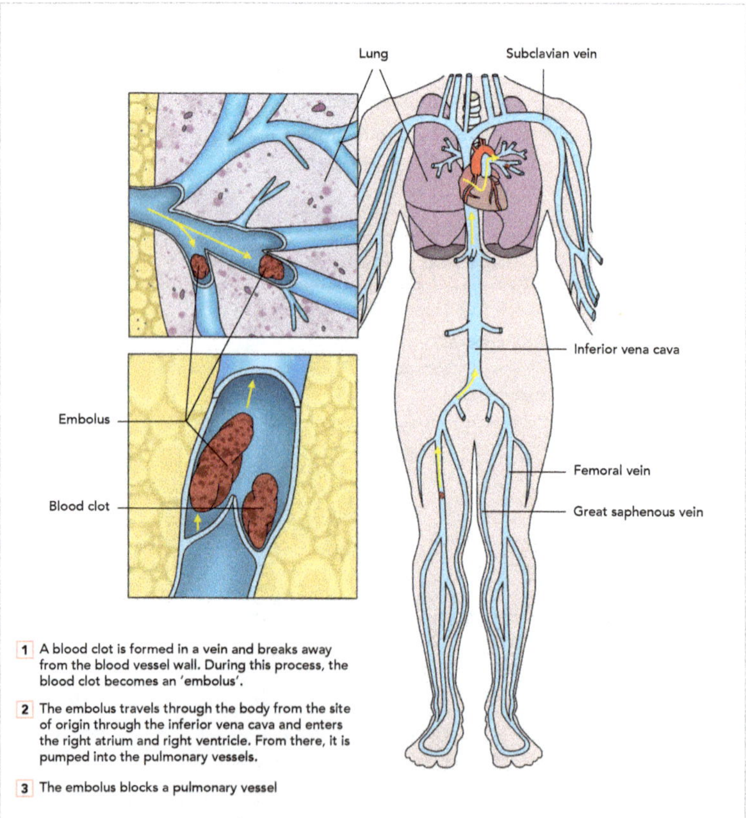

Figure 70 // Pulmonary embolism

As a result of the double lung circulation, there is often remarkably little ischaemia of the structures located beyond the embolism. This is because the bronchial arteries ensure oxygenation of the lung tissue. Small zones of infarction can occur distally, but this is considered secondary in importance to the hypoxaemia.

CLINICAL SIGN	POINTS
Age >80y	1
Past medical history: malignancy	1
Chronic cardiopulmonary disease	1
Heart rate ≥110/min Systolic BP <100 mmHg	1
Saturation <90%	1
Low risk	0
High risk	≥1

Table 122 // Simplified pulmonary embolism severity index (sPESI). Class 1-2: low mortality, class 3-5: high mortality.

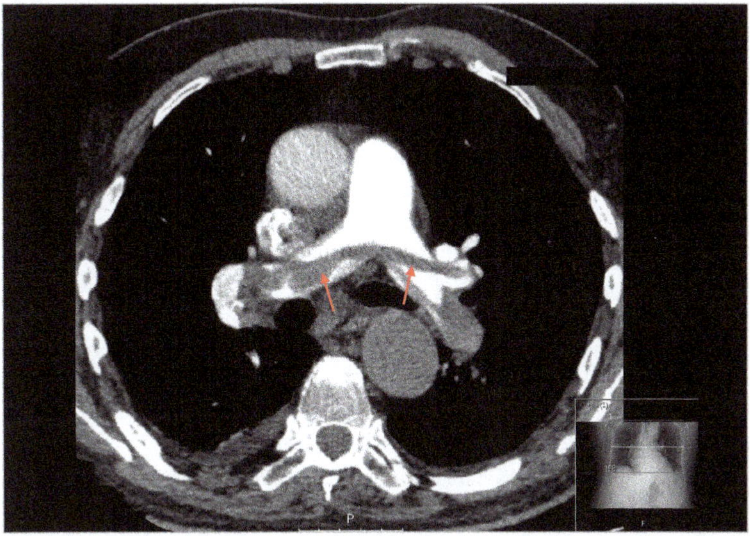

Figure 71 // CTA with a double pulmonary embolism (see red arrows)

> **Virchow's triad** consists of endothelial damage, stasis of blood flow and hypercoagulability (viscosity) of the blood. This triad is significant in the development of thrombosis.

Surgery

Abdominal aortic aneurysm (AAA)

D A dilatation of the abdominal aorta, in which the diameter of the abdominal aorta is >3.0 cm (normal diameter of infra-renal aorta ±2.0 cm, 95% <3.0 cm). Often a AAA is discovered as a coincidental finding in abdominal imaging studies. The Crawford classification (see Figure 72 is used to describe the extent of the thoracoabdominal aortic aneurysms.

E Prevalence of 0.3-5%, ♂>♀, peak incidence age 70-80

Ae Factors that are probably involved in the development and progression of AAA: proteases, inflammatory mediators, genetic factors

R
- Smoking, hypertension, hypercholesterolaemia, atherosclerosis, connective tissue diseases, advanced age, ♂, positive FHx
- Protective factors: ♀, DM

Hx Asymptomatic (++), symptomatic AAA: rupture may present as shock, diffuse abdominal pain, distention (life-threatening event). Furthermore, back pain, flank pain, fever (−), general malaise (−) may occur.

PE Pulsating abdominal mass (+)

Dx
- Asymptomatic AAA - abdominal ultrasound: evaluate diameter of aneurysm
- Symptomatic AAA - CTA: dimensions, anatomy of the aneurysm, evaluation of treatment options (endovascular/open)

Tx
- Stop smoking
- Ultrasound monitoring: annually for diameter 4.0 to 4.9 cm, if the diameter reaches ≥5.5 cm (♂) or ≥5.0 cm (♀), or the expansion rate is rapid, treatment is required.

Statin, platelet aggregation inhibitor, antihypertensives if necessary

- Endovascular aneurysm repair (EVAR) or open/conventional surgery in which a vascular prosthesis is inserted
- For rupture (AAAA: Acute AAA): emergency surgery

P Depending on the diameter of the aneurysm, 50% of patients who suffer a rupture will die before reaching the ER (see Table 123)

! Beware of an aneurysm rupture

$$\text{Wall tension} = \frac{\text{transmural pressure x radius}}{\text{2 x wall thickness}}$$

Formula 2 // Laplace's Law

Laplace's Law (see Formula 2): radius of a blood vessel ↑ or blood pressure ↑ → the wall tension of a blood vessel ↑.
Wall thickness ↓ → wall tension ↑.
Aneurysm → local radius of blood vessel ↑ and wall thickness ↓ → wall tension ↑↑ → blood vessel tears.

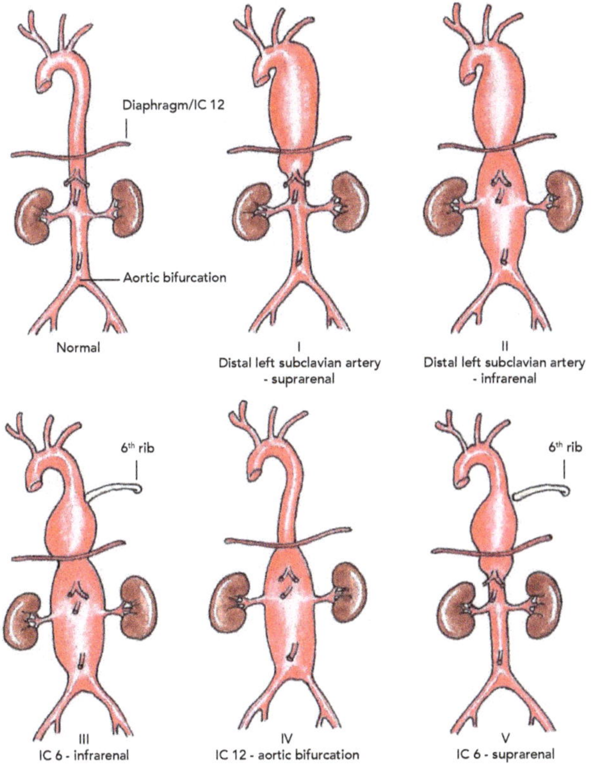

Figure 72 // Crawford classification: the classification of various types of thoracoabdominal aortic aneurysms

CATEGORISATION OF THORACIC ANEURYSMS	COURSE	PERCENTAGE OF TAAS
Ascending aorta	From the aortic valve to the brachiocephalic artery	80%
Aortic arch	Each thoracic aneurysm in which the brachiocephalic artery, left common carotid artery and/or left subclavian artery is/are involved	10%
Descending aorta	Distal to left subclavian artery	40%
Thoracoabdominal aorta	Both the thoracic and abdominal aorta are involved	4-10%

Table 123 // Categorisation of thoracic aneurysms

Acute appendicitis

D Acute appendicitis is an acute inflammation of the vermiform appendix.

E Incidence: 229,9:100,000 per year (worldwide), mostly between the ages of 5-45

Ae Obstruction of the appendiceal lumen → stasis of mucus → distention of serosa → vascular congestion → vascular congestion → ischaemia → necrosis → perforation → peritonitis

R ♂>♀

Hx Initial diffuse periumbilical pain (visceral peritoneum irritation) localising to the right lower quadrant (RLQ) (parietal peritoneum irritation) within ±12-24h, anorexia (80%), nausea/vomiting, fever (40%), diarrhoea, malaise, urinary frequency or urgency

PE
- McBurney's point tenderness: RLQ guarding (see Figure 73)
- Rovsing's sign: RLQ pain elicited by palpation of the left lower quadrant
- Psoas sign: pain elicited on flexing the right hip with stretched leg against resistance
- Obturator sign: RLQ pain on passive internal rotation of the right hip with the hip and knee flexed

Dx
- Traditionally a clinical diagnosis
- Labs: Leucocytes ↑, CRP ↑, urinalysis (usually normal), urine/serum B-hCG (usually normal)
- Abdominal ultrasound: distended appendix (>6 mm diameter), possible appendicolith, and abnormally increased echogenicity of the peri-appendiceal fat

- CT-scan preferably with contrast: enlarged appendix (>6 mm diameter), appendiceal wall thickening (>2 mm), peri-appendiceal fat stranding, appendiceal wall enhancement, possible appendicolith
- Consider MRI in young infants and pregnant patients, in sick patients or for persistent suspicion whilst repeated ultrasound remains inconclusive

Tx Nil per os

IV fluids, AB IV, analgesics

Appendectomy (gold-standard), laparoscopy preferred over open approach

P Mortality rate in developed countries (0.09-0.24%) varies from resource-limited countries (1-4%)

! Risk of perforation → peritonitis → sepsis

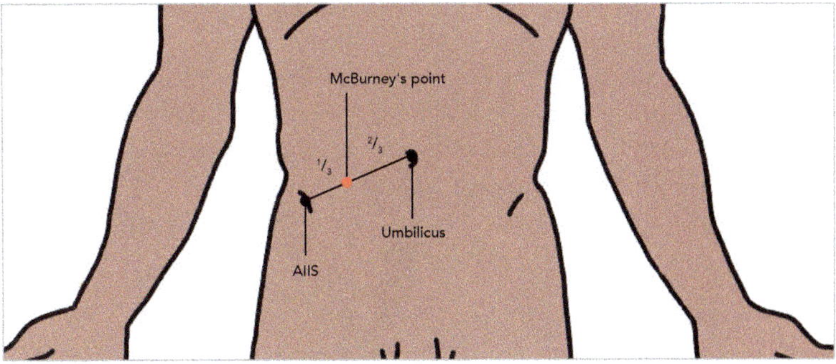

Figure 73 // McBurney's point
AIIS: Anterior inferior iliac spine

Acute cholecystitis

D Acute cholecystitis is an acute inflammation of the gallbladder, mostly due to obstruction of the cystic duct (see Figures 37 and 74).

E 6-11% of patients with symptomatic gallstones

Ae Cystic duct obstruction → gallbladder distention → inflammation and oedema of gallbladder wall → secondary bacterial infection of bile and gallbladder wall → ischaemic necrosis → perforation

R Cholecystolithiasis

Hx Prolonged (4-6h), steady, and severe pain in the right upper abdomen, anorexia, nausea, vomiting, fever, Boas' sign + (pain under right scapula), previous biliary colic

PE T ↑, HR ↑, signs of peritoneal irritation (guarding and rebound pain, muscular defense, pain during transportation), Murphy's sign + (pain upon palpation of the gallbladder during inhalation and patient holds their breath, low sensitivity)

Dx
- Labs: detect infection/inflammation (CRP ↑, WBC ↑ (left shift), ESR =/↑ (with chronic cholecystitis), liver function tests =/↑)
- Ultrasound: detect cholecystitis (gallstones, thickened wall (>4 mm), ultrasound-positive Murphy's sign, dilatation of the common hepatic duct (>5 mm))

Tx
Wait-and-see: consult surgeon, consider analgesics and AB, followed at a later stage if necessary by elective laparoscopic cholecystectomy

Initial care: IV fluid therapy, pain control (NSAIDs, opioids)

- Laparoscopic cholecystectomy (immediate or deferred), possibly in combination with AB
- Ultrasound-guided percutaneous drainage

P Mortality rate is estimated to be 3%

! Complications: gangrenous cholecystitis, perforation, emphysematous cholecystitis, cholecystoenteric fistula, gallstone ileus

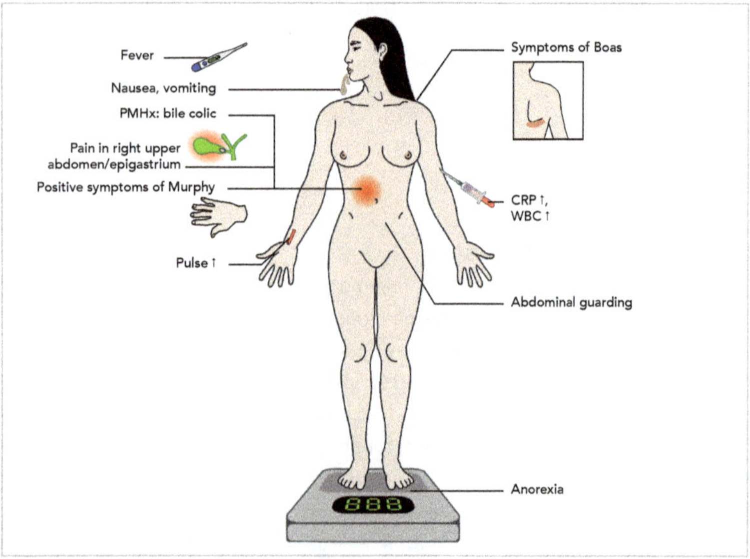

Figure 74 // Cholecystitis

Acute compartment syndrome

D Acute compartment syndrome is characterised by increased pressure within a confined fascial compartment, leading to tissue ischaemia.

E ♂: 7.3:100,000, ♀: 0.7:100,000 per year

Ae Bleeding due to vascular damage or coagulation disorder/ vascular permeability with swelling due to e.g. post-ischaemic phase after trauma and shock ↑ → compartment pressure ↑ → obstruction of venous outflow and collapse of arterioles → tissue perfusion ↓ → oxygen supply ↓ → irreversible tissue damage (necrosis) to muscles and nerves after 4-6h of ischaemia

R Long bone fracture (tibial shaft fracture (1-10% incidence of acute compartment syndrome), bandage or cast too tight, ischaemia, thermal injury, bleeding diathesis (i.e. haemophilia), central lines (e.g. extracorporeal membrane oxygenation (ECMO)), postoperative patients

Hx
- Early features: tense "wood-like" feeling, pain disproportional to injury, swelling
- Late features: neurological deficits, impaired perfusion
- The 6 Ps of acute limb ischaemia are seldom all present in early acute compartment syndrome

PE
- Inspection: observe for skin lesions, swelling, colour changes (pallor/redness)
- Palpation: observe temperature, tense compartment with a "wood-like" feeling, diminished sensation, usually pulse remains present
- Function: pain with passive stretch of muscles in the affected compartment, muscle weakness, paralysis (late sign)

Dx
- Diagnosis is based on clinical findings
- Invasive compartment pressure measurement: if suspected acute compartment syndrome with equivocal clinical findings (>30 mmHg indicated acute compartment syndrome and need for fasciotomy)
- Labs: CK ↑ may suggest muscle breakdown from ischaemia, damage, or rhabdomyolysis
- X-ray: if a fracture is suspected

Tx Remove constrictive dressings/splints, elevate the limb

Systemic analgesia

Fasciotomy (emergency surgery)

P
- Depends mainly on how quickly it is diagnosed and treated
- Fasciotomy <6h: almost 100% recovery; <12h: $^{2}/_{3}$ have normal limb function

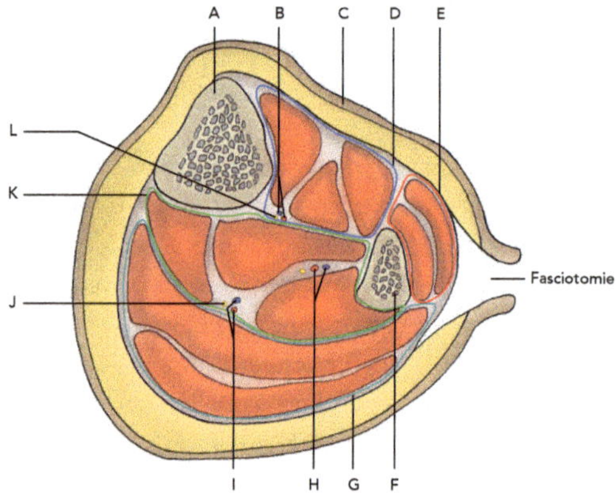

Figure 75 // Compartments of the lower leg

A: Tibia **B:** Anterior tibial artery/vein **C:** Skin **D:** Anterior tibial compartment **E:** Peroneal compartment **F:** Fibula **G:** Superficial posterior compartment **H:** Fibular artery/vein **I:** Posterior tibial artery/vein **J:** Tibial nerve **K:** Deep posterior compartment **L:** Deep fibular nerve

6 Ps of acute limb ischaemia:

- **P**ain
- **P**allor
- **P**araesthesias
- **P**oikilothermia
- **P**ulselessness
- **P**aralysis

Acute intestinal ischaemia

D Acute intestinal ischaemia, also referred to as acute mesenteric ischaemia, is a situation in which the blood supply to the intestines is acutely and severely reduced.

E Incidence: 16:100,000 per year

Ae
- Embolus emanating from a thrombus released from the left atrium, the LV, heart valves or proximal aorta → occlusion of the intestinal arteries (often the superior mesenteric artery, due to this vessel being less angular than the aorta). Often two arteries are completely occluded, due to progression of pre-existing atherosclerosis, often in patients with a history of chronic splanchnic syndrome.

- Mesenteric arterial embolism (50%), non-occlusive mesenteric ischaemia (NOMI) (20-30%), mesenteric arterial thrombosis (15-25%), mesenteric venous thrombosis (5%)
- In the case of venous mesenteric ischaemia, this can be primary (20%) or secondary (80%) as a result of hypercoagulability
- NOMI is primarily related to cardiac surgery and haemodialysis (hypotension). Cardiac surgery → irreversible, persistent vasoconstriction of the intestinal vascular bed.
- See Table 124

R Smoking, DM, hypertension, hyperlipidaemia, cardiac arrhythmias, heart valve disease, infectious endocarditis, recent myocardial infarction, ventricular aneurysm, aortic stenosis, and aortic aneurysm → risk of embolism ↑, patients with peripheral arterial vascular disease → risk of occlusion caused by thrombus ↑, advanced age and low cardiac output → risk of embolic occlusion ↑

Hx Acute severe abdominal pain, vomiting, nausea, risk of hypovolaemia ↑ (thirst ↑, diuresis ↓, vomiting, later hypovolaemic shock)

PE No obvious abdominal abnormalities, except severe pain in right lower abdomen (++), HR ↑, BP ↓

Dx
- Labs: WBC ↑ (due to volume depletion) or ↓ (due to GI bleed), Hct ↑, amylase ↑, blood gas (metabolic acidosis), lactate (↑ only in first hours, non-specific after that window), D-dimer ↑ (can also be due to other inflammatory or infectious diseases), I-FABP ↑ (intestinal fatty-acid binding protein) (I-FABP ↑ reflects specifically on the intestinal mucosa, no ↑ with other forms of ischaemia)
- Abdominal X-ray: pneumatosis, free air, bowel distension (non-specific for detecting acute intestinal ischaemia)
- Abdominal CT with arterial and venous contrast phase (diagnostic for acute intestinal ischaemia): occlusion 1-3 mesenteric arteries, thickened intestinal wall, gas in portal system, pneumatosis intestinalis

Tx Nil per os, NG tube

- Oxygen, anticoagulant (heparin in acute phase), no vasopressors due to exacerbations of ischaemia, broad spectrum AB, PPI
- Haemodynamic stability, correction of electrolyte abnormalities

- Surgery: exploration, resection of necrotic bowel, revascularisation, damage control
- Endovascular revascularisation: thrombectomy, angioplasty
- It is possible to opt for a primary endovascular access in stable patients without clinical or radiological signs of advanced intestinal ischaemia

P Acute mesenteric ischaemia mortality rate: >60% (mesenteric venous thrombosis: lower mortality, better recognition, and earlier treatment)

> In a patient >60y with sudden severe abdominal pain, without obvious indications in the PE (pain often appears disproportional with regard to the PE) and Dx, the working diagnosis is acute intestinal ischaemia until proven otherwise.

CAUSE	NATURE AND PERCENTAGE
Arterial	Thrombosis (50%), embolism (10%)
Venous	15%
Non-occlusive mesenteric ischaemia	25%
Other	Trauma, vasculitis, radiotherapy, strangulation (volvulus or hernia)

Table 124 // Causes of acute intestinal ischaemia

> An **embolism** is a clot of any type of material (blood clot, cholesterol plaque, fat body, foreign body, bacterial clump, etc.) that can cause an obstruction of a blood vessel beyond the site where it originated, whilst a **thrombus** is a blood clot that causes an obstruction at the site where it forms.

Aortic dissection

D Aortic dissection is a condition in which the tunica intima of the aorta is damaged to such an extent that blood accumulates between the tunica intima and the other layers of the aorta. It is an acutely life-threatening condition, due to the risk of aortic rupture and/or ischaemia of other organs. The types of aortic dissection are categorised according to the Stanford classification (A or B), or the DeBakey classification (type I, II, IIIa and IIIb) (see Figure 76). Dissections can also be categorised as acute (up to two weeks), sub-acute (two to six weeks), and chronic (after 6 weeks).

E Incidence 0.5-3:100,000 per year, 75% of cases 40-70y, ♂>♀

Ae Mechanical and hydrostatic pressure ↑, degeneration of the vessel wall (e.g. as a result of hypertension, pre-existing connective tissue abnormalities, Marfan syndrome), iatrogenic damage (e.g. cardiac catheterisation), unknown predisposing factors → intimal tear, usually in the ascending aorta and near the left subclavian artery, where the pressures are high → development of "true" and "false" lumen

R Hypertension (most common), connective tissue disorders, bicuspid aortic valve, aortic aneurysm, cocaine use, ♀:♂ = 1:2

Hx Sudden, stabbing chest pains radiating to the back and between the shoulder blades

PE Diastolic murmur precordial with aortic valve regurgitation caused by dissection continuing to the annulus, possible difference in BP left and right, heart rate deficit, neurological deficits, tamponade

Dx
- Chest X-ray: widened mediastinum and/or widened aortic contour
- ECG
- In case of suspected aortic dissection: urgent TTE, POCUS, or chest and abdominal CT without contrast and with arterial/venous contrast (gold standard)

Tx Type-A dissections or type-B dissections that develop complications (e.g. imminent rupture, impaired circulation (end organ ischaemia), persistent pain, or increasing pleural effusion), if possible: thoracic endovascular aortic repair (TEVAR) or artificial prosthesis through open thoracotomy

Type-B dissections: IV beta blockers and vasodilators adjusted according to BP and urine output, on a monitored ward (e.g. ICU)

P Mortality rate: 20-30% (depends on type of dissection and on treatment)

! Risk of dissecting aneurysm with conservative treatment of an aneurysm: dilatation

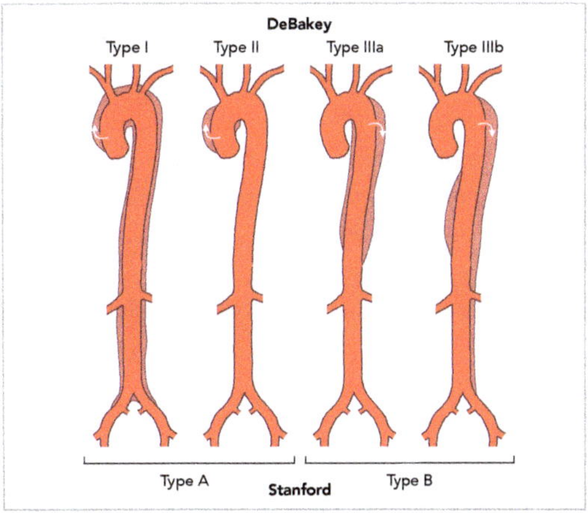

Figure 76 // Stanford and DeBakey classifications
DeBakey **Type I:** dissection arises in the ascending aorta up to the aortic arch, the descending aorta is often also involved; **Type II:** dissection is limited to the ascending aorta; **Type IIIa:** dissection arises in the descending aorta (from left subclavian artery) to above the diaphragm; **Type IIIb:** dissection arises in the descending aorta (from left subclavian artery) to below the diaphragm.

Necrotising fasciitis

D Necrotising fasciitis is a rare form of cellulitis usually caused by group A (e.g. *Streptococcus pyogenes*), a mixed infection, or in some cases (e.g. immunocompromised patients) a fungal infection. It is a fulminant infection, characterised by necrosis of all skin layers, fascia, and muscle that can develop into a life-threatening condition within hours.

E Incidence 0.3-15:100,000 per year worldwide

Ae *Streptococcus pyogenes*, mixed infection, or fungal infection

R DM, obesity, impaired immune system, liver disease, drug abuse

Hx Excruciating, disproportional pain, systemic septic signs, rapid expansion of redness, and swelling, sometimes crepitus upon palpation (due to gas in underlying tissues, esp. in *Clostridium* spp. infection)

PE
- P Mainly limbs but can occur everywhere
- A Solitary
- S Regional, rapidly increasing in size
- S Variable
- O Ill-demarcated erythema initially, well-demarcated bullae, and ulcerations later
- N Red, lesions quickly turn grey-blue with blistering and black necrosis
- E Erythematous macules with bullae, necrosis, and ulcerations

Dx
- Labs (possible findings): CRP ↑, WBC ↑, Hb ↓, Na ↓, creatinine ↑, glucose >180 mg/dl
- X-ray: subcutaneous gas/emphysema in *Clostridium* spp.
- Consider CT with IV contrast: gas in subcutaneous soft tissue, potentially fluid collections

Tx
- AB IV in consultation with microbiologist
- Analgesia for oain management
- Immunoglobulin IV for streptococcal toxic shock syndrome

Clinical suspicion warrants immediate surgical exploration and debridement of necrotic tissue with daily dressing

P Mortality 25%

!
- Always consider necrotising fasciitis in cases of extremely painful cellulitis unresponsive to ABx
- Treatment differs in case of fungal infection

Consider necrotising fasciitis in patients presenting with extreme pain for a relatively small infection and a rapid infection process. Often, a sharply-defined erythema may be present. Draw a line with a marker and note the time. Necrotising fasciitis is primarily distinguished from a simple erythema because it can progress at a rapid rate, marked by extreme pain and rapid infection progression.

Urology

Acute urinary retention (AUR)

D AUR is the inability to pass urine voluntarily. It is the most common urological emergency.

E Most frequently in males >60y. Over a 5y period, present in 10% of males >70y, 1:13 (♀:♂).

Ae Obstructive (most common, i.e. benign prostate hyperplasia), infectious, inflammatory, pharmacological, neurological

R
- ♂, ↑ age, obesity, DM, high alcohol consumption, physical inactivity
- History of prostate disease, pelvic or prostate surgery, radiation or pelvic trauma

Hx Inability to pass urine, lower abdominal and/or supra-pubic discomfort or pain, distress, acute decreased/altered consciousness in older patients

PE
- Abdominal inspection (bladder >1L is visible), abdominal percussion (bladder >300 mL can be percussed)
- Rectal examination: evaluate prostate (♂), assess sphincter tone, detect rectal mass or faecal impaction

Dx
- Labs: urinalysis and urine culture, HbA1c (exclude diabetes as potential cause), serum PSA to exclude prostate carcinoma (♂)
- Bladder and renal ultrasound: >150 mL in patients unable to void suggests urinary retention → assess kidneys for hydronephrosis
- More than 100-150 mL of residual urine after an attempt to urinate is considered a retention

Tx Alpha blockers

Treatment of the underlying cause

Prompt bladder decompression if >2 unsuccessful voiding trials: if urethral catheterisation fails, consider supra-pubic catheterisation

P Recurrence in 70% <1y

! • Complications: renal failure (AKI, obstructive nephropathy), chronic urinary retention, polyuria
• Beware of polyuria if hydronephrosis is present: polyuria might suggest ATN

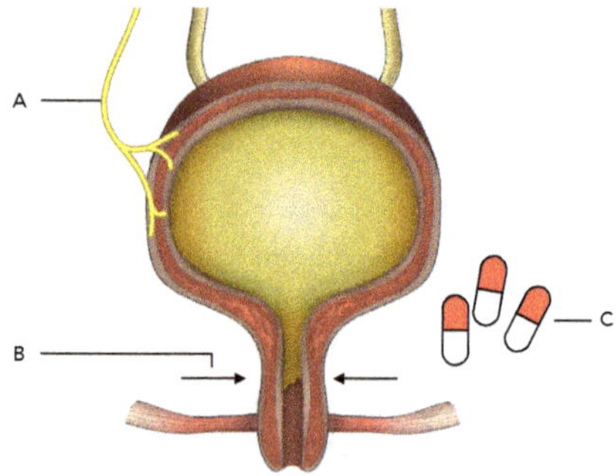

Figure 77 // Bladder retention: possible causes
A: Neurogenic bladder **B:** Obstructive cause (including BPH, urethral stricture) **C:** Medicinal

Urolithiasis

D Urolithiasis is used as an umbrella term (presence of stones in the urinary tract). Nephrolithiasis refers to the presence of stones in the kidneys or the pyelocaliceal system. Uterolithiasis refers to the presence of stones in the ureters. Cystolithiasis refers to the presence of stones in the bladder. 70-80% of the stones consist of calcium oxalate.

E Prevalence varies globally (1-15%), in Asia 1-5%, in Europe 5-9%, and in North America 7-15%

Ae Fluid intake ↓, genetic, infections

R • ♂, positive FHx, history of urolithiasis, primary hypoparathyroidism (hypercalciuria), obesity, gout (↑ uric acid), IBD, status following Roux-en-Y bypass surgery, anatomical variation (horseshoe kidney), high animal protein intake, high calcium and oxalate intake, high salt and sugar intake
• Chronic urinary retention (e.g. benign prostatic hyperplasia (BPH) (++)) → cystolithiasis

Hx Acute colic in the flank and back, possibly radiating to the groin and scrotum/vulva, nausea, vomiting, haematuria, dysuria, pollakiuria

PE T =/↑, BP = (↓ with sepsis) costovertebral angle tenderness

Dx
- Urine stick: erythrocytes ⊕, pH ↓ (calcium/phosphate in stones) / ↑ (uric acid in stones)
- Labs: eGFR, Ca^{2+} =/↑, uric acid =/↑
- Ultrasound of urinary tract: hydronephrosis, possible pyelocaliceal concretions, or concretions in proximal ureters or ostia
- Abdominal CT without contrast to detect kidney stones (gold standard in acute setting): presence of concretions, localisation, density, size (for prognosis of spontaneous passage or indication for lithotripsy)
- Retrograde uropyelography: to assess passage through ureters in scheduled double J stent placement

Tx
- Normal recommended daily fluid intake
- Prevention: fluid intake 2.5-3 L/d, avoid high calcium intake, salt restriction, restrict animal protein (oxalate)

- Stop colic: NSAIDs (diclofenac IM/IV/rectal), if inadequate effect morphine SC/IM
- Other analgesia: NSAIDs oral, morphine oral, alpha blocker for distal ureter stone >5 mm

For low probability of spontaneous stone passage, persistent obstruction with renal function impairment, or pain despite adequate analgesia:
- Ureterorenoscopy (URS) with stone extraction or laser lithotripsy (in OR)
- Extracorporeal ShockWave Lithotripsy (ESWL) if stone is visible on ultrasound or abdominal X-ray
- Percutaneous nephrolitholapaxy (PNL) for kidney stones >2 cm

P
- Risk of recurrence 50%
- Chance of spontaneous stone passage ±80%

! Complication: urosepsis. In (impeding) urosepsis: collect urine cultures, ABx, insert nephrostomy catheter or double J stent (if passage through ureters is possible).

> A high calcium intake is known to increase the risk of urolithiasis. However, the general population tends to have a low calcium intake, which also increases the risk of kidney stones. It is recommended to maintain a normal calcium intake while reducing oxalate consumption.

Palliative care

Palliative care is an approach that improves the quality of life for patients and their loved ones facing a life-threatening condition, such as cancer, HF, COPD or dementia. It aims to prevent and alleviate suffering through early identification and careful assessment and treatment of physical, psychosocial, and spiritual issues.

WHO definition of palliative care:

- Provides relief from pain and other distressing symptoms;
- Affirms life and regards dying as a normal process;
- Intends neither to hasten nor postpone death;
- Integrates the psychological and spiritual aspects of patient care;
- Offers a support system to help patients live as actively as possible until death;
- Offers a support system to help the family cope during a patient's illness and their own bereavement;
- Uses a team approach to address the needs of patients and their families, including bereavement counselling, if indicated;
- Will enhance quality of life, and may also positively influence the course of illness;
- Is applicable early in the course of illness, in conjunction with other therapies that are intended to prolong life, such as chemotherapy or radiation therapy, and includes those investigations needed to improve understanding and management of distressing clinical complications.

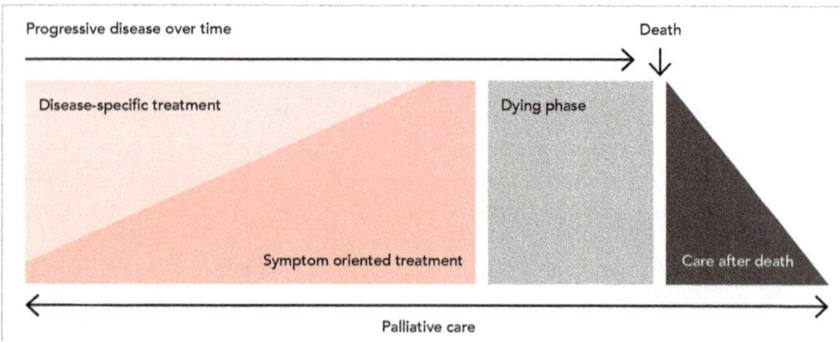

Figure 78 // Palliative care

> Although 63% of western and 26% of central and eastern European countries have a standalone national palliative care plan, many countries do not have national health policies and systems that include palliative care.

Surprise question

A tool used to identify the palliative phase is the surprise question. If a patient's medical condition worsens, a doctor or nurse might ask the surprise question. A negative response prompts a shift from primarily curative to a more palliative approach, focusing on the patient's comfort. It's important to engage in conversation with the patient and their loved ones about their wishes and needs during this phase. Assess their readiness for this conversation and their ability to process the information.

> Surprise question: 'Would it surprise me if this patient were to pass away in the next 12 months?'

Final stage of life

In the final stage of life, in patients whose passing is anticipated in the near future, vital organ systems begin to deteriorate. A cascade of events ensues, ultimately leading to death.

- Kidney and liver dysfunction → metabolic disturbances and a cytokine-mediated catabolic process → anorexia-cachexia syndrome → muscle weakness and overall frailty
- Cardiac function ↓ → organ perfusion and urine production ↓
- Cerebral ischaemia and hypoxia → sensitivity to partial CO_2 pressure → consciousness, reflexes, central respiratory drive ↓
- Eventually, Cheyne-Stokes breathing occurs: a pattern of gradually increasing and decreasing breaths followed by apnoeas. The frequency of apnoeas increases at the moment of death.

> In the final stage of life, morphine can be used to alleviate pain or breathlessness. It's important to communicate that morphine does not cause the patient's death. However, drowsiness is a significant side effect of morphine.

SYMPTOM	INFORMATION
Pain	• Explain to relatives about the interpretation and signals that may indicate pain but do not always have to be a signal of pain • Signals that may indicate pain include frowning, groaning, or increased motoric restlessness • Unexpected, uncontrollable pain is rare in the final stage of life
Rattling	• Explain to relatives that rattling is caused by the drying of saliva and that patients are typically not bothered by audible breathing due to their often reduced consciousness • Assure loved ones that rattling is not a sign of respiratory disease
Dyspnoea	• Explain dyspnoea and Cheyne-Stokes respiration • Weakness of the respiratory muscles contributes to dyspnoea in the dying phase • Accumulation of CO_2 → consciousness ↓ → perception of dyspnoea ↓ • Explain that choking almost never happens • Choking occurs only with specific pathology (e.g. obstruction of the large airways by a tumour)
Nausea/ vomiting	• Explain the lack of thirst and hunger during the dying phase • Nausea and vomiting during the dying phase of life are uncommon, however existing complaints can continue
Terminal agitation/ delirium	• Explain terminal restlessness and myoclonia due to the dying phase, which is often not an expression of discomfort • Be aware of an underlying cause of restlessness (e.g. bladder retention or obstipation)
Anxiety	• It is important to distinguish between anxiety and delirium • Be aware that physical complications can be a reason for fear during the dying phase
Urination and defaecation	• Being confined to bed and the use of opioids pose a risk of micturition and defaecation problems • Clearly indicate that the patient can experience this and may let the urine or faeces flow
Dry mouth	Explain that a dry mouth cannot be prevented or remedied by artificial fluid administration

Table 125 // Symptoms, providing information and treatment during the final stage of life

TREATMENT

- Patient still conscious: treat pain in consultation with the patient in accordance with the WHO pain ladder. If the patient is having difficulty swallowing, choose non-oral dosage forms
- Patient unconscious: titrate pain medication based on pain signals in accordance with the WHO pain ladder
- Skin perfusion during dying phase ↓, a SC or IV administration of morphine is preferred instead of transdermally

- If there is a high risk of mucus formation, you can consider scopolamine (you have to start treatment before it is present)
- Adjusting body position: lateral position (provided this is comfortable for the patient)
- Avoiding suctioning (leads to gagging, coughing and mucus production ↑)

- Morphine
- If morphine is insufficient after increasing the dose, then benzodiazepines can be added
- Corticosteroids (e.g. COPD) and diuretic medication (e.g. HF) are continued as long as possible

- Discontinue non-contributory medication
- Ensure a comfortable body position for the patient
- Moisten the mouth
- Antiemetics
- In case of an ileus: consider octreotides, scopolamine or stomach tube
- In case of hiccups: medication such as baclofen

- Guarantee peace and safety: ensure a quiet and low-stimulus environment
- Medication for terminal delirium
- During the dying phase, patients can still hear for a long time (despite the fact that they often no longer respond) and they are often calmed by the voices of their relatives

- If necessary, involve a spiritual counsellor
- Benzodiazepines
- Anxiety can also be a side effect of opioids

- Consider a bladder catheter (♂ consider a condom catheter, this has fewer side effects compared to a normal catheter)
- Consider an enema, however this could be an extra burden for the patient, so consider this carefully

- Good oral hygiene
- Regularly moisten the mucous membranes

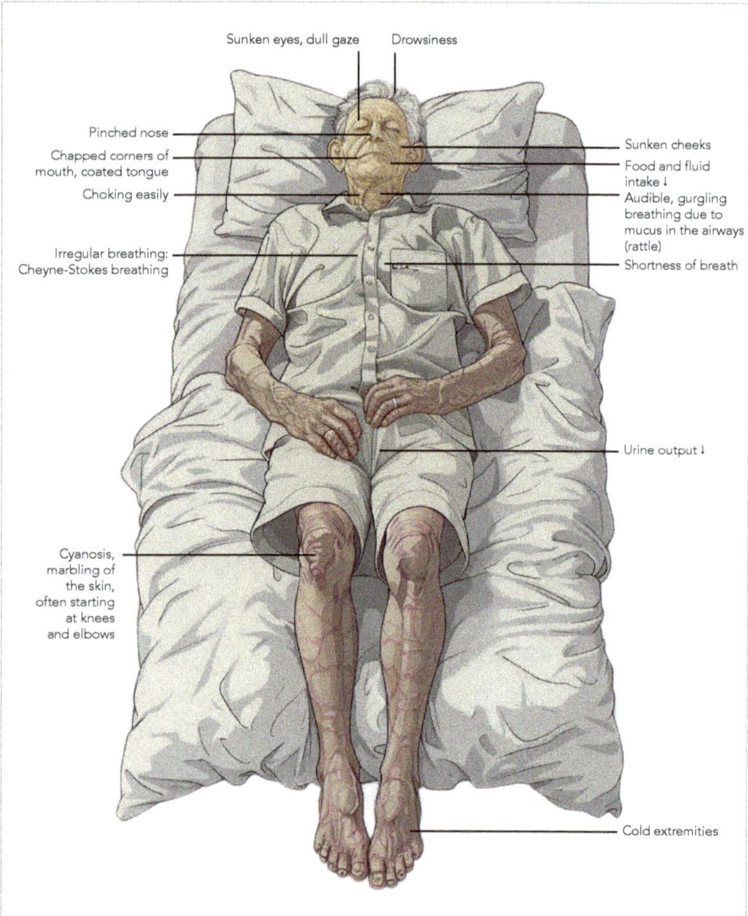

Figure 79 // Characteristics of a dying body

Signs of impending death may include:

- Karnofsky Performance Status ≤30
- Clinical Frailty Score 8 or 9
- Urine output ↓
- Food and fluid intake ↓
- Tachycardia accompanied by a weak pulse
- Cold extremities, cyanosis, marbling of the skin

- Level of consciousness ↓, drowsiness ↑
- Terminal delirium
- Audible, gurgling breathing due to mucus in the airways (rattle)
- Irregular breathing: Cheyne-Stokes breathing
- Pinched nose, sunken eyes
- The patient themselves indicating that death is near

Medical examination after death

In most countries, death must be confirmed by a physician. This confirmation is typically performed by a qualified physician who conducts an examination to confirm that the individual has passed away. The physician assesses the patient for signs of life, such as breathing and heartbeat, and checks for other physiological indicators of death, such as lack of response to stimuli. Following this examination, the physician can issue a death certificate officially confirming the death. This process may vary depending on the legal requirements and cultural practices of the country in question.

> Accurate documentation is essential. Asystole or the absence of breathing alone is insufficient. Definitive signs of death, such as rigor mortis or livor mortis, should be reviewed and recorded. If a non-natural cause of death is suspected, a full examination of the body, with the patient fully undressed, should be conducted.

Frequently asked questions (FAQ)

General

Although the novice junior doctor will primarily have concerns about recognising and treating critically ill patients during their initial shifts, the (often non-urgent) questions posed by ward nurses in daily practice can be just as challenging. Of course, every newly graduated medical student knows that hyperglycaemia should be treated with insulin, but most beginners do not know exactly how much insulin to administer and what to watch out for. This chapter offers practical suggestions for the "Frequently asked questions" (FAQ) during on-call shifts.

> Local protocols are the main guidelines for your actions. For quick access, save local protocols on your computer.

> As soon as your telephone or pager rings, grab a pen and paper and write along.

> For every phone call, decide whether this is something that you need to tackle **immediately yourself**, can **delegate** (e.g. to the admissions coordinator, on-call supervisor, or intern), can **schedule** (comment in the chart for the day shift and handover), or **need to take note of** (a short note in the chart should suffice).

> Make a **short note** in the chart about the telephone consultation during your shift. This will make it clear to the ward doctor on duty the following day that somebody contacted the ward.

Questions relating to medication prescriptions

Questions relating to medication prescriptions are very common: the nurse can consult you about home medication that is missing from the admissions list, apparently incorrect dosages, unclear indications and/or not having access to a certain substance.

"The patient uses metformin at home, but it is not on the list. Can you write a prescription?"

"The patient has been prescribed 50 mg metoprolol once daily, but the patient uses 100 mg/d at home. Can you adjust the prescription?"

"The pharmacist just called to say that they cannot dispense pravastatin. Can you prescribe an alternative?"

- First consider whether this question needs to be answered by the night shift, or whether it can be postponed until morning rounds. If it sounds like an urgent question to you, then check the hospital information system whilst discussing the question.
- If the nurse's findings appear to be correct, try to find out whether this is a deliberate, conscious change (any changes and relevant considerations are often listed under "treatment").
- However, if you cannot confirm the nurse's findings (the prescribed medication corresponds to the documented home medication and there are no notes describing any changes), then your colleague may have based the decision on an outdated/incorrect medication list. In that case, check whether prescribing the medication is something that absolutely must be done during your shift and check that there are no contra-indications.

Questions relating to anticoagulant policy

"Can you adjust the dose of acenocoumarol?"

You will encounter coumarins regularly on medication lists, particularly with elderly patients. At the start of the treatment, the INR is checked every few days to determine whether the clotting value is within the target range (depending on the indication). Once values are stable and predictable, the time between checks can be extended.

- Check what the patient is using coumarins for (and which target INR range needs to be maintained).
- Check explicitly whether the coumarins need to be continued during the hospitalisation or if you have to bridge a (temporary) stop.
- If continuation is required, check whether an INR has recently been determined.

- If a recent INR is available and this falls within the target range, then continue the previous schedule and ask the nurse to make a note for the morning rounds.
- If a recent INR is not available, check the dosage instructions together with the course of the INR over the preceding period. If the INR was reasonably stable at a certain dosage schedule and there are no reasons to assume that the INR has deviated significantly (e.g. clinical deterioration, initial phase after suspending treatment for a procedure), then continue the dosage schedule of the past few days for the next dose (use the patient's own dosing schedule for newly admitted patients, check with the patient) and request INR determination for the following day. Make a note about this in the chart and ask the nurse to ensure that this is discussed during the doctors' rounds the next day.

Questions relating to analgesia

See section *Pharmacological treatment* for more information about bridging and analgesia.

Pain is acceptable when the patient says that it is acceptable, the patient is not impeded in breathing/coughing/movement and the patient has a pain score <4. If the patient is impeded in their breathing/coughing/movement and has a pain score ≥4, then extra analgesia should be prescribed until the pain reaches an acceptable level.

Questions relating to nausea

"My patient is nauseous, what can I give him?"

- Take complaints of nausea seriously, as vomiting poses a risk of aspiration.
- Check whether this is a new symptom and why the patient could be nauseous and then try to remove this trigger if possible. Is there a logical reason for the patient to feel nauseous, considering the reason for admission? For example, is the patient recovering from a recent surgical procedure or actively being treated with chemotherapy?
- Is this a side effect of another medication? In that case, check whether an alternative could be used.

- Check which antiemetics are used in your centre and follow the local protocols (often a specific type of antiemetic is preferred in the situations described above).

Questions relating to diabetes regulation

"My patient has a glucose of 16.3, what extra injections can I give him?"

During hospitalisation, hyperglycaemia is more likely to occur due to illness, even in people without diabetes mellitus. In addition, certain medications could influence the blood glucose levels as well (e.g. prednisone). Patients being treated with oral blood glucose-lowering agents can generally use a scheduled "standard" extra injection (see Table 126). Note that the dose recommendation "before bedtime" (BB) is lower than the dose recommendations for the rest of the day! If the total daily dosage exceeds 40 units (all units of insulin per day added together), then the standard schedule will often need to be increased to achieve an adequate therapeutic effect. In that case, request a consultation from the internist during daytime.

EXAMPLE OF STANDARD ADDITIONAL INJECTION SCHEDULE FOR NOVORAPID	GLUCOSE 10-12 MMOL/L	GLUCOSE 12-15 MMOL/L	GLUCOSE 15-20 MMOL/L
Insulin daily dose 0-40U	2U (BB = accept deviation)	4U (BB = 2U)	6U (BB = 4U)

Table 126 // Example of standard additional injection schedule for Novorapid with maximum total daily dosage of insulin at 40 units. BB = before bedtime

"My patient needs to remain nil per mouth, what should I do with the insulin?"

The diabetes policy surrounding procedures depends on the urgency of the procedure (acute/scheduled) and the patient's own treatment regimen (see example in Table 127).

EXAMPLE OF DIABETES REGULATION SURROUNDING ACUTE/SCHEDULED PROCEDURES	BLOOD GLUCOSE-LOWERING TABLETS	INSULIN
Acute procedure	• Stop tablets • Administer glucose pre-op if <6 mmol/L • Restart own medication when patient resumes normal diet • Monitor the GDC	• Stop own insulin • Start continuous infusion of glucose/insulin • Restart own medication when patient resumes normal diet • Monitor the GDC
Scheduled procedure	• Skip morning dose • Administer glucose pre-op if <6 mmol/L • Restart own medication when patient resumes normal diet • Monitor the GDC	• Glucose BB ≥6 mmol/L: normal evening dose of long-acting insulin • Glucose BB <6 mmol/L: reduce evening dose by at least 4U • Skip morning dose of insulin • Start continuous infusion of glucose/insulin • Restart own medication when patient resumes normal diet

Table 127 // Example of diabetes regulation surrounding acute/scheduled procedures GDC = glucose daily curve, BB = before bedtime

"My patient has a hypo, what should I do now?"

- If the patient is still conscious, administer dextrose, followed by 15-20g carbohydrates (e.g. a sandwich), repeat if necessary.
- For severe hypoglycaemia: administer 10g glucose as a slow bolus IV (10g = 100 mL glucose 10% = 20 mL glucose 50%: expected increase of 2 mmol/L per 10g) and check glucose <10 min, repeat if necessary. Once the patient has recovered, ensure that he eats some long-acting carbohydrates (e.g. a sandwich).
- If oral or IV administration of glucose is not possible (yet), give 1 mg glucagon IM. There is no point in repeating this.
- In the case of hypoglycaemia caused by sulphonyl urea derivatives (e.g. gliclazide, glibenclamide), this course of action should be followed by clinical observation and - if necessary - a continuous glucose infusion, due to the long half-life of these preparations.
- If the hypoglycaemia is detected before the night, consider skipping the patient's usual dose of long-acting insulin or at least reduce this dose significant-

ly, depending on how high the standard dose is.

- Once the hypoglycaemia has been corrected, determine why the hypoglycaemia occurred (e.g. changes in dietary instructions, tapering of prednisone) and adjust the treatment accordingly.

Questions relating to the IV fluids policy

"The patient has returned from the CT, what setting should I put the infusion pump on?"

Various imaging techniques make use of IV contrast. There is a risk of contrast nephropathy (also called post-contrast acute kidney damage), particularly in patients whose renal function is already reduced. This damage can be (partially) prevented by giving patients generous hydration surrounding the examination.

- Patients with an eGFR <30 mL/min/1.73m^2 are at increased risk of contrast nephropathy when IV contrast is administered. In addition, vascular disease, diabetes mellitus, administration of a larger total quantity of contrast agent (e.g. for angio-intervention), advanced age (>75y) and the excretion of light chains in the urine as a result of Waldenström macroglobulinaemia/multiple myeloma can all contribute to an increase in the risk.
- Keep in mind that patients at risk of contrast nephropathy are often also at risk of fluid overload (e.g. due to underlying cardiovascular disease).
- Suspend diuretics, metformin and NSAIDs 24h prior to the examination.

Sample schedule of pre-hydration and post-hydration with sodium bicarbonate

- Before the scan: 3 mL/kg/h NaBic 1.4% for 1h.
- After the scan: 1 mL/kg/h NaBic 1.4% for 6h.

"Ms Jones' IV has failed, does she need a new IV?"

- Check whether the indication for the IV is still relevant (volume supplementation, IV medication, etc.).
- You can introduce an IV catheter using ultrasound.

"My patient has a positive fluid balance of 1250 cc."

Sometimes you will receive a phone call about an abnormal fluid balance (patient's input e.g. intake, IV, tube feeding vs. patient's output e.g. urine output, drain production, sweating). Take "insensible losses" into consideration; a positive balance of several hundred cc can easily be explained by the fluid lost via the airways and the skin. Indications for keeping track of the fluid balance include e.g. haemodynamic instability, fluid overload and imposed fluid restrictions.

- Check whether the abnormal fluid balance is bothering the patient. For example, does the patient feel short of breath and/or unable to lie flat (beware of fluid overload)? You should take action if the patient is presenting clinical signs of fluid overload or hypovolaemia.
- Keep in mind that a fluid balance can never be tracked with 100% accuracy. Check whether the registration appears realistic (critically inspect the recorded output) and trust your clinical judgement in this regard. In addition to the fluid balance, patients are often weighed daily for verification purposes.

Questions relating to abnormal observations

"My patient is passing very little urine, what is acceptable?"

- What does the caller mean by "very little" and how was this measured? First try to gauge the urine production objectively.
- Sometimes a patient has not passed urine spontaneously yet, but a bladder scan reveals that the bladder contains a generous volume of urine. You can consider a wait-and-see approach for this patient, particularly if their haemodynamic status does not reveal any signs of hypovolaemia. Ask the nurse to call again if the patient has not urinated spontaneously within two hours.
- Treat the patient soon if they exhibit clinical signs of hypovolaemia. Order a formal recording of the fluid balance from that point onwards.
- Once the oliguria has been confirmed objectively, order an indwelling catheter with urine meter - if this is not already in position - and ask the nurse to empty the collection bag every hour and record the production.
- Once the oliguria has been confirmed, check for any underlying causes of the oliguria (check the course of the blood pressure and heart rate, check the fluid balance if available and evaluate the course of the serum creatinine).

Although various reference materials recommend a target diuresis of 0.5 mL/kg/h, recent studies demonstrate that the blood pressure is the main determinant for the ultimate result of the case. In other words, you should base your decisions primarily on the blood pressure (aim for a MAP >65 mmHg) and do not continue giving the patient fluids if he has not achieved the recommended target diuresis yet.

The bladder scan measures fluid in the abdominal cavity. In case of fluid in the abdominal cavity due to other problems (e.g. ascites), an incorrect estimate is given. Urine production may be low in the first few hours after spinal anaesthesia.

"My patient's saturation seems to be dropping lower and lower, at the start of the evening it was 96%, now it's at 93%. Yesterday his saturation was fine at 99%. Shall I give him a nasal cannula?"

Although the nurse has not specifically requested it, these patients are often entitled to a formal assessment by the on-call physician.

- Ask the nurse to perform observations every hour for the time being (respiration rate, saturation, heart rate, blood pressure, AVPU, temperature), have the patient sit upright and encourage them to take several deep breaths. In the meantime, the patient in this case can also be started on oxygen (target saturation 94-98%). The frequent observations will also monitor the effect of this intervention.
- Ensure that all the required materials for lab sample collections are prepared (see the section *The treatment of a patient with dyspnoea*).
- Ask the nurse to call you sooner if they feel something is wrong/notice a deterioration in the vital signs. Give the nurse fixed limits, to provide certainty about when to contact you.

"The fluid challenge has been administered, but the patient's blood pressure is still 90/52 mmHg. What do you want me to do?"

- In this case, the intervention that was probably agreed upon over the telephone at an earlier stage has not produced the desired response. If this was not discussed with you, ask for additional information (reason for admission, other checks, etc.) according to the SBAR.
- Check on the patient yourself as soon as possible and call the ERT for a consultation sooner rather than later.

"My patient has a MEWS of 6."

- Check why the nurse has arrived at this score for the patient (abnormal blood pressure or heart rate, low saturation, reduced consciousness, or a combination of abnormal values), the number itself does not provide sufficient information to draw up a treatment plan.
- Check whether this is an acute or gradual deterioration/change, to determine the urgency of this request.
- Take the nurse's gut feeling into consideration when determining the level of urgency.
- Provide instructions over the telephone for the initial care on the ward (see section *Treatment of a patient with...*) and go and check on the patient yourself as soon as possible.

"The observations are fine, but something feels off. Can you come and have a look?"

Both the nurse's "sense that something is off" and the underlying subjective signs are proven early predictors of a clinical deterioration. When assessing a patient, do not base your decisions solely on the objective measurement values, but include the subjective signs and the nurse's feeling that something is off.

Nurses may struggle to describe this feeling, particularly if the vital signs do not support that feeling. You can help the nurse to clarify this feeling by asking additional questions.

- Ask the nurse to perform observations every hour for the time being (respiration rate, saturation, heart rate, blood pressure, temperature).

- Ask the nurse to call you sooner rather than later if they feel something is wrong/notice a change in the vital signs.
- Finish what you are doing and try to check on the patient as soon as possible after that.
- Use the checklists to assess the trends in the MEWS.

Questions relating end-of-life care

"My patient does not seem comfortable, can you come and have a look?"

- Always check on the patient as soon as possible if they experience pain, dyspnoea or restlessness. You have to realise that this is a moment in which you - as the doctor on call - can really make a difference for the patient and his loved ones.
- If you are informed that a patient is close to death, go to the patient at the start of your shift and introduce yourself to any loved ones who are there. This is often greatly appreciated and will make it easier for you when you return at a later time to confirm the patient's death.
- In general, you should always follow the local protocols.

> Palliative sedation is the deliberate lowering of the patient's consciousness by administration of sedatives, aimed at alleviating their suffering. This is a decision made by the doctor, based on the patient's wishes. Prerequisites for palliative sedation are:
> - Presence of refractory symptom(s) (pain, dyspnoea, delirium).
> - Expertise and consensus of the treatment team: consult external experts where necessary (e.g. palliative consultation team) and/or moral deliberation.
> - Use of sedation in accordance with the wishes of the patient and his loved ones. It is important to differentiate between a request for palliative sedation and a request for euthanasia.
> - The life-expectancy is <2 wk (only for deep and continuous sedation).

- The decision-making process surrounding palliative sedation must be recorded in the patient's medical file. All healthcare professionals involved in the patient's care must be informed.

- The following risk factors of the patient must be taken into consideration when determining the dose of midazolam, as these can result in stronger sedation: age >60y, weight less than 60 kg, renal and/or hepatic impairment, decreased albumin and co-medication.
- The dose of the sedative is an estimate. Patients can be so weak that the dose that is administered is a relatively high dose. Warn the patient that death may come quickly after administration of the dose.

"My patient has died, can you conduct a post-mortem examination?"

A post-mortem examination must be performed on every patient. Anyone can conclude that a patient has died, but only the treating doctor or coroner can conduct a post-mortem examination and determine the cause of death. The treating doctor can immediately issue a certificate if he is convinced that the patient died a natural death. If this is not the case, then the municipal coroner will conduct the post-mortem examination.

A **post-mortem examination** must include the following aspects:

- Confirming the person's identity
- External examination of the body
- Investigate the circumstances surrounding the death
- Confirm the date and place of death
- Determine the nature of the death: natural/non-natural
- If possible, determine the cause of death

- **Natural death:** death due to spontaneous illness, including a complication of a medical treatment performed "according to best practices". Issue a death certificate.
- **Non-natural death:** death as a direct or indirect result of an accident, act of violence or other external causes (e.g. a hip fracture after a fall, resulting in the patient dying as a result of the operation), negligence or intent by another party, or suicide. This relationship is not restricted in time, the cause of death may have taken place years prior (e.g. death caused by pneumonia as a result of a traumatic spinal cord injury that occurred 15y ago). Consult the municipal coroner sooner rather than later if you have any doubts.

- Explain to any family members who are present that a death in the hospital needs to be formally confirmed by a doctor and that this will take about one or two minutes. Ask the family if they want to be present (not everyone does).
- Verify the absence of heart sounds by listening for at least 30 seconds and simultaneously feeling for the carotid pulse (this often seems excessive, but plays an important role in confirming the death for any family members present).
- Check for the presence of post-mortem changes: extreme paleness (within minutes), dilated, deformable pupils (within minutes), lack of muscle tone (within minutes), post-mortem lividity (livor mortis, see Figure 80, occurs within two hours (within 24 hours blanchable, after 24 hours non-blanchable)), stiffness (rigor mortis, within three hours), cooled body, dehydration (yellow-brown colour, sunken eyes, dark spots in the sclera (Sommerse spots/tache noir, see Figure 81)).
- After confirming the death, offer your condolences to any loved ones present.
- Discuss the need for autopsy and donation.

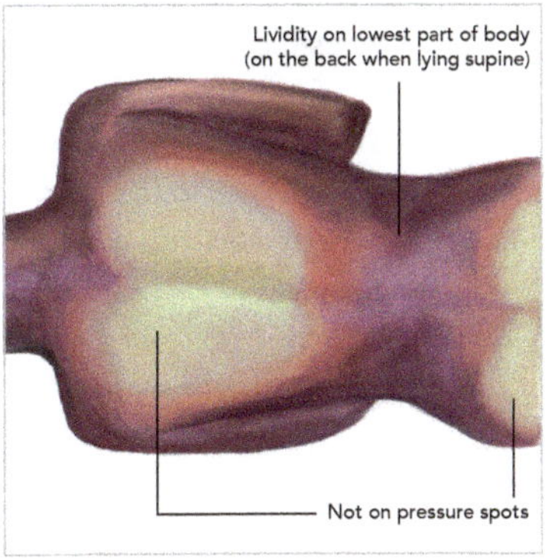

Figure 80 // Livor mortis

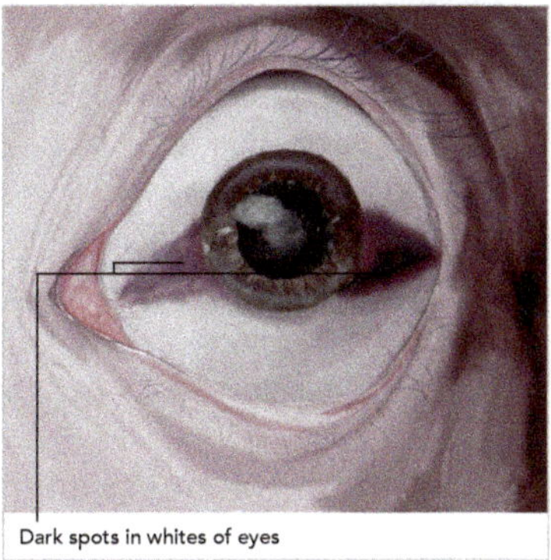

Figure 81 // Sommerse spots/tache noir

Follow local protocols when completing the death forms.

Request to speak to the patient and/or family

"I have Mr Jones' family here. They would like to speak to the doctor."

The evening or night shift is not the best time to conduct family meetings, unless the patient's current situation gives reason for this. Because there are often fewer doctors working, you are more likely to be disturbed during your conversation. As the on-call doctor, you are not familiar with the details of the case, meaning that you are not the best person to be speaking to.

"I have Mr Evans on the phone. He has a fever and was instructed to contact the ward if this happened."

- Briefly speak to the patient over the telephone and estimate whether evaluation in the hospital is indicated (a patient will not call for no reason, so have the patient come in for assessment sooner rather than later).
- If assessment is indicated, give the patient further instructions about where and when to present and - depending on the nature of the symptoms - to call the emergency number in the event of an acute deterioration in symptoms.
- If your assessment is that it is not safe for the patient to travel to the hospital using their own mode of transport, then an ambulance needs to be arranged. The control room has a dedicated number for healthcare professionals to discuss such indications. This can be delegated to the nurse.
- Register the patient with the ED (see section *Treatment of a patient with...*).

Consultation following an incident/calamity

An incident is an unintended or unexpected event relating to the quality of care and which has resulted, could have resulted or could potentially result in injury of the patient. If the injury is severe or fatal, this is referred to as a calamity as defined in the relevant legislation.

"Ms Davis has fallen out of bed. Can you come and have a look?"

See section *Management of a patient with...* for more information about the treatment of a patient after a fall out of bed.

"I mistakenly gave the Augmentin intended for Mr Sullivan to Ms Majors."

- Go and check on the patient as soon as possible if you suspect an incident/ potential calamity.
- Check if the incorrectly administered medication can cause serious negative damage to the patient that you need to control or treat.
- Speak openly and honestly to the patient and/or contact person about what has happened.
- Be mindful of the colleagues involved and support each other.
- Lastly, in consultation with those involved, write a report in the internal incident reporting system.

"I just had a needle-stick accident with a used IV needle."

Needle-stick accidents occur with some regularity. During a needle-stick accident, blood (or another body fluid) from the patient (the source) enters the body of the exposed person via a sharp object (e.g. injection needle). Needle-stick accidents can cause the transmission of hepatitis B virus (HBV), hepatitis C virus (HCV) and HIV. Therefore, it is important that you know how to act in such a situation.

- Allow the wound to bleed (do not stem the flow of blood) and rinse the wound with lukewarm water, preferably under a running tap. Next, the wound needs to be disinfected with a skin disinfectant (e.g. 70% alcohol).
- Ask what happened (preferably asking the exposed person themselves) and estimate the risk of viral transmission (none, low or high) (see Table 128 and 129).
- If the incident has no or a negligible risk of viral transmission, you do not need to take any further action at this point. You should always make a formal report to your supervisor.
- In the case of low-risk accidents, measures are only required against HBV. If the exposed person has been fully vaccinated and checks after vaccination re-

vealed a sufficiently high titre, then the exposed individual is protected against HBV. Non-responders are not protected and should receive additional protection. Immediately consult with the occupational health physician/on-call infectious disease specialist, depending on the agreements in your centre.

- In the case of high-risk accidents, measures are required against HBV, HCV and HIV. If possible, serological testing of the course should be prioritised. Explain to the patient what has happened and ask for their consent (although most patients will be happy to oblige, most will be surprised about an HIV test). Remember that the patient has the right "not to know" and can therefore decide whether he wants to hear the result of the HIV test or not. Immediately consult with the occupational health physician/on-call infectious disease specialist, depending on the agreements in your centre.

For more information about needle-stick/sharps and splash accidents, consult the freely accessible online guidelines by the national health security agency.

NATURE OF THE ACCIDENT	RISK ESTIMATE
Injury caused by injection needle used subcutaneously (insulin needle/heparin needle)	Low
Injury caused by injection needle used for intramuscular injection, without visible blood from source	Low
Injury caused by injection needle used for intramuscular injection, with visible blood from source	High
Injury caused by suture needle used for intracutaneous or subcutaneous sutures, without visible blood from source	Low
Injury caused by suture needle used for intracutaneous or subcutaneous sutures, with visible blood from source	High

Table 128 // Examples of common needle-stick accidents in the hospital

RISK ESTIMATE	HBV	HCV	HIV
None	Negligible risk of transmission/no risk		
Low	Low risk of transmission	Negligible risk of transmission	
High	High risk of transmission	Risk of transmission is not negligible	

Table 129 // Explanation of risk estimate

Questions regarding hospitalisation/discharge

"Mr Saunders has just been admitted via the ED and I don't have instructions yet."

In this case, the "instructions" usually refer to the treatment plan (frequency of observations, IV prescriptions, etc.). Check the electronic patient record and discuss the treatment considerations listed there, so that the nurse can proceed.

Tips & tricks

This brings us to the last section of this pocket guide. In addition to all the advice already provided, we want to give you a few tips for your first shift from "peers", supervisors and nurses.

The manual to this pocket includes settling-in instructions. These settling-in instructions include suggestions for the use of this pocket guide, aimed at maximising the efficiency of your learning process and settling-in period. If you have not consulted these instructions yet, then our first suggestion would be to do that now.

Preparations for your first shift

Some departments offer a formal settling-in programme, others expect you to learn as you go. Either way, it is important that you - as a novice doctor - start your first shift feeling confident. Discuss with your mentor or a supervisor what you need to do to achieve this.

Several tips for the settling-in period:

- Check whether an orientation document or manual is available and read it;
- Check whether any mandatory courses need to be completed prior to your first shift (e.g. ALS, ATLS, FCCS, MedicALS, etc.) and register for these in consultation with the study programme administrator;
- Get to know your way around the ward: find out where you can find the nurses, patient rooms, emergency medication and the resuscitation cart;
- If you also have to cover (part of) the ED during your on-call shifts, arrange shadowing/orientation days in the ED: get to know the department, the board, the registration procedure for new patients and the computer systems (sometimes these differ from other departments);
- Spend a day shadowing the consultant: know your way around the hospital (using maps or route numbers) and the logistics, gain an understanding of which problems can be transferred to the day shift or the outpatients' clinic;
- Ensure that you have access (both digitally and physically) to everything that you need. Open the resuscitation cart on your ward, so that you will know where everything is in any future resuscitation setting;

- Ask a fellow junior doctor if they have a list of useful telephone numbers that they can share with you (also see Appendix 1: *Contact details*);
- Determine which diseases and procedures are common in your specific context and look up the relevant guidelines and protocols;
- Check the admission chart not only for **what** it contains, but also **how** this is written, including the short notes relating to contact with the on-call junior doctor, so that you know what is expected of you in terms of charting;
- Have specific agreements in place with your mentor or a supervisor:
- Schedule a number of progress meetings during your orientation period (e.g. a short meeting every two weeks, at a time that you would be seeing each other anyway) and formulate your personal learning objectives based on these meetings;
- Schedule an observation so that you can receive targeted feedback.

Tips to apply during your first shift

During a busy shift, it is vital that you maintain oversight and prioritise correctly. Select a system that works for you (e.g. an A4 piece of paper in your pocket). If you feel that you are losing sight of the overall picture, sit down with your notes and take a few minutes to prioritise, checking with your supervisor via the telephone if necessary. The following tips can help you with time management:

- A complete handover takes time but is ultimately more efficient, less time searching for information and you can create to-do lists and priorities during the handover;
- An ED patient does not always have priority, a request from the ward may be more urgent;
- Immediately complete any tasks that you can complete within three minutes. If you require more time: prioritise and tell the caller when you expect to get around to it. Keep to the agreed time-frame, or let the other person know if there is a delay;
- The novice doctor can sometimes have an underdeveloped sense of urgency, simply due to lack of experience. Be open to suggestions from the nurse about this;
- Pro-actively visit your ward(s) and/or agree that you will drop by before the end of your shift and are available to answer any questions. This may save you a lot of phone calls during your shift, allowing you to work more efficiently;
- It may seem efficient to postpone your charting, but this is not the case. Adopting the motto "better done than perfect", it is best to record as much information as possible in the chart **immediately**.

During your on-call shift, you will notice - even more so than usual - that good communication and cooperation with the people around you is useful and increases job satisfaction. A number of tips in this regard:

- Introduce yourself, both to the doctors and the nurses, rather introduce yourself once too often than not often enough;
- Nurses often have more experience than you do. Take them seriously in their knowledge and skills, as this will benefit both you and the patient. As the doctor, you have final responsibility for the medical treatment at all times;
- Often the nurse will already have taken action if a patient is deteriorating. When the nurse calls the doctor, they are not doing this for no reason;
- Even when the pressure increases, try to remain available and accessible;
- Answer your phone by stating your first and last name and explicitly mention your position. This allows the caller to check that they are speaking to the correct person. Also listen attentively to how the other healthcare professional introduces themselves. When answering a phone call, always write down the caller's name and number, so that you can easily return this colleague's call;
- Be open about your level of experience, as this allows nurses and supervisors to gauge how best to support you during the shift. Consider contacting the supervisor in question to let them know that this will be your first shift.

In situations where you feel that you are unqualified, you should state this clearly to your fellow junior doctors and supervisor. Recognising and being able to speak up about your limitations is a sign of professionalism and will give the supervisor confidence in you.

- Keep the lines of communication short: opt for a verbal response where possible, this has been proven in practice to be more efficient than indirect communication via the patient records or via an intern/student. Go and consult with the radiologist in person once in a while, that will be greatly appreciated.
- Sit with the nurses during one of your breaks. This will allow you to learn more about each other, which will absolutely be of use when working together during emergency situations.

Sometimes personal circumstances affect our ability to perform at work. Examples include relationship problems, lack of sleep due to a sick child, or - on a much simpler level - that sandwich that you wanted to eat for hours ago or that trip to the toilet that you have had to postpone several times due to the ED being so busy. It seems obvious, but that does not make it any less true: to care for others, you need to take care of yourself first! Try to be open with your colleagues about anything that could affect your performance. This will allow them to be on the lookout for potential problems and to support you where necessary. Listen to yourself. Unfortunately burnout is a very common problem amongst junior doctors.

Tip for after your first shift

- Get some sleep and then treat yourself to breakfast in a nice café and reflect on your shift. Be proud of yourself, you did it!

REFLECTION ON FIRST SHIFT

Appendices

Appendix 1: Morning handover and consultation with supervisors

Many novice doctors struggle to gauge when they should consult with their supervisor. Although this varies per specialism (and sometimes even per supervisor), we can formulate several general guidelines (see Table 134). Verify the agreements with your supervisor prior to your on-call shift.

SITUATION
Doubt/risk of exceeding your own limitations and/or competencies
Patient assessed in the ED, consult with supervisor prior to proposed discharge or admission to the hospital
Called in to consult on a patient. Discuss treatment recommendation with supervisor before informing the requesting party.
Unexpected/unforeseen events (e.g. death of patient, sudden clinical deterioration, (potential) calamity)
Lack of expected response to implemented intervention(s)
(Impending) unacceptable time spent in the ED by patient due to increasing pressure on the ED

Table 134 // General agreements regarding consultation with the supervisor

Combining several less urgent questions can help to reduce the number of contacts with the supervisor, thus saving time. However, this can also result in - for example - patients spending an unnecessary amount of time in the ED. Weigh these factors when determining the best time to consult your supervisor.

Table 135 describes situations for which each supervisor and/or specialism may have a different view. Use this table as a guideline for making working arrangements with your supervisor.

SITUATION
Prior to requesting a consultation (with the exception of the ERT)
Prior to requesting an expensive/risky diagnostic test (e.g. ultrasound, CT, endoscopy)
Prior to administration of newly prescribed medication (e.g. analgesia, sleeping tablets)
Feedback on effect of intervention (e.g. response to fluid challenge)
Feedback on scheduled diagnostic examination (e.g. result of serum potassium for a patient receiving IV potassium supplementation)
Feedback on expected death
In preparation of the handover

Table 135 // Any additional agreements regarding consultation with the supervisor

Consult with your supervisor according to the SBAR structure. Formulate a **"what if" plan.**
Example:

- "What if the blood pressure does not increase in response to the fluid challenge?" plan: request ERT.
- "What if the potassium is lower than 3.5 mmol/L during the scheduled check?" plan: increase supplementation to... etc.

Formulating such a plan will result in far fewer consultations with your supervisor during your shift. Ask your colleagues to formulate a "what if" plan too when they hand their patient over to you. Often the ward doctor can quite easily provide some suggestions for anticipated situations. Making these plans yourself will take a lot of time during your on-call shift, because you will first need to study the case.

- In the weeks prior to your on-call shift, prepare yourself by observing the junior doctor on-call during the night. It is not enough to simply listen to the information that the on-call junior doctor is presenting during the handover, you should also listen to how the information is being presented. Is there a certain order to the handover (e.g. hospitalised patients first, then the consultations and lastly the patients being discharged to home), is each case structured in the same way, how does the doctor answer questions posed by staff members present, etc.;

- Limit yourself to the essence of the case. The more (irrelevant) details you present, the greater the risk that you will fail to bring your point across. If the person listening is missing any information, they will actively ask for it;
- Draw up a handover template for yourself, using your observations (see adjacent example). This template may look different for admissions than for patients who were sent home after assessment in the ED. Using the same wording each time makes it much easier to perform a brief and concise handover. Practise your handover skills when handing over to the night shift and ask your colleague for feedback;
- Try to organise the cases in an order that is logical to you when handing over to your shift. Keep your template in mind for each patient during the handover and ask your colleague for any missing information, this will save time in your preparations later;
- Prepare the handover at the earliest opportunity. Use the first quiet moment that you have, because you never know what will happen and time may unexpectedly be limited;
- Ask your supervisor to give you targeted feedback on your handover.

Example of handover template

Admitted for [*specialism*] **on** [*ward*]*:* **Mr/Ms** [*patient surname*], [*age in years*].

Patient presented [*to ED/for consultation/via the outpatients' clinic*] [*after referral by their GP/as a self-referral*] **with** [*chief complaint*]. [*Staccato description of the primary survey, including effects of interventions, if critically ill at time of presentation, otherwise continue immediately with a summary of the secondary survey*].

History of [*brief description of chief complaint + additional symptoms*] **since** [*date/time*]. **Physical examination reveals** [*concise description of relevant findings*].

The labs include [*summarise relevant values*].

The ECG reveals [*overall conclusion in one sentence*].

The [*chest X-ray/CT/ultrasound, etc.*] reveals [*concise description of relevant findings*]. **Due to suspected** [*working diagnosis*] **the patient was admitted to** [*ward*] **for** [*concise summary of treatment*].

Points of attention for today are [*summarise any items that – for example – the ward doctor needs to take action*].

Appendix 2: Clinical Human Factors

"A team of experts does not make an expert team". Unfortunately, bringing together a group of experienced, well-trained healthcare providers does not automatically lead to the formation of high-performing teams. Performance is ultimately determined by a combination of latent conditions (work conditions, safety systems, organisational culture), and individual actions (worker behaviour, technical and non-technical skills).

Non-technical skills (also known as behavioural skills) are defined as the 'social, cognitive, and personal resource skills that complement technical skills'. The role of non-technical skills in contributing to safe and effective care is widely recognised. These skills allow professionals and thereby teams, to excel. Establishing a culture where professionals feel encouraged to ask for help and share ideas and concerns without fear of embarrassment or retribution, known as psychological safety, is also important in this regard.

Newly graduated doctors tend to struggle with the application of non-technical skills, reporting difficulties regarding, for example, working with different collaborators, task prioritisation when confronted with a heavy workload, clinical decision making and performing under pressure. Further adding to their struggles, newly graduated doctors seem hesitant to call for help for a number of different reasons.

For newly graduated doctors to 'become part of the team' and feel safe and supported to speak up and ask for help when needed, some understanding of team dynamics and the concept of psychological safety is essential. Therefore, this chapter aims to provide a quick overview of the basics of non-technical skills and psychological safety, as a starting point for further exploration of these important topics.

Social skills

First, what makes a group of people a team? In a team, individuals with specific expertise work together as equals and in mutual dependence to achieve a common goal. Good teamwork requires effective communication, insight into the roles and responsibilities of other team members, team situational awareness, and the willingness to help others. One team member will take on the role of team leader. The responsibilities of a team leader include task allocation, information management, facilitating clinical decision making, and team support.

The other team members (followers) may be expected to execute tasks in a timely and thorough manner, share their insights and speak up when necessary.

Ideally, the role of team leader is taken on by the team member best equipped to handle the situation at hand. In multidisciplinary medical teams, however, the role of team leader is almost always (implicitly) assigned to the doctor. One could debate whether this approach is desirable. Think, for example, of the newly graduated cardiology trainee who is automatically appointed leader of the resuscitation team, whilst the ICU nurse (in this case a licenced Advanced Life Support instructor with 30y of clinical experience) operates the crash trolley. If you don't feel comfortable being in the lead, you may suggest a decision, followed by: "does everyone agree", or "are there any suggestions". This way, you include all team members in the decision process.

Cognitive skills

Situational awareness can be described as "the mental image that results from the accumulation of sensory information (perception), interpretation of its meaning and the predictions made based on this interpretation". Situational awareness is influenced by individual factors such as knowledge, prejudices and memory, and system factors such as care complexity and workload. Maintaining situational awareness might be challenging for newly graduated doctors.

Situational awareness is the foundation of good decision making. Different patterns in decision making can be distinguished. The distinction between pattern recognition and hypothetico-deductive reasoning is one that is widely recognised.

Intuitive, unconscious recognition of patterns allows for fast decision making, but is also prone to error. Hypothetico-deductive reasoning, in contrast, is conscious and deliberate, taking more time but also less likely to produce mistakes. Consider acute HF as an example. This is a diagnosis that experienced doctors will recognise having taken one look at the patient. Acute HF is in their 'pattern library', so to say. For newly graduated doctors, this might well be a diagnosis they have never encountered before, making clinical presentation harder to interpret, slowing down the process of decision making and adding to their cognitive load.

The use of cognitive tools such as checklists and standardised approaches can decrease cognitive load and facilitate the decision-making process. Fatigue, stress and extraneous cognitive load, on the other hand, often negatively influence this process.

Personal skills

Newly graduated doctors are often apprehensive about working on-call. It's important to realise that performing under pressure is a skill which, like any other skill, can be practised. Learning to register and regulate one's response to pressure will help to improve performance.

How much pressure someone experiences when confronting certain circumstances varies from person to person. How someone responds to pressure depends on how they assess the situation (cognitive appraisal). Perceiving a situation as difficult or challenging, but feasible, helps to create a state of 'high-performance flow'. The Yerkes-Dodson law (see Figure 82) describes the effect of pressure on performance: mild pressure improves performance, too much pressure impedes performance.

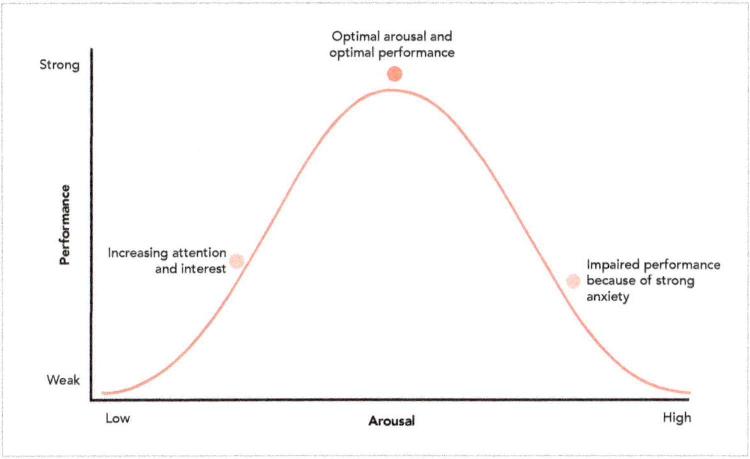

Figure 82 // Interaction between pressure and performance, based on Yerkes-Dodson law (1908)

> There are various strategies to optimise performance under pressure. Prevention plays a big role. Starting a shift well rested and with confidence that support is available at all times, will help you cope better with pressure. Being able to register where you are on your pressure curve and regulate your response to pressure to return to your flow state, for instance by using specific breathing techniques, are important skills to manage your response to pressure whilst on call.

Psychological safety

When working in an environment where the problems presented are more complex, consequences of mistakes may be great, and professionals are dependent on one another, psychological safety is crucial to achieve good results. Psychological safety is defined as "the shared belief that no one will be punished or humiliated for speaking up with ideas, questions, concerns, or mistakes". Put differently, professionals must be willing to take an interpersonal risk. A lack of psychological safety in these contexts leads to a higher risk of error, and a mental burden for professionals.

Unfortunately, hierarchy and educational status can threaten perceived levels of safety, especially when these concepts are intuitively translated as inequality. When teams encourage help-seeking behaviour by creating a safe environment, this helps to support learning and improve quality of care.

References

You can find the online list of references we used while crafting this pocket by scanning the QR code.

Illustrations & figures

Illustrators

Yente S. Beentjes: *figures 80, 81, and modification figure 47*
Hebe T.A. Boerhout: *figure 61*
Dagmar Bouwer: *figure 18*
Cas van Cruchten: *figures 17, 49, 57, 65, and 70*
Gulizar Durak: *figures 44, 45, and 47*
Astrid A.H. Feikema: *figure 52*
Dite L.C. de Jong: *figures 58 and 64*
Didi D.J. Juin: *figure 46*
Koen L.C. Ketelaars: *figures 8, 9, 10, 11, 12, 13, 19, 20, 21, 22, 23, 24, 28, 32, 35, 39, 42, 50, 53, and 76*
Rosalie C. Krijl: *figures 1 and 62*
Kiki van Langen: *figure 72*
Juliëtte M.E. Linskens: *figures 48, 75, and 77*
Kim A.M. van den Nobelen: *figures 36 and 40*
Belle van Rosmalen: *figures 56, 59, 60, and 66*
Laura Sanchez: *figures 30, 43, 51, 67, and 74*
Carlijn Sturm: *figures 37 and 73*
Isabel Versmissen: *figures 38 and 69*
Linda Xie: *figures 14, 15, and 78*

Sources

01. Photos cover and About us: www.ivarpel.nl
02. Figures 2, 3, 4, 5, and 6: Compendium Medicine©, photographer Seren Demirbilek, BSc
03. Figure 7: Dutch Resuscitation Council
04. Figures 16, 31, 41, 54, 55, and 68: Gwendolyn Vuurberg, MD, PhD
05. Figures 25, 33, and 34: Huidziekten.nl
06. Figure 26: Janeway-lesion-4 / DeNanneke / https://www.flickr.com/pho-tos/58146070@N07/8621673442 / CC BY 2.0 (https://creativecommons.org/licenses/by/2.0/)
07. Figure 27: Grosspathology of subacute bacterial endocarditis involving mitralvalve. / CDC / https://commons.wikimedia.org/wiki/File:Haemophilus_parainfluenzae_Endocarditis_PHIL_851_lores.jpg / Public domain
08. Figure 29: Chest radiograph of a lung with Kerley B lines / Mikael Häggström / https://commons.wikimedia.org/wiki/File:Chest_radiograph_of_a_lung_with_Kerley_B_lines_-_annotated.jpg / CC0 1.0 Universal Public Domain Dedication (https://creativecommons.org/publicdomain/zero/1.0/)
09. Figure 63: Prof. M. Maas, MD, PhD, radiologist Amsterdam University Medical Center, Amsterdam and M.M. Cabri, MD, PhD candidate radiology Amsterdam University Medical Center, Amsterdam
10. Figure 71: SADDLE PE / Glitzy queen00 at English Wikipedia / https://commons.wikimedia.org/wiki/File:SADDLE_PE.JPG / Public domain
11. Figure 79: generated using AI (Midjourney.co) by Delano Sanches, MD, BSc
12. Figure cover and beginning pages: Anique Baten, MD, educational advisor medical training, Radboud University Medical Center, Nijmegen

Epilogue

Through the collaborative effort of an incredible team consisting of students, illustrators, graphic designers, and medical specialists, with this pocket we have successfully translated our vision into reality. Our goal was to ensure that you, as students and doctors, have access to essential information – literally at your fingertips, regardless of your location.

Veerle Smit (L) & Romée Snijders (R)

A heartfelt thank you, Demi and Carlijn, for spearheading the publication of our sixth English pocket! We extend our gratitude to Gwendolyn, for her comprehensive involvement in the Acute Medicine project. To Luisa, Endry, and Edward – what an incredible journey we have embarked upon together! Your contributions and enthusiasm have been instrumental every step of the way. This has been an intense yet uniquely rewarding process, for which we also want to thank the editors of the previous edition: Anique and Carlijn.

We are enormously grateful to all the medical professionals who provided valuable feedback and content support, elevating the quality of the text. Your contributions were integral to achieving this result.

This pocket could not have turned out so visually successful without all the illustrators – also often medical students – who collaborated on this pocket. Thanks to our team for their exceptional ability to comprehensibly cover the specialty in their graphic work.

We gratefully acknowledge our graphic heroes, Maria and Ivana, whose efforts gave this pocket its recognisable *Compendium Medicine* look. Special thanks also go to Vera, Melanie, Pauline, Qin-ty, and Delano for ensuring the smooth functioning of the entire process.

Last, a sincere thank you to all our colleagues who have *Compendium Medicine* on their bookshelves. Your support has been indispensable in realising our dreams.

We are incredibly proud of this team and hope to see you again soon, in or outside the hospital!

Amsterdam, February 2025

Veerle Smit, MD & Romée Snijders, MD
Doctors and founders of *Compendium Medicine*

Compendium
Together for

Medicine
Healthcare

About us

As medical students, we felt overwhelmed by the amount of medical knowledge available. An overview was lacking. Fueled by this need for change, we embarked on a journey that has now brought together over 500 students and doctors to create the entire *Compendium Medicine* book series. Our mission is to help and connect healthcare professionals globally by providing accessible knowledge.

The bigger picture

In 2015, at VU University in Amsterdam, the Netherlands, our paths crossed as we were both pursuing our medical educations. The vast sea of medical knowledge overwhelmed us, highlighting the need for a comprehensive overview. We were surprised by the isolated efforts of every hospital and university, each working on its own 'island', publishing individual books and reference works instead of fostering collaboration.

Motivated to make a difference, we envisioned a solution: a comprehensive guide encompassing all 36 subspecialties, enriched with figures, icons, charts, and mnemonics. Our vision was clear – our books had to be visual, concise, and to the point. With a dedicated team of students and doctors, we started writing an encyclopedia using our unique method. *Compendium Medicine* was born!

Book series

Following almost two years of dedicated effort, the first edition achieved sold-out status even before its official launch: a remarkable start to the ongoing rollercoaster journey. The most rewarding aspect of this experience has been – and still is – the overwhelmingly positive feedback from medical students and specialists. Our narrative caught the attention of prominent Dutch and Belgian newspapers and journals, leading to invitations to feature on popular talk shows on national television.

Compendium Medicine book series

Our white-coat pockets

One year later, both of us had started our clinical rotations. We recognized a common challenge faced by many peers: the need for quick and easy access to practical information. In response, we started creating our first series of pockets – concise yet comprehensive pocket-sized booklets designed to provide essential and practical information during a shift.

A period of many milestones followed. Our team expanded every month: from authors to medical specialists, from ambassadors to illustrators. With a growing number of followers on social media, a real community was born. With this team, we worked incredibly hard on new pockets as well as new additions like flashcards and pocket cards. As of now, we have launched a total of 20 different pockets!

Compendium Medicine pockets

Expanding our mission globally

With the experience gained over the past years, we are committed to making a positive impact on medical students and healthcare professionals worldwide. This new phase kicked off with the distribution of our *Radiology* pocket to all continents. We were amazed to have reached readers from over 92 countries! Their positive feedback was instrumental in propelling us forward, and we are excited to present our sixth pocket in English: *Acute Medicine*. And this is just the beginning: we are actively working on bringing more pockets to you!

Romée Snijders & Veerle Smit

Doctors and founders of *Compendium Medicine*

Compendium Compass

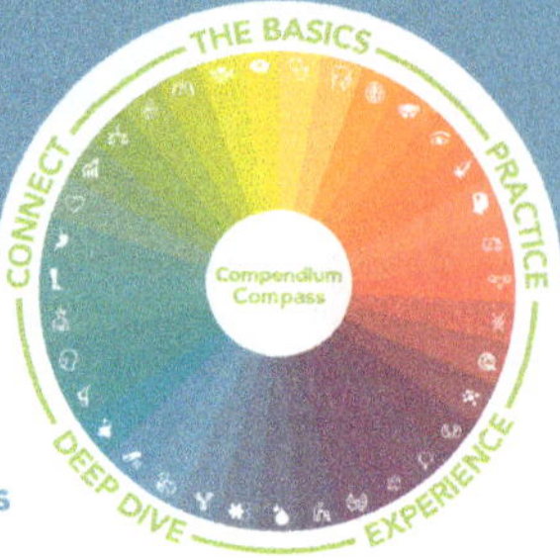

We believe that on your journey from medical student to retirement you continuously navigate these five steps. The Compendium Compass assists you along the way.

1 THE BASICS

Start at the foundation. Explore all 36 medical specialisms through our comprehensive series, featuring clear diagrams, tables, and illustrations. Visit our website for additional details.

2 PRACTICE

Reinforce your foundational knowledge with our *Compendium Medicine* App and through our social media platforms! The app, which can be downloaded from the Apple and Android app stores, enables you to practice questions on a daily basis and participate in the monthly challenge.

Scan this QR code for more information.

3 EXPERIENCE

Learn on-the-go by carrying our pockets and pocket cards with you on the ward, during your shifts and rounds, anytime. Our first pockets are already available worldwide, with many more to come. See below for details!

4 DEEP DIVE

Explore medical knowledge through extensive reading, immersing yourself in a variety of literature, guidelines, and the latest scientific articles.

5 CONNECT

Interested in connecting with individuals in your field? Become a member of our community through our social media platform – a network of students, physicians, specialists, and other healthcare professionals.

Abbreviations

NH_3	ammonia
AAA	abdominal aortic aneurysm
AAAA	acute AAA
AATD	alpha-1 antitrypsin
AB	antibiotic
ABCDE	Airway, Breathing, Circulation, Disability, Exposure
ABG	arterial blood gas
ABI	ankle-brachial index
AC	acromioclavicular
ACE	angiotensin-converting enzyme
ACNES	anterior cutaneous nerve entrapment syndrome
ACQ	asthma control questionnaire
ACS	acute coronary syndrome
ADC	apparent diffusion coefficient
ADH	antidiuretic hormone
AED	automatic external defibrillator
AF	atrial fibrillation
AKI	acute kidney injury
ALP	alkaline phosphatase
ALS	Advanced Life Support
ALT	alanine transaminase
AMBU	artificial manual breathing unit
AP	anteroposterior
APACHE	Acute Physiology And Chronic Health Evaluation
aPPT	activated partial thromboplastin test/time
AR	aortic valve regurgitation
ARDS	acute respiratory distress syndrome
AS	aortic valve stenosis
AST	aspartate aminotransferase
ATN	acute tubular necrosis
AUD	alcohol use disorder
AUR	acute urinary retention
AV	atrioventricular
AVM	arteriovenous malformation
AVPU	Alert, Voice, Pain, Unresponsive
BAL	bronchoalveolar lavage
BB	before bedtime
BE	base excess
BE-FAST	Balance, Eyes, Face, Arms, Speech, Time
Bi-PAP	bilevel positive airway pressure
BISAP	bedside index of severity in acute pancreatitis
BLS	Basic Life Support
BMI	body mass index
BP	blood pressure
BPH	benign prostatic hyperplasia
Ca^{2+}	calcium
CAA	cerebral amyloid angiopathy
CABG	coronary artery bypass graft
CAG	coronary angiography
CAM	confusion assessment method
CAP	community acquired pneumonia
CBD	common bile duct
CBF	cerebral blood flow
CBV	cerebral blood volume
cc	cubic centimeter
CCTA	cardiac computed tomography angiography
CCU	coronary care unit
CK	creatine kinase
CKD	chronic kidney disease
Cl^-	chloride anion
CMV	cytomegalovirus
CN	cranial nerve
CNS	central nervous system
CO	cardiac output
CO	carbon monoxide
CO_2	carbon dioxide
COPD	chronic obstructive pulmonary disease
COVID	Corona virus disease
COW	computer on wheels
CP	chest pain
C-PAP	continuous positive airway pressure
CPR	cardiopulmonary resuscitation
CRP	C-reactive protein
CRT	capillary refill time
CSF	cerebrospinal fluid
CT	computed tomography
CTa	CT angiography
CTCA	CT coronary angiogram
CTP	CT perfusion
CTPA	computed tomography pulmonary angiography
CTR	cardiothoracic ratio
CTV	CT venography
CVP	central venous pressure
DAPT	dual antiplatelet therapy
DHF	decompensated heart failure
DIC	disseminated intravascular coagulation
DKA	diabetic ketoacidosis
DM	diabetes mellitus
DOAC	direct oral anticoagulants
DOS	Delirium Observation Screening
DVT	deep vein thrombosis
DWI	diffusion-weighted imaging

EBV	Epstein-Barr virus
ECG	electrocardiogram
ECMO	extracorporeal membrane oxygenation
ED	emergency department
EDH	epidural haematoma
EDTA	ethylenediaminetetraacetic acid
EEG	electroencephalography
EF	ejection fraction
e-FAST	extended focused assessment with sonography for trauma
eGFR	estimated glomerular filtration rate
EMG	electromyography
EMV	eye, motor and verbal response
ENT	ear, nose and throat
EPO	erythropoietin
ERCP	endoscopic retrograde cholangiopancreatography
ERT	emergency response team
ESR	erythrocyte sedimentation rate
ESWL	extracorporeal ShockWave Lithotripsy
etc.	et cetera/and others
$etCO_2$	end-tidal CO_2
EUS	endoscopic ultrasound
EVAR	endovascular aneurysm repair
FABP	fatty-acid binding protein
FAQ	Frequently Asked Questions
FCCS	fundamental critical care support
FER	forced expiratory rate
FEV1	forced expiratory volume in 1 second
FFD	filtering face piece
FHx	family history
FiO_2	O_2 fraction
FLAIR	fluid-attenuated inversion recovery
FVC	forced vital capacity
GABA	gamma-aminobutyric acid
GCS	Glasgow Coma Scale
GDC	glucose daily curve
GGT	gamma-glutamyltransferase
GHB	gamma hydroxybutyrate
GI	gastrointestinal
GLP-1	glucagon-like peptide
GOLD	Global Initiative for Chronic Obstructive Lung Disease
GP	general practitioner
HACEK	Haemophilus species, Aggregatibacter actinomycetemcomitans, Cardiobacterium hominis, Eikenella corrodens, Kingella kingae)
HAP	hospital acquired pneumonia
Hb	heamoglobin
HBV	hepatitis B virus
HCO_3^-	bicarbonate
HCV	hepatitis C virus
HELLP	haemolysis, elevated liver enzyme levels and low platelet levels
HET	high energy trauma
HF	heart failure
HFmrEF	heart failure with mildly reduced ejection fraction
HFpEF	heart failure with preserved ejection fraction
HFrEF	heart failure with reduced ejection fraction
HHS	hyperosmolar hyperglycaemic state
HIV	human immunodeficiency virus
HLA	human leukocyte antigens
HR	heart rate
HSV	herpes simplex virus
Ht	haematocrit
HUS	hemolytic uremic syndrome
i.e.	id est/in other words
IBD	inflammatory bowel disease
IBS	irritable bowel syndrome
ICA	intralesional corticosteroid administration
ICD	implantable cardioverter defibrillator
ICS	intercostal space
ICS	inhaled corticosteroids
ICU	intensive care unit
IE	infective endocarditis
IM	intramuscular
INR	international normalised ratio
IO	intraosseous
IT	information technology
ITP	immune thrombocytopenia
IV	Intravenous
IVT	IV thrombolysis
JC	John Cunningham
JVD	jugular vein distention
K^+	potassium
kHz	kilohertz
kPa	kilopascal
LABA	long acting B adrenoceptor agonist
LBBB	left bundle branch block
LDH	lactate dehydrogenase
LLL	left lower lobe
LMWH	low molecular weight heparin
LP	lumbar puncture
LSD	lysergic acid diethylamide
LUL	left upper lobe
LV	left ventricle
LVEF	left ventricular ejection fraction
LVH	left ventricular hypertrophy

LVOTO	left ventricular outflow tract obstruction
MAP	mean arterial pressure
MCH	mean corpuscular haemoglobin
MCHC	mean corpuscular haemoglobin concentration
MCV	mean corpuscular volume
MEWS	modified early warning score
mg	miligram
Mg^{2+}	magnesium
mL	milliliter
mmHg	millimetres of mercury
MOF	multi-organ failure
MR	mitral valve regurgitation
MRA	mineralocorticoid receptor antagonist
MRCP	magnetic resonance cholangio pancreatography
MS	mitral valve stenosis
MTT	mean transit time
N/A	non applicable
Na^{+}	sodium
NaCl	sodium chloride
NG	nasogastric
NIBP	non-invasice blood pressure measurement
NIHSS	National Institutes of Health Stroke Scale
NIPPV	non-invasive positive pressure ventilation
NIV	non-invasive ventilation
NOMI	non-occlusive mesenteric ischaemia
NPO	nil per os/nothing by mouth
NRM	non-rebreather mask
NRS	numeric rating scale
NSAID	non-steroidal anti-inflammatory drug
NSTEMI	non-ST elevation myocardial infarction
NTM	non-tuberculous mycobacteria
NYHA	New York Heart Association
O_2	oxygen
OAC	oral anticoagulant
OPA	oropharyngeal airway
OSAS	obstructive sleep apnoea syndrome
Pa	partial pressure
PA	posterior-anterior
PAD	peripheral artery disease
PCA	patient controlled anaesthesia
PCI	percutaneous coronary intervention
PCr	protein creatinine ratio
PEA	pulseless electrical activity
PEARRL	Pupils Equal and Round, Reactive to Light
PEEP	positive end-expiratory pressure
PESI	pulmonary embolism severity index
PET	positron emission tomography
pH	potential of Hydrogen
PID	pelvic inflammatory disease
PJP	pneumocystis jirovecii pneumonia
PLT	platelet count
PMR	polymyalgia rheumatica
PMx	past medical history
PNL	percutaneous nephrolitholapaxy
PO_4^{3-}	phosphate
POCUS	point of care ultrasonography
PPE	personal protective equipment
PPI	proton pump inhibitors
PRBCs	erythrocytes
PSA	prostate-specific antigen
PSI	pneumonia severity index
PSP	primary spontaneous pneumothorax
PT	prothrombin test/time
PTC	percutaneous bile duct drainage
PTH	parathyroid hormone
PVR	peripheral vascular resistance
RABT	Revised Assessment of Bleeding and Transfusion
RAS	renin angiotensin system
RAST	radioallergosorbent test
RBBB	right bundle branch block
RBC	red blood cell
RCA	right coronary artery
RDW	red blood cell distribution width
RFRT	renal function replacement therapy
RLL	right lower lobe
RLQ	right lower quadrant
RML	right middle lobe
ROM	range of motion
ROS	O_2 radicals
ROSC	return of spontaneous circulation
RR	respiratory rate
RS	respiratory syncytial
RSVP	Reason, Story, Vital signs, Plan
RTA	renal tubular acidosis
RTIC	reticulocyte count
RUL	right upper lobe
RUQ	right upper quadrant
RUSH	rapid ultrasonography for shock and hypotension
RV	right ventricle
SABA	short acting B adrenoceptor agonist
SAH	subarachnoid haemorrhage
SBAR	Situation, Background, Assessment, Recommendation
SBP	systolic blood pressure

www.ingramcontent.com/pod-product-compliance
Lightning Source LLC
Chambersburg PA
CBHW050520240926
51846CB00003B/634
9789083374024